D0437894

Criminology

CRIMINOLOGY

Second Edition

Richard Quinney
Brown University

Little, Brown and Company
Boston Toronto

Library of Congress Catalog Card No.: 78-70244

First Printing

Published simultaneously in Canada
by Little, Brown & Company (Canada) Limited

Printed in the United States of America

Book Editor: Tina Samaha
Designer: Anna Post
Art Editor: Tina Schwinder

ACKNOWLEDGMENTS

Illustrations: Page 2 Springer/Bettmann Film Archive. *Page 27* Donald Young. *Page 34* Springer/Bettmann Film Archive. *Page 48* Reprinted by permission of the Chicago Tribune–New York News Syndicate. *Page 68* United Press International Photo. *Page 76* Lee Romero/Sygma. *Page 91* The Bettmann Archive, Inc. *Page 104* Wide World Photos. *Page 114* Tyrone Hall/Stock, Boston. *Page 123* Arthur Grace/Sygma. *Page 144* The Library of Congress. *Page 162* United Press International Photo. *Page 183* Wide World Photos. *Page 190* Donald Dietz/Stock, Boston. *Page 198* Wide World Photos. *Page 211* New York Times Pictures. *Page 220* Charles Harbutt/Magnum. *Page 236* Wide World Photos. *Page 249* Wide World Photos. *Page 264* Martin Dain/Magnum. *Page 268* Rhode Island Historical Society. *Page 291* Copyright © 1975 DC Comics Inc. *Page 304* Francis Miller © Time, Inc. *Page 312* David Omar White. *Page*
(Continued on page 425)

Preface

Our lives, our view of the world, and our way of knowing about crime have undergone considerable change in recent years. The revised edition of *Criminology* reflects the changes that have taken place. In *The Social Reality of Crime* (1970), and in the first edition of *Criminology* (1975), I tried to provide a reorientation to criminology, basing the study on revised assumptions about capitalist society in the United States. The purpose of *Criminology* continues to be a new understanding of crime.

Crime has acquired a different meaning for us as events have forced a reconsideration of the nature of crime in capitalist society. A perspective based on a constructionist view of reality or an instrumental class analysis is no longer sufficient. Rather, our understanding of contemporary experience depends on a critical–Marxist analysis of the structure of reality. The discussion in *Criminology* examines crime in the political economy of the United States.

The constituent elements of crime are covered, including the law, the offender, the forms of crime, law enforcement and criminal justice, and punishment and correction. Crime is viewed historically and structurally in relation to the development of capitalist society.

I have tried to present my critical understanding of crime in order to inform and to furnish ideas that aim toward a transformation of society. Our understanding contributes to a way of life, a politics of being in the world.

Contents

THE STUDY OF CRIME

I

Theory and Method in Criminology

1

Can you imagine a world without crime? What would our lives be like without criminals and criminal justice? With all the policies and programs, the political words and deeds, the rhetoric on law and order steadily belaboring it, completely eliminating crime would deny part of our experience. Crime and its control are basic to the way of life in the United States.

We begin our study of crime with anticipation, seeing a chance to learn about a subject close to our imagination and experience. Our interest increases when we begin to apply critical analysis to our conventional wisdom — the opinions we daily read and hear — about crime. Stripping away superficial layers, we find that sometimes that which is apparent in this knowledge is not always real. Myths, half-truths, imaginative stories about crime have obscured truth and reality.

First we should see what it is about crime that interests us. For some of us crime may have taken concrete form — we may have been the object of criminal laws and the system that administers criminal justice. Or we may have been the victims of violent or exploitative acts of a criminal nature. Then too, crime has entered our imaginations in one way or another all our lives. We have grown up in a world of crime.

We understand crime, then, at the same time as we begin to understand ourselves; we cannot adequately understand crime in the United States unless we do examine ourselves. And to know any phenomena or events of this world, crime in particular, we need to relate our own and our nation's biographies to the past and to present experiences.

We grow up in a world of shared meanings. The most consequential of these form everyday folklore or myths and are spread today by the mass media: radio, magazines, newspapers, movies, and television. At an impressionable age (and, in fact, all through our lives) we are drawn into a fictional world, a commercialized fiction that for us sometimes becomes a reality. Crime, criminals, and the law are probably the commonest and most vivid images molded into our lives as we grow up. Even as adults we are faced with these portrayals of crime, which is big business in commercial communications.

What ideas and characters have shaped the way your mind and imagination handle crime? The differences among people, of course, have a lot to do with your generation. But whether your views on law and crime are shaped by a Lone Ranger, a Perry Mason, or a Colombo, you have been developing an understanding, real or fanciful, of crime. Whether you grew up on Dick Tracy, Gangbusters, Dragnet, Mod Squard, or Police Story, you have been creating your own world of crime, helped along by others.

Before going further you might give some thought to your own conception of crime — what is it; what does it mean to you? You are likely to find that you have had a conception of crime that is partly obscured. For me, growing up in the forties and fifties, the Lone Ranger was a screen through which I viewed the world. Three nights a week we sat by the radio listening to the latest adventures of the masked man as he pursued badmen and criminals. We waited anxiously for good to triumph over evil. My world was made real by this frontier character. Now, confronting this earlier world and demystifying — removing the layers of myth and fiction from — these experiences, I am able to gain a better understanding of crime in the United States.[1]

DEVELOPMENT OF CRIMINOLOGY

Criminology as the "scientific" study of crime grew in reaction to turmoil and disorder in the European countries. The early theorists in criminology and the other social sciences were disturbed by the many rebellions and revolutions in the eighteenth and nineteenth centuries. It was their hope that the new sciences could discover the natural laws on which society had grown and provide a program for finding social tranquility.

Criminology began with a conservative ideology, a preference for keeping ideas and conditions as they are, opposing new ideas and change. Looking for the laws of social order, the rules that arranged people into a society, criminologists have favored current social arrangements. Anything that appears to threaten this social order, such as crime, strikes them as violating the "natural laws" of society. Instead of looking upon crime as a response to current conditions, they have treated it as endangering the established society. We can trace criminology's theoretical development by following its attempts to explain crime as it affects the social order.[2]

The most important ideas in criminology before the nineteenth century came from thinkers in the group commonly called the "classical school." It was the high point of eighteenth-century humanitarian rationalism, and came along just before scientific methods were first used in studying human behavior. Such writers as Cesare Beccaria, Jeremy Bentham, and Samuel Romilly studied the relationship between citizens and the state's legal structure.[3] Reacting against contemporary legal practices, these writers objected to inconsistencies in the way criminal law was administered, proposing reforms more in keeping with their conception of human life. Bentham's slogan, "the greatest happiness of the greatest number," proposed utility as the scale against which to measure all goodness. In practice, a rational system of criminal justice, following reason, not intuition and emotion, was established to protect the new capitalist society.

Modern criminology began in the 1830's when crime was first studied as a social, not an individual phenomenon.[4] During the early and middle years of the nineteenth century, scholars in Europe gathered and analyzed statistics as a source of facts on crime. Alexander von Oettingen of Germany devoted his *Moralstatistik* to the problem of measuring facts recorded earlier about crimes. In Belgium, statisticians such as Adolphe Quetelet studied crime's social characteristics as they could be seen in criminal statistics. A. M. Guerry, in charge of judicial statistics for Paris, analyzed rates of crime for the regions of France. Several Italian socialists also actively observed crime. During this period, journals were established to publish these studies and an international criminological association was founded.

English interest in the ecological distribution of crime, the number of crimes reflecting connections between criminals and their environments, was very active between 1830 and 1860.[5] Industrialization and the growing cities led several English writers to examine the social problems brought about by these changes, especially crime. Rawson W. Rawson published "An Inquiry into the Statistics of Crime in England and Wales" in the *Journal of the Statistical Society of London*. Joseph Fletcher, Rawson's successor as honorary secretary of that society, reported on English crime rates in relation to social characteristics of geographical areas. Henry Mayhew, a founder of *Punch*, an English humor magazine, made detailed ecological analyses of crime in London, published as *London Labour and London Poor*.

A large study later in the century was Charles Booth's *Life and Labour of the People of London*. Booth was a merchant, shipowner, and manufacturer who, though he benefited from industrialization, was aware that the social conditions it brought about were not ideal. His biographers observe that "Booth appears to be a true Victorian insofar as he acclaimed the positive values of industrial and commercial enterprise, but sought at the same time to devise methods of combating the evils that had resulted from it."[6] A practical man, Booth believed that social policy should be guided by facts, and he set out to gather them. He used scientific inquiry in an attempt to solve social problems.

Americans were inclined to think crime, sin, pauperism, and immorality were equally bad. Even when crime was recognized as distinct from other social events, it was usually thought of as an ill that should be no part of social life; it fell into the embrace of nineteenth-century reformers' attempts to reduce the number of social problems within the context of existing social arrangements.

Many people in positions of authority saw that they needed knowledge to guide their endeavors and supply them with rational grounds for implementing reform — that was the strongest stimulus behind the social-science movement in the second half of the century. Social science could supply knowledge to be used for reform, an important idea in the academic community.[7] Criminology was one of the first courses offered by the new social science departments.

Crime was also studied as a social phenomenon by people doing prison and welfare work. One of these early groups of criminologists saw crime as produced by the "disharmonious" way in which social forces or institutions of society worked: "When these institutions were not soundly constructed, or when their functions were not realized competently and responsibly, and when the patterns of behavior characteristic of groups of people differed from predominating standards, crime was a natural consequence."[8]

Crime grew rapidly along with the growing cities. Several authors wrote late in the nineteenth century about the urban crime problem. Charles Loring Brace devoted his life to organizing charities, finding the causes of crime in the way of life led by much of the urban population. In *The Dangerous Classes of New York*, Brace described in great detail the conditions of life among various groups. At the same time, Edward Crapsey described several types of crime in *The Nether Side of New York*. His theory was that crime had developed in the city because communities were not integrated and corruption permeated the political structure.

Other writers added religious ideas from the social gospel movement. Several Protestant leaders (among them Washington Gladden in *Applied Christianity and the Social Order*) argued for a religion that would adjust Christianity to the world's problems. This movement, like others of the time, helped shape ideas about social problems, including crime. Crime was viewed as a pathology that resulted from an industrial society devoid of human and religious values.

Another European system of ideas that greatly molded criminology's development culminated in the "positive school" of criminology. According to positivism, society can be described and understood by the application of methods of the physical sciences. Particularly among Italian criminologists, positivists used the point of view and methodology (rules and procedures) of the natural sciences, and emphasized determinism of conduct: every criminal act is inevitable because physical and environmental conditions predestine it.

Cesare Lombroso synthesized this line of thought in *L'uomo delinquente*, published in 1876, a vivid presentation of his theory about the criminal's physical inferiority. The criminal was born that way, a throwback to a more primitive and savage man. In a speech at the Congress of Criminal Anthropology at Turin in 1906, Lombroso recalled his discovery:

> In 1870 I was carrying on for several months researches in the prisons and asylums of Pavia upon cadavers and living persons, in order to determine upon substantial differences between the insane and criminals, without succeeding very well. Suddenly on the morning of a gloomy day in December, I found in the skull of a brigand a very long series of atavistic anomalies, above all an enormous middle occipital fossa and a hypertrophy of the vermis, analogous to those that are found in inferior invertebrates. At the sight of these strange anomalies, as a large plain appears under an inflamed horizon, the problem of the nature and of the origin of the criminal seemed to be resolved; the characters of primitive men and of inferior animals must be reproduced in our time.[9]

Lombroso later modified his thoughts on the born criminal, including many environmental factors in his theory on the causes of crime. Other Italian positivists, especially Enrico Ferri and Raffaele Garofalo, also began to emphasize various kinds of related factors.

Beyond these theories, the positivists proposed a kind of responsibility for crime based on the needs of society rather than the offender's free will and moral guilt. Ferri clearly stated their position on the individual's responsiblity to society: "Man is always responsible for every one of his acts, for the sole reason that he lives in society, and for as long as he does so."[10] It was the individual's duty to adjust to the state's demands.

Later in their careers, both Ferri and Garofalo adapted themselves to Mussolini's fascist regime. Their political alignment may not have been accidental or a matter of practical compromise; George B. Vold writes that positivism's general orientation is consistent with totalitarianism:

> The end of Ferri's career, assent to Fascism, highlights one of the implications of positivistic theory, namely, the ease with which it fits into totalitarian patterns of government. It is centered on the core idea of the superior knowledge and wisdom of the scientific expert, who, on the basis of his studies, decides what kind of human beings his fellow men are who commit crime, and who, on the basis of this knowledge and scientific insight, prescribes appropriate treatment without consent from the person so diagnosed (i.e., the criminal). There is an obvious similarity in conception of the control of power in society between positivism and the political reality of centralized control of the life of the citizen by government bureaucracy indifferent to democratic public opinion.[11]

In this century's first decades new explanations of crime were erected on many bases. The early theorists felt that the individual offender's characteristics were most important. Writings by the Italian positivists were being translated, directly influencing a number of American criminologists.[12] Lombroso's influence continued to appear in works through 1850.[13] Developing criminology discarded most of Lombroso's biological emphasis, though his positivism was accepted. Gustav Aschaffenburg severely criticized Lombroso's biological theory in *Crime and Its Repression* for American criminologists. Using data from Germany, he considered many individual and social factors as causes of crime.

The crushing blow to Lombrosian theory was evidence from Charles Goring in his statistical study of 3,000 male convicts, *The English Convict*. With data he collected as a medical officer at Parkhurst Prison, Goring sought "to clear from the ground the remains of the old criminology, based upon conjecture, prejudice, and questionable observations," and "to found a new knowledge of the criminal upon facts scientifically verified; such facts and inferences yielding, by virtue of their own established accuracy, unimpeachable conclusions."[14] He concluded that there is no "born" criminal type and that crime is not inherited, turning criminologists to study psychological characteristics, especially defective intelligence, as a cause of criminal behavior.[15]

Criminologists rebelled against the practice of explaining that crime is caused by just one factor such as shape of the skull, or low intelligence, and began to look for multiple causes. Their search for factors or variables, measuring and correlating them to criminal behavior, also reflected the trend toward empiricism (depending on experience and observation, not theory) in the social sciences. One of the first empirical studies was William Healy's *The Individual Delinquent*, in which he considered many factors that varied greatly and formed complex combinations. The multiple-factor approach was also used by Cyril Burt in *The Young Delinquent,* attributing a percentage of causative importance to each of the factors. The multiple-factor approach is still found today in such works as Sheldon and Eleanor Glueck's *Unraveling Juvenile Delinquency*.

The most recent individualistic trend in studying crime is found in psychiatry. Most psychoanalytic theories take crime as a form of substitute behavior (replacing a thwarted or repressed behavior with another that may be more dangerous or criminal).[16] Such works include Ben Karpman's *The Individual Criminal,* Robert Lindner's *Rebel Without a Cause,* David Abrahamsen's *Who Are the Guilty?* and Franz Alexander and Hugo Staub's *The Criminal, the Judge, and the Public.*

The sociological study of crime moved very slowly in the United States in the early 1900's. With today's hindsight, we can see that early sociologists studied crime from numerous questionable assumptions and did not specifically aim at social matters. One of the first works on crime by a sociologist, Frances A. Kellor's *Experimental Sociology,* was actually a study of physical differences (height of forehead, length of ears, width of mouth, nasal index) between women criminals and women students. In its introduction by C. R. Henderson, one of the first sociologists at the University of Chicago, expressed a moralism tempered by relativism (belief that all knowledge is relative and none can be absolutely true), hinting too at the adventure the early sociologists felt in the new social science: "The university cannot neglect any phase of social life. As in astronomy the study of perturbations in the movements [disturbances in the orbits] of known bodies leads to the discovery of new worlds, so in social science the investigation of evil brings us nearer to an understanding of the good and helps us on the path upward."[17]

The study of crime as a social phenomenon during this period was also affected by evolutionary theory, particularly social Darwinism — the superior (rich and powerful) social classes win the struggle for survival. This theoretical orientation to crime was best displayed in Arthur C. Hall's *Crime and Its Relation to Social Progress.* Franklin H. Giddings, first professor of sociology at Columbia University, set the tone in the introduction, suggesting that as civilization evolves some behaviors must be defined as criminal, adding that defining immorality as criminal in the legal code "is one of the most powerful means by which society in the long run eliminates the socially unfit, and gives an advantage in the struggle for existence to the thoughtful, the considerate, the far-seeing, the compassionate; so lifting its members to higher planes of character and conduct."[18]

Maurice Parmelee, perhaps more than any other person as the century began, brought about the union of sociology and criminology. In *The Principles of Anthropology and Sociology in Their Relations to Criminal Procedure,* he found some favorable ideas in Lombroso's theory, suggesting a sociological criminology. In 1918, he was the first American to attempt a comprehensive exposition of criminological knowledge in his *Criminology,* analyzing the social sources of crime. Nevertheless, he found it necessary to discuss evolution, the physical environment, "criminal traits," and the "organic basis of criminality." His work, despite these faults, represents the transition in the United States from an eclectic study (many varieties of explanations combined) of crime to a sociological explanation for its causes.

During the twenties and thirties a sociological criminology was advanced by sociologists at the University of Chicago. Albion W. Small, founder and head of the first university sociology department in the United States (Chicago), gathered a distinguished group. With broad ability and scope, they created a sociological tradition with the study of crime as one of its principal goals. Their theme was that criminal behavior is similar to any other social behavior.

A major influence on the students of crime at the University of Chicago was the work of Robert E. Park. With a colleague, E. W. Burgess, he suggested studying the spatial (geographic) distribution of social phenomena in the city.[19] Students of Park and Burgess examined the relationship of deviant behaviors (differing from accepted social standards) to urban growth and ecological patterns. Frederick M. Thrasher, in his study of 1,313 gangs in Chicago, argued that groups of boys in "interstitial areas" of the city could, by participation, become unified delinquent groups.[20]

Clifford R. Shaw and his collaborators, studying distribution of delinquency rates, found, among other things, that delinquency was concentrated in deteriorated parts of the city and that the areas of high delinquency consistently held high rates despite changes in population.[21] In a number of case studies, including *The Jack-Roller: Natural History of a Delinquent Career,* and *Brothers in Crime,* Shaw shifted from physical factors in the environment to the cultural environment and social participation. He suggested that slum youths participate in a culture that prescribes or encourages delinquent behavior.

By the late thirties, three distinct conceptions of crime had been formulated into theories: differential association, social structure and anomie, and cultural conflict. Edwin H. Sutherland gave the first in the 1939 revision of his popular textbook, *Principles of Criminology.* In his "theory of differential association," Sutherland offered an explanation of crime (an individual's behavior becomes criminal mostly because of steady association with criminals) that would replace the multiple-factor approach and go beyond the simple enculturation explanation of crime (we learn crime along with the traditional elements of our culture).[22] He provided an integrative (unifying) theory for criminology, assuming that the many diverse factors and correlates (parallels) of crime are important as far as they affect an individual's associations and learning. Postulating that criminal behavior is learned in primary association with others, relatively isolated from opposing values, it continues to serve as one of the major theoretical perspectives in criminology.

At the same time as Sutherland was presenting his theory, Robert K. Merton published his now famous article, "Social Structure and Anomie."[23] Elaborating upon Emile Durkheim's description of how aspiration or ambition appears and regulatory norms or standards break down, Merton sought to explain the kinds and amounts of deviation in society. An explanation for crime will be found in society's social and cultural structure, not in the individual. He went beyond other conceptions of social disorganization, suggesting different "modes of adaptation" to society. With his theory he tried to explain both the behavior of individuals and the rates of crime.

A third theory, with the idea of cultural conflict (usually conflict between groups of diverse cultural backgrounds), was presented by Thorsten Sellin in *Culture Conflict and Crime.*[24] Sellin believed that conflict stirred by cultural differences could arise in several ways, each of its forms being potentially related to crime. One conflict develops in a growing civilization and another from contact between the divergent codes of different cultures. Sellin found support for his theory by reviewing research on criminal behavior among immigrants, both of foreign birth and the second generation. In all cases, he saw crime as a matter of conflict between norms of conduct, of which legal norms are one form.

Theoretical developments in criminology since World War II have extended the perspectives formulated at the end of the thirties.[25] An important change in recent years is the attention that has been given to the legal process. Such subjects as formulation of criminal law, law enforcement, administration of criminal justice, criminal behavior patterns, and social reaction to crime are built on the thesis that crime is a socially defined phenomenon as contained specifically in the legal codes.[26] Crime is being viewed as part of the conflict and change in the social, political, and economic structure of society.

The most significant development since 1970 is a critical-Marxist criminology following the system of philosophical analysis devised by Karl Marx (1818–1883), with which we can critically examine our common assumptions about crime. Crime is understood in relation to the historical development and contemporary operation of capitalist society. This is the criminology that will guide our understanding of crime in this book.

RESEARCH METHODS AND MODES OF INQUIRY

Criminologists examining their methodology — their techniques, rules, and methods for studying crime — try to make their work less complex by dividing it into general categories, the traditional "research methods" of criminology. Very generally the kinds of methodologies used in studying crime are: (1) statistics on the characteristics of crime; (2) statistics on traits and conditions of criminals; (3) the individual case study of criminals; (4) the study of the criminal in the natural setting of the everyday world; and (5) the experimental method.[27]

Actual research is much more complicated than these categorical methods indicate. All research is essentially a process, requiring choices at many stages during the research. The methods are many and are combined in various ways during the research. Methodological decisions are made on such diverse matters as the kind of research case to be used, the type of research population and sample, the sources of data to be collected, the techniques for gathering data, and the methods for analyzing the research findings.

The design that organizes the research is just the first problem in criminological work; research findings must be related to a body of theory. At all stages there is an interplay between theory and research. In fact, it is often the theory of crime chosen by the researcher that determines which methods will be used in the research.

Ultimately, however, the student of crime has to work with much broader assumptions than those needed for research about ontology (the philosophical study of *being*) and epistemology (study of *knowledge*). That is, the criminologist is constantly faced with assumptions (ideas assumed true without proof, consciously recognized or not) about reality and the grounds of knowledge which shape the accumulating facts about crime. What we know as criminology is formed more by such assumptions, including our own values and ideology, than by the concrete methods of research: the research methods are inextricably linked to the criminologist's notions about the world.

When we discuss research on crime, we can divide the different approaches into more general forms, *modes of inquiry* (which I will explain) containing assumptions about research and reality: (1) the positivist, (2) the social constructionist, (3) the phenomenological, and (4) the critical. From the last we will develop a critical understanding of crime.[28]

Positivism

The positivist mode of inquiry follows a simple epistemology that absolutely separates the knower from the known, assuming that objectivity is possible, that they can judge by facts or observable phenomena, unhampered by the emotion or bias of subjectivity, because they believe that an order exists independent of the observer. The observer's cognitive apparatus (intellectual ways of getting knowledge about perceptions or ideas) ideally does not affect the nature of what is known. With enough knowledge, accumulated systematically, the scientist could predict future events and control their occurrence. An orderly universe could be established by knowledge and by manipulating the external world.

With their mechanistic conception about how social facts are related (entirely by physical and material laws), positivists usually present their explanations as governed by causality, the connection between cause and effect. They do not examine, nor do they even consider the philosophical assumptions by which the observer operates.[29] Nor do they accept that the explanation depends upon the kinds of things investigated, or that it requires describing the unique context in which every event occurs. Likewise, positivists refuse to recognize that to assess and make statements about human actions is to engage in a moral endeavor; they see their activity as "value free," free from the biases of the observer.

The intellectual failure of positivism is that it is not reflective — the positivist makes little or no attempt to examine or even question the metaphysics or methods of inquiry, to turn the activity of explanation back upon itself, to be introspective, looking inside the self.

Positivist thought has also failed politically because it accepts the status quo, the way things are. Positivists do not question the established order, just as they do not examine scientific assumptions. The official reality, the ideology that emphasizes bureaucratic organization, modern technology, centralized authority, and scientific control, is the one within which positivists operate and which they accept, support, and take for granted.[30]

Criminologists who have adhered to positivism consequently have devoted almost all their efforts to established interests. Traditionally they have concentrated on the violator of criminal law, not the legal system itself.[31] They usually try to solve the crime problem by changing the lawbreaker, not the legal system. Recently some criminologists, realizing that law itself is problematic, open to question, have turned to the study of the law.[32] But for the most part even these studies have been based on the positivist mode of thought.

Following the positivist mode of inquiry, criminologists have developed their own wisdom about social and political life, but their research

Drawing by Niculae Asciu; © 1974 The New Yorker Magazine, Inc.

and theory have done little more than provide a rationale for the established order, the status quo. No social theory that would allow for human liberation from oppression of any kind has been found, and it now seems that positivistic thought cannot provide liberating conceptions of human existence. Instead, we must turn to alternative modes of inquiry.

Social Constructionism

Social constructionist thought begins with a recognition of philosophical idealism, an ontology that questions the existence of an objective reality apart from the individual's imagination. Social constructionists assume that objects cannot exist *independently* of our minds; that they are ideas, not things; and that any reality is important only as long as it can be perceived. The epistemological assumption is that observations are based on mental *constructions* instead of raw apprehension of the physical world. The social constructionist is primarily interested not in the correspondence between "objective reality" and observation, but in that between observation and the utility of such observation in understanding our own subjective, multiple worlds.

Following these assumptions, the social scientist's constructs have to be founded upon the world created by social actors. Alfred Schutz conceptualized the problem: "The constructs of the social sciences are, so to speak, constructs of the second degree, that is, constructs of the constructs made by the actors on the social scene, whose behavior the social scientist has to observe and explain in accordance with the procedural rules of his science."[33] The world that is important to the social constructionist, then, is the one created by the social actions of human beings by interaction and communication with others. This *social reality* involves the social meanings and the products of the subjective world of everyday life.[34]

The social constructionist mode of inquiry is a major advance over positivist thought in the crucial area of reflexivity, in turning back to consider its own techniques. The social constructionist questions the process by which we know, instead of taking it for granted; reflects on our activity as observer, using to advantage the social and personal character of observation. But this reflexivity does not extend to a political position, and possible political action, a shortcoming inherent in this mode of inquiry.

Moreover, social constructionist thought generally concentrates on the world of meanings created by social actors. It emphasizes, especially in ethnomethodological studies (which are meant to describe the actual world, the environment, of social actors), the construction of social order. Such concentration often ignores a world of events and structures independent of the social actor's consciousness. This is the conservative side of social constructionist thought, making it inadequate for a critical perspective.

Therefore, it is often necessary to revise or reject the world as some social actors conceive it. Social constructionists do give us the beginnings for examining multiple versions of reality, which might allow us to transcend the official reality, and ultimately, our current existence. But they fail to provide a yardstick for judging whether one reality has more good in it than another. Social relativism (refusing to take a value position) prevents a critical understanding of the social world.

The social constructionist perspective, however, has given new vitality to the study of crime. Departing significantly from positivist studies, social constructionists have turned to the questionable legal order. Crime and other stigmatized or banned behaviors are examined first as categories created and imposed upon some persons by others.[35] Crime exists because the society constructs and applies the label *crime*. Criminal law, too, is not separate from society, but is itself a construction, created by those who are in power. The administration of justice is a human social activity that is constructed as various legal agents interpret and impose their order on those they select for processing. The social reality of crime is thus a procedure whereby conceptions of crime are constructed, criminal laws are established and administered, and behaviors are developed following these definitions of crime.[36]

Social constructionist thought stops here, although, to be sure, it is critical in its own way.[37] It offers the libertarian ideal that individuals should not be controlled by others, that people must be free to pursue their potential, that social order is created for political purposes. Nevertheless, it does not show what a new world should look like, and without such an image our understanding of reality lacks a critical perspective.

Phenomenology

Phenomenological inquiry departs markedly from the positivistic and social constructionist inquiries in its basic intention. The other modes of thought are aimed at explaining social life, but phenomenological thought begins by examining how we understand the world. Explanation as a form of thought is itself examined.

Phenomenologists, though they differ considerably among themselves, generally agree that our knowledge of the physical world comes from our experiences. But, they continue, when we talk about the physical world we are not limited by our actual experiences; we are able to talk about *possible* experiences, and so we alter our perception of things in the world. As long as a physical object exists in the world, it is possible to perceive it. We are capable of perceiving the essence of things.

Phenomenological thought attempts to transcend commonly assumed knowledge about the world and our place in it. It allows us to remove ourselves momentarily from our concrete experiences. The German philosopher Martin Heidegger describes this kind of thought: "Meditative thinking demands of us not to cling one-sidedly to a single idea, nor to run down a one-track course of ideas. Meditative thinking demands of us that we engage ourselves with what at first sight does not go together at all."[38] A compartment that enables us to keep open the meaning hidden in the world, in the arrangements of modern society, is described by Heidegger as "openness to the mystery." By this openness and a "releasement toward things," in meditative thinking, we seek our true nature. And, Heidegger writes, "They grant us the possibility of dwelling in the world in a totally different way. They promise us a new ground and foundation upon which we can stand and endure in the world of technology without being imperiled by it."[39]

It is in the transcendental thinking of the phenomenologists that we find the inspiration for moving beyond the conventional wisdom of the age, including our contemporary knowledge of crime and the legal order. Instead of *reifying* the social order (treating it as if it had concrete existence), or giving an account of ordered existence, the movement is toward transcending our experience. This is a necessary step as we begin to act in a way that will demystify the social world. The primary interest is not in developing a new social science (still a reified science) but in creating a new existence, free of all reifications.

Phenomenological thought by itself, however, is incomplete for attaining our objectives. Although it provides a drastic and necessary move beyond the other modes of thought, it lacks the critical edge that would allow us to truly transcend the present, in life as in mind.[40] Phenomenology does make us question the assumptions by which we know and by which we live. This is its major achievement. But we need a philosophy that will allow us to actively change the existing order. We thus turn to the development of a critical philosophy.

A Critical Mode of Inquiry

A critical mode of inquiry is a radical philosophy — one that goes to the roots of our lives, to the foundations and the fundamentals, to the essentials of consciousness.[41] In rooting out presuppositions we are able to assess every actual and possible experience. The operation is one of demystification, removing the myths created by the official reality. Conventional experience is revealed as a reification of the social order, exposing the underside of official reality.

The classical philosophical tradition holds the attitude that ideas are to inform and shape actions, that life is to be enlightened by thought. Conceived in this way, thought itself is necessarily critical. In fact, the chief characteristic of thinking, Hannah Arendt writes in an essay on thinking and moral considerations, is that it interrupts all doing, all ordinary activity.[42] We are momentarily removed from our worldly associations; it is as though we entered into a different existance. Arendt adds that "thinking, the quest for meaning — rather than the scientist's thirst for knowledge for its own sake — can be felt to be 'unnatural,' as though men, when they begin to think, engage in some activity contrary to the human condition."[43] She concludes that only with thought that is aimed toward ideals (with the desiring of love, wisdom, beauty, and justice) are we prepared with a kind of thought that promotes a moral existence. Only when we are filled with what Socrates called *eros*, a love that desires what is not, can we find what is good.

Without critical thought we are bound to the only form of social life we know — the current one. We are not then free to choose a better life; our only activity further supports the system in which we are bound. Our current cultural and social arrangements, supported as they are by the bureaucratic-technological system of production and distribution, are a threat to individual freedom — including the freedom to know that this system is oppressive and may be altered. Such a system can keep opposition from growing within it. In aspiring to the rewards that the system holds out to us, we are unable to consider an alternative existence. Such is the message of Herbert Marcuse in his discussion of the "one-dimensional" character of our present reality.[44] Only by negating the present system can we experience something else.

A critical philosophy lets us break with the ideology of the age, for built into critical thinking is the ability to think negatively. This *dialectical* form of thought, by being able to entertain an alternative, allows us to question current experience and better understand what exists.[45] Instead of merely looking for an objective reality, we are interested in negating the established order, which will make us better able to understand what we experience. By applying this dialectic in our thought we can comprehend and surpass the present.

Moreover, dialectical thinking moves us to reconstruct our lives. In order to reject something we must have some idea of what things could be like. Here a critical philosophy must ultimately develop a Marxist perspective. In the Marxian notion of the authentic human being we are provided with a concrete image of the possible. Current realities are judged by how much they alienate human beings. The imagery is transcendental, rising above common thought to attain what is natural to us by removing that which obstructs our lives. It is in contradicting an oppressive existence, between what exists and what is authentically human, that we understand our reality and collectively act to bring about a liberating existence.

To think in a Marxian fashion is to be genuinely critical, requiring the fullest extent of our critical resources. In developing our critical capacities, we are rediscovering and recreating a form and body of thought grounded in Marxian analysis. Marxism is the one philosophy of our time that takes as its focus the oppression produced by a capitalist society. It is the one form of analysis that is historically specific, that is related to concrete time and place, and locates the problems of the age in relations between the economic classes.[46] A Marxist critique provides, most important, a form of inquiry that allows us to transcend in thought and action that kind of existence.

Contrary to both liberal and orthodox interpretations, Marxism is highly creative thought, open to the interpretation of each generation. And with the changes in capitalism itself, from industrial capitalism to advanced monopoly capitalism, new and critical readings of Marx are necessary. Critical thought makes possible a new understanding of Marx in each age, which is also to say, a new understanding of Marx makes critical thought possible.

CRIMINOLOGY AND CRIME CONTROL

The study of crime must begin with a critical understanding of criminal law and crime control. Because the law *officially* defines behavior as criminal, it is necessary to examine how criminal law works in society. Early students of criminal law focused on sociological jurisprudence, utilizing a particular notion of social order. Gradually a criminology developed that further mystified the actual operation of the criminal law. We gain an understanding of the criminal law — and the definition of crime — as we critically examine these perspectives. A critical understanding of criminal law will allow us eventually to develop a Marxist theory of crime.

Sociological Jurisprudence

The study of criminal law had its origin in a legal philosophy known as "sociological jurisprudence." Around 1900, several legal scholars began to consider the social nature of law. An Austrian, Eugen Ehrlich, in particular distinguished between the "positive law" and the "living law."[47] The positive law can be effective only when it corresponds to the living law; that is, when legal codes are based on underlying social norms, or real life. In other words, law is to be understood as part of the social order.

Similar thoughts developed a little later in the United States. The early sociologists incorporated law into their theoretical frameworks. E. A. Ross referred to law as "the most specialized and highly furnished engine of control employed by society."[48] Lester F. Ward, advocate of government control and social planning, foresaw a day when legislation would undertake to solve "questions of social improvement, the amelioration of the condition of all the people, the removal of whatever privations may still remain, and the adoption of means to the positive increase of the social welfare, in short the organization of human happiness."[49] The possibility of social reform, by legal means available to the state, was also emphasized by Albion W. Small.[50]

The early sociologists' ideas directly influenced the school of legal philosophy that developed into a major force in legal thought — sociological jurisprudence. Roscoe Pound, its principal figure, drew from those sociologists when he asserted that law should be studied as a social institution.[51] Pound thought of law as a specialized form of social control that brings pressure to bear on each person "in order to constrain him to do his part in upholding civilized society and to deter him from antisocial conduct, that is, conduct at variance with the postulates of social order."[52]

Pound argued that law is not merely a complex of rules and procedures, and called for the study of "law in action," not law in the books. For some purposes it may be useful to view law as separate from society, developing according to its own internal logic and proceeding along its own lines. But law also simultaneously reflects society and influences it. In a social sense, law is both social product and social force. Pound's juristic approach, however, took law as both a product and a force in a very special way. In jurisprudence, law as a social product reflects the consciousness of the whole society. This *consensus* model in criminal law holds that: "The state of criminal law continues to be — as it should — a decisive reflection of the social consciousness of a society. What kind of conduct an organized community considers, at a given time, sufficiently condemnable to impose official sanctions, impairing the life, liberty, or property of the offender, is a barometer of the moral and social thinking of a community."[53]

At the heart of Pound's sociological jurisprudence was his theory of interests, according to which the law functions for socially worthwhile purposes. He looked upon law as reflecting the needs of the well-ordered society:

> For the purpose of understanding the law of today I am content to think of law as a social institution to satisfy social wants — the claims and demands involved in the existence of civilized society — by giving effect to as much as we may with the least sacrifice, so far as such wants may be satisfied or such claims given effect by an ordering of human conduct through politically organized society. For present purposes I am content to see in legal history the record of a continually wider recognizing and satisfying of human wants or desires through social control; a more embracing and more effective securing of social interests; a continually more complete and effective elimination of waste and precluding of friction in human enjoyment of the goods of existence — in short, a continually more efficacious social engineering.[54]

The interests Pound had in mind would maintain and, ultimately, improve the capitalist social order. His was a teleological as well as a consensus theory: some interests must be fulfilled for the good of the whole society, and these are to be achieved through law; only the right law could develop in a civilized society.

According to the theory of interests, therefore, the legal order is created in society to regulate and adjust the conflicting desires and claims. Law provides the framework within which individual and group life is carried on, according to the postulates of social order. A legal historian writes, "The law defines the extent to which it will give effect to the interests which it recognizes, in the light of other interests and of the possibilities of effectively securing them through law; it also devises means for securing those that are recognized and prescribes the limits within which those means may be employed."[55] The law, we are told, is an instrument that controls interest according to the requirements of social order.

Sociological jurisprudence has greatly influenced legal philosophy. Pound's assumptions have been accepted by sociologists, but few have attempted to revise his theory of interests. Any revision has to move beyond these pluralist assumptions, critically examining how the capitalist class imposes its interests on the society, in spite of some diversity of interests among elite groups. Then too, we have to consider law as a consequence of class interests, not merely an instrument that functions outside of interests to resolve conflicts between them. Criminal law is an instrument of the capitalist state and represents the interest of the capitalist class.

Legalistic Criminology

Legalistic definitions of crime — determined by the legal codes — have dominated criminology. The importance of the legal notion was dramatized in the early thirties when Jerome Michael and Mortimer J. Adler reported on the state of knowledge in criminology.[56] Critical of past research on the etiology (causes) of criminal behavior, they suggested that it was the criminal law that defined criminology's scope and boundaries:

> If crime is merely an instance of conduct which is proscribed by the criminal code, it follows that the criminal law is the formal cause of crime. That does not mean that the law produces the behavior which it prohibits, although . . . the enforcement or administration of the criminal law may be one of the factors which influence human behavior, it means only that the criminal law gives behavior its quality of criminality.[57]

Michael and Adler observed that "the most precise and least ambiguous definition of crime is that which defines it as behavior which is prohibited by the criminal code" and, further, that "this is the only possible definition of crime."[58]

A strong adherent of legally defining crime was a sociologist trained in the law, Paul W. Tappan. Though he advocated explaining an offender's behavior, Tappan warned, "Our definitions of crime cannot be rooted in epithets, in minority value judgments or prejudice, or in loose abstractions."[59] He recognized that a person is a criminal only because his or her behavior has been defined as criminal by the state. Answering his own question, "Who is the criminal?" Tappan went so far as to propose that "only those are criminals who have been adjudicated as such by the courts."[60]

Several criminologists have since called for a legalistic conception of crime. C. Ray Jeffery, reviewing diverse definitions of crime, suggested that crime should be studied within the framework of the criminal law, from which we could ascertain under what conditions behavior becomes defined as criminal and how legal codes interact with other normative (standard-imposing) systems.[61]

Vold also illustrated how important criminal law is to the study of crime, observing the dual problem of explanation in criminology:

> Crime always involves both human behavior (acts) and the judgment of definitions (laws, customs, mores) of fellow human beings as to whether specific behavior is appropriate and permissible, or is improper and forbidden. Crime and criminality lie in the area of behavior that is considered improper and forbidden. There is, therefore, always a dual problem of explanation — that of accounting for the behavior, as behavior, and equally important, accounting for the definitions by which specific behavior comes to be considered as crime or non-crime.[62]

Considering this dual question further, Austin T. Turk wrote that the distinctly criminological problem is the study of criminality.[63] He argued that the criminal status of people and behavior, and an explanation of such criminality, is the only explanation of crime. Because the legal definition of behavior determines what is regarded as criminal, the criminologist has to study how criminal law is formulated and administered.[64]

Sociology of Criminal Law

Sociologists and other social scientists have become interested in making the law a subject of scientific, empirical research. Social science and law have converged in a movement that defines and combines their mutual interests.[65] To ensure the exchange of ideas between the disciplines attending to legal matters, the Law and Society Association was formed in 1964. In the first issue of its journal, the editor described the new convergence, remarking that "during the past decade, each of the social sciences has found it necessary to face legal policy issues of highest relevance to the disciplines themselves and to the society as a whole."[66]

The research resulting from this convergence and from recent research in criminology form the basis for the sociology of criminal law, which has gathered a body of empirical research in a relatively short time. Most of the research is dominated by the positivistic mode of thought. The legal system is taken for granted, and research is aimed at explaining how the system operates, with studies on how laws are formulated, enforced, and administered.[67] Few ask why law exists, whether law is indeed necessary, or what a just system would look like. If they consider the value of justice, it is the equitability of the system that interests them, not whether the system's very existence is just. They may suggest changes in particular laws, but the legal system itself is to remain intact.[68] And they may point to inadequacies in the administration of justice, but their prescriptions for change are simply more technical and efficient procedures.

Even the research that departs from the positivistic mode avoids critically analyzing the present system. Social constructionist thought, as found in ethnomethodological studies, may suggest that the administration of criminal law consists of the construction of official reality by those in positions of power.[69] But this research fails to help us reach a position from which we could analyze reality by holding up to it a higher ideal of human justice. A critique of the legal order in advanced capitalist society is missing from the sociology of criminal law. Without an image of what could be, that sociology has no possibility of understanding even the current reality.

The theoretical perspective that sociology does have accepts the legal order, and treats law as the realization of rationality. Furthermore, the legal order can be strengthened and made more efficient by applying scientific methods. In an essay on the sociology of law, Philip Selznick writes that "legal reasoning cannot but accept the authority of scientifically validated conclusions regarding the nature of man and his institutions. Therefore, inevitably, sociology and every other social science have a part in the legal order."[70] This sociology — narrowly construed as the scientific study of law — not only studies law but supports the legal order; their fates are tied together.

As presently conceived and practiced, a sociology of criminal law cannot break out of the established ideology and ask critical questions about the legal order. It can only confirm the order that is and exacerbate the problems of society.

Contemporary Criminology

Criminology today, including the theories and practices of what is to be done about crime, supports current institutions at the expense of human freedom and social revolution.[71] Criminologists ask the question: "What causes crime?" The answer is usually sought in the study of the "criminal." That is, the sources of crime are believed to be located in the person who violates the law, not in the society that produces criminal activity. This emphasis has meant that legal order and political theory have been ignored. To critically understand and question the current society has traditionally remained outside the scientific and ideological interests of criminologists.

Thus, contemporary criminology serves the interests of the capitalist system. By pursuing a narrow scientific model and following their own unexamined assumptions, criminologists find their interests tied to those of the state and the capitalist ruling class. It is argued that the term *criminology* "should be used to designate a body of *scientific* knowledge about crime."[72] This definition of criminology is closely associated with attempts to control crime. In fact, criminology is strengthened by practical applications in the field of corrections. As Stanton Wheeler writes, referring to the common interests of corrections and criminology: "The movement toward professionalism in the practicing fields should lead to an increased number of competent and skilled practitioners and the recognition of need for more systematic research on crime and its control. Increased public attention to problems of delinquency and crime, particularly as reflected in increased budgets for prevention and research efforts, may attract a larger number of social scientists to problems of delinquency and crime."[73]

Moreover, crime control and scientific prediction go hand in hand. Science and politics are united: "If control and prediction in experimentation are integral goals of research and, regardless of the substantive area, if analysis proceeds by means of the scientific method, then we may include within the scope of criminology any correctional research that embraces these goals and this method."[74] Scientific criminology and the state's correctional aims are mutually supportive.

We are told in criminology textbooks that not only is criminology a body of verified principles about crime but that "criminology is concerned with the immediate application of knowledge to programs of social order and crime control."[75] We are informed that theoretical knowledge is increased in the efforts at social control. A critical criminology would depart significantly from the control interests of current scientific criminology.

The theories and practices of criminologists tend to take the capitalist system of institutions for granted.[76] Furthermore, criminal behavior is regarded as being the result of such problems in the environment as lack of opportunity and improper socialization. The proposed solutions call for ameliorating these conditions. As the social science staff of the National Commission on Violence wrote on a solution to crimes of violence: "The perspective advocated here accepts the present system as the framework within which changes should be made. It does not call for total change; it does not denounce major institutions in their entirety. It argues, rather, that there are significent defects in the operating social insitutions."[77]

Social amelioration is combined with belief in rationalizing crime control, bringing to it modern, efficient techniques. Law enforcement is to be improved, and the administration of justice is to be made more efficient. The liberal has faith that crime will be reduced by spending more money, conducting more research, and developing new technology.[78]

The conventional criminologist, following the ideology dominant in the capitalist system, turns to the capitalist state as the ultimate agency to control crime. Therefore, the state, with the assistance of its "experts" (especially criminologists and correctional workers), is to intervene in the criminal process by instituting not only various forms of imprisonment, but a host of programs to rehabilitate and reintegrate the offender into the dominant society.[79] During these efforts, the social and economic system is to be protected and preserved.

Crime control, being mostly a social problem, may appear to be beyond the scientists' skills. Indeed, many aspects of the problem do fall outside their scope. The experience of science in the military, however, suggests that a fruitful collaboration can be established between criminal justice officials on one hand and engineers, physicists, economists, and social and behavioral scientists on the other. In military research organizations these different professionals, working with military officers in interdisciplinary teams, have attacked defense problems in new ways and have provided insights that were new even to those with long military experience. Similar developments appear possible in criminal justice.[80]

The technological and ameliorative approaches to crime control, however, are being reinforced by a new emphasis on punishment. Theories and policies are being proposed that seek to control crime without drastically altering the established order, returning to punishment as the appropriate response to crime. While Marxian theory begins to provide a critique of the crisis in capitalist society, creating a politics as well, punitive theory and practice seek intellectual and policy solutions attempting to preserve the dying order.[81]

Hence, much current research by sociologists and criminologists is aimed at establishing "certainty" and "swiftness" of punishment as indispensable in deterring crime.[82] Legal and philosophical works also argue that the purpose of the criminal sanction is to deter criminal acts, which is accomplished by administering punishment for noncompliance to the legal code of the existing order.[83] Overall these works are to make deterrence (*punishment*) "morally tolerable." Although the traditional split between liberal and conservative may yet distinguish responses on some issues, when it comes to crime control it is the practical possibility of deterring crime that characterizes the modern debate. As the "rehabilitation" ideal proves itself bankrupt in practice, liberals and conservatives alike (all within the capitalist hegemony or dominance) resort to any form of crime control that seems effective in preserving the established order.

This kind of criminology offers us a defense of punishment. But, more to the point, it is a defense of punishment that is to be applied within our unique historical context, in protecting social order based on late capitalist development. Punishment becomes the solution when vision is confined within the problem itself. With ideas such as these, combined with the criminological research that seemingly gives a semblance of support, we have the construction of a reality that accepts the social order as it stands. Rather than an alternative order, based on a different conception of human nature, political economy, and social justice, we are presented with schemes that merely justify further repression within the established order. The solutions being offered can only exacerbate the conditions of our existence. We need, in clear contrast, a critical understanding of crime and control of crime in contemporary society.

A CRITICAL-MARXIST CRIMINOLOGY

The critical-Marxist criminology that is appearing today departs sharply from the dominant criminology.[84] This new critical criminology — to be developed in this book — is founded on the Marxist approach to social reality, understanding social life in relation to the underlying mode of production and class struggle. This criminology mainly focuses on the relation of the economic system to the production of crime. A materialist analysis of criminality and crime control is required.

Breaking sharply with traditional criminology, the new criminology challenges the dominant assumptions that criminologists and the agents of crime control have long followed. This challenge begins with the definition of crime itself. In contrast to the traditional definition, "Radicals see as a starting point the notion of human rights to self-determination, dignity, food and shelter, and freedom from exploitation, or criminogenic systems, such as imperialism, racism, capitalism and sexism, because they promote inherently repressive relationships and social injury."[85] The solution to crime is thus predicated on transforming society, on constructing socialist political and economic institutions. In its broadest sense, the new criminology involves a move toward redefining crime and criminal justice.

During the early part of this century in the United States, the literary and political journal Masses *waged an assault against the cultural and economic establishment, breaking down the assumptions on which conventional life rested. The journal was allied with the socialist movement and opened the way for radical changes in artistic tastes and political practice. The artists and intellectuals who worked on* Masses *were committed to shaping art and criticism into instruments of political consciousness. Art Young, an artist who grew up in a small Wisconsin town, critically portrayed in* Masses *the workings of the capitalist system. His drawing of the mammon of capitalism, appearing in 1912 and shown above, depicts the struggle for food, shelter, and clothing under capitalism. Life under the capitalist order generated fear of the lack of the necessities of life and fostered the worship of money. Art and social criticism are revolutionary forms in the struggle for a socialist society.*

According to critical criminology, as capitalist society is further threatened by its own contradictions, as capitalism continues to develop, criminal justice is increasingly used in the attempt to maintain domestic order. To remove the oppression of capitalist conditions would mean a radical change in our present class structure and in our present political economy. The crimes of those who profit from the present system, particularly those of criminal syndicates, of political conspiracy by government officials, and of American corporations in business operations, are the product of a capitalist society. In the view of Marxist criminologists, whether criminal law and law enforcement are directed against the working class or against those who profit from the political and economic arrangements, the purpose of capitalist criminal justice is to protect and strengthen the capitalist system.

As we work toward developing a new criminology we will gain an understanding of crime in capitalist society by covering the diverse facets of crime: from the legal system in theory to the law in action, from the theories of criminologists to the social reality of crime, from the "criminal's" world to that of legal authority, from the traditional approaches of crime control to the radical notions of social existence. We can do this by recognizing the nature of the society in which we live, the character of our times, and our own place in the past, present, and future history of the United States.[86]

The success of this venture will be in our ability, yours and mine, to examine our common experiences critically. An understanding of crime will be realized as we start to act in ways that give meaning to our experience. Our imaginations will be altered as we change our ways of thinking and our ways of living. In this manner we will begin to create a critical life.

NOTES

1. Richard Quinney, "There's a Lot of Folks Grateful to the Lone Ranger: With Some Notes on the Rise and Fall of American Criminology," *The Insurgent Sociologist,* 4 (Fall 1973), pp. 56–64.
2. A more extensive discussion of the development of criminology is found in Richard Quinney and John Wildeman, *The Problem of Crime: A Critical Introduction to Criminology,* 2nd ed. (New York: Harper & Row, 1977), Chapter 3.
3. Cesare Beccaria, *Essay on Crime and Punishment,* 1st American ed. (New York: Stephen Gould, 1809); Jeremy Bentham, *An Introduction to the Principle of Morals and Legislation,* corrected ed. (Oxford: Clarendon Press, 1823); Coleman Phillipson, *Three Criminal Law Reformers: Beccaria, Bentham, Romilly* (London: J. M. Dent, 1923).
4. Willem A. Bonger, *Introduction to Criminology,* trans. Emil Van Loo (London: Methuen, 1936). Also see C. Berneldo de Quirós, *Modern Theories of Criminality,* trans. Alfonso de Salvio (Boston: Little, Brown, 1911).
5. Yale Levin and Alfred R. Lindesmith, "English Ecology and Criminology of the Past Century," *Journal of Criminal Law, Criminology and Police Science,* 27 (March-April 1937), pp. 801–816.
6. T. S. Simey and M. B. Simey, *Charles Booth, Social Scientist* (London: Oxford University Press, 1960), p. 4.
7. Floyd N. House, *The Development of Sociology* (New York: McGraw-Hill, 1936), pp. 331–337.

8. Ellen Elizabeth Guillot, *Social Factors in Crime: As Explained by American Writers of the Civil War and Post Civil War Period,* published Ph.D Dissertation (Philadelphia: University of Pennsylvania, 1943), p. 172.

9. Quoted in Charles Goring, *The English Convict: A Statistical Study* (London: His Majesty's Stationery Office, 1913), p. 13.

10. Quoted in Quirós, *Modern Theories of Criminality,* p. 16.

11. George B. Vold, *Theoretical Criminology* (New York: Oxford University Press, 1958), pp. 35–36.

12. Arthur MacDonald, *Criminology* (New York: Funk and Wagnalls, 1892); August Draehms, *The Criminal, His Personnel and Environment: A Scientific Study* (New York: Macmillan, 1900); Philip A. Parson, *Crime and the Criminal* (New York: Alfred A. Knopf, 1926).

13. E. A. Hooton, *The American Criminal: An Anthropological Study* (Cambridge: Harvard University Press, 1939); William H. Sheldon, *Varieties of Delinquent Youth* (New York: Harper, 1949); Sheldon and Eleanor Glueck, *Physique and Delinquency* (New York: Harper, 1956).

14. Goring, *The English Convict,* p. 18.

15. Henry Goddard, *Human Efficiency and Levels of Intelligence* (Princeton: Princeton University Press, 1920); Carl Murchison, *Criminal Intelligence* (Worcester, Mass.: Clark University Press, 1926); Simon H. Tulchin, *Intelligence and Crime* (Chicago: University of Chicago Press, 1939).

16. See Michael Hakeem, "A Critique of the Psychiatric Approach to Crime and Correction," *Law and Contemporary Problems,* 23 (Autumn 1958), pp. 650–682.

17. Frances A. Kellor, *Experimental Sociology* (New York: Macmillan, 1901), pp. ix–x.

18. Arthur C. Hall, *Crime and Its Relation to Social Progress* (New York: Columbia University Press, 1902), p. xi.

19. Robert E. Park, ed., *The City* (Chicago: University of Chicago Press, 1925).

20. Frederick M. Thrasher, *The Gang* (Chicago: University of Chicago Press, 1927).

21. Clifford R. Shaw, *Delinquency Areas,* with Frederick M. Zorbaugh, Henry D. McKay, and Leonard S. Cottrell (Chicago: University of Chicago Press, 1929).

22. Edwin H. Sutherland, *Principles of Criminology,* 4th ed. (Philadelphia: J. B. Lippincott, 1947), pp. 6–7.

23. Robert K. Merton, "Social Structure and Anomie," *American Sociological Review,* 3 (October 1938), pp. 672–682. An excellent critique is found in Alex Thio, "A Critical Look at Merton's Anomie Theory," *Pacific Sociological Review,* 18 (April 1975), pp. 139–158.

24. Thorsten Sellin, *Culture Conflict and Crime* (New York: Social Science Research Council, 1938).

25. See, for example, Austin T. Turk, *Criminality and Legal Order* (Chicago: Rand McNally, 1969); Robert L. Burgess and Ronald L. Akers, "A Differential Association-Reinforcement Theory of Criminal Behavior," *Social Problems,* 14 (Fall 1966), pp. 128–147; Melvin L. DeFleur and Richard Quinney, "A Reformulation of Sutherland's Differential Association Theory and a Strategy for Empirical Verification," *Journal of Research in Crime and Delinquency,* 3 (January 1966), pp. 1–22; Daniel Glaser, "Criminality Theories and Behavioral Images," *American Journal of Sociology,* 61 (March 1956), pp. 433–444; Walter C. Reckless, Simon Dinitz, and Barbara Kay, "The Self Component in Potential Delinquency," *American Sociological Review,* 22 (October 1957), pp. 566–570; Marshall B. Clinard, ed., *Anomie and Deviant Behavior* (New York: Free Press, 1964); Albert K. Cohen, *Delinquent Boys* (New York: Free Press, 1955); Richard A. Cloward and Lloyd E. Ohlin, *Delinquency and Opportunity* (New York: Free Press, 1960).

26. For example, see Abraham S. Blumberg, *Criminal Justice* (Chicago: Quadrangle Books, 1967); Marshall B. Clinard and Richard Quinney, *Criminal Behavior Systems: A Typology,* 2nd ed. (New York: Holt, Rinehart and Winston, 1973); Donald R. Cressey, *Theft of the Nation* (New York: Harper & Row, 1969); Don C. Gibbons, *Changing the Lawbreaker* (Englewood Cliffs, N.J.: Prentice-Hall, 1965); Daniel Glaser, *The Effectiveness of a Prison and Parole System* (Indianapolis: Bobbs-Merrill, 1964); Edwin M. Lemert, *Human Deviance, Social Problems, and Social Control* (Englewood Cliffs, N.J.: Prentice-Hall,

1964); Arthur Niederhoffer, *Behind the Shield* (Garden City: Doubleday, 1967); Richard Quinney, ed., *Crime and Justice in Society* (Boston: Little, Brown, 1969); Jerome H. Skolnick, *Justice Without Trial* (New York: Wiley, 1966).

27. Edwin H. Sutherland and Donald R. Cressey, *Criminology*, 8th ed., (Philadelphia: J. P. Lippincott, 1970), pp. 61–70. Also see Donald R. Taft and Ralph W. England, Jr., *Criminology*, 4th ed. (New York: Macmillan, 1964), pp. 70–74.

28. The following discussion is adapted from my book *Critique of Legal Order: Crime Control in Capitalist Society* (Boston: Little, Brown, 1974), pp. 2–15.

29. See A. R. Louch, *Explanation and Human Action* (Berkeley: University of California Press, 1969).

30. See John H. Schaar, "Legitimacy in the Modern State," in Philip Green and Sanford Levinson, eds., *Power and the Community: Dissenting Essays in Political Science* (New York: Vintage Books, 1970), especially pp. 303–308.

31. See C. Ray Jeffery, "The Structure of American Criminological Thinking," *Journal of Criminal Law, Criminology and Police Science*, 46 (January 1956), pp. 658–672.

32. For example, see the research studies in Ronald L. Akers and Richard Hawkins, eds., *Law and Control in Society* (Englewood Cliffs, N.J.: Prentice-Hall, 1975); and Richard Quinney, ed., *Crime and Justice in Society* (Boston: Little, Brown, 1969).

33. Alfred Schutz, "Concept and Theory Formation in the Social Sciences," in Maurice Nathanson, ed., *Philosophy of the Social Sciences* (New York: Random House, 1963), p. 242.

34. See Alfred Schutz, *The Problem of Social Reality: Collected Papers, I* (The Hague: Martinus Nijhoff, 1962); and Peter L. Berger and Thomas Luckmann, *The Social Construction of Reality* (Garden City, N.Y.: Doubleday, 1966).

35. Howard S. Becker, *Outsiders: Studies in the Sociology of Deviance* (New York: Free Press, 1963).

36. Richard Quinney, *The Social Realty of Crime* (Boston: Little, Brown, 1970).

37. Critiques of the labeling perspective in sociology and criminology are found in Erich Goode, "On Behalf of Labeling Theory," *Social Problems*, 22 (June 1975), pp. 570–583; Dean Manders, "Labelling Theory and Social Reality: A Marxist Critique," *The Insurgent Sociologist*, 6 (Fall 1975), pp. 53–66; Peter K. Manning, "Deviance and Dogma," *British Journal of Criminology*, 15 (January 1975), pp. 1–20; Anthony C. Meade, "The Labeling Approach to Delinquency: State of the Theory as a Function of Method," *Social Forces*, 53 (September 1974), pp. 83–91; Prudence Rains, "Imputation of Deviance: A Retrospective Essay on the Labeling Perspective," *Social Problems*, 23 (October 1975), pp. 1–11; and Charles Wellford, "Labelling Theory and Criminology: An Assessment," *Social Problems*, 22 (February 1975), pp. 332–345.

38. Martin Heidegger, *Discourse on Thinking*, trans. John M. Anderson and E. Hans Freund (New York: Harper & Row, 1966) p. 53.

39. Ibid.

40. Critiques of the phenomenological perspective in sociology are found in Scott C. McNall and James C. M. Johnson, "The New Conservatives: Ethomethodologists, Phenomenologists, and Symbolic Interactionists," *The Insurgent Sociologist*, 5 (Spring 1975), pp. 49–66; and Alex Thio, "The Phenomenological Perspective of Deviance: Another Case of Class Bias," *The American Sociologist*, 9 (August 1974), pp. 146–149.

41. See Richard M. Zaner, *The Way of Phenomenology: Criticism as a Philosophical Discipline* (New York: Pegasus, 1970), especially pp. 112–113, 117, 196, and 203.

42. Hannah Arendt, "Thinking and Moral Considerations," *Social Research*, 38 (Autumn 1971), pp. 417–446.

43. Ibid., p. 424.

44. Herbert Marcuse, *One-Dimensional Man* (Boston: Beacon Press, 1964), p. 9.

45. Herbert Marcuse, *Reason and Revolution* (Boston: Beacon Press, 1960), pp. vii–xiv and 3–29.

46. Jean-Paul Sartre, *Search for a Method*, trans. Hazel E. Barnes (New York: Alfred A. Knopf, 1963). Also see David Horowitz, "Marxism and Its Place in Economic Science," *Berkeley Journal of Sociology*, 16 (1971–72), pp. 46–59; Bertell Ollman, *Alienation: Marx's Conception of Man in Capitalist Society* (London: Cambridge University Press, 1971).

47. Eugen Ehrlich, *The Fundamental Principle of the Sociology of the Law,* trans. W. Moll (Cambridge: Harvard University Press, 1936).

48. E. A. Ross, *Social Control* (New York: Macmillan, 1922), p. 106 (originally published in 1901).

49. Lester F. Ward, *Applied Sociology* (Boston: Ginn, 1906), p. 339.

50. Albion W. Small, *General Sociology* (Chicago: University of Chicago Press, 1925).

51. The relationship between early American sociologists and the development of Pound's sociological jurisprudence is discussed in Gilbert Geis, "Sociology and Jurisprudence: Admixture of Lore and Law," *Kentucky Law Journal,* 52 (Winter 1964), pp. 267–293. Also see Edwin M. Schur, *Law and Society* (New York: Random House, 1968), pp. 17–50.

52. Roscoe Pound, *Social Control Through Law* (New Haven: Yale University Press, 1942), p. 18. Earlier statements by Pound are found in Roscoe Pound, *An Introduction to the Philosophy of Law* (New Haven: Yale University Press, 1922); Roscoe Pound, *Outline of Lectures on Jurisprudence* (Cambridge: Harvard University Press, 1928).

53. Wolfgang Friedmann, *Law in a Changing Society* (Harmondsworth, England: Penguin Books, 1964), p. 143.

54. Pound, *An Introduction to the Philosophy of Law,* pp. 98–99.

55. George Lee Haskins, *Law and Authority in Early Massachusetts* (New York: Macmillan, 1960), p. 226.

56. Jerome Michael and Mortimer J. Adler, *Crime, Law and Social Science* (New York: Harcourt, Brace, 1933).

57. Ibid., p. 5.

58. Ibid., p. 2.

59. Paul W. Tappan, *Crime, Justice and Correction* (New York: McGraw-Hill, 1960), p. 10.

60. Paul W. Tappan, "Who Is the Criminal?" *American Sociological Review,* 12 (February 1947), p. 100.

61. C. Ray Jeffery, "The Structure of American Criminological Thinking," *Journal of Criminal Law, Criminology and Police Science,* 46 (January-February 1956), pp. 658–672.

62. Vold, *Theoretical Criminology* pp. v–vi. For recent discussions of these dual problems, behavior and definition, see David J. Bordua, "Recent Trends: Deviant Behavior and Social Control," *Annals of the American Academy of Political and Social Science,* 369 (January 1967), pp. 149–163; Jack P. Gibbs, "Conceptions of Deviant Behavior: the Old and the New," *Pacific Sociological Review,* 9 (Spring 1966), pp. 9–14; Ronald L. Akers, "Problems in the Sociology of Deviance: Social Definitions and Behavior," *Social Forces,* 46 (June 1968), pp. 455–465.

63. Austin T. Turk, "Prospects for Theories of Criminal Behavior," *Journal of Criminal Law, Criminology and Police Science,* 55 (December 1964), pp. 454–461.

64. Richard Quinney, "Crime in Political Perspective," *American Behavioral Scientist,* 8 (December 1964), pp. 19–22. This perspective is utilized and developed in Stuart L. Hills, *Crime, Power, and Morality: The Criminal-Law Process in the United States* (Scranton, Pa.: Chandler, 1971).

65. See Gilbert Geis, "Sociology, Criminology, and Criminal Law," *Social Problems,* 7 (Summer 1959), pp. 40–47.

66. Richard D. Schwartz, "From the Editor," *Law and Society Review,* 1 (November 1966), p. 6.

67. For a critique of this research, see Elliott Currie, "Sociology of Law: the Unasked Questions," *Yale Law Journal,* 81 (November 1971), pp. 134–147. The positivist position is defended in Donald J. Black, "The Boundaries of Legal Sociology," *Yale Law Journal,* 81 (May 1972), pp. 1086–1100.

68. Norval Morris and Gordon Hawkins, *The Honest Politician's Guide to Crime Control* (Chicago: University of Chicago Press, 1970); Herbert L. Packer, *The Limits of the Criminal Sanction* (Stanford: Stanford University Press, 1968).

69. An excellent critique on some of this research is found in Nanette J. Davis, *Sociological Constructions of Deviance: Perspectives and Issues in the Field* (Dubuque, Iowa: Wm. C. Brown, 1975). Also see: Alvin W. Gouldner, "The Sociologist as Partisan: Sociology and the Welfare State," *The American Sociologist,* 3 (May 1968), pp. 103–116; Alexander

Liazos, "The Poverty of the Sociology of Deviance: Nuts, Sluts, and Perverts," *Social Problems,* 20 (Summer 1972), pp. 103–120; Alex Thio, "Class Bias in the Sociology of Deviance," *The American Sociologist,* 8 (February 1973), pp. 1–12.

70. Philip Selznick, "The Sociology of Law," in Robert K. Merton, Leonard Broom, and Leonard S. Cottrell, Jr., eds., *Sociology Today* (New York: Basic Books, 1959), p. 126.

71. See Richard Quinney, "From Repression to Liberation: Social Theory in a Radical Age," in Robert A. Scott and Jack D. Douglas, eds., *Theoretical Perspectives on Deviance* (New York: Basic Books, 1972), pp. 317–341.

72. Marvin E. Wolfgang, "Criminology and the Criminologist," *Journal of Criminal Law, Criminology and Police Science,* 54 (June 1963), p. 155.

73. Stanton Wheeler, "The Social Sources of Criminology," *Sociological Inquiry,* 32 (Spring 1962), pp. 158–159.

74. Wolfgang, "Criminology and the Criminologist," p. 159.

75. Edwin H. Sutherland and Donald R. Cressey, *Criminology,* 9th ed. (Philadelphia: J. B. Lippincott, 1974), p. 3.

76. See David M. Gordon, ed., *Problems in Political Economy: An Urban Perspective* (Lexington, Mass.: D. C. Heath, 1971), pp. 9–11, 275–276.

77. *Crimes of Violence,* vol. 12, A Staff Report Submitted to the National Commission on the Causes and Prevention of Violence, Donald J. Mulvihill and Melvin M. Tumin, Co-Directors (Washington, D.C.: U.S. Government Printing Office, 1969), p. 727.

78. Such are the recommendations in the President's Commission on Law Enforcement and Administration of Justice, *The Challenge of Crime in a Free Society* (Washington, D.C.: U.S. Government Printing Office, 1967).

79. See, for example, the recommendations in National Commission on the Causes and Prevention of Violence, *Crimes of Violence,* vol. 12, pp. 753–787; and President's Commission on Law Enforcement and Administration of Justice, *The Challenge of Crime in a Free Society,* passim.

80. President's Commission on Law Enforcement and the Administration of Justice, *Science and Technology,* Task Force Report Prepared by the Institute for Defense Analysis (Washington, D.C.: U.S. Government Printing Office, 1967), p. 2.

81. For further documentation and discussion, see Richard Quinney, *Class, State and Crime: On the Theory and Practice of Criminal Justice* (New York: David McKay, 1977), chapter 1.

82. For example, Theodore G. Chiricos and Gordon P. Waldo, "Punishment and Crime: An Examination of Some Empirical Evidence," *Social Problems,* 18 (Fall 1970), pp. 220–217; Maynard L. Erickson and Jack P. Gibbs, "Specific Versus General Properties of Legal Punishments and Deterrence," *Social Science Quarterly,* 56 (December 1975), pp. 390–397; Charles H. Logan, "General Deterrent Effects of Imprisonment," *Social Forces,* 51 (September 1972), pp. 64–73; Matthew Silberman, "Toward a Theory of Criminal Deterrence," *American Sociological Review,* 41 (June 1976), pp. 442–461; Robert V. Stover and Don W. Brown, "Understanding Compliance and Non-Compliance with Law: The Contributions of Utility Theory," *Social Science Quarterly,* 56 (December 1975), pp. 363–375; Charles R. Tittle, "Crime Rates and Legal Sanctions," *Social Problems,* 16 (Spring 1969), pp. 409–423; Charles R. Tittle and Charles H. Logan, "Sanctions and Deviance: Evidence and Remaining Questions," *Law and Society Review,* 7 (Spring 1973), pp. 371–392.

83. Ernest van Den Haag, *Punishing Criminals: Concerning a Very Old and Painful Question* (New York: Basic Books, 1975); Norval Morris, *The Future of Imprisonment* (Chicago: University of Chicago Press, 1974); James Q. Wilson, *Thinking About Crime* (New York: Basic Books, 1975); Franklin E. Zimring and Gordon J. Hawkins, *Deterrence: The Legal Threat in Crime Control* (Chicago: University of Chicago Press, 1973).

84. The beginnings of a new criminology are found in, among other places, Barry Krisberg, *Crime and Privilege: Toward a New Criminology* (Englewood Cliffs, N.J.: Prentice-Hall, 1975); Tony Platt, "Prospects for a Radical Criminology in the United States," *Crime and Social Justice,* 1 (Spring-Summer 1974), pp. 2–10; Richard Quinney, ed., *Criminal Justice in America: A Critical Understanding* (Boston: Little, Brown, 1974); Charles E. Reasons, ed., *The Criminologist: Crime and the Criminal* (Pacific Palisades, Calif.: Goodyear,

1974); Ian Taylor, Paul Walton, and Jock Young, eds., *Critical Criminology* (London: Routledge & Kegan Paul, 1975).

85. Dorie Klein and June Kress, "Any Woman's Blues: A Critical Overview of Women, Crime and the Criminal Justice System," *Crime and Social Justice*, 5 (Spring-Summer 1976), p. 36. Also see Herman and Julia Schwendinger, "Defenders of Order or Guardians of Human Rights?" *Issues in Criminology*, 5 (Summer 1970), pp. 123–157; Clayton A. Hartjen, "Legalism and Humanism: A Reply to the Schwendingers," *Issues in Criminology*, 7 (Winter 1972), pp. 59–69; Gene Grabiner, "The Limits of Three Perspectives on Crime: 'Value-Free Science,' 'Objective Law,' and State 'Morality,' " *Issues in Criminology*, 8 (Spring 1973), pp. 35–48.

86. See Richard Quinney, "The Production of a Marxist Criminology," *Contemporary Crises*, 2 (July 1978), pp. 277–292.

Ideology and the Image of Crime

2

The social and economic order of capitalist society is secured in various ways. One of the traditional means is the coercive force of the state, including legal control. More subtly, capitalist society expands its influence by perpetuating a particular conception of reality. In establishing a bourgeois hegemony or dominance the order of society is legitimated or justified and secured.

Every society is founded on and supported by some ideology or body of ideas that establishes and justifies its order. But the ideology that prevails in capitalist society is inevitably that of the capitalist ruling class. Karl Marx observed about the ideological hegemony of the ruling class that the ruling ideas are exlusively those of that class.

> The ideas of the ruling class are in every epoch the ruling ideas, i.e. the class which is the ruling *material* force of society, is at the same time its ruling *intellectual* force. The class which has the means of material production at its disposal, has control at the same time over the means of mental production, so that thereby, generally speaking, the ideas of those who lack the means of mental production are subject to it. The ruling ideas are nothing more than the ideal expression of the dominant material relationships, the dominant material

relationships grasped as ideas; hence of the relationships which make the one class the ruling one, therefore, the ideas of its dominance.[1]

The ideology we are concerned about here develops in a capitalist society to secure domestic order. It is the ideology of crime, a primary form of control in capitalist society and an extension of the prevailing capitalist ideology. Criminal policy particularly reflects the capitalistic outlook and interests. The framework for dealing with domestic disorder is always that of the ruling class, which means that criminal policy is articulated or expressed within the capitalist framework; in subscribing to the general capitalist ideology, the public usually accepts the policies of the state. We are led to believe that the legal system is for the benefit of us all. The objective reality is quite different, however; the ideology serves the state and the ruling class, supporting capitalist economic interests.

It is usual in any discussion of crime to ignore the fact that our image of crime is a part of the prevailing ideology. Such lack of awareness supports the official capitalist picture of reality. If we are to rise above the official reality in thought and practice, we must recognize that the capitalist order is an ideology. Gabriel Kolko suggests, "The pervasiveness of this ideological power in American society and its measurable influence on mass culture, public values, and political opinions is the most visible reality of modern American life to the contemporary social analyst."[2] We can understand the social and economic order in the United States only when we recognize that the ideology is dominant and how it is related to the capitalist class.

What then is the ideology of crime in the United States? And how has it come to prevail in the society? First, it prevails simply because alternatives to the capitalist order are not perceivable within the present framework. Few suggest a society without a capitalist legal order. Second, the conscious efforts of the capitalist ruling class make it prevail. Through the various means of communication the ruling class and its bureaucracies systematically present the bourgeois ideology to the public by indoctrination.[3] By selectively presenting one view of reality, and by rejecting alternatives to it, the ruling class (with the assistance of organizations that serve it) present an ideology to the public as *the* reality.

Whether this representation is a deliberate effort to shape public consciousness or a general conception of the world, an ideological hegemony prevails. Although the public may qualify this ideology and adhere to it inconsistently, the ideology provides an abstract version of reality.[4] We model our lives and actions on the established vision of reality.

Only as we begin to develop a critical imagination — questioning the system — do we go beyond the dominant ideology. The purpose of a critical criminology is to demystify the capitalist ideology of crime, and to remove the aura of legitimacy from it. Then, examining our attitudes toward crime and control of crime, we begin to consider other possibilities. Likewise, as we investigate the image of crime presented in the official statistics on crime, we begin to understand the ideology of crime in the United States. We realize that we have been presented only one image of crime — and that another social reality of crime is possible in capitalist society.

INVESTIGATIONS OF CRIME

The public is often made dramatically aware of the problem that is crime. The alarm fluctuates from one period to another, each providing a new "crime wave."[5] How and why are these waves manufactured? The answer can be found in part in the interests of the classes that have something to gain from constructing a reality that includes aroused fear and anxiety about crime.

Concerted efforts to heighten public worries about crime are often managed by appointing committees to investigate some problem that authorities feel is currently an epidemic of crimes. Crusades on crime have been organized explicitly to promote a specific ideology of crime. Realities of crime are shaped by such periodic investigations.

In the last sixty years many crime commissions have been organized in communities for such investigations. In 1920, civic groups in Cleveland (headed by the Cleveland Bar Association) commissioned a survey of crime. The report concentrated on the machinery of criminal justice.[6] At about the same time the Chicago Crime Commission was established in response to a sensational case in which a four-man gang killed two armed guards carrying a factory payroll. To this day the Chicago Crime Commission is looking into crime and criminal justice. Both in the past and recently, other cities have established commissions to investigate aspects of the crime problem.[7]

New York City has seen innumerable investigations. One of the earliest organizations was the Society for the Prevention of Crime, started in 1878; it brewed a religious fervor under its leader, the Reverend Charles Henry Parkhurst. In the twenties, when a crime wave was the principal topic of conversation, the society engaged the public by sponsoring an essay contest on how best to reduce crime. Professor Franklin H. Giddings and a panel of prominent citizens awarded the first prize of $2,500 to a former police captain and the second prize of $500 to a police detective. The winners proposed to curb crime by criticizing the police commissioner, recommending that parole be eliminated, and suggesting that prisoners' heads be shaved and that they wear striped uniforms.

Committees and citizens' groups then concentrated on specific forms of crime and deviance in New York City, especially prostitution and organized crime. Criminal justice in the city received attention in the thirties when the Appellate Court appointed the Seabury Commission. Graft and corruption in the city government were exposed, but city officials, as could be expected, denounced and then ignored the investigation. Mayor Jimmy Walker responded by condemning those who called for further investigations as "slanderers of the fair name of the City we love."[8]

State as well as local crime commissions have investigated crime. In 1925 the Missouri Bar Association called a meeting of civic and business leaders to enlist their support for a statewide survey of crimes. Research covered law enforcement, prosecution, penal sanctions, and corrections.[9] Although they recommended changes in the criminal justice system, few were implemented. These proposals would have destroyed political machines in metropolitan areas. Corrupt and inefficient systems of criminal "justice," as well as crime, are not terribly serious when the interests of those who hold political power are at stake.

Similar commissions, with similar results, completed their tasks in other states during this period.[10] The conclusion we can draw from all these efforts is that crime commissions have been appointed primarily for political reasons. Politicians would like to give their constituents the idea that something is being done about crime. But when the commissions' recommendations go against the politicians' interests, legislation is more likely to be restricted to controlling "the criminal" than to reforming the criminal justice system. Yet everyone can be happy with the results of a criminal investigation. Civic, business, and professional groups have displayed activity; the researchers have carried out their study; politicians have fought crime without upsetting the political apparatus; and nothing has changed. All has been accomplished by appointing a crime commission.[11]

Until recent times, the major national experiment with an investigation of crime was the Wickersham Commission, formally titled the National Commission on Law Observation and Enforcement. Chaired by former United States attorney general George W. Wickersham, it was established by an act of Congress in 1929. From the beginning, it fulfilled a campaign promise by Herbert Hoover to conduct a thorough inquiry into the enforcement of laws prohibiting manufacturial sale of alcoholic beverages.

Things had been going rather badly for the prohibition laws — they seemed to be unenforceable, and the lack of enforcement was making a mockery of the American legal system. In response the commission, with a large staff of researchers, assistants, and writers, completed a report that ran to fifteen volumes.[12] The material extended beyond enforcing prohibition laws to the causes of crime, crime among the foreign born, child offenders, statistics on crime, the cost of crime, criminal courts, deportation, criminal procedure, and penal institutions.

Recommendations on its primary subject, enforcing prohibition laws, were confused and contradictory, revealing the commissioners' desire to satisfy opposing interests. The federal government could rest satisfied at finding no recommendations for repealing the prohibition laws, but the public was told that the laws were unenforceable. Prohibition soon ended nevertheless, partly of its own exhaustion.

Crime commissions of recent years, however, have carried greater influence. These are closely tied to the society's power structure and have large technical staffs, representing the most respected institutions. Organized on bureaucratic patterns, they have some permanence and continuity, and a chance to implement their proposals. Their activities are also made known to most of the public. Through mass communications, we are all presented the image of crime as a national problem. The whole population is alerted to a social reality of crime that is being constructed by state-appointed commissions.

THE WAR ON CRIME

It was in the middle of the sixties, on March 9, 1966, that the president told the nation:

> The problems of crime bring us together. Even as we join in common action, we know there can be no instant victory. Ancient evils do not yield to easy conquest. We cannot limit our efforts to enemies we can see. We must, with equal resolve, seek out new knowledge, new techniques, and new understanding.[13]

The resolve to make "war on crime" had been confirmed less than a year before (July 23, 1965) in Lyndon Johnson's executive order establishing the President's Commission on Law Enforcement and Administration of Justice.

The president's crime commission was composed of 19 commissioners, 63 staff members, 175 consultants, and hundreds of advisors. During the investigation, it called three national conferences, conducted five national surveys, held hundreds of meetings, and interviewed tens of thousands. A number of publications came from the commission and its staff. Several task force reports were made on specific subjects and field surveys reported the research findings. The investigation is summarized in *The Challenge of Crime in a Free Society.*[14] The general report also contains the commission's recommendations — more than 200 specific proposals.

Appointing the commission was an expedient political move.[15] During the presidential campaign of the previous year, Barry Goldwater had campaigned on "lawlessness." Although he lost the election, the theme was ingrained in the public's reality of crime. President Johnson, recognizing the fears upon which the lawlessness idea played, reacted by organizing something very American: a commission that would identify a broad evil, a thorough study of that problem, and proposals that would offend no one. A "war on crime" would also divert the public's attention from a nasty and unpopular war abroad to a common evil at home.

The commission was composed of "men and women of distinction," most of them uninformed about the problem they were supposed to analyze. All the commissioners, however, had a private interest in analyzing the crime problem. In typical consensus style, the commission was a careful balance of recognized constituencies: members from the law-enforcement establishment, lawyers, judges, the mayor of New York, a publisher, a university president, a couple of law professors, a civil-rights leader, a woman attorney, and the president of the League of Women Voters. Although the group covered a range of opinion about crime, the report was noncontroversial and clearly within the bounds of the political and legal establishment.

The commission's recommendations reflect the "liberal" thinking of the time, and its conclusion that crime can be reduced by "vigorously" pursuing these objectives:

> First, society must seek to prevent crime before it happens by assuring all Americans a stake in the benefits and responsibilities of American life, by strengthening law enforcement, and by reducing criminal opportunities.
>
> Secondly, society's aim of reducing crime would be better served if the system of criminal justice developed a far broader range of techniques with which to deal with individual offenders.
>
> Third, the system of criminal justice must eliminate existing injustices if it is to achieve its ideals and win the respect and cooperation of all citizens.
>
> Fourth, the system of criminal justice must attract more people and better people — police, prosecutors, judges, defense attorneys, probation and parole officers, and corrections officials with more knowledge, expertise, initiative, and integrity.
>
> Fifth, there must be much more operational and basic research into the problems of crime and criminal administration, by those within and without the system of criminal justice.

Sixth, the police, courts, and correctional agencies must be given substantially greater amounts of money if they are to improve their ability to control crime.

Seventh, individual citizens, civic and business organizations, religious institutions, and all levels of government must take responsibility for planning and implementing the changes that must be made in the criminal justice system if crime is to be reduced.[16]

By spending enough energy and money, the commission reasoned, crime can be abolished without significantly altering American institutions.

Certainly the president's crime commission did not suggest major changes in the legal system. It expected the causes of crime to be found in individuals ("criminals") and in social conditions. That criminal law might itself be the "cause" of crime was not considered. No justification was offered for using the criminal law as a sanction or penalty for human behavior.[17] The criminal law as a force in defining and perpetuating crime was not conceived of as part of the problem. Crime is not that which the law defines as criminal, but an evil that exists in spite of the law. Such evil, according to the president's commission, can be eradicated in an ultimate victory over crime.

The president's crime commission provided an explicit ideology on the reality of crime. The war on crime was now a political weapon to accomplish the objectives of the capitalist class. Moreover, the social reality of crime constructed for us had long since begun to create real events. An ideology of crime was leading to a definite kind of social order. Its implications are gradually being fully realized in the United States.

PUBLIC OPINION ABOUT CRIME

Fear of crime is prominent in this ideology. When the social order is caught up in crisis, emphasis on crime is escalated. And the state's increased use of the criminal sanction at such times is bound to the need to convince the public that its own interests are endangered. Though citizens are indeed the victims of criminal acts, the official ideology construes some forces as causing this victimization and not others, and suggests specific ways of taking action. The official ideology, the one that is presented to the public, stresses and rationalizes the interests and policies of the ruling class. The public is thereby diverted from developing critiques and solutions that would threaten the governing order. True public consciousness is avoided.

Crime became a major concern in the sixties that continues unabated in the seventies, officially and publicly. One observer of the phenomenon reports:

> Sometime during the 1960's — it is not easy to pinpoint just when — crime emerged as a predominant public issue. By the end of the decade, some polls revealed that the public ranked crime as the most serious problem facing our society — above the Vietnam war, race relations, and inflation. Certainly there have been other times in our history when this issue has aroused great anxiety, and this is hardly the first time that politicians have exploited America's chronic apprehension that the moral order is breaking down. Nevertheless, at least in its magnitude, the current reaction to crime is unprecedented.[18]

The problem for us in a critique of crime is to understand the relation between increased uneasiness about crime and the social and economic order.

Generally two kinds of explanations are found for the sharp rise in public concern about crime.[19] The first suggests an irrational response by the public to the rapid social changes supposed to have taken place since the mid-1960's. According to the second, the public's reaction to crime is justified by the increasing crime rate. The establishment of the president's crime commission in 1965 was justified by explanations of these kinds. And the crime commission even subjected the public reaction to study: "A chief reason that this Commission was organized was that there is widespread public anxiety about crime. In one sense, this entire report is an effort to focus that anxiety on the central problem of crime and criminal justice. A necessary part of that effort has been to study as carefully as possible the anxiety itself."[20] The president's crime commission and the resulting Omnibus Crime Control and Safe Streets Act were also justified — officially — by the public's fears about crime.

For a critical understanding of the public's reaction to crime, however, we need to recognize that public opinion cannot be separated from the ideology fostered by government officials and members of the ruling class. Public opinion is seen as formed by official indoctrination and ideological manipulation — by and for those who rule and govern. It is not to be doubted that public concern about crime is widespread and has increased sharply in recent years. National public opinion polls and surveys indicate not only that crime is perceived by the public as one of the most serious domestic problems (see Table 2.1) but that a majority of people are greatly concerned about their personal safety and private property.[21] Moreover, the fear of crime has affected people's lives and has prompted the public to alter their behavior and activities. Most important from the official ideological standpoint, however, are the attitudes that people share on control of crime. It is here that officials would like the public to agree that

TABLE 2.1 What Do You Regard as Your Community's (Your City's) Worst Problem? (Views of Residents of Cities 500,000 and Over)

Crime	21%
Unemployment	11
Transportation/traffic	7
Education	6
Poor housing/slums	5
High cost of living	5
Drugs	4
High Taxes	4
Unsanitary conditions	3
Ineffective police	3
Juvenile delinquency	3
Lack of civic pride	3
Other problems	28
Don't know/No answer	5
	108%*

* Total adds to more than 100 per cent since some persons named more than one problem.

SOURCE: George Gallup, "Crime Named More Often Than Economic Problems as Top City Problem," *The Gallup Poll,* July 27, 1975, p. 3.

action is needed and that the policies made and the actions taken deserve popular support. Though the public may be fearful about crime, even independent of official ideology, it is in actions against crime that the officials desire public opinion to support government policies. Public opinion must be shaped, if necessary, to rationalize official policies of crime control. With the appropriate public opinion, official policies can be instituted without seeming to exploit the public or to serve the narrow interests of the ruling class.

Public attitudes toward control of crime generally *have* been favorable to the government's war on crime. Although the public attributes an increase in crime to lowering moral standards, most people would depend on the police and similar agencies for controlling crime. Along with reliance on law enforcement the public's attitude toward the police is generally positive. According to opinion polls, most of the public has a high opinion of their work. A poll in 1967 showed that 77 percent of the public had a "great deal" of respect of the police, 17 percent had "some" respect, and only 4 percent had "hardly any" respect.[22] Similarly, a survey in 1975 of people in the large cities of the nation by the National Crime Survey (for LEAA) showed that 81 percent of those interviewed thought the police were doing an average to good job of enforcing the law.[23]

In spite of some criticism, the public generally relies on the police for control of crime. We are also willing to give the police much scope in their efforts to control crime. A majority (73 percent) of those interviewed in Washington, D.C. agreed that the police have the right to act tough when they deem it necessary.[24] More than half (56 percent) thought that police dogs should be used more often. In the national survey, 52 percent of the respondents believed that the police should have more power, and 42 percent that police should risk arresting an innocent person rather than risk missing an offender.[25]

The public also believes repressive measures, not changed social conditions, are the most effective means of controlling crime, which shows in opinions about court actions. A Gallup survey poll found that 74 percent of adults believe the courts do not deal harshly enough with criminals.[26] Only 5 percent said that courts in their area deal "too harshly" with criminals, whereas 13 percent agreed that treatment by the courts is "about right." Further evidence of the public's desire to crack down on crime was that 58 percent of the respondents in another poll agreed it was a good idea to give a double sentence to anyone who commits a crime with a gun.[27] Similarly, 71 percent of the sample believed it is a good idea to deny parole to a person convicted of crime a second time.

The public would deal severely with offenders according to another national survey asking the best way of dealing with an adult convicted of a specific crime.[28] The alternative sentences for a list of seven crimes from embezzlement to murder were probation, a short prison sentence with parole, or a long prison sentence. Probation found little favor. Considering each of the crimes, only about a quarter of the respondents felt that probation was an appropriate sentence. Only for prostitution, judged more harshly by women than men, did as much as 26 percent of the public feel that probation should be used.[29]

A similar pattern appears in a national survey with questions on prisons and corrections.[30] More than half the adults polled felt that the prison system was doing a good job in helping to deal with the problem of crime. Most believed in the prison's worth as a form of punishment, an even larger proportion (72 percent) felt that rehabilitation should be the main emphasis in the prison. A more recent Gallup poll found public support for the death penalty the highest in two decades, with 65 percent of those polled favoring the death penalty.[31]

These and many other polls and surveys of public attitudes toward crime and crime control tell us that these findings have to be read along with the official ideology, including that on crime and control of it. The correspondence between public opinion and official ideology and policy is striking. But I suggest we put aside the traditional assumption that official policy reflects public opinion, and see that officials use public opinion for their own advantage and that, at the same time, government officials and members of the ruling class manipulate public opinion to suit the policies they are establishing. It is to be expected that public opinion and official ideology are now similar. A critical public intelligence would spell a different attitude and approach to crime and criminal justice.

Public opinion about crime is conventionally thought to be a major force in determining criminal policy, but with power and economics as they are in the United States, the opposite is closer to the truth. It is criminal policy and official ideology that shape public opinion about crime. Also, public opinion is shaped by government officials and members of the ruling class. Public attitudes about law and order are influenced greatly by the statements and actions of the president, the attorney general, the director of the FBI, the administrator of LEAA, executives of large corporations, Congressmen, local officials, lawyers of the American Bar Association, members of government commissions, and so on. The public, because of the support an authoritarian political system demands, tends to follow the words and deeds of government officials and successful professional men and businessmen. Whenever "responsible" leaders utter conclusions and formulate policies we are expected to follow. Such is the force of modern government and such is the way in which public opinion is formed.

And if public opinion should give way, that is, if it should no longer conform to government policies, the government would nevertheless continue to carry out its program. In the end public opinion shows itself as a mere façade for state and capitalist interests. Kolko writes:

> We must confront anew the meaning of the concept of consensus or public opinion and the way it operates in the policy process. On one hand the seemingly shared beliefs, values, and consensus in society appear more critical than any single interest. But the fact that a ruling class makes its policies operate even when the mass of society ceases to endorse them, and that the voluntaristic and occasionally enforced social goals benefit individuals rather than all of society, is a central reality most analysts perpetually exclude from a descriptive explanation of American society.[32]

Official policy continues even when public consensus withers away.

Public opinion therefore is based on the ideological hegemony of the capitalist class — on the ideology of the small but ruling element of society. The capitalist class shapes the way we think as well as the way we are governed. All this serves the interests of the minority, but ruling class. Until we create a critical imagination, to be shared by all, public opinion about crime can do little more than reflect the capitalist ideology. As we consciously experience both the oppression of the crimes against us and the oppression of the capitalist system that generates crime, we begin to form a public consciousness of the truth about crime in capitalist society.

IDEOLOGY IN THE MASS MEDIA

How is the official ideology of crime translated into public opinion? Most of us at some time directly experience the force of that ideology, but there are more subtle and continuous ways of transmitting it. The most important means in an advanced technological society is mass communications. Each day the citizenry is presented messages from the media. We see images of law and order, or simply portrayals of the "real" America, daily in the newspapers, on the radio, in books and magazines, and on the television screen. Whether the format is "entertainment," news broadcasts and articles, or statements by government officials and community leaders, a message is conveyed about the official reality. A world is presented for us to believe in.

The ruling class does not simply dictate the substance of social reality in the media of mass communications. Indeed, in modern capitalist countries communications are not the official mouthpiece of the state; a diversity of views is presented, some even opposing the interests of government and the ruling class. Yet in spite of the diversity, a general reality is conveyed; in spite of some freedom of expression the current order is legitimated.

> The importance and value of this freedom and opportunity of expression is not to be underestimated. Yet the notion of pluralist diversity and competitive equilibrium is, here as in every other field, rather superficial and misleading. For the agencies of communication and notably the mass media are, in reality, and the expression of dissident views notwithstanding, a crucial element in the legitimation of capitalist society. Freedom of expression is not thereby rendered meaningless. But that freedom has to be set in the real economic and political context of these societies; and in that context the free expression of ideas and opinions *mainly* means the free expression of ideas and opinions which are helpful to the prevailing system of power and privilege.[33]

Although the media are not explicitly engaged in transmitting an official ideology, that ideology is nevertheless portrayed to the exclusion of alternative realities. There may be a variety of viewpoints, and controversies may be presented, but the general framework of the prevailing system serves as the boundary of expression. Hence, "the fact remains that the mass media in advanced capitalist societies are mainly intended to perform a highly 'functional' role; they too are both the expression of a system of domination, and a means of reinforcing it."[34]

The media presentations about crime, whether as fiction or reality, are based on general acceptance of the prevailing social and economic order. And on such a basis the portrayals of crime and crime-fighting inevitably adhere to the legal system and the necessity of controlling crime. Crime is viewed in the media as a threat to the American way of life, and the right of the state to intervene in controlling crime is presented as the only legitimate reality. This is the ideology presented by officials when they appear in the media, and this is the message in most of the fictional accounts of crime and the law.

The content of the mass media must therefore be understood in terms of the underlying ideology and the presentation of a particular reality. The media are usually criticized for such things as the lack of good programming, commercialism, excessive violence, and the like. And the indictment is justified. "But that indictment also tends, very often, to understate or to ignore the specific ideological content of these productions and the degree to which they are used as propaganda vehicles for a particular view of the world."[35] The specific ideological content of mass media portrayals of crime is shown, for example, in popular detective fiction:

> Furthermore, it is worth noting that much of the "message" of the mass media is not diffuse but quite specific. It would of course be ridiculous to think of such authors as Mickey Spillane and Ian Fleming (to take two writers whose sales have been astronomical) as political writers in any true sense. But it would also be silly to overlook the fact that their heroes are paragons of anti-Communist virtues and that their adventures, including their sexual adventures, are more often than not set in the context of a desperate struggle against subversive forces, both alien and home-grown. As has been said about the anti-communism of the Spillane output, "it is woven into the texture of assumptions of the novel. Anyone who thinks otherwise is taken to be either treasonable or hopelessly naive." This kind of crude "ideology for the masses" does not permeate the whole field of "mass culture"; but it permeates a substantial part of it in most media. Nor of course is the rest of "mass culture" much permeated by counter-ideological material. There are not, on the whole, many left-wing and revolutionary equivalents of James Bond. It may be that the *genre* does not lend itself to it; and the political climate of advanced capitalist societies certainly does not.[36]

How crime is to be fought — and the fact that it is necessary to fight crime — is clearly portrayed in a variety of media presentations. The portrayals are strikingly similar, however, whether presented as Dick Tracy (p. 48) and Superman cartoons, the Lone Ranger and the Green Hornet radio series, or the latest detective thrillers on television. Crime is to be "stamped out"; crime fighters pursue crime impersonally and with anonymity; methods and techniques beyond the law are used, including se-

cret decoder rings, electronic devices, entrapment, and murder — anything that gets results; and the world is divided into "good guys" and "bad guys." Being raised on the games called cops and robbers or cowboys and Indians, we all are prepared to be on the side of law and order. It is the "white hat," not the "black hat" that we must wear. The "forces of evil" are to be wiped out, and good is to win over bad. No wonder we grow up seeking solutions to problems by law and order, looking to the FBI and LEAA.

The media have been effective in disseminating a narrow view of crime and control. Beginning in the twenties, with cartoons and radio, definite themes about the world of crime began to be presented to the American public. A new American hero, continuing to this day, carried specific themes:

> A new breed of American heroes — SUPER crime-fighters — was inked on drawing boards and a tradition was born. As these new heroes were created and continued in the media — the comic strips, the comic ("funny") books, radio, television, and the wide screen of the neighborhood theatre — several themes emerged about the nature of the crime problem, the crime fighters and the criminals.
>
> These themes have been generally consistent over time and in the various media and may have produced a "Dick Tracy mentality" in the minds of our citizenry.
>
> The "Dick Tracy mentality" — born in frustration — includes the following concepts:
>
> 1. The crime-fighter is no mere mortal, but rather a SUPER crime-fighter.
> 2. The criminal is distinctive, unique, readily identifiable, and different.
> 3. The best way to stamp out crime is through the use of gimmicks and hardware.
> 4. Good always triumphs over evil; crime does not pay.
> 5. Members of ethnic minorities may fight crime, but only in a supporting role.
> 6. Violence is central to the crime problem.
> 7. Uniforms, costumes, and masks provide the crime-fighter with anonymity and identity, and conceal any emotional involvement in crime-fighting.
> 8. Operating outside the law is appropriate in dealing with major crimes and criminals.
> 9. There are two kinds of people in society — good guys and bad.[37]

When content of the media has been subjected to systematic investigation, a uniform presentation of crime and its control has consistently shown up. As the National Commission on the Causes and Prevention of Violence (formed in 1968) found, in one of the research investigations for which it contracted, dramatic presentations on television make a world of violence — more than 80 percent of the programs contained some form of violence.[38] Violence occurred most often, however, in programs with a crime-western-action-adventure story. And to no one's surprise, collision between the forces of law and lawlessness made up a quarter of television drama. High proportions of violent acts were committed by and against both criminals and agents of the law. Eighty-two percent of the criminals and 80 percent of the lawmen were engaged in some violence. In other words, when crime was featured, the programs nearly always displayed violence. And violence by the agents of the law was usually portrayed as justified.

The message for the television viewer is that crime is commonplace and that it must be fought, even with violence itself. That most crime in the real world does not involve violence is ignored, and a reality is portrayed that is quite the opposite. But crime is presented as violent and a great danger to social order, so that the viewer is expected to believe in the worthiness of the lawmen's or lawwomen's cause. Crime, like the enemy, is to be fought in any way.

News coverage on television presents its own version of reality, not so very different from that of television dramatic programs. When the commission on violence turned to coverage of news, government influence on the media was specifically questioned. The ideal for the media has always been the libertarian belief in the right of free expression unfettered by government intervention. "Objective journalism" is the goal, with a "balancing" of viewpoints. The media industry projects the ideology that diversity is being achieved, primarily because of its own professionalism and its attempt to maintain "independence and integrity" from government control.

> Professional pride and morale, high standards of performance, and maintenance of the public interest — all are dependent on continuing diversity in the channels of expression. Where the pressure for improvement comes through the channels of government, there is an inevitable threat to independence and integrity and thus to professionalism, high standards, and the public interest. Herein lies the dilemma which must be faced in any effort to raise the level of the mass media and thus to improve the quality of life in America.[39]

This argument totally neglects to tell the public that as long as the media are in the hands of corporate power, removed from those who receive their communications (the public), government regulation and interference have little meaning. So long as communications are controlled by corporate power and journalists are supported by business interests, recommendations that suggest "balanced coverage" still encourage media presentations that are well within the official reality. The way the media are controlled is in large part the message; the substance of the media establishes one reality in place of any other.

As a major American industry, the mass media are not separate from the interests of the state and the ruling class. The mass media industry, in fact, is a solid part of the business and government establishment. Media have, as the violence commission euphemistically put it, "an economic base."

Media, like other social institutions, cannot exist without an economic base, and accordingly are big business in the United States. Daily newspapers are a $7 billion-a-year industry, of which about $5 billion is from advertisers' investments and $2 billion is the direct revenue from the public. Television is supported by $3 billion a year which is paid by advertisers for time and production. Radio yearly draws $1 billion. Magazines are a $2.5 billion industry, with $1.3 billion accounted for by advertising. Book publishing grosses $2.4 billion and motion picture theaters $1.8 billion each year.[40]

These concrete influences make the media industry protectors of the status quo.[41] As partners with government and the rest of the corporate business world, the mass media inevitably present an ideology that supports and preserves the established system. Being capitalist enterprises, the mass media are bound by the same contingencies as other corporations. Failure of the capitalist system would also mean the end of the mass media industry. Those who own and control the mass media therefore agree ideologically with the rest of the ruling class. And this ideology is ultimately presented to the public in network programming.

Just as important as the ownership and control of the mass media in assuring ideological hegemony is the way in which the media are supported — by advertisers. Advertisers, themselves members of the capitalist ruling class, strongly influence the content of the mass media. And the influence need not be direct:

The direct political influence of large advertisers upon the commercial media need not be exaggerated. It is only occasionally that such advertisers are able, or probably even try, to dictate the contents and policies of the media of which they are the customers. But their custom is nevertheless of crucial importance to the financial viability, which means the existence, of newspapers and, in some but not all instances, of magazines, commercial radio, and television. That fact may do no more than *enhance* a general disposition on the part of these media to show exceptional care in dealing with such powerful and valuable interests. But that is useful too, since it provides a further assurance to business interests in general that they will be treated with sympathetic understanding, and that the "business community" will, at the least, be accorded a degree of indulgence which is seldom if ever displayed towards the labour interest and trade unions: *their* displeasure is a matter of no consequence at all.[42]

Advertising revenue from the large corporations of the capitalist system suggests a favorable portrayal of the world that supports this system.

Finally, the government, in its own ways, exerts pressure on the media. The state and its agencies "now make it their business, ever more elaborately and systematically, to supply newspapers, radio, and television with explanations of official policy which naturally have an apologetic and tendentious character. . . . The state, in other words, now goes in more and more for 'news management,' particularly in times of stress and crisis, which means, for most leading capitalist countries, almost permanently; and the greater the crisis, the more purposeful the management, the evasions, the half-truths, and the plain lies."[43]

All this means that the mass media carry an ideology that supports the capitalist system. The media, as an integral part of the capitalist system, effectively present us with an ideology of law that enforces the existing order. Daily a social reality of law and order is constructed for us, according to the interests of the capitalist ruling class.

USE AND MEANING OF CRIMINAL STATISTICS

The social reality of crime is also perpetuated by systematically applied statistics on crime. These are collected by agencies of the state ultimately for political use. That which can be counted and recorded is more amenable to social control. Moreover, criminal statistics collected by these agencies are often the primary data for criminological research and indicators of the actual amount of crime in society. Ways of using criminal statistics accordingly arouse controversy among criminologists. Much of the problem is in the way they are collected, but just as important is the true meaning of criminal statistics.

The meaning and use of statistics on crime depends greatly on the prior ideological assumptions of those using them. We can distinguish at least three approaches to the meaning and use of such statistics: the conservative, the liberal, and the critical.[44] The conservative's approach to criminal statistics grows from classical assumptions about human behavior: statistics on crime reflect willful and willing conscious human choices to violate the social contract, the theory that government must depend on the consent of the governed. Crime is freely chosen behavior, a victory of passion over reason. Criminal statistics, therefore, are thought of as *actual* measures of offense against a reified social contract, the ideal given concrete existence. Politically, such a use of statistics on crime boils down to an expectation that criminal behavior is all but randomly distributed through the social structure and that all equally need to be controlled. But the lower classes have more need for external control, for the crime concentrated in this segment of society reflects a weaker commitment to the social contract.

The liberal in approaching criminal statistics considers the social and psychological bases of behavior. That is, the liberal conception has all behavior determined extensively by a complex of social and psychological forces beyond the individual's control and sometimes even recognition.

This world view embraces positivist, not classical assumptions about human nature and behavior, and liberal criminology must therefore know what empirical research can reveal to us by way of statistical measures about the causes of criminal behavior. What causal factors should be investigated? This approach to the meaning and use of criminal statistics sees them as indicators of the variables that determine people to commit crime.

Finally, a critical criminology would employ statistics on crime in a radically different manner. Critical theorists argue that, for all the criticisms that have been leveled at statistics, they "can fruitfully be used as evidence of the underlying trends occurring in the wider social structure."[45] Among other things, criminal statistics can be read and used as evidence of efforts by the capitalist ruling class to apprehend and prosecute members of the working class who threaten the established order. Criminal statistics also indicate how tightly the society must control and punish the behavior that cannot be solved without making basic changes in the social and economic structure. Ultimately statistics on crime must be understood in their political context.

Most statistics on crime available to the public and to criminologists come from official sources, that is, from the statistics gathered by agencies of the government.[46] In fact, criminologists often equate criminal statistics with official statistics. Keeping the source of these statistics in mind, we have this definition:

> By criminal statistics we mean (a) uniform data on offenses or offenders expressed in numerical terms; (b) derived by official agencies (police, prosecutors, courts, penal institutions, etc.) from their records; (c) classified, tabulated, and analyzed in order to establish relationships between or among the classes of items tabulated; and (d) published — preferably annually — in a uniform manner.[47]

The regular collection of official criminal statistics by governmental agencies has not had a noteworthy history. The state of New York started to collect judicial statistics in 1829. Eventually, during the nineteenth century, twenty-four other states adopted the practice. The statistics were derived from reports sent by state attorneys or clerks of criminal courts to state officials; the results of this collection are summarized here:

> To sum up the situation existing at the end of the period 1829 to 1908, twenty-five states were collecting judicial statistics and twenty-three states statistics of prisoners, an impressive total were it not that with rare exceptions both kinds of statistics were of very doubtful value, serving no scientific purpose. Police statistics were mentioned occasionally in laws but that is about as far as they got. The Federal Government had tried from time to time in a half-

hearted way to collect judicial criminal statistics, also police statistics, but failed in each attempt. Its efforts to collect statistics of prisoners had, however, met with reasonable success. In the 1904 report, the earlier mistake of making the statistics relate solely to a point of time was rectified but the length of time intervening between the statistical inquiries was discouragingly long.[48]

The official statistics available for use in criminological research are collected by federal, state, and local governments, and the sources may be further divided according to the administrative stages at which the statistics are compiled. The criminal statistics criminologists most commonly use are based on the reports of local police departments, gathered by the federal government. In 1927, at a convention of the International Association of Chiefs of Police, a Committee on Uniform Crime Reports was appointed. Two years later the committee published a guide for collecting police statistics titled *Crime Reporting: A Complete Manual for Police.* In 1930, the FBI took over the system of reporting police statistics and issued the first bulletin of the *Uniform Crime Reports* (UCR), which was published monthly at first, then quarterly until 1944, and semiannually until 1957. Since 1958 the reports have been issued annually, with quarterly preliminary reports.

Judicial statistics are compiled and published from prosecutions, dismissals, acquittals, convictions, prison sentences, fines, and probations. In 1932, the United States Bureau of the Census began to publish such statistics for state courts, but discontinued the task in 1947. Some states continue to collect their own court statistics, but the great variations in collection procedures make state comparisons nearly impossible. For federal figures, the Adminstrative Office of the United States Courts publishes an *Annual Report* compiling the judicial statistics of the federal courts. Figures on juvenile delinquency, appearing as judicial statistics on youths who appear before selected local courts, have been published since 1946, under the direction of the Children's Bureau of the United States Department of Health, Education and Welfare, in a series known as *Juvenile Court Statistics.*

Statistics on prisoners have been published annually since 1926 in *National Prisoner Statistics.* Under the direction of the United States Department of Justice, this report includes information on the number of commitments to state and federal penal institutions as well as information on prison populations and discharges. Since 1972, the Bureau of the Census, acting as the collecting agent for LEAA, has compiled the statistical data for the National Prisoners Statistics Program, with the annual report being titled *Prisoners in State and Federal Institutuions.* The Federal Prison System also issues an annual report which provides statistical data on those convicted of violating federal laws. Several state departments of correction issue periodic reports on prisoners in their jurisdictions.

Still other sources of criminal statistics include reports from other governmental and private agencies, such as: *Vital Statistics in the United States,* which incorporates the reports of homicides submitted by local coroners; special reports occasionally published by the United States Treasury Department; reports of special offenses against the Federal Deposit Insurance Corporation; information on some federal violations reported in the *Annual Report of the Attorney General of the United States;* records of burglaries and robberies committed against member banks of the American Bankers Association; reports of state departments of public welfare; and special surveys and reports of historical interest, such as *Criminal Justice in Cleveland* of 1922, *The Missouri Crime Survey* of 1926, *The Illinois Crime Survey* of 1929, the *Survey of the Administration of Justice in Oregon* of 1932, and the series of reports in the state of New York in the late twenties by the Commission on the Administration of Criminal Justice.[49]

The most recent, and probably most influential and important, source of criminal statistics is the National Crime Panel. This is a newly devised empirical instrument, with enthusiastic official support by the state, for measuring crime not only across the nation but also locally in selected metropolitan centers. Under the actual administration of the Bureau of the Census and sponsored by the LEAA, the panel measures victimizing of individuals, households, and commercial establishments. It gathers nationwide data on characteristics of victims, relationship between victim and perpetrator, time and location of offense, degree and amount of injury or loss suffered, and whether or not the incident was reported to the police: "Because the Panel measures victimizations not reported to the police, in addition to those that come to official attention, it is expected to produce rates of victimization higher than those previously documented."[50] The panel is a direct result of the recommendations made by the 1967 LEAA in its report entitled *The Challenge of Crime in a Free Society*.

CRIMINAL STATISTICS AS MEASURES OF CRIME

Most criminal statistics have been gathered for purposes other than those of a specific criminological research project, so that the appropriate use of criminal statistics by the criminologist is an important issue. All criminal statistics, of course, represent the operations of agencies charged with administering criminal law. Most criminologists, and the general public for that matter, have attempted to use criminal statistics as measures of the "actual amount of criminality" in a geographical area or the country as a whole.

When criminal statistics are used in assessing the "true" incidence of criminality, criticism about the methods of collecting criminal statistics may indeed be valid. Pessimistic appraisals are relevant *if* criminal statistics are used to indicate actual criminality, as described here:

> Since around 1920, a great deal of effort has been put forth in different parts of the United States, and at various levels of government, toward the production of useful criminal statistics. But despite all of this work, there has not been produced in the United States any systematic collection of information on crime which furnishes the factual information desired, or which is comparable to the criminal statistics of many other countries.[51]

> The statistics about crime and delinquency are probably the most unreliable and most difficult of all social statistics. It is impossible to determine with accuracy the amount of crime in any given jurisdiction at any particular time. Some behavior is labeled "delinquency" or "crime" by one observer but not by another. Obviously a large proportion of all violations goes undetected. Other crimes are detected but not reported, and still others are reported but not officially recorded. Consequently any record of crimes, such as crimes known to the police, arrests, convictions, or commitments to prison, can at most be considered an "index" of the crimes committed. But these "indexes" of crime do not maintain a constant ratio with the true rate, whatever it may be. We measure the extent of crime with elastic rulers whose units of measurement are not defined.[52]

Such criticisms have led to numerous suggestions and recommendations to improve the collection of criminal statistics, especially the procedures used for the *Uniform Crime Reports.*[53] One obvious difficulty in using available criminal statistics as indexes of criminality is the lack of uniform reporting. Because of our political organization, each of the fifty states is a separate political jurisdiction. Each state has its own constitutional provisions, penal codes, courts, criminal procedures, and systems of law enforcement. Furthermore, in each state criminal law is not centrally administered but is, instead, a local activity. This political decentralization throws unpredictable variation into the recording of criminal offenses and makes information on criminal offenses hard to compare from state to state and from one locality to another within states.[54]

Thorsten Sellin some time ago described how "the value of a crime rate for index purposes decreases as the distance from crime itself in terms of procedure increases."[55] That is, police records measure incidence of criminal offenses more reliably than arrest statistics do, arrest statistics are more reliable than court statistics, and court statistics are better than prison statistics. The implication is that many offenses are "lost" between recording by police and prosecution. Aware of these discrepancies, criminologists usually prefer records made by police to those from other sources for inferences about how plentiful criminality is. The principal source of such information is the statistics on "crimes known to the police." Found in the annual *Uniform Crime Reports,* these list the offenses recorded by police departments of approximately 8,000 jurisdictions. For the annual report, the records of the local police departments are grouped into twenty-nine categories of offenses. Seven of the categories (murder and nonnegligent manslaughter, forcible rape, robbery, aggravated assault, burglary, larceny of $50 and more, and auto theft) are combined and designated "Index of Crime" by the FBI. Shown in Table 2.2 is the index from the *Uniform Crime Reports* for 1976. Readers of this and other tables in the *Uniform Crime Reports* should not regard the FBI categories as the only forms of crime or regard them as representing the "actual" amount of crime.

We can see how the statistics shrink as they move from one step of law enforcement to another in the difference between "crimes known to the police" and "crimes cleared by arrest." Furthermore, the discrepancy between crimes known to have occurred and arrests connected with the known crimes varies widely from one category of offenses to another. The police count a clearance when they have identified someone they believe is the offender of a known offense, have sufficient evidence to charge the person, and actually take him or her into custody (Figure 2.1). Arresting one person can conceivably clear several crimes, or, on the other hand, *several* persons may be arrested in clearing one known offense.

The statistics may be drastically reduced between known crimes and convicted persons received in prisons, as C. C. Van Vechten found in an early study analyzing "criminal case mortality" in several jurisdictions.[56] Distinguishing seven levels of criminal procedure, he found that, for all the crimes known in the District of Columbia, 35.7 percent resulted in offenses cleared, 10.0 percent in persons charged, 7.5 percent in judicial prosecutions, 5.9 percent in convictions, 3.7 percent in sentences to prison, and 3.6 percent in prisoners received from the courts. The clear decrease from first procedural level to last demonstrates how misleading criminal statistics far removed from the offense itself can be in measuring the "actual" amount of criminality.

Perhaps the most critical problem in using official criminal statistics to indicate the incidence of criminality, even when "offenses known to the police" are employed, is that some unknown amount of criminality never comes into the public record. For assorted reasons many criminal offenses are never reported to the police, or when reported are not recorded by

TABLE 2.2 Index of Crime—United States, 1976

Area	Population[1]	Crime Index Total	Violent[2] crime	Property[2] crime	Murder and non-negligent man-slaughter	Forc-ible rape	Robbery	Aggravated assault	Burglary	Larceny-theft	Motor vehicle theft
United States Total	214,659,000	11,304,788	986,578	10,318,210	18,784	56,730	420,214	490,850	3,089,789	6,270,822	957,599
Rate per 100,000 inhabitants		5,266.4	459.6	4,806.8	8.8	26.4	195.8	228.7	1,439.4	2,921.3	446.1
Standard Metropolitan Statistical Area	157,146,114										
Area actually reporting[3]	98.1%	9,409,605	857,683	8,551,922	14,823	48,681	398,530	395,649	2,546,637	5,148,347	856,938
Estimated total	100.0%	9,544,150	864,830	8,679,320	14,935	49,154	400,554	400,187	2,586,480	5,221,644	871,196
Rate per 100,000 inhabitants		6,073.4	550.3	5,523.1	9.5	31.3	254.9	254.7	1,645.9	3,322.8	554.4
Other Cities	25,062,777										
Area actually reporting[3]	94.0%	1,031,851	62,652	969,199	1,229	3,175	11,963	46,285	239,185	681,571	48,443
Estimated total	100.0%	1,096,237	66,634	1,029,603	1,331	3,356	12,781	49,166	254,083	723,943	51,577
Rate per 100,000 inhabitants		4,374.0	265.9	4,108.1	5.3	13.4	51.0	196.2	1,013.8	2,888.5	205.8
Rural	32,449,109										
Area actually reporting[3]	89.1%	605,201	49,448	555,753	2,177	3,827	6,060	37,384	226,144	298,413	31,196
Estimated total	100.0%	664,401	55,114	609,287	2,518	4,220	6,879	41,497	249,226	325,235	34,826
Rate per 100,000 inhabitants		2.047.5	169.8	1,877.7	7.8	13.0	21.2	127.9	768.1	1,002.3	107.3

[1] Population is Bureau of the Census provisional estimate as of July 1, 1976.

[2] Violent crime is offenses of murder, forcible rape, robbery, and aggravated assault. Property crime is offenses of burglary, larceny-theft, and motor vehicle theft.

[3] The percentage representing area actually reporting will not coincide with the ratio between reported and estimated crime totals, since these data represent the sum of the calculations for individual states which have varying populations, portions reporting and crime rates.

SOURCE: Federal Bureau of Investigation, *Uniform Crime Reports, 1976* (Washington, D.C.: U.S. Government Printing Office, 1977), p. 36.

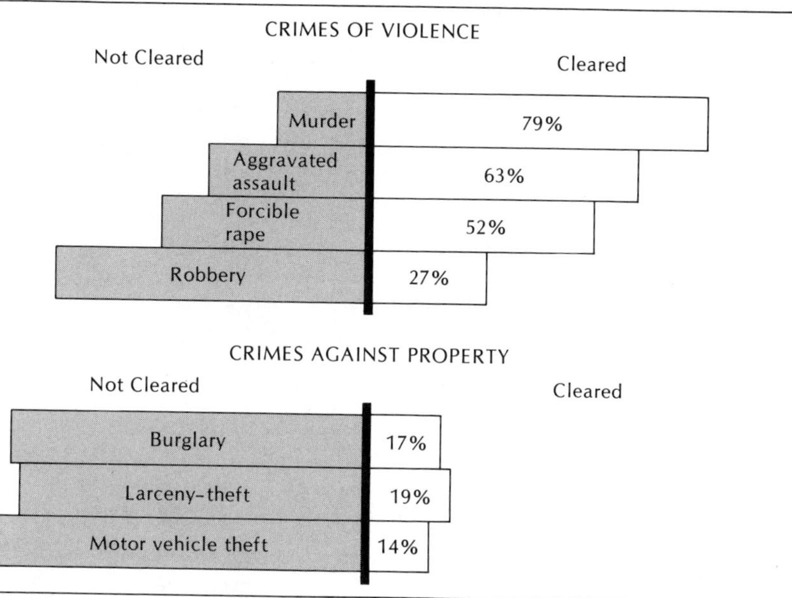

Source: Federal Bureau of Investigation, *Uniform Crime Reports, 1976* (Washington, D.C.: U.S. Government Printing Office, 1977), p. 161.

FIGURE 2.1 Crimes Cleared by Arrest, 1976

them. Any violation of the criminal law carries a probability that it will come to the attention of law-enforcement agencies. Some reasons why an offense will not be reported or recorded are: (1) Some offenses are known only to the offender and are not likely to be reported. (2) Because they lack knowledge of the criminal law, victims and witnesses may not report criminal violations. (3) Witnesses to an offense may not want to report the offense because of inconvenience, embarrassment, fear, or lack of interest in law enforcement. (4) The victim or witness may be afraid of being implicated in the violation or in other violations if investigated. (5) The victim or witness may fear reprisal if the criminal offense is reported. (6) Friends and relatives may try to protect the offender and therefore will not report the offense. (7) The victim may fear unfavorable publicity and embarrassment. (8) Social values and public opinion do not favor full enforcement of some criminal laws. (9) Some criminal offenses are not readily visible to the general public or law-enforcement agencies. (10) Law-enforcement agencies may wish to conceal some criminal offenses.[57] The National Crime Panel's survey of victimization in eight cities yielded the percentages, shown in Table 2.3, of reasons given by victims for not reporting personal, household, and commercial victimizations.

A "hidden criminality" has been uncovered in a number of studies in criminology. Examining how official statistics measure juvenile delinquency, Sophia M. Robinson noticed that about a third of the behavior problems known to New York City agencies did not become court cases.[58] Other researchers studying boys in a special counseling program saw that many were "unofficial delinquents." The juvenile offenses were known by some authorities but were handled informally.[59] When Texas college students reported on delinquent behavior they committed in their high school and college years, Porterfield found that the amounts and forms of their delinquent behavior were similar to that for which other juveniles had been officially processed in court.[60] The college students, with their advantageous backgrounds, had not been referred to court for their illegal acts; the other juveniles, however, had been officially handled.

More recently, Short and Nye compared the self-reported juvenile behavior of students in three midwestern high schools and three western high schools with the reported delinquency of juveniles in a western training school.[61] Among the things they found were extensive delinquent conduct among the noninstitutional students and similarities between the institutionalized and noninstitutionalized students in self-reported delinquent conduct. Other recent studies using the self-reporting technique have investigated differences according to social class, sex, race, religion, family relations, and rural-urban residence.[62]

Adult criminality also is much more widespread than the official criminal statistics show. Wallerstein and Wyle published in 1947 responses by New York residents (1,020 men and 678 women) to a questionnaire with

TABLE 2.3 Reasons Given for Not Reporting Victimizations

	Personal	*Household*	*Commercial*
Nothing could be done; lack of proof	34	38	37
Not important enough	28	32	33
Police would not want to be bothered	5	7	4
Too inconvenient or time-consuming	3	2	5
Private or personal matter	6	5	–
Did not want to become involved	–	–	1
Fear of reprisal	2	1	0
Reported to someone else	10	3	8
Other and not available	12	12	12
	100%	100%	100%

SOURCE: National Crime Panel, *Crime in Eight American Cities, Advance Report* (Washington, D.C.: U.S. Department of Justice, 1974), p. 6.

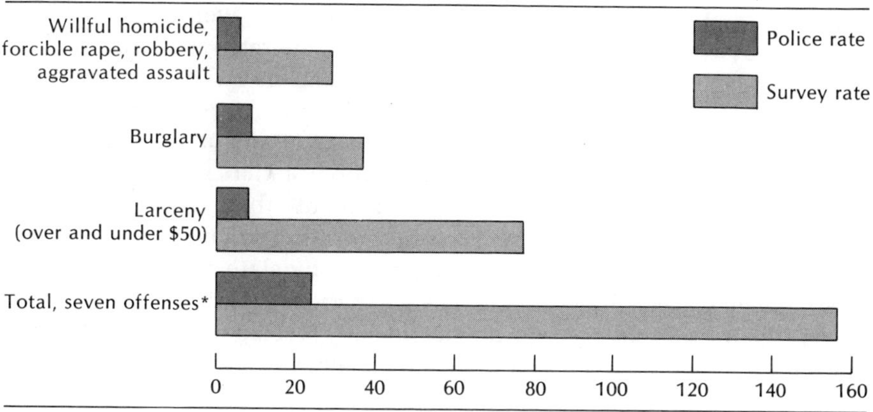

*Willful homicide, forcible rape, robbery, aggravated assault, burglary, larceny (over and under $50), and motor vehicle theft.

Source: President's Commission on Law Enforcement and Administration of Justice, *The Challenge of Crime in a Free Society* (Washington, D.C.: U.S. Government Printing Office, 1967), p. 21.

FIGURE 2.2 Estimated Rates of Offense: Comparison of Police and Bureau of Social Sciences Research Survey Data for Three Washington, D.C., Precincts (Rates per 1,000 Residents 18 Years or Over)

49 offense categories.[63] They were asked to check the offenses they had committed. Ninety-one percent admitted to one or more of the offenses. The men had committed on the average 18 of the offenses and the women averaged 11 offenses each. Of the men, 89 percent admitted to larceny, 85 percent to disorderly conduct, 49 percent to assault, and 35 percent to concealed weapons. Among the women, 83 percent admitted to larceny, 81 percent to malicious mischief, 76 percent to disorderly conduct, 74 percent to indecency, and 39 percent to auto misdemeanors.

A national survey conducted for the president's commission by the National Opinion Research Center (NORC), asking whether anyone in their household had been a victim of crime, estimated the rate of crimes against the person to be twice as high as that of the UCR and more than three times as high for property crimes.[64] An even more dramatic survey of unreported crime was reported in three Washington precincts. As Figure 2.2 shows, for offenses against individuals the number reported in the survey, depending on the offense, was from three to ten times greater than that in the police statistics. Certainly the actual amount of crime in the United States today is several times higher than reported in the UCR.

The most recent evidence that official statistics indicate only part of the real number of crimes is in the reports of the National Crime Panel's victimization studies.[65] Presented in Table 2.4 is the average rate of victimization by type of offense in selected cities. The rates are considerably higher than reported in the previous official statistics on the crime rate in cities.

Even more important, many of the most frequent and dangerous crimes are not collected in the official sources of criminal statistics.[66] These crimes occur in commerce and industry, management-labor relations, union management, income-tax reporting, and social security and public administration. Most of these offenses are dealt with by state and federal regulatory agencies, and the statistics covering them are in their files and reports. Such criminal records do not usually become a part of official criminal statistics. If we rely on the traditionally collected criminal statis-

TABLE 2.4 Average Victimization Rates for Persons Age 12 and Over, by Type of Victimization, in Eight Selected American Cities*

Type of victimization	*Average rate per 1000*
Crimes of violence	51
Rape and attempted rape	2
Robbery	19
Robbery and attempted robbery with injury	6
Serious assault	3
Minor assault	2
Robbery without injury	8
Attempted robbery without injury	6
Assault	30
Aggravated assault	14
With injury	5
Attempted assault with weapon	9
Simple assault	16
With injury	4
Attempted assault without weapon	12
Crimes of theft	91
Personal larceny with contact	9
Purse snatching	3
Attempted purse snatching	1
Pocket picking	5
Personal larceny without contact	82

* (Average rate per 1000 population age 12 and over, based on surveys during the months July through November 1972 of victimizations during the previous 12 months.)

SOURCE: Adapted from National Crime Panel, *Crime in Eight American Cities, Advance Report* (Washington, D.C.: U.S. Department of Justice, 1974), p. 11. The eight cities are: Atlanta, Baltimore, Cleveland, Dallas, Denver, Newark, Portland, and St. Louis.

Note: Detail may not add to total shown because of rounding. In general, small differences between any two figures in this table are not statistically significant because of sampling.

tics we obscure these and other prevalent crimes. We can say then that official statistics serve better as indicators of the state's response to specific kinds of offenses than as a way of measuring the amount of criminality in society.

POLITICS OF CRIME RATES

Using the official statistics on crime to measure incidence of criminality is a questionable practice. Furthermore, if we criticize the criminal statistics and advocate better crime-reporting procedures, we accept the assumption that official statistics can tell us the real amount of crime. Nevertheless, these official statistics are still used as indicators of criminality in society. Numerous studies have taken official statistics to draw conclusions about the *extent* of crime and delinquency and the *characteristics* of offenders.[67]

Conclusions often reached by those who use official statistics are (1) the crime rate is higher than it "should be," and (2) the crime rate has continued to increase since World War II. The student of crime, and the entire public, will continue to be reminded periodically that the crime rate for the current year is higher than that of previous years. Newspapers report as news the releases of the annual *Uniform Crime Reports*. We are reminded by the FBI that our crime rate continues to increase. Figure 2.3 from the UCR is typical of the graphic description regularly presented to the public. Once we know that the crime rate is increasing, we are expected to experience collective alarm. The reader is not usually, however, given the additional information that no one is certain what the criminal statistics mean. They may mean only that law-enforcement procedures change from year to year. The crime rate may not reflect the actual amount of crime so much as it does the way in which police departments operate and change their operations.

In other words, it may well be that the wrong question is being asked of our criminal statistics. Official statistics, first, represent only a fraction of some unknown amount of offensive behavior in a geographical area. In this use of statistics is much "hidden criminality." Second, because most human behavior can at some time be defined as criminal at one stage or another of criminal procedure by those with the authority to do the defining, the statistics reflect the policies and behaviors of the agencies administering criminal law.

Let us broaden our conception of official criminal statistics to include the fact that criminal statistics also represent the defining of behavior as criminal. Then, instead of assuming that criminal statistics indicate only

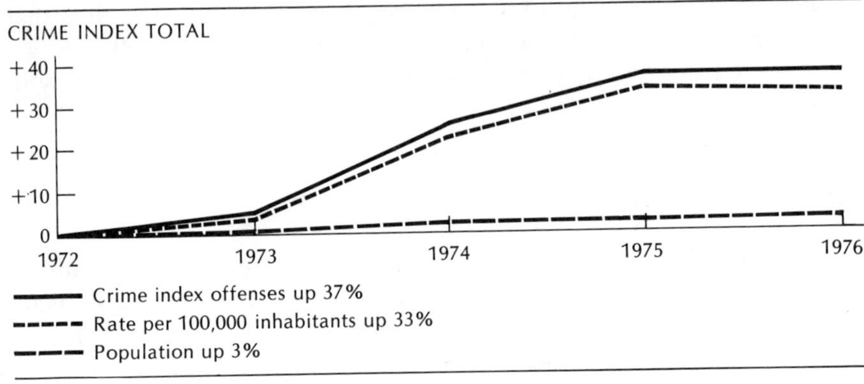

Source: Federal Bureau of Investigation, *Uniform Crime Reports, 1976* (Washington, D.C.: U.S. Government Printing Office, 1977), p. 34.

FIGURE 2.3 Increase in Crime Rate, 1972–1976, by Percentage of Change over 1972

the *incidence of criminal behavior* in a population, we will assume as well that criminal statistics reflect differences in the *administration of criminal law.*[68] These two conceptions of criminal statistics may not necessarily be regarded as mutually exclusive. A third meaning of the statistics is that they reflect a combination of the first two conceptions, a mixture of the *incidence of criminality and the administration of criminal law.* It has been shown that this combination of reasons for particular crime rates operates in the statistics on drug arrests. The study found that although there were distinct trends and distributions by time and place for the drug offenses, these patterns were shaped by systematic biases in the operations of police assigned to the narcotics division. These biases, including the general climate of social control, interaction between the law-enforcement agencies, and social organization of the agencies, "distorted the validity of drug arrest rates as measures of drug use activity to unknown degrees."[69] These systematic biases, furthermore, were changeable, making analysis of trends impossible. Although the arrest rates reflect in some way the illegal use and sale of drugs, the rates can be better understood as the combined behavior of the offenders and the agencies of control.

A fourth meaning of criminal statistics is that they indicate the *socially recognized volume of crime.* They are the society's production figures. Whether there is more or less "actual" criminality, strict or lenient administration of criminal law, or some combination of criminality and administration, is not the issue. Why do societies and their agencies report, manufacture, or produce the volume of crime that they do?

With a similar notion in mind, Donald R. Cressey has suggested that the kind of reporting system that is devised in a society is useful for the varying personnel controlling, treating, and preventing crime. A vagueness in criminal statistics is useful because it decreases the wide range of ideological and theoretical commitments of the many who deal with criminals. He suggests a "sociology of crime reporting":

> The kind and amount of statistics compiled on crime and delinquency are, in a very real sense, an index of social concern about crime and delinquency. Why do we report and compile what we do? What pressures are there on workers in the field to report some deviations and not others? What pressures are there for and against establishment of uniform categories for reporting and compilation? Why do we ask the personnel who are in direct contact with criminals to look at what they look at?[70]

For us, then, the meaning of criminal statistics is clear: they represent the kind and quantity of crime recognized in the society at a particular time. Crime rates are ultimately political.

Crime rates finally have to be understood for their political construction and the political uses they serve. It is for political purposes that criminal statistics are gathered and for political needs that criminal statistics are recorded and interpreted. For that reason, American crime rates are subject to great manipulation, from their inception to their use. It is impossible to know from any statistic the "true" rate of crime. Whether crime is increasing or decreasing in the United States is a question that can never be answered objectively without considering the politics of the times.

Crime rates, therefore, are used to justify or instigate a multitude of political (including social and economic) interests. With high crime rates the police rationalize the need for more personnel and equipment. But they cannot drastically reduce the rates without jeopardizing further appropriations.[71] The police have an interest in maintaining both a high and a low rate of crime.

Arrest rates are also political in the kinds and amounts of offenses recorded for various categories of the population. In the United States, the racism and sexism inherent in the social and economic structure is reflected and reified in the gathering and reporting of criminal statistics. The statistics on race and crime indicate that, for their proportion in the population, blacks are arrested between three and four times as frequently as whites. Although blacks comprise about one-ninth of the population, they account for more than a quarter of the offenses.[72] Similarly, judicial and prison statistics show that blacks have a higher risk of being arrested, convicted, and imprisoned. Although these rates represent a reaction of blacks to subordination, class conflict, economic exploitation, and discrimination, they also reflect the overall tendency of the agencies of the law to arrest and convict blacks more readily than whites.[73] To overrepresent the amount of crime by blacks is to make a political statement: that blacks are inferior (at least socially) and that they must be further controlled. Racism is thereby maintained by the legal system, in the recording and reporting of crime rates.

Likewise, the increase in crime among women, especially in economic and financial offenses, partly reflects the woman's changing role, and at the same time the continuing barriers produced by sexism.[74] Changes in the arrest rates of women do not necessarily indicate a real rise or decline in the illegal activity of women, though. Rather, as Dorie Klein and June Kress observe, "it may reflect the political situation in or growth of law-enforcement circles, different organization of the date, changes in arrest categories, and altered perceptions of women offenders by the police."[75] Sexism in the United States affects both the social position of women in the society and the extent to which they are arrested and recorded as criminals. The resulting crime rates are, once again, political.

The crime rate is political also in the official sense, when the crime rate is quoted in the political campaigns of politicians. Promising to reduce the crime rate, Barry Goldwater, Republican presidential candidate, introduced "law and order" into the 1964 campaign. The rhetoric was escalated by candidates in the 1968 presidential campaign. Each developed his own version of law and order as a battle cry. Richard Nixon, then the Republican candidate, touched it off in his acceptance speech at Miami, charging that "some of our courts in their decisions have gone too far in weakening the peace forces as against the criminal."[76] In even greater detail, Nixon presented his position on law and order in a paper, "Toward Freedom from Fear." His position was clear: "Just as justice dictates that innocent men go free, it also means that guilty men must pay the penalty for their crimes. It is this second part of justice to which the nation must begin to address itself in earnest. . . . By now Americans, I believe, have learned the hard way that a society that is lenient and permissive for criminals is a society that is neither safe nor secure for innocent men and women."[77]

The 1968 Democratic candidate, Hubert Humphrey, responded by promising to halt "rioting, burning, sniping, mugging, traffic in narcotics, and disregard for law." But he added that "the answer lies in reasoned effective action by our authorities, not in attacks on our courts, our laws, or our Attorney General."

The former governor of Alabama, George Wallace, running as an independent candidate, took the extreme position on the law-and-order issue. His solution was simple: free the police of all restraint. Wallace repeated his position everywhere he went, usually bringing the house down with the message: "If you walk out of this hotel tonight and someone knocks you on the head, *he'll* be out of jail before *you're* out of the hospital, and on Monday morning they'll try the policeman instead of the criminal. That's right, we're going to have a *police* state for folks who burn the cities down. They aren't going to bury any more cities." The law-and-order issue was becoming a racist euphemism for suppressing the demands of blacks in the urban ghettoes.

The law-and-order issue, with its own variations, was repeated in the presidential election of 1972. This time, Richard Nixon, the incumbent, explicitly used statistics on crime to bolster his position, but this time he argued that the crime rates were actually *decreasing* during his administration. George McGovern, the Democratic candidate, refuted Nixon's use of criminal statistics. A "numbers game" was being played with the Ameri-

Employing technological advances in crime detection, a police radio dispatcher instantly checks an auto license number by computer. The auto license number goes directly to a regional computer center and to the national crime information center in Washington, D.C. Within seconds the information on the automobile appears in type on the television screen.

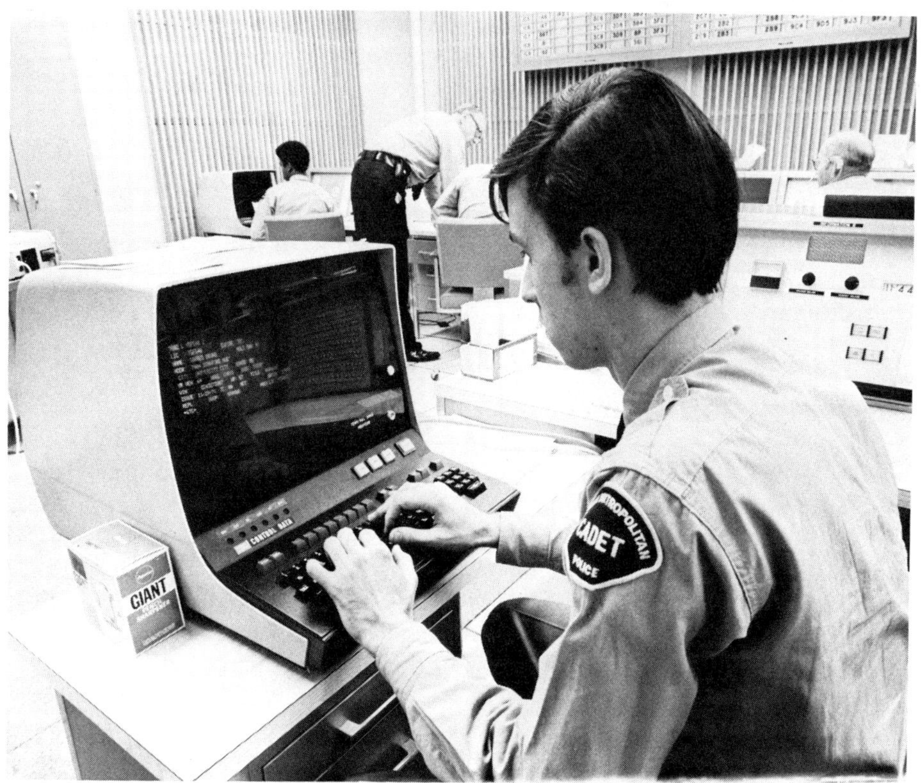

can crime rates. McGovern nevertheless found it necessary to offer similar law-and-order programs to control crime. Crime control now was clearly a means for keeping the established order from being destroyed. By the 1976 presidential campaign, all candidates were united on the theme of "fair and uniform punishment" for criminals. The new model of justice, ensuring the certainty of punishment, was now a political platform agreed upon by all politicians of the established order.

The ultimate use of criminal statistics for political ends is currently being planned and implemented. By improving the techniques of national surveys, as first used in research for the president's crime commission, the government is developing a system for continuously monitoring crime. The objective, however, is not merely to get a more nearly complete record of otherwise unreported crime, but to gather information that can be used to devise more effective means of law enforcement. An administrative official of the Information and Statistics Service (of the LEAA) observed about these new statistical methods: "Actually, under-reporting is only of marginal interest to our study. We are attempting to design a statistical methodology that will allow us to continuously monitor the characteristics of crime in the country; who are the victims; what is the genesis of a certain type of crime; where, how and when does it occur? These are the questions we want answers to, to provide tools for planning responses by police and other social agencies."[78]

We are well on the road to a national crime data reporting system. A national data bank, from which information can be retrieved instantly, will be the most rational and political device for controlling the population. The use of criminal statistics has progressed to its ultimate purpose, to protect the interests of the capitalist social and economic order in the United States.

DEMYSTIFYING THE IDEOLOGY OF CRIME

As we have shown, ideology shapes our image of crime. Contrary to conventional wisdom, an ideology not only exists but is extremely important in promoting the current social and economic arrangements. The capitalist system, in fact, depends on this ideology. It is another, and the most subtle, way of controlling the social order — by controlling the minds of the people. An ideology, reinforced daily in mass communications, serves the capitalist ruling class in dominating the minds and lives of the rest of the population.

An important part of this ideology is the belief that the legal system we now have is the most appropriate means for establishing order. Crime control, that is, preservation of domestic order, is supposedly for the "public interest." The ideology of crime is made more palatable to us by including rhetoric on civil liberties. That we are often granted due process before the law supposedly is enough to warrant our allegiance to the capitalist legal system. Even when we are given the right of civil disobedience, we are nevertheless expected to accept the punishment for transgressing the law. And when civil disobedience becomes too great a threat to the established order, it too must cease. All of this is for the purpose of preserving "the society."

Only a new consciousness will free us from the hold of the capitalist ideology. As long as our minds and our lives are dominated by this ideology, we are not free to create a new existence. A critical understanding is the beginning of a new life. An alternative existence is possible when we allow ourselves to demystify the capitalist ideology and its imposed reality.

NOTES

1. Karl Marx and Frederick Engels, *The German Ideology*, C. J. Arthur, ed. (New York: International Publishers, 1970), p. 64.

2. Gabriel Kolko, *The Roots of American Foreign Policy* (Boston: Beacon Press, 1969), p. 26. Also see David Horowitz, "Introduction," in David Horowitz, ed., *Corporations and the Cold War* (New York: Monthly Review Press, 1969), pp. 14–16.

3. See Ralph Miliband, *The State in Capitalist Society* (New York: Basic Books, 1969), p. 182.

4. See Joseph Femia, "Hegemony and Consciousness in the Thought of Antonio Gramsci," *Political Studies*, 23 (March 1975), pp. 29–48. Also see Leonard Salamini, "Gramsci and Marxist Sociology of Knowledge: An Analysis of Hegemony-Ideology-Knowledge," *Sociological Quarterly*, 15 (Summer 1974), pp. 359–380.

5. See Yale Kamisar, "When the Cops Were Not 'Handcuffed,' " *The New York Times Magazine*, November 7, 1965, p. 34.

6. Roscoe Pound and Felix Frankfurter, eds., *Criminal Justice in Cleveland* (Cleveland: Cleveland Foundation, 1922).

7. See Ralph G. Murdy, *Crime Commission Handbook* (Baltimore: Criminal Justice Commission, 1965), pp. 15–35. Also E. Connor, "Crime Commissions and Criminal Procedure in the United States since 1920," *Journal of Criminal Law, Criminology and Police Science*, 21 (May 1930), pp. 129–144; Allen Eaton, *A Bibliography of Social Surveys* (New York: Russell Sage Foundation, 1930); A. F. Kuhlman, ed., *A Guide to Material on Crime and Criminal Justice* (New York: H. W. Wilson, 1929); Virgil Peterson, *Crime Commissions in the United States* (Chicago: Chicago Crime Commission, 1945).

8. William B. Northrop, *The Insolence of Office — the Story of the Seabury Investigations* (New York: G. P. Putnam's Sons, 1932), p. 54.

9. Missouri Association for Criminal Justice, *The Missouri Crime Survey* (New York: Macmillan, 1926).

10. Illinois Association for Criminal Justice, *The Illinois Crime Survey* (Chicago: IACJ, 1929); Wayne Morris and Ronald H. Beattie, *Survey of the Administration of Justice* (Eugene: University of Oregon Press, 1932).

11. On the political nature of government commissions, see Anthony Platt, "The Poli-

tics of Riot Commissions, 1917–1970," in Anthony Platt, ed., *The Politics of Riot Commissions* (New York: Macmillan, 1971), pp. 3–43.

12. See especially National Commission on Law Observance and Enforcement, *Report on the Enforcement of the Prohibition Laws of the United States* (Washington, D.C.: U.S. Government Printing Office, 1931).

13. President Lyndon B. Johnson, Message to the Congress, March 9, 1966.

14. President's Commission on Law Enforcement and Administration of Justice, *The Challenge of Crime in a Free Society* (Washington, D.C.: U.S. Government Printing Office, 1967).

15. See Isidor Silver, "Crime and Punishment," *Commentary*, 45 (March 1968), pp. 68–73; Isidor Silver, "Introduction," *The Challenge of Crime in a Free Society* (New York: Avon, 1968), pp. 17–36.

16. President's Commission on Law Enforcement and Administration of Justice, *The Challenge of Crime in a Free Society*, p. vi.

17. Herbert L. Packer, "Copping Out," *New York Review of Books*, 9 (October 12, 1967), pp. 17–20).

18. Frank F. Furstenberg, Jr., "Public Reaction to Crime in the Streets," *The American Scholar*, 40 (Autumn 1971), p. 601.

19. Ibid., pp. 601–602.

20. President's Commission on Law Enforcement and Administration of Justice, *The Challenge of Crime in a Free Society*, p. 49.

21. See President's Commission on Law Enforcement and Administration of Justice, "Public Attitudes Toward Crime and Law Enforcement," *Task Force Report: Crime and Its Impact — An Assessment* (Washington, D.C.: U.S. Government Printing Office, 1967), pp. 85–95; and James Garofalo, *Public Opinion About Crime: The Attitudes of Victims and Nonvictims in Selected Cities* (Albany, N.Y.: Criminal Justice Research Center, 1977).

22. George Gallup, "U.S. Public Gives Police Big Vote of Confidence," *The Gallup Report* (Princeton, N.J.: American Institute of Public Opinion, August 30, 1967).

23. James Garofalo, *The Police and Public Opinion: An Analysis of Victimization and Attitude Data From 13 American Cities* (Albany, N.Y.: Criminal Justice Research Center, 1977), p. 11. An earlier survey is found in Phillip H. Ennis, *Criminalization in the United States: A Report of a National Survey*, President's Commission on Law Enforcement and Administration of Justice, Field Survey II (Washington, D.C.: U.S. Government Printing Office, 1967), pp. 52–72.

24. Albert D. Biderman, Louise A. Johnson, Jennie McIntyre, and Adrianne W. Weis, *Report on a Pilot Study in the District of Columbia on Victimization and Attitudes Toward Law Enforcement*, President's Commission on Law Enforcement and Administration of Justice, Field Survey I (Washington, D.C.: U.S. Government Printing Office, 1967), pp. 144–419.

25. Ennis, *Criminalization in the United States*, pp. 58–60.

26. *The Washington Post*, January 16, 1973, p. A3.

27. *The New York Times*, February 16, 1969, p. 47.

28. Louis Harris and Associates, *The Public Looks at Crime and Corrections* (Washington, D.C.: Joint Commission on Correctional Manpower and Training, 1968), pp. 11–12.

29. Research on public attitudes toward crime control is found in John E. Conklin, "Criminal Environment and Support for the Law," *Law and Society Review*, 5 (November 1971), pp. 247–265; Sarah L. Boggs, "Formal and Informal Crime Control: An Exploratory Study of Urban, Suburban, and Rural Orientations," *Sociological Quarterly*, 12 (Summer 1971), pp. 319–327; Jennie McIntyre, "Public Attitudes Toward Crime and Law Enforcement," *Annals of the American Academy of Political and Social Science*, 374 (November 1967), pp. 41–44; Don C. Gibbons, "Crime and Punishment: A Study in Social Attitudes," *Social Forces*, 47 (June 1969), pp. 391–397; Craig L. Boydell and Carl F. Grandstaff, "Public Opinion Toward Legal Sanctions for Crimes of Violence," *Journal of Criminal Law and Criminology*, 65 (March 1974), pp. 113–116; Simon Dinitz, "Progress, Crime, and the Folk Ethic: Portrait of a Small Town," *Criminology*, 11 (May 1973), pp. 3–21; Michael J. Hindelang, "Public Opinion Regarding Crime, Criminal Justice, and Related Topics," *Journal of Research in Crime and Delinquency*, 11 (July 1974), pp. 101–116; Gregory Johnson and John

Newmeyer, "Pleasure, Punishment and Moral Indignation," *Sociology and Social Research*, 59 (January 1975), pp. 82–95; Charles W. Thomas, Robin J. Cage, and Samuel C. Foster, "Public Opinion on Criminal Law and Legal Sanctions: An Examination of Two Conceptual Models," *Journal of Criminal Law and Criminology*, 67 (March 1976), pp. 110–116. Related theoretical issues are presented in Richard L. Henshel and Robert A. Silverman, eds., *Perception in Criminology* (New York: Columbia University Press, 1975).

30. Louis Harris and Associates, *The Public Looks at Crime and Corrections*, pp. 7–9.

31. George Gallup, "Support for Death Penalty at Highest Point in Two Decades," *The Gallup Poll* (Princeton, N.J.: American Institute of Public Opinion, April 29, 1976).

32. Kolko, *The Roots of American Foreign Policy*, pp. xii–xiii.

33. Miliband, *The State in Capitalist Society*, p. 220.

34. Ibid., p. 221.

35. Ibid., p. 226.

36. Ibid., pp. 226–227.

37. Robert M. Carter, "Where Have All the Crime-Fighters Gone?" *Gunsmoke Gazette*, 1 (January-February, 1972), p. 9.

38. National Commission on the Causes and Prevention of Violence, *Violence and the Media* (Washington, D.C.: U.S. Government Printing Office, 1969), pp. 311–339.

39. Ibid., p. 184.

40. Ibid., p. 169.

41. These influences are discussed in Miliband, *The State in Capitalist Society*, pp. 227–235.

42. Ibid., p. 231.

43. Ibid., p. 232.

44. Ian Taylor, Paul Walton, and Jock Young, "Advances Toward a Critical Criminology," *Theory and Society*, 1 (Winter 1974), especially pp. 455–460.

45. Ibid., p. 454. On criminal statistics, see also Roger Hood and Richard Sparks, *Key Issues in Criminology* (New York: McGraw-Hill, 1970), especially Chapter 1.

46. Sources of criminal statistics are discussed in, among other places, Ronald H. Beattie, "Sources of Statistics on Crime and Correction," *Journal of the American Statistical Association*, 54 (September 1959), pp. 582–592; Walter A. Lunden, *Facts on Crimes and Criminals* (Ames, Iowa: Art Press, 1961); James A. McCafferty, "Prisoner Statistics — National and State," *Proceedings of the American Statistical Association* (1960), pp. 25–33; Edward B. McConnell, "Judicial Criminal Statistics," *National Probation and Parole Association Journal*, 3 (July 1957), pp. 250–262; Edward E. Schwartz, "Statistics of Juvenile Delinquency in the United States," *Annals of the American Academy of Political and Social Science*, 261 (January 1949), pp. 9–20.

47. Thorsten Sellin, "The Measurement of Criminality in Geographic Areas," *Proceedings of the American Philosophical Society*, 97 (April 1953), p. 163.

48. Louis N. Robinson, "History of Criminal Statistics, 1908–1933," *Journal of Criminal Law, Criminology and Police Science*, 24 (May-June 1933), p. 126. Also see C. E. Gehlke, "Development of Criminal Statistics in the Past Century," *Proceedings of the American Prison Association* (1931), pp. 176–190.

49. These and other surveys are discussed in Virgil Peterson, *Crime Commissions in the United States* (Chicago: Chicago Crime Commission, 1945).

50. National Crime Panel, *Crime in Eight American Cities*, Advance Report (Washington, D.C.: U.S. Department of Justice, 1974), p. iii.

51. Ronald H. Beattie, "Problems of Criminal Statistics in the United States," *Journal of Criminal Law, Criminology and Police Science*, 46 (July-August 1955), p. 178.

52. Edwin H. Sutherland and Donald R. Cressey, *Criminology*, 9th ed. (Philadelphia: J. B. Lippincott, 1974), p. 25.

53. See, for example, Peter P. Lejins, "Uniform Crime Reports," *Michigan Law Review*, 64 (April 1966), pp. 1011–1030; David J. Pittman and W. F. Handy, "Uniform Crime Reporting: Suggested Improvements," *Sociology and Social Research*, 46 (January 1962), pp. 135–143; Sophia M. Robinson, "A Critical View of the Uniform Crime Reports," *Michigan Law Review*, 64 (April 1966), pp. 1031–1054; Thorsten Sellin, "The Uniform

Criminal Statistics Act," *Journal of Criminal Law, Criminology and Police Science,* 40 (March-April 1950), pp. 679–700; Leslie T. Wilkins, "New Thinking in Criminal Statistics," *Journal of Criminal Law, Criminology and Police Science,* 56 (September 1965), pp. 277–284; Marvin E. Wolfgang, "Uniform Crime Reports: A Critical Appraisal," *University of Pennsylvania Law Review,* 111 (April 1963), pp. 708–738; Eugene Doleschal, *Criminal Statistics,* Crime and Delinquency, Monograph Series, National Institute of Mental Health (Washington, D.C.: U.S. Government Printing Office, 1972); David Seidman and Michael Couzens, "Getting the Crime Rate Down: Political Pressure and Crime Reporting," *Law and Society Review,* 8 (Spring 1974), pp. 457–493.

54. Ronald H. Beattie, "Criminal Statistics in the United States — 1960," *Journal of Criminal Law, Criminology and Police Science,* 51 (May-June 1960), pp. 49–65. Uniformity does seem possible for reporting homicides, as shown in Michael J. Hindelang, "The Uniform Crime Reports Revisited," *Journal of Criminal Justice,* 2 (1974), pp. 1–17.

55. Thorsten Sellin, "The Basis of a Crime Index," *Journal of Criminal Law, Criminology and Police Science,* 22 (September-October 1931), p. 346.

56. C. C. Van Vechten, "Differential Criminal Case Mortality in Selected Jurisdictions," *American Sociological Review,* 7 (December 1942), pp. 833–839.

57. Based on Marshall B. Clinard, *Sociology of Deviant Behavior,* rev. ed. (New York: Holt, Rinehart and Winston, 1963), pp. 20–21; and Thorsten Sellin, *Research Memorandum on Crime and the Depression* (New York: Social Science Research Council, 1936), pp. 69–70.

58. Sophia M. Robison, *Can Delinquency Be Measured?* (New York: Columbia University Press, 1936).

59. Fred J. Murphy, Mary M. Shirley, and Helen L. Witmer, "The Incidence of Hidden Delinquency," *American Journal of Orthopsychiatry,* 16 (October 1946), pp. 686–696.

60. Austin L. Porterfield, *Youth in Trouble* (Fort Worth, Texas: Leo Potishman Foundation, 1946).

61. James F. Short, Jr., and F. Ivan Nye, "Extent of Unrecorded Juvenile Delinquency: Tentative Conclusions," *Journal of Criminal Law, Criminology and Police Science,* 49 (November-December 1958), pp. 296–302.

62. Among the studies are Ronald L. Akers, "Socio-Economic Status and Delinquent Behavior: A Retest," *Journal of Research in Crime and Delinquency,* 1 (January 1964), pp. 38–46; John P. Clark and Eugene P. Wenninger, "Socio-Economic Class and Areas as Correlates of Illegal Behavior among Juveniles," *American Sociological Review,* 27 (December 1962), pp. 826–834; Robert A. Dentler and Lawrence J. Monroe, "Social Correlates of Early Adolescent Theft," *American Sociological Review,* 26 (October 1961), pp. 733–743; Maynard L. Erickson and Lamar T. Empey, "Court Records, Undetected Delinquency and Decision-Making," *Journal of Criminal Law, Criminology and Police Science,* 54 (December 1963), pp. 456–469; F. Ivan Nye and James F. Short, Jr., "Socioeconomic Status and Delinquent Behavior," *American Journal of Sociology,* 63 (January 1958), pp. 381–389; Albert J. Reiss and Albert Lewis Rhodes, "The Distribution of Juvenile Delinquency in the Social Class Structure," *American Sociological Review,* 26 (October 1961), pp. 720–732; Harwin L. Voss, "Socio-Economic Status and Reported Delinquent Behavior," *Social Problems,* 13 (Winter 1966), pp. 314–324; Leroy C. Gould, "Who Defines Delinquency: A Comparison of Self-Reported and Official-Reported Indices of Delinquency in Three Racial Groups," *Social Problems,* 16 (Winter 1969), pp. 325–336; Michael J. Hindelang, "Age, Sex, and the Versatility of Delinquency Involvements," *Social Problems,* 18 (Spring 1971), pp. 522–535; Jay R. Williams and Martin Gold, "From Delinquent Behavior to Official Delinquency," *Social Problems,* 20 (Fall 1972), pp. 209–227; Joseph Harry, "Social Class and Delinquency: One More Time," *Sociological Quarterly,* 15 (Spring 1974), pp. 294–301; Gary J. Jensen and Raymond Eve, "Sex Differences in Delinquency: An Examination of Popular Sociological Explanations," *Criminology,* 13 (February 1976), pp. 427–448. Some of the studies of self-reported delinquency are summarized in Robert H. Hardt and George E. Bodine, *Development of Self-Report Instruments in Delinquency Research: A Conference Report* (Syracuse, N.Y.: Syracuse University Youth Development Center, 1965).

63. James S. Wallerstein and Clement J. Wyle, "Our Law-Abiding Law-Breakers," *Probation,* 25 (April 1947), pp. 107–112.

64. President's Commission on Law Enforcement and Administration of Justice, *The*

Challenge of Crime in a Free Society, p. 21. For an analysis of the research, see Albert D. Biderman, "Surveys of Population Samples for Estimating Crime Incidence," *Annals of the American Academy of Political and Social Science*, 374 (November 1967), pp. 16–33.

65. Some of the victimization surveys are analyzed in Wesley G. Skogan, "Citizen Reporting of Crime: Some National Panel Data," *Criminology*, 13 (February 1976), pp. 535–549; and John B. Cordrey, "Crime Rates, Victims, Offenders: A Victimization Study," *Journal of Police Science and Administration*, 3 (March 1975), pp. 100–110.

66. Harry Manuel Schulman, "The Measurement of Crime in the United States," *Journal of Criminal Law, Criminology and Police Science*, 57 (December 1966), pp. 485–486.

67. See, for example, John C. Ball, Alan Ross, and Alice Simpson, "Incidence and Estimated Prevalence of Recorded Delinquency in a Metropolitan Area," *American Sociological Review*, 29 (February 1964), pp. 90–93; E. Jackson Baur, "The Trend of Juvenile Offenses in the Netherlands and the United States," *Journal of Criminal Law, Criminology and Police Science*, 55 (September 1964), pp. 359–369; Joseph W. Eaton and Kenneth Polk, *Measuring Delinquency* (Pittsburgh: University of Pittsburgh Press, 1961); Thomas P. Monahan, "On the Incidence of Delinquency," *Social Forces*, 39 (October 1960), pp. 66–72; Austin L. Porterfield, "A Decade of Serious Crimes in the United States: Some Trends and Hypotheses," *American Sociological Review*, 13 (February 1948), pp. 44–54; Thorsten Sellin, "Crime," *American Journal of Sociology*, 47 (May 1942), pp. 898–906; Thorsten Sellin, "Crime and Delinquency in the United States: An Overview," *Annals of the American Academy of Political and Social Science*, 339 (January 1962), pp. 11–23; Harry Willbach, "The Trend of Crime in New York City," *Journal of Criminal Law, Criminology and Police Science*, 29 (May-June 1938), pp. 62–75. For rates in a particular city, see Victor Eisner, *The Delinquency Label: The Epidemiology of Juvenile Delinquency* (New York: Random House, 1969).

68. Such an approach to criminal statistics is suggested in John I. Kitsuse and Aaron V. Cicourel, "A Note on the Uses of Official Statistics," *Social Problems*, 11 (Fall 1963), pp. 131–139; Donald J. Newman, "The Effect of Accommodations in Justice Administration on Criminal Statistics," *Sociology and Social Research*, 46 (January 1962), pp. 144–155; Stanton Wheeler, "Criminal Statistics: A Reformulation of the Problem," *Journal of Criminal Law, Criminology and Police Science*, 58 (September 1967), pp. 317–324.

69. Lois B. DeFleur, "Biasing Influence on Drug Arrest Records: Implications for Deviance Research," *American Sociological Review*, 49 (February 1974), p. 102.

70. Donald R. Cressey, "The State of Criminal Statistics," *National Probation and Parole Association Journal*, 3 (July 1957), pp. 240–241. A similar view is presented in Albert D. Biderman and Albert J. Reiss, Jr., "On Exploring the 'Dark Figure' of Crime," *Annals of the American Academy of Political and Social Science*, 374 (November 1967), pp. 1–15.

71. Michael E. Milakovich and Kurt Weis, "Politics and Measures of Success in the War on Crime," *Crime and Delinquency*, 21 (January 1975), pp. 1–10.

72. See Marvin E. Wolfgang, *Crime and Race: Conceptions and Misconceptions* (New York: Institute of Human Relations, 1964), pp. 31–35; and Gilbert Geis, "Statistics Concerning Race and Crime," *Crime and Delinquency*, 11 (April 1965), pp. 142–150. On the crime rates of native Americans, see Charles E. Reasons, "Crime and the Native American," in Charles E. Reasons and Jack L. Kuykendall, eds., *Race, Crime and Justice* (Pacific Palisades, Calif.; Goodyear, 1972), pp. 79–95.

73. See Guy B. Johnson, "The Negro and Crime," *Annals of the American Academy of Political and Social Science*, 271 (September 1941), pp. 93–104; Earl R. Moses, "Differentials in Crime Rates Between Negroes and Whites Based on Comparisons of Four Socio-economically Equated Areas," *American Sociological Review*, 12 (August 1947), pp. 411–420. The argument that the excess of black arrest rates over white rates results from greater concentration of blacks in the lower class and their higher rate of unemployment is in Edward Green, "Race, Social Status, and Criminal Arrest," *American Sociological Review*, 35 (June 1970), pp. 476–490. The full effect of racism on behavior of blacks and discrimination in arrests is presented in John A. Davis, "Blacks, Crime, and American Culture," *The Annals*, 423 (January 1976), pp. 89–98; and Robert Staples, "Black Crime, White Racism, and American Justice: An Application of the Colonial Model to Explain Crime and Race," *Phylon*, 36 (March 1975), pp. 14–22.

74. On the changing crime rates of women, see Rita J. Simon, "American Women and

Crime," *The Annals*, 423 (January 1976), pp. 31–46. Also Rita James Simon, *The Contemporary Woman and Crime*, Crime and Delinquency Monograph Series, National Institute of Mental Health (Washington, D.C.: U.S. Government Printing Office, 1975). Excellent critiques of research on the criminality of women are found in Dorie Klein, "The Etiology of Female Crime: A Review of the Literature," *Issues in Criminology*, 8 (Fall 1973), pp. 3–30; and Dale Hoffman Bustamante, "The Nature of Female Criminality," *Issues in Criminology*, 8 (Fall 1973), pp. 117–136.

75. Dorie Klein and June Kress, "Any Woman's Blues: A Critical Overview of Women, Crime and the Criminal Justice System," *Crime and Social Justice*, 5 (Spring-Summer 1976), p. 41.

76. Quoted in Fred J. Cook, "There's Always a Crime Wave — How Bad's This One?" *The New York Times Magazine*, October 6, 1968, p. 38. The quotations from the other presidential candidates are also in Cook's article.

77. Quoted in Albert J. Reiss, "Crime, Law and Order as Election Issues," *Trans-action*, 5 (October 1968), p. 3.

78. *The New York Times*, April 27, 1973, p. 1.

CRIMINAL LAW

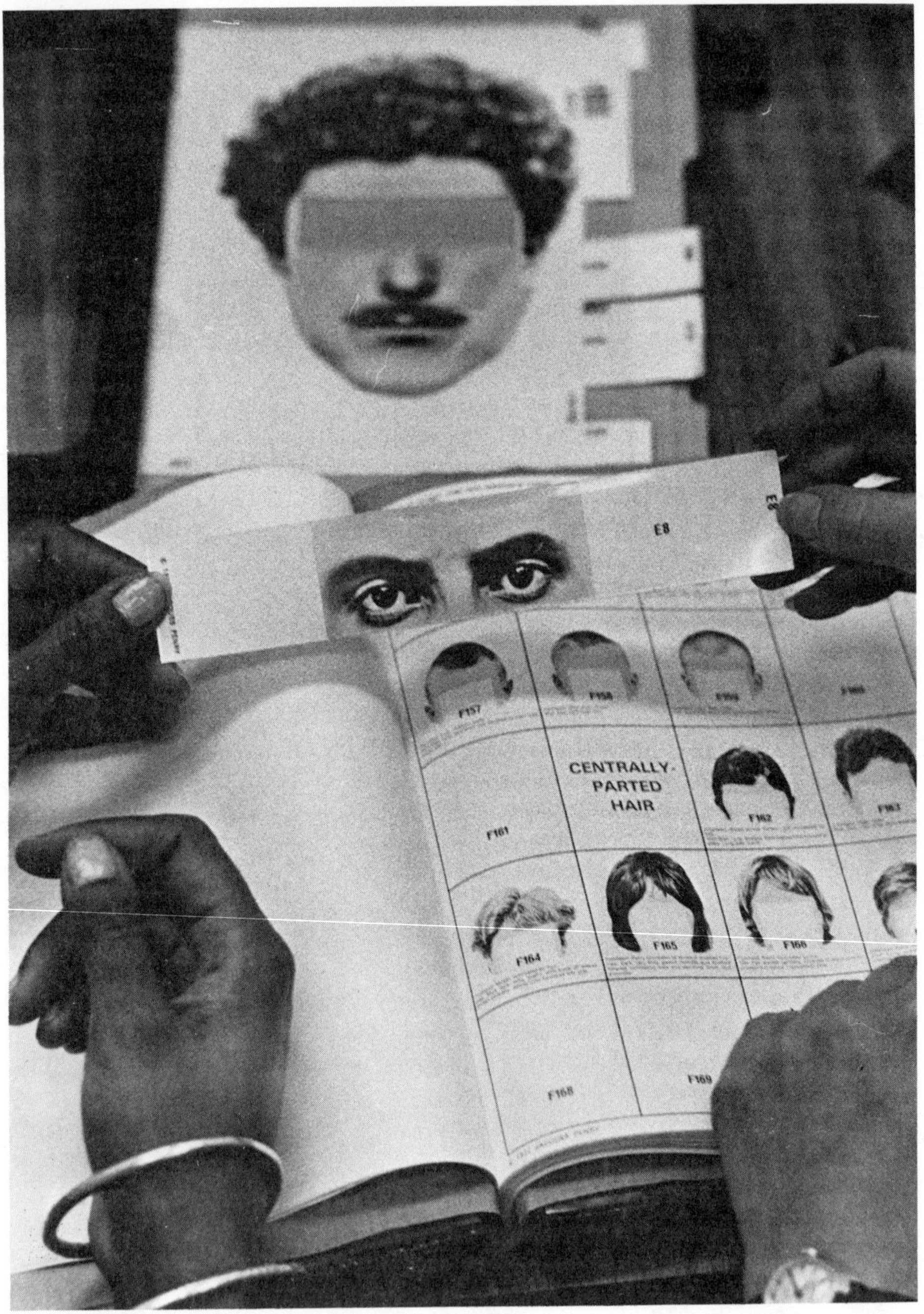
E8
F157
CENTRALLY-
PARTED
HAIR
F161
F164
F165
F168
F169

Legal Order and Crime Control

3

Our analysis of crime begins when we recognize that crime is a material problem. In fact, the phenomenon we should consider is not crime itself, but the history of how the capitalist economy developed and how it operates. To study crime we must investigate such natural products and contradictions of capitalism as inequality, racism, sexism, poverty, unemployment, and the continuing economic crisis burdening the capitalist state. Ultimately, to understand crime we must know how the political economy of capitalist society developed.

A capitalist class society arises when the system of production is owned and controlled by one segment of the society, excluding another from ownership and control. All production requires ownership of some kind, but in some systems ownership is private, not social or collective. In these economies social relations depend on domination of some and subjection of others.[1]

All social life in capitalist society, including everything associated with crime, depends on the economic conditions imposed by production and the struggle between classes produced by these conditions. In other words, in capitalist society the life and behavior of any group in the society, or any member of a group, is affected by the conflict in class relations, which in turn is produced by the capitalist system of production.

The capitalist system must be reproduced continuously, which it does by expedients that range from establishing ideological hegemony to further exploiting labor, from creating public policy down to coercively repressing the population. Most explicitly it is the *state* that secures the capitalist order. With all its schemes and mechanisms, the capitalist class is able to dominate. And by creating a legal order within the state, the capitalist system protects and reproduces itself.

This legal order determines the behavior that is officially defined as crime in the United States. The legal order provides the context for administering and enforcing criminal law. Composed of statutes, court opinions, and administrative rulings, law is also a step-by-step process, which includes the making of legal decisions by agents of the state. In substance and in process, criminal law in the modern state is the regulating of human conduct by those who have the authority to act in the society's name.

LEGAL ORDER OF THE STATE

Conventional wisdom, the knowledge all of us pick up in every day communications, is built on belief in the need for a state and the inevitability of law. These assumptions are so ingrained that we may never think about them. Yet, the state and its legal order intimately shape the reality of our lives.

> More than ever before men now live in the shadow of the state. What they want to achieve, individually or in groups, now mainly depends on the state's sanction and support. . . . It is possible not to be interested in what the state does; but it is not possible to be unaffected by it. The point has acquired a new and ultimate dimension in the present epoch: if large parts of the planet should one day be laid waste in a nuclear war, it is because men, acting in the name of their state and invested with its power, will have so decided, or miscalculated.[2]

Our failure to recognize how deeply the state influences our lives has kept us from understanding why we have a legal order and how it continues to survive. Unquestioning belief in the state prevents us from analyzing the state and seeing it as a coercive instrument used by an economically dominant class.[3] Such an examination would raise critical questions about the state and the legal order. They are inseparable; to understand one is to understand the other.

Historically the capitalist state is produced by a political economy that depends on division into classes. With an economy built by one class exploiting another, a political form was needed that would perpetuate that kind of order. When capitalism appeared, with class divisions and class struggle, the state became necessary. A new stage of development, Frederick Engels observes, called for creation of the state:

> Only one thing was wanting: an institution which not only secured the newly acquired riches of individuals against the communistic traditions of the gentile order, which not only sanctified the private property formerly so little valued, and declared this sanctification to be the highest purpose of all human society; but an institution which set the seal of general social recognition on each new method of acquiring property and thus amassing wealth at continually increased speed; an institution which perpetuated, not only this growing cleavage of society into classes, but also the right of the possessing class to exploit the non-possessing, and the rule of the former over the latter.
>
> And this institution came. The state was invented.[4]

The state arose to protect and promote the interests of the dominant class, which owns and controls the means of production. It is a device for controlling the exploited class, the class that labors, for the benefit of the ruling class. Modern civilization, as epitomized in capitalist societies, is founded on exploitation of one class by another. Moreover, the capitalist state is oppressive not only because it supports the interests of the dominant class but because it is responsible for the design of the whole system within which that class dominates and the working class is dominated.[5] The capitalist system of production and exploitation is secured and reproduced by the capitalist state.

The state's coercive force, embodied in law and legal repression, is the traditional means of maintaining the social and economic order. Contrary to conventional wisdom, law, instead of representing community custom, is an instrument of the state that serves the interests of the developing capitalist ruling class. Law appeared as capitalism arose, as Stanley Diamond writes: "Law arises in the breach of a prior customary order and increases in force with the conflicts that divide political societies internally and among themselves. Law *and* order is the historical illusion; law versus order is the historical reality."[6] Law and legal repression are, and continue to serve as, the way of enforcing the interests of the dominant class in the capitalist state.

It is through the legal system, then, that the state forcefully protects its interests and those of the capitalist ruling class. Control of crime becomes the coercive means of checking threats to the social and economic order, threats that result from a system of oppression and exploitation. As a way of controlling the behavior of the exploited population, crime control is accomplished by many methods, strategies, and institutions. The state, especially through its legislative bodies, establishes official policies for controlling crime. The administrative branch of the state establishes and enforces crime control policies, usually setting the design for the whole nation. Specific agencies of law enforcement, such as the FBI and the recent Law Enforcement Assistance Administration, determine how crime will be controlled. And the state, with its Department of Justice, can officially repress the "dangerous" and "subversive" elements in the population.

Altogether, these state institutions attempt to rationalize the legal system by applying the advanced methods of science and technology. And whenever any changes are to be attempted to reduce the incidence of crime, rehabilitation of the individual or reform within institutions is suggested. Drastically altering the society and the crime control establishment would alter the capitalist system beyond recognition. Modern capitalist society, with its state and legal order, is the one least likely to serve as a guide for building a humane society.

DEVELOPMENT OF CRIMINAL LAW

The criminal law is a political and economic phenomenon. It began at the same time as the political state of capitalist society was being created. In early societies custom prevailed, and injuries to wronged people were handled by the family and the community. Criminal law was devised only when this custom of managing private or community wrong locally was replaced by the principle that the state is injured when one of its subjects is harmed. The community's right to deal with wrongdoing was taken over by the state as "representative" of the people; the state could now act by means of the criminal law to protect its own interests.

Criminal law as we know it today in the Western world came into being in several political environments, the most important of which were Greece, Rome, England, and early America. We can follow its development in the political and economic structure of the new states.

Criminal Law and Democracy in Ancient Greece

The decisive step in forming criminal law was taken in Athens at the beginning of the sixth century B.C. Solon, appointed *nomothete* (lawgiver or legislator), with dictatorial powers, instituted formal enactments giving every citizen the right of action in prosecution applying to some offenses. Greek society was in the throes of a political crisis. Solon's enactments, which formed the basis for the criminal law developing in Greece, were part of an attempt to solve the crisis and rehabilitate Greek government.

A number of facts have been established about the Athenian political struggle.[7] All functions of government were exclusively in the hands of the *eupatrids*, a hereditary class of Athenian aristocrats. The inferior orders of citizens, the peasant proprietors (the *georgi*) and the artisans (the *demiurgi*), could have no part in the government except by attaching themselves to a member of the aristocracy. Below these was the lowest class of freemen, the propertyless population (variously named *thetes, hectemori,* and *pelatae*), who had few rights and many of whom were no better off than serfs. Still lower were the slaves, without rights of any kind.

The class and political structure in Athens consisted of an oligarchy (government by the few) of the wealthy and privileged that ruled over a large proletariat (the nonpossessing, working class). The lower classes were politically subjugated and subjected to economic exploitation. This oppression, accompanied by the proletariat's increasing economic strength, eventually spurred discontent among those excluded from government. The ruling aristocrats reacted with compromise:

> In such a situation the alternative to revolution and perhaps tyranny was compromise, and this the ruling class, or some of them, were wise enough to see. And we must believe that these wiser men were keenly alive to the menace which confronted them in the presence of a prosperous alien population, chafing under the denial of the political rights to which their economic strength entitled them, ready at the first opportunity to fan into the flame of revolution the smouldering discontent of the native proletariat.[8]

The political compromise that arose from class conflict in ancient Greece was a beginning for the criminal law of the Western world. The step toward criminal law gave citizens some protection from one another and sometimes from government itself. By legal reform, as an alternative to possible revolution, Solon and his council set up courts, provided for appeal from the decisions of magistrates, and gave citizens the right to initiate prosecutions. The foundations of democratic government and criminal law occurred together in a mutually supportive relationship.

Victory was far from complete for the people of Athens, however.

> The democratic republic itself operated as a social dictatorship. It was the domination of a citizen minority who alone exercised political rights over the noncitizen majority of women, slaves and foreigners. And even within the boundaries of the citizen body, the wealthier elements dominated.[9]

A ruling class of slaveholders and rich merchants governed this early political democracy. The new criminal law served the interests of the dominant class in the democratic state.

Criminal Law in the Roman Empire

Criminal law developed slowly among the Romans. Although eventually they distinguished between *civilis* (private, civilian rights) and *criminalis* (criminal laws), law in Rome was devoted primarily to private legal matters and civil procedure. When a criminal law did develop, its principal business was trying offenses against the state and punishing such offenders. The Romans were efficient administrators of their empire, and not students and practitioners of justice.

The law of the Twelve Tables in the middle of the fifth century B.C. was based on the injured party's right to private vengeance. Punishment was inflicted by the state, however, for crimes committed directly against the commonwealth. Although most provisions in the Twelve Tables, as codifications of Roman customary law (the unwritten rules of the people), rested on private law, the Twelve Tables were originally created as a safeguard for part of the population. In effect the Twelve Tables protected the plebeians or common people against unfair treatment by the patricians or aristocrats.[10]

As Rome grew from a rural community to a powerful city-state, the "private criminal law" of the Twelve Tables was not enough.

> The "private criminal law" of the Twelve Tables reflected the conditions of a primitive commonwealth of modest dimensions and rustic character. It was bound to prove increasingly inadequate as Rome developed into a metropolis dominated by powerful social tensions; and the growth of the urban proletariat and of the slave population was certainly accompanied by a rise in criminality which demanded vigorous measures for the maintenance of public security.[11]

During the third century B.C. and the beginning of the second century, a criminal jurisdiction with courts was established to control those engaged in such politically threatening activities as violence, treason, arson, poisoning, carrying weapons, and stealing state property.[12]

The criminal law that appeared late in the Roman Republic was created mainly to protect the state itself. Protection of the individual's rights was not a vital part of Roman law. Criminal law was created by the interests that could be best satisfied by maintaining a strongly controlled political regime.

Criminal Law in England

Criminal law could come to be only as the state achieved political domination, allowing law to be established and administered in the name of a centralized governmental authority. For Anglo-American law, this evolution came in England late in the eleventh century and continued throughout the twelfth.[13] With the Norman invasion of England in 1066 and strong rule by the Norman kings, the old tribal-feudal system of law was replaced by a criminal law that lay in the hands of a central authority, the Crown. Before that the territory we now know as England was divided into separate units with their own laws. These legal systems could not foster a criminal law.

The Anglo-Saxons' law was originally a system of tribal justice. Each tribe, as a group of kinsmen, was controlled by its own chief and armed warriors who met for, among other duties, passing laws. Any wrong was regarded as against or by the family; and the family atoned for or carried out the blood feud if an offense occurred between kinship groups (between groups of people related by blood).

By the tenth century, England was divided into six or eight large kingdoms. Civil wars among local tribes had brought some political consolidation. The leaders accepted Christianity, which provided not only a spiritual unit but, as in the Roman Catholic Church, centralized control. In the reorganization, tribal chiefs were replaced by kings who became both military leaders and landlords. As feudalism changed the organization of Saxon society between the eighth and eleventh centuries, the blood feud was replaced by a system of compensation for offenses. Eventually the kinship group's collective responsibility was absorbed by the kingdom. Compensation for offenses became the domain of the king, lord, or bishop, rather than the kinship group. One of King Aethelred's laws made it a breach of the king's peace to resort to the feud before compensation had been demanded from the offender or his family.[14]

With the Norman invasion of England and the reign of the Norman kings the old tribal-feudal system of law disappeared and a new system appeared in England. When William had conquered England he proclaimed himself the "supreme landlord" of all England. By this move, implemented by the Domesday Survey, he redistributed the land, with the Norman nobles at the top, and placed all social relationships on land tenure, under his control. William took another important step, separating state law from canon (church) law. But the most important move in William's time toward a criminal law was unifying England under one head, the "king of England."

The administratively able Norman kings developed centralized legal institutions, creating several courts to place law under the jurisdiction of the king's government. Writs (orders written by the courts) were devised by which cases could be carried out of baronial courts into the king's courts. Itinerant judges were sent into the various "hundreds" and "shires" to administer the king's laws. By the end of Henry II's reign (1154 to 1189), the law of England was in the Crown's hands. A court of "common law" was established to apply the ancient and universal body of unwritten law to give justice to all people. A new procedure and a new conception of offenses had been created.[15] For the first time some offenses were regarded as clearly violating the peace of king and country. England had a criminal law.

English criminal law came about to protect particular interests, primarily those of the king. The criminal law placed the affairs of his subjects under his jurisdiction. The powerful landholders and the church could no longer freely create and administer law in their own courts. Law that affected the nation was now the king's law; the nation's interests were those of the king.

Eventually after many centuries the English monarch's power diminished and finally vanished when parliamentary government was created. Today, because of the political unification in the eleventh and twelfth centuries and the creation of criminal law at the same time, a common law survives. Its justice continues to be more common for some people than for others.

Law for the New Propertied Class

Laws to protect private property were soon established in England. The change from an agricultural economy to a new order based on industry and trade required legal structure to protect the interests of the new economic class. Before the fifteenth century the Western world had no legal conception of theft. During that century, in England, the modern law of theft was officially formulated into criminal law. It was shaped by changing social conditions, and especially by pressing economic interests. Defining theft as a crime solved a legal problem that arose within that historical context.

The English decision responsible for the legal concept of theft was pronounced in 1473, in the Carrier's Case, documented and interpreted by Jerome Hall in his book *Theft, Law and Society*.[16] The facts of the case are these: the defendant was hired to carry bales of goods to Southampton; instead of fulfilling his obligation, he carried the bales to another place, broke them open, and took the contents. The man was apprehended and charged with felony.

The most illustrious judges of the time discussed the case at length. Although the defendant was finally held guilty by a majority of the judges, a portentous legal problem developed during the proceedings. Before the case arose, the common law recognized no criminality in a person who came legally into possession of something and "converted" it to his own use. The reasoning followed in the common law was that the owner of transported goods was responsible for protecting himself by employing trustworthy employees. In this case, the legal problem was *stare decisis* ("following previous decisions"), in which the judges regarded themselves as bound by the common law.

Until the Carrier's Case it had been agreed that although trespass (taking property from one who is in possession of it) was an essential element of larceny, a person in possession of property could not commit a trespass upon that property. Because a bailee (an employee who is trusted with property) has possession, larceny could not technically be committed by such an employee. The judges, however, departed from precedent by introducing a new idea that could neither be found among the legal rules nor logically derived from them. For the judges held that "breaking bulk" terminated the bailment, that such property at once reverted to the bailor's possession, and that removing it from the bales supplied the trespass. Hall observes: "By this refinement the door was opened to admit into the law of larceny a whole series of acts which had up to that time been purely civil wrongs."[17] Law was being made by judges in the Carrier's Case by departing from and renouncing precedents from the common law.

An important question is which forces were active in creating a new legal concept. Hall outlines the changes that were occurring in fifteenth-century England. These, coupled with social conditions and institutions, made a change in the law of theft convenient. To begin with, in the political realm, the courts were subservient to the wishes of Edward IV; the special interests of the Crown therefore were protected by the courts. Among the king's interests that received the favor of the courts were the royal commercial activities, including trade with merchants on the continent. Edward was himself a merchant and carried on many private ventures.

Economic conditions were especially important for the decision reached in the Carrier's Case: a commercial revolution was taking place in England and Europe. The old feudal structure resting on an agricultural economy was giving way to a new order based on industry and trade. Also, "(1) the complainant was an alien merchant; (2) he had a covenant with the kings which provided safe passage for him and his goods; (3) the property taken is described as being within bales, and weighing twenty pounds; (4) the defendant was a carrier; (5) and he was to deliver the merchandise at Southampton."[18]

Hall contends that the complainant was a foreign merchant (probably

Italian) whose trade was desired by the Crown. Such foreign merchants were subject to special risks: local merchants were naturally hostile toward foreign trade. Moreover, foreign merchants were handicapped in transporting goods because they were uncertain of finding trustworthy carriers who would not abscond with the goods. The king attempted to relieve the situation by issuing covenants of safe-conduct through the country.

The merchandise taken by the bailee in the Carrier's Case was probably wool or cloth, or both, usually transported in bales. Also, Southampton was a principal port for shipping these goods, for trade with Latin countries in particular. All these deductions mean that "the interests of the most important industry in England were involved in the case."[19]

Conditions in fifteenth-century England directly affected the decision in the Carrier's Case:

> We are now in a position to visualize the case and the problem presented to the judges as a result of the legal, political and economic conditions described above. On the one hand, the whole complex aggregate of political and economic conditions described above thrusts itself upon the court. The more powerful forces of the time were inter-related very intimately and at many points: the New Monarchy and the *nouveau riche* — the mercantile class; the business interests of both and the consequent need for a secure carrying trade; the wool and textile industry, the most valuable, by far, in all the realm; wool and cloth, the most important exports; these exports and the foreign trade, this trade and Southampton, chief trading city with the Latin countries for centuries; the numerous and very influential Italian merchants who bought English wool and cloth inland and shipped them from Southampton. The great forces of an emerging modern world, represented in the above phenomena, necessitated the elimination of a formula which had outgrown its usefulness. A new set of major institutions required a new rule. The law, lagging behind the needs of the times, was brought into more harmonious relationship with the other institutions by the decision rendered in the Carrier's Case.[20]

The Carrier's Case of 1473 vividly demonstrates how changing social conditions and new class interests bring about the formulation of criminal law. The decision provided the framework for further developing the law of theft. Eventually, as banking and the use of paper currency grew, the law was expanded to include the act of embezzlement by clerks, officers, and the like. A parliament in the eighteenth century passed an embezzlement statute to protect mercantile interests.

The legal protection of property continues to be in the interest of the propertied class. Protecting private property became a basic purpose of criminal law in the new capitalist state. To this day a large portion of criminal law in the United States is devoted to protecting the property of the dominant economic class.

English Common Law in the American Colonies

The early criminal laws of the American colonies developed within the tradition of the English common law. The English charters for founding settlements in the New World provided that the laws established in the settlements should not be contrary to the laws of England. During the American colonial period, colonial statutes that were counter to the English common law could be disallowed by the Crown's Privy Council, the supreme legislative body. In addition, the decisions of the provincial courts were subject to appeal by the Privy Council where any radical departure from the common law could be corrected.[21] But in spite of these provisions for controlling the American colonies in accord with the political and economic interest of the Crown and stockholders in the companies that founded some American colonies, local interests shaped the early American criminal laws.

Some local conditions in the American colonies made English legal practices irrelevant or impractical. Even the vast differences in settlement and development within colonies would foster divergences in their legal systems.[22] Except for England's primary political interest in controlling its colonies, the colonies were relatively free to establish and administer their own legal systems.

The criminal laws that grew up in the colonies, however, did not depart substantially from English common law.[23] The interests embodied in it became instrumental in formulating American criminal law. Several forces, beyond the standards set by the Crown, were at work to ensure continuance of English common law in America. A vital one was that the early settlers coming from the mother country were deeply imbued with the ideas and traditions of the common law. Another was adherence to the liberal ideal of democracy. The natural-law conception of inherent rights as human beings inspired the Declaration of Independence (1776) as it had the British Bill of Rights (1689).[24] John Locke's formula, "life, liberty, and property" (later broadened to include the pursuit of happiness), was an underlying value for American law. The English common law was exalted and perpetuated in nineteenth-century America by the popularity of such codifications as Sir Edward Coke's *Institutes* and Sir William Blackstone's *Commentaries on the Laws of England.* One more force made the interests of English common law the same as those of American law: attempts by lawyers to adapt the common law to American conditions.[25] Although they ran into much conflict with their colleagues, American lawyers were generally successful in asserting England's legal heritage against provincial interests.

All these forces combined to produce an American law incorporating the class interests of English common law. Political independence did not signify new beginnings in law. How can we best describe early legal development in the United States? It supported the interests of an emerging capitalist class in the development of a capitalist society.

Law in the Expansion of the United States

As the United States expanded, several legal problems became apparent. One was the legal status and control of the native Americans, the Indians. Another was legal regulation of the people in territories that did not yet have their own law. The third problem, at times related to the others, was controlling the expanding labor force, including many slaves.

The English Crown did not recognize the sovereign right of the native Indians, acknowledging only their right of occupancy in the land.[26] Because the continent had no written rules, any law established in America was to be imposed by the Crown or by the colonial settlers according to standards set by the Crown. As the law evolved, any offense against the colony by Indians outside colonial territory was administered by tribal leaders. But for Indians within the territory, cases were tried in colonial courts. The Indians subject to colonial law were judged not by their own customary law but according to the English settlers' interests. Law was being used to dispossess the Indians of their own lands.[27]

Later a new problem arose in formulating and administering law in the western Indian territory. The federal government sent agents and legal officers into the expanding territories. Infantry troops first brought "law" to the Indian territories in the west, carrying out treaties and government policy — moving the Indians from their land. Courts were established to settle disputes between whites and Indians.

When the United States Court for the Western District of Arkansas was created at Fort Smith, and Judge Isaac C. Parker was appointed, a new phase of law and order arrived on the frontier. On May 2, 1875, Judge Parker arrived in Fort Smith to take over the federal district court of the territory. His task was to control the Indians and to put an end to the "outlawry" of the breed of men who have since become western folk heroes. Judge Parker quickly acquired his reputation as "the hanging judge." In his twenty-one years on the bench at Fort Smith, he heard 13,490 cases and convicted 9,454 persons, of whom 344 were tried for offenses punishable by death. Of the 344 cases, 165 were convicted and 160 of these were sentenced to the gallows. Seventy-nine were eventually hanged, two were killed attempting to escape, and two more died in jail awaiting execution. Judge Parker saw it all as his mission:

> During the twenty years that I have engaged in administering the law here, the contest has been one between civilization and savagery, the savagery being represented by the intruding criminal class. The United States government, in its treaties from the days of Andrew Jackson, stipulated that this criminal element should be kept out of the country, but the treaties have only been made to be broken. . . . Thus this class keeps on increasing; its members marry, and the criminal population keeps ever growing larger. . . . At the present time there seems to be a criminal wave sweeping over the country, the like of which I have not yet seen before.[28]

Judge Parker, according to his sympathetic biographer, "had taken pardonable pride in eradicating lawlessness from his jurisdiction. He had taught the criminal class to fear the law and respect the rights and property of peaceful citizens, and had helped the Indian advance to a higher civilization."[29]

In the fast-growing western mining camps some kind of order was needed to resolve the conflicts between miners and the disputes over land and mining rights. As yet no territorial or state governments had been formed to create and administer law. In this void a "local law" appeared among the miners to regulate their own interests.[30] A popular sovereignty was created in the mining territory to formulate and administer its own form of law. The miners' customs, or local laws, spread through the western territories. Eventually, when states were formally established, the miners' local laws were enacted into statute law or incorporated into the legal precedents of court decisions. In the nineteenth century miners' economic interests were formulated into laws that still apply in the twentieth century.

All this time a country expanding both geographically and economically required a labor force to carry out the productive work for the capitalist class. Excluding the Indians from their own lands provided the new propertied class with the territory they needed to accumulate capital. But they also needed a legal order that would ensure a supply of workers, both native labor and that imported from Europe and Asia. The laborers likewise had to be controlled on the plantations, in the factories, and in their own communities. Criminal law served the new capitalist class in securing these objectives.

Even in colonial times much of the population was a controlled labor force, usually handled as indentured servants.[31] Unfree labor, both white and black, provided labor power for the rising bourgeoisie. Gradually black slaves were imported explicitly for exploitable labor.[32] By 1775 the black slave population reached about half a million, and grew steadily over the next century. Throughout the colonial period immigrants from

Europe and Asia were brought in to work in the factories. Alongside the new capitalist class grew a working class that was employed in a wide range of capitalist production, from rural agriculture to urban industry. A criminal law subsequently developed to contain the class struggle that was now predominant in American capitalist society.

The law was formulated and then systematically administered against workers to establish a docile labor force. Moreover, the criminal law was used to make sure that anyone believed to be inferior to the members of the capitalist class — especially blacks, Orientals, Indians, and poor whites — stayed in their place. The law, supported by white racism, excluded people from rights legally shared by the bourgeoisie. Indians and Chinese were not allowed to testify in court, and were restricted from owning land. Slave codes prevented blacks from testifying in court; and blacks (free and slave alike) were barred from some occupations.[33] Special criminal sanctions aimed at blacks were devised for those violating a host of laws. "Throughout the past," Haywood Burns writes, "the racism of American society has been reflected in its legal system."[34]

Today, the most explicit racial distinctions are gone from the criminal codes. Nevertheless, "there is much about the law today that may not be racist on its face but is racist in its impact."[35] Covert racism still taints judicial and administrative discretion. In making arrests, prosecuting, adjudicating, sentencing, and executing, race is still very much a factor in the legal system. The poor and the nonwhite are subordinated legally as well as socially in the United States. In fact, the law is used to enforce the patterns of social life that characterize capitalist society.

Legal Order and the Rise of Corporate Capitalism

The legal order of the United States changed and adapted as the nation grew economically. Each stage of economic development requires a specific kind of legal order to ensure the dominance and continuance of the new capitalist system. The main contradictions inherent in each stage of development must somehow be resolved. Criminal law is one of the primary ways of maintaining the social order, managing the problems (including criminality) caused by structural conditions, and helping the capitalist system grow further.

Each new stage in the economy, conditioned by the preceding movements of history, brings about its own forms of social reality — and related problems of existence. Each period requires, in turn, a definite kind of legal order. Early in American history, the legal order was a collection of laws imported from the Old World, modified to meet the needs of an agricultural economy. Gradually as the mercantile economy grew and the

In an engraving of the 1880s titled "His First Offense," a man accompanied by his family stands humbly in a courtroom before lawyers, jury, and judge. Most likely a laborer, dressed appropriately for the occasion, the defendant receives the benevolent attention of the court. The engraving captures the image of justice in the period of industrializing capitalism, when a social and economic order was being established for further capitalist accumulation.

national state was formed, laws were made in the courts and in the legislative bodies that regulated this growth and protected it from disruption.

For the first hundred years of nationhood the United States resisted large-scale capitalist production. Independant production of commodities predominated; farmers, artisans, small manufacturers and other petty producers were the mainstay of the economy.[36] Only as northern capitalists acquired property and as immigrant labor power was imported from abroad did capitalism finally appear in the United States. It came when capitalists won the battle over who was to control the labor power of the population. The economy could now develop along capitalist lines, whereby those who own the means of production (the capitalist class) can exploit the labor of those (the working class) who do not own and control the means of production. A criminal law gradually formed, ensuring this structural arrangement.

And then the American political and economic system moved from early mercantile capitalism (up to Jackson's presidency), to laissez-faire capitalism (climaxing after the Civil War), to maturing industrial-corporate capitalism.[37] Today we are in a stage of late, advanced capitalism in the United States. The current meaning of criminal law can be understood as part of capitalism today. The meaning of criminal law at one time or another in the past also has to be understood according to the stage of capitalism's development. Only by investigating and analyzing law's part in the development of capitalism do we understand the contemporary legal order.

LEGISLATING CRIME CONTROL

As capitalism grew in the United States, the state's intervention expanded in all political, economic, and social realms. The present stage of advanced capitalism requires a highly rational and efficient legal order instituted and administered by the state. This kind of order, emphasizing control of crime, is now an essential part of the political economy.

During the 1960s the legal order entered a new stage of development.[38] Early in the decade the nation's problems were simply and conveniently concentrated on one domestic enemy — crime. Crime and fear of it were crucial in political campaigns. The federal government assumed a new role, launching the "war on crime." In a presidential message to the 89th Congress in 1965, Lyndon Johnson declared that "we must arrest and reverse the trend toward lawlessness."[39] Suggesting that "crime has become a malignant enemy in America's midst," the president charted a course that would use legal control and law enforcement: "This active combat against crime calls for a fair and efficient system of law enforcement to deal with those who break the law. It means new priority to the methods and institutions of law enforcement."

The problem was conceived to be a national one, and crime prevention and crime fighting were to be intensified at all levels of government. The federal effort, Johnson continued, would consist of "(1) increased federal law enforcement efforts, (2) assistance to local enforcement efforts, and (3) a comprehensive, penetrating analysis of the origins and nature of crime in modern America." The president appointed a commission — the President's Commission on Law Enforcement and Administration of Justice — to study the crime problem and to make recommendations for action. Hearings were held by the Senate Judiciary Committee, and legislation to control crime was subsequently enacted.

Today the government undertakes control of crime by national laws and enforcement agencies. The federal government, especially through its legislative bodies, establishes official policies of control. Since 1968, Congress has enacted several crime bills that reveal how it felt the established order was being challenged, as in the statement opening one of the crime bills:

> Congress finds that the high incidence of crime in the United States threatens the peace, security and general welfare of the Nation and its citizens. To prevent crime and to insure the greater safety of the people, law enforcement efforts must be better coordinated, intensified, and made more effective at all levels of government.
>
> Congress finds further that crime is essentially a local problem that must be dealt with by State and local governments if it is to be controlled effectively.
>
> It is therefore the declared policy of the Congress to assist State and local governments in strengthening and improving law enforcement at every level by national assistance. It is the purpose of this title to (1) encourage States and units of general local government to prepare and adopt comprehensive plans based upon their evaluation of State and local problems of law enforcement; (2) authorize grants to States and units of local government in order to improve and strengthen law enforcement; and (3) encourage research and development directed toward the improvement of law enforcement and the development of new methods for the prevention and reduction of crime and the detection and apprehension of criminals.[40]

Not only was the war on crime intensified by this legislation, but the federal government stimulated local governments to engage in the battle by creating the LEAA, with large amounts of financing and guidance.

President Johnson sounded the call in a message to Congress in 1967, warning the legislators that "crime — and the fear of crime — has become a public malady," and reminded them of their "duty to seek its cure."[41] Johnson's legislative proposals gave Congress the opportunity to further define the problem. Hearings were held by the Senate Subcommittee on Criminal Laws and Procedures and by the House Judiciary Committee, providing the framework for defining the problem of crime in modern words, and suggesting stricter law enforcement, more limited rights for defendants, and use of the most recent technology in the war on crime. The Senate Committee's chairman, John McClellan, opened the hearings on March 7, 1967, by stating that "It is quite probable that these hearings and the bills we will be considering will mark the turning point in the struggle against lawlessness in this nation."[42] The survival of the state and the social and economic order (the "society") seemed to be at stake:

"The rate of increase in crime cannot continue if our society is to remain safe and secure and our people protected against the ravages of crime."

These efforts culminated in the Omnibus Crime Control and Safe Streets Act of 1968. The new crime legislation initially assisted state and local governments by making law enforcement and criminal administration more effective — in trying to ensure domestic order more effectively. By the time the bill was passed it carried several amendments in a deliberate attempt to overturn Supreme Court decisions that supposedly "coddled criminals" and "handcuffed the police." All voluntary confessions and eyewitness identifications — regardless of whether a defendant had been informed of his rights to counsel — could be admitted in federal trials. State and local law-enforcement agencies were given broad permission to tap telephones and engage in other forms of eavesdropping. Law-enforcement officials were permitted these practices without a court order. Anyone convicted of "inciting a riot or civil disorder," "organizing, promoting, encouraging, or participating in a riot or civil disorder," or "aiding and abetting any person in committing" such offenses would be disqualified for employment by the federal government for five years. The legislation was a clear attempt to control by means of the criminal law any behavior that might seem to threaten established order.

The government has continued enacting crime-control legislation. The Congress and the presidency have worked together to construct a comprehensive program for controlling crime.[43] Several congressional committees — including four Senate committees, five House committees, and two appropriations committees — actively formulated policies on control of crime. From these efforts came a crime bill for the District of Columbia, drug control legislation, a bill on organized crime, and proposals for future legislation. There is no sign that the administration and the Congress will cease their interests and activities in controlling crime.

In July 1970, President Nixon signed into law the District of Columbia crime bill. Crime there had become a symbolic issue for the president and Congress, deserving an exemplary program for controlling crime. This bill has new laws of regulation and these potentially repressive measures:

> Authorization for "no-knock" searches, under which a policeman with a warrant could force his way into a building without announcing his presence or identifying himself if there was reason to believe evidence inside would otherwise be destroyed.
>
> Preventive, or pretrial, detention, under which a defendant could be jailed without bail for up to 60 days if a hearing established that he might commit further crimes if he were released.
>
> Establishment of a mandatory five-year sentence upon a second conviction for a crime of violence in which the defendant was carrying a gun.

Authorization for wiretaps by the police with court approval, but restricting their use when the communication involved was between physician and patient; attorney and client; clergyman and parishioner; or husband and wife.[44]

The bill not only regulates crime in the District of Columbia, but, as Attorney General Mitchell suggested, is a model for all the states.

The government's crime control was further advanced in October 1970 by the Organized Crime Control Act. Although labeled an "organized-crime" bill, its provisions apply to many kinds of offenses.[45] Fundamental procedural policies cover such matters as grand-jury powers, illegally obtained evidence, long sentences, self-incrimination, and due process of law. Grand juries are instructed to issue reports on noncriminal misconduct by an appointed public official, with little safeguard for the accused against reports made by the grand jury. Federal judges are authorized to impose an additional sentence of up to 25 years on a class of so-called "dangerous special offenders." The sentence can be imposed upon a convicted person in a hearing before a judge rather than in a jury trial. The bill also revises the laws dealing with immunity of a witness from prosecution and other procedural safeguards, to overcome some problems in gathering evidence.

Soon after the organized crime bill came the Comprehensive Drug Abuse Prevention and Control Act. Like the organized crime bill, the new law covered activities related only superficially to drug control and suspended some constitutional rights. Witnesses could be forced to testify in almost any federal case; new provisions were made for admitting wiretapping evidence; grand-jury powers were extended; search and seizure without warrant were expanded; and special offenders could be given extended sentences by judges. Drug control, like control over other criminal activities, had become an excuse for Congress and the presidency to control anything that seemed to threaten the social order.

The government continues to expand its crime control program. As the seventies began, the Senate could praise itself for passing a good share of legislation for the program. Of twenty proposed anticrime measures, thirteen had already been passed by the Senate by January 1970. The Senate majority leader, Mike Mansfield, could state: "After the passage of these bills, we may then direct ourselves to the more difficult tasks of identifying and addressing ourselves to the task of eradicating the causes of criminal behavior."[46] Even if the government turned to the conditions that underlie behavior defined as criminal, it is unlikely that the system that makes crime possible would get a critical examination. There would be no critique of the American capitalist system.

Legislation on crime control continues to be enacted by the state to control problems that cannot be solved within the framework of advanced capitalism. The innovations and reforms in crime control (now called "criminal justice") combine the traditional conservative and liberal approaches to social problems into an overall system of criminal justice. Whether the specific programs, strategies, and techniques of criminal justice are explicitly repressive and coercive, or more subtle and seemingly more humanistic, the purpose is a system of control for preserving late capitalism.

The direction that criminal justice is taking is indicated in the revision of the criminal code of the federal government. It is taken from a criminal code written by the National Commission on Reform of Federal Criminal Laws and modified by subsequent amendments. In practice the new crime bill, first known as S-1, and then as S-1437, provides the legal basis for further repression by the capitalist state.[47] Not only is state control broadened in these and other proposals, with political expression by citizens further restricted, but the state is permitted to legally perform criminal acts in protecting the capitalist order.

Even when the crimes of government agencies are exposed, as in the recent disclosures of illegal surveillance, political assassination, covert operations, and the like by the Central Intelligence Agency (CIA) and the FBI, the government response is not to prevent these criminal acts but to strengthen the agencies and the security of their secrets.[48] In fact, some of the current proposals, a number of which can be instituted merely by executive order, give law-enforcement agencies a legal basis for some domestic activities that, when conducted in the past, have been done either illegally or with questionable authority. That which the capitalist state regards as a threat to its interests and its survival is subject to control through the state's own criminal (but legalized) methods. This is criminal justice under advanced capitalism.

The most ominous consequence of the revised federal code is the expanded jurisdiction of the federal government over crime and criminal justice. Control of crime and the criminal justice system are being developed, coordinated, and increasingly administered by the federal government. As the highest level of the capitalist state, the federal government becomes the ultimate political authority in the late stages of capitalist development.

Yet, even these measures of criminal justice cannot provide an enduring solution to the problem of crime. Strengthening the system of criminal justice only strengthens the larger system that generates crime in the first place. To deal with crime within the capitalist framework, by furthering legal repression, is to accept the inevitability of crime and to submit to the system that produces crime. The only real solution to crime is to be found in the class struggle. It is a political struggle against capitalism.

NATIONAL LAW ENFORCEMENT

Control of crime under advanced capitalism in the United States consists of much more than the efforts made by local police departments and criminal courts. Indeed, control is being determined increasingly by the federal government. The middle sixties began a great change in law enforcement and administration of justice. Responding to the threats against American institutions, the federal government took the leadership in controlling crime. Pursuing its war on crime, it created an apparatus for controlling crime unparalleled in world history. We must examine this rationalized, coordinated, and scientifically advanced national system for controlling crime.

The modern state creates a complex of bureaucratic agencies as it establishes control over the population. These agencies carry out the objectives of state authority, and also solidify and protect the economic interests that underpin the state. An adequate picture of the state control of crime must therefore take into account what these bureaucratic agencies do. The state bureaucracies and the people who function within them reinforce the state's political and economic objectives.

The United States federal government had long shied away from interfering in local law-enforcement activities, but by the mid-sixties the time was ripe for a program that would give national direction to law enforcement. At President Johnson's urging, in a special message to Congress on February 6, 1967, greater federal efforts and expenditures for law enforcement were suggested "to strengthen the system and to encourage the kind of innovations needed to respond to the problems of crime in America."[49] Congress responded by creating the Office of Law Enforcement Assistance, within the Department of Justice. The new agency supported projects including "training, research and demonstration efforts to prevent and control crime; to improve law enforcement, corrections, courts and other criminal justice agencies; and to assist these agencies in recruiting and upgrading personnel."[50]

But this was only the beginning. By 1968 Congress had passed the Omnibus Crime Control and Safe Streets Act, in which a major provision (Title I) created the Law Enforcement Assistance Administration (LEAA). As an agency within the Department of Justice, to replace and supersede the Office of Law Enforcement Assistance, LEAA assumed a broader and more pervasive plan of federal involvement in law enforcement and crime control. Support for the enlarged program came from all quarters, because domestic security was the name of the game.

The LEAA has grown steadily, although some decline in funding is likely to take place. During its first year it received a congressional appropriation of $63 million. The budget increased sharply to $268 million in 1970, and was further increased to $529 million in 1971. By 1977 the budget had gone up to $753 million; and there has been yearly funding of $800 million for 1978 and 1979.[51] In preparing one of the annual reports, the administrator of the LEAA, citing the generous appropriations, advised the president and the Congress on the mission and success of his agency:

> The mission of LEAA is to reduce crime and delinquency by channeling Federal financial aid to state and local governments, to conduct research in methods of improving law enforcement and criminal justice, to fund efforts to upgrade the educational level of law enforcement personnel, to develop applications of statistical research and applied systems analysis in law enforcement, and to develop broad policy guidelines for both the short and long-range improvement of the nation's Criminal Justice System as a whole.[52]

Most of the LEAA's budget goes to states and localities for the fight against crime. Officially, this is the objective:

> State and local governments receive the bulk of LEAA aid. To be effective, law enforcement planning and action programs must be broad and comprehensive. Congress recognized that the most meaningful primary unit to accomplish improvements is the state. Within this framework, the state and its cities can increase cooperation; there can be greater coordination among police, courts, and corrections. The bulk of the LEAA budget therefore goes in block grants to the 50 states, which in turn re-allocate most of those funds to their city and county governments.[53]

Nevertheless, though the states are the units for receiving block grants, "the goal of the LEAA program is across-the-board improvement of the Nation's criminal justice system." Thus, we are told, "For the first time in our history, all levels of government and all parts of the criminal justice system are working together in a coordinated, nationwide approach to the urgent problems of crime and criminal justice."[54]

To carry out its program "more effectively and efficiently," the LEAA has gone through several bureaucratic reorganizations. The function of the agency's headquarters in Washington now "is largely to develop and implement policy guidelines, to channel Federal funds to the states, to undertake research, to provide special assistance to states in such areas as applied systems analysis, and to provide technical assistance."[55] In other words, LEAA seems to be trying to maximize the possibility of building a comprehensive national program for controlling crime, under the guise of decentralization. Each state, however, in order to receive the grants and technical assistance of the LEAA, has had to set up a comprehensive law-enforcement agency. And to be eligible for federal funds, each state agency must annually draw up a law-enforcement plan, which must in turn be approved by the LEAA, for "comprehensive state-wide law enforcement improvements in police, courts, and corrections."

Along with encouraging, or forcing, state governments to develop law-enforcement plans, the LEAA awards federal funds to state and local governments for developing programs to improve and strengthen law enforcement, gives funds for training law-enforcement agents, and supports research and the development of methods for improving law enforcement and reducing crime. These programs are administered in the three operating divisons of the LEAA: the Office of Criminal Justice Assistance, the National Institute of Law Enforcement and Criminal Justice, and the Office of Operations Support. In other words, a nationally sponsored program for controlling crime has been created. At the same time, a huge bureaucracy has been created not only in Washington but in every state. It is some encouragement for those who fear governmental repression that much of the funds and energies of the LEAA are used up merely keeping these bureaucracies going. The potential effectiveness of the LEAA is necessarily limited by its bureaucracy.[56]

But the aims are specific and of lasting consequence. In testimony before the Legal and Monetary Affairs Subcommittee of Congress, the administrator of the LEAA, Jerris Leonard, made clear the government's objectives in the war on crime:

> For the future, reducing crime nationally will not be an easy job. It will not be cheap, in either labor or money. But it can be done, and the present LEAA program must be the major vehicle for doing it.
>
> For those without blinders, unmistakable signs of progress already are evident. Many more will become apparent if we can have unmatched dedication by local, state, and federal officials; responsible assistance from the Congress, whose Judiciary Committees gave LEAA a remarkably sound bill of health following extended hearings last year.
>
> In many ways, American citizens are safer now than they were three years ago. A year from now, they will be safer than they are today. The decade of the 1960s ended as the most lawless in our history. The decade of the 1970s can end with crime long since under control, if we are not diverted from our task by phantoms.[57]

The system of criminal justice more explicitly controls that which cannot be remedied by other programs or social services in the economy. The police, the courts, and the penal agencies — the entire criminal-justice system — expands to cope as a last resort with the problems of the capitalist economy.[58] And as the contradictions of capitalism increase, this system becomes a preventive institution as well as a control and corrective agency. State expenditures on criminal justice absorb a larger share of the state's budgetary expenses. Criminal justice as a social expense of the state necessarily expands with the further development of capitalism.

CRIME CONTROL BY THE DEPARTMENT OF JUSTICE

The federal government concentrates its crime control efforts within the agencies in the Department of Justice (Figure 3.1). With the principal forces of crime control now centralized in the Justice Department, the possibility of controlling the citizenry is considerable. Not only is the Justice Department engaged in law enforcement and administration of justice, it is establishing the policies for controlling crime as well. Legal repression by the state becomes necessary as the ultimate attempt to deal with problems that cannot be solved under the conditions of advanced capitalism.

The Federal Bureau of Investigation

Control of crime has traditionally been handled by the Justice Department's Federal Bureau of Investigation. Since its creation by a secret executive order in Theodore Roosevelt's administration, the FBI has evolved into a national police and investigative force with 9,000 special agents, a clerical staff of 10,000, 59 regional offices, and hundreds of local "resident offices."[59] But more significant still is the FBI's involvement beyond simply investigating violations of federal law: it specializes in gathering domestic intelligence and protecting internal security. Its history is one of controlling "domestic subversion," from investigating spy activities in wartime, to pursuing communists, to suppressing radical political action in recent years. Under its long-time former director, J. Edgar Hoover, the FBI became a self-perpetuating bureaucracy that, though occasionally criticized, sometimes operates beyond public control for the benefit of itself and the government.[60] Those who expected the FBI to change after Hoover died in 1972 ignored the FBI's bureaucracy and the service it performs for the state in maintaining domestic security.

Over the years the FBI has been able to extend its activities in surveillance by legislative enactments overturning Supreme Court decisions. Since the mid-sixties the FBI has freely engaged in electronic eavesdropping, court-ordered and otherwise.[61] Each year the telephones of tens of

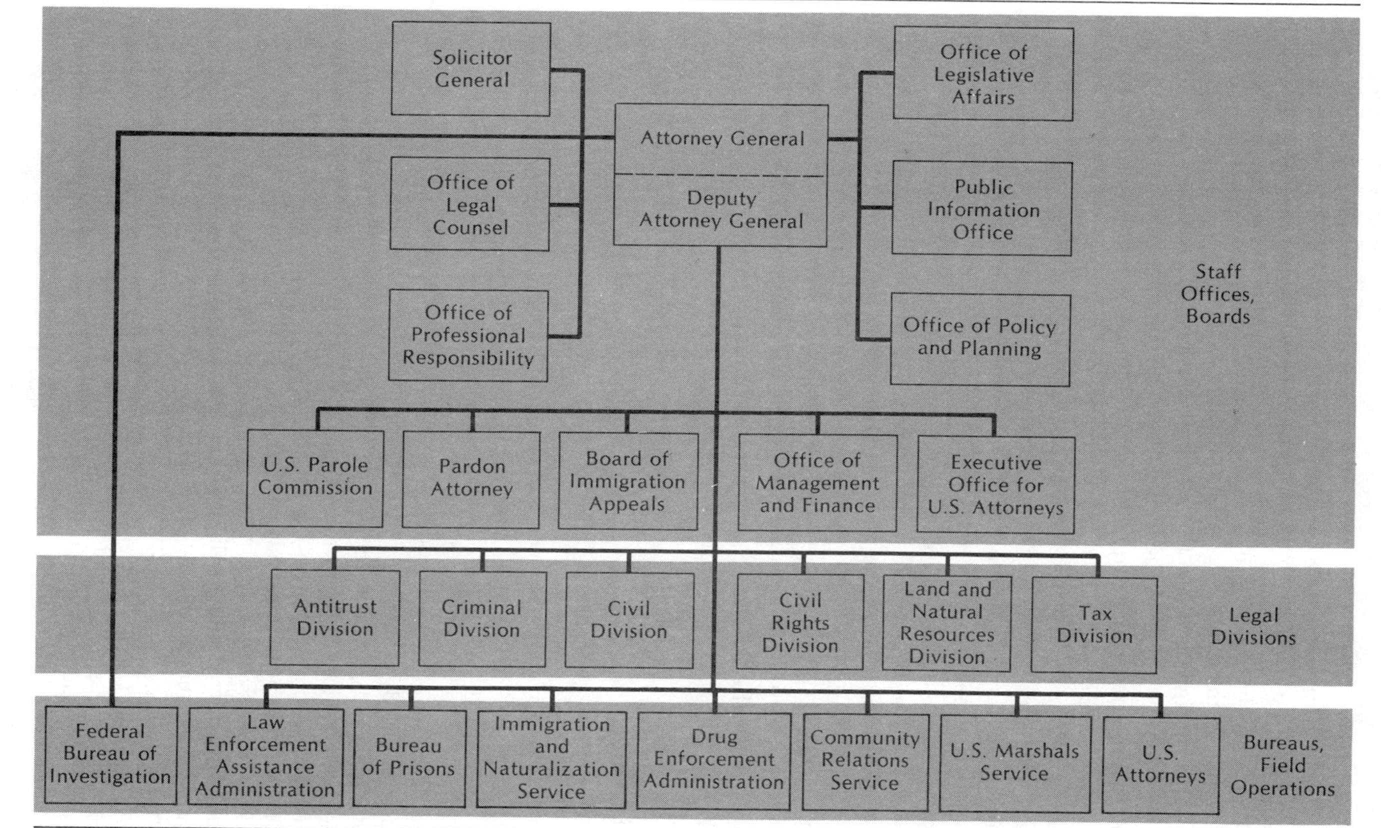

Source: *Annual Report of the Attorney General of the United States, 1976* (Washington, D.C.: U.S. Government Printing Office, 1977), p. v.

FIGURE 3.1 United States Department of Justice

thousands of citizens are wiretapped, at a cost of about $5 million for this operation alone. Using the title "national security," the FBI legally and illegally justifies the wiretaps. Defending the government's inherent right to listen in on dissident domestic groups, Deputy Attorney General Richard Kleindienst maintained that no distinction can be made between Americans and foreigners when the aim is to destroy the government: "It would be silly to say that an American citizen, because he is an American, could subvert the government by actions of violence or revolution and be immune from, first, identification, and second, prosecution."[62]

In the early seventies it came as a shock to many Americans that the government was spying on them. In a Senate investigation led by the Subcommittee on Constitutional Rights (chaired by Sam J. Ervin, Jr.), it was disclosed that several government agencies, the FBI included, were heavily involved in obtaining intelligence information on hundreds of thousands of law-abiding yet suspect citizens. With the justification that domestic security is in jeopardy, the government is building a "national data bank," or "criminal justice information center," for instantly retrievable intelligence information on "persons of interest." The government's purpose is to avert internal subversion and threats to the domestic order. Upon discovering the existence and extensiveness of such surveillance, *The New York Times* reported to its readers:

> The Government is gathering information on its citizens in the following reservoirs of facts:
>
> A Secret Service computer, one of the newest and most sophisticated in Government. In its memory the names and dossiers of activists, "malcontents," persistent seekers of redress, and those who would "embarrass" the President or other Government leaders are filed with those of potential assassins and persons convicted of "threats against the President."
>
> A data bank compiled by the Justice Department's civil disturbance group. It produces a weekly printout of national tension points on racial, class and political issues and the individuals and groups involved in them. Intelligence on peace rallies, welfare protests and the like provide the "data base" against which the computer measures the mood of the nation and the militancy of its citizens. Judgments are made; subjects are listed as "radical" or "moderate."
>
> A huge file of microfilmed intelligence reports, clippings and other materials on civilian activity maintained by the Army's Counterintelligence Analysis Division in Alexandria, Va. Its purpose is to help prepare deployment estimates for troop commands on alert to respond to civil disturbances in 25 American cities. Army intelligence was ordered earlier this year to destroy a larger data bank and to stop assigning agents to "penetrate" peace groups and civil rights

organizations. But complaints persist that both are being continued. Civilian officials of the Army say they "assume" they are not.

Computer files intended to catch criminal suspects — the oldest and most advanced type with the longest success record — maintained by the Federal Bureau of Investigation's National Crime Information Center and recently installed by the Customs Bureau. The crime center's computer provides 40,000 instant, automatic teletype printouts each day on wanted persons and stolen property to 49 states and Canada and it also "talks" to 24 other computers operated by state and local police departments for themselves and a total of 2,500 police jurisdictions. The center says its information is all "from the public record," based on local and Federal warrants and complaints, but the sum product is available only to the police.

A growing number of data banks on other kinds of human behavior, including, for example, a cumulative computer file on 300,000 children of migrant farm workers kept by the Department of Health, Education and Welfare. The object is to speed the distribution of their scholastic records, including such teacher judgments as "negative attitude," to school districts with larger itinerant student enrollments. There is no statutory control over distribution of the data by its local recipients — to prospective employers, for example.[63]

The war is here at home; domestic security is at stake.

A national intelligence network has been constructed. Started as a $45 million LEAA pilot project called SEARCH (Systems for Electronic Analysis and Retrieval of Criminal Histories), it has grown into a computerized "criminal justice information center," operated by the FBI. The information includes not only official records, such as an individual's arrest record (regardless of the eventual disposition of the case), but information compiled from other sources as well. The computerized intelligence system contains information derived from informants, wiretaps, employers, and the like.[64]

The intelligence-gathering network functions through separate computer centers set up by each state. All records, criminal and otherwise, will be stored and then transmitted to the FBI for filing in the National Crime Information Center (NCIC).[65] Each locality decides how much and what kind of information to feed into its computer; and all the information, regardless of its validity or legality, is pumped into the national computer in Washington.

With the national intelligence system in operation, law-enforcement agents have instant access to information on any person they regard as "suspicious." The national state has a system that enables government agents to control domestic order. In the name of combating crime, the state is now able to obtain information on as many people as it wants to and make it instantly available for use against them. This new anticrime

In waging the war on crime, "satellite" scanners such as this have been developed and installed to keep an "eye" on potential shoplifters. The images from the camera are stored on video tape for purposes of arrest and prosectuion.

technology, in the form of a computerized data bank, has threatening implications, even from a constitutional standpoint.

> The new technology has made it literally impossible for a man to start again in our society. It has removed the quality of mercy from our institutions by making it impossible to forget, to understand, to tolerate. . . . The undisputed

> and unlimited possession of the resources to build and operate data banks on individuals, and to make decisions about people with the aid of computers and electronic data systems, is fast securing to executive branch officials a political power which the authors of the Constitution never meant any one group of men to have over all others.[66]

The modern system of criminal justice, aided by science and technology, becomes the state's ultimate political instrument. Criminal justice is being used in the attempt to preserve the capitalist system.

Controlling Domestic Order

The war on crime began as a governmental attack on "crime in the streets," The presidential and congressional elections of 1964 and 1968 capitalized on the rising crime rate in America. Each candidate blamed the problem on the others. Richard Nixon, in the election of 1968, committed himself to a full-scale attack on the problem. Blaming the rising crime rate on the incumbent administration, he had to deal with lawlessness as soon as he entered the White House. The greatest threat to law and order now seemed to be the protests against the war in Vietnam, the draft system, and racial injustice. With his attorney general, John Mitchell, and ready assistance by Hoover and the FBI, he turned public attention to these politically dissident actions as the really serious crimes facing the nation.

Shortly after the president took office, the attorney general announced that he intended to prosecute "hard-line militants," such as those who crossed state lines "to incite riots" on college campuses. The attorney general told the nation, citing evidence collected by the FBI, that "a great deal of evidence has been collected on this aspect of campus disorders," and that "I would say this is a very serious component."[67] A few days later, the assistant attorney general announced to the public that he was prepared to prosecute such militants under the newly enacted antiriot law. "These statements," Richard Harris writes in his study of the early years of Nixon's Department of Justice, "on top of a promise by Deputy Attorney General Kleindienst to go after 'radical, revolutionary, anarchistic kids,' suggested that the Department now fully shared Hoover's conviction that most of the trouble in the country was caused by a few radicals and that if they were locked up everything would be fine again."[68]

The government was prepared therefore to launch a concerted drive against political dissent, expressed in thought, word, or deed. Political dissent was now defined as criminal by a legal structure created for that purpose and meant to provide for its control. Attacks began to be carried out by the government. A trial was held against the "Boston Five" for conspiring to interfere with the operations of the Selective Service System by organizing public rallies, writing and circulating dissident statements, and encouraging draft-age men to resist the draft.[69] Similarly, the government prosecuted the "Chicago Eight" for conspiring to cross state lines, during the 1968 Democratic Convention, with intent to incite a riot and commit some illegal act. The "Oakland Seven" were charged with conspiracy to commit the misdemeanors of trespass and resisting arrest in a stop-the-draft demonstration. The "Harrisburg Seven" were tried for, among other things, a plot to kidnap presidential advisor Henry Kissinger. Daniel Ellsberg was tried for passing Pentagon documents to the press. And Black Panther groups were harassed in various ways, including raids and killing by local and federal agents. Political action against the government, or against its policies, had been defined as such a threat to the regime that dubious criminal charges and repressive acts had to be undertaken.

The government has continued to use many legal weapons in attempting to secure domestic order. Although the conspiracy law has not been upheld in higher appeals courts, the law with its ensuing trials has nevertheless stifled dissent. In addition to the conspiracy prosecutions, false raids on private premises, and invasions of human rights, the government has resorted to tactics available in the legal system. A "preventive detention" law has been enacted to detain "dangerous" persons. As a pretrial detention measure, defendants can be confined to jail by a judge's decision, being denied the right to bail. And the mass arrest has been used to detain large numbers of political demonstrators. In the May Day demonstration of 1971 in Washington, nearly 13,000 were rounded up and confined in jails and special camps. Although most of the charges were later dropped, the government had stopped a protest against itself. These tactics do not usually result in successful prosecutions, however, and often are judged unconstitutional.

A new use of the grand jury symbolizes the administration's initiative in crime control: "The nationwide grand jury network is emerging as a 'chosen instrument' of an Administration strategy to curb dissent and to intimidate and demoralize radicals. This strategy is so effective because federal prosecuting officials — who themselves have no power of subpoena — are using the coercive powers of the grand jury for police and intelligence purposes."[70] The federal grand jury operation is directed and coordinated by the Internal Security Division (ISD) of the Department of Justice. It reviews thousands of FBI reports about radical activities, determining violations of statutes. Further information is provided by the Justice Department's Interdivisional Intelligence Unit (IDIU), now a broad intelligence system that observes and collects data on many radical activities. With this information, grand juries are activated by the government to hold secret sessions on suspected criminal or subversive activities. Thus, the grand jury has been reformed from a "people's panel," sometimes used to curb prosecutions, to a tool for prosecuting political behavior. Further intelligence information is secured by these grand juries from testimony, without the protection of counsel, and may subject witnesses to jail sentences for contempt or get them charged with a crime.

The new enemy in American society is the "criminal." Replacing the red menace (internal communism) as the threat to domestic security, is crime. Not only the conventional attacks on private property (robbery and burglary), or the crimes against person (murder and assault), but anything that is regarded as a threat to the established order is being handled as a crime — civil disobedience, verbal expression of political dissent, and organized protest of various forms.

From a critical perspective, the new era is more than another instance of government officials imposing their own will. In the late stages capitalism must use repression to maintain order. Such a system, based on an advanced capitalist political economy, can survive only by increasing its use of repression. The legal system has long been a means for establishing order, but in the last few years we have experienced its use as the final weapon in protecting the social order. The capitalist system is being perpetuated by the state's use of legal power, not by instituting changes that are necessary for achieving a just and humane society.

THE NEW JUSTICE MODEL

The modern criminal justice movement is initiated and supported by the state to rationalize the mechanisms of social control. The larger purpose is to secure a capitalist order that is in grave crisis, perhaps in its final stage of development. The criminal justice system will surely be modified in response to further problems generated by late capitalism. Technological as well as ideological solutions will be attempted. There will be greater efforts to plan criminal justice, to achieve a comprehensive system of criminal justice.[71] Not only will the traditional agencies of the law be systematized, involving the police and the courts, but more of the agencies of criminal justice will be integrated into unified systems. Already several states and regions have unified and consolidated their apparatus for crime control, forming superagencies of criminal justice.[72]

A new form of crime control (or criminal justice) is coming to be in this era of late capitalism. A move is on also to institute alternatives to legal processing. In the Report of the National Advisory Commission on Criminal Justice Standards and Goals, (sponsored by the LEAA), it is being recommended that cases be diverted from the courts, and new agencies ("non-criminal-justice institutions") are to deal with cases formerly handled by the police and the courts.[73] The criminal justice system is freed to deal with serious offenses against the state and the economy and, at the same time, subjects much social behavior to surveillance and control by the state. Criminal justice is expanding, and will make further changes for greater control within the capitalist order.

This "new-justice model" is represented in the influential report of the Committee for the Study of Incarceration.[74] Called *Doing Justice*, it combines the work of lawyers, philosophers, historians, and social scientists over several years. Using the language of punitive reform, the report is to create a "fairer and less brutal penal system." The criminal sanction of punishment (mainly the length of prison sentences) is to be limited, but the aim of the report is nevertheless to provide a rationale for punishment. Instead of questioning the society's quality in the first place, a scheme of punishment is designed to serve the ends of society as it is. In proposing a justice for the present and the future, there is a return to the justice of the past.

> Some of our conclusions may seem old-fashioned. To our surprise, we found ourselves returning to the ideas of such Enlightenment thinkers as Kant and Beccaria — ideas that antedated notions of rehabilitation that emerged in the nineteenth century. We take seriously Kant's view that a person should be punished because he deserves it. We argue, as both Kant and Beccaria did, that severity of punishment should depend chiefly on the seriousness of the crime. We share Beccaria's interest in placing limits on sentencing discretion.[75]

Moreover, punishment itself is defended for its deterrent effect and according to the value that those who are defined as criminal *deserve* to be punished. The penalty is deserved for seriousness of the past conduct of the "criminal" and seriousness of the act. Rehabilitation (or any attempt to change behavior) is rejected in favor of a penalty for the behavior. The sentencing system of criminal justice becomes technically rational: "Graded levels of seriousness would be established, and the guidelines would specify which offense categories belong to which seriousness level."[76] Such is reform at the present stage of capitalist development.

There is, however, a clear alternative to the notion of justice in the new model of criminal justice. The new model is a limited historical version of justice. The "new" justice in fact combines two specific notions: justice as protecting acknowledged "rights" within the current order and justice as distributing punishment according to what one "deserves." The new justice model dispenses justice (that is, punishment) to preserve the capitalist social order and according to what the offender deserves in pursuing rational action. This notion of justice is appropriate for the capitalist order; it assumes a hierarchy of rights and competitive social relations.

The new model of justice (which is actually a mixture of old justice), contrasts sharply with the idea of justice as distribution according to *need.* The latter form of justice is appropriate for a society based on cooperative social relations, a communal society, and a developing socialist society.[77] Behind it is the assumption that human beings behave (or are capable of behaving) cooperatively and altruistically, without financial rewards or penal sanctions. Although not likely to be found in capitalist societies, this notion of justice nevertheless has its own tradition. It is found in early and more recent communal and religious movements, with elements present in socialist countries today.

As capitalist society continues to develop its own contradictions and crises, the contrasts between divergent conceptions of justice become evident. In the recent theories and practices of criminal justice we are witnessing an attempt to reestablish a justice appropriate to a former age, which ignores historical development, but one that would seemingly preserve the contemporary capitalist order.

Class struggle today, however, is also a struggle for social justice. Beyond the conventional notions of crime and punishment is the creation of a new social order. The extent of justice is being questioned and also its kind and under what conditions it is to prevail. Now we are beginning to attend to a socialist sense of justice.

NOTES

1. See Richard C. Edwards, Michael Reich, and Thomas E. Weisskopf, eds., *The Capitalist System: A Radical Analysis of American Society,* 2nd edition (Englewood Cliffs, N.J.: Prentice-Hall, 1978).
2. Ralph Miliband, *The State in Capitalist Society* (New York: Basic Books, 1969), p. 1.
3. Karl Marx, *Selected Writings in Sociology and Social Psychology,* trans. T. B. Bottomore (New York: McGraw-Hill, 1964), pp. 222–223.
4. Frederick Engels, *The Origin of the Family, Private Property, and the State* (New York: International Publishers, 1942), p. 97.
5. David A. Gold, Clarence Y. H. Lo, and Erik Olin Wright, "Recent Developments in Marxist Theories of the State," *Monthly Review,* 27 (November 1975), pp. 36–51.
6. Stanley Diamond, "The Rule of Law Versus the Order of Custom," *Social Reserach,* 38 (Spring 1971), p. 71.
7. George M. Calhoun, *The Growth of Criminal Law in Ancient Greece* (Berkeley: University of California Press, 1927).
8. Ibid., p. 52.
9. George Novack, *Democracy and Revolution* (New York: Pathfinder Press, 1971), p. 32.

10. Hans Julius Wolff, *Roman Law: An Historical Introduction* (Norman, Okla.: University of Oklahoma Press, 1951), pp. 54–61. Also Barry Nicholas, *An Introduction to Roman Law* (Oxford: Oxford University Press, 1962), pp. 208–209.

11. Wolfgang Kunkel, *An Introduction to Roman Legal History and Constitutional History* (Oxford: Oxford University Press, 1966), p. 61.

12. Erich S. Gruen, *Roman Politics and the Criminal Courts, 149–78* B.C. (Cambridge: Harvard University Press, 1968).

13. C. Ray Jeffery, "The Development of Crime in Early English Society," *Journal of Criminal Law, Criminology and Police Science*, 47 (March-April 1957), pp. 647–666.

14. See F. L. Attenborough, ed., *The Laws of the English Kings* (Cambridge: Cambridge University Press, 1922).

15. G. O. Sayles, *Medieval Foundation of England* (London: Methuen, 1966), chap. 21. Also John W. Jeudwine, *Tort, Crime and Police in Medieval Britain* (London: Williams and Norgate, 1917), especially chapters 7 and 8.

16. Jerome Hall, *Theft, Law and Society*, 2nd ed. (Indianapolis, Ind.: Bobbs-Merrill, 1952).

17. Ibid., p. 10.

18. Ibid., p. 19.

19. Ibid., p. 31.

20. Ibid., p. 33.

21. Roscoe Pound, "The Development of American Law and Its Deviation from English Law," *Law Quarterly Review*, 67 (January 1951), pp. 49–66.

22. Julius Goebel, Jr., "King's Law and Local Custom in Seventeenth Century New England," *Columbia Law Review*, 31 (March 1931), pp. 416–448.

23. See Edwin C. Surrency, "Revision of Colonial Laws," *American Journal of Legal History*, 9 (July 1965), pp. 189–202; Elizabeth Caspar Brown, *British Statutes in American Law, 1776–1836* (Ann Arbor: University of Michigan Law School, 1964).

24. See Carl J. Friedrich, "Rights, Liberties, Freedoms: A Reappraisal," *American Political Science Review*, 57 (December 1963), pp. 841–854; Roscoe Pound, *The Formative Era of American Law* (Boston: Little, Brown, 1938).

25. Perry Miller, *The Life of the Mind: From the Revolution to the Civil War* (New York: Harcourt, Brace and World, 1965), pp. 99–265.

26. W. Stitt Robinson, "The Legal Status of the Indian in Colonial Virginia," *Virginia Magazine of History and Biography*, 61 (July 1953), pp. 247–259.

27. See Wilcomb E. Washburn, "The Moral and Legal Justifications for Dispossessing the Indians," in James Morton Smith, ed., *Seventeenth-Century America: Essays in Colonial History* (Chapel Hill, N.C.: University of North Carolina Press, 1959), pp. 15–32.

28. Quoted in Glenn Shirley, *Law West of Fort Smith: Frontier Justice in the Indian Territory, 1834–1896* (New York: Collier Books, 1961), p. 146.

29. Ibid., p. 180. Further material on frontier law is found in Lawrence M. Friedman, *A History of American Law* (New York: Simon and Schuster, 1973), pp. 295–383.

30. For one of the few studies of law in the mining territory, see Charles Howard Shinn, *Mining Camps: A Study in American Frontier Government* (New York: Harper and Row, 1965), originally published 1884.

31. See Richard B. Morris, *Government and Labor in Early America* (New York: Octagon Books, 1965); and Marcus W. Jernegan, *Laboring and Dependent Classes in Colonial America, 1607–1773* (Chicago: University of Chicago Press, 1931).

32. Herbert Aptheker, *The Colonial Era* (New York: International Publishers, 1966), pp. 7–49; and Edmund S. Morgan, *American Slavery, American Freedom: The Ordeal of Colonial Virginia* (New York: W. W. Norton, 1975).

33. Haywood Burns, "Racism and American Law," in Robert Lefcourt, ed., *Law Against the People: Essays to Demystify Law, Order and the Courts* (New York: Random House, 1971), pp. 38–54.

34. Ibid., p. 49.

35. Ibid., p. 50.

36. James O'Connor, "The Twisted Dream," *Monthly Review*, 26 (March 1975), pp. 46–53.

37. Douglas F. Dowd, *The Twisted Dream: Capitalist Development in the United States Since 1776* (Cambridge, Mass.: Winthrop, 1974), pp. 42–48.

38. For a detailed discussion of the crime control effort in this period, see Richard Quinney, *Critique of Legal Order: Crime Control in Capitalist Society* (Boston: Little, Brown, 1974).

39. "Crime, Its Prevalence, and Measures of Prevention," Message from the President of the United States, House of Representatives, 89th Congress, March 8, 1965, Document No. 103.

40. "Omnibus Crime Control and Safe Streets Act," Public Law 90–351, *United States Statutes at Large,* 1968, vol. 82 (Washington, D.C.: U.S. Government Printing Office, 1969), pp. 197–198.

41. See Richard Harris, *The Fear of Crime* (New York: Praeger, 1969).

42. "Controlling Crime Through More Effective Law Enforcement," Hearings Before the Subcommittee on Criminal Law and Procedures of the Committee on the Judiciary, United States Senate, 90th Congress (Washington, D.C.: U.S. Government Printing Office, 1967), p. 1.

43. See Herbert L. Packer, "Nixon's Crime Program and What It Means," *The New York Review of Books,* 15 (October 22, 1970), pp. 26–37.

44. *The New York Times,* July 24, 1970, p. 1. See District of Columbia Committee, "Anti-Crime Proposals," *Hearings* Before the Select Committee on Crime, U.S. House of Representatives, 91st Congress (Washington, D.C.: U.S. Government Printing Office, 1970).

45. "Organized Crime Control," *Hearings* Before the Subcommittee on Criminal Laws and Procedures of the Committee on the Judiciary, United States Senate, 91st Congress (Washington, D.C.: U.S. Government Printing Office, 1970).

46. *Congressional Record,* Vol. 16, Part 2, 91st Congress, January 28, 1970 (Washington, D.C.: U.S. Government Printing Office, 1970), p. 1690.

47. See Frank Wilkinson, "The Era of Libertarian Repression — 1948 to 1973: From Congressman to President, with Substantial Support from the Liberal Establishment," *University of Akron Law Review,* 7 (Winter 1974), pp. 280–309; and Thomas I. Emerson, "The 'Criminal Code Reform Act of 1977,' " (Washington, D.C.: National Committee Against Repressive Legislation, 1977).

48. See Robert L. Borosage, "The Tyranny of 'Intelligence,' " *The Nation,* 222 (March 13, 1976), pp. 296–299.

49. See Joseph C. Goulden, "Tooling up for Repression: The Cops Hit the Jackpot," *The Nation,* 211 (November 23, 1970), pp. 520–533.

50. Law Enforcement Assistance Administration, *Grants and Contracts Awarded under the Law Enforcement Assistance Act of 1965,* Fiscal Year 1966–1968 (Washington, D.C.: U.S. Government Printing Office, 1969), p. 1.

51. Law Enforcement Assistance Administration, *Sixth Annual Report of LEAA,* Fiscal Year 1974 (Washington, D.C.: U.S. Government Printing Office, 1974), pp. 1–5; Law Enforcement Assistance Administration, *The Law Enforcement Assistance Administration: A Partnership for Crime Control* (Washington, D.C.: U.S. Government Printing Office, 1976), p. 15; and LEAA *Newsletter* 6 (June-July 1977), p. 1.

52. *Third Annual Report of the Law Enforcement Assistance Administration,* Fiscal Year 1971 (Washington, D.C.: U.S. Government Printing Office, 1972), p. ii.

53. Law Enforcement Assistance Administration, *A Program for a Safer, More Just America* (Washington, D.C.: U.S. Government Printing Office, 1971), p. 3.

54. Law Enforcement Assistance Administration, *Safe Streets: The LEAA Program at Work* (Washington, D.C.: U.S. Government Printing Office, 1971), p. i.

55. *Third Annual Report of the Law Enforcement Assistance Administration,* p. iii. Also see the LEAA *Newsletter,* 1 (July 1971), pp. 1–6.

56. See "Crime Program Held Inefficient," *New York Times,* April 11, 1972, p. 14.

57. Quoted in the LEAA *Newsletter,* 2 (November 1971), p. 8.

58. On the social expenses of the state, see James O'Connor, *The Fiscal Crisis of the State* (New York: St. Martin's Press, 1973), pp. 150–178. The social expense of criminal justice is analyzed in Richard Quinney, *Class, State, and Crime: On the Theory and Practice*

of Criminal Justice (New York: Longman,1977), pp. 107–144. Also see Gregory McLauchlan, "LEAA: A Case Study in the Development of the Social Industrial Complex," *Crime and Social Justice,* 4 (Fall-Winter 1975), pp. 15–23.

59. For the FBI's history, see Fred J. Cook, *The FBI Nobody Knows* (New York: Macmillan, 1964); and Sanford J. Unger, *The FBI* (Boston: Little, Brown, 1976). On the history of the Department of Justice, see Homer Cummings and Carl McFarland, *Federal Justice* (New York: Macmillan, 1937).

60. Hank Messick, *John Edgar Hoover* (New York: David McKay, 1972); Ralph de Toledano, *J. Edgar Hoover: The Man and His Times* (New Rochelle, N.Y.: Arlington House, 1973); Pat Watters and Stephen Gillers, eds., *Investigating the FBI* (New York: Doubleday, 1973).

61. Tom Wicker, "A Gross Invasion," *The New York Times,* December 19, 1971, p. E11.

62. Quoted in the NCCD *Newsletter,* 50 (May-June 1971), p. 15.

63. Ben A. Franklin, "Federal Computers Amass Files on Suspect Citizens," *The New York Times,* June 28, 1970, p. 42. On the army's surveillance of the population, see *The New York Times,* January 18, 1971, p. 1; September 7, 1971, p. 39. Also "Army Surveillance of Civilians: A Documentary Analysis," Subcommittee on Constitutional Rights, Committee on the Judiciary, United States Senate, 92nd Congress, 2nd Session (Washington, D.C.: U.S. Government Printing Office, 1972).

64. Jeff Gerth, "The Americanization of 1984," *Sundance Magazine,* 1 (April-May 1972), pp. 58–65. Also see Lawyers' Committee for Civil Rights Under Law, *Law and Disorder III: State and Federal Performance under Title I of the Omnibus Crime Control and Safe Streets Act of 1968* (Washington, D.C., 1973).

65. Michael Sorkin, "The FBI's Big Brother Computer," *The Washington Monthly,* 4 (September 1972), p. 24.

66. Senator Sam J. Ervin, Jr., as quoted in Goulden, "Tooling up for Repression," p. 528. Also see 'Federal Data Banks, Computers and the Bill of Rights," *Hearings* Before the Subcommittee on Constitutional Rights of the Committee on the Judiciary, Part I, United States Senate, 92nd Congress (Washington, D.C.: U.S. Government Printing Office, 1971).

67. Quoted in Richard Harris, *Justice: The Crisis of Law, Order and Freedom in America* (New York: E. P. Dutton, 1970), p. 186.

68. Ibid. Also see John T. Elliff, *Crime, Dissent, and the Attorney General: The Justice Department in the 1960's* (Beverly Hills, Calif.: Sage Publications, 1971).

69. On this trial and other political trials, see *Trials of the Resistance* (New York: Vintage Books, 1970).

70. Frank J. Donner and Eugene Cerruti, "The Grand Jury Network: How the Nixon Administration Has Secretly Perverted a Traditional Safeguard of Individual Rights," *The Nation,* 214 (January 3, 1972), p. 5.

71. See, for example, James E. Frank and Frederic L. Faust, "A Conceptual Framework for Criminal Justice Planning," *Criminology,* 13 (August 1975), pp. 271–296; Daniel Glasser, *Strategic Criminal Justice Planning,* National Institute of Mental Health, Center for Studies of Crime and Delinquency (Washington, D.C.: U.S. Government Printing Office, 1975).

72. National Institute of Law Enforcement and Criminal Justice, *Recent Criminal Justice Unification, Consolidation and Coordination Efforts* (Washington, D.C.: Law Enforcement Assistance Administration, 1976); Daniel Skoler, "State Criminal Justice Superagencies," *State Government,* 49 (Winter 1976), pp. 2–8. Resistance to unification is indicated in David Weinstein, "Judicial Independence in the Computer Age," *Judicature,* 59 (March 1976), pp. 372–378.

73. National Advisory Commission on Criminal Justice Standards and Goals, *A National Strategy to Reduce Crime* (New York: Avon Books, 1975). A critique of the report is found in David W. Neubauer and George F. Cole, "A Political Critique of the Court Recommendations of the National Advisory Commission on Criminal Justice Standards and Goals," *Emory Law Journal,* 24 (Fall 1975), pp. 1009–1036.

74. Andrew Von Hirsch, *Doing Justice: The Choice of Punishments,* Report of the Committee for the Study of Incarceration (New York: Hill and Wang, 1976).

75. Ibid., p. 6.

76. Ibid., p. 99. Further support for the new justice model, regarding mandatory sentencing, "flat time," and the like, is provided in the Report of the Twentieth Century Task Force on Criminal Sentencing, *Fair and Certain Punishment* (New York: McGraw-Hill, 1976).

77. David Miller, "The Ideological Backgrounds to Conceptions of Social Justice," *Political Studies*, 22 (December, 1974), pp. 387–399.

Criminal Laws in the United States

4

Within the general legal order of the United States the specific criminal laws regulating conduct of individuals and groups are formulated, enforced, and judicially administered. These criminal laws are shaped within the society's social, political, and economic structure. The overall purpose behind the criminal laws is to preserve and perpetuate the social and economic order.

What, then, are these criminal laws? How are they formulated in a capitalist society? An understanding of American criminal law presupposes a theory of the capitalist political economy, including the class structure of the society and the organization of the state.

We begin, following the Marxist interpretation, by seeing the state as intimately tied to civil society, especially to the class structure. The state rests on the material, economic base of society, characterizing the capitalist state as the managing committee of the capitalist ruling class. But the state is more than a mere instrument of the capitalist class; it is itself a social reality.[1] The state provides a framework for the class structure inherent in the capitalist mode of production. Be aware of the difference between a theory of the state as an *instrument* of class domination and the state as a *coordinating agency* responsible for the administrative operations of capitalist society.[2] The theories currently being formulated are addressed to these problems and themselves reflect the changing state under advanced capitalism.

The recent formulations of the state go beyond the notion taking the state and its policies as direct outcomes of manipulations by the ruling class. The structuralist theory describing the functions the state performs to reproduce capitalist society as a whole is also expanding. Likewise, the Hegelian-Marxist perspective emphasizing consciousness and ideology is being made more concrete, materialist, and historical.[3] The complexity of the state's apparatus in late capitalism is becoming evident.

The problem in examining criminal laws is trying to link the class structure of advanced capitalism to the capitalist state. The starting point, Claus Offe writes, is the class-character of the state.[4] How is the capitalist state really a *capitalist* state and not merely a state in capitalist society? As he investigates the internal structure of the capitalist state, Offe shows that several "selective mechanisms" within the state apparatus either keep anticapitalist interests out of state policy or ensure that capitalist interests are included in state policy. These structural features "put the State in a position to formulate and express class-interests more appropriately and circumspectly than can be done by representatives of the class — in the form of isolated units of capital."[5] The state thereby provides the conditions necessary for continued accumulation of capital. Moreover, in periods of political crisis, as the selective mechanisms begin to break down the state is forced to rely more and more on *repression* to maintain its class character. By acting negatively it attempts to exclude interests and forces that oppose or threaten the capitalist system. Class structure is translated into political power in the structure and operation of the capitalist state.

In its United States form the advanced capitalist state is not simply an instrument for promoting the interests of a ruling class. The state instead secures the whole order of capitalism, protecting and sanctioning "a set of *rules* and *social relationships* which are presupposed by the class rule of the capitalist class. The state does not defend the interests of one class, but the common interests of all members of a *capitalist class society*."[6] Under late capitalism, the state is a complex apparatus that provides the general design to ensure survival of the capitalist system.

The substantive criminal law, then, is a part of the state apparatus. It is enacted and administered by the state to promote the capitalist system. Although specific interests are represented when the laws are actually formulated, with interests often conflicting, the general purpose of the criminal law is to ensure the dominance of the system.

With this understanding, we can examine some of the criminal laws regulating realms of conduct in the United States. We begin with laws early in the country's formation, specifically the religious and political sides of criminal law. As business, and much later, the large corporations became essential to American capitalism, criminal laws were formulated to promote the nation's economic interests. Many realms of conduct have come under the control of criminal law, including private and public morality. Again, the purpose is to promote the capitalist social order in the United States.

RELIGIOUS FOUNDATIONS

Along the shores of the tidewater basin later called Boston Harbor, a Puritan community was established in 1630. Although the Massachusetts Bay Colony was chartered as a commercial enterprise, its settlers' objectives were clearly religious and social. From the time the Puritans landed, their chief aim, Governor John Winthrop said, was to build "a City upon a Hill," a society that would be an example of godliness to the world. Religious interests were dominant in creating a social and legal order in early Massachusetts.

The colony carried on the political traditions of England, from which the settlers had come. Among these were the belief that government is made to regulate imperfect human being, that political leaders must be obeyed, and that the welfare of the whole is more important than that of the individual. Puritanism drew as well from the medieval imagery of piety, doom, and sin.[7] Out of these older ideas the Puritans developed a conception of living by a covenant: government had originated in a compact among the people. But more than this, the power of the state was legitimate because it was government conforming to God's decree. "Thus, in subjecting themselves to a state that was divinely approved, the people also subjected themselves to obedience to God."[8]

The Puritans, adhering to the covenant, took the word of God as a basis for establishing government and society in Massachusetts Bay. They saw themselves as an elite chosen by God to represent Him on earth. But most important for government, they considered the positions to which the leaders were elected in the colony as ordained by God. Once elected, the governor and the magistrates were granted power by divine authority. As "Gods upon earth," the leaders must be obeyed for the covenant to be kept. Winthrop forcefully expressed this idea to the Puritans: "The determination of law belongs properly to God: He is the only lawgiver, but He hath given power and gifts to man to interpret his laws; and this belongs principally to the highest authority in a commonwealth, and subordinately to other magistrates and judges according to their several places."[9] The covenant's logical conclusion was rule by a few for the interests they deemed appropriate: "The government of Massachusetts was thus a dictatorship of a small minority who were unhesitantly prepared to coerce the unwilling to serve the purposes of society as they conceived it."[10]

The early history of Massachusetts Bay Colony shows a continuing problem about the place of law in a religious community.[11] The early settlers resolved the problem with a legal structure built on biblical authority. The Scriptures were a most appropriate source for establishing a government according to God's word. In 1635 the General Court of the colony ordered work to begin on a legal code. By 1641 a brief bill of rights, known since as the Body of Liberties, was passed. Finally, in 1648, a comprehensive code of law, known as "Laws and Liberties," was adopted. The code, first of its kind in the English-speaking world, was a compilation of constitutional guarantees, provisions for the conduct of government, trade, military affairs, and relations between church and state, as well as the substantive law of crime, tort, property, and domestic relations. At the beginning of the code was the Epistle that dramatically related the laws of the colony to religious principles in the Old Testament Scriptures:

> So soon as God had set up Political Government among his people Israel he gave them a body of laws for judgment both in civil and criminal causes. These were brief and fundamental principles, yet withall so full and comprehensive as out of them clear deductions were to be drawn to all particular cases in future times.[12]

The code was a unique effort to order life and conduct in accordance with the ideals of Puritanism.

The biblical influence in the law formulated for the colony is most clearly observed in the criminal laws of the code. All punishable by death, they included idolatry, witchcraft, blasphemy, bestiality, sodomy, adultery, rape, treason, false witness with intent to take life, cursing or smiting a parent, stubbornness or rebelliousness of a son against his parents, and homicide committed with malice aforethought, by guile or poisoning, or in anger or passion. Most of the provisions, as well as other enactments, were annotated by some chapter and verse from the Old Testament, and several had biblical phrases. Compare this provision from the law with its counterpart in the Old Testament on rebellion of the son:

> *Code of 1648:* If a man have a stubborn or REBELLIOUS SON, of sufficient years and understanding (viz) sixteen years of age, which will not obey the voice of his Father, or the voice of his Mother, and that when they have chastened him will not harken unto them: then shall his Father and Mother being

> his natural parents, lay hold on him, and bring him to the Magistrates assembled in Court and testifie unto them, that their Son is stubborn and rebellious and will not obey their voice and chastisement, but lives in sundry notorious crimes, such a son shall be put to death.
>
> *Deuteronomy 21:18–21:* If a man have a stubborn and rebellious son, which will not obey the voice of his father, or the voice of his mother, will not harken unto them: Then shall his father and his mother lay hold on him, and bring him out unto the elders of his city and unto the gate of his place; And they shall say unto the elders of his city, This our son is stubborn and rebellious, he will not obey our voice; he is a glutton, and a drunkard. And all of the men of his city shall stone him with stones, that he die. . . .[13]

Other criminal laws contain words, clauses, or phrases taken directly from the Old Testament:

> Thus, the witchcraft provision defined a witch as one that "hath or consulteth with a familiar spirit" in terms of Leviticus 20:27 and Deuteronomy 18:11, which speak respectively of one "that hath a familiar spirit" and of "a consulter with familiar spirits." Again, it is prescribed in Leviticus 20:15 and 16 that "if a man lie with a beast, he shall surely be put to death: and you shall slay the beast," and a similar punishment was provided "if a woman approach unto any beast and lie down thereto"; by comparison, the bestiality law of Massachusetts states that "If any man or woman shall LYE WITH ANY BEAST, or bruit creature, by carnal copulation; they shall surely be put to death: and the beast shall be slain, and buried, and not eaten." In the same chapter of Leviticus, 20:13, it is stated that "If a man also lie with mankind, as he lieth with a woman, both of them have committed an abomination"; the colony law against sodomy prescribes that "if any man LYETH WITH MAN-KINDE as he lieth with a woman, both of them have committed abomination. . . ." In Exodus 21:16 it is declared that "he that stealeth a man, and selleth him, or if he be found in his hand, he shall surely be put to death; in Massachusetts law, "If any man STEALETH A MAN, or Mankinde, he shall surely be put to death." Finally, the colonial provision that "if any child, or children . . . shall CURSE, or SMITE their natural FATHER, or MOTHER: he or they shall be put to death," is paralleled by Exodus 21:15 and 17, to the effect that "he that smiteth his father, or his mother. . . . And he that curseth his father, or his mother, shall surely be put to death."[14]

There can be no doubt that the religious principles of the Old Testament were one of the cornerstones for the Puritans' criminal law. The Bible's authority served as a justification for the law's provisions. The law was God's word enacted on earth.

The purpose of law for the Puritans was to accomplish God's will in a society bound by a religious and political covenant. The state's authority was thus religiously condoned. Carrying that theory to its conclusion, the state's welfare, not that of the individual, was its chief interest. Law and government, therefore, have the power to coerce individuals according to the interests of those who hold power: "The end of law as viewed by the colonists was less alien to our own conceptions than a first impression might suggest. In politically organized society, law operates as a restraint on individual action for the benefit of some other individual or of the group as a whole."[15] The state's authority now had a religious and moral basis, which continues to support criminal laws in the United States.

PROTECTING THE POLITICAL ORDER

Our early criminal codes, primarily religious, equated sin with crime. The laws punished religious offenses, such as idolatry, blasphemy, and witchcraft. Offenses against persons or property were declared offenses against God. Prosecution for religious infractions practically disappeared after the Revolution, but increased for economic and disorderly offenses.

The prerevolutionary notion that criminal law was meant to enforce the community's morals and religion shifted gradually to include the post-revolutionary view that criminal law is to protect property and physical security. The state became actively involved, using the criminal law, in promoting stability of the social order.[16] Political acts against the state and its economy also were controlled by the criminal law. No longer worried about sinners, the new state elite "feared organized groups of malcontents bent upon reconstruction of society. . . . In short, their fear was that the economically underprivileged would seek material gain by banding together to deprive more privileged persons of their wealth and standing."[17] Criminal law had one purpose: to promote order in a new society.

Protecting the political order has become a primary characteristic of the capitalist state. Creating criminal laws preserves the political and economic system. The struggles and conflicts between holders of power, their foes, and contenders for political power take many forms. Criminal laws are formulated in the attempt to control or eliminate the political foe from competition.[18] As political weapons, these laws limit the political action of those who appear to jeopardize the established order's stability and survival.

The state's ideology, claimed to be a political democracy, maintains a paradox with two opposing ideals. The state claims the power to govern but grants the freedom that may result in words and actions against the state. The opposing ideals coexist with the unspoken agreement that "the majority agrees to tolerate the criticism and dissent of the minority (or minorities), while the minority agrees to seek power only through persuasion and political activity, not through violence."[19] In the abstract, the majority is not to persecute the minority and the minority is not to express dissent by revolution.

The boundaries and definitions of political freedom are by no means constant in any society, however; the latitude of dissent that may be regarded as legitimate varies from one time to another. During some periods extensive and loud dissent may be tolerated, but in others it may be suppressed by the criminal law.

Political expression is especially restricted during periods of conflict and crisis. Expecting a political emergency, the government is likely to take action to protect the political order. The events that led to the American Revolution illustrate how criminal law may be used to maintain the desired political order. England as the imperial nation tried to hold its political control over the colonies. A natural antagonism separated the rulers of England and a rising bourgeoisie in the American colonies.[20] At the same time as this struggle was going on the British government was faced with other problems, including administration of its territorial acquisitions elsewhere in North America and a mounting debt at home. To organize a more efficient administration, Britain made several demands on the colonies, such as the trade and revenue acts passed in Parliament, which tightened control over the colonies. At the same time, however, the colonies were developing a revolutionary ideology and a new nationalist spirit. Britain's attempt to demand more of the colonies and the Americans' growing desire for freedom of economic and political action produced a sharp clash of interests.[21] After insurrections and a war, the colonies won their independence.

One of the devices the British government used to establish and preserve its own political order in the colonies was substantive criminal law. The law of treason applied against the colonists began in a statute enacted in the time of Edward III, making it a crime to plot or imagine the death of the king, to adhere to the king's enemies, to give them aid and comfort, or to levy war against the king. The law of seditious libel was also used to control public criticism of British efforts, though how much they resorted to it to control dissent is debated.[22] But ironically, each of the colonies formulated similar laws to protect its own political interests. These political criminal laws were almost identical to the English laws that were being imposed on them.

The English common law on political crime was eventually adopted by the states and the federal government. It seemed oppressive in the hands of the British but it was now a law for Americans to impose on those who appeared to endanger their government. The federal government in 1798 enacted the Sedition Act to punish anyone who uttered or published statements against the government of the United States.[23] The Federalists (a political party led by Alexander Hamilton), to curtail loyalty to the British, applied this instrument to suppress the activities (considered pro-French) of the opposition Republican party.[24]

The law of treason was shaped by American fears of British Loyalists during and immediately after the Revolution. Drawing upon English common law once again, the Americans formulated and utilized treason laws against those who aided the British or fled to the enemy.[25] After the Declaration of Independence, the state legislatures enacted anti-Loyalist laws. "Test acts" compelled a declaration of loyalty from those who appeared to be indifferent or enemies of the Revolution. They also had laws (1) disenfranchising the Loyalists or removing them from office, (2) suppressing, quarantining, and exiling Loyalists, (3) providing for the crime of adhering to Great Britain, and (4) amercing (subjecting to arbitrary punishment), taxing, or confiscating the property and estates of Loyalists.[26] In most states Loyalists were legally defined as traitors.

All the states today have criminal laws to prevent subversion of the political order. This order is not always clearly defined in the state laws, although most agree on which kinds of behavior are subversive:

> There can no doubt be general agreement that, at the very least, subversive activities include (1) the use of violent or otherwise unconstitutional means to change this country's political or economic institutions; (2) the commission of espionage, sabotage, and other crimes of stealth in behalf of foreign enemies or domestic cliques; (3) the bearing of arms against the United States, and other affirmative behavior in aid of hostile forces; and (4) the entry into a conspiracy to perform these acts or the actual though unsuccessful attempt to do them. Conduct of these types is unquestionably within the reach of criminal laws in every American state.[27]

Numerous federal statutes also have been created to control subversive activity. The Espionage Act of 1917 made it a crime to "willfully make or convey false reports or false statements with intent to interfere with the operations or success of the military or naval forces of the United States." A 1918 amendment to the Espionage Act broadened the proscriptions in words reminiscent of the Sedition Act of 1798. The Voorhis Act of 1940 required persons and organizations that act as agents of foreign powers to register with the government. The Smith Act of 1940 forbade advocating the overthrow of the government. The Internal Security Act of 1950 (McCarran Act) required communist and communist-front organizations to register and strengthened other legislation on subversion. The Immigration and Nationality Act of 1952 (McCarran-Walter Act) provided for deporting resident aliens because of disloyal beliefs and associates. The Communist Control Act of 1954 required Communist party members to register with the attorney general. Loyalty and security programs have been initiated and blacklist procedures have been established as well.

Political expression is an especially delicate matter in the United States.

Criminal law stands ready to secure the capitalist political economy through control of the labor force, as illustrated by the presence of state police during the miner's strike of 1978.

Compared to other peoples with representative governments, Americans seem particularly intolerant of social and political differences.[28] This intolerance is expressed by withholding civil rights from some social and political minority groups, religious groups, racial and ethnic groups, and political dissenters. Criminal laws and rulings have been formulated to handle these differences. Specific behaviors that political minorities may commit out of conscience have been made illegal. Along with the many acts defined as subversive (by the groups in power), attempts to express dissatisfaction with nuclear testing, civil defense, racial discrimination, and war have been subject to criminal action. Volumes of laws have helped suppress dissent and protest. Demonstrators for racial civil rights and other causes have been arrested on such charges as disorderly conduct, breach of peace, parading without a permit, trespassing, loitering, and violating fire ordinances. Other laws have gotten hundreds arrested for refusing to pay income taxes used for military purposes, for picketing military bases, for engaging in student protests, and for refusing to register for the draft.

The criminal laws written to control perceived threats to the state are patently political. The political regime is to be protected from any internal or external danger. The law upholds the state. Even when procedural guarantees such as due process (the right to established legal procedure) and civil disobedience (defiance of the law out of moral conscience) are recognized, the law can be qualified at every point to maintain the status quo.

Nowhere is this qualification of law better illustrated than in the laws on military conscription. United States involvement in Southeast Asia brought new light to this matter. Those of draft age who could show absolute pacifism on religious grounds could avoid military service. There may well be constitutional grounds to support broader, selective conscientious objection, but until such a right is legally recognized, those who claim it are defined as criminal.[29]

Conspiracy and related laws are among the best examples of the government's attempt to ensure its own survival. Legal cases, especially like that of the Boston Five (a "conspiracy" to aid in violating the Selective Service Law) and the Chicago Eight (demonstrators during the 1968 Democratic Convention), show how far the government will go in using the criminal law to ward off apparent political dangers. In these cases dubious charges have been made, the most questionable being "conspiracy." As a political weapon, the conspiracy law requires merely that the prosecution show that the defendants conspired, or rather, communicated in some way about a demonstration, draft resistance, or whatever. The prosecution need not show that the defendants actually engaged in overt acts, but merely that they said something. Among other things, whether or not the defendants are convicted, the conspiracy law is an effective form of political harassment whereby those who threaten the system can be detained for long periods at great personal expense.

The so-called antiriot laws accomplish similar objectives for the state. Six of the eight Chicago defendants were prosecuted under a newly formulated federal antiriot act, making it a felony to travel in interstate commerce with intent to incite or participate in a riot. "Riot" is defined in the statute as any assemblage of three or more persons, in which at least one threatens injury to another person or property. The act was conceived in response to the ghetto riots of the sixties. Speaking for an earlier version of the law, this statement by a congressman from Georgia illustrates that the act was a simplistic attempt to solve urban disorders by striking at the "outside agitators" supposedly behind the outbreaks of civil disorder:

> There is impressive evidence that many of the riots which have been plaguing our cities have been incited by persons who have been traveling from one city to another, deliberately stirring up trouble. We have all heard that in so many instances, preceding a riot, an outside agitator has appeared in the community to harangue an audience concerning the grievances. Sometimes those grievances have been real, sometimes they have not. But real or not, often the speeches of these agitators have been criminally inflammatory, and often in clear violation of our laws against inciting to riot.[30]

Such thinking gets laws of consequence enacted.

The most insidious yet blatant tactic used by the government against its citizens (including its political offenders) is the refusal to publicly and legally recognize such an act as political crime. Its reason lies in the Anglo-American doctrine of legalism: obedience to the law is a moral absolute.[31] Because opposition to the government could not be legally *and* morally recognized in this tradition, political crime could not be incorporated into the law. Political offenders have usually been dealt with under "nonpolitical" laws. The political offender has been handled officially in the same way as the conventional offender. To admit political crime into domestic jurisprudence would be to recognize the limitations of liberal (democratic elitist) democracy. Such a philosophy of government, enhanced by substantive criminal law, supports the capitalist system.

PROMOTING AMERICAN BUSINESS

Toward the end of the nineteenth century an antimonopoly movement against economic domination by large corporations gathered in response to new economic conditions. It was accompanied by a body of doctrine on the problem of monopoly as resolvable only by government intervention. Subsequent action by the federal government brought an innovation in criminal law, that is, the state is responsible for protecting the national economic order from private interests within that order. This departure from the traditional scope and purpose of the criminal law meant that the law not only protected private property but also helped maintain a specific kind of national economy. American capitalism was secured, not threatened, by the new legal regulations.

A tradition for antitrust legislation was already in the common law of England and America.[32] The common-law precedents had established that specific commercial activities were to be restricted by law. Yet the common-law doctrine as applied by the individual states was not effective in controlling the monopolies growing in the United States. Broad interpretation by state courts of the interstate commerce clause of the Constitution and the first article of the Fourteenth Amendment allowed many corporations to expand greatly beyond state borders and to receive the federal government's protection. Because no federal common law regulated monopolies, the need for federal antitrust legislation was clear.

Opposition to trusts and monopolies was aroused in several segments of the society. Diverse groups, not always with compatible ideologies, agitated for antimonopoly legislation.[33] Some groups were gravely worried about the corporations that were ruthlessly exploiting national resources for their own profit-making ventures. Labor was hostile to powerful corporations, finding itself at a distinct disadvantage in bargaining with them. Small businessmen feared possible ruin because of the wealth and facilities concentrated in gigantic corporations. Declining farm prices were attributed to the growth of large corporations. The Populist party actively supported agrarian antagonism toward big buiness. A farmer expressed the antimonopoly spirit of the period, relating monopoly to "progress":

> Progress which the possessors of the good things of earth call innovation, progress the cardinal principle of this democracy of the people, will go on as all history shows. It must be through continual strife, for progress is but a contest still going on in spite of the death chants, the impenetrable armor, and the resisting spirit of self; a contest which has been going on through earth's long day, and will still go on until evening — until the mighty purposes of creation are accomplished, and the many are entitled to preeminence over the few in the view of the earth as they are now entitled in the eye of heaven. This is what the great democracy of the people demands. That is what the antimonopoly movement means.[34]

In the 1880's, monopolies were attacked in the name of the theory and practice of laissez-faire economics, which supported enterprise free from government interference. A challenge was presented to the long-entrenched classical economies. Individual radicals were influential also, such as Wendell Phillips and Peter Cooper, and the writings of Henry George, Edward Bellamy, and Henry Demarest Lloyd reached wide audiences. President Cleveland brought the issue to the front in a tariff message of 1887 and stressed it with even greater urgency in the following year: "As we view the achievements of aggregated capital we discover the existence of trusts, combinations and monopolies, while the citizen is struggling far in the rear or is trampled to death beneath an iron heel. Corporations which should be carefully restrained creatures of the law and servants of the people, are fast becoming the people's masters."[35] That year the platforms of both major political parties pledged to oppose trusts and monopolies.

Widespread opposition to monopolies brought on the Sherman Act of 1890. Drafted primarily by Senator John Sherman of Ohio, the law declared: "(1) Every contract, combination in the form of trust or otherwise, or conspiracy, in restraint of trade or commerce among the several States, or with foreign nations is hereby declared to be illegal. . . . (2) Every person who shall monopolize, or attempt to monopolize . . . any part of the trade or commerce among the several States or with foreign nations, shall be deemed guilty of a misdemeanor. . . ." To combine in restraint of trade and to monopolize became public offenses. The federal government was empowered to proceed by criminal action against violations of the law.

Broadly, the interest to be protected in the law was the nation's economic order. Supporters of antitrust legislation did not, for the most part, aim to alter the economic order, but to protect the free-enterprise system. "The interest to be protected was the maintenance of a competitive economy based on private enterprise. The State did not mean to become owner or entrepreneur, but it felt compelled to use its legislative, administrative, and judicial machinery for the protection of the economic well-being of the community as a whole — as conceived by a liberal economic philosophy — and to defend it against powerful industrial and commercial interests."[36]

Further legislation and measures for more strictly enforcing antitrust laws followed. During the Theodore Roosevelt administration particular attention went to regulating corporations. Roosevelt's intentions were clear, to work within the capitalist system:

> In dealing with the big corporations we call trusts, we must resolutely purpose to proceed by evolution and not by revolution. . . . Our aim is not to do away with corporations; on the contrary these big aggregations are an inevitable development of modern industrialism. . . . We can do nothing of good in the way of regulating and supervising these corporations until we fix clearly in our minds that we are not attacking the corporations, but endeavoring to do away with any evil in them. We are not hostile to them; we are merely determined that they shall be so handled as to subserve the public good."[37]

Legislation and court rulings during the "progressive era" of increasing government regulation of business, the first fifteen or twenty years of this century, actually protected and strengthened business in America. During that period, as new laws were established, big business triumphed. Gabriel Kolko analyzed the enactment of laws regulating the railroad and meatpacking industries:

> There were any number of options involving government and economics abstractly available to national political leaders during the period 1900–1916, and in virtually every case they chose those solutions to problems advocated by the representatives of concerned business and financial interests. Such proposals were motivated by the needs of the interested business, and political intervention into the economy was frequently merely a response to the demands of particular businessmen. In brief, conservative solutions to the emerging problems of an industrial society were almost uniformly applied. The result was a conservative triumph in the sense that there was an effort to preserve the basic social and economic relations essential to a capitalist society, an effort that was frequently consciously as well as functionally conservative.[38]

The regulations were influenced and shaped by the largest companies, trying to control competition from the smaller companies and to ensure better markets for the large companies.

The crowning achievement for corporate business was the Federal Trade Commission (FTC), which ruled out "unfair methods of competition." Business and politics became one. "The business community knew what it wanted from the commission, and what it wanted was almost precisely what the commission sought to do. No distinction between government and business was possible simply because the commission absorbed and reflected the predominant values of the business community."[39]

The legislation and actions of the New Deal, in Franklin D. Roosevelt's administration, added much governmental planning and protection for the capitalist economy. Yet in spite of the antitrust legislation and enforcement since the Sherman Act of 1890, the purpose was clearly to protect the capitalist system from abuse, not to create a new type of economic order. Franklin Roosevelt was not the socialist the public thought and feared; he represented and promoted capitalist enterprise:

> It would be a mistake to assume that this socialization was developed entirely at the expense of private enterprise. Indeed it is certain that the New Deal did more to strengthen and to save the capitalist economy than it did to weaken or destroy it. That economy had broken down in many nations abroad, and its collapse contributed to the rise of totalitarian governments which completely subordinated business to the state. The system was on the verge of collapse in the United States during the Hoover administration, and it is at least conceivable that had that collapse been permitted to occur, it might have been followed by the establishment of an economy very different from that to which Americans were accustomed. Historically Franklin Roosevelt's administration did for twentieth-century American capitalism what Theodore Roosevelt's and Wil-

son's had done for nineteenth-century business enterprise: it saved the system by ridding it of its grosser abuses and forcing it to accommodate itself to larger public interests. History may eventually record Franklin D. Roosevelt as the greatest American conservative since Hamilton.[40]

The attack upon corporations, beginning in the latter part of the nineteenth century and still going, has not been against business but has been inspired and led by the business interest itself. Economic regulation has been enacted and administered for the benefit of the capitalist economic system. The capitalist state, with the legal order as its apparatus, seeks to ensure continuation of the capitalist system in the United States.

THE HEALTH INDUSTRY

The legal safeguards for the public's health are similar to those found in corporate legislation. Government has imposed more and more controls on the manufacture and sale of food and drugs. Criminal laws and commissions have been created to protect our health. The food and drug industry interests, however, receive more protection from these controls than does the public interest.

Through the first half of the nineteenth century the United States was chiefly an agricultural nation and purity of food and safeness of drugs had to be watched by the family. During this period the principle *caveat emptor* ("let the buyer beware") prevailed. In the industrial era after the Civil War, the economy began to grow in complexity. Many new products were introduced and the consumer was further removed from the producer. Standards for judgment became uncertain. *Caveat emptor* was eventually replaced by another attitude that favored protecting the consumer. Now the blame for poor food and drug standards fell on the manufacturer or distributor. The new value, *caveat vendor* ("let the seller beware") was reinforced in legislation, making producer and distributor responsible for quality.

Food and drugs were being produced and shipped in ever larger amounts, multiplying possibilities for spoilage, adulteration, and misrepresentation. The public gradually was made aware that adulteration was a problem by bulletins and reports, by purchasing the products, and by reading popular books, articles, and newspaper editorials. The Division of Chemistry of the Department of Agriculture, under Dr. Harvey W. Wiley, was especially effective in defining the abuses as a threat to public welfare. His dramatic "poison-squad" experiments showed that some food preservatives were harmful and dangerous. The division also showed that a new interstate business was thriving in patent (nonprescription) medicines, some of them of questionable value.

Now that the public was aware of dangers in the food and drugs they were consuming, conflicts arose over a solution.[41] State and federal legislative measures were proposed, but opposition was strong because interest groups, usually consumer and producer, had different values. The first attempts to pass legislation were instigated by the interest groups to protect their products from competition they thought unfair. Early bills that were passed consequently applied to one or two products and not to the basic problem, adulteration and misrepresentation of food and drugs.

Not until the 1880s was the first federal pure food and drug legislation introduced for the public benefit. These measures, however, were defeated: "It and other efforts like it were defeated by a durable alliance of quacks, ruthless crooks, pious frauds, scoundrels, high-priced lawyer-lobbyists, vested interests, liars, corrupt members of Congress, venal publishers, cowards in high office, the stupid, the apathetic, and the duped."[42] Opposing such interests as these, defenders of the public's interest could have small hope.

From 1880 to 1906 more than 150 pure food and drug bills were introduced in Congress. Most were heard of no more after introduction, and the few that were approved were minor.[43] But continued pressure from the popular press and opinions from congressional constituents overcame apathy, and in 1906 the Federal Food and Drug Act was passed by both House and Senate. The act declared it unlawful to manufacture in any territory, or to introduce into any state, any adulterated or misbranded food or drug. Offending products were to be seized and criminal penalties were provided for anyone found guilty of violating the act's provisions.

The need for revising the act, however, became apparent shortly after its passage. The absence of control over advertising was an especially large loophole for evading the spirit of the law, and the labeling requirements permitted extravagant and unwarranted therapeutic claims for a product. Also, the 1906 act contained no provisions on cosmetics or safe and effective health devices. In spite of amendments in 1912 (the Sherley amendment) and 1919 (the New Weight Act), impure and unsafe foods and drugs had not been effectively controlled by law.

A renewed effort was made to regulate food and drugs. Further awareness of the problem was provided in such popular works as Kallet and Schlink's *100,000,000 Guinea Pigs* and Lamb's *American Chamber of Horrors.*[44] Consumer organizations were formed and consumer research groups were established. After Franklin D. Roosevelt took office in 1933 a committee was appointed to draft new legislation.

A bill to correct the deficiencies in the 1906 law was introduced in 1933. The expected attacks came. Particularly active in opposing it was the organization representing the patent-medicine interests (nonprescription commercial preparations), the United Medicine Manufacturers of America. The organization tried to block the bill with a drive involving "Seven Plans," which would:

> (1) Secure cooperation of newspapers in spreading favorable publicity; (2) enlist all manufacturers and wholesalers to instruct customers through their salesmen; (3) secure the pledge of manufacturers, wholesalers, advertising agencies, and all other interested affiliates to address letters to Senators to gain their promise to vote against the bill; (4) line up with other organizations, such as the Drug Institute, Proprietary Association, National Association of Retail Druggists, to make a mass attack on the bill; (5) enlist the help of carton, tube, bottle, and box manufacturers; (6) ridicule organizations favoring the bill; and (7) convey by every means available — radio, newspapers, mail, and personal contact — the alarming fact that if the bill is adopted, the public will be deprived of the right of self-diagnosis and self-medication.[45]

But the public interest succeeded, at least in theory. The Federal Food, Drug, and Cosmetic Act was enacted in 1938, requiring, among other things, more effective methods for controlling false labeling and advertising. Informative, specific labeling was definitely required. False advertising of foods, drugs, and cosmetics was prohibited, with more severe penalties for violating the law. And authority was established for setting standards for the identity, quality, strength, and purity of drugs. In 1951, the Durham-Humphrey amendment to the act was passed, placing stricter controls on the dispensing of drugs.

Other special federal laws were enacted to govern the manufacture and marketing of some classes of drugs (narcotics, marijuana, biological products). Still other laws regulated such activities as weighing, measuring, and mailing foods and drugs.[46] The federal laws were complemented by state laws also regulating manufacturing, labeling, and advertising, but in addition overseeing pharmacy.[47]

The federal government showed continued interest in providing the public with safe and pure foods by an inquiry into the drug industry at the beginning of the sixties. Presumably interested in the broad problem of administered prices, the Senate Subcommittee on Antitrust and Monopoly under Chairman Estes Kefauver touched on such topics as the high cost of drugs, the flood of new drugs released each year, the multiple trade names for identical chemicals and compounds, advertising and promotion of drugs, safety and efficacy of drugs, and violation of antitrust laws by drug manufacturers.[48] The hearings strongly criticized the amount of money drug manufacturers spend on advertising and promotion compared to what they spend for research. After the hearings, amid strong opposing pressure from the large pharmaceutical houses and their lobbying organizations, Congress passed the Kefauver-Hart Drug Act in 1962. This act was not successful on regulating drug prices, but it did secure provisions for stricter control of testing, labeling, and advertising of drugs.

Although the drug act of 1962 corrected many abuses in the drug industry, the problems remain. The federal agency that is supposed to regulate the food and drug industry, the Food and Drug Administration (FDA), is closer to the industry's interests than to the general public's needs. In fact, the public is kept insulated from the activities of the FDA, which has the benign attitude "that the public is primarily an ignorant and hysterical mob from whom any suggestions of danger must be kept at all cost."[49] The attitude is fostered by the FDA's general faith in the food industry, assuming that the industry voluntarily ensures the safety and quality of food it produces and distributes. Because of this mistaken belief, the FDA is not able to advance the public interest:

> In the place of sustained action to advance health by helping to improve the American diet, the FDA substitutes a naive faith that the way American food is produced, preserved, and distributed is exceptionally fine. It maintains this faith in the face of increasing scientific evidence that chemical additives can be extremely dangerous, that the vitamin content of the American diet is deteriorating, that saturated fat in food may be a contributing factor to more than 70 percent of all American deaths, and that American food is getting filthier. Faith has a way of withstanding fact. But while the FDA goes through the ritualistic exercise that it passes off as regulation, it is the food consumer who is injured.[50]

In other words, the FDA is not able to effectively enforce the laws on consumer protection. Not only does it lack the inclination, but it does not have the knowledge and techniques to detect and enforce violations. It is far behind the advances made by the food industry.

> As a result, between 1950 and 1965 the food industry went through its period of fastest growth almost completely unmonitored. In that time a brand new series of problems — including the hazards involved with the chemical environment through the use of food additives, the threat of food contamination becoming nationwide through a modern mass-distribution system, the monitoring of dangerous pesticide residues in widely distributed foods, the introduction of brand new synthetic foods made up entirely of chemicals — developed without serious and effective attention from the FDA.[51]

Clearly the food and drug industry is regulated to the advantage of the industry itself. To assume that such criminal laws protect the public's welfare is to misunderstand criminal law in American society. Regulatory criminal law protects the national economy.

REGULATING OCCUPATIONAL PRACTICE

Legal regulation of occupations has a long and uneven history. The beginnings are to be found among the medieval guilds. Their licensing practices were designed to protect the members' economic interests and the community from harmful economic and trade activities. By the beginning of the nineteenth century, professional and occupational licensing was well established in America, especially for law and medicine. Later in the century the laws were greatly modified, and many were repealed, following the laissez-faire philosophy. But with the eventual founding of national and state occupational associations, regulations were once again established.

These associations were meant mostly to promote the interests of the occupations, often to protect one occupation from encroachment by another. On the regulation of health professions, Ronald L. Akers writes:

> The foundings of state associations were often for the express purpose of promoting occupational legislation, sometimes in a defensive move to prevent other, already established, professions from regulating them. The New Jersey Pharmaceutical Association (1870), for instance, was formed only after steps were undertaken by the medical society of New Jersey to force legislative measures on "all dispensers of medicines" in the state. Within a week of the formation of the New York Optical Society (1896), a bill to regulate the practice of refracting opticians (the early denotation of optometrists) was introduced in the New York legislature. Securing passage of a medical practice act was one of the main reasons for the organization of the Virginia Medical Society. The initial organization of each of the five professions in Kentucky was shortly followed by the enactment of a practice act. Since its organization, each association has been the driving force in legislation regulating practice in its own field.[52]

By 1900 all the established professions had their own laws, reacting to pressure from their associations. The occupational associations, not the general public, have been responsible for the laws that regulate the occupations. To this day, the statutes and administrative codes that regulate occupations and professions are made by themselves, representing their own parochial interests. Especially through their associations, they have a monopoly on the lawmaking that affects their operations.

> The state association, in conjunction with the examining board, initiates moves for legislation, decides what provisions should be added, deleted, or

changed, drafts preliminary and final proposed bills, persuades a legislator to introduce the bill, and works for its passage throughout the time it is being considered. If proposed practice legislation comes from any other direction, the association will oppose it and work for its defeat.[53]

Each occupation attempts to protect itself from competition by other occupations. Of the relationship among five health professions in one state, this was observed:

> The general picture of the context of conflict among the five professions in Kentucky can be summarized as follows: Chiropractic and optometry generally do not oppose one another but have not made any apparent efforts to cooperate with and support one another. Medicine, dentistry, and pharmacy in recent times have not actively opposed one another and, in fact, are members of an allied group of health professions. Medicine and chiropractic consistently oppose each other, and sometimes optometry and medicine engage in political combat. Medicine, dentistry, and pharmacy occasionally all oppose certain aspects of chiropractic's legislation. Secondarily, they may be politically opposed to optometry. Medicine and dentistry seem to cooperate more closely than any other two groups, and they seldom oppose pharmaceutical legislation, although not always wholeheartedly supporting it. Finally, each profession experiences conflict with additional groups besides the other four health professions.[54]

The professions with the greatest organizational resources and cohesive structures are the most successful in gaining legislation that favors their own interests. That some occupations have the power to overwhelm other groups is a basic fact in legislative politics. All this passes for maintaining high standards of service for the public good.

Especially created agencies, not police and prosecutors, enforce and administer occupational laws. The administrative hearing of cases, rather than trial procedures, closely approximates juvenile court procedures. The actions are more often remedial, using injunctions instead of directly punishing the offender by fine or imprisonment. The distinction becomes apparent when we consider that an apprehended burglar or robber is punished by a jail sentence, a fine, or probation, whereas a doctor may be punished by revoking his license, a lawyer by disbarment, or a businessman by a government warning or injuction, civil damages, or suspending his license to do business.

Regulation of the medical profession displays clearly how occupational laws are enforced and administered. Most states have a special administrative agency for regulating medical practice laws. In New York State, a board of examiners is appointed by the regents of the state, composed of medical practitioners, appointed by the governor with the consent of the state senate. It issues licenses and is responsible for disciplining members, which may consist of revoking licenses after a hearing. Only as a last resort are cases turned over to the state's attorney general for criminal prosecution.

The physicians are almost free agents. Their license is a lifetime certificate to practice mostly at their own discretion. When violations of laws on medical practice are detected, the state board is not fast to act. Self-discipline among doctors is more illusory than real.

> Within the profession itself the disciplining of colleagues has little support; physicians do not like to police their fellows, and this reluctance is reflected at every level of organized medicine. At that, the strongest penalty a medical society or hospital staff can levy is expulsion. But removal from a society or hospital has no bearing on the doctor's license; though unacceptable to his peers, the offender retains his legal privilege to treat patients. Moreover, just as the profession is slow to prosecute violators within its own ranks, so also is it loath to pursue the cause of more effective laws. As a result, the inadequate statutes currently on the books are likely to remain unamended for the foreseeable future.[55]

Yet malpractice suits and other cases do arise in the medical profession and sometimes reach the courts. At least 2,000 professional-liability claims are brought against doctors for malpractice each year. The Law Department of the American Medical Association estimates that at least one malpractice claim has been filed against 18 percent of the doctors in private practice. The judgments and settlements in malpractice cases total about $50 million each year.[56]

But the malpractice plaintiff, the patient who brings suit, meets strong resistance taking a case before the court.[57] Many courts even obstruct the plaintiff by requiring testimony by medical witnesses. Doctors who testify are very likely to sympathize with their fellow doctors. Doctors and hospital staffs are known to tamper with medical records, if such tampering will reflect favorably on the defendant's case. Just as false or biased testimony may be given in malpractice suits, so too may records be altered.

Because occupations and professions are an integral part of the American economy, it is to be expected that they, as well as their practitioners, will receive favorable treatment under the criminal law. Not only does the law protect these groups, it makes their activity possible. The criminal law promotes the welfare of these groups more than it does the public that is subject to their activities. The larger political economy of the United States is secured in the legal regulation of occupations and professions.

PSYCHIATRY AND SEXUAL-PSYCHOPATH LAWS

Some criminal laws, not unlike our other social passions and conveniences, have times of increased popularity. Fashion in law was at work when, in the late thirties and on into the fifties, more than half the states enacted "sexual-psychopath" laws. The statues varied somewhat from one state to another, but generally defined the sexual psychopath as "one lacking the power to control his sexual impulses or having criminal propensities toward the commission of sex offenses."[58] The laws provided that a person diagnosed as a sexual psychopath be confined for an indefinite period in a state hospital for the insane. Why were these laws enacted then, and what social interests were involved in their formulation?

Sexual-psychopath laws responded in part to public anxiety about serious sex crimes. Like the somewhat comparable "habitual-offender" laws that swept the country earlier, the sexual-psychopath laws were a partial solution to a condition that was being defined as a social problem.[59] Consequently, as the legal system characteristically does, it created a new law to solve a problem.

The problem of the sex offender, as defined by the public, was based on propositions most of which were false or at least questionable:

> Namely, that the present danger to women and children from serious sex crimes is very great, for the number of sex crimes is large and is increasing more rapidly than any other crime: that most sex crimes are committed by "sexual psychopaths" and that these persons persist in their sexual crimes throughout life; that they always give warning that they are dangerous by first committing minor offenses; that any psychiatrist can diagnose them with a high degree of precision at an early age, before they have committed serious sex crimes; and that sexual psychopaths who are diagnosed and identified should be confined as irresponsible persons until they are pronounced by psychiatrists to be completely and permanently cured of their malady.[60]

But once the public had been aroused, partly by press coverage of a few spectacular sex crimes, and partly by a misinformed conception of the sex offender, sexual-psychopath legislation followed as the answer to the problem.

Yet the public's worry about sex offenses could not be effective in formulating criminal law without organizing action groups within the community. Concrete pressure for sexual-psychopath legislation was provided in most states by committees, most of which were guided by psychiatrists. These committees presented sexual-psychopath bills to the public and to the legislatures as the most scientific and enlightened method of protecting society against dangerous sex criminals. It is pointed out by Edwin H. Sutherland that "the psychiatrists, more than any others, have been the interest group in back of the laws."[61] A committee of psychiatrists and neurologists in Chicago wrote the bill that became the sexual-psychopath law of Illinois. In Minnesota all the members of the governor's committee except one were psychiatrists.

That these laws were predominantly formulated by psychiatrists accounts for most of their substance. Because a common assertion among psychiatrists is that serious sex crimes are the result of emotional or mental pathology, or that all psychological defectives have actual or potential sexual abnormalities, it is little wonder that the laws stipulated that sex offenders be handled as psychologically disturbed and treated as patients. But the psychiatric interest in formulating the laws was also a matter of private economics.

Their interest in the legislation was, nevertheless, reinforced by the more general movement promoting the treatment of all offenders. Also, many professionally trained persons employed in corrections have believed that emotional traits are the explanation for crime. Treating the criminal as a patient, therefore, was consistent with the aims of those engaged in applying these laws.

In spite of the rush to enact sexual psychopath laws, the tendency has been not to enforce them, for several reasons:

> One is that the laws were passed in a period of panic and were forgotten after the emotion was relieved by this action. A second reason is that the state has no facilities for the care and custody of sexual psychopaths; the state hospitals are already crowded with psychotic patients. A third reason is that the prosecutor and judge, anxious to make records as vigorous and aggressive defenders of the community, favor the most severe penalty available and are unwilling to look upon serious sex criminals as patients. They use the sexual psychopath laws only when their evidence is so weak that conviction under the criminal law is improbable. Finally, it is reported that defense attorneys have learned that they can stop the proceedings under this law by advising their clients to refuse to talk to the psychiatrists. The psychiatrists can make no diagnosis if those who are being investigated refuse to talk.[62]

But perhaps, writes Paul W. Tappan, "the greatest saving grace has been the almost uniform lack of enforcement that has followed their enactment."[63] The sexual-psychopath laws depart from some of the most fundamental conceptions of criminal law. Most important, the Anglo-American legal doctrine of *nulla crimen sine lege,* prohibiting prosecution without clearly specified substantive norms, is denied by most of the sexual-psychopath statutes. Because the individual may be adjudged either without a criminal charge or without a finding of guilt, merely by diagnosis that he or she is a sexual psychopath, due process is ignored. Furthermore, the "sexual psychopath" is so vaguely and variously defined by psychiatrists that a great deal of variation in diagnoses and much discretion in administration of the law results.

> There appears to be no agreement as to the syndromes of aberration that justify special treatment. Indeed, hospital authorities handling cases of alleged

sex psychopaths committed to them by the courts discover a wide spread of psychological types — many who are normal, along with neurotics, psychotics, epileptics, feebleminded, alcoholics, and constitutional types. Agreement among authorities is often difficult enough to attain for purposes of classifying individuals where traditional and fairly precise clinical categories are involved; consensus is impossible in the no man's land of psychopathic personality. The hazard inherent in the substantive definitions of these statutes is manifest upon inspection; the psychopathology is defined by such nondiscriminating terminology as "impulsiveness of behavior," "lack of customary standards of good judgment," "emotional instability," or "inability to control impulse." The cases adjudicated under these criteria display varied forms of personality organization and a widely assorted sexual symptomatology, a significant proportion of which is in fact normal behavior viewed from either a biological or statistical point of view.[64]

And in some jurisdictions persons may be adjudicated without having a criminal charge placed against them and without it being established that a crime has been committed. "Thus individuals who are nonpsychotic and nondefective, against whom no charge has been laid, may be confined for long periods in hospitals that lack both the space and the treatment facilities to handle them. By the simple expedient of shifting jurisdiction to civil courts, these legislators have made it possible to commit minor deviates who are not insane to psychiatric institutions where they do not belong."[65]

We have no reason to believe that such legislation will not recur. Law has its element of fashion when formulated and administered within some larger ideology and fostered by the interests of a group representing the dominant ideology. Establishing official policies in the name of the common good, and under the guise of scientific knowledge, is always a force in formulating some types of criminal law. In capitalist society the need for creating a humane society is not commonly found in the criminal law.

ECONOMICS IN THE SUNDAY-SALES LAW

Since Sunday became different from other days of the week, interests have been effective in guarding it by criminal law. Until fairly recent times religious interests determined the legal meaning of the Sabbath. Today, however, Sunday is regulated by the law because of influence wielded by social and economic interests.

Sunday closing laws, or "blue laws," (often printed on blue paper), started with the command from Mount Sinai: "Ye shall keep the Sabbath therefore; for it is holy unto you: every one that defileth it shall surely be put to death" (Exodus 31:14). The command gained legal character in A.D. 321 when Emperor Constantine, after his own conversion to Christianity, issued an edict requiring all work to cease on the day that was settled by law to be the Sabbath.[66] Numerous statutes regulating activities on Sunday were later enacted in England. In 1237, Henry III forbade attendance at markets on Sunday; the Sunday showing of wools at the market was banned by Edward III in 1354; in 1409, Henry IV prohibited some games on Sunday; Henry VI proscribed Sunday fairs in churchyards in 1444 and four years later made unlawful all fairs and markets and all showing of goods or merchandise; Sunday bodily labor was disallowed by Edward VI in the mid-sixteenth century; and Sunday sports and amusements were restricted in 1625 by Charles I. The early English Sunday laws were aimed at frequenting markets, participating in commercial activity, laboring, and engaging in amusements on Sunday.

The American colonies wasted little time in enacting Sunday laws. The colonial Sunday laws, however, were similar to the later English statute of Charles II (29 Charles II, c. 7, 1677). The law stated:

> For the better observation and keeping holy the Lord's day, commonly called Sunday; be it enacted . . . that all the laws enacted and inforce concerning the observation of the day, and repairing to church thereon, be carefully put in execution; and that all and every person and persons whatsoever shall upon every Lord's day apply themselves to the observation of the same, by exercising themselves thereon in the duties of piety and true religion, publicly and privately; and that no tradesman, artificer, and workman, laborer, or other person whatsoever, shall do or exercise any worldly labor or business or work of their ordinary callings upon the Lord's day, or any part thereof (works of necessity and charity only excepted) . . . and that no person or persons whatsoever shall publicly cry, show forth, or expose for sale any wares, merchandise, fruit, herbs, goods, or chattels, whatsoever, upon the Lord's day, or any part thereof. . . .

This law added to the earlier statutes compulsory worship and church attendance on Sunday. The idea was evident in the 1610 statute of the Virginia colony, which made church attendance compulsory, for both the morning and afternoon services.[67] Such laws were to benefit the churches of the colonies, just as they had been meant to protect the established church in England.

Most states today have Sunday laws among their statutes. Some others have no statewide law, but leave the option to cities and counties. The substance of all these laws no longer relates to church attendance, but to other diversions likely to occur on Sunday, such as labor, amusement, and sales. The change in the substance of Sunday law is indicated in the statutes of New York State. The first Sabbath law of New York, included in conditions of the Burgomaster of New Amsterdam of 1656, required the

Scriptures to be read in public by a hired schoolmaster. Shortly after, in 1644, the "Duke of York laws" were issued to regulate worship on Sunday. The forerunner of the present Sunday law, however, was an act of 1695 that forbade labor on Sunday. The act continued in effect until 1788, when it was adopted as part of the laws under the state constitution. Revisions were made in 1813, 1830, and 1909, but the body of the act remained. Today the statute prohibits on Sunday acts "which are serious interruptions of the repose and religious liberty of the community." In New York, as in other states, the law of church attendance has shifted to a law restricting work on Sunday. Sunday law became "closing" law.

Sunday closing law, needless to say, is a confusing hodgepodge of standards and applications. The laws are sporadically and selectively enforced in local settings. However obsolete these laws may seem, formulation and administration of them has been revived:

> The Sunday blue laws are unfair and seem to serve no useful function in our society today. However, due to their antiquity, they are well established and widespread, although seldom enforced. In addition to their ages, their widespread incorporation and continuation are due to a large degree to various pressure groups. Their incorporation probably had its basis in the religious pressure elements, and their continuance, in the pressure groups representing the retail sellers' associations.[68]

New pressure groups with other than religious interests have been effective in revising Sunday laws. Secular and economic rather than religious interests are in control, accompanied by such rationales as relaxation, leisure, and recreation. Work schedules now require customers to shop seven days a week, 24 hours a day, and competition among merchants makes an extended opening necessary.

The action of pressure groups on Sunday legislation can be seen in recent amendments to the statutes, changing the wording to include the private interests of specific groups.[69] In 1957 the Massachusetts Sunday law was amended to allow frozen custard stands to operate on Sunday. The frozen-custard lobby got the ice-cream sales clause expanded to permit the sale on Sunday of "frozen dessert mixes." Likewise, local pressure groups in Massachusetts were active in changing the Sunday statute to permit selling fishing bait on Sunday. Pressure groups in New York too were able to have the Sunday law expanded, allowing roadside stands to sell farm products. And in Arkansas, laws make it permissible to sell film, flashbulbs and batteries, but not cameras or projectors; and in some New Jersey counties one can buy jackets, tennis shorts, ski pants, and fishing boots, but not shirts or dresses. In some New Jersey counties it is also legal to sell disposable diapers but not washable ones. In the state of New

York the Appeals Court changed the law to permit on Sunday the sale of windshield wiper blades, ski wax, take-out fried chicken, and thousands of other items.[70] The ruling makes it profitable for discount stores and supermarkets to remain open on Sunday.

The Automobile Dealers Association has influenced several states to amend their Sunday sales laws on selling automobiles on Sunday. The action was inspired by the combination of the traditional Sunday pleasure drive with Sunday shopping on the superhighway. Sunday drivers were finding it convenient to purchase autos from the automobile dealers on the highways. Auto dealers within the city limits, beyond the highways, could not compete with the highway auto dealers. Into this crisis stepped the Automobile Dealers Association, dominated by downtown dealers, successfully lobbying to prohibit the sale of autos on Sunday. A similar phenomenon has restricted the sale of other kinds of merchandise in the large discount stores also on the superhighways. Downtown businesses have succeeded in having local statutes amended or enforced to curb competition from businesses with easy access to the affluent Sunday driver.

The United States Supreme Court in 1960 heard an appeal from the Maryland Court of Appeals. The Maryland State Court had convicted and fined employees of a large department store on a highway in Anne Arundel County for selling on Sunday a looseleaf binder, a can of floor wax, a stapler, staples, and a toy. The Maryland State Court had ruled that the conduct of the employees violated a Maryland statute forbidding the sale on Sunday of all merchandise, except the retail sales of tobacco products, confectioneries, milk, bread, fruit, gasoline, oils, greases, drugs, medicines, newspapers, and periodicals. After hearing the case the Supreme Court upheld (on May 29, 1961), in McGowan v. Maryland, the conviction of the Maryland State Court.

The Supreme Court's principal argument in McGowan v. Maryland was that although Sunday law originated for religious purposes, today the law is maintained for secular pursuits:

> In the light of the evolution of our Sunday Closing Laws through the centuries, and of the more or less recent emphasis upon secular considerations, it is concluded that, as presently written and administered, most of them, at least, are of secular rather than of a religious character, and that presently they bear no relationship to establishment of religion, as those words are used in the constitution of the United States.[71]

Furthermore, the opinion continues, secular interests may be served on Sunday: "The present purpose and effect of most of our Sunday Closing Laws is to provide a uniform day of rest for all citizens; and the fact that this day is Sunday, a day of particular significance for the dominant Christian sects, does not bar the State from achieving its secular goals." It was argued too that "the present purpose and effect of the statute here involved is not aid to religion but to set aside a day of rest and recreation." Finally, on the issue of religious liberty, Chief Justice Warren, in writing the majority opinion, observed that Sunday law does not violate constitutional rights: "People of all religions and people with no religion regard Sunday as a time for family activity, for visiting friends and relatives, for late sleeping, for passive and active entertainments, for dining out, and the like."[72]

The Supreme Court in its decision has therefore recognized that "Sunday closing legislation no longer exclusively represents religious interests."[73] That it now represents economic interests is recognized in the court's decision, in the remark that the recent Sunday laws of such states as New Jersey were reformulated because of pressure from labor groups and trade associations. The Court said too that modern Sunday legislation in England was promoted by such interest groups as the National Federation of Grocers, the National Chamber of Trade, the Drapers' Chamber of Trade, and the National Union of Shop Assistants.

A criminal law, then, as shown in the Sunday laws, may be intended for a particular interest at one time and then amended and implemented at another time for other class interests. Sunday law, in existence for hundreds of years for religious reasons, was never officially negated. But social conditions have changed and the economy has shifted; it is used for new purposes. In a capitalist economy the state must continuously intervene to adjust the economic marketplace, to make legitimate the "free-enterprise" system. Sunday-sales law has become such a device in the economic development of the United States.

ORIGINS OF JUVENILE JUSTICE

The legal system not only regulates the daily affairs and various enterprises of adults, but also intervenes in the lives of juveniles. In fact, especially in the United States over the last two centuries, delinquent behavior of youths has been seen as a threat to social order. In the popular imagination the child's conduct is a prerequisite for the orderly progress of civilization. The delinquent child, we are told, is a sure sign that society is about to collapse. The New York Children's Aid Society warned in the middle of the last century: "It should be remembered that there are no dangers to the value of property, or to the permanency of our institutions, so great as those from the existence of such a class of vagabond, ignorant, ungoverned children."[74]

Over the years in the United States a large number and great range of laws have been formulated to guide the behavior of the young. Many programs have been instituted both to punish and reform the wayward child. Yet, a larger purpose than merely regulating the delinquent conduct of youths has been behind all these laws and programs. Alexander Liazos writes, "All of the programs through the years have aimed at control and discipline of the poorer classes; they have tried to resocialize the boys and girls of the poor, working class, and minority groups so they would accept the place capitalism (in its various forms) chose for them."[75] Certainly the programs have not been intended to change the social and economic conditions that consign working-class youths to their position in life. Today it is still mainly the children of the poor and the working class who are processed through the juvenile-justice system.

The aim behind juvenile justice, then, besides the attempt to control delinquency and recidivism, is to integrate the children of the working class into the bottom of the social and occupational world. The class structure of capitalist society is maintained:

> Especially for the boys, this has meant socializing them to fit into a disciplined labor force and accepting low-level unskilled or semi-skilled jobs, with few making it to higher jobs and positions so as to perpetuate the belief that "anybody can make it if they work hard enough." Whereas private boarding schools send the sons of the upper classes into the ruling positions of the society, the institutions and programs for delinquents send many of their graduates to lower (but still "respectable") occupations (others remain unemployed or end up in prisons).[76]

Juvenile justice has gone through several stages in the effort to secure the class structure. The approaches have ranged from preaching and teaching to the use of psychological and therapeutic techniques, with discipline and confinement always present. In the first part of the nineteenth century, children were placed in houses of refuge, given moral training, and taught the value of being industrious. The New York House of Refuge proposed in 1824 that its inmates would be "put to work at such employments as will tend to encourage industry and ingenuity, taught reading, writing, and arithmetic, and most carefully instructed in the nature of the moral and religious obligations."[77] Youthful inmates were assigned jobs, such as making chairs, shoes, clothing, and soap; and in some states their labor was let out to contractors. A total environment was established for the young: "Life in the houses of refuge was rigid, with a neverending round of work and duties. Work, housekeeping, school, and other duties left no free time at all. Punishment was severe: privation of

Boys making shoes at the New York House of Refuge about 1870. The early reformatory in the United States, as today, trains working class youth for jobs that further exploit their labor and perpetuate the class system.

recreation, solitary confinement, bread and water diet, and corporal punishment."[78]

During the middle years of the nineteenth century family living was emphasized as a way of preventing and controlling delinquency. The family-like "cottage system" was created within juvenile institutions and children were placed in "foster-home" families outside the reformatory. Later in the century some reforms were made in the employment of inmates, such as abolishing the contract system and changing some of the work conditions. Nevertheless, the focus was still industrial, moral, and social training for the unfortunate, teaching them to make an "honest living."[79]

By the end of the nineteenth century a major reform in juvenile justice was taking place. In 1899 the Chicago juvenile court was created as a separate court for processing youths under 17 years of age, closed to the public and with no need for lawyers. Although court proceedings were changed for delinquents, the goal of justice remained the same: controlling socialization of youths within the class structure. The modern system of juvenile justice has many of its roots in the penal and judicial reforms of this period.

Anthony Platt documented and analyzed the creation of the modern juvenile-justice system within the "child-saving" movement.[80] He found that during the progressive era, "the modern system was systematically organized to include juvenile courts, probation, child guidance, clinics, truant officers, and reformatories. The child-saving movement — an amalgam of philanthropists, middle-class reformers and professionsals — was responsible for the consolidation of these reforms."[81] Privileged intellectuals and professionals recognized during this period that far-reaching economic, political, and social reforms were needed to restore order and stability to the society.

As Platt writes, "The child-saving movement tried to do for the criminal justice system what industrialists and corporate leaders were trying to do for the economy — that is, achieve order, stability and control while preserving the existing class system and distribution of wealth."[82] Moreover, "The child-saving movement was not simply a humanistic enterprise on behalf of the lower classes against the established order. On the contrary, its impetus came primarily from the middle and upper classes who were instrumental in devising new forms of social control to protect their privileged positions in American society."[83] The system of justice that resulted was a liberal reform, bringing about a new and more expansive form of social control, meant to preserve the social order.

During this century the system has grown into a large and complex bureaucratic organization, staffed by judges, prosecutors, public defenders, probation and parole officers, counselors, and correction personnel. The system's design continues to be two-pronged: some strategies are benevolent and ameliorative and others are explicitly coercive and authoritarian.

The most significant recent reform in juvenile justice is the "constitutional domestication" of the juvenile court.[84] The United State Supreme Court in 1967 recognized the constitutional argument that the juvenile court violates guarantees of due process and stigmatizes youths. The Court delivered an opinion in the Gault case, establishing guidelines for future juvenile proceedings. Juveniles now have the right to be notified of the charges against them, to have legal counsel, to cross-examine witnesses, and the privilege against self-incrimination. The decision, though hailed as a landmark in juvenile justice, generates only a few modest alterations in the arrangements for handling delinquents, "Whereas the Gault decision may introduce some measure of due process in juvenile court, it also runs the risk of making juvenile court more orderly and efficient at the expense of substantive fairness."[85] Furthermore, even the implementation of due process falls far short of the ideal suggested by the Supreme Court.[86] Juveniles today often get the same discriminatory treatment in court that they get outside in the home and in the school.

In the meantime new programs of punishment and correction are devised for dealing with delinquents. Present programs range from mandatory imprisonment to community-based corrections and diversion from the juvenile-justice system. But present programs and trends, though they differ in language and form, resemble those of the past in most essentials. Liazos concludes: "They still try to fit the children of the poorer classes into the bottom of society and dead-end jobs. The changes are in style, not in function. Capitalism, which demands the existence of a disciplined, exploited working force, is not questioned."[87]

CONTROLLING MORALITY AND THE SOCIAL ORDER

When morality is controlled, the more material aspects of society are controlled at the same time. That is, laws on private and public morality reflect the desire to preserve all aspects of life. If the moral base of social and economic life should be threatened, then the social and economic order itself might give way. Laws regulating sexual activities, drinking, use of drugs, and the like are enacted to control the whole environment, even the most intimate moments of one's life.

A great many American laws are meant to control personal behaviors contrary to the morals that some in the community hold. Many of these criminal laws are kept on the books, without serious or uniform enforcement, because they reflect a popular sense of reprobation or condemnation. The behaviors they prohibit are regarded, at least by some, as wrong and unworthy of the society. The criminal laws meant to protect morality and public order include those which regulate some kinds of sexual conduct, prostitution, homosexuality, abortion, drinking, the use of drugs, and public behaviors defined by such names as "public nuisance," "loitering," "trespassing," and "vagrancy."

Regulating Sexual Conduct

Much of the anxiety about public order has to do with controlling sexual conduct, which in Anglo-American society is based on a fairly rigid conception of appropriate sexual expression. Our moral sense carries strong Puritan overtones. To be moral in America is to be *sexually* discreet. Likewise, a sex bias is evident in the laws that regulate sexual conduct in favor of males.

The range of sexual conduct covered by law is so extensive that the law makes potential criminals of most of the adolescent and adult population.[88] One of the principal reasons for such complete control over sexual behavior is to protect a specific kind of family system that preserves the institutions in our society. A great number of state laws seek to control acts that might otherwise endanger the chastity of women before marriage, such as the many laws on rape (statutory and forcible), fornication, incest, and sexual deviance of juveniles. The criminal laws on adultery also are intended to protect the family by preventing sexual relations outside the marriage bond.[89] The Puritans of Massachusetts Bay Colony gave sexual relations within the family so much importance that they made adultery a crime punishable by death. Other criminal laws today as in the past regulate sexual relations of family members. These laws help preserve the cherished monogamous (one mate at a time) family pattern.

Some of our criminal laws on sexual behavior were formulated to protect specific aspects of marriage and family life in the larger social order. Several southern states enacted laws to prevent marriage between blacks and whites. In 1967, however, the Supreme Court ruled that an antimiscegenation statute of Virginia was unconstitutional. Such "slavery laws" had been formulated originally to ensure the enslaved status of blacks and in more recent times have been used to maintain segregation of the races.

Another type of criminal law, also enacted early in Virginia, pertained to bastardy among women of the lower ranks. It was instituted not only for a moral purpose but was to ensure maximum work from domestic servants.

> Having paid a very high price for their labor, their masters, not unnaturally, were opposed to their entering a relationship which was quite certain to lead to interruptions in their field work, perhaps, at the very time their part in that work would be most valuable, if not wholly indispensable. Not only would the birth of children make it necessary for them to lie by for a month or more, but it might even result in their deaths, and the complete loss of the money invested by the planter in their purchase.[90]

Also, blame for the offense could be placed on the servant woman overpowered by the advances of her masters.

Criminal laws have also been formulated to prevent exposing members of the society to that which is regarded by some as lewd or obscene. The Comstock Act of 1873 stands in American criminal law as a landmark in the control of obscenity. Before that time the common law was not clear on the issue. In fact, obscenity was not considered to be a problem before the nineteenth century, but by the middle of that century it had been given an identity by the Victorian Age.[91] Several segments of the population became interested in protecting women and the young. Finally, in 1873, under pressure for a statutory law, the Comstock Law was enacted, providing for censorship of literature and other printed matter that might come into the hands of the innocent.

Today well-organized groups, such as the National Organization for Decent Literature, continue to pressure courts and legislatures for statutes and decisions regulating obscenity. Countering this move are recommendations for relaxing the legal controls over obscene materials in this country.[92] These, in turn, meet severe reactions, with President Nixon suggesting that proposals condoning pornography "would increase the threat to our social order as well as to our moral principles."[93]

The interest in controlling "obscene" materials was supported in the 1973 Supreme Court decision, Miller v. California, establishing new standards for judging the content of books, magazines, plays, and movies. This new decision abandons the 1957 ruling, in Roth v. United States, which had allowed sexual materials that were of "redeeming social value." The new decision gives communities and states the power to determine what is obscene, without reference to a national standard. State and local courts may now punish the printing or sale of works that appeal to "prurient interest in sex." Such judgment is to be based on "contemporary community standards." Giving new direction to obscenity law, the Supreme Court is allowing the local power structure in the community to establish standards that will protect its own established order.

Prostitution, Homosexuality, and Abortion

The laws on prostitution vary greatly throughout the country. In most states solicitation is a misdemeanor punished by a fine or a jail sentence of one year. Repeated apprehensions, however, may result in a charge of felony. In some states laws control not only solicitation by prostitutes but also those who exploit and patronize prostitutes. Prostitution may be defined as a crime, but the conduct is frequent in all societies. The laws remain, however, representing what some in the society expect in the ideal moral order. The Wolfenden Report of England perhaps best expressed the reasons for the continued legal regulation of prostitution:

> If it were the law's intention to punish prostitution per se, on the ground that it is immoral conduct, then it would be right that it should provide for the punishment of the man as well as the women. But that is not the function of the law. It should confine itself to those activities which offend against public order and decency or expose the ordinary citizen to what is offensive or injurious; and the simple fact is that prostitutes do parade themselves more habitually and openly than their prospective customers, and do by their continual presence affront the sense of decency of the ordinary citizen. In so doing they create a nuisance which, in our view, the law is entitled to recognize and deal with.[94]

There are moves in the United States to revise the laws on prostitution. Supposedly to make the statutes less discriminatory toward women, some suggest reducing the penalties and including the male patrons in the law. But some groups, especially community leaders and law-enforcement agents, would like to "clean up" some areas in the cities. Pamela Roby, studying the revision of the New York State law on prostitution, documents that the final law is written by the groups that have the most power and resources to shape public policy.[95] In the end it is not the class interests of the prostitute that are being considered in the law, but the interests of those who make the law. Their order prevails through the criminal law.

Criminal penalties for homosexual acts in the United States have been severe. Some states provide for ten or more years of imprisonment. In actuality, however, relatively few are arrested for homosexual acts and when penalties are administered they usually are lenient. A moral connotation is still attached to homosexuality by many people, though the trend may be toward removing some homosexual acts from the list of crimes. In 1955 the American Law Institute concluded that homosexual behavior between consenting adults in private should be removed from the criminal law.[96] The state of Illinois, revising its penal code in 1961, adopted the institute's recommendation. Similar legal reforms are currently under consideration, although other states have been relectant to revise their homosexual statutes.

In a 1976 ruling, however, the United States Supreme Court decided that states may prosecute and imprison people for committing homosexual acts even when both parties are consenting adults and the act occurs in private.[97] The ruling sharply departs from the ten-year trend in which the high court had increasingly expanded the constitutional right of privacy. In effect, the Supreme Court decided that the right to privacy does not include the right of willing adult homosexuals to engage privately in their sexual conduct. Although the ruling does not require states that have repealed the sodomy prohibition to reinstitute it, it lessens the pressure on other states to repeal their laws.

Maintaining the prohibition against homosexual behavior is a symbolic if not real attempt to preserve the behavior regarded as basic to the American way of life — heterosexual love and marriage, the nuclear family of parents and children, and the sanctity of the traditional home. These institutions are so closely tied to the capitalist political economy that any harm caused to them is a sign of the collapse of the established order. Whether the connection is necessary is one question, but belief in the tie keeps its hold over criminal law in the United States.

Abortion has long been defined as a crime. Taking a life is a moral offense, but the question of whether or not life is taken when an abortion is performed is subject to debate. Various groups have exerted pressure to have their views represented in an appropriate abortion law.[98] Legal reform has taken place in England in part through the well-organized activities of the Abortion Law Reform Association. Similar proposals for reform have been advanced in the United States. The Planned Parenthood Federation called for a law that would recognize therapeutic abortion for psychological, eugenic, and humanitarian purposes. The American Law Institute proposed a model abortion code with similar provisions. Such legalization schemes have been opposed primarily by the Roman Catholic Church.[99]

The contemporary legal solution to the abortion controversy was reached at the beginning of 1973, when the United States Supreme Court handed down its landmark ruling on abortion.[100] States may prohibit abortions only during the last ten weeks of pregnancy, after the fetus has become "viable" or likely to survive on its own if prematurely delivered. The Court's decision in effect repeals most of the nation's abortion laws.

Drinking and Drunkenness

Although drinking itself is not a crime, being drunk in public view may result in a criminal arrest. Criminal laws have been formulated to handle those who openly disturb the public order.[101] The person who drinks excessively may be apprehended simply because he or she is disturbing a community's sense of propriety or because being intoxicated may lead to other acts of public nuisance or disturbance. To become intoxicated and exuberant in one's own home is proper middle-class behavior, but to be drunk in the public is to violate the puritanical standards of moral strength and personal discipline.

It is likely that public drunkenness will not be treated as crime in the future. A legal change has occurred already. In 1966 the United States

Court of Appeals for the District of Columbia ruled that a chronic alcoholic cannot be convicted of the crime of public drunkenness. Because the defendant under a drunkenness charge "has lost the power of self-control in the use of intoxicating beverages," the court held, the defendant lacks criminal intent to be guilty of a crime and cannot therefore be punished under the criminal law. Similar rulings and legislative measures may eventually eliminate a vast number of criminal offenses.

The current trend in the law on drinking and drunkenness in part extends the forces that repealed the Eighteenth Amendment to the Constitution in 1933. That was the end of the "great experiment" known as prohibition, which had been established by the Volstead Act and ratified by the Eighteenth Amendment in 1920. It has been observed that the movement to ban drinking and the liquor trade was an assertion of the rural Protestant mind against the urban culture that grew up at the end of the nineteenth century and the beginning of the twentieth.[102] For a significant portion of the population prohibition meant stamping out sin in an evil society. The rural element was temporarily successful in enacting prohibition legislation, but succumbed within thirteen years to the inevitable.

Amid resentment against drinking and what it represented, specific interest groups were active in the movement that led to legislation. The Prohibition party was founded in 1869 as a third political party to deal with the problem of drinking. Later, such organizations as the Anti-Saloon League and the Women's Christian Temperance Union crusaded against alcohol and the saloon. Their lobbying brought about state and local temperance legislation. The "dry" lobby groups exerted great pressure against legislators. The Anti-Saloon League could "With the menace of thousands of votes cast at the next election against any legislator who dared to vote against a dry measure . . . make the representatives of the people vote against their personal wet convictions."[103] The dry interest groups, with other forces in American society at the time, brought about formal enactment of prohibition:

> In this way, the Eighteenth Amendment and the Volstead Act became the law of the land. Through the many roots of prohibition — rural mythology, the psychology of excess, the exploited fears of the mass of the people, the findings of science and medicine, the temper of reform, the efficiency of the dry pressure groups, their mastery of propaganda, the stupidity and self-interest of the brewers and distillers, the necessary trimming of politicians, and the weakness of the elected representatives of the people — through all these channels the sap of the dry tree rose until the legal prohibition of the liquor trade burst out new and green in the first month of 1920. The roots had been separate; yet they were all part of a common American seed. They combined and contributed to the

strength of the whole. The Anti-Saloon League, bent on its particular reform, was the heir and beneficiary of many interactions in American life. As the drys stood on the threshold of victory at the opening of the twenties, they could see manifest destiny in the success of their cause. They seemed to be the darling army of the Lord. Behind them appeared to lie one mighty pattern and purpose. Before them hung the sweet fruits of victory.[104]

But prohibition was to fail both as law and as a noble experiment. An outdated morality could not be enforced by criminal law. Rural interests were replaced by the interests of a new social order.

> The old order of the country gave way to the new order of the cities. Rural morality was replaced by urban morality, rural voices by urban voices, rural votes by urban votes. A novel culture of skyscrapers and suburbs grew up to oust the civilization of the general store and Main Street. A technological revolution broadcast a common culture over the various folkways of the land. It is only in context of this immense social change, the metamorphosis of Abraham Lincoln's America into the America of Franklin Roosevelt, that the phenomenon of national prohibition can be seen and understood. It was part of the whole process, the last hope of the declining village. It was less of a farce than a tragedy, less of a mistake than a proof of changing times.[105]

The new morality, permitting the use of alcohol, nevertheless has its material basis. In the growth of the advanced political economy in the United States, manufacture and sale of alcohol have become big business. Moreover, the recreation and night-club industry profits; organized crime is allowed to traffic legally and illegally in the liquor trade; and a large part of the consuming population is pacified in its daily existence. Drinking and drunkenness are an integral part of American society.

Law of Vagrancy

Vagrancy has been a crime in nearly every one of the United States. Because the state statutes had their heritage in English law, the common-law meaning of "vagrancy" is either stated or implied in the statutes: a vagrant is an idle person, beggar, or person wandering without being able to give a good account of himself or herself. Most important is the person's character: "Vagrancy is the principal crime in which the offense consists of being a certain kind of person rather than in having done or failed to do certain acts."[106]

Vagrancy laws are widely used in the community to detain questionable and suspicious persons. They and their enforcement are aimed at potential criminals, are used sometimes in place of other charges, and often are the means for ridding the community of those who do not meet the standards set by the respectable members.

The crime of vagrancy derives from early English laws that came into existence during the fourteenth century in response to changing social conditions.[107] The first full-fledged vagrancy law was enacted in 1349, making it a crime to give alms to able-bodied, unemployed persons and establishing that such persons would be criminally punished. The law and supplementary statutes were formulated, after the Black Death (the great epidemic of bubonic plague in the 1330s) and the flight of workers from landowners, to supply needed labor: "There is little question that these statutes were designed for one express purpose: to force laborers (whether personally free or unfree) to accept employment at a low wage in order to insure the landowner an adequate supply of labor at a price he could afford to pay."[108]

Changing social conditions in England made it unnecessary to enforce the vagrancy statutes. But by the sixteenth century, with increased emphasis on commerce and industry, vagrancy law was revived. Because of changes in the social structure, the law shifted from regulating labor to controlling criminal activities. It developed gradually in early English society:

> These laws were a legislative innovation which reflected the socially perceived necessity of providing an abundance of cheap labor to landowners during a period when serfdom was breaking down and when the pool of available labor was depleted. With the eventual breakup of feudalism the need for such laws eventually disappeared and the increased dependence of the economy upon industry and commerce rendered the former use of the vagrancy statutes unnecessary. As a result, for a substantial period the vagrancy statutes were dormant, undergoing only minor changes and, presumably, being applied infrequently. Finally, the vagrancy laws were subjected to considerable alteration through a shift in the focal concern of the statutes. Whereas in their inception the laws focused upon the "idle" and "those refusing to labor" after the turn of the sixteenth century an emphasis came to be upon "rogues," "vagabonds," and others who were suspected of being engaged in criminal activities. During this period the focus was particularly upon "roadmen" who preyed upon citizens who transported goods from one place to another. The increased importance of commerce to England during this period made it necessary that some protection be given persons engaged in this enterprise and the vagrancy statutes provided one source for such protection by refocusing the acts to be included under these statutes.[109]

In other words, the formulations and changes in the statutes on vagrancy were made in accordance with changes in the political economy.

With minor variations the vagrancy statutes remained the same through the seventeenth and eighteenth centuries. They were adopted by American colonies and states for the same purposes they performed in English society. Today the laws continue to provide a way of controlling persons and activities regarded as undesirable in the community, particularly those who might endanger private property and threaten order.

The vagrancy laws are being evaluated and questioned, however. One writer states, "The time is surely at hand to modernize the vagrancy concept or, better yet, to abandon it altogether for statutes which will harmonize with notions of a decent, fair, and just administration of criminal justice, and which will at the same time make it possible for police departments to discharge their responsibilities in a reasonable manner."[110] A significant change in the law has been made in the state of New York. In 1967 the New York Court of Appeals ruled unconstitutional a statute of 1788 that provided for arresting people with no visible means of support.[111] The court ruled that the law "constitutes an overreaching of the proper limitations of the police power." Furthermore, the court said that the statute has little use "other than, perhaps, as a means of harassing, punishing or apprehending suspected criminals in an unconstitutional fashion." The old statute was declared unconstitutional, as interfering with citizens' liberty to conduct themselves as they see fit as long as they do not interfere with the rights of others. Such repeal, which is occurring in other states as well, will end use of laws of the vagrancy type to enforce community order. Undoubtedly other ways of maintaining public order, legal or extralegal, will be substituted for vagrancy law.

Controlling Drugs

Before the turn of this century there was no significant legislation on manufacturing or distributing narcotic drugs. But then states and the federal government enacted laws to control them. This legislation of morality required a shift in the conception of drug use and a different way of handling the problem. Drug users were moved from one category to another, from a problem shared by the general population to one belonging to the lower classes, the "unrespectable" part of society.[112]

The Harrison Act, passed by Congress in 1914, defined users of specific drugs as criminals. In technical language it required that all drug-handlers be registered and that the fact of securing drugs be made a matter of record.[113] But in the act's interpretation, court rulings in specific cases, and supplementary laws, criminal sanctions were provided for the unauthorized possession, sale, or transfer of drugs. The states too have enacted antinarcotics laws. In the United States, penalties for violating drug laws have become more severe in recent years. Possessing narcotics is now a felony instead of a misdemeanor.

Drug laws not only have defined users as criminals but have created public suspicion and fear of drug users and addicts. Today using any drug

— addictive or not, a narcotic, marijuana, or a psychedelic — arouses a public response that will almost certainly bring a call for legislation. Much of this atmosphere has been created by the Federal Bureau of Narcotics, responsible for administrative decisions that are the basis for most of the drug legislation.[114] The Bureau of Narcotics has defined its interests as total restriction of drugs and complete enforcement of the law. These interests have become the standards by which the public now views and officially acts upon the use of drugs. The addict is defined in the law as a criminal, is dealt with officially as a criminal, and is looked on by many as a criminal.[115]

Great Britain's policy on drugs differs sharply from ours. In England drug addiction is considered a medical rather than a legal problem; the addict is not regarded as a criminal. The Dangerous Drug Act of 1920 defined the addict as a patient who may receive drugs upon the medical discretion of a physician.[116] Addicts in England do not have to resort to criminal activities to maintain a supply of drugs. Because of the British approach it is now being argued, primarily by academicians, that the American policy on use of drugs is unsound and that to deal more effectively with the problem official policy should be changed. Lindesmith has made several proposals: (1) antinarcotics laws should be written so that addicts do not have to violate them solely because they are addicts; (2) drug users are admittedly handicapped by their habit but should be encouraged to engage in productive labor even when they are using drugs; (3) cures should not be imposed upon narcotics victims by force but should be voluntary; (4) police officers should be prevented from exploiting drug addicts as stoolpigeons just because they are addicts; and (5) heroin and morphine addicts should be handled according to the same principles and moral precepts applied to barbiturate and alcohol addicts because the three forms of addiction are similar.[117]

Other policies are being instituted to control the "drug problem." There is a trend to handle drug addiction as a disease — the addict is "sick." Substitute drugs, such as methadone, are being administered to addicts as a further means of pacifying them and controlling their behavior. The federal government has established new laws, such as the Comprehensive Drug Control Act of 1970. Use of drugs, according to the former President Nixon, has "assumed the dimensions of a national emergency."[118]

The state, defining drug use and addiction as a problem, has conditioned the public to respond by condemning the drug user, not questioning the kind of social order that makes use of drugs a viable alternative to everyday reality. We are taught to believe that the problem is in the drug user's morality or physical condition, not in the pathology of the capitalist order.

Behind the criminalization of drug use and addiction, in spite of the myths, is the state's response to the material conditions of the capitalist economy. The real effort is not so much controlling drug use, but preserving the labor market. As John Helmer argues, blatant class conflicts during periods of acute economic crisis have determined the criminal status of drugs through the nation's history.[119] By identifying drugs especially with Chinese, Mexicans, and blacks, each measure of control reflects a fear of economic competition by aliens in the work force, and not a fear of drugs.

The reasons for controlling drugs are in the material forces of capitalist society. The order is secured by legislating morality, making moral order and economic order inseparable; they serve each other.

NOTES

1. See Amy Beth Bridges, "Nicos Poulantzas and the Marxist Theory of the State," *Politics and Society*, 4 (Winter 1974), pp. 161–190.
2. Anthony Giddens, *The Class Structure of the Advanced Societies* (New York: Harper & Row, 1975), p. 51.
3. These traditions are presented in David A. Gold, Clarence Y. H. Lo, and Erik Olin Wright, "Recent Developments in Marxist Theories of the State," *Monthly Review*, 27 (October 1975), pp. 29–43.
4. Claus Offe, "Class Rule and the Political System: On the Selectiveness of Political Institutions," mimeo., 1973. (A translation of Chapter 3 of *Strukturprobleme des kapitalistischen Staates*, Frankfurt: Suhrkamp, 1972.)
5. Ibid., p. 8.
6. Claus Offe and Volker Ronge, "Theses on the Theory of the State," *New German Critique*, No. 6 (Fall 1975), p. 139. Also see Nicos Poulantzas, "On Social Classes," *New Left Review*, No. 78 (March-April 1973), pp. 27–54.
7. See Perry Miller, *The New England Mind: The Seventeenth Century* (New York: Macmillan, 1939).
8. George Lee Haskins, *Law and Authority in Early Massachusetts* (New York: Macmillan, 1960), p. 44.
9. Quoted in Richard B. Morris, *Studies in the History of American Law*, 2nd ed. (New York: Joseph M. Mitchell, 1959), p. 35.
10. Haskins, *Law and Authority in Early Massachusetts*, pp. 44–45.
11. See Kai T. Erikson, *Wayward Puritans: A Study in the Sociology of Deviance* (New York: John Wiley, 1966), pp. 54–64. Also see Edwin Powers, *Crime and Punishment in Early Massachusetts* (Boston: Beacon Press, 1966).
12. Quoted in Haskins, *Law and Authority in Early Massachusetts*, p. 145.
13. Ibid., p. 146.
14. Ibid., pp. 146–147.
15. Ibid., p. 225.
16. David J. Rothman, *The Discovery of the Asylum* (Boston: Little, Brown, 1971), especially pp. 57–58.
17. William E. Nelson, "Emerging Notions of Modern Criminal Law in the Revolutionary Era: An Historical Perspective," *New York University Law Review*, 42 (May 1967), p. 463. Also see Roger Lane, "Crime and Criminal Statistics in Nineteenth-Century Massachusetts," *Journal of Social History*, 2 (Winter 1968), pp. 156–163.
18. See Otto Kirchheimer, *Political Justice: The Use of Legal Procedure for Political Ends* (Princeton: Princeton University Press, 1961).

19. Paul B. Horton and Gerald R. Leslie. *The Sociology of Social Problems,* 3rd ed. (New York: Appleton-Century-Crofts, 1965), pp. 632–633.

20. Herbert Aptheker, *The American Revolution* (New York: International Publishers, 1960), pp. 9–23.

21. Lawrence Henry Gipson, *The Coming of the Revolution, 1763–1775* (New York: Harper and Row, 1954). Also see George Adrian Washburne, *Imperial Control of the Administration of Justice in the Thirteen Colonies, 1684–1776* (New York: Columbia University Press, 1923). On resistance among American colonists, see Pauline Maier, *From Resistance to Revolution: Colonial Radicals and the Development of American Opposition to Britain, 1765–1776* (New York: Random House, 1972).

22. Harold L. Nelson, "Seditious Libel in Colonial America," *American Journal of Legal History,* 3 (April 1959), pp. 160–172; and Frederick S. Siebert, *Freedom of the Press in England, 1476–1776* (Urbana: University of Illinois Press, 1952).

23. Leonard W. Levy, *Freedom of Speech and Press in Early American History: Legacy of Suppression* (New York: Harper and Row, 1963); James Morton Smith, "The Sedition Law, Free Speech, and the American Political Process," *William and Mary Quarterly,* 9 (October 1952), pp. 497–511.

24. Herbert L. Packer, "Offenses Against the State," *Annals of the American Academy of Political and Social Science,* 339 (January 1962), pp. 77–89.

25. Bradley Chapin, *The American Law of Treason: Revolutionary and National Origins* (Seattle: University of Washington Press, 1964); J. Willard Hurst, "Treason in the United States," *Harvard Law Review,* 58 (December 1944), pp. 226–272; 58 (February 1945), pp. 395–444; and 58 (July 1945), pp. 806–857.

26. Claude H. Van Tyne, *The Loyalists in the American Revolution* (New York: Macmillan, 1902), especially Appendix C.

27. Walter Gellhorn, "A General View," in Walter Gellhorn, ed., *The States and Subversion* (Ithaca: Cornell University Press, 1952), p. 359.

28. Herbert H. Hyman, "England and America: Climates of Tolerance and Intolerance," in Daniel Bell, ed., *The Radical Right* (Garden City, N.Y.: Doubleday, 1963), chap. 12.

29. Norman Redlich and Kenneth R. Feinberg, "Individual Conscience and the Selective Conscientious Objector: The Right Not to Kill," *New York University Law Review,* 44 (November, 1969), pp. 875–900.

30. Quoted in Peter and Deborah Babcox and Bob Abel, eds., *The Conspiracy* (New York: Dell, 1969), pp. 28–29.

31. B. L. Ingraham and Kazuhiko Tokoro, "Political Crime in the United States and Japan: A Comparative Study," *Issues in Criminology,* 4 (Spring 1969), pp. 145–170. A more general discussion is in Mark C. Kennedy, "Beyond Incrimination: Some Neglected Facets of the Theory of Punishment," *Catalyst,* No. 5 (Summer 1970), pp. 1–37.

32. Hans B. Thorelli, *The Federal Antitrust Policy: Origination of an American Tradition* (Baltimore: Johns Hopkins Press, 1955), pp. 9–53.

33. Ibid., pp. 54–163. In addition, see Lawrence M. Friedman, *A History of American Law* (New York: Simon and Schuster, 1973), pp. 384–408.

34. Quoted in Arthur P. Dudden, "Men Against Monopoly: The Prelude to Trust-Busting," *Journal of the History of Ideas,* 18 (October 1957), p. 593.

35. Quoted in Samuel Eliot Morison and Henry Steele Commager, *The Growth of the American Republic,* vol. 2 (New York: Oxford University Press, 1950), p. 143.

36. Wolfgang Friedmann, *Law in a Changing Society* (Harmondsworth, Eng.: Penguin Books, 1964), p. 161.

37. Quoted in Morison and Commager, *The Growth of the American Republic,* vol. 2, p. 391.

38. Gabriel Kolko, *The Triumph of Conservatism: A Reinterpretation of American History, 1900–1916* (New York: Free Press, 1963), p. 2.

39. Ibid., p. 278.

40. Morison and Commager, *The Growth of the American Republic,* vol. 2, p. 630.

41. A natural history of the social problem of food adulteration is in Donald J. New-

man, "A Study of the Criminal Nature of Pure Food Law Violations," unpublished M.A. thesis, University of Wisconsin, 1952.

42. Morton Mintz, *The Therapeutic Nightmare: A Report on Prescription Drugs, the Men Who Take Them, and the Agency That Controls Them* (Boston: Houghton Mifflin, 1965), p. 41.

43. For these and later laws, see Stephen Wilson, *Food and Drug Regulation* (Washington, D.C.: American Council of Public Affairs, 1942).

44. Arthur Kallet and F. J. Schlink, *100,000,000 Guinea Pigs* (New York: Vanguard Press, 1933); Ruth deForest Lamb, *American Chamber of Horrors* (New York: Farrar and Rinehart, 1936).

45. From Mintz, *The Therapeutic Nightmare*, pp. 45–46.

46. Thomas W. Christopher and Charles W. Dunn, *Special Federal Food and Drug Laws* (New York: Commerce Clearing House, 1954).

47. David H. Vernon and Franklin M. Depew, *General State Food and Drug Laws* (New York: Commerce Clearing House, 1955). For a study of how occupational laws are formulated according to characteristics and efforts of the occupations, pharmacy included, see Ronald L. Akers and Richard Quinney, "Differential Organization of Health Professions: A Comparative Analysis," *American Sociological Review*, 33 (February 1968), pp. 104–121.

48. U.S. Congress, Senate, Subcommittee of the Committee on the Judiciary, *Hearings Before the Subcommittee on Antitrust and Monopoly*, 86th Congress, 1st and 2nd Sessions, Parts 14–22, 1959–1960; U.S. Congress, Senate, Subcommittee of the Committee on the Judiciary, *Report of the Committee on the Judiciary*, "Antitrust and Monopoly Activities, 1960," Report No. 167, 87th Congress, 1st Session, 1961: U.S. Congress, Senate, Subcommittee of the Committee on the Judiciary, *Report of the Committee on the Judiciary*, "Administered Prices: Drugs," Report No. 448, 87th Congress, 1st Session, 1961.

49. James S. Turner, *The Chemical Feast* (New York: Grossman, 1970), p. 209.

50. Ibid., p. 81.

51. Ibid., p. 43.

52. Ronald L. Akers, "The Professional Association and the Legal Regulation of Practice," *Law and Society Review*, 2 (May 1968), p. 465.

53. Ibid., p. 467.

54. Ibid., p. 476. Also see Ronald L. Akers, "Professional Organization, Political Power, and Occupational Laws," unpublished Ph.D. dissertation, University of Kentucky, 1966.

55. Howard R. and Martha E. Lewis, *The Medical Offenders* (New York: Simon and Schuster, 1970), p. 21.

56. Ibid., p. 24. For related research on disbarment of lawyers, see Kenneth J. Reichstein, "Ambulance Chasing: A Case Study of Deviation and Control within the Legal Profession," *Social Problems*, 13 (Summer 1965), pp. 3–17.

57. Lewis, *The Medical Offenders*, pp. 312–320.

58. See Alan H. Swanson, "Sexual Psychopath Statutes: Summary and Analysis," *Journal of Criminal Law, Criminology and Police Science*, 51 (July-August, 1960), pp. 215–235.

59. Habitual offender laws are discussed in Paul W. Tappan, "Habitual Offender Laws in the United States," *Federal Probation*, 13 (March 1949), pp. 28–31.

60. Edwin H. Sutherland, "The Diffusion of Sexual Psychopath Laws," *American Journal of Sociology*, 56 (September 1950), pp. 142–148.

61. Ibid., p. 145.

62. Edwin H. Sutherland, "The Sexual Psychopath Laws," *Journal of Criminal Law, Criminology and Police Science*, 40 (January-February, 1950), pp. 543–554.

63. Paul W. Tappan, "Sex Offender Laws and Their Administration," *Federal Probation*, 14 (September 1950), p. 33.

64. Ibid., p. 33.

65. Ibid., p. 34.

66. For a history of Sunday laws, see Abram H. Lewis, *A Critical History of Sunday Legislation from 321 to 1888 A.D.* (New York: D. Appleton, 1888); and George E. Harris, *A Treatise on Sunday Laws* (Rochester, N.Y.: Lawyers' Cooperative, 1892).

67. Sunday laws in America are discussed in Alvin W. Johnson, "Sunday Legislation," *Kentucky Law Journal*, 23 (November 1934), pp. 131–166; and Warren L. Johns, *Dateline Sunday, U.S.A.: The Story of Three Centuries of Sunday-Law Battles in America* (New York: Taplinger, 1967).

68. Eugene P. Chell, "Sunday Blue Laws: An Analysis of Their Position in Our Society," *Rutgers Law Review*, 12 (Spring 1958), p. 520.

69. Chell, "Sunday Blue Laws," pp. 511–512.

70. Tom Goldstein, "New York Appeals Court Voids Sunday Sale Bans," *The New York Times*, June 18, 1976, p. 1.

71. McGowan v. Maryland, in 366 *United States Reports* (October term, 1960), p. 421.

72. McGowan v. Maryland, pp. 451–452.

73. McGowan v. Maryland, p. 435.

74. Charles Loring Brace, *The Dangerous Classes of New York and Twenty Years' Work Among Them* (New York: Wynkoop and Hallenbeck, 1972), p. 321.

75. Alexander Liazos, "Class Oppression: The Functions of Juvenile Justice," *The Insurgent Sociologist*, 1 (Fall 1974), p. 2.

76. Ibid., p. 8.

77. Ibid. Original quoted in Robert H. Bremner, ed., *Children and Youth in America: A Documentary History*, Vol. I: 1600–1865 (Cambridge, Mass.: Harvard University, 1970), p. 679.

78. Ibid., p. 9.

79. Ibid., pp. 10–11.

80. Anthony M. Platt, *The Child Savers: The Invention of Delinquency* (Chicago: University of Chicago Press, 1969); and Anthony Platt, "The Triumph of Benevolence: The Origins of the Juvenile Justice System in the United States," in Richard Quinney, ed., *Criminal Justice in America: A Critical Understanding* (Boston: Little, Brown, 1974), pp. 356–389.

81. Platt, "The Triumph of Benevolence: The Origins of Juvenile Justice in the United States," pp. 366–367.

82. Ibid., p. 367.

83. Ibid., p. 368.

84. Ibid., pp. 387–389.

85. Ibid., p. 388.

86. Anthony Platt and Ruth Friedman, "The Limits of Advocacy: Occupational Hazards in Juvenile Court," 116 *Pennsylvania Law Review* (1968), pp. 1156–1184; and Anthony Platt, Howard Schechter, and Phyllis Tiffany, "In Defense of Youth: A Case Study of the Public Defender in Juvenile Court," *Indiana Law Journal*, 43 (1968), pp. 619–640.

87. Liazos, "Class Oppression: The Functions of Juvenile Justice," p. 14.

88. See Morris Ploscowe, "Sex Offenses: The American Legal Context," *Law and Contemporary Problems*, 25 (Spring 1960), pp. 217–225; also, Gerhard O. W. Mueller, *Legal Regulation of Sexual Conduct* (Dobbs Ferry, N.Y.: Oceana, 1961).

89. Morris Ploscowe, *Sex and the Law* (Englewood Cliffs, N.J.: Prentice-Hall, 1951), pp. 136–164.

90. Philip Alexander Bruce, *Social Life in Old Virginia* (New York: Capricorn Books, 1965), p. 45 (originally published in 1910).

91. Henry H. Foster, Jr., "The 'Comstock Load' — Obscenity and the Law," *Journal of Criminal Law, Criminology and Police Science*, 48 (September-October, 1957), pp. 245–258.

92. *The Report of the Commission on Obscenity and Pornography* (New York: Bantam Books, 1970).

93. *The New York Times*, October 25, 1970, p. 71.

94. The Wolfenden Report, *Report of the Committee on Homosexual Offenses and Prostitution* (New York: Stein and Day, 1963), pp. 143–144.

95. Pamela A. Roby, "Politics and Criminal Law: Revision of the New York State Penal Law on Prostitution," *Social Problems*, 17 (Summer 1969), pp. 83–109.

96. See Martin Hoffman, *The Gay World* (New York: Basic Books, 1968), pp. 77–97.

97. Lesley Oelsner, "Justices Decline to Remove the Curb on Homosexuals," *The New York Times*, March 30, 1976, p. 1.

98. See Edwin M. Schur, *Crimes Without Victims* (Englewood Cliffs, N.J.: Prentice-Hall, 1965), pp. 11–66.

99. An excellent coverage of the abortion controversy is in Daniel Callahan, *Abortion: Law, Choice and Morality* (New York: Macmillan, 1970).

100. *The New York Times*, January 23, 1973, p. 1.

101. These offenses are discussed in Irwin Deutscher, "The Petty Offender: A Sociological Alien," *Journal of Criminal Law, Criminology and Police Science*, 44 (January-February, 1954), pp. 592–595; David J. Pittman and C. Wayne Gordon, *Revolving Door* (New York: Free Press of Glencoe, 1958); and Earl Rubington, "The Chronic Drunkenness Offender," *Annals of the American Academy of Political and Social Science*, 315 (January 1958), pp. 65–72.

102. Andrew Sinclair, *Era of Excess: A Social History of the Prohibition Movement* (New York: Harper and Row, 1964).

103. Ibid., p. 105.

104. Ibid., p. 170.

105. Ibid., pp. 5–6. Laws, such as that on prohibition, are discussed as responses to the lack of consensus on norms in Joseph R. Gusfield, "Moral Passage: The Symbolic Process in Public Designations of Deviance," *Social Problems*, 15 (Fall 1967), pp. 175–188.

106. Forrest W. Lacey, "Vagrancy and Other Crimes of Personal Condition," *Harvard Law Review*, 66 (May 1953), p. 1203. Also see Caleb Foote, "Vagrancy-Type Law and Its Administration," *University of Pennsylvania Law Review*, 104 (March 1956), pp. 603–650.

107. William J. Chambliss, "A Sociological Analysis of the Law of Vagrancy," *Social Problems*, 12 (Summer 1964), pp. 67–77. Also George Rusche and Otto Kirchheimer, *Punishment and Social Structure* (New York: Columbia University Press, 1939), pp. 32–41.

108. Chambliss, "A Sociological Analysis of the Law of Vagrancy, p. 69.

109. Ibid., p. 76.

110. Arthur H. Sherry, "Vagrants, Rouges, and Vagabonds — Old Concepts in Need of Revision," *California Law Review*, 48 (October 1960), p. 567.

111. *The New York Times*, July 8, 1967, pp. 1 and 9.

112. Troy Duster, *The Legislation of Morality: Laws, Drugs, and Moral Judgment* (New York: Free Press, 1970), pp. 3–28.

113. Alfred R. Lindesmith, *The Addict and the Law* (Bloomington: Indiana University Press, 1965), chap. 1.

114. See Alfred R. Lindesmith, "Federal Law and Drug Addiction," *Social Problems*, 7 (Summer 1959), pp. 48–57; Howard S. Becker, *Outsiders: Studies in the Sociology of Deviance* (New York: Free Press, 1963), pp. 135–146; Donald T. Dickson, "Bureaucracy and Morality: An Organizational Perspective on a Moral Crusade," *Social Problems*, 16 (Fall 1968), pp. 143–156.

115. Charles E. Reasons, "The Addict as a Criminal," *Crime and Delinquency*, 21 (January 1975), pp. 19–27; Charles E. Reasons, "The Politics of Drugs: An Inquiry in the Sociology of Social Problems," *Sociological Quarterly*, 15 (Summer 1974), pp. 381–404.

116. Alfred R. Lindesmith, "The British System of Narcotics Control," *Law and Contemporary Problems*, 22 (Winter 1957), pp. 138–154; Edwin M. Schur, *Narcotic Addiction in Britain and America: The Impact of Public Policy* (Bloomington: Indiana University Press, 1962).

117. Lindesmith, *The Addict and the Law*, p. 270. Legalization of marijuana use has recently been recommended by the National Commission on Marijuana and Drug Abuse, *Marijuana: A Signal of Misunderstanding* (Washington, D.C.: U.S. Government Printing Office, 1972). An analysis of the class interests operating in the liberalization of marijuana law is provided in John F. Galliher, James L. McCartney, and Barbara E. Baum, "Nebraska's Marijuana Law: A Case of Unexpected Legislative Innovation," *Law and Society Review*, 8 (Spring 1974), pp. 441–455.

118. *The New York Times*, June 18, 1971, p. 1.

119. John Helmer, *Drugs and Minority Oppression* (New York: Seabury Press, 1975).

PATTERNS OF CRIME

ATTICA
CORRECTIONAL
FACILITY

Crimes of the State

5

The capitalist system generates its own patterns of crime. For a critical-Marxist understanding of these we begin by examining the capitalist political economy. The class struggle endemic to capitalism is characterized by a dialectic between domination and accommodation. Those who own and control the means of production, the capitalist class, attempt to secure the order by various forms of domination, especially control of crime by the state. Those who do not own and control the means of production, the working class, must accommodate to and resist capitalist domination in many ways.

The contradictions of developing capitalism increase the intensity of class struggle and thereby: (1) the need to dominate by the capitalist class and (2) the need to accommodate and resist by the class exploited by capitalism, the working class. Most of the behavior in response to domination, including the actions of the oppressed that are defined as criminal by the capitalist class, is a product of the capitalist system of production. During capitalist appropriation of labor, for the accumulation of capital, conditions are established calling for behaviors that may be defined as criminal by the capitalist state. These behaviors become eligible for crime control when they disturb or threaten the capitalist order in some way.

But the major crimes in the United States are those which occur during domination. By various schemes and mechanisms, including domination by the state, the capitalist system is reproduced. And in this domination crimes are carried out. It is a contradiction of capitalism that some of its own laws must be violated to secure the system. Not only is this contradiction heightened during times of crisis, making for increased crimes of domination, but the crimes change with the further development of capitalism.

These crimes, committed by the state, the capitalist class, and the agents of the capitalist system, are the crimes of domination. The crimes most characteristic of capitalist domination are those which occur during state control. They include the felonies and misdemeanors that law-enforcement agents, especially the police, carry out in the name of the law, usually against persons accused of other violations. Violence and brutality have become a recognized part of police work. These crimes of control are added to subtler crimes in which agents of the law violate the civil liberties of citizens, as in the many forms of surveillance, the use of provocateurs (agents of the law who provoke people into acts that in turn can be dealt with by the law as crimes), and the illegal denial of due process.

Then there are the crimes of the government itself, committed by the elected and appointed officials of the capitalist state. The Watergate crimes, carried out to perpetuate a governmental administration, are the most publicized instances of these crimes. Other offenses too are committed by the state against persons and groups who would seemingly threaten national security. Included here are the crimes of warfare and political assassination of foreign and domestic leaders.

Finally, many social injuries are committed by the capitalist class and the capitalist state that are not usually defined as criminal in the legal code. These systematic actions, involving denial of basic human rights (resulting in sexism, racism, and economic exploitation) are an integral part of capitalism and are important to its survival.

CRIMES AGAINST CITIZENS' RIGHTS

The state commits crimes in numerous areas involving human rights. The civil-rights movement showed how government officials violate the law to keep the system intact. Court decisions and legislative acts have made some of the behaviors illegal, even when committed by officials of the state. We have come to realize that many of our civil liberties are being narrowed by those who are supposed to guarantee these rights. In the name of "law and order," legal agents have slighted laws designed to protect such rights as free speech, assembly, and due process. Federal

"Yes, Mr. And Mrs. America — This Is Your Life"

agents have violated the law in their surveillance and in their quest for evidence usable in criminal prosecution. Local police, too, have been accused of blatantly violating human rights, as well as the conventional laws of murder and assault, in running the affairs of state.[1]

The United States Constitution guaranteed some rights that are not to be infringed upon. Governmental surveillance, according to Supreme Court rulings, is illegal in most situations. Such techniques as unreasonable search and seizure, interrogation, wiretapping, and various forms of electronic surveillance have been declared unconstitutional except in specified cases. Nevertheless, government agents continue to use these forms of surveillance, a fact dramatically brought to public attention by the disclosure that the Army was obtaining information on 18,000 civilians.[2]

It has been disclosed that several governmental agencies, especially the FBI and the CIA, also are heavily engaged in obtaining information about law-abiding citizens by these means.[3] The investigations of the Watergate crimes have uncovered how much citizens are being denied their civil liberties in the name of "national security," and the many criminal techniques (including burglary) the government uses to obtain information. Agencies of the state, including the presidency, may also resort to espionage and sabotage against citizens, obtaining information illegally and even falsifying records and documents. Among the disclosures was the plan approved by President Nixon for gathering domestic intelligence. Blackmail and extortion have been used against individuals and organizations, as in the threat of income-tax prosecutions if funds were not "donated" for campaign and other expenses. Some of these activities, such as burglary by agents of the FBI in gathering information for the presidency, have been going on for many years. These are not only unconstitutional but also violate criminal codes. It is always problematical, however, whether these crimes will be prosecuted, because the government itself would have to do the prosecuting.

A classic strategy used by a state to promote its own security is the criminal law, which it wields against those who appear to threaten the state's existence. The state traditionally responds by establishing a legal system that defines as "criminal" any conduct that threatens it, and denying the citizen's rights of dissent. These "political crimes" form a significant part of legal history, especially in recent years.[4] This use of criminal law is usually illegal; the laws are illegal in formulation and inevitably result in criminal means of enforcement.

In the sixties and seventies the state has gone through many political trials to promote its own interests. Those who objected to war in Southeast Asia were sometimes harassed and prosecuted. "Rioters" in the ghettos, rebelling against the abuses they suffer, have been subjected to laws by the state, which has used many old laws, or created new ones, to control dissent. Law-enforcement agencies and the judiciary have tried to prosecute those who apparently threaten the state. Later, however, trials pending for years, after harassment of the defendants, were thrown out of court because of the means the government used to prosecute them. Charges against such groups as the Chicago Seven, the Harrisburg Seven (the Berrigan case), the Daniel Ellsberg and Anthony J. Russo, Jr. case, and the Gainesville Eight were dropped because the police, the prosecution, or the court used criminal techniques in conducting them.[5]

Yet the extent to which the state has used criminal means to maintain its sense of order continues to be uncovered. Some violations of citizens' rights that have been disclosed indicate that the FBI committed murder in raids against members of the Black Panther Party; that the FBI kidnapped radicals and burglarized their homes and offices; that the FBI has carried out wiretaps and surveillance against citizens at the behest of all six presidents from Franklin D. Roosevelt to Richard M. Nixon; that the CIA has subverted the political process in such countries as Iran and Chile, including assistance in the overthrow and murder of Salvador Allende; and that the FBI and CIA were involved in the attempted assassination of Fidel Castro in Cuba during the administration of John F. Kennedy.[6]

More revelations came out in findings by a ten-month investigation of the intelligence agencies by the Senate Select Committee on Intelligence Activities. These disclosures, so numerous and so complex that they have been likened "to reading the Federal Budget or contemplating the number of stars in the solar system," have been sorted out to include the findings below:

> The Central Intelligence Agency illegally opened 215,000 letters in one of four mail intrusion projects. Totals in the three other projects are not known. The agency, too, in clear violation of its charter, conducted domestic surveillances, sought data from the National Security Agency and prepared dossiers on Americans.
>
> The National Security Agency scanned virtually every overseas telephone call and cable from 1967 until 1973 to locate communications of 1,680 American citizens involved in political dissent, suspected of being narcotics traffickers or feared to be potential threats to the President.
>
> The Federal Bureau of Investigation has publicly acknowledged that it committed 238 burglaries aimed at domestic dissidents. Bureau officials estimate that 700 others may have been carried out against foreign espionage targets or foreign embassies. The bureau has also acknowledged that, like the CIA, it also opened mail, in eight projects in as many cities. It has not made public how many letters it opened and photographed. In addition, the bureau operated a counterintelligence program against such dissidents as the Ku Klux Klan, the

Socialist Workers party and the Black Panthers. Agents used forged letters and made anonymous telephone calls, among other techniques, to harass those they could not charge with a crime.

The Internal Revenue Service set up dossiers on 8,585 political activists and 2,873 political organizations. It traded information with the CIA and the FBI.

Military intelligence units collected political intelligence and spied on domestic dissidents from 1967 until 1970 and prepared dossiers on a broad range of American citizens.[7]

No one knows how many people in the United States, as well as in other countries, have been deprived of their civil rights by these actions. All these and many more, as crimes of domination, have been committed by the state to secure the capitalist system.

CONVENTIONAL CRIMES IN LAW ENFORCEMENT

The police have traditionally been the governmental agents most exposed to opportunities for committing conventional felonies and misdemeanors while enforcing the law. Crimes by the police have been documented throughout the history of law enforcement in American communities. A study of police operations in Washington, Boston, and Chicago reported that "27 percent of all the officers were either observed in misconduct situations or admitted to observers that they had engaged in misconduct."[8] The forms of crime included shaking down traffic violators, accepting payoffs to alter sworn testimony, stealing from burglarized establishments, and planting weapons on suspects. Documented elsewhere are illegal raids against innocent persons, participating in narcotics traffic, and extorting money from the prostitution business.[9] The Knapp Commission of New York City found that well over half the police force in that city are engaged in some form of crime and corruption.[10] The activities range from accepting bribes to selling stolen articles, from selling heroin to tapping telephones illegally, from blackmail to murder.

Violence is part of police work, and brutality is often used in making an arrest. Investigating police abuses in New York City, Paul Chevigny found that the police will make an arrest to cover up an assault committed against the suspect, concealing their own violence by arresting and charging the citizens with some offense.[11]

Crimes by the police can be understood if we look at how the police work. The police recruit, during his training, adopts a very definite outlook on his work and develops a justification for using specific procedures in the line of "duty." He learns an ideology that later affects his work:

> The policeman finds his most pressing problem in his relationships to the public. His is a service occupation but of an incongruous kind, since he must discipline those whom he serves. He regards the public as his enemy, feels his occupation to be in conflict with the community, and regards himself to be a pariah. The experience and the feeling give rise to a collective emphasis on secrecy, an attempt to coerce respect from the public, and a belief that almost any means are legitimate in completing an important arrest. These are for the policeman basic occupational values. They arise from his experience, take precedence over his legal responsibilities, are central to an understanding of his conduct, and form the occupational concepts within which violence gains its meaning.[12]

Many of the illegal activities of the ordinary policeman are prescribed and supported by group norms of rules and expectations of behavior among policemen. Research has shown that criminal practices of police are patterned by an informal "code": "It was found that the new recruits were socialized into 'code' participation by 'old timers' and group acceptance was withheld from those who attempted to remain completely honest and not be implicated. When formal police regulations were in conflict with 'code' demands among its practitioners, the latter took precedence."[13]

In fact, the policeman may give little thought to the legality of his own actions when he is enforcing other laws. The law that is meant to protect the citizen from abuses by government authorities is more likely to be regarded by the policeman as an obstacle to law enforcement. "For him, due process of law is, therefore, not merely a set of constitutional guarantees for the defendant, but also a set of working conditions which, under increasingly liberal opinions by the courts, are likewise becoming increasingly arduous."[14] From the policeman's standpoint, the public's civil liberties impede his performance on the job. That is how the law is sometimes broken by its enforcers.

The opportunity for unlawful behavior among the police is especially acute in the black community and in political protests. Here the police already have their own group norms prescribing some illegal behavior and providing support for it. Several studies have shown that the majority of policemen are hostile and prejudiced toward blacks, which can impair their ability to always keep their behavior lawful.[15] In the ghetto riots of the late sixties, police violence was common.

Police handling of political protesters also has often been violent and illegal. The police response to the demonstrations at the 1968 Democratic National Convention in Chicago has been described as "unrestrained and indiscriminate police violence."[16] These confrontations increase the chances for violence because of the views the police share about protesters. That is, "organized protest tends to be viewed as the conspiratorial product of authoritarian agitators — usually 'Communists' — who mislead otherwise contented people."[17] Such ideas, combined with frustration and anger, provide ready support for harsh police actions. And because the police look on most people they find in these situations as already guilty, they think their own methods of control and apprehension are appropriate — no matter how criminal these methods may be.

Homicides committed by police against citizens have increased in recent years, especially the killing of black men by the police.[18] Police also sometimes kill one another, often because of mistaken identity. All these occurrences are a result of the tendency in law enforcement to employ more sophisticated and deadly weapons. Police departments in several states are adopting soft-headed, hollow-nosed bullets (the "dumdum"). These bullets, wounding more seriously and killing more often, have been banned in some international treaties in an attempt to limit the conduct of war.

Police engaged in enforcing narcotics laws are especially prone to commit crimes in their work. The conventional crimes they commit range from taking illegal bribes to dealing in drugs themselves.[19] Other offenses by narcotics agents include theft of seized property, illegal searches and seizures, and criminal violence in enforcing the law. These violations occur in enforcement of a prohibition (drug use and sale) that is also an integral part of American society. Crime by the enforcers of such a contradictory criminal law are to be expected.

Other agents of the law, such as the officials who guard and "correct" conventional offenders, also violate the law in their work. These crimes correspond closely to the objectives of security and punishment. Prison guards, in particular, are to do whatever is necessary to maintain security in the prison.

These crimes are documented only when a crisis happens. Several crimes committed by correctional workers became known to the public following prison riots in New York City jails.[20] The inmates were responding to the harsh conditions in the jails, including excessive bail, overcrowding, and months of being confined without indictment or trial. After the revolt had been ended peacefully by negotiations between the inmates and the mayor's office, correctional officers systematically beat the prisoners in the courtyard of one of the jails. The beatings were recorded in photographs and eyewitness accounts. A reporter for the *Daily News* described what he saw:

> It was a gruesome scene. About 250 prisoners were sitting on the grass. Behind them, 30 Correction Department guards were lined up, all of them holding weapons — ax handles, baseball bats, and night sticks. One inmate was dragged out a doorway onto a loading platform and five guards attacked him with their clubs. They battered his head and blood flowed over his face and body. He was kicked off the platform and several other guards pounded him again with their clubs. His limp form then was lifted off the ground and thrown into a bus as another prisoner was hauled out and belted across the back with a club. Then more clubs rained down on him until he was motionless and bloodsoaked. He too was thrown into the bus. Another man was pushed out, his hands above his head. A bat caught him in the stomach and he doubled over. More clubs came down on his spine. Eight guards were slugging away at one time. A fourth prisoner emerged but the guards seemed to let go of him. He began running but the guards kicked him over and over. Some more prisoners got the same treatment.[21]

As it often turns out with such incidents, three weeks after the beatings the district attorney announced that eight inmates were indicted and all guards exonerated.

The results of crimes committed by agents of the law are usually predictable: the charges are dropped, the defendants are cleared, or, at most, an official may be dismissed. Although three students were killed and several more injured at Orangeburg State College in 1968, the South Carolina highway patrolmen who fired the shots were cleared of wrongdoing. Similar events and results were to occur later at Jackson State College in Mississippi.

Likewise, at Kent State University in 1970, National Guardsmen killed four students, and then were freed of blame. Instead, a state grand jury indicted twenty-five persons in connection with campus protests. The grand jury indicted no guardsmen because they "fired their weapons in the honest and sincere belief and under circumstances which would have logically caused them to believe that they would suffer serious bodily injury had they not done so." (No evidence of the sniper fire that they feared could be found.) The "major responsibility" for the events at Kent State, the grand jury continued, "rests clearly with those persons who are charged with the administration of the university." The university administration, the report asserted, had fostered "an attitude of laxity, overindulgence and permissiveness," and faculty members had placed an "over-emphasis" on "the right to dissent."[22] The idea that the government could be at fault was never entertained by the grand jury.

The September 1971 killings at Attica prison in New York State demonstrate violence by the state; more than forty were killed by state troopers when the prisoners demanded prison reforms.[23] Fearing that the rebellion threatened law and order, Governor Rockefeller ordered in the troopers who fired upon and killed prisoners and their guards. Actions such as these are beginning to be understood by the public; crime by the state is becoming a part of the public consciousness.

CRIMES OF PROVOCATION

The ideology of the American state promotes the myth that law enforcement is a neutral force intended to maintain the democratic process.

> The history of America contradicts this official image of neutrality and equal justice. The pattern is clear: when women tried to vote and Labor claimed its right to organize, at the beginning of this century, police were used as poll-watchers, as strike-breakers, and as shock troops by those who held industrial power; in the 1950's as black people began a new round in their centuries-old struggle for equal protection, police were once again used to defy the Constitution in the name of states' rights and public order; in the 1960's police again and again were sent in to disperse hundreds of thousands of citizens peacefully exercising their First Amendment rights to protest an unconstitutional war in Southeast Asia. All this time, on a day to day, face to face level the typical law enforcement slogan "to protect and to serve" meant one thing to the powerful or the passive and another to the powerless or the dissident.[24]

The practice in which a law-enforcement agency uses a policeman or an informer to encourage or plan actions that violate the law is itself a crime. Yet, we are now realizing this practice is common. The crime of informers becoming agents provocateurs and encouraging or committing illegal acts is widespread. Instances include these:

> One of the people most involved in encouraging the violence that accompanied the Chicago Democratic Party Convention was actually an undercover police officer; two members of a national peace committee who always tried to push the group into confrontations with the police were both police provocateurs; a young man who provided a bomb to blow up a Seattle U.S. Post Office was an FBI and city police informer; another FBI informer burned buildings at the University of Alabama; police agents tried to incite violence at Yale University during the demonstrations of May 1971; a Chicano activist in Los Angeles who attempted to provoke his group into terrible acts of violence was an informer for the Treasury Department; the Weatherman group in Ohio was infiltrated by an informer who won a position for himself through advocacy of the most extreme forms of violence; the Black Panther Party "Minister of Defense" in Los Angeles, who helped bring about a shootout with the police, was actually a police informer; a New York City undercover police officer tried to convince a

veterans' peace group that it should use violent tactics; another police provocateur, who had vandalized a state college campus, attempted to convert a San Diego peace march into a pitched battle with police; in upstate New York, an informer, who was on the FBI payroll, tried to set up a class to teach students at Hobart University how to make and use bombs; informers working for the FBI and local police set up a bombing attempt in Mississippi in an effort to kill two KKK members; a Chicago police informer provided the false tip which led to the killing of two Panther leaders there; a police informer led an illegal SDS sit-in at an Illinois college and later — claiming he was a Weatherman — helped to hurl the president of the college off the stage; a police informer attempted to force a militant Seattle group into taking on violent activities; two men who had led the shutting of a massive gate at Ohio State University and set off a violent confrontation with the police, were officers of the state highway patrol; and the false report claiming guns were stored in the Black Muslim Temple in Los Angeles came from a paid police informer, who claims he was instructed to make the report so that the police who employed him would have an excuse to raid the temple.[25]

Such accounts appear endless, making us realize that in attempting to protect itself the state systematically engages in acts of provocation. Persons and groups thought to be threats to the system have found themselves harassed by surveillance. Violent criminal acts are committed against them in the name of law and order. Law-enforcement agents have raided the homes of blacks, probably in response to acts of provocation by agents provocateurs among the Black Panthers.[26] It was also exposed in the trial of the San Quentin Six that an agent provocateur was involved in the assassination of revolutionary prison organizer George Jackson in an alleged escape from San Quentin prison. The ex-informer from the Los Angeles Police Department was participating in the general plot to infiltrate, disrupt, and destroy black radical organizations.[27] Plans and actions like these are systematically practiced to eliminate any group that does not accept the state's legitimacy; it is, after all, supposed to be guardian of the national interest.

How far will the state go to protect its own interests? Recently revealed plans might have imposed martial law in the United States if a plot involving the 1972 Republican Convention, which was to be held in San Diego, had come off:

The plan entailed planting a number of agents-provocateurs both inside and outside the 1972 Republican Convention in San Diego. Agents were to infiltrate the groups planning demonstrations against the war and poverty. At the time of the demonstrations these agents were to provoke street battles with the police surrounding the convention hall; meanwhile, agents inside the convention hall were to have planted explosives, timed to blow up simultaneously with the "riot in the streets." The result, he [Louis E. Tackwood] claimed, would be to create a nation-wide hysteria that would then provide President Richard M. Nixon with the popular support necessary to declare a state of national emergency; the government could then arrest all "radicals," "militants," and "left-wing revolutionaries."[28]

In the Watergate crimes we recognize the full authoritarian possibilities in the modern state. The break-in at the Democratic National Convention headquarters (in the Watergate apartment complex) was much more than a mere burglary and installation of electronic listening devices. The invading team was discovered putting forged documents *into* the files. They also had incendiary and bomb manufacturing devices and implements.

> One thing was perfectly clear: this espionage mission was involved with far more than eavesdropping. As the investigation of the event unfolded during the 1972 presidential campaign, it became clear that Watergate was but the tip of the iceberg. Hundreds of thousands of dollars and scores of men were revealed as part of a national network for political espionage, sabotage and provocation. The contacts for the provocateurs who were recruited turned out to be men from the White House, some of the President's closest advisors.[29]

Crimes of provocation come from the highest sources.

CRIMES OF WAR

Criminologists, content to study criminal acts by individuals against society, have neglected international incidents that are also criminal, in which the state itself or its agents are implicated. One of these is war, today entirely a governmental function. War is, obviously, violence. Many violent acts that are forbidden without question in peacetime are accepted as necessary in wartime. Some acts of this kind, though, go beyond even the laws that nations have accepted as governing their behavior at war. These are crimes of war.

Sociologists, confronted with these acts, conveniently ignore them, suggesting that they are not "crimes" as they define them, that these acts are not a system of behavior, or that only history can determine which acts are crimes. They fail to realize that these acts (1) are covered by the criminal laws, (2) can be systematic, integral parts of a political and economic system, and (3) are crucial in a nation's history. If we do not consider such crimes, we abdicate both our integrity as scholars and our responsibility as human beings.

An elaborate body of international laws covers the crimes of war. The laws of war are of ancient origin, and up to the eighteenth century were mostly preserved by unwritten tradition.[30] Gradually the laws were codified and courts were established to try violations of the laws. In the last hundred years international laws and treaties have firmly codified an international law of war. The United States is party to twelve conventions pertinent to land warfare, including the detailed Geneva Conventions of 1949. The most authoritative and encompassing statement of war crimes is in the chapter of the International Military Tribunal at Nuremberg where war crimes are defined as

> Violations of the laws or customs of war which include, but are not limited to, murder, ill-treatment or deportation to slave-labour or for any other purpose of civilian population of or in occupied territory, murder, or ill-treatment of prisoners of war or persons on the high seas, killing of hostages, plunder of public or private property, wanton destruction of cities, towns or villages, or devastation not justified by military necessity.[31]

"The laws of warfare are part of American law, enforceable in American courts, not only because the United States is party to most of the major multilateral conventions on the conduct of military hostilities but also because the laws of warfare are incorporated in international customary law, which under the Constitution is part of American law."[32] The United States also recognizes that the laws of war apply to us in the Field Manual of the Department of the Army. The Manual makes it clear that the international laws are also "the supreme law of the land," and that "the law of war is binding not only upon States as such but also upon individuals and, in particular, the members of their armed forces."[33] The international laws of war are part of American law, and may be enforced against both civilians and soldiers, by national or international courts.

Now, let us see how international law can be applied to a country that committed monstrous criminal acts in a long war: the United States in Southeast Asia. We assume that the nation and its representatives discussed here are guilty of these crimes. How are they guilty, and how can the international courts prove their guilt and bring the guilty to trial?

At the Nuremberg war crimes trials in Germany after World War II, Chief Prosecutor Justice Jackson of the United States Supreme Court declared: "If certain acts and violations of treaties are crimes, they are crimes whether the United States does them or whether Germany does them. We are not prepared to lay down a rule of criminal conduct against others which we would not be willing to have invoked against us." Years later many believed the United States had put itself in the respondent's position. But those who level the charge of war crimes against the United States are not the obvious victors. The countries in Southeast Asia, though continually advancing their own condition, are not yet in a position to conduct a war crimes trial. And other nations have not been inclined to convene an international trial. Nevertheless, the words of Justice Jackson are coming back to haunt many Americans.

Our century has been dominated by a single view of reality: the liberal view, which may have been the source of both our problems as a nation and our inability to understand these problems. So it is that the war in Southeast Asia and the crimes associated with it may be made understandable by another theory of reality, socialist theory. What did liberals predict about our involvement in Southeast Asia?

> Did they predict that the American government, continuously advised by university professors, would persist for several years in methods of warfare and of pacification that are criminal in international law and custom, and that are modeled on communist methods? Did they predict that the American government, in pursuit of its presumed strategic interests, would prop up, by fire-power and money, any puppet, however repressive, provided only that he would not have dealings with Russia and China? Did they anticipate that the principles of the Nuremberg trials and pledges to international order would be brought into contempt so soon and by a democracy?[34]

The liberal theory always held that the Vietnam war was, at most, a mistake. The socialist theory, scoffed at by most intellectuals in the late fifties and early sixties, suggested another meaning. Rather than viewing the war as an accident or miscalculation, an event that would cease with immediate American withdrawal, that theory predicted the United States would extend the war.

What the United States did in Southeast Asia was a logical outcome of policies that have long existed. That the United States has intervened in the affairs of other nations has been taken for granted. Its right to interfere in the development of these countries, including the right to suppress national revolts, has been patently accepted. To overthrow revolutionary governments and to replace them with military dictatorships has been recognized as good foreign policy. Instead of questioning a foreign policy that is guided by corporate capitalism, in which national interests are defined as business interests, liberals have proclaimed this arrangement. And these arrangements and ideas helped bring about the Vietnam war.

The dramatic disclosure of a massacre involving more than 500 civilians in the My Lai #4 hamlet of Son My village raised the first serious consideration of war crimes by the United States in the Vietnam war. That disclosure, not made until several months after the March 16, 1968 massacre, suggested other war crimes over a long time:

> The official policies developed for the pursuit of belligerent objectives in Vietnam appear to violate the same basic and minimum constraints on the conduct of war as were violated at Songmy. B-52 pattern raids against unde-

fended villages and populated areas, "free bomb zones," forcible removal of civilian populations, defoliation and crop destruction and "search and destroy" missions have been sanctioned as official tactical policies of the United States government. Each of these tactical policies appears to violate the international laws of war binding upon the United States by international treaties ratified by the U.S. government with the advice and consent of the Senate. The overall conduct of the war in Vietnam by the U.S. armed forces involves a refusal to differentiate betweeen combatants and noncombatants and between military and nonmilitary targets.[35]

The implications of Son My are far-reaching. The United States government seems to have pursued official policies of warfare that constitute war crimes: "It would, therefore, be misleading to isolate the awful happening at Songmy from the overall conduct of the war. It is certainly true that the perpetrators of the massacre at Songmy are, if the allegations prove correct, guilty of the commission of war crimes, but it is also true that their responsibility is mitigated to the extent that they were executing superior orders or were even carrying out the general lines of official policy that established a moral climate in which the welfare of Vietnamese civilians is totally disregarded."[36]

Let us, then, examine some of the specific acts by the United States government in Southeast Asia that are defined as criminal in the international laws of war.

Murder and Ill-Treatment of Civilians

The Son My massacre of civilian men, women, and children took place in a standard American military operation. Trying to trap a Vietcong unit, an American brigade (C Company of Task Force Baker) killed almost every villager they could lay hands on, although no opposition or hostile behavior was encountered.[37]

The tragedy of Son My cannot obscure the fact that the killing of civilians by American forces became an every day occurrence in Vietnam. Estimates have suggested that American or South Vietnamese forces killed or wounded ten civilians for every Vietcong.[38] Civilian casualties in South Vietnam ran into the hundreds of thousands. The Kennedy Subcommittee on Refugees estimated that there were about 300,000 casualties in 1968. According to a conservative estimate for the years 1965 to 1969, 1,116,000 South Vietnamese civilians were killed and 2,232,000 were wounded; between a fifth and a quarter of the population was killed or wounded by military operations in the war. Not included in these figures are the unknown number of casualties from disease and malnutrition brought on by the war. Likewise, these figures do not include the casualties suffered by the civilians of North Vietnam, many by massive bombing. Thousands of other civilians were killed as the war was "wound down."

Destruction of Nonmilitary Targets

The United States engaged in heavy aerial bombardment in Vietnam. The bomb tonnage exceeded that delivered in all the allied bombing in Europe and Asia during World War II. By February 1969, 3,200,000 tons of bombs had been dropped on an agricultural country slightly larger than New York State: 180 pounds of bombs for every man, woman, and child in Vietnam, or 25 tons of bombs for every square mile of North and South Vietnam.[39]

The strictly legal question is whether or not these bombs fell on military objectives:

> Under the traditional approach to the war-crimes concept, no legal issue is presented with respect to the bombing of genuinely strategic military targets such as factories, ammunition depots, oil refineries, airports, and — particularly in the Vietnam context — roads, bridges, viaducts, railroad tracks, trucks, trains, tunnels, and any other transportation facilities. Furthermore, we assume that accidental and incidental damage to nonmilitary and nonstrategic targets is not a war crime.[40]

But the kind of bombing carried out by the United States government appears to have been quite different; it is accused of carrying out a deliberate, nonaccidental bombardment of nonmilitary targets. In North Vietnam, B-52 bombers were said to have continuously attacked schools, churches, hospitals, private homes, dikes, and dams.[41]

In South Vietnam, bombing of rural villages was a standard military policy. Any area could be more or less indiscriminately bombed. "While such strategy violates all international law regarding warfare and is inherently genocidal, it also adjusts to the political reality in South Vietnam that the NLF is and can be anywhere and that virtually the entire people is America's enemy."[42] Military policy turned an entire nation into a target.

Murder and Ill-Treatment of Prisoners of War

The laws of war on treatment of prisoners of war are precise: it is a war crime to murder or torture prisoners.

> According to the Nuremberg precedents, captors may not shoot prisoners even though they are in a combat zone, require a guard, consume supplies, slow up troop movements, and appear certain to be set free by their own forces

in an imminent invasion. The Hague Conventions of 1907 require that prisoners be humanely treated, and the Geneva Convention of 1949 prohibits "causing death or seriously endangering the health of a prisoner of war." In particular it stipulates that "no physical or mental torture, nor any other form of coercion, may be inflicted on prisoners of war to secure from them information of any kind whatever."[43]

Yet there are numerous reports of the murder and ill-treatment of prisoners by American military forces as well as by the American trained and supported South Vietnamese Army.[44] Detailed accounts have been given of the beheading and shooting of wounded prisoners and of torture. Instead of incarcerating prisoners, execution is often carried out at the time of capture. Some combat soldiers characterized these actions as "everyday things," "expected" combat behavior, and "standard operating policy." Violations of the international laws of war become an issue of American military policy.

Other Crimes

American armed forces, working with the Army of South Vietnam, sprayed more than 100 million pounds of herbicidal chemicals on about half (5 million acres) of the arable land in South Vietnam. The object was "to defoliate trees affording cover for enemy forces and to kill certain plants, including rice, which furnished food for Vietcong forces and their civilian supporters.[45] In addition, 14 million pounds of CS gas which incapacitates combatants and civilians was used. In other words, the United States relied extensively on chemical warfare in Vietnam and later in Cambodia.

The Geneva Gas Protocol of 1925 states that the "use in war of asphyxiating, poisonous or other gases, and of all analogous liquids, materials, or devices, has been justly condemned by the general opinion of the civilized world," and prohibits the use of such weapons. Even with the most limited interpretation of the protocol, as lethal devices, the liquids and sprays used by the United States in Southeast Asia were in violation of international law.[46] Napalm too was widely used in Vietnam and surrounding countries.

In officially conducting a war against the population of Vietnam, the United States and some of its leaders could be charged with genocide, a crime against humanity, covered by international treaties and for which all but two of the defendants at Nuremberg were convicted.

"The case for these stark accusations is based on the conclusions that both South Vietnam and the United States violated the Geneva Declaration of 1954 by hostile acts against the North, unlawful rearmament, and refusal to carry out the 1965 national elections provided for in the Declaration, and that the United States likewise violated the United Nations Charter by bombing North Vietnam."[47] The United States attempted to legitimize its war by claiming that self-defense measures were required in response to armed attacks.

World Justice

Only a few war-crimes violations have been prosecuted, and these by military courts. Lieutenant William Calley stood a court-martial trial for his part in killing civilians at Son My. It became clear at the trial that Calley was being used as a scapegoat for decisions made by others at higher levels of command. But crucial questions about individual responsibility were raised during the trial.[48] According to the Nuremberg principles and the Army's Field Manual, members of the armed forces are bound to obey only *lawful* orders; orders violating international law are not to be obeyed. Moreover, questions were raised about war crimes by the United States, and according to international law, those who make and administer these policies must be held responsible. In the Tokyo War Crimes Trial, the defendant, General Yamashita, was convicted and executed for failing to restrain his troops from committing crimes against civilians in the Philippines during the closing months of World War II. That trial established for international law that "A leader must take affirmative acts to prevent war crimes or dissociate himself from the Government. If he fails to do one or the other, then by the very act of remaining in a government of a state guilty of war crimes, he becomes a war criminal."[49]

The grounds are considerable, therefore, for regarding policy-makers and those who administer policy as war criminals. One noted legal scholar, Telford Taylor, chief counsel for the prosecution at Nuremberg, suggests that with the precedents in international law, several civilian leaders and military officers could be held criminally responsible for their acts.[50] The political leaders (including Rusk, McNamara, Bundy, and Rostow), as well as the military leaders, such as the Joint Chiefs of Staff (especially General Westmoreland), should have borne responsibility for the war crimes in Southeast Asia.

To invoke the law, if it could be done beyond the manipulations of the regime itself, is probably to expect too much of legal institutions. The war crimes of the United States cannot be probed adequately in a court-martial proceeding when the responsibility lies higher. It seems more critical to develop a moral and political judgment on our recent history.[51]

A national or international board of inquiry may be the most appropriate way to deal with war crimes. The main objective of this approach, as Richard Falk argues, is to achieve a measure of rectitude by *moral clarification.* Moreover:

> Such a focus is not punitive, the idea is not to catch, convict and punish individuals, but to expose, clarify, and repudiate their conduct. Such an enterprise can only be effective if it represents as authoritative a collective judgment of mankind as a whole reached in a proceeding that was fair, but honest. Americans concerned at once with avoiding any deepening polarization at home, and with renouncing crimes committed on their behalf, should join together in calling for an *external* process of inquiry and judgment, perhaps in the form of a specially constituted U.N. Commission of Inquiry. For Americans of conscience this is the time for neither insurgency, nor silence.[52]

In the end, everyone is responsible for the acts of government. It is the responsibility of all peoples of the world to remove the oppression of national empires and to achieve world justice and human liberation.

WATERGATE — BENEATH AND BEYOND

From the time the offices of the Democratic National Committee in the Watergate buildings in Washington, D.C. were broken into in June 1972, Americans gradually became aware of crimes committed by the state, its leaders and officials, and those hired to commit criminal acts. Acts of spying and sabotage were directed from the White House, whose purpose (as former President Nixon said) was to "stop security leaks and to investigate other sensitive matters."[53] As the disclosures multiplied, crimes far beyond Watergate were exposed.

Still more crimes were committed as the investigations went forward, to cover up the criminal world that made Watergate possible or necessary. The name "Watergate" came to include not only a plot within the president's reelection committee and the coverup activities, but all the schemes the state and its leaders resorted to.

Watergate uncovered a "second government" in the United States, or perhaps better, a previously unsuspected form of influence and control spreading through the government. Watergate was but the tip of a coolly rational iceberg; the real forces lay in the political depths below.

Beneath Watergate is a government with "a combination of vast and complicated interlocking forces, pulling in the CIA here and organized crime there, using politicians one time and émigré thugs the next, which seems to regard government as a tool for financial enrichment."[54] These operations are usually beyond the reach of citizens. "Other scandals —

whether called by that name in the press or not, as with the Watergate 'caper' — are also sure to follow, for it seems obvious that the kind of milieu in which the president has chosen to immerse himself will continue to produce policies self-serving at best, shady at average, and downright illegal at worst, and that at least some of this will break through to public attention."[55] This power will not be washed away by investigations, prosecutions, or new administrations; the underside of the United States is likely to reign for some time, until politics and economics can be changed.

The secret government's clandestine operations tell us of the forces involved in established politics and economics. These operations are connected with government and business agencies; when discovered they are covered by lies. A pattern visible in these spy and sabotage operations consists of the agents who reappear in many of the same assignments. A list of the men indicted in the Watergate break-in reveals some of the complex criminal operations in the American state, and the key roles played by the CIA and the FBI.

Bernard L. Barker (alias Frank or Fran Carter). Half-Cuban American who lived in Cuba for a number of years and left after Castro's revolution. Former employee of the Central Intelligence Agency and reported to have had a role in the abortive Bay of Pigs invasion of Cuba. Founded Barker Associates, a Miami real estate firm, in 1971.

Virgilio R. Gonzalez (alias Raul or Raoul Godoy or Goboy). Cuban who emigrated to United States at time of Castro's rise. Employed as locksmith.

Eugenio R. Martinez (alias Gene or Jene Valdes). Former pro-Castro Cuban legislator. Exile reportedly active in anti-Castro movement. Said to have been associated with CIA. Member of Barker's real estate firm.

James W. McCord, Jr. (alias Edward J. Warren and Edward J. Martin). Former FBI agent. CIA employee for 19 years until retirement in 1970. Salaried security coordinator for the Republican National Committee and Nixon's reelection committee until day after his arrest.

Frank A. Sturgis (alias Frank Angelo Fiorini, Edward J. Hamilton and Joseph DiAlberto or D'Alberto). Reportedly former American gun-smuggler for Castro, later active in anti-Castro Cuban exile activities, including Bay of Pigs invasion. Said to have had extensive links with CIA. Described as an associate of Barker.

E. Howard Hunt, Jr. CIA employee, 1949–70. Reportedly had key role in 1961 Bay of Pigs invasion. Writer of spy novels. Part-time consultant to White House counsel Charles W. Colson from 1970 until March 29, 1972. Consultant projects included declassification of the Pentagon Papers and intelligence work in narcotics enforcement.

G. Gordon Liddy. Former FBI agent. Special assistant to assistant Treasury Secretary, 1969–1971, when he was reportedly fired for unauthorized activities. Joined White House staff in July 1971 and said to have suggested bugging *The New York Times* during Pentagon Papers controversy. Joined Nixon re-election

Walking to their White House offices in 1971 are President Richard Nixon and his chief-of-staff H. R. Haldeman. In 1972 the Watergate crimes were uncovered. Subsequently, Haldeman and other presidential assistants and officials were tried and sentenced, while Nixon resigned in 1974 and went into exile at his California estate.

committee in late 1971, where he was finance counsel at time of Watergate break-in. Dismissed by Mitchell for refusing to answer FBI's questions.[56]

As the Watergate investigation proceeded, it seemed clear that these men were agents for criminals much higher in the American business and political establishment. This and other events of recent years suggest not isolated incidents, but a conspiracy led by powers within the United States. An observer with close ties to the intelligence establishment said: "A look at the power and history of the fifteen years lying behind Watergate — at the CIA and the espionage establishment tied to Gordon Liddy's bungling burglars and the bright young men who proposed Gestapo-like plans for the White House — suggests that there was indeed a conspiracy — possibly one whose reach extended beyond CREEP [Committee to Re-elect the President] and even the White House itself."[57] Other events, involving foreign as well as domestic operations, may be similarly connected.

Inquiries into Watergate and the subsequent coverup disclosed many other alliances and related criminal operations, connecting the United States government, organized crime, and clandestine intelligence networks. Not the least of these discoveries is the connection between some of the Watergate figures, agencies, and operations and past political assassinations. The assassinations of John Kennedy, Martin Luther King, Robert Kennedy, and the attempted assassination of George Wallace were likely conspiratorial plots to maintain control over the established political and economic system by the groups, persons, and forces that arranged Watergate.[58] From the assassination of John Kennedy in Dallas to the Watergate burglary in Washington, a single path appears to be traceable.

The path of crime led finally to the highest level of the government, the presidency itself. Politics, business, and organized crime are tightly intertwined in the circle of people and events around the career of Richard Nixon. In an extensive investigation, a researcher uncovered information about Nixon's business and organized crime dealings in Florida and the Caribbean since the late forties:

> Nixon visited Miami numerous times in the late forties, contrary to all of his official biographies. While there, he yachted with Richard Danner, Bebe Rebozo, and Tatum "Chubby" Wofford of the syndicate-controlled Wofford Hotel. Danner also had mob connections at that time.
>
> Nixon has invested in two southern Florida land deals; others involved in both projects have had links with organized crime. Two men in particular — Leonard Bursten and Nathan Ratner — have had business connections with organized crime.
>
> Nixon concealed his ownership of a Key Biscayne lot for four years until a mortgage held by another Lansky associate, Arthur Desser, was paid off.
>
> Nixon's closest friend, Bebe Rebozo, was a war profiteer in the early forties in the tire recapping business. Three of his associates served on the Dade County tire allocation board, in clear violation of OPA regulation No. 3C-118. At the same time Nixon was working in the legal interpretations unit of the OPA in Washington, D.C.
>
> Nixon technically concealed his employment with the OPA until he was President.
>
> Nixon is linked to the "Havana Connection" — a funnel for organized crime and reactionary Cuban politics. Indictees in the Watergate case also figure in this connection.
>
> Nixon has received campaign contributions from two men who have had direct connections to organized crime.
>
> Nixon has appointed a number of men, including John Connally, William Rogers, and Will Wilson, who have indirect ties to organized crime.

The mob-favored Miami National Bank was the chief creditor in a bankruptcy case which led to a $300,000,000 suit, still pending, against Nixon and other members of his New York law firm for their alleged part in skimming over $5,000,000 off the bankrupt firm's accounts.

Nixon's rise to wealth and power has required the silent loyalty of a wide range of personalities whose names only occasionally surface in the glare of scandal — with good reason. Richard Nixon would not be where he is today were it not for his uncanny ability to thrive on political crisis. As much as anything else it is his self-proclaimed poker-playing instincts — the cautious, calculating, close-mouthed style and the ability to keep a stone face in rough as well as smooth times — that has carried Nixon to the Presidency.[59]

The full extent of crime in the American state is beginning to surface; some of the criminal associations and dealings were revealed by Watergate. The Nixon administration's operations this time overstepped the bounds of trickery and deceit acceptable in American politics, and the administration was called to account for *some* of its criminal acts.

Watergate, however, is but one reflection of the growing crisis in the American state and in the capitalist economy upon which it rests. Concentration of power, corruption, repression, and crime will continue to be a part of the state as corporate and financial power require a strong state to ensure their dominance in a failing capitalist economy.

Centralized state power must increasingly be used to implement domestic and foreign policies in support of the capitalist system. Watergate was one administration's attempt to secure that concentration by working around the established institutions of the federal bureaucracy and bypassing the pluralistic processes of the Congress and the two major political parties.[60] The removal of the Nixon entourage from the White House has done nothing to solve the structural problems which confront the capitalist state and which continue to shape the state's policies.

With no satisfactory structural solutions to the current crisis, repression by the state and crimes of the state continue to be a reality. Such measures will be used in an effort to suppress the class struggle that continues in a society that cannot solve its problems within a capitalist political economy. A critical understanding of the state and the crimes it commits begins the thought and practice that move us beyond the present reality of the United States.

NOTES

1. For documentation on some of these crimes, see Jethro K. Lieberman, *How the Government Breaks the Law* (New York: Stein and Day, 1972); Theodore L. Becker and Vernon G. Murray, eds., *Government Lawlessness in America* (New York: Oxford University Press, 1971).

2. Richard Halloran, "Army Spied on 18,000 Civilians in Two-Year Operation," *The New York Times*, January 18, 1971, pp. 1 and 22.

3. The documentation is extensive. See, for example, reports of the congressional committees, such as the hearings conducted by the Senate Subcommittee on Constitutional Rights and the hearings of the Senate Watergate Committee. Also see daily coverage by *The New York Times.* Analysis is provided in several articles in *Society,* 12 (March-April 1975).

4. See Marshall B. Clinard and Richard Quinney, *Criminal Behavior Systems: A Typology,* 2nd ed. (New York: Holt, Rinehart and Winston, 1973), pp. 154–186.

5. Homer Bigart, "Berrigan Case: A Strategy That Failed," *The New York Times,* April 9, 1972, p. E2; John Kifner, "Court in Chicago Frees 5 in 1968 Convention Case," *The New York Times,* November 23, 1972; "Ellsberg Case: Defendants Freed, Government Convicted," *The New York Times,* May 13, 1973, p. E1; John Kifner, "Eight Acquitted in Gainesville of G.O.P. Convention Plot," *The New York Times,* September 1, 1973, p. 1.

6. John Kifner, "F.B.I. Sought Doom of Panther Party," *The New York Times,* May 9, 1976, p. 1; Nicholas M. Horrock and John M. Crewdson, "F.B.I. Men Linked to 70's Kidnapping of Domestic Radical," *The New York Times,* June 25, 1976, p. 1; Nicholas M. Horrock and John M. Crewdson, "F.B.I. Burglaries Said to Be Sifted by Justice Aides," *The New York Times,* June 24, 1976, p. 1; John M. Crewdson, "Burglaries in '73 Conceded by F.B.I.," *The New York Times,* July 1, 1976, p. 1; Nicholas M. Horrock, "Car Burnings and Assaults on Radicals Linked to F.B.I. Agents in Last 5 Years," *The New York Times,* July 11, 1976, p. 20; Nicholas M. Horrock, "F.B.I. is Accused of Political Acts for 6 Presidents," *The New York Times,* December 4, 1975, p. 1; I. F. Stone, "The Threat to the Republic," *The New York Review of Books,* 23 (May 27, 1976), pp. 3–4; Seymour M. Hersh, "Aides Say Robert Kennedy Told of C.I.A. Castro Plot," *The New York Times,* March 10, 1975, p. 1.

7. Nicholas Horrock, "Public Disclosures of Lost Privacy," *The New York Times,* November 1, 1975, p. E5. Also see John M. Crewdson, "Intelligence Panel Finds F.B.I. and Other Agencies Violated Citizens' Rights," *The New York Times,* April 29, 1976, pp. 1 and 31–33. Further description of the covert and illegal counterintelligence program of the FBI is in Nelson Blackstock, *Cointelpro: The FBI's Secret War on Political Freedom* (New York: Random House, 1976). Also see Morton H. Halperin, Jerry J. Berman, Robert L. Borosage, and Christine M. Marwick, *The Lawless State: The Crimes of the U.S. Intelligence Agencies* (New York: Penguin Books, 1976); and David Wise, *The American Police State: The Government Against the People* (New York: Random House, 1976).

8. David Burnham, "Misconduct Laid to 27% of Police in Three Cities' Slums," *The New York Times,* July 5, 1968, p. 1.

9. Fred J. Cook, "How Deep Are the Police in Heroin Traffic?" *The New York Times,* April 25, 1971, p. E3; Andrew H. Malcolm, "Violent Drug Raids Against the Innocent Found Widespread," *The New York Times,* June 25, 1973, p. 1; Ralph Blumenthal, "Officer in Albany Says Fellow Police Joined in Thievery," *The New York Times,* September 21, 1973, p. 1; Ralph Blumenthal, "Brothel Boss Tells of Albany Bribes," *The New York Times,* September 25, 1973, p. 39.

10. *The Knapp Commission Report on Police Corruption* (New York: George Braziller, 1972).

11. Paul Chevigny, *Police Power: Police Abuses in New York City* (New York: Random House, 1969), pp. 136–146.

12. William A. Westley, "Violence and the Police," *American Journal of Sociology,* 59 (July 1953), p. 35.

13. Ellwyn R. Stoddard, "The Informal 'Code' of Police Deviancy: A Group Approach to 'Blue-Coat Crime,' " *Journal of Criminal Law, Criminology and Police Science,* 59 (June 1968), p. 212. Also see Barbara Raffel Price, "Police Corruption: Analysis," *Criminology,* 10 (August 1972), pp. 161–176; Julian B. Roebuck and Thomas Barker, "A Typology of Police Corruption," *Social Problems,* 21 (No. 3, 1974), pp. 423–437; and Meyer S. Reed, Jerry Burnette, and Richard R. Troiden, "Wayward Cops: The Function of Deviance in Groups Reconsidered," *Social Problems,* 24 (June 1977), pp. 565–575.

14. Jerome H. Skolnick, *Justice Without Trial: Law Enforcement in Democratic Society* (New York: John Wiley, 1966), p. 202.

15. See Donald J. Black and Albert J. Reiss, Jr., "Patterns of Behavior in Police and Citizen Transactions," in the President's Commission on Law Enforcement and Administration of Justice, *Studies in Crime and Law Enforcement in Major Metropolitan Areas,* vol. 2, Field Surveys III (Washington, D.C.: U.S. Government Printing Office, 1967), pp. 132–139.

16. The Walker Report to the National Commission on the Causes and Prevention of Violence, *Rights in Conflict* (New York: Bantam Books, 1968), p. 1.

17. Jerome H. Skolnick, *The Politics of Protest* (New York: Ballantine Books, 1969). Also see Rodney Stark, *Police Riots* (Belmont, Calif.: Wadsworth, 1972).

18. Paul Takagi, "A Garrison State in 'Democratic' Society," *Crime and Social Justice,* 1 (Spring-Summer 1974), pp. 27–33.

19. Peter K. Manning and Lawrence John Redlinger, "Invitational Edges of Corruption: Some Consequences of Narcotic Law Enforcement," in Paul Rock, ed., *Drugs and Politics* (New York: E. P. Dutton, 1976).

20. Paul L. Montgomery, "Crisis in Prisons Termed Worst Mayor Has Faced," *The New York Times,* October 15, 1970, p. 1.

21. Quoted in Jack Newfield, "The Law is an Outlaw," *The Village Voice,* December 17, 1970, p. 1.

22. John Kifner, "Jury Indicts 25 in Kent Disorder; Guard is Cleared," *The New York Times,* October 17, 1970, p. 1.

23. *Attica,* The Official Report of the New York State Special Commission on Attica (New York: Bantam Books, 1972).

24. Citizens Research and Investigation Committee and Louis E. Tackwood, *The Glass House Tapes* (New York: Avon Books, 1973), p. 259.

25. Paul Jacobs, "Informers, the Enemy Within," *Ramparts,* 12 (August-September, 1973), pp. 53–54.

26. Other cases of provocation against the Black Panthers are presented in Paul Chevigny, *Cops and Rebels: A Study of Provocation* (New York: Random House, 1972). On the sociological implications of provocation, see Gary T. Marx, "Thoughts on a Neglected Category of Social Movement Participant: The Agent Provocateur and the Informant," *American Journal of Sociology,* 80 (September 1974), pp. 402–442.

27. Karen Wald, "Quentin Jury Hears of Plot," *Guardian,* May 5, 1976, p. 5. The full account is in Jo Durden-Smith, *Who Killed George Jackson?* (New York: Alfred A. Knopf, 1976).

28. Citizens Research and Investigation Committee and Louis E. Tackwood, *The Glass House Tapes,* p. 42.

29. Ibid., p. 173.

30. Telford Taylor, *Nuremberg and Vietnam: An American Tragedy* (Chicago: Quadrangle Books, 1970), pp. 19–41.

31. Nuremberg Principle VI, clause b. The full text can be found in *The Nation,* January 26, 1970, p. 78.

32. Anthony A. D'Amato, Harvey L. Gould, and Larry D. Woods, "War Crimes and Vietnam: The 'Nuremberg Defence' and the Military Service Register," *California Law Review,* 57 (November 1969), p. 1058.

33. U.S. Department of the Army, *The Law of Land Warfare,* Field Manual No. 27–10, 1956. On the applicability of the international law of warfare to an undeclared war in Vietnam, the Manual clearly states: "As the customary law of war applies to cases of international armed conflict and to the forcible occupation of enemy territory generally as well as to declared war in its strict sense, a declaration of war is not an essential condition of the application of this body of law. Similarly, treaties relating to 'war' may become operative notwithstanding the absence of a formal declaration of war."

34. Stuart Hampshire, "Russell, Radicalism, and Reason," *New York Review of Books,* 15 (October 8, 1970), p. 3. Also see Noam Chomsky, *American Power and the New Mandarins* (New York: Vintage Books, 1969).

35. Richard A. Falk, "War Crimes and Individual Responsibility: A Legal Memorandum," *Trans-action*, 7 (January 1970), pp. 33–34.

36. Ibid., p. 34.

37. Richard Hammer, *One Morning in the War: The Tragedy at Son My* (New York: Coward-McCann, 1970). Also see Seymour H. Hersh, *My Lai, 4: A Report on the Massacre and its Aftermath* (New York: Vintage Books, 1970); and Josephy Goldstein, Burke Marshall, and Jack Schwartz, eds., *The My Lai Massacre and Its Cover-Up: Beyond the Reach of Law?* (New York: The Free Press, 1976).

38. Edward S. Herman, *Atrocities in Vietnam: Myths and Realities* (Philadelphia: Pilgrim Press, 1970), pp. 43–45.

39. Ibid., pp. 54–60.

40. D'Amato, Gould, and Woods, "War Crimes and Vietnam," pp. 1081–1082.

41. John Gerassi, *North Vietnam: A Documentary* (Indianapolis: Bobbs-Merrill, 1968).

42. Gabriel Kolko in Erwin Knoll and Judith Nies McFadden, eds., *War Crimes and the American Conscience* (New York: Holt, Rinehart and Winston, 1970), p. 57.

43. D'Amato, Gould, and Woods, "War Crimes and Vietnam," p. 1075.

44. For some of the sources of documentation, see ibid., pp. 1077–1081.

45. Arthur W. Galston in Knoll and McFadden, eds., *War Crimes and the American Conscience*, p. 69.

46. D'Amato, Gould, and Woods, "War and Crimes and Vietnam," pp. 1091–1093.

47. Taylor, *Nuremberg and Vietnam*, pp. 96–97.

48. See *The New York Times*, December 20, 1970, p. 8.

49. Falk, "War Crimes and Individual Responsibility," p. 39.

50. Taylor, *Nuremberg and Vietnam*, pp. 154–207. Also *The New York Times*, January 9, 1971, p. 3.

51. See the Proceedings of the Russell International War Crimes Tribunal, *Against the Crime of Silence* (Flanders, N.J.: O'Hare Books, 1968). Also Bertrand Russell, *War Crimes in Vietnam* (New York: Monthly Review Press, 1967).

52. Richard A. Falk, in *The New York Times Book Review*, December 27, 1970, p. 14.

53. On the Watergate events, see J. Anthony Lukas, *Nightmare: The Underside of the Nixon Years* (New York: Viking Press, 1976).

54. Kirkpatrick Sale, "The World Behind Watergate," *The New York Review of Books*, 20 (May 3, 1973), p. 14.

55. Ibid., p. 15.

56. *Congressional Quarterly Almanac*, 1972, vol. 28 (Washington, D.C.: Congressional Quarterly, Inc., 1972), p. 91.

57. L. Fletcher Prouty, "Watergate and the World of the CIA," *Ramparts*, 12 (October 1973), p. 50.

58. Much of the evidence is summarized in Mae Brussell, "Why Was Martha Mitchell Kidnapped?" *The Realist*, No. 93 (August 1972), pp. 1, 27–47.

59. Jeff Gerth, "Nixon and the Mafia," *SunDance*, 1 (November-December, 1972), p. 32. Also see Hank Messick, *Lansky* (New York: Berkley Medallion Books, 1973); Lucian K. Truscott IV, "The Rebozo Connection," *The Village Voice*, 18 (August 30, 1973), pp. 1, 24–34; "Nixon and Organized Crime," NACLA's *Latin America and Empire Report*, 6 (October 1972), pp. 3–17.

60. San Francisco Bay Area Kapitalistate Group, "Watergate, or the Eighteenth Brumaire of Richard Nixon," *Kapitalistate*, No. 3 (Spring 1975), pp. 3–24.

AJAX PRESSES

Crimes of the Economy

6

The economic structure of capitalist society generates its own forms of crime. An economy based on accumulation of capital by a capitalist class that owns and controls the means of production produces crimes as it secures the economic order. Among these crimes of economic domination are those committed against workers in the economy and economic crimes of individual businessmen and professionals against the public. Others are committed by corporations, from price-fixing and misrepresentation in advertising to fraudulent financial manipulations and pollution of the environment. Finally, in a capitalist economy, the operations of organized crime become linked to the economy and the state in the attempt to ensure survival of the capitalist system.

CRIMES AGAINST THE WORKER

Underlying all the capitalist crimes is appropriation of the worker's labor power. The worker creates a value several times greater than the labor power purchased by the capitalist. The excess value produced by the worker over the value of labor power is the *surplus value,* which is appropriated by the capitalist. The worker has the right to possess the whole of this value. Surplus value as a form of exploitation, however, is essential to capitalism, being the source from which capital is accumulated and production is expanded.

Work as purposeful action, guided by conceptual thought, is the distinct product of humankind.[1] Under capitalism, however, labor is dominated and shaped by alien forces, namely the accumulation of capital. The capitalist invents means of increasing the output of the worker's labor power. Harry Braverman writes: "The means he employs may vary from the enforcement upon the worker of the longest possible working day in the early period of capitalism to the use of the most productive instruments of labor and the greatest intensity of labor, but they are always aimed at realizing from the potential inherent in labor power the greatest useful effect of labor, for it is this that will yield for him the greatest surplus and thus the greatest profit."[2] With work dominated by new relations of production, with workers being forced to sell their labor power to another, the human quality of work has been surrendered. The labor has become the province of the capitalist: work has become *alienated.*

The worker in capitalist society is alienated in many ways: powerless within the bureaucratic organization of work; work that is meaningless because it is fragmented and impersonal; isolation from other workers; and estrangement from the act of work itself.[3] Karl Marx observed about the worker in capitalist production, "The *alienation* of the worker in his product means not only that his labor becomes an object, assumes an *external* existence, but that it exists independently, *outside himself,* and alien to him, and that it stands opposed to him as an autonomous power. The life which he has given to the object sets itself against him as an alien and hostile force."[4] The activity of the worker, therefore, is for the benefit and profit of the capitalist ruling class, not to satisfy the worker's social and psychological needs. Alienation of workers from ownership and control of production means that little satisfaction can be obtained from work itself: work is only to earn wages. "Thus in capitalist society production is carried on in an atmosphere of hostility or indifference, by a mass of workers who have lost all stake or concern for the process."[5]

Worker alienation sometimes impels the worker to commit crimes against the system. In the factory, property may be removed. Such "pilfering," however, is very selective, indicating moral compunction even in crimes against the alienating bureaucracy.[6] To take property from the company is to gain at least some control over the product of one's work.

Crimes against the work situation reflect a struggle, conscious, or not, against exploitation of the worker's life and activity. Workers often engage in specific political actions against their employers:

> On the assembly lines of the American automobile industry, this revolt extends as far as clandestine acts of sabotage against a product (the automobile body) which appears to the worker as the detestable materialization of the social uselessness and individual absurdity of his toil. Along the same lines is the less extreme and more complex example of miners fighting with admirable perseverance against the closing of the mines where they are exploited under inferior human and economic conditions — but who, individually, have no difficulty in recognizing that even if the coal they produced were not so bad and so expensive, their job, under the prevailing conditions, would still be abominable.[7]

These defensive actions by workers are likely to become even more politically motivated and organized in the future. For a contradiction is built into the capitalist economy: increased economic growth necessitates the kind of labor that further alienates workers from their needs. Further economic expansion can bring only increased crimes of survival. A worker struggle revolves around the contradiction of capitalist growth and alienation in the work place.

OCCUPATIONAL AND PROFESSIONAL CRIME

Most economic crime consists of both exploiting others and surviving within the system. People in many occupations and professions survive and profit in their work by taking part, in small ways or massively, in criminal activities, some of them harming those who receive their services. The small businessman who shortchanges the customer is committing an illegal and harmful act against the public. The failing lawyer who arranges to fix a case engages in a criminal act in attempting to survive in the profession.

Crimes in occupations and professions must be understood as part of the economic system's structure and culture. The norms and values that prevail in the pursuit of economic gain also regulate the activity by members of occupations and professions. Many activities defined as criminal, some of them just recently made criminal, follow closely the dominant patterns of legitimate behavior. A popular ideology supports such crimes as embezzlement:

> "Honesty is the best policy, but business is business"; "It is all right to steal a loaf of bread when you are starving"; "All people steal when they get in a tight spot." Once these verbalizations have been assimilated and internalized

by individuals, they take a form such as: "I'm only going to use the money temporarily, so I am borrowing, not stealing," or "I have tried to live an honest life but I've had nothing but troubles, so to hell with it."[8]

A symbiotic relationship or close association connects occupational crime and the organization of capitalist society. We know because of the discovery that doctors are committing offenses regularly, using the medical insurance system.[9] Not only are they obtaining money excessively and illegally for services supposedly rendered, but they are violating income-tax laws in doing it. A Treasury official told Congress that more than one doctor of every three who receives substantial income by treating patients under the Medicare and Medicaid programs is cheating on his or her income tax. Figures on this tax evasion came out in an investigation of tax returns filed by 11,000 doctors who received $25,000 or more in Medicare and Medicaid payments in 1968. Because about 65 percent of the income received by doctors in the United States (estimated as $11.6 billion in 1968) comes from health plans, the violations amount to a sizable sum. Needless to say, without the health plans doctors would have to find money elsewhere if they wanted to maintain their large incomes. The American Medical Association continues to lobby for such plans, rather than support an extensive medical program that would assure everyone of care, though it would possibly reduce the doctors' yearly income.

The relationship of occupational crime to the economic structure is found in most other occupational and professional activities as well. The automobile industry, a key part of the American economy, is a classic example. Criminal conduct in selling and servicing automobiles is built into the market structure of the automobile manufacturing industry. Much of the auto dealer's fraudulent behavior is forced on him by the manufacturer. This is the relationship that sets up the possibility of criminal behavior:

> While only four domestic manufacturers of cars remain, their products are distributed through 30,000 dealers with facilities scattered throughout the United States. Technically, the dealer is an independent businessman. Rarely, however, does he have the capital to acquire more than a fraction of the value of property involved in the dealership. The rest is supplied by the manufacturer, and although the dealer may increase his ownership, may keep him dependent on the manufacturer for a long time. Further, he operates under a restrictive agreement, terms of which are set by the manufacturer.[10]

Auto dealers must meet minimum sales responsibilities, a requirement that often leads to fraudulent warranties. They also engage in unscrupulous sales tactics and other behaviors of questionable legality, including high finance charges, parts pushing, service gouging, forcing accessories, and phony repairs. These behaviors are closely allied to the dominant patterns of doing business in the United States, to a "criminogenic market structure." A limited number of manufacturers who sit at the pinnacle of an economically concentrated industry establish a policy that creates a market structure causing dependent industry participants at lower levels to engage in illegal activity. "Thus, criminal activity, in this instance, is a direct consequence of legally established market structure."[11]

Offenders in occupations and professions usually regard themselves as respectable citizens, not as criminals. Because the offender is in a legitimate occupation, it is difficult to conceive that any activity in that occupation could be a crime. In fact, a noncriminal self-conception is one essential element in this form of crime. Those who violate financial trust, such as embezzlers, are able to engage in such behavior only when they can describe their own conduct in a way that allows them to adjust their opinion of themselves as trusted persons with their concepts of themselves as users of entrusted funds or property.[12] These violators thus define their situations by rationalizations enabling them to regard their violations as essentially noncriminal. They think of their behavior as merely "borrowing," justified by unusual circumstances or a nonsharable problem that can be resolved by violating their position of trust.

Likewise, the life of the occupational or professional offender is not organized around a criminal role. That person has many roles, the most prominent being that of respected citizen. The reputations of occupational offenders have been observed in several studies. In an examination of the most flagrant World War II price and rationing violations in which criminal prosecution was instituted, fewer than one violator in ten had a criminal record.[13] The person pursuing an occupation or profession, although at times violating the criminal law, is in a legitimate occupation that is not usually subjected to criminal investigation.[14] In career and life style, the occupational offender can hardly be distinguished from the nonoffender.

More and more of the crime in legitimate occupations and professions is being documented. In recent years, several crimes like these have been publicized: illegal operation and financing of nursing homes for the aged; murder of hospital patients by doctors and nurses; Congressmen using public funds for vacation travel and to employ women for sexual exploitation; and exchanging by judges and lawyers of political favors for business deals.[15] These are only the most notorious and best-publicized cases. That which is done in the name of business and gainful employment is usually beyond the reach of the law. Yet these crimes cost much more in social harms than the conventional crimes that receive most of the everyday publicity.

Since Edwin H. Sutherland introduced the idea of white-collar crime, most studies of occupational crime have documented the behavior of occupational offenders in their group associations.[16] Occupational crimes have been explained according to the principle of differential association: criminal behavior is learned from others who define the behavior favorably and in isolation from those who do not. In some occupations members may even learn specific techniques by which the law can be violated, and build up such rationalizations as "business is business," or "good business demands it." This diffusion of illegal practices is spread from someone already in the occupation to new people, and from one business establishment, political machine, or white-collar group to another. The majority of black-market violations in the United States by businessmen appear to begin in behavior learned in association with others.[17] Unethical and illegal practices are circulated in the trade as part of a shared view of the situation, and rationalizations to support these violations of law are transmitted by this differential association. Types of violations are picked up in conversations with businessmen and from descriptions in trade journals and the press.

Each occupation or profession has its own group norms about the possibility of illegal behavior. Moreover, occupational crimes are related to the structure of the occupation in which the offender is engaged and to the offender's roles in the occupation. The importance of the occupation's structure and the offender's role has been shown in a study of violations by retail pharmacists in filling prescriptions.[18] Because retail pharmacy consists of divergent occupational roles, professional and business, pharmacists experience the problem of adapting to one of several "occupational role organizations," which produce different tendencies toward filling of prescriptions. Pharmacists with such an organization that includes an orientation to the professional role are bound by a system of occupational control that includes guides for compounding and dispensing prescriptions. Pharmacists who lack the professional orientation to pharmacy are not bound by the occupational controls. The business-oriented pharmacists are interested in the general goal of business, monetary gain. They subscribe to the popular belief in business that self-employment gives independence and freedom from control. The professional norms, as incorporated in the prescription laws, give litte control over the occupational behavior of pharmacists who prefer the business role. Other occupations and professions have their own norms and structures for violating criminal law.

To engage in business or professional life in the United States is to follow the basic patterns of capitalist society. An economy of competition and success, as well as economic gain, promotes a form of life emphasizing the rightness of any activity pursued in the interest of one's business or occupation. Consequently, "respectable" members of society engage in criminal activities, crimes usually not traditionally considered by them or most of the public as criminal. Public consciousness, however, is now beginning to recognize and understand these crimes.

CORPORATE CRIME

The problem that is crime finds its ultimate expression and source in the country's corporate economy. Even under criminal law, much of it enacted just recently, the corporation and its officials are liable for a whole range of harms committed against people. We recognize today that some parts of our lives and our environment are being victimized by corporations. Both public reaction and criminal law are defining many corporate activities as criminal.

Crimes by corporations reflect the underlying political economy. In modern times, in the United States, "economic power is concentrated in the hands of a relatively few supercorporations that are now moving toward dominance in the world economy to match their position in the domestic economy."[19] Not only is the economy determined by corporate power, but the state itself increasingly serves the corporate economy. Crimes of exploitation inevitably flow from this system of domination and expansion. The relation of the corporate economy to this exploitation is vividly described:

> Our nation is being poisoned with the ultimate threat of extinction by pollution and destruction of our environment, the main factor in which is the plunder of our natural resources. Everybody appears agreed on this. There is a widespread tendency to blame this dangerous situation on science and technology. But the real source of the problem must be sought elsewhere. It lies in the very nature of the social system under which we are forced to live.
>
> The main impulse of our social system is the quest for profit. The result is unplanned, anarchic production, which allows the pollution and indiscriminate plunder of our natural resources. The ones responsible are the monopolies, the corporations, who have made enormous profits while they pollute and destroy our environment. It is estimated that hundreds of billions of dollars will be needed just to remedy the pollution and destruction wrought by the monopolies and their predecessors.
>
> The major victims are the working people, who suffer from the effects of pollution every minute of their lives.[20]

We have taken our existence for granted. The dominant ideology is a firm belief that economic growth and technological application are the surest way to progress. The crimes resulting from this ideology and prac-

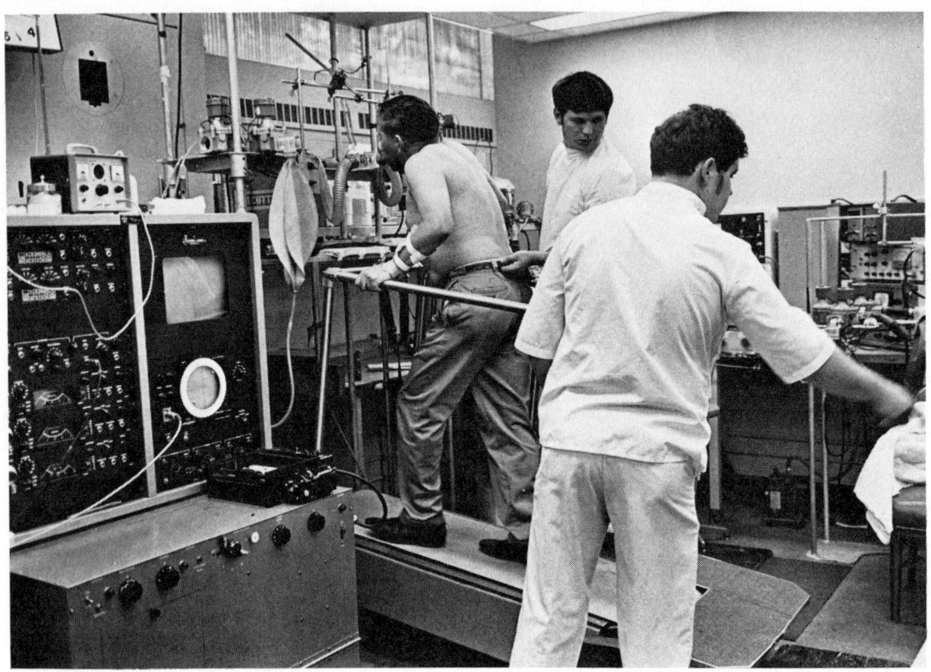

In a regional clinic in Appalachia, a miner undergoes blood, heart, and breathing tests for the detection of pneumoconiosis — the occupational disease caused by inhalation of coal and dust particles. Those who live with the disease, developed by years of working under dangerous and criminal conditions, call it "black lung."

tice are many, including pollution of air, water, and land, adulteration and poisoning of food, and frauds against the consumer. Another of these crimes is the high accident rate and hazardous conditions in factories and mines:

> This mass murder, because it takes place within the industrial processes, has always been acceptable to capitalist society as necessary and normal. Workers' lives have always been expendable for the corporations. Sixty die from industrial accidents every day. Thousands are maimed and crippled. This industry cannot deny. In spite of the overwhelming evidence to the contrary, the coal companies still try to deny that the black lung disease, from which hundreds of thousands of coal miners have died, is related to the unhealthy conditions in their coal mines. Corporations in other industries are no different. On the scale of profits, human lives are worthless.[21]

About 100,000 workers die each year in the United States from exposure to health hazards on the job, and many others become seriously ill. These occupation-spawned diseases include lung ailments, such as miner's black lung and brown lung among textile workers, cancer, heart disease, damage to the nervous system, and countless poorly known illnesses.[22] They can be caused by perhaps only a few years or as much as a lifetime of exposure to the thousands of industrial chemicals, radiation, excessive noise, vibration, and a generally stressful work environment. The corporations that perpetrate these criminal acts against the worker are among the most important and respected in the country, including the Anaconda Aluminum Company, Union Carbide, Mobil Oil, Chrysler, Ford Motor, Bethlehem Steel, and Minnesota Mining — these are just a few of the largest offenders.[23]

The death toll and disease from working in these corporations is in fact preventable. "The technology exists which could reduce the exposure to all hazardous substances to safe levels or to eliminate them entirely."[24] It is cheaper for corporations not to take these measures, however. The ultimate reason for the deaths and the diseases is the drive of corporations to extract as much profit as possible from the workers. Public attention is slowly focusing on the operation of corporations as workers combat the crimes that are being committed against them.

The relationship between corporate crime and the economy is obvious in still other ways, such as the fraudulent methods corporations use to promote their products to the consumer. Corporate advertising is one of the most sophisticated forms of fraud, an integral part of the production and distribution system. Moreover, "any sensitive observer of the American scene recognizes that modern mass advertising at its heart represents a kind of institutionalization of deception and misrepresentation. Indeed many perceptive social critics insist it is nothing less than an enormous swindle — albeit a somewhat genteel one."[25] The prevalence of these violations is indicated in the report that a third of the nation's manufacturers of prescription drugs are violating federal laws prohibiting false and misleading advertising.[26] The drug companies spend approximately $2.4 billion producing drugs and between $600 and $800 million on advertising and promotion. Among the violations are the extending or distorting of claims for usefulness beyond that approved in the product's final printed labeling; quotes from studies used to imply improperly that the study represents a much larger and general experience with the drug; data from papers that report no side effects, ignoring contrary evidence from much better research; and ads constructed from data once valid but rendered obsolete or false by more recent research. Not only is the promotion criminal, but the public's health and safety are endangered. Many American products, as prescribed in the advertisements, cause thousands of injuries and deaths to consumers each year.[27]

Hardly a day passes without some fresh exposure of corporate bribery, abuse of funds, tax manipulations, and the like. Bribery of both government officials and potential customers by corporations has become a standard part of the operating cost of almost every large corporation.[28] It revealed that the Allied Chemical Corporation, which does well over $2 billion in business a year, paid out $335,750 over four years to the purchasing agent of just one of its domestic customers to guarantee its favored position. Another major scandal involves the multi-billion-dollar beer industry, which the Securities and Exchange Commission began investigating for payoffs to purchasing agents by some of the country's largest beer producers. And it was discovered that the Lockheed Corporation has been paying millions to business officials in other countries to receive purchasing contracts. It is evident that these scandals are not mere mischances in an otherwise well-ordered economy, but a widely used form of business in the operation of monopoly capitalism. "One of the inevitable consequences of this kind of bribery is an acceleration in the tendency towards monopoly as larger companies drive their competitors out of business by making use of their enormous resources."[29]

Strong legal actions are not usually taken against these corporations or their officers. When they are initiated, it is usually by administrative agencies, and they are not a significant problem for the corporation. For often, even after long litigation, the only penalty is a modest fine against the corporation or an insignificant sentence for an official. But companies are usually given advance notice of their violations; they may be asked simply to modify their advertising claims, or to alter or withdraw their product. Court action may be only a last resort. Only fundamental change in the political economy will make possible a solution to corporate crime.

When corporations and their officials violate the criminal law they have appropriate rationalizations for their conduct. They are able to maintain a noncriminal self-conception, as in this testimony by a Westinghouse executive in an antitrust case brought against the heavy electrical equipment industry:

> *Committee Attorney:* Did you know that these meetings with competitors were illegal?
>
> *Witness:* Illegal? Yes, but not criminal. I didn't find that out until I read the indictment. . . . I assumed that criminal action meant damaging someone, and we did not do that. . . . I thought that we were more or less working on a survival basis in order to try to make enough to keep our plant and our employees.[30]

An official of the Ingersoll-Rand Corporation said, "It is against the law." But he added, "I do not know that it is against public welfare because I am not certain that the consumer was actually injured by this operation."

Considering testimony by corporate offenders in the electrical-equipment cases, Gilbert Geis offers an explanation that says much about the offenders' rational character and their decision to violate the law:

> For the conspirators there had necessarily to be a conjunction of factors before they could participate in the violations. First, of course, they had to perceive that there would be gains accruing from their behavior. Such gains might be personal and professional, in terms of corporate advancement toward prestige and power, and they might be vocational, in terms of a more expedient and secure method of carrying out assigned tasks. The offenders also apparently had to be able to neutralize or rationalize their behavior in a manner in keeping with their image of themselves as law-abiding, decent, and respectable persons. The ebb and flow of the price-fixing conspiracy also clearly indicates the relationship, often overlooked in explanations of criminal behavior, between extrinsic conditions and illegal acts. When the market behaved in a manner the executives thought satisfactory, or when enforcement agencies seemed particularly threatening, the conspiracy desisted. When market conditions deteriorated, while corporate pressures for achieving attractive profit-and-loss statements remained constant, and enforcement activity abated, the price-fixing agreements flourished.[31]

Corporate crimes are now being recognized, and the character of the corporation itself as an offender is being understood. The nation's leading corporations are committing destructive criminal acts systematically and repeatedly; not randomly and occasionally, but as a standard operating procedure. To ensure profits at minimal expense, these corporations are wilfully engaging in crime. As legal entities, they, and some of the corporate officials who make decisions, are criminal.

Crime by corporations receives support from similar and even competing individuals and businesses. Law-breaking becomes a normative pattern in some corporations, and norms for violation are shared among corporations and their executives. Corporate officials learn the values, motives, rationalizations, and techniques favorable to specific kinds of crime. Many businessmen may even, for a large part of their day, be isolated from law-abiding definitions of business conduct. Further, businessmen are often shielded from criticism, and may find some support for their activities in the mass media. Then too, business executives associate chiefly with other businessmen, both at work and in their social activities, so that all implications of corporate crime are removed from their own scrutiny.

Corporate crime requires that the participants organize. They may have a comparatively simple reciprocal relationship in a business transaction or go in for more complex illegal activities among several large corporations. The latter may include not just one other corporation, but many corporations and subsidiaries. The illegal activity may be quite informally organized, as in false advertising; it may be simply organized though deliberate, as in black-market activities; or it may be complex and involved, as in antitrust violations.

How extensive group involvement and rational planning are in corporate crime is indicated in the antitrust crimes of the electrical-equipment corporations:

> The offenders hid behind a camouflage of fictitious names and conspiratorial codes. The attendance roster for the meetings was known as the "Christmas card list" and the gatherings, interestingly enough, as "choir practice." The offenders used public telephones for much of their communication, and they met either at trade association conventions, where their relationship would appear reasonable, or at sites selected for their anonymity. It is quite noteworthy, in this respect, that while some of the men filed false travel claims, so as to mislead their superiors regarding the city they had visited, they never asked for expense money to places more distant than those they had actually gone to — on the theory, apparently, that whatever else was occurring, it would not do to cheat the company.[32]

The corporate officials would even draw lots to determine who would submit the pricing bids. Promotions within the corporation depended on the officials' willingness to go along with these schemes. Price-fixing, in other words, has become an established way of corporate life.

Operations in the food industry, finally, dramatically illustrate how much corporate support goes to criminal practices.[33] This is the largest retail industry in the country; the corporations in it are moving toward monopoly of some products. Ninety-five per cent of the breakfast food is produced by four firms (Kellogg, General Foods, General Mills, Quaker Oats). Other large corporations got into the food conglomerates: the Greyhound Corporation took over Armour Foods, International Telephone and Telegraph absorbed Continental Bakery, and so forth. The food business is, of course, a giant industry whose goal is making a profit rather than promoting the consumer's health. And the governmental agency, the Food and Drug Administration, is defender of the industry's interests, more than advocate for the public.

The food industry then is relatively free to engage in wholesale deception, misrepresentation in advertising, misbranding, and sale of dangerous foods. Hazardous chemicals can be added to foods despite inadequate research on their effects. Food preservatives and additives are used to increase the industry's profits, harming the consumer's health.

Crimes by corporations are crimes against the people. Enormous social harms are committed by the economy of monopoly capitalism. Yet as capitalism continues to develop, corporations must accumulate more capital and expand, raising profits by whatever means in order to survive. A consequence is increasing use of criminal operations — against the population, as well as against other corporations, the government, and the society.[34] The capitalist economy becomes criminal in itself.

ORGANIZED CRIME

The economy in capitalist society not only creates and perpetuates criminal activity in business and corporate enterprise, but fosters a kind of crime organized explicitly for economic gain by criminal activities. More concretely, "Organized crime is a continuing conspiracy to gain money and power without regard for law by utilizing economic and physical force, public and private corruption, in an extension of the free-enterprise system."[35] Organized crime is an illegal business enterprise.

The principal feature that differentiates organized crime from other crimes of business is the degree to which the objective to profit from crime is itself rationalized.[36] Organized crime's objective is to serve the interests of the thousands who have organized themselves into criminal enterprises. Criminal organizations, with their divisions of labor, their permanence, and their ability to escape the law, are businesses that make crime profitable in the economy.

Organized crime in the United States is a phenomenon of the twentieth century. During the frontier period, outlawed activities were carried out on a modest scale by roving criminal groups. In the cities, groups gained control of illegal activities in their localities, such as gambling, prostitution, distribution of beer and liquor, and rackets. After the turn of the century, organized crime expanded into more activities and larger geographical areas. It often provided a way of channeling disadvantaged minorities into remunerated but illegal enterprises.[37]

One event brought about the greatest change in organized crime: prohibition, forbidding by law the sale and distribution of alcoholic beverages. Because of the Eighteenth Amendment, adopted in 1920, and the supporting Volstead Act, organized crime was able to provide the illegal services and commodities demanded by millions of citizens. Conflict and widespread violence among organized adult gangs were inevitable as rival groups competed to serve the public. The strongest gangs finally won dominance. These organized groups, because of the large sums of money they amassed and the elaborate organization they achieved, continued in illegal activity after the amendment was repealed.

The modern era of organized crime is represented by the crime syndicate. Organized crime has expanded so much that leaders coordinate illegal activities across state and regional boundaries. Now organized crime has expanded into many legitimate businesses and occupations. Contrary to popular belief, the national crime syndicate is not limited to Italians in the Mafia.[38] The national crime syndicate, as organized in 1934, is still today a "combination," the Mafia being a minor part of the syndicate. The leader and genius behind the syndicate, in fact, is Meyer Lansky, a man of Jewish background who has been a leader in organized crime since the 1930s. The history of the syndicate combines efforts by Irish, German, Jewish, and, more recently, Cuban exiles. The syndicate today controls the drug market and gambling, but is expanding into an international organization of crime.[39]

The character of the political economy does not stop organized crime from continuing expansion. Organized crime, like legitimate business, works for maximum returns with minimum expenditure by efficient organization and skilled management. The difference is that legitimate business operates within the law some of the time and organized crime operates outside the law most of the time. Organized crime seems more significantly affected by economic facts of supply and demand, and the fads in consumer habits, than by legislation and sporadic attempts at formal control.

Organized crime receives a great deal of toleration in the United States because of its close relationship to legitimate business. A criminologist concluded:

> Organized crime must be thought of as a natural growth, or as a developmental adjunct to our general system of private profit economy. Business, industry, and finance all are competitive enterprises within the area of legal operations. But there is also an area of genuine economic demand for things and services not permitted under our legal and social codes. Organized crime is the system of business functioning in the area. It, too, is competitive, and hence must organize for its self-protection and for control of the market.[40]

Organized crime provides illegal services and products to business, government, and public. It continues without undergoing a great deal of legal action because of its relationship to the political economy.

Control of Criminal and Legitimate Business

Organized crime has traditionally made illicit behavior its business, such as gambling, prostitution, loan sharking, extortion and racketeering, and narcotics, but gambling has been the largest source of revenue. It includes lotteries, off-track horse-betting, numbers games, dice games, and illegal casinos. Few organized gambling operations in large cities are separate from such operations. Bets may be a quarter or a very large sum and the profits for organized crime are enormous, up to hundreds of millions of dollars. Gambling operations are very complex.

> Most large-city gambling is established or controlled by organized crime members through elaborate hierarchies. Money is filtered from the small operator who takes the customer's bet, through persons who pick up money and slips, to second-echelon figures in charge of particular districts, and then into one of several main offices. The profits that eventually accrue to organization leaders move through channels so complex that even persons who work in the betting operation do not know or cannot prove the identity of the leader. Increasing use of the telephone for lottery and sports betting has facilitated systems in which the bookmaker may not know the identity of the second-echelon person to whom he calls in the day's bets. Organization not only creates greater efficiency and enlarges markets, it also provides a systematized method of corrupting the law enforcement process by centralizing procedures for the payment of graft.[41]

Loan sharking, lending money at rates higher than the legally prescribed limit, is another major source of profit. Much of the money for lending comes from gambling operations. Loans are made to small businessmen whose channels of credit are closed, gamblers, narcotics users, politicians, and others who need money to cover their expenses or debts.

Narcotics sales are organized like a legitimate importing-retailing business, distributing drugs through several levels to the street peddler. Because of severe penalties, organized crime is less involved in retail business, leaving that to individual pushers.

> The large amounts of cash and the international connections necessary for large, long-term heroin supplies can be provided only by organized crime. Conservative estimates of the number of addicts in the nation and the average daily expenditure for heroin indicate that the gross heroin trade is $350 million annually, of which $21 million are probably profits to the importer and distributor. Most of this profit goes to organized crime groups in those few cities in which almost all heroin consumption occurs.[42]

Organized crime groups extend their control to many other kinds of products and services. The wholesaling of perishable products, such as fruit, vegetables, and fish, is often held by racketeers. Racketeering, the systematic extorting of money from individuals or organizations, is prevalent in laundry businesses, cleaning establishments, trucking, loading businesses, and among such workers as motion-picture operators, bartenders, waiters, truck drivers, and retail clerks. These organizations are especially vulnerable to the rackets. One of the simplest forms of this type of racketeering is the protection racket: individuals or organizations are "protected," by paying fees regularly, for the privilege of operating without being injured, damaged, or destroyed by the organized criminals. This kind of operation is not exclusive of other forms of racketeering, but may be used as one means of controlling services and commodities.

Racketeering has operated successfully in controlling some groups of organized labor. It uses schemes such as infiltrating labor unions, extorting money from employees for union cooperation, and cheating the members of the union by not paying them union wages or misusing union welfare and pension funds. Workers may be forced to pay high fees and dues to find and hold jobs. Union leadership may be taken over by organized criminals. A large part of union operating funds may go to organized crime. Furthermore, money may be extorted from employers; strikes are often threatened as a way of controlling them. The building trades are particularly vulnerable to racketeering because they need to purchase materials at crucial times and to complete projects by scheduled dates.

To its control of criminal activities, organized crime has added infiltration into legitimate businesses by illegal means and by large investments. Organized crime has at times, of course, used legitimate business as a front for other criminal activities. More recently, however, it has found a major source of income in legitimate business. Organized crime has a vested monopoly in some legitimate enterprises, such as cigarette-vending machines and jukeboxes. Criminals own many enterprises, such as real estate brokerages, retail firms, restaurants and bars, hotels, automobile agencies, trucking companies, food companies, linen-supply outlets, garbage-collection routes, and other such services. The Kefauver Committee found that organized crime had infiltrated about fifty types of legitimate business, including advertising, the amusement industry, the automobile industry, banking, insurance, jukebox distribution, the liquor industry, loan businesses, the oil industry, radio stations, real estate, and scrap surplus sales.[43]

Organized crime invests some of its profits from illegal services in legitimate businesses, giving it a legitimate source of profits and also helping to avoid prosecution. The organizational arrangement involves full-time business consultants, accountants, and attorneys. Control of businesses is secured by (1) investing concealed profits acquired from gambling and other illegal activities, (2) accepting business interests as payments for the owner's gambling debts, (3) foreclosing on usurious loans, and (4) using forms of extortion. A favorite operation is placing a business it has acquired into fraudulent bankruptcy after taking its assets.[44]

Structure of Organized Crime

Like any other large business enterprise, organized crime requires a structure of positions with a hierarchy of command. Atop the pyramid are powerful leaders, the "lords," who make the important decisions and run the organization. They maintain a master-serf relationship over others in the feudal structure. A middle echelon of gangsters, henchmen, and lieutenants carry out the leaders' demands. At the bottom of the structure are those marginally associated with organized crime — narcotics peddlers, prostitutes, bookies, runners — who deal directly with the public. The structure is held together by a chain of command, personal loyalties, a moral code, alliances with rival groups, and hostility toward conventional society.

The hierarchic structure of organized crime makes generalizing about its members' careers difficult. Some have specialized training, as in law and accounting, and are directly recruited. Others are given university training as young men, with the idea that they will join the syndicate. "Cosa Nostra members occupying the higher echelons of organized crime are orienting their sons to the value of education, if only as a part of the general move toward respectability . . . they are sending their sons to college to learn business skills, on the assumption that these sons will soon be eligible for 'family' membership."[45] Many organized criminals have careers like those of conventional offenders, associating with young gang members and having a long series of delinquencies and crimes. Instead of ending their careers in their early twenties, however, they continue their criminal activities in association with organized criminals.

Organized crime may thus provide a person with the opportunity for a lifetime career in crime. Selecting a career in organized crime, instead of other criminal careers, apparently depends on social conditions where the person lives.[46] Little is known, however, about the criminal's specific mobility from one position to another once he is a part of the hierarchy of organized crime. Career histories are not usually available because of the secrecy in the work. There are indications, however, that as organized crime has moved from the bootlegging and prostitution rackets of the twenties and thirties into gambling, usury, and control of legitimate businesses, the need for expertise in management operations grows and security and secrecy are needed less because the new operations are more in the open. Organized crime syndicates, therefore, are growing looser, more flexible, and more creative, rewarding those in the organization who display the ability to make profits.

Progression into organized crime increasingly isolates the offender from conventional society. Despite variations according to the person's location in the hierarchy, most organized offenders are committed to the world of crime. Most of their activities continually violate the law. But by self-justification, in part from contempt for the rest of society, they maintain an appropriate self-image. Underworld leaders may, however, choose to live segmented lives, retiring to seclusion and pseudo-respectability.[47] They remain committed, nevertheless, to the world of crime, where they receive their prestige and power, and are provided with a luxurious life.

Throughout their careers those in organized crime associate regularly with other offenders. These associations and the support they give are provided by the very characteristics of organized crime. The crime syndicate, organized to maintain a large-scale business enterprise for coordinating and controlling products and services, ensures the association of persons involved in similar illegal activities.

All organized criminals more or less observe a code of behavior. The code is highly developed and extends into areas such as maintaining internal discipline and power of leadership. It involves "(1) *intense loyalty* to the organization and its governing elite, (2) *honesty* in relationships with members, (3) *secrecy* regarding the organization's structure and activities, and (4) *honorable behavior* which sets members off as morally superior to those outsiders who would govern them."[48] Loyalty, respect, honor, and absolute obedience are expected of all members. Compliance is helped by custom, material rewards, and violence, either by beating or execution. No subordinates should interfere with the leader's interests, they should not inform the police, and, if necessary, they should go to prison to protect those in power in the organization.

> Although the code of organized criminals is purportedly for the protection of "the people," it is administered and enforced for the protection of each boss. Since the boss of a "family" has the most to lose if the organization is weakened through an attack by outsiders, he enthusiastically promotes the notion that an offense against one is an offense against all. Moreover, this same principle protects the boss from his own underlings. The principle gets transformed so that it deals with matters of safety rather than matters of offense — the safety of all depends upon the safety of each. Since each conforming member is guaranteed a livelihood without fear of encroachment by other members or by nonmembers, each member must be "protected." This transformation, of course, authorizes the boss to take extreme measures to insure his own safety by crushing any plot or potential plot against him by his underlings. The principle also encourages informing. Despite the code's admonition to be tight-lipped, one is guilty by association if he does not report that a member has injured him or another member. By promulgating the idea that "We are all equals in matters of defense," the boss makes lower-status workers his "boys," who henceforth are

dependent upon his paternalism. Organized criminals frequently refer to some subordinate, who might be fifty years old, as "the kid." A boss who can establish that he will assist his followers when they have been offended or when they are in need has gained control over these men. They become indebted to him. They are obligated to reciprocate, in the name of "honor" and "loyalty," thus enhancing his privileged position. The saying is, "If you don't respect the boss, no one will respect you."

Those aspects of the code which prohibit appealing to outside authorities for help and justice also serve to concentrate power in the hands of the few and, hence, to enable leaders to exploit followers. The ruler of an organized-crime unit, whether it be an entire Cosa Nostra "family" or a thirty-man lottery enterprise, has three classes of enemies — law-enforcement officers, outsiders who want his profits, and underlings. The code protects him from all of them.[49]

The continued existence of organized crime depends on maintaining permanent immunity from interference by law-enforcement agencies. It is achieved in several ways.[50] First, the leaders of organized crime are not usually arrested and prosecuted, because they stay behind the scenes of operation. Gangland activity therefore cannot be readily traced to its leaders. Second, persons lower in the hierarchy of organized crime, if arrested, are likely to be released by action from their superiors. Such release and avoidance of prosecution and punishment are ensured by the technique popularly known as the "fix." People not directly involved in criminal activity — law-enforcement officials, judges, doctors, businessmen, and others — may at times provide services needed to protect organized criminals.

A third way of acquiring immunity is buying political power with contributions to political organizations. Elected officials may owe their election to organized criminals. Regular payoffs to officials provide protection for organized crime, which may be permanently immune to law enforcement because of political graft and corruption. Fourth, because it provides the public with illicit and desired services, such as prostitution, gambling, and narcotics, public toleration gets it some immunity from arrest and prosecution.

Immunity can also be found in the functioning of the law itself. Laws and enforcement procedures have not been especially successful in coping with organized crime. Its survival and continuance are possible because legal action is kept at a minimum. Lack of effective legislation and weak law enforcement also reflect public toleration of organized crime.

Finally, by infiltrating legitimate business, organized crime is able to evade the law. It often operates behind a legitimate façade obscuring its operation and making its detection difficult. Also, racketeering escapes the law because intimidated businessmen must contend with reprisal if they report it. And organized crime and legitimate business may assist one another, as in regulating prices of commodities or enforcing labor contracts. Interdependence between the underworld of crime and the upperworld of business ensures that both systems will be maintained. Mutual assistance, accompanied by the profit motive, provides ensured immunity.

Organized crime has grown into a huge business in the United States and is an integral part of the political economy. Enormous amounts of illegitimate money are passed annually into socially acceptable endeavors. An elaborate corporate and financial structure is now tied to organized crime. Moreover, organized crime and the business world are intimately related to the state's political organization. In capitalism's late stage of development, organized crime has an important role.

CRIME, BUSINESS, AND THE STATE

Crime as an economic enterprise depends on the symbiotic alliance between politics and business, which in turn enhances all three realms. In fact, in many areas of the United States political economy, the distinctions between criminal and legitimate activity are becoming obsolete. Criminal politics and criminal business, corrupt politicians and political officials serving business, threaten to become an institutional arrangement. Crime is reaching into the highest levels of politics and business; it is becoming nationalized.

Roughly since prohibition, an unseen alliance has gradually developed in the United States, entangling organized crime, politicians, public officials, and agencies of law enforcement and administration of justice. Organized crime has become a part of politics, and politics has infiltrated organized crime. Organized criminals have found it necessary to get into politics to protect their operations from governmental interference. Their liaison with public officials is a passport to immunity from the law, preventing interruptions to their business, which is amassing large economic gains. People in politics discover that involvement in organized crime furnishes lucrative financial rewards. Collaboration with organized crime also gives the political system a way of controlling the country's social and economic organization. The political, economic, and criminal realms are increasingly becoming one.

The known examples illustrating how deeply business and politics are involved in crime are overwhelming. Small cities as well as large ones

In May 1967 James Marcus, New York City Commissioner of Water Supply, Gas, and Electricity, accompanied by Mayor John Lindsay, turned on the water to refill Jerome Park Reservoir. A year later Marcus pleaded guilty to crimes that involved the cooperation of organized crime, business, and city government.

have their own cases of systematic crime. A few documented cases will show this tainted, self-sustaining relationship. In Reading, Pennsylvania, we can see how a syndicate controlled an entire community:

> Operating in conjunction with a local underworld figure, most of the municipal administration from the mayor on down was corrupted. As a result, the biggest illegal still since Prohibition was tied into the city water supply, the biggest red-light district on the East Coast was set up, and biggest dice game east of the Mississippi, within an easy drive of either Philadelphia or New York, was launched. Nothing was done for the city. Industry started leaving; downtown Reading became an eyesore. When murmurs of public discontent grew too loud, mob-controlled "reformers" were promptly whisked on the scene. As the city steadily began to wither, a Justice Department task force noticed that the only sign of civic improvement was new parking meters. The

company involved in the installation of these meters had a history of kicking back to municipal governments to get the business. It was this thread that eventually unraveled the whole mess, but until outside aid arrived, the local citizenry was truly helpless.[51]

A New York City official helped organized crime infiltrate city politics and economics:

The manner in which organized crime may effectively sink its claws into public officials can be seen in the case of James L. Marcus, former Commissioner of Water Supply, Gas and Electricity in New York City and a close advisor and member of Mayor Lindsay's inner circle. Deeply in debt from business investments and Wall Street plunges, Marcus was referred by a business associate to Anthony Corallo, a reputed lieutenant in the Thomas Lucchese Cosa Nostra "family" with a reputation as a labor racketeer and loan shark. Paying interest to Corallo on cash loans said to be at an annual rate of 104 percent, Marcus sank further in debt, and was finally pressured into doing business "favors" to the Cosa Nostra loan shark and his associates. The result was a tangled web of rigged municipal contracts, bribes, and illegal real-estate deals. In 1968, Marcus pleaded guilty to taking a $16,000 kickback in return for awarding an $835,000 city contract to clean a Bronx reservoir and received a fifteen-month sentence for his part in this and several other conspiracies.[52]

Collusion further plagued Newark:

Illustrative of this wide scope of political corruption is perhaps the city of Newark, New Jersey, which in 1969 was rocked by a major scandal involving public officials, law enforcement agents, and organized crime. In the first of two mass indictments, a federal grand jury charged the mayor, Hugh Addonizio, with income-tax evasion and sixty-six counts of extortion involving a share in payoffs totalling $253,000 from a business firm that had contracts with the city. Also included in the indictments were eleven current or former city officials and a reputed prominent member of the Cosa Nostra. Barely a day before this action by the grand jury, a series of gambling raids by some 100 FBI agents (apparently sparked by information derived from wiretaps) in Newark and surrounding suburbs resulted in scores of arrests and led to another mass indictment of fifty-five persons. Almost a dozen of those indicted were reported to be Cosa Nostra members, including Simone Rizzo DeCavalcante, alleged boss of one of the six Cosa Nostra "families" in the New York metropolitan area. (This huge interstate operation, extending as far as Troy, New York, reportedly brought the syndicate $20 million a year.) The indictments of these gambling figures also charged that some of them had "solicited and obtained" tipoffs from Newark city police on any impending gambling raids.[53]

Lasting control over a city by organized crime, with a relationship between local politicians and business, is documented in a study of "Wincanton," pseudonym for an eastern industrial city controlled by a crime syndicate for the last fifty years. The Stern syndicate, operating gambling enterprises in the city, was able "to put cooperative politicians in office, to buy off those who occupied strategic enforcement positions, and to implicate most city officials in various forms of corruption so completely that they would be unable to turn upon him."[54] City officials have added to their syndicate payoffs by demanding bribes from individuals and companies doing business with the city. Many city, state, and federal laws were violated, and the law-enforcement apparatus was under illegal control. Only those not involved in the established politics and business of the community, namely, the majority of the citizens, were excluded from this arrangement. The city had a local ruling class, deeply involved in and dependent on crime.

Similar associations between city officials, members of organized crime, and business leaders were found in a western city. Investigating corruption there, William Chambliss observed that the arrangement has become institutionalized in the city.

> I have argued, and I think the data demonstrate quite convincingly, that the people who run the organizations which supply the vices in American cities are members of the business, political, and law enforcement communities — not simply members of a criminal society. Furthermore, it is also clear from this study that corruption of political-legal organizations is a critical part of the lifeblood of the crime cabal. The study of organized crime is thus a misnomer; the study should consider corruption, bureaucracy, and power. By relying on governmental agencies for their information on vice and the rackets, social scientists and lawyers have inadvertently contributed to the miscasting of the issue in terms that are descriptively biased and theoretically sterile. Further, they have been diverted from sociologically interesting and important issues raised by the persistence of crime cabals. As a consequence, the real significance of the existence of syndicates has been overlooked; for instead of seeing these social entities as intimately tied to, and in symbiosis with, the legal and political bureaucracies of the state, they have emphasized the criminality of only a portion of those involved. Such a view contributes little to our knowledge of crime and even less to attempts at crime control.[55]

Further evidence indicates how closely crime, business, and politics collaborate. In a recent investigation, which resulted in the murder of the reporter, it was disclosed that fraudulent land deals in Arizona were being perpetrated by a collusion of organized criminals, businessmen, and politicians.[56] Land fraud is a huge business, involving many elements in the society's economic and political organization. Other investigations have revealed the link between organized crime, big businesses, and labor leaders.[57] The murder of former Teamster union head James R. Hoffa by organized crime, in part over control of the International Brotherhood of

Teamsters pension fund, has revealed more of these connections.[58] New revelations are certain to follow.

That the intimacy binding crime, economics, and politics has reached the national level shows dramatically in events of recent years. Resignation by a vice president of the United States was startling evidence of how high the infection has climbed. Vice President Spiro T. Agnew resigned from that office after pleading no contest — the equivalent in law of a guilty plea — to a charge of income-tax evasion, and permitted the court to publish evidence that he had extorted bribes for a decade.[59] From the time he was county executive in suburban Baltimore until he reached the second highest national office, Agnew received cash in kickbacks and payments from engineers who wanted government business.

In return for his bargained plea, Mr. Agnew was assured that the government would drop all other prosecution against him.[60] He was free to proclaim his innocence of any wrongdoing, and the court settled for a sentence of three years of unsupervised probation and a fine of $10,000. Now a convicted felon, he was also (unlike most felons) free to pursue his private life, which undoubtedly would include business as well as pleasure. The state once again remained relatively exempt from a searching examination. The public, however, had one more indication — this time from the top — about the close relationship among crime, economics, and politics.

Moreover, we are finally beginning to realize that government officials are not only involved in criminal activities, usually related to organized crime, but that crime is actually a part of government in the United States. Policies are established by the national government for reasons of crime. Both government and crime, and the business associated with them, are aided by their mutual interdependence. The evidence of recent years reveals the state to be considerably different from the common image of the democratic state.

Investigations are uncovering some of the instances of collusion among organized crime, business, and the national state. One discovered organized crime at work in policies toward revolutionary Cuba.[61] Distressed that Fidel Castro tossed organized crime operations out of Cuba, closing down gambling casinos and brothels, syndicate figures and Cuban right-wing exiles cooperated with the CIA in planning and executing the attempted Bay of Pigs invasion and the subsequent attempts to assassinate Castro. Some of these same people and forces surfaced later in the crimes of Watergate. Similarly, it has been found that the government of Salvador Allende in Chile was weakened by the intelligence and espionage work of one of the largest corporations in the United States and the world, the International Telephone and Telegraph Company.[62] To protect its interest in Latin America, ITT collaborated with the United States government to prevent a socialist government from succeeding in Chile. The United States government, supporting the capitalist system, collaborates with large corporations to maintain the "free" world.

The connection among crime, business, and the state continues to be covered up by the federal government's law-enforcement agencies. The FBI has long tried to perpetuate the idea that organized crime is limited to a few persons of Italian descent and that there is no such thing as a national crime syndicate.[63] To disclose a nationwide criminal conspiracy would require the FBI to investigate and expose gangster friends and supporters deeply involved in business and politics. Likewise the CIA has concealed its part in international covert and criminal operations.

Going beyond the national boundaries, we recognize that this country by its economic and political policies commits crimes against millions in other parts of the world. Because the American political economy depends on continuing expansion, and that expansion is naturally limited within the United States, it is necessary to exploit the people and resources of other countries.[64] Those peoples and countries most subject to imperialism are of the underdeveloped world. In fact, the logic of capitalist expansion involves systematic exploitation of other countries. For the United States to continue its development, other nations must remain underdeveloped, their resources being appropriated by the United States.

We now have a better idea of crime in the United States, committed by the country in cooperation with business and organized crime. From the accumulation of evidence, we know how far crime reaches in the United States: "The gray area between crime and business and politics deepened and widened until in the 1970's it is impossible to say where one ends and the other begins."[65] We need critical understanding of this kind to start looking for the thoughts and actions that will provide an alternative to a future built on the association of crime, business, and the state.

NOTES

1. Karl Marx, *The Grundrisse*, ed. by David McLellan (New York: Harper & Row, 1971), pp. 132–143.

2. Harry Braverman, *Labor and Monopoly Capital: The Degradation of Work in the Twentieth Century* (New York: Monthly Review Press, 1974), p. 56.

3. Robert Blauner, *Alienation and Freedom* (Chicago: University of Chicago Press, 1964), chap. 1.

4. Karl Marx, *Early Writings*, trans. and ed. by T. B. Bottomore (New York: McGraw-Hill, 1963), pp. 122–123.

5. Harry Braverman, "Work and Unemployment," *Monthly Review*, 27 (June 1975), p. 20.

6. Donald N. M. Horning, "Blue-Collar Theft: Conceptions of Property, Attitudes Toward Pilfering, and Work Group Norms in a Modern Industrial Plant," in Erwin O. Smigel and H. Laurence Ross, eds., *Crimes Against Bureaucracy* (New York: Van Nostrand Reinhold, 1970), pp. 46–64.

7. André Gorz, *Strategy for Labor: A Radical Proposal*, trans. Martin A. Nicolaus and Victoria Ortiz (Boston: Beacon Press, 1964), pp. 57–58.

8. Donald R. Cressey, "The Respectable Criminal," *Trans-action*, 3 (March-April, 1965).

9. See *The New York Times*, September 22, 1970, p. 1; Richard D. Lyons, "Fraud and Waste in Medicaid Found in Senate Report," *The New York Times*, August 30, 1976, pp. 1 and 14.

10. William N. Leonard and Marvin Glenn Weber, "Automakers and Dealers: A Study of Criminogenic Market Forces," *Law and Society Review*, 4 (February 1970), p. 411.

11. Harvey A. Farberman, "A Criminogenic Market Structure: The Automobile Industry," *Sociological Quarterly*, 16 (Autumn 1975), p. 456.

12. Donald R. Cressey, *Other People's Money* (New York: Free Press, 1953).

13. Marshall B. Clinard, *The Black Market: A Study of White Collar Crime* (New York: Holt, Rinehart and Winston, 1952), p. 295.

14. Further characteristics of occupational crime are discussed in Harold E. Pepinsky, "From White Collar Crime to Exploitation: Redefinition of a Field," *Journal of Criminal Law and Criminology*, 65 (June 1974), pp. 225–233; and Gerald D. Robin, "White-Collar Crime and Employee Theft," *Crime and Delinquency*, 20 (July 1974), pp. 251–262.

15. Reported in, among other places, John L. Hess, "The Eternal Nursing Home Inquiries," *The New York Times*, May 30, 1976, part IV, p. 6; M. A. Farber," 'Dr. X' Indicted in Jersey in 5 Deaths from Curare," *The New York Times*, May 20, 1976, p. 1; Nicholas M. Horrock, "U.S. Investigating Charges on Hays," *The New York Times*, May 25, 1976, p. 1; Tom Goldstein, "DiFalco, Saypol Accused of Plot to Trade Favors," *The New York Times*, May 14, 1976, p. 1; Tom Goldstein, "Cunningham and a Judge Indicted by Nadjari Jury; 2nd Charge Names Partner," *The New York Times*, May 27, 1976, p. 1.

16. Edwin H. Sutherland, "White-Collar Criminality," *American Sociological Review*, 5 (February 1940), pp. 1–12.

17. Clinard, *The Black Market*. Also see the selections in Gilbert Geis, ed., *White-Collar Criminal: The Offender in Business and the Professions* (New York: Atherton Press, 1968).

18. Richard Quinney, "Occupational Structure and Criminal Behavior: Prescription Violation by Retail Pharmacists," *Social Problems*, 11 (Fall 1963), pp. 179–185.

19. Daniel R. Fusfeld, "The Rise of the Corporate State in America," *Journal of Economic Issues*, 6 (March 1972), p. 1. Also see Paul A. Baran and Paul M. Sweezy, *Monopoly Capitalism: An Essay on the American Economic and Social Order* (New York: Monthly Review Press, 1966); Frank Pearce, "Crime, Corporations and the American Social Order," in Ian Taylor and Laurie Taylor, eds., *Politics and Deviance* (Harmondsworth, Eng.: Penguin Books, 1973), pp. 13–41.

20. Gus Hall, *Ecology: Can We Survive under Capitalism?* (New York: International Publishers, 1972), p. 7.

21. Ibid., p. 34.

22. Joel Swartz, "Silent Killers at Work," *Crime and Social Justice*, 3 (Summer 1975), p. 15.

23. Documentation is found in Rachel Scott, *Muscle and Blood: The Massive, Hidden Agony of Industrial Slaughter in America* (New York: E. P. Dutton, 1974).

24. Swartz, "Silent Killers at Work," p. 20.

25. Edwin M. Schur, *Our Criminal Society: The Social and Legal Sources of Crime in America* (Englewood Cliffs, N.J.: Prentice-Hall, 1969), p. 168.

26. *The New York Times*, May 26, 1966, p. 1.

27. Morton Mintz, "There's No Bloody Place Like Home," *The Progressive*, 34 (September 1970), pp. 22–24.

28. See Irwin Silber, "Corruption Is Not the Exception," *Guardian*, July 7, 1976, p. 21; August 30, 1976, pp. A1 and A2.

29. Ibid.

30. Gilbert Geis, "The Heavy Electrical Equipment Antitrust Cases of 1961," in Marshall B. Clinard and Richard Quinney, *Criminal Behavior Systems: A Typology* (New York: Holt, Rinehart and Winston, 1967), p. 144.

31. Ibid., pp. 150–151.

32. Ibid., p. 143.

33. James S. Turner, *The Chemical Feast* (New York: Grossman Publishers, 1970), pp. 82–106.

34. Further discussion of corporate crime is provided in Marshall B. Clinard and Richard Quinney, *Criminal Behavior Systems: A Typology*, 2nd ed. (New York: Holt, Rinehart and Winston, 1973), pp. 206–223.

35. A definition given by the New York Joint Legislative Committee on Crime, as quoted in Hank Messick and Burt Goldblatt, *The Mobs and the Mafia* (New York: Thomas Y. Crowell, 1972), p. ix. A similar definition is found in Mark H. Haller, "Urban Crime and Criminal Justice: The Chicago Case," *Journal of American History*, 57 (December 1970), p. 623.

36. Donald R. Cressey, *Criminal Organization* (New York: Harper & Row, 1972), pp. 1–17.

37. See Francis A. J. Ianni with Elizabeth Reuss-Ianni, *A Family Business: Kinship and Social Control in Organized Crime* (New York: Russell Sage, 1973). A historian, Mark Haller, points out that various ethnic groups and blacks have participated in organized crime and that it has served as a means of upward mobility for some of the Italian, Irish, Polish, and Jewish immigrants and for some of those of black ancestry. See Mark H. Haller, "Organized Crime in Urban Society: Chicago in the Twentieth Century," *Journal of Social History*, 5 (Winter 1971–1972), pp. 210–234.

38. See Hank Messick, *Lansky* (New York: G. P. Putnam's Sons, 1971); Messick and Goldblatt, *The Mobs and the Mafia*, pp. 181–204. The origin and operation of the Mafia in Sicily are analyzed in Anton Blok, *The Mafia of a Sicilian Village, 1860–1960: A Study of Violent Peasant Entrepreneurs* (New York: Harper & Row, 1974). Also see Robert T. Anderson, "From Mafia to Cosa Nostra," *American Journal of Sociology*, 71 (November 1965), pp. 302–310.

39. Questions about the origin and structure of organized crime are raised and discussed in these sources: Joseph L. Albini, *American Mafia — Genesis of a Legend* (New York: Appleton-Century-Crofts, 1971); John F. Galliher and James A. Cain, "Citation Support for the Mafia Myth in Criminology Textbooks," *The American Sociologist*, 9 (May 1974), pp. 68–74; William Chambliss, "On the Paucity of Original Research on Organized Crime: A Footnote to Galliher and Cain," *The American Sociologist*, 10 (February 1975), pp. 36–39; Dwight C. Smith, Jr., *The Mafia Mystique* (New York: Basic Books, 1975).

40. George B. Vold, *Theoretical Criminology* (New York: Oxford University Press, 1958), p. 240.

41. President's Commission on Law Enforcement and Administration of Justice, *The Challenge of Crime in a Free Society* (Washington, D.C.: U.S. Government Printing Office, 1967), p. 189.

42. Ibid.

43. U.S. Senate Special Committee to Investigate Organized Crime in Interstate Commerce, *Third Interim Report*, 2nd Session, 81st Congress, 1950 (Washington, D.C.: U.S. Government Printing Office, 1950), p. 171. Also see Estes Kefauver, *Crime in America* (New York: Greenwood Press, 1951).

44. Donald R. Cressey, *Theft of the Nation: The Structure and Operations of Organized Crime in America* (New York: Harper & Row, 1969), pp. 99–107.

45. Ibid., pp. 241–242.

46. See Solomon Kobrin, "The Conflict of Values in Delinquency Areas," *American Sociological Review*, 16 (October 1951), pp. 653–661; Irving Spergel, *Racketville, Slumtown, Haulburg: An Exploratory Study of Delinquent Subcultures* (Chicago: University of Chicago Press, 1964).

47. See Virgil W. Peterson, "The Career of a Syndicate Boss," *Crime and Delinquency*, 8 (October 1962), pp. 339–354.

48. Cressey, *Theft of the Nation,* p. 171.
49. Ibid., pp. 186–187.
50. See Clinard and Quinney, *Criminal Behavior System,* pp. 237–238.
51. Peter Maas, *The Valachi Papers* (New York: G. P. Putnam's Sons, 1968), p. 274. Quoted in Stuart L. Hills, *Crime, Power, and Morality: The Criminal-Law Process in the United States* (Scranton, Pa.: Chandler, 1971), p. 121.
52. Hills, *Crime, Power, and Morality,* pp. 121–122.
53. Ibid., p. 123.
54. John A. Gardiner, *The Politics of Corruption: Organized Crime in an American City* (New York: Russell Sage Foundation, 1970), pp. 22–23.
55. William J. Chambliss, "Vice, Corruption, Bureaucracy, and Power," *Wisconsin Law Review,* 1971 (No. 4, 1971), pp. 1172–1173.
56. Robert Lindsey, "Organized Crime Spreads to Fast-Growing Arizona," *The New York Times,* June 14, 1976, p. 34.
57. See the series of investigative articles by Seymour M. Hersh in collaboration with Jeff Gerth, "The Contrasting Lives of Sidney R. Korshak," *The New York Times,* June 27, 1976, p. 1; "Korshak's Power Rooted in Ties to Labor Leaders," *The New York Times,* June 28, 1976, p. 1; "Major Corporations Seek Korshak's Labor Advice," *The New York Times,* June 29, 1976, p. 1; "Korshak Again the Target of a Federal Investigation," *The New York Times,* June 30, 1976, p. 1.
58. Wallace Turner, "Pension Fund of Teamsters Scanned for Clues on Hoffa," *The New York Times,* August 12, 1976, p. 50.
59. See Anthony Ripley, "After the Defiance, Guilt and Resignation," *The New York Times,* October 14, 1973, p. E2.
60. "How Agnew Bartered His Office to Keep from Going to Prison," *The New York Times,* October 23, 1973, p. 1.
61. Hank Messick, *John Edgar Hoover* (New York: David McKay, 1972), pp. 172–176. Also see Nicholas M. Horrock, "Files Fail to Link Mafia to C.I.A. in '61 Castro Plot," *The New York Times,* May 20, 1975, p. 1.
62. North American Congress on Latin America, "Secret Memos from ITT," *Latin America & Empire Report,* 6 (April 1972), pp. 1–23.
63. Messick, *John Edgar Hoover,* pp. 190–191.
64. See Paul Baran, *The Political Economy of Growth* (New York: Monthly Review Press, 1962); Harry Magdoff, *The Age of Imperialism* (New York: Monthly Review Press, 1969); William A. Williams, *The Tragedy of American Diplomacy* (New York: Dell Publishing, 1962).
65. Messick, *John Edgar Hoover,* p. 254.

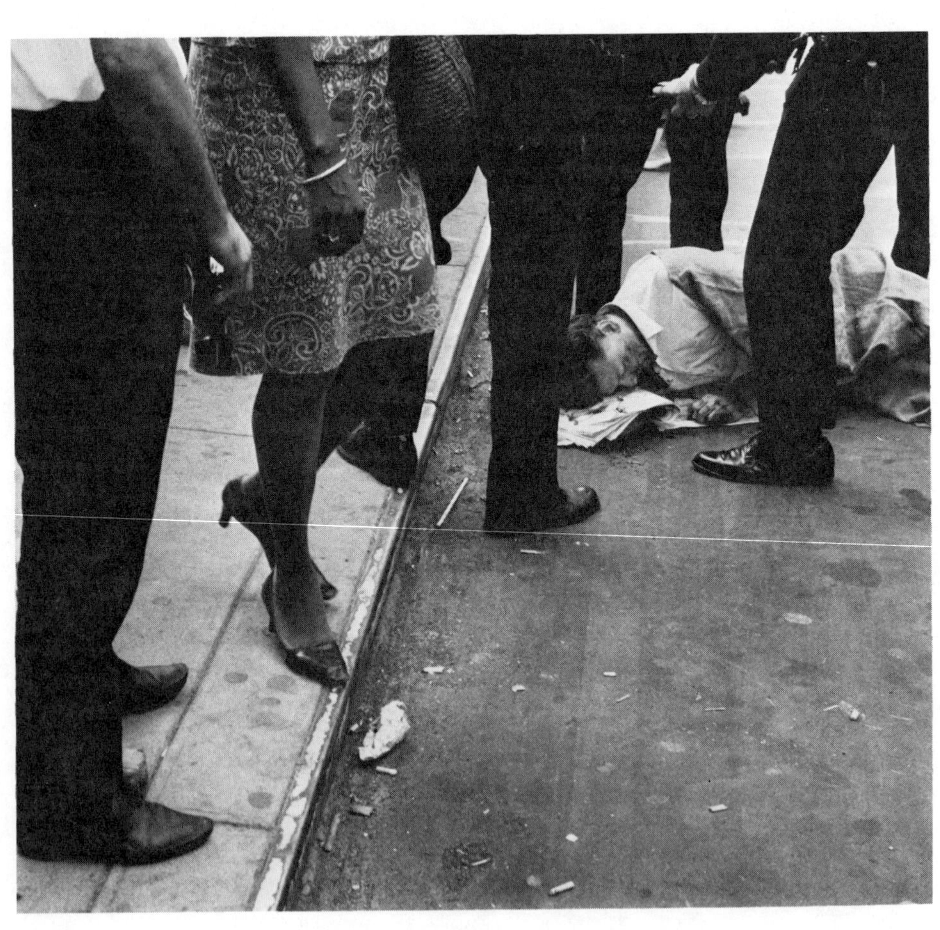

Conventional Crime

7

Accommodation and resistance to the conditions of capitalism are basic to the class struggle. Those who do not own or control the means of production must adapt to the conditions of capitalism. Actions by those who are exploited and oppressed are mostly accommodations or resistance to the conditions produced by the capitalist system of production. Criminality among people who do not own the means of production is action (conscious or otherwise) in the class struggle. Crime, with its many historical variations, is an integral part of class struggle in the development of capitalism.

As we read the limited and brief discussion by Karl Marx and Frederick Engels, criminals outside the capitalist class are usually viewed as among the *lumpenproletariat,*[1] oppressed, unproductive workers lacking class consciousness; they are parasitical in that they do not contribute to the production of goods, and they create a livelihood out of commodities produced by the working class.[2] Most criminal activity in accommodation expresses false consciousness, an apolitical expression, an individualistic reaction to the forces of capitalist production.

Many crimes of accommodation are of this *lumpen* type. Nevertheless, these actions occur within capitalist oppression, stemming from the system of production. Much criminal behavior is parasitical, including burglary, robbery, drug dealing, and hustling of various sorts.[3] These crimes against property, although pursued because of the need to survive, reproduce the capitalist system. The actions are nevertheless antagonistic to the capitalist order. Most police activity is directed against these "conventional" crimes.

Personal crimes are another type, usually directed against members of the same class. These are the conventional criminal acts of murder, assault, and rape. They are pursued by those already personally brutalized by the conditions of capitalism. These actions occur in immediate situations that are themselves the result of more basic accommodations to capitalism. Beyond these lumpen crimes are actions carried out mainly by the working class resisting the capitalist system.

Criminologists have devoted most of their theorectical and research work to the conventional crime. In theories they have sought to explain the behavior of those who commit these crimes. Critically analyzing crime in capitalist society we recognize that conventional crime is but one part of the crime problem. Examining conventional crime now allows us to understand the full extent of crime — and its integral part — in the social and economic structure of the United States.

ECOLOGY OF CONVENTIONAL CRIME

The rates of conventional crime in capitalist society form patterns of geographic or ecological distribution. In general, despite variations from one category of offenses to another, crime rates in the United States are higher in urban areas than in rural areas, higher in larger cities than in smaller cities, and higher in the center of cities than farther from the center.[4] Moreover, the high rates of crime and delinquency are found in areas with substandard and oppressive conditions.

Ecological patterning of crime reflects the larger class struggle in the society's overall political economy. In a class-divided, capitalist society, all aspects of life are affected by the ownership and control of the means of production by the capitalist class. The working class, the poor, and the oppressed minorities are constantly in conflict and struggle with the capitalist class. Included in this basic antagonism is the struggle for living space and for living conditions. Those who own and control the means of production have different access — because of their economic and political power — to property and housing.[5] The conflict and struggle that locate people geographically also produce the geographic distribution of crime rates. Behavior patterns develop in class conflict *and* definitions of criminal behavior are imposed on those who lack power by those who possess power. The ecological variations in crime rates may be examined in the way the class struggle operates in the political economy of capitalist society.

Regional Differences

The amounts and types of crime vary broadly from one region to another. An early student found that some offenses displayed a gradient or slope throughout the country.[6] Murder was concentrated in the southeastern states, going down to the north and west, and robbery was concentrated in the mid-central states, with rates decreasing on either side of a line running through the center of the United States. Essentially the same patterning of offenses was found several years later; some offenses showed more of a regional concentration.[7]

The regional variation in crime rates can be readily observed in the annual reports of offenses known to the police. In the 1976 report, as summarized in Table 7.1, the East South Central region had the lowest crime rate, and the Pacific region had the highest. In the specific offense categories, the East South Central region had the highest murder rate. The Pacific region had the highest rate of forcible rape, aggravated assault, and burglary; the Middle Atlantic region had the highest robbery rate; New England had the highest motor-vehicle theft rate and the Mountain region had the highest larceny rate. On the other hand, New England had the lowest rates in the country for murder and forcible rape; the West North Central region had the lowest rate of aggravated assault; the West North Central region had the lowest rates of robbery and burglary; and the East South Central had the lowest rates of larceny and motor-vehicle theft.

These variations can be explained partly by different cultural behaviors, with relative probabilities of being defined as criminal, according to regions of the country. There are, first, regional variations in normative systems and behavior patterns. In the South a tradition of violence, including prescriptions on the use of weapons, accompanied by a code of personal honor, provides the background for behavior patterns that have a good chance of being defined as criminal.[8] The relationship of whites and blacks in the South leads to conflict both within the two groups and between them. In some regions of the country, the effects of class struggle may at times be more pronounced.

Second, opportunity for some activities varies according to region. The high rate of property offenses in the West is in part a result of the casual style of living, the openness of the region, and the availability of prop-

TABLE 7.1 Index of Crime by Regions, 1976 (Rate per 100,000 population)

Region	*Crime index*	*Murder*	*Forcible rape*	*Robbery*	*Aggravated assault*	*Burglary*	*Larceny*	*Motor-vehicle theft*
New England	5,196.7	3.2	14.8	129.6	164.2	1,468.2	2,538.9	877.8
Middle Atlantic	5,144.9	8.2	22.2	340.1	222.5	1,439.7	2,542.8	569.4
East North Central	5,164.2	8.5	25.0	205.5	191.1	1,236.7	3,050.5	446.9
West North Central	4,335.1	4.6	19.6	103.2	136.3	1,094.0	2,684.5	292.9
South Atlantic	5,171.5	10.9	27.4	164.9	302.5	1,424.3	2,950.7	290.7
East South Central	3,587.9	12.2	20.9	107.1	202.1	1,094.4	1,897.3	253.9
West South Central	4,931.5	11.4	28.1	121.2	202.2	1,383.3	2,869.1	316.4
Mountain	6,322.4	7.1	29.7	115.7	239.9	1,712.5	3,841.1	376.2
Pacific	6,940.4	8.9	42.0	238.0	312.6	2,047.5	3,705.5	585.9

SOURCE: Adapted from Federal Bureau of Investigation, *Uniform Crime Reports,* 1976 (Washington, D.C.: U.S. Government Printing Office, 1977), pp. 38–43.

erty.[9] Opportunities for activities that may be defined as burglary, robbery, larceny, and theft vary from one region to another. Finally, regions differ in expectations of enforcement and administration of criminal law. Behavior patterns vary regionally, therefore, in both the conduct that may be defined as criminal and the behaviors that get the conduct defined as criminal.

Moreover, as recent studies have shown, structural and situational factors are becoming more important in accounting for the regional variations in crime rates. In a study of homicide rates, Colin Loftin and Robert H. Hill have found that such factors as inequality of income and unemployment explain much of the variation in homicide rates between the South and other regions of the country.[10] Other studies show that variation in crime rates between the South and non-South appears to be waning.[11] The socioeconomic features that characterize all regions of the country are growing in importance. As the class struggle increases under advanced capitalism, and our critical analysis indicates it is doing so, the rates of crime become more uniform throughout the country. The regional variations that remain reflect structural variations in the class struggle and the different geographic distributions of the struggle between classes.

Rural and Urban Differences

One of the most consistent findings in the ecology of crime is that crime rates are higher for urban than rural areas and that they increase with size of city. Urban areas have higher rates for all major offenses, except murder. The greatest differences in rates between rural and urban areas are for crimes against property, and the differences are less apparent for crimes against the person. The rates for all categories of offense increase progressively with each category of city size.

Differences in offense rates between rural and urban areas can be accounted for by variation in the cultures and structures of the two areas. Rural areas have traditionally had comparatively few behavioral norms and social processes conducive to behaviors that may be defined as criminal.[12] Gang activity in rural areas has been relatively limited. The possibilities for learning techniques and motivations for committing criminally defined activities are not as readily available in rural as in urban areas. Also, the structural characteristics of urban areas and large cities are conducive to criminal behavior and the legal processing of crime.[13]

On the other hand, opportunities for carrying out such property offenses as robbery, burglary, larceny, and auto theft are much greater in urban than in rural areas, and become even more prevalent in large cities. Urban areas (especially the larger cities) provide the cultural and structural environments for developing behavior patterns that may result in criminally defined activities.

But most important for the variation in crime rates between rural and urban areas and according to the size of city is the uneven distribution of class conflict. Its extent increases with the size of city, exacerbating living conditions. Furthermore, the struggle between classes has not traditionally been focused in the rural parts of the country. The intensifying class struggle in the larger cities increases the rates of urban crime. Capitalist development is most pronounced in the city, and it is in the largest cities of capitalist society that crime is most prevalent.

Variations within Cities

Studies over several decades have documented fairly consistent patterns in crime and delinquency rates in American cities. Research by members of the "Chicago school" established that the highest offense rates generally occur in low-rent areas near the center of the city and that the rates decrease farther out.[14] Such studies have shown too that the relative rates of crime and delinquency are maintained within the city in spite of changes in population.

The distribution of offense rates is related to social characteristics of areas within cities. In several sources we see the conclusion that offense rates of areas are related to (1) socioeconomic conditions, (2) housing and family characteristics, and (3) degree of ethnic and racial segregation. In Baltimore, delinquency rates of census-tract areas were associated with the percentage of owner-occupied housing and the ratio of nonwhites to whites.[15] Similar findings appear in the distribution of offense rates in Washington, D.C., Detroit, and Indianapolis.[16] Using somewhat different analyses and theoretical assumptions, others have found that similar variables are related to the ecology of crime and delinquency in Seattle, San Diego, Lexington (Kentucky), and Houston.[17] Such findings continue to accumulate. The important problem, however, is accounting for the relationships between social characteristics of the areas and their offense rates.

Behavior patterns that may conflict with legal definitions necessarily develop within the city's ecological areas. Initially such behavior among adolescents may be inspired by no more insidious purpose than adventure and recreation. Frederick M. Thrasher found some time ago in his classic studies of gangs in parts of Chicago that children forming play groups engage in activities that may be defined as illegal.[18] In time, conflict with other groups in the neighborhood and contact with other values may bring the members into activities such as stealing from stores, robbery, and aggressive acts against other gangs.[19] Violent gang activity may become a collective response of adolescents in slums to the problems of living in such areas of the city.

Diversity of cultural traditions in ecological areas, and juxtaposition of the traditions, appear to be significant in developing the types and amounts of criminally defined activities. Where adult activity is fairly stable and organized, adolescent behavior usually takes on the same qualities.[20] Where adult patterns are not so integrated, juvenile activities (some of which may be defined as delinquent) are unorganized and more violent.

Extending this formulation, some criminologists have suggested that different types of adolescent "subcultures" appear in relation to the "criminal" and "noncriminal" patterns integrated in the neighborhood.[21] Where adult patterns are integrated, the subcultures of adolescents will be "criminal" and the gangs will engage in theft, extortion, and similar activities to achieve status and income. In unintegrated areas, characterized by transiency and instability, "conflict" patterns develop. Where neither criminal nor noncriminal traditions are available to youths, a "retreatist" solution relying on drug use and sensual experiences will appear. Whatever the merit of such a conceptualization, different behavior patterns develop in the city according to the social and cultural structure of the areas.[22]

All behavior patterns, then, develop within definite geographic areas. The patterns differ not only in content but in the probability that they will be defined as criminal. According to a critical analysis, the forms and amounts of crime in any area are produced by conflict between behavior patterns of the community and the patterns represented by those who own and control the important resources of the society, including the power to formulate and impose the criminal law. The traditional studies of the ecology of crime, as in the "Chicago school," have assumed the community was breaking down and individuals were failing to adjust to urban life.[23] The traditional approach has failed to analyze and criticize the effects — including the rising crime rates — of the class conflict generated by a developing capitalist society. By ignoring the larger movements, mainly the class struggle in the political economy of capitalism, those doing ecological studies have generally failed to understand the meaning of the geographic distribution of crime.

Crime, with its ecological variations, reflects the class struggle that accompanies the development of capitalism. The crime rates indicate the differences in class conflict as located in its geographic context. Because class conflict varies ecologically, rates of crime are distributed differently according to the ecological areas of the city and the nation.

CONVENTIONAL CRIMINAL BEHAVIOR

To understand conventional crime we also need to examine the origin and personal meaning of the behavior that is defined as criminal. Much theory and research in criminology is devoted to studying the behavior of "the criminal." Such studies include: (1) the human construction of meaningful social action, (2) the learning of behavior patterns in association with others, and (3) the personal effect of legal processing on those who are defined as criminal. A critical criminology recognizes that all these occur in the class struggle in capitalist society.

Personal Action and Social Conditions

The social psychology of the conventional criminal is a way of analyzing how people create patterns of action that provide a source of personal identity and a basis for social behavior. In short, personal patterns of action are the essence of a life that is both human and social.

The assumption is that human actions are purposive and meaningful. This humanistic conception suggests that people develop an awareness of self by being members of society, and subsequently engage in personal actions, breaking from the established order.[24] Conformity is very much a matter of choice, and nonconformity may be consciously pursued. It is thus *against* something that the self can appear.[25]

By conceiving of the person as able to reason and choose courses of action, we may see human life as changing and becoming, not merely being.[26] The kind of environment that we develop shapes our ability to be creative. Not only are we shaped by our physical, social, and cultural experiences, but we attempt to select what we are to experience and develop. Situations that people find undesirable may lead to actions and self-conceptions opposed to the established order. It may not be unusual, therefore, to find that actions that result from such patterns are defined by those in power as criminal. A great deal of traditionally defined criminal behavior has been a response by individuals and groups to situations considered inadequate for attaining specific objectives.[27] Calculated violation of the law may be a rational solution to socially structured problems. Protest and resistance against unjust conditions and policies may be most appropriately pursued in activities that violate criminal laws.

The *social-action* frame of reference, the basis for the humanistic conception, is drawn from the work of several writers.[28] Max Weber originally suggested that "Action is social insofar as, by virtue of the subjective meaning attached to it by the acting individual (or individuals), it takes account of the behavior of others and is thereby oriented in its own course."[29] Human behavior is *intentional,* has *meaning* for the actors, is *goal-oriented,* and takes place with an *awareness* of behavior's consequences.

Because people engage in social action, a *social reality* is created: interacting with others, we construct a meaningful world of everyday life.

> It is the world of cultural objects and social institutions into which we are all born, within which we have to find our bearings, and with which we have to come to terms. From the outset, we, the actors on the social scene, experience the world we live in as a world both of nature and of culture, not as a private but as an intersubjective one, that is, as a world common to all of us, either actually given or potentially accessible to everyone; and this involves intercommunication and language.[30]

Social reality consists of both our social meanings and the products of our subjective world. We construct activities and patterns of actions as we attach meaning to everyday existence.[31] Social reality is both a *conceptual reality* and a *phenomenal reality.* Having constructed social reality, we find a world of meanings and events that is real to us as conscious social beings.

Marxian theory, however, allows us to understand the relationship between human action and social conditions. In an often quoted line, Karl Marx observed: "Men make their own history, but they do not make it as they please; they do not make it under circumstances chosen by themselves, but under circumstances directly encountered, given, and transmitted from the past."[32] Instead of assuming that human beings are, on the one hand, the products of external conditions or, on the other, totally free agents, this theory proposes a dynamic and dialectical interplay between social circumstances and our ability to act independently. We are, in a sense, the products of our own culture, but we are also historical agents who shape the circumstances that we encounter.[33] Our consciousness and our actions come out of a historical struggle to realize ourselves within our social relationships. We make our history and initiate our actions, but we do it all in a social and historic environment that conditions our immediate possibilities.

In this environment each person seeks a meaningful existence. In the abstract, the paths to salvation are many. But each of us is bound by the social space we occupy in our own time in history. The alternatives at our command are limited. Our horizons are set by what we see as the possibilities of being human and by the opportunities structured around us.

The patterns of action that people develop for themselves are solutions to the problems of being socially human. Each person's actions, including a patterning of self-images and overt behaviors, are shaped by relationships with others. In a socially structured environment, with the help of our friends (and others), we create a meaningful life.

The substance of a person's action is problematic. Though the content of the actions is shaped by our social and cultural location in society, actions are ultimately the responsibility of each person.[34] But the name that will be given the behavior is also an enterprise of others. And the names are often simplistic: "good" or "bad," "virtuous" or "sinful," "law-abiding" or "criminal." Personal actions are thus constructed in part by the reactions of other people. The person may develop a way of behaving — including a supporting style of life — that takes its reference from criminal definitions. Criminal definitions not only provide behavior with the quality of criminality, but also assist in living a life.

Learning and Association

All of us, whether or not we are at times defined as criminal, act in patterns learned in our social and cultural settings. In a class society, we have normative systems as points of reference for personal behavior. Because we are differently located in the society according to social classes, we learn behavior selectively. The content of our learning depends greatly on our position in the society. Therefore, learning of behavior is structured and selective; a class-divided society has *differential learning structures*.

In his search for understanding of criminal behavior, Edwin H. Sutherland may be credited with the most systematic formulation of how behavior patterns are learned.[35] His argument was that people acquire patterns of criminal behavior in the same way as they acquire patterns of lawful behavior, by interacting with others in communication. The learning includes techniques for committing offenses as well as the specific direction of motives, attitudes, and rationalizations. The motives and rationalizations, in turn, are learned from favorable or unfavorable definitions of the law. It follows, from Sutherland's proposition of "differential association," that you become delinquent or criminal because you learn more definitions favorable to violating the law than those unfavorable to violating it.

Shared meanings are provided for most by membership in some kind of social group. According to *reference-group* terminology, social groups furnish members with a frame of reference to organize perceptions and experiences.[36] People act, then, in reference to the perspectives of their groups. Furthermore, their actions are in part an attempt to preserve and enhance social status within their groups. Consequently, we can look for an explanation for variations in people's behavior in their group experiences.

The theory of *differential association,* as formulated by Sutherland, provides such an explanation of "criminal" behavior.[37] We acquire our behavior during associations with others. Some of us, however, become criminal because our associations involve an excess of definitions favorable to violating the law. The learning of "criminal" behavior patterns is not fundamentally different from other kinds of socialization, during which the individual is differentially exposed to various norms about some socially significant form of behavior.[38]

A problem in the theory of differential association is that few systematic guides are provided for empirically verifying the theory. Formulated at a high level of abstraction, the theory has not been testable with empirical data. At best, it has been subject to only partial testing by research on the variables of association, including the frequency, duration, priority, and intensity of association. These limited studies, nevertheless, have shown that people who associate with delinquents (however defined) report or engage in more alleged delinquent behavior than those who associate with others.[39]

There is more to learning criminally defined behavior than simple association with other people, however. Not only are other processes involved, but association itself is complex. The theory has been reconceptualized by Daniel Glaser in an image of role playing.[40] The differential association idea is first replaced by that of *differential identification.* All persons, accordingly, identify with others, that is, they view their own behavior from the perspective of other people. Moreover, most identify with both "criminal" and "noncriminal" persons, by direct association, by reference to criminal roles portrayed in mass media, or as a negative reaction to forces opposed to crime. "The theory of differential identification, in essence, is that a person pursues criminal behavior to the extent that he identifies himself with real or imaginary persons from whose perspective his criminal behavior seems acceptable."[41] Thus, people who engage in criminally defined behavior identify with and consequently direct their actions toward those who are behaving similarly. All factors are important, in this theory, depending on how much they affect the choice of the others from whose perspective one views his or her own behavior. Our choices vary, and so accordingly do our behaviors.

According to this perspective, the individual engages in behavior, some of which may be defined as criminal or delinquent, rationally and voluntarily. In any situation the individual acts according to her or his own evaluation of the situation with reference to others. In the language of learning theory, social actions are conceptualized as *operant* behavior, that is, behavior emitted in the presence of specified conditions and maintained by its consequences. In other words, the behavior is stimulated by expecting a specific response. Social relations are maintained by the consequences they produce for the interacting parties. It has been argued that criminally defined behavior is also operant behavior: "Criminal behavior is maintained by its consequences, both material and social."[42] The criminally defined behaves in order to produce a desired effect, whether it is acquiring money, harming another person, or changing current conditions. Actions (some of which may be defined as criminal) are pursued for their personal and social consequences.

Among the considerations that affect a decision to act in a specific way is the *commitment* to contingency interests.[43] That is, a person may consider the consequences of some line of action for interests no more than indirectly associated with the present situation. Acting persons may have "commitments to conformity: not only fear of the material deprivations and punishments which might result from being discovered as an offender but also apprehension about the deleterious consequences of such a discovery on one's attempts to maintain a consistent self-image, to sustain valued relationships, and to preserve current and future statuses and activities."[44] According to this notion, those who have strong commitments to law-abiding behavior are not likely to engage in actions that have a high probability of being defined as criminal. The consequences would not be to their advantage.[45]

But for most, commitment to the legal code and its specific laws is not a stable and constant matter. People vary in their commitments during their lives and, furthermore, qualify their commitments according to the immediate context of their actions. Delinquents *drift,* David Matza suggests, between standards of conduct. "The delinquent transiently exists in a limbo between convention and crime, responding in turn to the demands of each, flirting now with one, now the other, but postponing commitment, evading decisions. Thus, he drifts between criminal and conventional action."[46]

Flexibility in their commitment to legal standards is used temporarily by delinquents, especially, to lessen the control of legal norms on their actions.[47] Persons violating the law are able at the same time to maintain some commitment to the standards of the law. Actions defined as either criminal or delinquent do not necessarily represent commitment to violation itself, but are more likely to be episodic actions calculated to produce specific consequences for the actors.

According to a theory of social control, delinquent and criminal acts generally occur when a person's "bond" to society is weak or broken. The conforming individual maintains an allegiance to conventional norms and practices, but the deviant is likely not to be attached to conventional ways.[48] Those who do not share in the rewards of the system, including those engaged in rejecting these "rewards," will behave in ways that will be defined as criminal by those who profit from the system.

Persons may behave, then, looking ahead to the consequences of their actions. The consequences they desire are socially learned. They act in association and identification with the group. With one's past behavior, present interests, and future hopes, actions are considered for their possible ramifications. Whether the actions will be defined as criminal by others may or may not be one of the things one considers when acting in a concrete situation.

Action Patterns and Legal Processing

Personal actions are symbolic for both the actors and the respondents. As interaction continues between parties, or as the actor confronts similar situations, the meanings of personal actions are more firmly established. Eventually we develop patterns of action in reference to our interactions with others. *Social reactions* of others are important in developing such patterns. In the reactions of others we learn to regard ourselves in a specific way. What we become, including how we behave, will depend very much on the way we have been and continue to be assessed and defined by others.

Most reactions of others are directed toward controlling personal actions.[49] These social reactions to behavior come from various sources. Generally, social reaction is found in the informal judgments of others in face-to-face encounters, and also in the organized formal control of private or public agencies. Both forms of reaction provide social definitions of a situation. The actions of some are singled out for special consideration by others during social reaction.

Although social reaction operates as social control, it is at the same time a means of *conferring* definitions on persons, probably producing the actions that are the object of control. That is to say, as others react negatively to your actions, you may begin to accept the definitions others have applied to you. This self-definition according to the definitions of others was pointed out some time ago in a discussion of how a community may react to a juvenile's adventurous behavior by eventually defining the child as bad. He or she responds by accepting the definition and acting in reference to it.

> From the community's point of view, the individual who used to do bad and mischievous things has now become a bad and unredeemable human being. From the individual's point of view there has taken place a similar change. He

has gone slowly from a sense of grievance and injustice, of being unduly mistreated and punished, to a recognition that the definition of him as a human being is different from that of other boys in his neighborhood, his school, street, community. This recognition on his part becomes a process of self-identification and integration with the group which shares his activities. It becomes, in part, a process of rationalization; in part, a simple response to a specialized type of stimulus. The young delinquent becomes bad because he is defined as bad and because he is not believed if he is good. There is a persistent demand for consistency in character. The community cannot deal with people whom it cannot define. Reputation is this sort of public definition.[50]

You are likely to become that which you are described as being.

Defining a person negatively, therefore, affects the person's definition of self and his or her subsequent actions. People may readily channel their efforts toward behaviors with a high potential for criminality because they have been defined as deviant in some way. Accordingly, much of the research and writing on offenders' physical characteristics can be reinterpreted as social definitions. The physical stereotypes of the criminal may often characterize specific offenders, but the relationship is not so much genetic as it is a self-fulfillment of others' perceptions and definitions. It may well be that some offenders conform to Lombroso's "stigmata" of overly small or large head, asymmetry of face, ears of unusual size, receding chin, and so forth.[51] People with such characteristics are not savage "throwbacks," however; they are people who are endowed with human characteristics, defined by others as deviant (both physically and socially); to be officially defined as criminal; and to engage in the behaviors consistent with the status they have been assigned.

Similarly, many of the notorious outlaws of the West may have had red hair.[52] Yet, being redheaded did not genetically make such men and women criminals. Rather the social definitions of others described redheaded people as deviant, making the consequence true. In the same way we may recognize the finding that delinquents often are mesomorphs (muscular, athletic, and aggressive).[53] Boys of such appearance and temperament are probably more likely than other boys to be recruited into juvenile gangs and to engage in behaviors that may readily be defined as delinquent. Physical characteristics are first socially defined, then self-defined in relation to social reactions, and subsequently shape personal actions. The interaction of physical characteristics, social reactions, and personal action is dramatically illustrated by Richard Speck, slayer of eight Chicago nurses in the summer of 1966. When finally arrested, Speck, who had been described as physically and personally unattractive, was identified by the tattoo on his arm, which read, "Born to raise hell."

The extent to which personal patterns of action develop in response to others' social reactions depends on how much the person accepts and adjusts to the assigned role. "Secondary deviation," as proposed by Edwin M. Lemert, suggests the transition that may occur in a person's self-conception and behavior as he or she is confronted with social reactions. The deviance imputed to a person remains "primary deviation" to that person as long as it is rationalized or otherwise dealt with as a socially acceptable role. As a person continues to act, and as social reactions are repeated and strengthened, deviation becomes secondary. Lemert writes:

> Secondary deviation refers to a special class of socially defined responses which people make to problems created by the societal reaction to their deviance. These problems are essentially moral problems which revolve around stigmatization, punishments, segregation, and social control. Their general effect is to differentiate the symbolic and interactional environment to which the person responds, so that early or adult socialization is categorically affected. They become central facts of existence for those experiencing them, altering psychic structure, producing specialized organization of social roles and self-regarding attitudes. Actions which have these roles and self attitudes as their referents make up secondary deviance.[54]

People develop such a position toward themselves and others because their identity and actions are organized around the deviance that others have imputed to them.

Defining a person as "criminal" is the extreme form of stigmatization. Criminal conviction — even confrontation with the police and judicial prosecution — modifies a person's identity and actions. The "criminalization of deviance" may thus force those engaged in specific kinds of behavior to redefine themselves and their actions.[55] Such public branding can lead a person to new situations and activities. The development of a new style of life, in turn, increases the probability of further criminal definition. By social reaction, then, in the form of legal processing, crime is again created and perpetuated. In the class struggle crime is constantly being produced.

CRIMES OF VIOLENCE

Violence is abstractly prohibited by the criminal law as well as by the moral values of the society. Broadly conceived, criminal violence is any harm-producing act. In practice, however, violence against other human beings is subject to many qualifications. Killing is a tactic in time of war, as long as the state has people it can define as the "enemy"; those killed or injured under wartime conditions exceed by thousands the numbers killed by civilian murder and assault. For a civilian to kill a fellow human

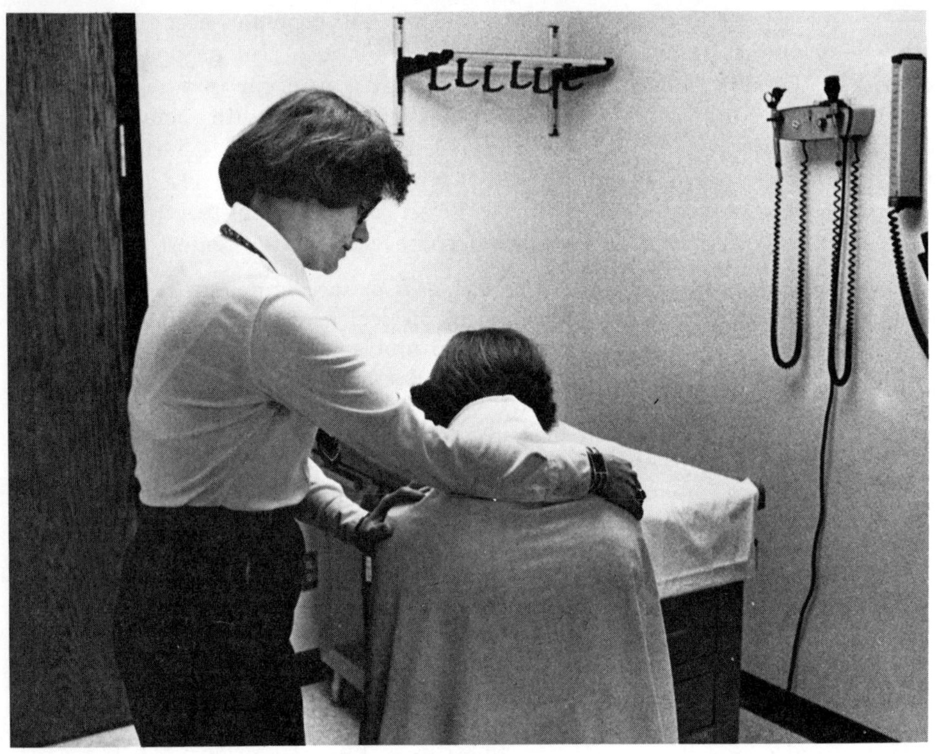

A counselor in a new Rape–Sexual Assault Care Center gives comfort and advice to a victim brought to the emergency room of a hospital.

being wilfully may warrant the death penalty or life imprisonment; for a soldier to do the same to the enemy warrants a medal for heroism. Far more people are killed or injured for reasons of state than by criminal violence.

Moreover, it is commonly assumed that violence mainly involves the conventional acts of murder, assault, and rape. Ignored in this assumption are the more frequent forms of violence, including the marketing of dangerous drugs, the illegal sale of contaminated or spoiled foodstuffs, death and injury from violation of housing and fire codes, death and injury from dangerous working conditions, and the violence resulting from gross traffic negligence.[56] Including the full range of harmful actions, we recognize that violence pervades the society. We also have a better view of who really kills and maims in the United States.

The United States has a violent history. With a developing capitalist economy, immigrant, working, and racial groups were thrown into fierce competition with each other.[57] The capitalist class fostered antagonism between the classes, pitting one group against another in the quest for economic survival. Built into this society, with class divisions, is the practice of violence.

The use of violence to solve personal and interpersonal problems varies considerably throughout the society. Violent crimes are closely linked to males, particularly young men; for many people maleness is equated with physical aggression. Male aggression can be a device to maintain supremacy over women, as it seems to be with forcible rape.

> Indeed, the existence of rape in any form is beneficial to the ruling class of white males. For rape is a kind of terrorism which severely limits the freedom of women and makes women dependent on men. Moreover, in the act of rape, the rage that one man may harbor toward another higher in the male hierarchy can be deflected toward a female scapegoat. For every man there is always someone lower on the social scale on whom he can take out his aggressions. And that is any woman alive.[58]

That cultural definitions of violence are important is revealed in the wide regional differences in criminal homicide. Homicide rates have consistently been highest in the southern region of the United States. There, cultural definitions promote personal violence in some situations and weapons are carried more in some areas. The pattern of violence in the South, one writer suggests, lies in historical factors such as the influence of slavery as a repressive system on the culture, the type of immigration (Scotch-Irish and fundamentalist), and, above all, "the development of a Southern world view that defines the social, political, and physical environment as hostile."[59]

Possessing weapons is a part of the culture of violence. A 1969 survey found that Americans have in their possession 90,000,000 firearms, including 24,000,000 handguns, 35,000,000 rifles, and 31,000,000 shotguns.[60] Forty-nine per cent of the 60.4 million American households reported owning firearms, or 2.2 firearms per household. Such ownership is highest in the South (59 per cent) and lowest in the East (33 per cent). A recent study finds that ownership of weapons, especially handguns, is highest in rural areas of the country, with ownership lowest in the largest cities.[61] Furthermore, counter to a common assumption, ownership of weapons is more characteristic of Protestant middle-income groups than of urban, working-class Catholics. Also more whites than nonwhites own weapons in the United States.

Firearms, usually handguns, are commonly used in the United States in crimes involving violence. In the ten years up to 1974, the number of homicides involving firearms increased by about 50 percent. Firearms permit greater range, more concealment, and attacks by people either unwilling or unable to overpower a victim by other means. When a gun is used the chances of death are five times greater than with a knife. The percentage of homicides and aggravated assaults involving firearms parallels that of firearm ownership; a Detroit study showed that firearms violence increased after an increase in handgun acquisition.[62] In the United States today about one in five serious assaults is committed with a firearm. More than 65 per cent of murder victims are killed by a gun.

Whatever the weapon, most murders and aggravated assaults are concrete responses, growing out of social interaction between one or more parties, to situations that come to be defined as requiring that violence be used. Violence may result from one argument or dispute or from a series of arguments, sometimes extending over years, between husband and wife, lovers, neighbors, or fellow employees. Verbalization in these arguments declines, and emotional reactions increase, until, in a final argument, a climax is built up, and one of the parties is injured or killed with a weapon.

Because of the interplay between persons in a situation leading to violence, the victim often "causes" his or her own death or serious injury. A Philadelphia study showed that more than one in four criminal homicides were precipitated by the victim, who first showed or used a deadly weapon or struck a blow in an altercation.[63] Victim-precipitated homicides were found to be significantly associated with blacks, victim-offender relationships involving male victims of female offenders, mate slaying, alcohol in the homicide situation or in the victim, and victims with a record of assault or arrest. Other homicides, not included in this figure, involved infidelity of a mate or lover, failure of the victim to pay a debt, and use of vile names by the victim in such a manner that the victim contributes to the homicide. Evidence from other cities and areas of the country likewise indicates how often violent crime is precipitated by the victim.[64]

Homicide and assault are similar in that both often involve interaction between relatives, friends, or acquaintances. Moreover: "The ostensible motives in homicide and assault are often relatively trivial, usually involving spontaneous altercations, family quarrels, jealous rages, and the like. The two crimes are similar; there is often no reason to believe that the person guilty of homicide sets out with any more intention to harm than the one who commits an aggravated assault. Except for the seriousness of the final outcomes, the major distinction is that homicides most often involve handguns while knives are most common in assault."[65] Although people in American cities often worry about physical assaults by strangers on the streets, personal violence is far less likely to come from a stranger.

According to a survey, about 70 percent of wilful killings, nearly two-thirds of aggravated assaults, and high percentages of forcible rapes are committed by family members and others previously known to the victims.[66]

A government survey of a 10 per cent random sample of offense and arrest reports in seventeen large cities found that only a fifth of assaults involved strangers, much higher even than the figure for homicide.[67] This study also found that one in four of 668 criminal homicides was between family members and 9 per cent involved other primary-group relationships, 15.4 per cent involved an acquaintance, and only 15.6 per cent were committed by strangers. Forcible rape, however, was found slightly more likely to be committed by a stranger (53 per cent), and the balance by people with whom the victim had some acquaintance.

A change appears to be occurring, however, in the traditional relationship between victim and offender in some parts of the country. For New York City murders in 1975, more than 33 percent involved a victim and an assailant unknown to each other.[68] The so-called "crime of passion," or murder arising from romantic or family quarrels, no longer are the most numerous homicides in the city. Instead, the proportion of murders by a stranger has been increasing in recent years. The urban dweller is becoming a potential victim with little control even over the immediate situation.

Another pattern in the conventional crimes of violence is that most of these crimes are *intraracial,* carried out against persons of one's own racial group: most homicides, aggravated assaults, and forcible rapes have whites victimizing whites and blacks victimizing blacks. In the study of seventeen large cities, it was found that 24 per cent of the homicides were between whites and 66 per cent between blacks.[69] As shown in Table 7.2, 6 per cent involved blacks killing whites and 4 per cent whites killing blacks. In a Houston study 97 per cent of the black victims were killed by blacks, 91 per cent of the white victims were killed by whites. Eighty-six per cent of the Latin-Americans were killed by other Latin-Americans.[70] In Chicago only 6.6 per cent of the criminal homicides were interracial, and of this small number 80 per cent involved the killing of whites by nonwhites.[71] A larger government survey of 1,493 aggravated-assault cases in seventeen large cities found that one-fourth of the assaults were between whites, 66 per cent between blacks, 8 per cent involved blacks attacking whites, and 2 per cent whites attacking blacks.[72] The study also found that 90 per cent of the forcible rapes were intraracial; of these 30 per cent were both white, 60 per cent were both black, 10 per cent were whites raping blacks, and less than 1 per cent were blacks raping whites.

Conventional violence is one of the many oppressions suffered by the poor and the working class in an exploitative, class-divided society. It is

TABLE 7.2 Characteristics of Victim and Offender by Sex, Race, and Age, Criminal Homicide in 17 Cities, 1967 (in percentages)[a]

	Sex of victim					
Sex of offender	*Male*		*Female*		*Total (victims)[b]*	
Male	62.3%		17.5%		79.8%	(455)[c]
Female	16.4		3.8		20.2	(115)
Total (offenders)[b]	78.7	(449)	21.3	(121)	100.0	(570)

	Race of victim					
Race of offender	*White*		*Negro*		*Total (victims)[b]*	
White	24.0%		3.8%		27.8%	(159)[c]
Negro	6.5		65.7		72.2	(412)
Total (offenders)[b]	30.5	(174)	69.5	(397)	100.0	(571)

	Age of victim							
Age of offender	*0–17*		*18–25*		*26 and over*		*Total (victims)[b]*	
0–17	3.3%		1.6%		4.2%		9.1%	(49)[c]
18–25	3.6		10.3		19.8		33.5	(182)
26 and over	3.5		6.7		47.0		57.4	(311)
Total (offenders)[b]	10.4	(56)	18.6	(101)	71.0	(385)	100.0	(542)

[a] Total of known criminal homicide victim-offender interactions, by sex, 570; by race, 571; by age, 542. Frequencies weighted according to total reported violent crimes for 1967, by type, in the 17 cities surveyed.

[b] Total row and column percentages may not exactly equal 100.0 per cent because of the weighting procedure and rounding.

[c] Numbers are given in parentheses.

SOURCE: *Crimes of Violence,* Vol. 11, A Staff Report Submitted to the National Commission on the Causes and Prevention of Violence, Donald J. Mulvihill and Melvin M. Tumin, Co-Directors (Washington, D.C.: U.S. Government Printing Office, 1969), p. 210.

finally in interpersonal relationships that the conditions and forces of capitalist society are made manifest. In the United States, violence against your own people becomes a personal solution to the problems produced by the larger society.

CRIMES AGAINST PROPERTY

Property crimes — especially larceny and burglary — are among the most important in capitalist society because they violate the value placed on private property. A value system that emphasizes property, however, contains its own contradictions about the violation of that property. Although property is cherished and protected, the desire to acquire it, by whatever means, is great too. The same normative system that protects the property stimulates the need to gain more of it. It is in this contradiction that crimes against property must be understood.

Those who engage in property crimes (probably a big portion of the population) differ in the extent to which they violate the criminal law in acquiring property, and in the proportion of their livelihood taken up by these crimes. And the offenders vary in their skills and techniques for commiting property offenses. Some offenders violate the law occasionally and others make a career of it. All believe in the importance of private property; their difference is in the frequency and degree to which they will violate the law to achieve that goal.

Most offenders who occasionally commit property crimes are relatively committed to the values of capitalist society. Naive check forgers "appear to have acquired normal attitudes and habits of law observance."[73] Adult department-store pilferers are generally "respectable" citizens who have little or no contact with criminal groups.[74] Juveniles caught joyriding (involving auto theft) either have no criminal record or none other than for auto theft and are likely to come from conventional middle-income neighborhoods.[75]

Occasional crimes against property may be simply a rejection of the dominant behavior patterns, especially of the value placed on law-abiding behavior, as in other forms of property crime. Much destruction of property by vandalism seems to be a way of challenging the high opinion of private property in our society. Evidence is increasing that dominant behavior patterns are not internalized or absorbed by all persons and groups and that many violators of laws are involved in a world of their own, relatively isolated from the dominant values of the society.[76]

The tentative and sporadic commitment to the dominant culture is evident among those who more regularly engage in property crimes, especially the juveniles. Delinquents do not completely reject the dominant values and norms of the society but neutralize them in violating the law. Such delinquents also make use of the "subterranean values" of the dominant society, using these as a code of behavior instead of reserving them for leisure-time activities. Being uncommitted, the delinquent "drifts" between delinquent and nondelinquent ways of life.[77]

In a society that values acquisition of property but is structured on economic inequality, property crime is inevitable. Criminal patterns may develop to solve the problem of acquiring that which is valued. Property crime is an integral part of a society that both values property and limits possibilities for obtaining it.

Careers of Property Offenders

The conventional property offender is generally a product of the areas of poverty in which juvenile gangs are active. Violent personal offenders come out of these areas, and also offenders who commit robbery and burglary. A government group reported that "Study after study in city after city in all regions of the country have traced the variations in the rates for these crimes. The results, with monotonous regularity, show that the *offenses,* the *victims,* and the *offenders* are found most frequently in the poorest, and most deteriorated and socially disorganized areas of cities."[78]

It is common for property offenders to begin their careers early in life as juvenile delinquents in a class-divided society. People from fifteen to seventeen years of age are the group most frequently arrested for burglaries, larcenies, and auto theft. In 1976, 51.6 per cent of those arrested for burglary were under eighteen, and 71.4 per cent were under twenty-one. For motor-vehicle left, 52.6 per cent were under eighteen and 71.6 per cent were under twenty-one. Comparable figures for robbery were 33.5 per cent under eighteen and 56.5 per cent under twenty-one.[79] A Philadelphia study showed that the highest arrest rates in the population for robbery were for ages 15 to 19 and 20 to 24.[80] The early histories of these offenders show truancy, destruction of property, street fighting, and delinquent gang membership. By the time they are young adults, they have had extensive contact with the law, and may have some experience in an institution.

As juvenile offenders progress into conventional career crime, they become more committed to crime as a way of life and develop a criminal self-conception. Because of repeated offenses and subsequent arrests and convictions, conventional offenders eventually identify with crime. Occasional property offenders who pursue criminal activity only sporadically experience vacillating self-conceptions. But for conventional criminals who regularly commit offenses, a criminal self-conception is almost inescapable. And because property offenders are dealt with rather severely before the law, by arrest and sentencing, such offenders readily come to regard themselves as criminals. The criminal record is a constant reminder that the person has been stigmatized by the society, and may promote a vicious circle in which the offender continues in a life of crime.

Conventional property criminals are likely to have a diversified offense record, committing a number of offenses that may include theft, larceny, robbery, and burglary. The amount of money in each offense is relatively small; the offenses provide a part of the offenders' livelihood; and they must be repeated regularly. Many people arrested for robbery have records in theft, not acts of violence. A Boston study of robbery suspects apprehended during half of 1968 showed that five times as many juveniles had been previously arrested for theft as for violent crimes.[81] National figures show that for suspects under seventeen the ratio is about 7 to 1. In a Philadelphia study of arrests for robbery it was reported:

> Using different types of indexes of prior police arrest record, our study reveals that when an offender has a previous record, he is much more likely to have a criminal profile of offenses against property than against the person. For example, only 4 percent of the offenders have a past profile of assault, but 45 percent have a pattern of robbery, larceny or burglary. There is no significant difference between Negro and white offenders in this respect; neither is there a difference in criminal background between the violent and non-violent robbers of our study. Robbers, thus, are not a special class, but are primarily thieves who occasionally, though rarely, use force to achieve their objects. The display of violence in this context is on the whole an isolated episode. It is general persistence in crime, not a widespread specialization in crimes of violence, which is the main characteristic of robbers.[82]

Because of their relative lack of skill and organization, property offenders are more likely than organized and professional criminals to be eventually arrested and imprisoned. Consequently, conventional property offenders form a large portion of the prison population — perhaps as many as half the inmates.[83] With similar offenders in mind, Don C. Gibbons said this about the career of these criminals:

> Many semiprofessionals spend a considerable part of their early adult years in penal institutions where they are likely to be identified as "right guys" or antiadministration inmates. It does not appear that conventional treatment efforts are successful in deflecting many of these persons away from continuation in crime. On the other hand, many of them ultimately do withdraw from crime careers upon reaching the early middle-aged period.[84]

When crime is pursued as a way of life, as it is by conventional property offenders, other ways of living are not readily available. Furthermore, the excitement and notoriety of a criminal career may seem more rewarding to the criminal than the hard work, mediocrity, and monotony provided by a respectable, law-abiding career. A group consciousness among criminals makes movement to a law-abiding life less comprehensible and desirable. By their early thirties, most conventional offenders, however, feel that a law-abiding career holds greater possibilities than a criminal career that has not been particularly successful. A relatively small number continue on to make professional careers of conventional crime.

A few juvenile-gang delinquents continue to engage in illegal activities as adults, particularly as adult conventional career criminals, but it is unclear why many of them discontinue criminal behavior in their mid-twenties or early thirties. One writer points out "it is much easier to determine why offenders continue in criminal careers than it is to understand what makes them quit."[85] As they grow older, they lose touch with deviant and criminal associates because of marriage and family responsibilities. Such a change in life is more important in breaking a criminal pattern than are attempts at rehabilitation in correctional institutions.

PROFESSIONAL PROPERTY CRIME

Under the appropriate conditions, work becomes criminal. Work is essentially a central activity of life, giving meaning to our daily existence. We are only relatively free, however, at specific times and places to choose the work that fulfills us personally and achieves social good. Much work, consequently, exploits others and is detrimental to the self. That *careers* are made of criminal work reflects the social, political, and economic order. The political economy, in other words, provides the framework for pursuing meaningful and socially constructive work, or for developing a career in crime. Work that is dictated solely by economic survival makes crime a rational and likely possibility in contemporary society.

These crimes pursued as occupations began as the European feudal order disintegrated. James A. Inciardi shows that a new group of dispossessed persons — a vagabond class — developed as the old order collapsed and a new capitalist economic order replaced it.[86] To survive, those displaced from the occupational structure, for whom a commercial and industrializing world had no room, invented alternative forms of economic subsistence. Around the urban centers, created by commerce and industry, criminality grew to be a life's work. Becoming firmly established in England during the eighteenth and nineteenth centuries, the social organization and operation of career crime were transported to fertile soil in the United States. To this day, crime as an economic way of life has prospered in a supportive environment. Crime followed legitimate business, often filling the gaps left by other forms of commerce.

Some people in capitalist society, then, continue to engage in highly specialized property crimes. Many of these professional criminals acquire large sums of money without being arrested or prosecuted. Their activities include picking pockets, shoplifting, sneak-thieving from stores, stealing from jewelry stores by substituting articles, stealing from hotel rooms, and miscellaneous rackets, such as passing illegal checks and extorting money from others engaged in illegal behavior.

Professional criminals come from economic backgrounds better than those of other conventional property offenders. A person entering a career of professional crime may continue to engage in legitimate employment until he is successful in crime. Professional criminals are also likely to begin their careers relatively late. Furthermore, once in professional crime, they continue in it for the rest of their lives. The confidence man's career has been summarized:

> The con man begins his special career at a much older age than other criminals, or perhaps it is better said that he continues his criminal career at a time when others may be relinquishing theirs. Unemployment occasioned by old age does not seem to be a problem of con men; age ripens their skills, insight, and wit, and it also increases the confidence they inspire in their victims. With age the con man may give up the position of the roper and shift to being an inside man, but even this may not be absolutely necessary. It is possible that cultural changes outmode the particular con games older men have been accustomed to playing and thereby decrease their earnings somewhat, but this seems unlikely. We know of one con man who is seventy years of age and has a bad heart, but he is still as effective as he ever was.[87]

Longevity in crime is attributable in part, of course, to the fact that very few professional criminals are ever arrested, brought to trial, convicted, or made to serve time in prison.

Professional offenders develop a philosophy of life to justify their actions and to enhance their self-images. They believe that all people are actually dishonest, and justify their behavior by believing all would violate the law if they had the skill and opportunity. Joseph "Yellow Kid" Weil, a successful confidence man, said of himself:

> The men I fleeced were basically no more honest than I was. One of the motivating factors in my action was, of course, the desire to acquire money. The other motive was a lust for adventure. The men I swindled were also motivated by a desire to acquire money, and they didn't care at whose expense they got it. I was particular. I took money only from those who could afford it and were willing to go in with me in schemes they fancied would fleece others.[88]

Professional offenders can justify their own behavior by the conduct of their victims, who, after all, have been willing to participate in an illegal act. Such rationalizations are shared and supported by professional offenders in their associations with one another.

Group associations are important among professional offenders, as indicated by the way in which people are recruited into the world of professional theft. Edwin H. Sutherland, in his study of the professional thief, found that recognition by other professional thieves is the essential quality.[89] Without that recognition, no knowledge and experience can provide the offender with the qualifications for a successful career built around the social role of the professional.

To be recognized by established professional thieves, selection and tutelage are necessary. Selection takes place as professional offenders come in contact with other offenders (amateur thieves, burglars), with those on the fringes of crime (pimps, "fences"), or with people in legitimate occupations. The contacts are made in places where professional offenders are working, in jails, or in places of leisure activities. Selection, which must be by mutual agreement between established and prospective professionals, is followed by a probationary period in which the neophyte learns the skills, techniques, attitudes, and values of the professional offender. The person assimilates standards of group morality, such as honesty among professionals and not informing on others. Gradually they become acquainted with other professional thieves. They eventually acquire the special language or argot by which members communicate.[90] With such knowledge and expertise, the person develops a life in a world that is shared with other professional offenders.

The social characteristics of other forms of professional crime differ somewhat from those of professional theft. Some professional criminals may work alone, and some are self-taught, requiring small learning or recognition. For fraudulent check writing, little training is necessary; the skills required are elementary. One professional offender's learning is described:

> He was first a check writer, which is a craft requiring little or no tutelage. It takes no great flash of wisdom to realize that people will give you money for a piece of paper or to realize that if you are going to depend on that for your livelihood, it might be more pleasant to use names other than your own. Highly skilled craft aspects, such as check raising, are now fairly rare. The problem in check passing is handling the person with the money you want, and that is dependent on personal style rather than technical skill. Check writing is a solitary profession, it is better done alone, it is one in which the worst thing that can happen is to become well-known. Check writers do not socialize very well; they may meet in jail, but they do not tend to hang around together outside.[91]

Check writing is not the only professional crime that can be successfully executed alone and without much training. Although professional shoplifters sometimes work in small troupes, many prefer to work alone.[92] Lemert found in his study of check forgers that these offenders carefully avoid contact and interaction with other criminals:

> Moreover, their preference for solitude and their secretiveness give every appearance of a highly generalized reaction; they avoid not only cooperative

crime but also any other kinds of association with criminals. They are equally selective and cautious in their contacts and associations with the noncriminal population, preferring not to become involved in any enduring personal relationships.[93]

And in armed robbery, when career offenders do have social organization, it is usually in the form of a partnership. Not a permanent association of offenders, group activity is smaller and more flexible:

> Hence there is little evidence in the social organization of robbers of group cohesion during periods of stress in the manner described by Sutherland. The robber's organization is a more fluid arrangement taking into account existing conditions; it is not conceived by those involved as a permanent group but more or less a loose confederation of individuals joined together for a specific purpose on a short-term basis. Among certain types of robbers specific role relationships do develop; however, these always are assumed to be temporary by the robbery participants even though the association is of some duration. When this type of social organization exists no provision need be made for incapacitated members; each member considers himself on his own.[94]

Professional property crimes, nevertheless, continue because the activity is related to other patterns in the society. Not only are professional criminals engaged in a full-time economic activity, but they provide services for other people. Many forms of professional crime, especially the confidence game, depend on cooperation by normally law-abiding people who serve as accomplices. Also involved are those who assist in "fixing" cases, including police, attorneys, and judges.[95] And the "fences" are needed in distributing stolen goods, providing the general public with desired products. Neal Shover found in his study of burglary that fences also educate the burglar about the merchandise, coach for mastery of criminal techniques, supply information on where to burglarize, and put burglars in contact with one another.[96]

The close association between professional crime and the dominant society is finally evident in the patterns of professional crime, and changes in these. A task force report by the president's crime commission found these associations and changes:

> As conditions in society change, certain criminal occupations become relatively unprofitable, and other opportunities develop. The nature of crime will tend to change accordingly. Criminal activity like legitimate business activity may respond to the market, to supply and demand curves, and to technological developments. Professional crime, guided by the profit motive, can be expected to be particularly responsive to such factors. One example is the reported decline in safecracking. This is apparently due in part to such factors as increased law enforcement surveillance and mobility, and improvements in the design of

safes. Undoubtedly the fact that safes no longer play an important role has also contributed to the decline — modern economic transactions involve the transfer of credits much more than the transfer of cash. Thus it may have become both more difficult and riskier to rob safes, and also less profitable. At the same time, more promising opportunities for crime have arisen. One of these is check-passing. The Commission's study learned that nearly every burglar nowadays is also in the check business. One professional burglar said that in one period of several weeks between burglaries he passed over $20,000 of stolen checks. A generation ago burglars did not even look for checks to steal.[97]

Other changes in professional crime, influenced by social and economic changes, include crimes related to the automobile, such as auto theft, auto stripping, and stealing from parked cars. Frauds in home improvement and insurance have also increased rapidly. In general, professional criminals are turning from picking pockets, confidence games, and bank robbery to other economic opportunities. In adapting to new technology, such as better safes, electronic alarms, and modern law-enforcement tactics, professional criminals (including bank robbers, safecrackers, and burglars) are showing that the criminal life is comparable in many ways to the structure and goals of "straight" society.[98] Professional crime, like legitimate activities in capitalist society, must alter its enterprises, diversify, and reorganize to remain solvent.

Although there are signs that career crime is in crisis, and adaption is necessary for its survival, other forms of crime (still pursued for economic reasons) probably will develop in the United States. A contradiction in an advanced capitalist society is the need for criminal, alienating, and exploitative activity in an economy that supposedly meets basic human needs. The future of crime and its forms in the United States ultimately rests on the kind of political economy that is created.

CRIMES OF PUBLIC ORDER

Most officially defined crimes are violations against public order. Among these offenses, defined as criminal in various ways, are prostitution, homosexuality, drunkenness, selling and using narcotics, gambling, traffic violations, disorderly conduct, and vagrancy. Although the differences in the behaviors are striking, all the offenses violate in some way the sense of public order established in the society.

Yet, much of the behavior of public-order offenders is consistent with the patterns dominant in the society. Users of drugs, prostitutes, homosexuals, traffic violators, excessive drinkers, and so on are not too different in their attitudes toward the society's general goals from those engaged in

In a drive to "clean-up" the tourist attraction area of Times Square in New York City, police plainclothesmen arrest an alleged prostitute, escorting her to their unmarked car.

legitimate behaviors. The prostitute's behavior is a response to the female role, representing the further exploitation of women.

> Prostitution is a blatant example of the sexual oppression of women. The sexual ideology and economic exploitation which force poorer women into criminal prostitution are pressures to which all women in our society are subject. . . . The socio-economic structure of our society has in fact served to perpetuate the profession and the ideology that women exist only to serve the pleasures and needs of men.[99]

Prostitution thus becomes a commercial enterprise with the same goals as those of many other occupations in our society.

Those who engage in homosexual behavior are taking part in a widely practiced sex behavior. The homosexual is involved in a community of friendships, some of which are as lasting as heterosexual arrangements.[100]

The use of drugs such as heroin and marijuana, though disapproved, has its counterparts in the frequent use of alcohol, cigarettes, tranquilizers for relaxation, barbiturates for sleeping and relaxation, and other minor drugs such as aspirin. Coffee and tea are also stimulant drugs that can have strong effects when consumed regularly in large quantities. Some idea of how widely the more accepted drugs are used is indicated by the manufacture each year of more than a million pounds of barbiturate derivatives in the United States, or the equivalent of twenty-four half-grain doses for each person in the country — enough to kill each of us twice.[101] In 1957 it was estimated that 7 per cent of the adult population was regularly using tranquilizers, sedatives, and drug stimulants; in 1967 one of four, or 27 per cent, was doing so.[102]

The economic considerations in many public-order offenses are readily apparent. Much of the behavior in these offenses provides an economic commodity for both those who offer the service or product and the dominant culture that receives it. Prostitution is closely allied to regular economic forces: "Our laissez-faire economy and its integration through a price system allows the relatively free operation of supply and demand whether it be commerce in grain futures or sex service."[103]

Drug addiction has an elaborate social and economic arrangement, a "survival system."[104] It consists of a "reproductive" system in which addicted persons must continually recruit new members to sell them drugs to support their own habit. The system has defensive communication, with its own argot for drugs, suppliers, and drug users, which must be learned by the initiates, and "neighborhood warning systems," in which addicts are protected by others. Supporting the habit requires a complex network of distribution for illegal drugs, a "circulatory" system that teaches addicts how to secure drugs. These are imported and wholesale distribution is made mostly by crime syndicates or other highly organized groups.[105]

Once addicted to a narcotic drug like morphine or heroin, an individual depends on a continuous supply, and this demand usually becomes the most important act of daily life. As they build up tolerance and need larger and more frequent dosages, the cost of supporting the addiction may be $40 or more a day. That is generally more than the addict can afford, forcing the addict to theft or other illegal activities simply to get an adequate supply.[106] Addicts often engage in stealing, burglary, "rolling drunks," or robbery to get enough money to buy drugs. They may break into hospitals and doctors' offices to steal drugs, turn to prostitution, or sell drugs and become "pushers" to get enough drugs for their own needs.

The widespread popularity of drugs in the United States supports a criminal population here and a whole class of speculators and growers in the drug-producing countries. The largest financial gains from crimes of public order, therefore, are made in manufacturing and selling narcotics. The large addicted portion of the population provides a lucrative business for those engaged with narcotic drugs in one way or another. Those who profit from the addiction of others are many, from manufacturers and sellers of narcotics to those who control narcotics. In the last category is the vast organization created to define, process, harass, confine, and "rehabilitate" the drug addict.[107] Criminal syndicates, politicians, the police, agency bureaucrats, and correctional workers have a symbiotic relationship, vividly described here:

> The real drug problem in America is that government narcotics bureaucracies and organized crime have had a status quo working relationship for decades. This arrangement denies legitimate opiate addicts reasonable access to their specific medicines. The black market for opiates consequently created serves to increase the number of addicts, not decrease it, serves only to increase the social disorientation of addiction, not cure it, serves to discredit helpless sick citizens, not minister to them. This arrangement increases the pain of addiction. This arrangement profits only Narcotics Control Agencies and Organized Crime Networks. Both depend on continued criminalization of addicts to maintain their complementary parasitic existences. Both groups have grown with the growth of the black market they have created. In this situation the medically sick junkie is a victim, treated like a Jew under Hitler, driven mad in the streets to seek relief from unendurable pain and social degradation imposed on him by police bureaucracy and organized crime.[108]

Offenses of the public order, like other kinds of crimes in capitalist society, are deeply embedded in the society's organization and operation. These are produced by a contradiction: if a society cannot provide a humane, unalienating existence, it must contend with activities that are defined as criminal. These crimes are at the same time a threat to the society and furnish needed services and commodities within the social order.

VICTIMS OF CRIME

All crimes have a victim. Specific acts, in fact, are defined as criminal because someone or something is conceived of as a victim. In this sense, the victim *precedes* the official definition of an act as criminal. If a victim cannot be related to a specific act, a criminal law is neither created nor enforced. A "victimless" crime can only be one that is defined after the fact by an outside observer.[109]

That every crime has a victim is recognized in the legal definitions of crime. One legal scholar described a crime as "any social harm defined and punishable by law."[110] The "social harm," of course, can be a physical injury to an individual, *if* the state feels that such an injury also threatens its social order, to the most diffuse harm that in some way is regarded as hurting the body social.

Obviously, law cannot regulate all conduct that could conceivably cause social harm. Only acts that cause harm to those able to make and enforce the law officially become crimes. And, similarly, when the social harms that are a part of the written law cease to be regarded by those in power as a harm to their interests, these laws are no longer enforced. Every act may conceivably involve a victim, but only the acts that threaten the welfare of capitalist society become crimes. Social harm, no matter how abstract, is a reality traditionally decided upon by those who rule.

The presence of a victim, then, the one *officially* designated, is an indication that the social order has been challenged. The victim, a concrete one, apart from the state itself, is held up as a defense of the social order.

Therefore, according to the criminal law and the traditional conception of victimization, *the victim* is the object of *conventional* crime. Someone is a victim when her or his property is stolen; murder is committed against another person in particular; and some crimes are committed against the community, or "public order." In all these crimes a victim is the rationale for the law that regulates conventional crime.

Even for conventional crimes, the victims are those who are already oppressed in the society. Except for auto theft, the victims of all the major conventional crimes are disproportionately in the lower income levels.[111] The highest victimization rates for murder, rape, robbery, aggravated assault, burglary, and larceny are in the $0 to $2,999 and $3,000 to $5,999 income brackets. Except for larceny, the highest rates of victimization are for blacks. The working class and blacks, in particular, are the major victims of conventional crimes.

Nevertheless, we are all victims of even more common crimes. The most dangerous and frequent are committed against all who are exploited by the state and its capitalist economy. The amount of crime and the number of victims expand tremendously when we recognize the true extent of criminal conduct in the United States. The most systematic and pervasive crimes are committed daily by those who sit in corporate and government offices. The victims are among the majority of the population that is the object of these actions. We are all victims of an exploitative, capitalist society.

A society that is based on racism, sexism, and other forms of human exploitation necessarily victimizes a large portion of the population. Even the conventional forms of violent crime, especially rape against women, personal violence within the family, and the suffering of children are an integral part of the social and economic order.[112] Women, blacks, native Americans, youths, and the poor are the ready victims of such a society. Violence against these groups is supported by the prevailing culture and economy of capitalist society. And the criminal-justice system itself becomes an instrument of class, sexist, and racist oppression.[113] Victimization is rooted in the systematic practices and ideologies of capitalist society in the United States.

Why we conceive of some persons as victims and others not as victims is a consequence of our common-sense assumptions. Our own character is indicated by the kinds of persons we single out as victims of crime. Those who make proposals for compensating victims are writing as much about themselves as they are about specific programs. And whenever the criminologist confronts the victim, a particular view of reality is presented.

It is no surprise then that other contenders for the category of victim are usually excluded from criminological attention, because it would take an alternative world view to conceive of them. Breaking out of the theory of reality that has dominated conventional thought, we would revise or at least expand our image of victimization and begin to conceive of other victims: those who suffer police force, war, the "correctional" system, state violence, racism and sexism, and oppression of any kind. These are the victims of a capitalist society.

To regard one group of persons as victims and another as non-victims is therefore an appeal to one's own consciousness. To argue that abortion is victimless is to exlude the living fetus as a victim. To regard the person who loses property as a victim is to value the sanctity of private property. To exclude civilians suffering from criminal war operations is to accept imperialist policies. To conceive of the person who is assaulted as a victim is to hold a view of proper social conduct. And to regard prisoners as criminals, not as victims of a system which places them there to begin with and which brutalizes them once they are there is to accept a particular notion of law and order.

That we do not usually regard ourselves as victims of an oppressive — and criminal — system says much about our own state of mind and our view of contemporary society. It is time that we critically investigate our own minds, our own theories of reality. Without doing so we run the risk of accepting the official reality. With a critical imagination, it is our task to expose that which negates the possibility of our personal and collective life.

NOTES

1. Karl Marx and Frederick Engels, *The Communist Manifesto* (New York: International Publishers, 1965; original, 1848), p. 20.

2. Paul Q. Hirst, "Marx and Engels on Law, Crime and Morality," *Economy and Society*, 1 (February 1972), pp. 49–52; Ian Taylor, Paul Walton, and Jock Young, *The New Criminology: For a Social Theory of Deviance* (London: Routledge & Kegan Paul, 1973), pp. 217–220.

3. Judah Hill, *Class Analysis: United States in the 1970's* (Emeryville, Calif.: Class Analysis, 1975), pp. 86–87.

4. Analyses of the ecological approach in criminology can be found in Terrence Morris, *The Criminal Area* (London: Routledge & Kegan Paul, 1958); Judith A. Wilks, "Ecological Correlates of Crime and Delinquency," in President's Commission on Law Enforcement and Administration of Justice, *Crime and Its Impact — An Assessment* (Washington, D.C.: U.S. Government Printing Office, 1967), pp. 138–156. Much of the research on the ecology of crime is in Harwin L. Voss and David M. Petersen, eds., *Ecology of Crime and Delinquency* (New York: Appleton-Century-Crofts, 1971). A radical critique of the ecological approach in criminology is found in Taylor, Walton, and Young, *The New Criminology*, pp. 110–125.

5. See John Rex and Robert Moore, *Race, Community and Conflict: A Study in Sparkbrook* (London: Oxford University Press, 1976).

6. Stuart Lottier, "Distribution of Criminal Offenses in Sectional Regions," *Journal of Criminal Law, Criminology and Police Science*, 29 (September-October 1938), pp. 329–344.

7. Lyle W. Shannon, "The Spatial Distribution of Criminal Offenses by States," *Journal of Criminal Law, Criminology and Police Science*, 45 (September-October 1954), pp. 264–274.

8. See Walter C. Reckless, *The Crime Problem*, 3rd ed. (New York: Appleton-Century-Crofts, 1961), pp. 69–70; H. C. Brearley, *Homicide in the United States* (Chapel Hill, N.C.: University of North Carolina Press, 1932); Raymond D. Gastill, "Homicide and a Regional Culture of Violence," *American Sociological Review*, 36 (June 1971), pp. 412–427; Sheldon Hackney, "Southern Violence," in Hugh Davis Graham and Ted Robert Gurr, eds., *The History of Violence in America* (New York: Bantam, 1969), pp. 505–527.

9. Wilks, "Ecological Correlates of Crime and Delinquency," pp. 150–151.

10. Colin Loftin and Robert H. Hill, "Regional Subculture and Homicide: An Examination of the Gastil-Hackney Thesis," *American Sociological Review*, 39 (October 1974), pp. 714–724.

11. Alvin L. Jacobson, "Crime Trends in Southern and Nonsouthern Cities: A Twenty-Year Perspective," *Social Forces*, 54 (September 1975), pp. 226–242; Howard S. Erlanger, "Is There a 'Subculture of Violence' in the South?" *Journal of Criminal Law and Criminology*, 66 (December 1976), pp. 483–490.

12. Marshall B. Clinard, "The Process of Urbanization and Criminal Behavior," *American Journal of Sociology*, 48 (September 1942), pp. 202–213; William P. Lentz, "Rural and Urban Differentials in Juvenile Delinquency," *Journal of Criminal Law, Criminology and Police Science*, 47 (September-October 1956), pp. 331–339; Theodore N. Ferdinand, "The Offense Patterns and Family Structures of Urban, Village, and Rural Delinquency," *Journal of Criminal Law, Criminology and Police Science*, 55 (March 1964), pp. 86–93; John P. Clark and Eugene P. Wenninger, "Socio-Economic Class and Area as Correlates of Illegal Behavior Among Juveniles," *American Sociological Review*, 27 (December 1962), pp. 826–834.

13. Richard Quinney, "Structural Characteristics, Population Areas, and Crime Rates in the United States," *Journal of Criminal Law, Criminology and Police Science*, 57 (March 1966), pp. 45–52.

14. Clifford R. Shaw and Henry D. McKay, *Delinquent Areas* (Chicago: University of Chicago Press, 1929); Clifford R. Shaw and Henry D. McKay, *Juvenile Delinquency and Urban Areas* (Chicago: University of Chicago Press, 1942).

15. Bernard Lander, *Toward an Understanding of Juvenile Delinquency* (New York: Columbia University Press, 1954).

16. Charles V. Willie and Anita Gershenovitz, "Juvenile Delinquency in Racially Mixed

Areas," *American Sociological Review,* 29 (October 1964), pp. 740–744; David J. Bordua, "Juvenile Delinquency and Anomie," *Social Problems,* 6 (Winter 1958–1959), pp. 230–238; Karl Schuessler, "Components of Variation in City Crime Rates," *Social Problems,* 9 (Spring 1962), pp. 314–323; and Roland J. Chilton, "Continuity in Delinquency Area Research: A Comparison of Studies for Baltimore, Detroit and Indianapolis," *American Sociological Review,* 29 (February 1964), pp. 71–83. Some of this research is analyzed in Gerald T. Slatin, "Ecological Analysis of Delinquency: Aggregation Effects," *American Sociological Review,* 34 (December 1969), pp. 894–907.

17. Calvin F. Schmid, "Urban Crime Areas: Part II," *American Sociological Review,* 25 (October 1960), pp. 655–678; Kenneth Polk, "Juvenile Delinquency and Social Areas," *Social Problems,* 5 (Winter 1957–1958), pp. 214–217; Richard Quinney, "Crime, Delinquency and Social Areas," *Journal of Research in Crime and Delinquency,* 1 (July 1964), pp. 149–154; Ronald W. Beasley and George Antunes, "The Etiology of Urban Crime" *Criminology,* 11 (February 1974), pp. 439–461; Kenneth R. Mladenka and Kim Quaile Hill, "A Reexamination of the Etiology of Urban Crime," *Criminology,* 13 (February 1976), pp. 491–506. A social-area analysis of offense rates in Indianapolis is reported in Roland Chilton and John P. J. Dussich, "Methodological Issues in Delinquency Research: Some Alternative Analyses of Geographically Distributed Data," *Social Forces,* 53 (September 1974), pp. 73–82.

18. Frederick M. Thrasher, *The Gang* (Chicago: University of Chicago Press, 1927). Also see William F. Whyte, *Street Corner Society* (Chicago: University of Chicago Press, 1943).

19. Lewis Yablonsky, *The Violent Gang* (New York: Free Press of Glencoe, 1962); Harold W. Pfantz, "Near-Group Theory and Collective Behavior: A Critical Reformulation," *Social Problems,* 9 (Fall 1961), pp. 167–174.

20. Solomon Kobrin, "The Conflict of Values in Delinquency Areas," *American Sociological Review,* 16 (October 1951), pp. 653–661.

21. Richard A. Cloward and Lloyd E. Ohlin, *Delinquency and Opportunity: A Theory of Delinquent Gangs* (New York: Free Press, 1960), pp. 161–186.

22. For further empirical works to support this position, see Irving Spergel, *Racketville, Slumtown, Haulburg: An Exploratory Study of Delinquent Subcultures* (Chicago: University of Chicago Press, 1964); Irving Spergel, "Male Young Adult Criminality, Deviant Values, and Differential Opportunities in Two Lower Class Negro Neighborhoods," *Social Problems,* 10 (Winter 1963), pp. 237–250; Albert J. Reiss, Jr. and Albert Lewis Rhodes, "The Distribution of Juvenile Delinquency in the Social Class Structure," *American Sociological Review,* 26 (October 1961), pp. 720–732; Sarah L. Boggs, "Urban Crime Patterns," *American Sociological Review,* 39 (December 1965), pp. 899–908. For an example of cross-cultural variations, see Lois B. De Fleur, "Ecological Variables in the Cross-Cultural Study of Delinquency," *Social Forces,* 45 (June 1967), pp. 556–570.

23. Excellent critiques are provided in Jon Snodgrass, "Clifford R. Shaw and Henry D. McKay: Chicago Criminologists," *British Journal of Criminology,* 16 (January 1976), pp. 1–19; and James T. Carey, *Sociology and Public Affairs: The Chicago School* (Beverly Hills, Calif.: Sage Publications, 1975).

24. For essentially this view of social psychology, see Peter Berger, *Invitation to Sociology: A Humanistic Perspective* (New York: Doubleday, 1963), chap. 6; Max Mark, "What Image of Man for Political Science?" *Western Political Quarterly,* 15 (December 1962), pp. 593–604; Dennis Wrong, "The Oversocialized Conception of Man in Modern Sociology," *American Sociological Review,* 26 (April 1961), pp. 183–193.

25. Tamotsu Shibutani, *Society and Personality: An Interactionist Approach to Social Psychology* (Englewood Cliffs, N.J.: Prentice-Hall, 1961), especially pp. 60, 91–94, 276–278. Also see S. F. Nadel, "Social Control and Self-Regulation," *Social Forces,* 31 (March 1953), pp. 265–273; Erving Goffman, *Asylums* (New York: Doubleday, 1961), pp. 318–320.

26. Richard A. Schermerhorn, "Man the Unfinished," *Sociological Quarterly,* 4 (Winter 1963), pp. 5–17; Gordon W. Allport, *Becoming: Basic Considerations for a Psychology of Personality* (New Haven: Yale University Press, 1955); Julian Huxley, *New Bottles for New Wines* (New York: Harper, 1957); John Lofland, *Deviance and Identity* (Englewood Cliffs, N.J.: Prentice-Hall, 1969).

27. On delinquency, for example, see Albert K. Cohen, *Delinquent Boys* (New York:

Free Press of Glencoe, 1955); Cloward and Ohlin, *Delinquency and Opportunity;* Harold W. Pfantz, "Near-Group Theory and Collective Behavior: A Critical Reformulation," *Social Problems,* 9 (Fall 1961), pp. 167–194; John P. Clark and Eugene P. Wenninger, "Goal Orientations and Illegal Behavior Among Juveniles," *Social Forces,* 42 (October 1963), pp. 49–59; Delbert S. Elliott, "Delinquency and Perceived Opportunity," *Sociological Inquiry,* 32 (Spring 1962), pp. 216–227; Judson R. Landis and Frank R. Scarpitti, "Perceptions Regarding Value Orientation and Legitimate Opportunity: Delinquents and Non-Delinquents," *Social Forces,* 44 (September 1965), pp. 83–91; Gerald Maxwell, "Adolescent Powerlessness and Delinquent Behavior," *Social Problems,* 14 (Summer 1966), pp. 35–47; John C. Quicker, "The Effect of Goal Discrepancy on Delinquency," *Social Problems,* 22 (October 1974), pp. 76–87. Also see Irving Louis Horowitz and Martin Liebowitz, "Social Deviance and Political Marginality: Toward a Redefinition of the Relation Between Sociology and Politics," *Social Problems,* 15 (Winter 1968), pp. 280–296; Richard Quinney, "A Conception of Man and Society for Criminology," *Sociological Quarterly,* 6 (Spring 1965), pp. 119–127.

28. Florian Znaniecki, *Social Actions* (New York: Farrar and Rinehart, 1936); Robert M. MacIver, *Social Causation* (Boston: Ginn, 1942); S. F. Nadel, *Foundations of Social Anthropology* (New York: Free Press, 1951); Talcott Parsons, *The Structure of Social Action* (New York: Free Press, 1949); Howard Becker, *Through Values to Social Interpretation* (Durham, N.C.: Duke University Press, 1950).

29. Max Weber, *Theory of Social and Economic Organization,* trans. by A. M. Henderson and Talcott Parsons (New York: Free Press, 1964), p. 88.

30. Alfred Schutz, *The Problem of Social Reality: Collected Papers* I (The Hague: Martinus Nijhoff, 1962), p. 53.

31. See Peter L. Berger and Thomas Luckmann, *The Social Construction of Reality* (Garden City, N.Y.: Doubleday, 1966).

32. Karl Marx, *The Eighteenth Brumaire of Louis Bonaparte* (New York: International Publishers, 1964).

33. See R. D. Laing and D. G. Cooper, *Reason and Violence: A Decade of Sartre's Philosophy, 1950–1960* (New York: Random House, 1971), pp. 49–51; Antonio Gramsci, *Selections from the Prison Notebooks,* ed. and trans. by Quintin Hoare and Geoffrey Nowell Smith (New York: International Publishers, 1972).

34. This "naturalistic" notion of social action is developed in David Matza, *Becoming Deviant* (Englewood Cliffs, N.J.: Prentice-Hall, 1969), pp. 3–14.

35. Edwin H. Sutherland, *Principles of Criminology,* 3rd ed. (Philadelphia: J. B. Lippincott, 1939).

36. See, for example, Tamotsu Shibutani, "Reference Groups as Perspectives," *American Journal of Sociology,* 60 (May 1955), pp. 562–569; Ralph H. Turner, "Role Taking, Role Standpoint and Reference Group Behavior," *American Journal of Sociology,* 61 (January 1956), pp. 316–328.

37. Edwin H. Sutherland, *Principles of Criminology,* 4th ed. (Philadelphia: J. B. Lippincott, 1947), pp. 1–9.

38. See Melvin L. DeFleur and Richard Quinney, "A Reformulation of Sutherland's Differential Association Theory and a Strategy for Empirical Verification," *Journal of Research in Crime and Delinquency,* 3 (January 1966), pp. 1–22. For a related discussion, see S. Kirson Weinberg, "Personality and Method in the Differential Association Theory: Comments on 'A Reformulation of Sutherland's Differential Association Theory and a Strategy for Empirical Verification,' " *Journal of Research in Crime and Delinquency,* 3 (July 1966), pp. 165–172.

39. See Albert J. Reiss, Jr. and A. Lewis Rhodes, "An Empirical Test of Differential Association Theory," *Journal of Research in Crime and Delinquency,* 1 (January 1964), pp. 5–18; James F. Short, Jr., "Differential Association and Delinquency," *Social Problems,* 4 (January 1957), pp. 233–239; James F. Short, Jr., "Differential Association as a Hypothesis: Problems of Empirical Testing," *Social Problems,* 8 (Summer 1960), pp. 14–25; Harwin L. Voss, "Differential Association and Reported Delinquent Behavior: A Replication," *Social Problems,* 12 (Summer 1964), pp. 78–85; Allen E. Liska, "Interpreting the Causal Structure

of Differential Association Theory," *Social Problems,* 16 (Spring 1969), pp. 485–492. Some of the findings are questioned in Reed Adams, "Differential Association and Learning Principles Revisited," *Social Problems,* 20 (Spring 1973), pp. 458–470; Maynard Erikson, "The Group Context of Delinquent Behavior," *Social Problems,* 19 (Summer 1971), pp. 114–129; and Michael J. Hindelang, "With a Little Help from Their Friends: Group Participation in Reported Delinquent Behavior," *British Journal of Criminology,* 16 (April 1976), pp. 109–125.

40. Daniel Glaser, "Criminality Theories and Behavioral Images," *American Journal of Sociology,* 61 (March 1956), pp. 433–444.

41. Ibid., p. 440. Empirical support for the theory of differential identification is found in Victor Matthews, "Differential Identification: An Empirical Note," *Social Problems,* 15 (Winter 1968), pp. 376–383.

42. C. R. Jeffery, "Criminal Behavior and Learning Theory," *Journal of Criminal Law, Criminology and Police Science,* 56 (September 1965), p. 300. Also see Robert L. Burgess and Ronald L. Akers, "A Differential Association-Reinforcement Theory of Criminal Behavior," *Social Problems,* 14 (Fall 1966), pp. 128–147. The theory subsequently has been applied to a wide range of deviant behaviors in Ronald L. Akers, *Deviant Behavior: A Social Learning Approach* (Belmont, Calif.: Wadsworth, 1973).

43. Howard S. Becker, "Notes on the Concept of Commitment," *American Journal of Sociology,* 66 (July 1960), pp. 32–40.

44. Scott Briar and Irving Piliavin, "Delinquency, Situational Inducements, and Commitment to Conformity," *Social Problems,* 13 (Summer 1965), p. 39.

45. Related research is found in Gary F. Jensen, " 'Crime Doesn't Pay': Correlates of a Shared Misunderstanding," *Social Problems,* 17 (Fall 1969), pp. 189–201; Gary F. Jensen, "Delinquency and Adolescent Self-Conceptions: A Study of the Personal Relevance of Infraction," *Social Problems,* 20 (Summer 1972); pp. 84–103; John R. Stratton, "Differential Identification and Attitudes Toward the Law," *Social Forces,* 46 (December 1967), pp. 256–262.

46. David Matza, *Delinquency and Drift* (New York: John Wiley, 1964), especially pp. 27–30. For related research, see Michael J. Hindelang, "The Commitment of Delinquents to Their Misdeeds: Do Delinquents Drift?" *Social Problems,* 17 (Spring 1970), pp. 502–509.

47. Gresham M. Sykes and David Matza, "Techniques of Neutralization: A Theory of Delinquency," *American Sociological Review,* 22 (December 1957), pp. 644–670.

48. Travis Hirschi, *Causes of Delinquency* (Berkeley: University of California Press, 1969), pp. 16–34.

49. See Edwin M. Lemert, *Social Pathology* (New York: McGraw-Hill, 1951), pp. 54–72; Alexander L. Clark and Jack P. Gibbs, "Social Control: A Reformulation," *Social Problems,* 12 (Spring 1965), pp. 398–415.

50. Frank Tannenbaum, *Crime and the Community* (New York: Columbia University Press, 1938), pp. 17–18.

51. Cesare Lombroso, *Crime: Its Causes and Remedies* (Boston: Little, Brown, 1911). Also see E. A. Hooton, *Crime and the Man* (Cambridge: Harvard University Press, 1937). For more recent research and interpretation, see Raymond J. Corsini, "Appearance and Criminality," *American Journal of Sociology,* 65 (July 1959), pp. 49–51.

52. Hans von Hentig, "Redhead and Outlaw," *Journal of Criminal Law, Criminology and Police Science,* 38 (May-June 1947), pp. 1–6.

53. William H. Sheldon, *Varieties of Delinquent Youth: An Introduction to Constitutional Psychiatry* (New York: Harper & Row, 1949). Also see Sheldon and Eleanor T. Glueck, *Physique and Delinquency* (New York: Harper & Row, 1956). The controversy over the XYY chromosomal constitution in relation to crime, especially the excessive body height attributed to people who have it, may be similarly resolved. On the evidence, see *Report on XYY Chromosomal Abnormality* (Chevy Chase, Md.: National Institute of Mental Health, Center for Studies of Crime and Delinquency, 1970). A critical discussion is found in Theodore Sarbin and Jeffrey Miller, "Demonism Revisited: The XYY Chromosomal Anomaly," *Issues in Criminology,* 5 (Summer 1970), pp. 195–208.

54. Edwin M. Lemert, *Human Deviance, Social Problems and Social Control* (Englewood

Cliffs, N.J.: Prentice-Hall, 1967), pp. 40–41. Material on self-conception in juvenile delinquency is in these reports on research: Walter C. Reckless, Simon Dinitz, and Ellen Murray, "Self-concept as an Insulator Against Delinquency," *American Sociological Review,* 21 (December 1956), pp. 744–746; Walter C. Reckless, Simon Dinitz, and Barbara Kay, "The Self Component in Potential Delinquency and Potential Non-Delinquency," *American Sociological Review,* 22 (October 1957), pp. 566–570; Frank R. Scarpitti, Ellen Murray, Simon Dinitz, and Walter C. Reckless, "The 'Good' Boy in a High Delinquency Area: Four Years Later," *American Sociological Review,* 25 (August 1960), pp. 555–558; Simon Dinitz, Frank R. Scarpitti, and Walter C. Reckless, "Delinquency Vulnerability: A Cross Group and Longitudinal Analysis," *American Sociological Review,* 27 (August 1962), pp. 515–517. Other research on self-conceptions of offenders includes Leon F. Fanin and Marshall B. Clinard, "Differences in the Conception of Self as a Male Among Lower and Middle Class Delinquents," *Social Problems,* 13 (Fall 1965), pp. 205–214; John W. Kinch, "Self-Conceptions of Types of Delinquents," *Sociological Inquiry,* 32 (Spring 1962), pp. 228–234; James F. Short, Jr. and Fred L. Strodtbeck, *Group Process and Gang Delinquency* (Chicago: University of Chicago Press, 1965), pp. 140–184. Critiques are found in Michael Schwartz and Sandra S. Tangri, "A Note on Self-Concept as an Insulator Against Delinquency," *American Sociological Review,* 30 (December 1965), pp. 922–926; Sandra S. Tangri and Michael Schwartz, "Delinquency Research and the Self-Concept Variable," *Journal of Criminal Law, Criminology and Police Science,* 58 (June 1967), pp. 182–190. A theory of socialization and self is formulated in James C. Hackler, "A Developmental Theory of Delinquency," *Canadian Review of Sociology and Anthropology,* 8 (May 1971), pp. 61–75. self is formulated in James C. Hackler, "A Developmental Theory of Delinquency," *Canadian Review of Sociology and Anthropology,* 8 (May 1971), pp. 61–75.

55. See Edwin M. Schur, *Crimes Without Victims* (Englewood Cliffs, N.J.: Prentice-Hall, 1965), pp. 5–7. Empirical support is found in Suzanne S. Ageton and Delbert S. Elliott, "The Effects of Legal Processing on Delinquent Orientations," *Social Problems,* 22 (October 1974), pp. 87–100. Further conceptualization is presented in Joseph W. Rogers and M. D. Buffalo, "Fighting Back: Nine Modes of Adaptation to a Deviant Label," *Social Problems,* 22 (October 1974), pp. 101–118; John R. Hepburn, "The Role of the Audience in Deviant Behavior and Identity," *Sociology and Social Research,* 59 (July 1975), pp. 387–405; Neal Shover, "Criminal Behavior as Theoretical Praxis," *Issues in Criminology,* 10 (Spring 1975), pp. 95–108.

56. Raymond J. Michalowski, Jr., "Violence in the Road: The Crime of Vehicular Homicide," *Journal of Research in Crime and Delinquency,* 12 (January 1975), pp. 30–43.

57. Richard Maxwell Brown, "Historical Patterns of Violence in America," in *Violence in America: Historical and Comparative Perspectives,* A Report to the National Commission on the Causes and Prevention of Violence, prepared by H. D. Graham and Ted R. Gurr (New York: Bantam Books, 1969), pp. 45–84. Some qualifications, especially on extent of violence on the frontier, are in W. Eugene Hollon, *Frontier Violence: Another Look* (New York: Oxford University Press, 1974).

58. Susan Griffin, "Rape: The All-American Crime," *Ramparts,* 10 (September 1971), p. 34. Research on rape is found in Menachem Amir, *Patterns in Forcible Rape* (Chicago: University of Chicago Press, 1971).

59. Sheldon Hackney, "Southern Violence," in *Violence in America,* p. 524.

60. National Commission on the Causes and Prevention of Violence, *Firearms and Violence in American Life,* A Staff Report prepared by George D. Newton and Franklin D. Zimring (Washington, D.C.: U.S. Government Printing Office, 1969).

61. James D. Wright and Linda L. Marston, "The Ownership of the Means of Destruction: Weapons in the United States," *Social Problems,* 23 (October 1975), pp. 93–107.

62. National Commission on the Causes and Prevention of Violence, *Firearms and Violence in American Life,* pp. 69–74.

63. Marvin E. Wolfgang, *Patterns in Criminal Homicide* (Philadelphia: University of Pennsylvania Press, 1958), p. 252.

64. Lynn A. Curtis, "Victim Precipitation and Violent Crime," *Social Problems,* 21 (April 1974), pp. 594–605.

65. National Commission on the Causes and Prevention of Violence, *To Establish Justice, to Insure Domestic Tranquility* (Washington, D.C.: U.S. Government Printing Office, 1969), pp. 25–26.

66. President's Commission on Law Enforcement and Administration of Justice, *The Challenge of Crime in a Free Society* (Washington, D.C.: U.S. Government Printing Office, 1967), p. 18.

67. *Crimes of Violence,* vol. 11, A Staff Report Submitted to the National Commission on the Causes and Prevention of Violence, codirectors Donald J. Mulvihill and Melvin M. Tumin (Washington, D.C.: U.S. Government Printing Office, 1969), pp. 216–219.

68. Selwyn Raab, "33% in New York Don't Know Killer," *The New York Times,* June 13, 1976, p. 1. Other emerging patterns are mentioned in Robert A. Silverman, "Victim-Offender Relationships in Face-to-Face Delinquent Acts," *Social Problems,* 22 (February 1975), pp. 383–393.

69. *Crimes of Violence,* vol. 11, p. 210.

70. Alex Pokorny, "A Comparison of Homicides in Two Cities," *Journal of Criminal Law, Criminology and Police Science,* 56 (December 1965), pp. 479–487.

71. Harwin L. Voss and John R. Hepburn, "Patterns in Criminal Homicide in Chicago," *Journal of Criminal Law, Criminology and Police Science,* 5 (December 1968), p. 502.

72. *Crimes of Violence,* vol. 11, p. 209.

73. Edwin M. Lemert, "An Isolation of Closure Theory of Naive Check Forgery," *Journal of Criminal Law, Criminology and Police Science,* 44 (October 1953), p. 298.

74. Mary Owen Cameron, *The Booster and the Switch: Department Store Shoplifting* (New York: Free Press, 1964), p. xii.

75. William E. Wattenberg and James Balistrieri, "Automobile Theft: A 'Favored-Group' Delinquency," *American Journal of Sociology,* 57 (May 1952), pp. 575–579.

76. Bertram Spiller, "Delinquency and Middle Class Goals," *Journal of Criminal Law, Criminology and Police Science,* 56 (December 1965), pp. 463–478. A vast literature comments on formation of delinquent patterns in relation to the dominant culture. See Walter B. Miller, "Lower Class Culture as a Generating Milieu of Gang Delinquency," *Journal of Social Issues,* 14 (November 3, 1958), pp. 5–19; Albert K. Cohen, *Delinquent Boys: The Culture of the Gang* (New York: Free Press of Glencoe, 1955). Critiques of the theory of the "delinquent subculture" are found in "Delinquent Subcultures: Sociological Interpretations of Gang Delinquency," *Annals of the American Academy of Political and Social Science,* 338 (November 1961), pp. 119–136; John I. Kitsuse and David C. Dietrick, "Delinquent Boys: A Critique," *American Sociological Review,* 24 (April 1959), pp. 208–215; Lamar Empey, "Delinquency Theory and Recent Research," *Journal of Research in Crime and Delinquency,* 4 (January 1967), pp. 28–42.

77. David Matza and Gresham M. Sykes, "Juvenile Delinquency and Subterranean Values," *American Sociological Review,* 26 (October 1961), pp. 712–719; Matza, *Delinquency and Drift.* Further research is in Benjamin G. Carmichael, "Youth Crime in Urban Communities: A Descriptive Analysis of Street Hustlers and Their Crimes," *Crime and Delinquency,* 21 (April 1975), pp. 139–148.

78. President's Commission on Law Enforcement and Administration of Justice, *The Challenge of Crime in a Free Society* (Washington, D.C.: U.S. Government Printing Office, 1967), p. 35. Italics added.

79. Federal Bureau of Investigation, *Uniform Crime Reports, 1976* (Washington, D.C.: U.S. Government Printing Office, 1977), p. 183.

80. Andre Normandeau, "Violence and Robbery: A Case Study," *Acta Criminologica,* 5 (1972), p. 77.

81. John E. Conklin, *Robbery and the Criminal Justice System* (Philadelphia: J. B. Lippincott, 1972), pp. 103–105.

82. Normandeau, "Violence and Robbery," p. 83.

83. A similar estimate is in Russell R. Dynes, Alfred C. Clarke, Simon Dinitz, and Iwao Ishino, *Social Problems: Dissensus and Deviation in an Industrial Society* (New York: Oxford University Press, 1964), p. 543.

84. Don C. Gibbons, *Changing the Lawbreaker: The Treatment of Delinquents and Criminals* (Englewood Cliffs, N.J.: Prentice-Hall, 1965), p. 105.

85. Walter C. Reckless, *The Crime Problem,* 3rd ed. (New York: Appleton-Century-Crofts, 1961), p. 164.

86. James A. Inciardi, *Careers in Crime* (Chicago: Rand McNally, 1975).

87. Edwin M. Lemert, *Social Pathology* (New York: McGraw-Hill, 1951), pp. 323–324.

88. Joseph R. Weil and W. T. Brannon, *"Yellow Kid" Weil* (Chicago: Ziff-Davis, 1948), p. 293.

89. Edwin H. Sutherland, *The Professional Thief* (Chicago: University of Chicago Press, 1937), pp. 197–228. Excellent background material is in Robert H. Vasoli and Dennis A. Terzola, "Sutherland's Professional Thief," *Criminology* 12 (August 1974), pp. 131–154.

90. David W. Maurer, *The Big Con* (New York: Signet Books, 1962); David W. Maurer, *Whiz Mob* (New Haven: College and University Press, 1964).

91. Bruce Jackson, *A Thief's Primer* (New York: Macmillan, 1969), p. 23.

92. Cameron, *The Booster and the Snitch,* pp. 40–45.

93. Edwin M. Lemert, "The Behavior of the Systematic Check Forger," *Social Problems,* 6 (Fall 1958), p. 143.

94. Werner J. Einstadter, "The Social Organization of Armed Robbery," *Social Problems,* 17 (Summer 1969), pp. 67–68. For research on professional burglary, see Neal Shover, "The Social Organization of Burglary," *Social Problems,* 20 (Spring 1973), pp. 499–514.

95. See Harry King, *Bag Man: A Professional Thief's Journey,* William J. Chambliss, ed. (New York: Harper & Row, 1972), especially pp. 97–108. Also Edwin H. Schur, "Sociological Analysis of Confidence Swindling," *Journal of Criminal Law, Criminology and Police Science,* 48 (September-October, 1957), pp. 296–304.

96. Neal Shover, "Structures and Careers in Burglary, *Journal of Criminal Law, Criminology and Police Science,* 63 (December 1972), pp. 550–549. Also see Carl B. Klockars, *The Professional Fence* (New York: Free Press, 1974).

97. President's Commission on Law Enforcement and Administration of Justice, *Crime and Its Impact — An Assessment* (Washington, D.C.: U.S. Government Printing Office, 1967), pp. 98–99.

98. Peter Letkemann, *Crime as Work* (Englewood Cliffs, N.J.: Prentice-Hall, 1973). Also Neal Shover, "The Social Organization of Burglary," *Social Problems,* 20 (Spring 1973), pp. 499–514.

99. Women Endorsing Decriminalization, "Prostitution: A Non-Victim Crime?" *Issues in Criminology,* 8 (Fall 1973), pp. 137–138. For a general discussion of prostitution today see T. C. Esselstyn, "Prostitution in the United States," *The Annals,* 376 (March 1968), pp. 123–135.

100. See Maurice Lexnoff and William Westley, "The Homosexual Community," *Social Problems,* 3 (1956), pp. 257–263; Donald W. Cory, *The Homosexual in America* (New York: Greenberg, 1951); D. J. Mercer, *They Walk in the Shadow* (New York: Comet Press, 1959); Gordon Westwood, *Society and the Homosexual* (New York: E. P. Dutton, 1953), chaps. 19–21; Michael Schofield, *Sociological Aspects of Homosexuality: A Comparative Study of Three Types of Homosexuals* (Boston: Little, Brown, 1965); Barry Dank, "Coming Out in the Gay World," *Psychiatry,* 34 (May 1971), pp. 180–197.

101. John C. Pollard, "Some Comments on Nonnarcotic Drug Abuse," paper presented at the Nonnarcotic Drug Institute, Southern Illinois University, Edwardsville, Ill., June 1967. Also see Carl D. Chambers and Leon Brill, "Some Considerations for the Treatment of Nonnarcotic Drug Abusers," Leon Brill and Louis Lieberman, eds., *The Treatment of Drug Addiction and Drug Abuse* (Boston: Little, Brown, 1970).

102. Hugh Parry, "Tranquilizer Users," *Wayfarers Magazine* (February 1969). Also see Henry L. Lennard, Leon J. Epstein, Arnold Bernstein, and Donald C. Ransom, *Mystification and Drug Misuse: Hazards in Using Psychoactive Drugs* (San Francisco: Jossey-Bass, 1971).

103. Edwin H. Lemert, *Social Pathology,* p. 246.

104. Seymour Fiddle, "The Addict Culture and Movement into and out of Hospitals," in Senate Committee on the Judiciary, Subcommittee to Investigate Juvenile Delinquency,

Hearings, Pt. 13, New York City, September 20–21 (Washington, D.C.: U.S. Government Printing Office, 1963), p. 3156.

105. See William J. Chambliss, "Markets, Profits, Labor and Smack," *Contemporary Crises*, 1 (January 1977), pp. 53–75.

106. Richard C. Stephens and Rosalind D. Ellis, "Narcotic Addicts and Crime: Analysis and Trends," *Criminology*, 12 (February 1975), pp. 474–488. Also see the essays in James A. Inciardi and Carl D. Chambers, eds., *Drugs and the Criminal Justice System* (Beverly Hills, Calif.: Sage Publications, 1974).

107. See Abraham S. Blumberg, "The Politics of Deviance: The Case of Drugs," *Journal of Drug Issues*, 3 (Spring 1973), pp. 105–114. Also Nicholas M. Regush, *The Drug Addiction Business* (New York: Dial Press, 1971).

108. Allen Ginsberg, "Abbie Hoffman — Political Poet," *Berkeley Barb*, October 5–11, 1973, p. 5.

109. For a more detailed discussion of victimization, see Richard Quinney, "Who is the Victim?" *Criminology*, 10 (November 1972), pp. 314–323.

110. R. M. Perkins, *Criminal Law* (Brooklyn, N.Y.: Foundation Press, 1957), p. 5.

111. President's Commission on Law Enforcement and Administration of Justice, *The Challenge of Crime in a Free Society*, p. 80.

112. Julia R. Schwendinger and Herman Schwendinger, "Rape Myths: In Legal, Theoretical, and Everyday Practice," *Crime and Social Justice*, 1 (Spring-Summer 1974), pp. 18–26; Kurt Weis and Sandra S. Borges, "Victimology and Rape: The Case of the Legitimate Victim," *Issues in Criminology*, 8 (Fall 1973), pp. 71–115; Murray A. Straus, "Sexual Inequality, Cultural Norms, and Wife-Beating," *Victimology*, 1 (Spring 1976), pp. 54–70; Herman Schwendinger and Julia R. Schwendinger, "Delinquency and the Collective Varieties of Youth, *Crime and Social Justice*, 5 (Spring-Summer 1976), pp. 7–25; and David F. Greenberg, "Delinquency and the Age Structure of Society," *Contemporary Crises*, 1 (April 1977), pp. 189–223.

113. Dorie Klein and June Kress, "Any Woman's Blues: A Critical Overview of Women, Crime, and the Criminal Justice System, *Crime and Social Justice*, 5 (Spring-Summer 1976), pp. 34–49; Robert Staples, "Black Crime, White Racism and American Justice: An Application of the Colonial Model to Explain Crime and Race," *Phylon*, 36 (March 1975), pp. 14–22.

LAW ENFORCEMENT AND CRIMINAL JUSTICE

POLICE

Police in the Community

8

Criminal justice is a principal feature of modern, advanced capitalist society. When a society cannot solve the social problems of its own creation, it must devise and implement policies for controlling the population. The state's control apparatus has become even more important in the development of capitalism in the United States. Policies of control, especially for crime, are an attempt to regulate problems and conflicts that otherwise can be solved only by social and economic changes that go beyond capitalist reforms. Criminal justice, as the euphemism for controlling class struggle and administering legal repression, becomes a major type of social policy in the advanced stages of capitalism.

An expanding system for criminal justice is the only way late capitalism has of "integrating" the population into the economic and political system. The notion that the social problems generated by capitalism can be solved becomes obsolete. Instead, problems such as crime are dealt with by following a *control* model. When the underlying conditions of capitalism cannot be changed — without changing the system itself — controlling the population oppressed by the social conditions is the only "solution." One theorist-strategist of the capitalist state says, we must "learn to live with crime," and the next important question is then "what constitutes an effective law-enforcement and order-maintenance system?"[1]

At all levels of the criminal-justice system new techniques of control are being developed and instituted. Not only has implementation of a military-hardware approach to criminal justice increased, but more recently subtler approaches have grown alongside it. A dual system deals harshly with some actions of the working-class population that are defined as criminal, by strong-arm techniques and punitive measures. Other actions are handled by gentler techniques such as diversion from the courts and community-based corrections. In general, whatever the current techniques, the model is designed for *pacification*. The population is not only to be controlled, but it is to accept this control. The authors of *The Iron Fist and the Velvet Glove* write about the developing law-enforcement aspects of the system:

> During the later 1960's the technical and managerial approach to police work represented by the military-corporate model came under increasing criticism. More sophisticated analyses of crime and urban disorder suggested that massive spending on military hardware, by itself, would not only fail to stop rising crime rates and urban discontent, but would probably serve to further alienate large sectors of the population. This approach stressed the need for the police to develop closer ties to the communities most heavily patrolled by them. The emphasis began to be placed less on paramilitary efficiency and more on insuring popular consent and acquiescence. The idea that police departments should engage in some sort of "community relations" had, of course, been around for some time, but community relations programs, in practice, were few, and those that did exist were generally regarded as ineffective window-dressing. The new emphasis, on the other hand, represented a serious attempt to supplement the growing technological prowess of the police with programs that could make the police role more acceptable to the people most affected by it.[2]

The capitalist state, in alliance with monopoly capital, must continually innovate in expanding the criminal-justice system.

DEVELOPMENT OF THE POLICE

Law enforcement in the community is crucial in maintaining the established social and economic order in the United States. The police institution developed in the nineteenth century to preserve the social order. The police were formed as a separate agency that could respond to the attacks being made on domestic order in the growing cities of Europe and the United States. The propertied classes feared the threat they felt from the "dangerous classes," the "agglomeration of the criminal, vicious, and violent — the rapidly multiplying poor of cities whose size had no precedent in history."[3]

The policed society relieved the propertied class of coercing the population by themselves. Police were a domestic force outside the military that would maintain domestic order. Mobs and riots, whether reacting to oppressive conditions or other impulses, could be contained by a separate police force, performing for the propertied classes.

The new police bureaucracy could penetrate society in a way impossible for military forces. Diffused throughout society, they could work at preventing crime by detecting and apprehending criminals. The convenience was more than technical: "The replacement of intermittent military intervention in largely unpoliced society by continuous professional bureaucratic policing meant that the benefits of police organization — continual pervasive moral display and lower long-term costs of official coercion for the state and propertied classes — absolutely required the moral cooperation of civil society."[4] The police had become an integral part of society, to be morally accepted by everyone. They were a garrison force, used constantly against the internal enemy.

The movement to a policed society can be traced from the constabulary system to the modern professional police.[5] In early England, local citizens were mutally responsible for maintaining law and order. Eventually local noblemen appointed constables to enforce the law. When the local areas, known as "hundreds," were grouped to form "shires," the office of the "shire-reeve" (later "sheriff") came into being. During the reign of Edward I (1272–1307) the first official forces were formed in the large towns of England. These "watch and ward" officers were charged with protecting property and arresting offenders between sunset and daybreak. In 1326 Edward II created the justices of the peace to assist the sheriff in policing the country, but the constable remained the primary law-enforcement officer in all the English towns.

As long as England was rural these law-enforcement officers were adequate. But by the middle of the eighteenth century, towns and cities had grown fairly large, and innovations in law enforcement were needed. One of the most important experiments was the appointment by Henry Fielding (he wrote *Tom Jones*) of a foot patrol, later known as the "Bow Street Runners," in the Bow Street magistracy of London. Such a small force could not, however, keep order in the city, and conditions were so critical that as the eighteenth century ended, committees in the House of Commons called for a better system of protecting the public. Finally, a committee of the Commons issued a report on the increase in crime and urged a change in the method of policing the metropolis. Sir Robert Peel introduced a police reform bill that was passed by Parliament in 1829.[6] The

Urban police forces were established to deal with the problems of industrial capitalism. Here a unit of the Providence, Rhode Island police department was photographed in 1904 in the courtyard of the police station.

Metropolitan Police Act established for London a police force separate from the old constabulary system and served as model for other cities in Great Britain.

The American colonies adopted the English system of law-enforcement officers.[7] American villages and rural areas had their night watchmen, constables, sheriffs, and justices of the peace. Early in the nineteenth century, American cities too established their own forces. London's police plan was adopted by New York in 1844, and in the next ten years similar police systems were organized in Chicago, Boston, and Philadelphia. By the early 1900's most cities in the United States had unified police forces.[8]

The professional police force was an attempt to control the behavior of those who rebelled against oppressive urban and industrial conditions. Capitalist industrialization increased the work force and the exploitation of workers in the factories and growing slums of the industrial cities. The police force, designed as an instrument of class domination, attempted to control the new industrial working class. In Buffalo, the wealthiest business interests were responsible for establishing the police force, to control disputes between business owners and workers over wages and working conditions.[9] The police force maintained an order beneficial to the new industrial capitalist class. Sidney Harring argued, "The preeminent force behind the creation of the police institution in the United States was the need of large-scale entrepreneurs to ensure the orderly control of workers during the era of capitalist industrialization."[10]

The police were now to prevent disorder, according to a preventive conception of law enforcement: "the police take the initiative and seek out those engaged in violating the law — those engaged in specific behaviors that are designated as illegal."[11] Preventing crime seemed a rational way of keeping public order. The objectives of the police force are the same today, only now the methods of law enforcement are aided by the latest in scientific and technological developments, plus bureaucratic management and the science of social behavior.

Law enforcement in the United States today, with half a million employed in approximately 40,000 law-enforcement agencies, cannot be treated as a unitary system. The duties vary, with at least five types of public law-enforcement systems, conforming roughly to the major levels of government: (1) the police agencies of the federal government; (2) the state police forces and criminal investigation agencies of the fifty states; (3) the sheriffs in more than 3,000 counties, plus a few county police forces that either duplicate the sheriff's police jurisdiction or displace it; (4) the police of a thousand cities and more than 20,000 townships and New England towns, to which must be added an unknown number of magisterial districts and county districts in the South and West; and (5) the police of 15,000 villages, boroughs, and incorporated towns, together with a small number of special-purpose forces serving public quasi-corporations and ad hoc districts.[12] Add to these the law-enforcement activities of private police agencies and you have a great many systems of law enforcement, related in their functions and at times overlapping in their jurisdictions.

And within the systems are specific police agencies. Some federal agencies have law-enforcement powers, such as the Federal Bureau of Investigation, the Secret Service, the Bureau of Narcotics, Post Office Inspectors, the Bureau of Internal Revenue, the Bureau of Customs, the Immigration Border Patrol, and the Alcohol Tax Unit of the Department of the Treasury. The federal government also maintains the United States Marshal as a law-enforcement agent whose duty it is to preserve order in the courtrooms, handle subpoenas and summonses, seize goods, transport prisoners, and serve as a disbursing officer.[13]

Law enforcement on the state level was not established in the United

States until the first part of this century. In 1905, Pennsylvania organized the first state police force; by World War II, all the states had followed. Today the state police forces perform such varied functions as patrolling highways, investigating fires, and inspecting property.[14] They also provide services to local police forces, including criminal identification, laboratory services, and communication services.

Outside public law enforcement is a type usually obscured from public view: *private police.* Private agencies such as Pinkerton's, Inc., came into being in the middle of the last century when private companies desired protection that civil police could not give them. Railroads, coal companies, and iron-ore companies employed their own police forces to suppress labor militancy, using the private police to break strikes of workers against the companies.[15] Today numerous kinds of businesses, industries, and institutions use private police to guard their property and promote their own welfare.

More than 3,000 private police agencies are currently engaged in privately enforcing criminal law. Expenditures on uniformed guards and private detective services amount to about $15 million a year.[16] And, contrary to our common knowledge, private police outnumber public police in most cities and states. The Pinkerton agency alone has a staff of nearly 30,000. Although private police do not usually make arrests, suspects they apprehend may be turned over to public police for official arrest and prosecution. The public and private police in the United States today cooperate in ways that increase the ability of the capitalist class to establish its rule and maintain control over the rest of the population.

REGULATION AND DISCRETION IN LAW ENFORCEMENT

The police, in the attempt to maintain the social and economic order, operate within a very tenuous framework of social and legal control. In fact, contrary to popular belief, few activities of the police are regulated by the law. Any regulation that does apply to them comes from decisions made by the courts. Developing independently of other judicial agencies, most police activity takes place outside legal control.

Most of the law regulating police behavior has formed from specific cases in which defendants have questioned the procedures used in their criminal convictions. Primarily by default, the Supreme Court has sought to provide a few legal guarantees to protect the person against actions by the state. The court has ruled on a number of issues directly related to law enforcement, such as arrest warrants, search and seizure, interrogation, confessions, wiretapping and eavesdropping, use of informers, and right of counsel. The assumption is that controlling police *mis*conduct will somehow regulate police behavior.

The Supreme Court decisions on law enforcement are generally founded on three provisions in the Constitution. The Fourth Amendment provides: "The right of the people to be secure in their persons, houses, papers, and effects, against unreasonable searches and seizures, shall not be violated, and no warrants shall issue but upon probable cause, supported by oath or affirmation, and particularly describing the place to be searched, and the persons or things to be seized." The Fifth Amendment provides that "no person . . . shall be compelled in any criminal case to be a witness against himself, nor be deprived of life, liberty, or property, without due process of law." And the Fourteenth Amendment provides that "no state shall . . . deprive any person of life, liberty, or property without due process of law, nor deny to any person within its jurisdiction the equal protection of the laws." Several Supreme Court decisions have come from the review of criminal cases in which these constitutional guarantees have been jeopardized.[17]

One of the first constitutional tests of law-enforcement practices confronted by the Supreme Court was in the Weeks v. United States case of 1914. In establishing the "exclusionary" rule in that case, the court ruled that evidence obtained by illegal means must be excluded from criminal procedure. With the McNabb v. United States case in 1943, the Supreme Court ruled confessions inadmissible if obtained by federal officers during an unlawful detention. The McNabb decision was elaborated upon in 1957 in Mallory v. United States. The court ruled that confessions are inadmissible when they are obtained from an arrestee who had not been properly brought before a magistrate. In 1961 the court ruled in Mapp v. Ohio that evidence obtained by unreasonable searches and seizures must be excluded from state and federal criminal trials. The Gideon v. Wainwright decision of 1963 ensured the right of counsel for defendants, which was further specified in 1964 in Massiah v. United States and Escobedo v. Illinois. The decisions of 1964 provide that the accused in custody may not be questioned until the request for legal counsel has been complied with. Specific guidelines for law enforcement and minimum procedural safeguards were established in 1966 in Miranda v. Arizona.

More recently, however, the courts have retreated from some of these decisions. In Harris v. New York, the Supreme Court withdrew some provisions of the Miranda decision, on the illegal obtaining of incriminating statements from the defendant. Likewise, recent crime bills and court decisions have in effect overturned some of the earlier court rulings.

But no matter what the extent of judicial regulation of police conduct, the court's influence on law enforcement is of little consequence. Even when the court rulings touch local police departments, there is hardly any effect on arrest practices. As in the Miranda case, data on interrogation of suspects by the police show that the police always have evidence apart from the interrogation itself.[18] And restrictions, when they are observed by the police, do not limit them in making an arrest and charging the suspect with a crime. The result is that the police are almost totally free to pursue their own course[19]. They are bound mainly by the rules of their own occupation and the interests of those they serve.

Contrary to any framework of legal control, then, much police behavior is a matter of *discretion*: how they act is determined by their own standards combined with the general objective of preserving domestic order. Still it is commonly assumed that the police are operating entirely according to a body of legal prescriptions.

Many assume too that the police fully enforce the criminal law by arresting all who violate the law. The ideal of *full enforcement* of the law is, in fact, preserved officially in formal law as well as in popular conception.[20] Criminal statutes are so stated as to imply that the duty of the police is to faithfully enforce all the laws, against everyone, in all circumstances, at all times. The stereotype of the police shows them as ministerial officers whose function it is to detect crime, gather evidence, and make arrests. Police themselves reinforce this conception by denying that decisions are involved in their work or that they have informal standards for making their decisions.

Full enforcement of criminal law, however, is far from possible because of numerous limitations and circumstances. First, a few *procedural* restrictions limit the enforcement of some laws. Second, *interpretational* latitude, resulting primarily from ambiguous wording in many statutes, permits much discretion on what a criminal offense is. Third, *technical* matters confound law enforcement, such as limited police time, personnel, and equipment for detecting and investigating crime. Fourth, *organizational* norms of local police departments are guides for both enforcement and nonenforcement of criminal law. Fifth, *ideological* orientations or values of policemen provide a basis for selective law enforcement. Sixth, *societal* pressures prevent full enforcement of some criminal laws. These pressures are a lack of correspondence between criminal statutes and current norms, failure of victims and the public to report offenses, and the harmful social consequences that might follow enforcement of some criminal laws. Whatever the reasons, law enforcement is a matter of decision-making, of discretion.

Most people continue to have little idea about the extent of discretionary decisions in law enforcement and little knowledge of the ways in which discretion operates. Police discretion rarely comes to the average citizen's attention. Only when we find ourselves in an encounter with the police do we realize how important police discretion is for us. "Solutions" such as these are being suggested:

> The first step is to evaluate police discretion from the sub-rosa position it now occupies; the role of police as decision-makers must be expressly recognized. Then, as has been found possible with respect to other administrative agencies, the areas in which discretion properly may be exercised must be delimited, principles to govern its exercise must be established, and effective means of control must be discovered.[21]

It is unlikely, however, that any solutions to the problem will be possible so long as the police are an agency apart from the community in which law enforcement takes place. But no matter what solutions are proposed and implemented, we must immediately recognize that discretion does exist and that it is basic to law enforcement in the United States. At a crucial stage in the legal process persons are defined as criminal because police act in some ways, not in others. Law enforcement is class-based and discretionary.

POLICING THE COMMUNITY

As traditionally conceived and currently practiced, the primary function of the police is to operate as a permanent presence in the community; they are employed to impose force or the threat of force in solving the problems that arise in the community. Their concrete activities may be diverse, but the objective is singular. Egon Bittner writes,

> Whatever the substance of the task at hand, whether it involves protection against an undesired imposition, caring for those who cannot care for themselves, attempting to solve a crime, helping to save a life, abating a nuisance, or settling an explosive dispute, police intervention means above all making use of the capacity and authority to overpower resistance to an attempted solution in the native habitat of the problem.[22]

The police enter situations requiring solutions that are "non-negotiably coercible."

Because of their conventional role in capitalist society, natural forces isolate the police from other members of the community.[23] By definition, police activity involves intruding upon the citizen's affairs, usually restricting one's freedom. Also, it is natural to separate from your life those who are charged with detecting and arresting members of the community. This response is reinforced by the fear and mistrust aroused by the police following experience with them. The police, in addition, have come to represent by their role and their behavior the forces of sanction and punishment.

The organization and procedure of police work isolate the police. The requirements of patrol, investigation, surveillance, and the like clearly separate the police from the public. Furthermore, most of their operating policies are beyond public scrutiny; they are secretive and known only to the police themselves. Isolation from the community is inevitable, because of what is conventionally expected of the police in capitalist society.

We must understand police activity in a context larger than law enforcement. Although the general purpose is to maintain a particular kind of domestic order, the day-to-day police activities in the community are quite varied. We may not go so far as to argue, as some have, that the police are "peace officers," unless this means preserving domestic order for the benefit of the dominant class in the community.[24] Yet it is true that the objectives of the police are not always accomplished by making an arrest. Indeed, in many situations other methods may be more appropriate for keeping order in the community.

Maintaining order often involves giving support to some members of the community while denying it to others, controlling one member but lending support to another. Many disputes are handled by police intervention, which has been documented in a study of the calls received at a metropolitan police department.[25] Nearly half were requests for assistance of some kind. The calls for support were about personal problems: requests for health services (ambulance escorts, investigation of accidents, suicide attempts), problems with children (complaints about trespassing or destructive behavior), and the problems of incapacitated persons. Other calls were requests for assistance in personal disputes and quarrels, violence or protection from potential violence, and requests for assistance about missing persons and behavior of youths. The police perform many actions that are not directly related to enforcing the law but to other aspects of maintaining order in the community.

The character of law enforcement varies among communities and from one area to another within a community. One of the most important reasons for these variations is found in the varying *expectations* of law enforcement in different kinds of communities. First, communities differ in the kinds of behavior that community members and the police think should receive criminal sanctions. The correspondence between the criminal law and the behavior actually condemned may vary too. In one community, or part of it, arrest of a violent spouse may be expected, though such an arrest would be entirely inappropriate elsewhere. Second, communities differ in their norms on seeking assistance from the police. One community may prescribe that complaints be made to the police, another may restrict the citizen's use of the police. Third, community attitudes toward the police affect both the use of the police by community members and the way in which police respond to situations in which law-breaking may be involved.

A significant characteristic affecting law enforcement is the community's homogeneity in cultural values, social class, race, and occupation. A homogeneous community has fairly well-defined expectations on appropriate community behavior, and its police will operate more consistently according to those shared expectations.

In a heterogeneous community, the police must operate by department procedures more than by community expectations. The police in a homogeneous community may detect more law violations, but they handle the cases informally, not by the formality of an arrest. Furthermore, in a homogeneous community violators of the law may be referred back to the community for disposition rather than to the legal process. Invoking the law may be the only way of maintaining order in the heterogeneous community. In the homogeneous community a wide scope of law-violating behavior is handled informally by the police, and in the heterogeneous community criminal sanctions are more readily applied to the same behaviors to accomplish the same objectives.

The relationship between community homogeneity and law enforcement is found in a study of how juvenile cases were handled by police in four communities in the Pittsburgh area.[26] The researcher investigated how police differentially selected juvenile offenders for court appearance, finding clear differences in the rates of juvenile arrests and court referrals in the four kinds of communities. The large industrial community ("Steel City") had a juvenile arrest rate of 37.3 for every 1,000 juvenile population, compared to 12.4 in the residential and commercial community ("Trade City"), 34.8 in the small industrial community ("Mill Town"), and 49.7 in the well-to-do residential community ("Manor Heights"). Further analysis of police records and interviewing of police confirmed the differences among communities.

Several patterns were found in the way juvenile offenders were handled in the four communities, apparently a function of relations between police and community. In general, the police in each community tried to reflect what they considered to be the community's attitudes toward delinquency. The researcher summarized the differences in arrests:

> (1) Where there exists an objective, impersonal relation between the police and the public, court referral rates will be high and there will be little discrimination with respect to seriousness of offense, race, and sex of the offender; (2)

> Where there exists a personal face-to-face relation between the police and the public, there will be more discriminations with respect to court referral of an arrested juvenile.[27]

The research showed that law enforcement is affected by the specific role of the police in the community, and that the relationship between community and police explains some of the differences in law enforcement from one community to another.

Law enforcement in rural areas seems to be especially influenced by the community's expectations and the role of law enforcement there. A study of the county sheriff's social role describes law enforcement in a rural area.[28] In "Star County" in southern Illinois, the sheriff was permitted (or expected) to use a great amount of discretion in law enforcement. His primary function was to conserve the peace, and peace was not always best preserved by making an arrest. A community organized on informal relations resorts to official sanctions only when other means are exhausted or for some reason are inappropriate. In rural communities, whenever possible, informal controls are used in place of law enforcement.[29]

In the final analysis, no matter what the community is like, the primary objective of the police is simply to maintain order in the community. Police behavior must therefore be understood as part of the class conflict in most communities.[30] By arrest and criminal charges, the police usually define as criminal those who threaten class arrangements in the community, thereby containing conflict — at the expense, of course, of the working class.

POLICE ORGANIZATION AND IDEOLOGY

The most significant organizing characteristic of law enforcement is the bureaucratic and military structure of the police. Police departments, structured like military institutions, give community law enforcement its special character. The military model is especially appropriate to law enforcement's purpose:

> Both institutions are instruments of force and for both institutions the occasions for using force are unpredictably distributed. Thus, the personnel in each must be kept in a highly disciplined state of alert preparedness. The formalism that characterized military organization, the insistence on rules and regulations, on spit and polish, on obedience to superiors, and so on, constitutes a permanent rehearsal for "the real thing."[31]

The mission is warlike and the organization is structured for that purpose.

The system is built on subordination and a chain of command.[32] Modernized metropolitan police departments also are organized as a centralized command system, with the communications center the principal source of structure. That is, each police department is divided into a number of units. Each has its specialized enforcement activity to perform.

The functional divisions of police departments follow the kinds of activities they handle: (1) traffic patrol and patrol of structural disorders, enforcing regulations that do not entail moral turpitude in those who break the law; (2) street patrol (including radio cars), especially in downtown areas, to control individual offenses in public places; (3) investigative work, generally responding to complaints; (4) undercover work, sometimes using fraud to get inside situations otherwise protected by privacy; and (5) quasi-military action, in which the problem is to apply coercion to control a public riot.[33] Criminal law is selectively enforced according to the different organizations and the normative expectations of the separate units within the police department. Each division develops and perpetuates its own system of law enforcement. This is especially evident in the special strike units of local police departments, currently known as SWAT (Special Weapons and Tactics).[34] Employing military weaponry and combat tactics, these units are used against domestic "enemies" who would disrupt the order of the society.

The "effectiveness" of the police in enforcing the law has much to do with the way in which the departments are organized.[35] In a study of a "nonprofessional" police department in an east-coast city and a "professional" department in a west-coast city, it was found that the nonprofessional department's members lacked a strong sense of urgency about police work and produced low rates of official actions against offenders.[36] In the professional department, however, infractions of the law were more likely to be detected and offenders were more likely to be arrested, producing a higher crime rate.

How much difference police organization and procedure can make in the rate of reported crime shows too in the yearly change of crime rates within cities. The annual fluctuations sometimes obviously result from changes in law-enforcement policy. Police departments do change policy in such matters as recording crime. During organizational change in the New York City Police Department in 1966, it was decided to change the procedure for recording statistics on crimes. The newly appointed chief inspector suggested that under the old system a great number of offenses either went unrecorded or were "downgraded" in the official reports. He estimated that roughly 60 per cent of the complaints of burglary had been officially recorded in the previous year as lesser crimes, such as petty larceny, or had been given a noncriminal label, such as lost property. "To insure factual recording of crime statistics," the inspector ordered that "there should be no discretion with regard to reporting a crime and no ambiguity with regard to categorizing a crime."[37] Needless to say, the burglary rate for the following year climbed. The new policy affected the imposing and recording of criminal definitions.

The effect of changed policy on the rate of crime is evident in the way in which traffic tickets are issued by the police. The rate for moving violations in eight cities was found to vary greatly.[38] The researcher concluded that the variations were caused by the police departments' policies and not the characteristics of the communities. Departments with high rates of traffic offenses had specialized policies for enforcing traffic laws. Pressure applied by the department administrator also got more traffic tickets issued. Departments with high rates of traffic violations include in their policies the quota system of law enforcement. Such departmental policies can affect the rate of crime.

Carrying out their special mandate in capitalist society has led police to develop their private occupational ideology. They have built an occupational culture with its own assumptions about everyday life and use it as a base for their strategies and tactics.[39] Much of their behavior is understandable when we know the job's context.

The police learn to behave according to this occupational ideology. During the training period, the recruit gradually adopts an outlook on work and justifications for the procedures and methods used in the line of "duty." Socialization of police recruits into the occupation is also affected by their backgrounds. A researcher studied police training for the New York City Police Department and found that candidates are drawn primarily from the lower middle class.[40] The recruits considered their new source of employment an upward step, but at the same time were convinced that police work was assigned lower prestige than other occupations by the general population. Because of similar socioeconomic status and career expectations, the recruits adapted similarly to their training. They also shared the belief, which grew stronger during their training, that the police lack the basic legal authority to effectively carry out their work.

After completing academy training and assignment to a local precinct, the police rookie is called upon to face the challenge of actual duty. Arthur Niederhoffer observes: "His reputation is made in the next few weeks and will shadow him for the rest of his police career: no matter where or when he is transferred, a phone call will precede his arrival, reporting the evaluation that was made of his handling of his first few important cases."[41] The new officer's principal challenge is the dilemma of choosing between the professional ideal of police work learned in the academy and the precinct's pragmatic approach. The "lock-them-up" philosophy of the precinct contradicts the professional orientation toward police work learned in the academy. It becomes obvious that every law on the book cannot be enforced and that the laws are, in fact, to be enforced with much discretion according to the norms of the department and neighborhood.

The occupational ideology learned by the police is formed by two characteristics of day-to-day work: danger and authority. These characteristics, Jerome Skolnick suggests, lead to a "working personality."[42] The combination frustrates any possibility of procedural regularity in law enforcement.

Socialization and experience within the occupation promote other personal attributes. In a study of the New York City Police Department, it was found that after appointment to the force many police become cynical. "When they succumb, they lose faith in people, society, and eventually in themselves. In their Hobbesian view the world becomes a jungle in which crime, corruption, and brutality are normal features of the terrain."[43] Cynicism is part of the occupational ideology, learned during socialization into the occupation, and an authoritarian personality usually follows during the police career. "The police occupational system is geared to manufacture the 'take charge guy,' and it succeeds in doing so with outstanding efficiency. It is the police system, not the personality of the candidate, that is the more powerful determinant of behavior and ideology."[44] In the United States, a police institution removed from the needs of working-class people in the community shapes law enforcement.

SELECTIVE LAW ENFORCEMENT

Within the class structure and police organization, making an arrest involves a number of social relations and personal perceptions. That which is defined as criminal is not so much behavior obviously violating a specific criminal law as it is a definition of circumstances in the encounter between interacting parties in a concrete situation. Few cases of law enforcement show clear evidence that a specific person is the "criminal." Usually it is only in the totality of the encounter that a decision is made to apply the criminal label to a person.

Encounter between Police and Citizens

The encounter can take place only when the police have been mobilized. That usually happens when private citizens act, not by police taking the initiative. They may be mobilized in several ways:

> Police departments refer to incidents or complaints that originate by mobilizing police units through the communications center as *calls-for-service, dis-*

patches, or *runs,* the first term referring to the citizen's call or complaint and the latter terms to the fact that a mobile unit is radio-dispatched to take the complaint. A request for police action made by a citizen personally appearing at the police station is referred to as a *station complaint* or a *citizen station mobilization.* All incidents arising in a field setting are commonly referred to as *on-view* incidents, but a distinction can be made among them. A direct, in-the-field, citizen request for police action, usually by flagging a patrol car or a call to an officer on the beat, is sometimes referred to as a *field complaint* or a *citizen field mobilization.* When an officer initiates contact and reports on an incident that occurs in his presence, it is referred to as an *on-view* mobilization. Any law violation occurring in an officer's presence that leads to an arrest with the officer as complainant is an *on-view arrest.*[45]

In 5,360 mobilization situations in Boston, Chicago, and Washington, D.C., 81 per cent of the mobilizations were dispatches, 14 per cent were on-views, and the remaining 5 per cent were citizen field mobilizations. Most important, nearly three-quarters of the mobilizations consisted of some kind of police-citizen interaction.[46] More often than not, then, the police are involved in criminal-defining situations because citizens report offenses.

The encounter between police and citizens in a situation potentially definable as criminal involves a number of social roles. Beyond the police we can see eight of these: complainant, member of complainant group, offender, member of offender group, victim, member of victim group, informant, and bystander. These roles may lead to a criminal arrest.

A *complainant* is a person who wants police action in response to what he sees as an "offense" of some kind; e.g., a man whose car has been stolen or a woman who complains about a noisy party is a complainant. A *member of a complainant group* is a person who supports or stands with the central complainant. An *offender* is either a person who is seen or treated as a possible violator of the law or as a person who is not fulfilling role obligations or expectations that the complainant regards as "legal." The first kind of offender is represented by a person accused of a larceny, the second by a man whose wife thinks he has been negligent in fulfilling his obligations as husband or head of the household. A *member of an offender group* is a person who supports or stands with the offender. A citizen is called a *victim* who needs or requests help or a service from the police in a situation that does not involve an "offense" or possible criminal violation of any kind, e.g., a sick or accidentally injured person. A *member of victim group* is a person who supports or is behaviorally concerned about a victim. The *informant* is a participant who gives information relative to the nature of any situation or incident but who does not support or stand with any of the more involved participants; he is, however, more than a mere guide or person who gives information only about the location of a situation. The *bystander* is nothing more than an onlooker.[47]

The most important social roles in the situations that may become defined as criminal are those of the policeman, the suspect, and the victim. The *victim,* when a crime is created, is not just the object of an offense, but may be the only person able to report the offense to the police so that an arrest can be made. In the studies for the President's Commission on Law Enforcement and Administration of Justice it was discovered that in only about half the cases of victimization did the victim report the offense to the police.[48] The tendency to report or not report varied according to the type of offense and the victim's characteristics. As shown in Table 8.1, the victims had several reasons for not reporting. The most common was a resigned belief that the police could do nothing about the incident, would not catch the offender, or would not want to be bothered. Many other nonreporting victims believed that the incident was not a police matter. These victims either did not want the offender to be known to the police or thought that the incident was a private affair. Other victims simply did not want to get involved with the police, to take the time or trouble to report the offense. Still others were afraid of possible reprisal by the offender and his friends or some other kind of loss. Finally, some did not notify the police because they were uncertain about what ought to be done. It is not always clear that a criminal offense has been committed or what procedure is proper for reporting an offense. For all these reasons, many possible criminal defining situations do not come to the attention of the police.[49]

The ultimate encounter that may lead to a criminal definition is between *police* and *suspect.* The encounter is guided by a conflict between opposing interests: (1) those of a person who wants to carry out some behaviors (some of which may conceivably violate the criminal law), and (2) those of the police officer who wants to prevent criminal violations and apprehend criminals. These opposing interests lead both parties to develop strategies, according to what one party expects of the other.[50] Each attempts to predict the other's behavior, at the same time trying to reduce the opponent's ability to predict his or her own moves.

Yet it is the police who have the ability to officially define a crime: in the encounter between police and citizen a social reality is being constructed.

> Whenever the police intervene in a situation, whether it be in response to a citizen request or on their own volition, they have at their disposal a wide range of alternative modes of action ranging from simply issuing orders or giving warnings through the making of arrests. In engaging in any or all of these activities, the police possess the sole official monopoly over the use of physical force, to the point of taking a human life. Through any one or a combination of

TABLE 8.1 Crime Reports to the Police: Victims' Most Important Reason for Not Notifying Police[a] (NORC Survey; in percentages)

		Reasons for not notifying police				
Crimes	*Percentage of cases in which police not notified*	*Felt it was private matter or did not want to harm offender*	*Police could not be effective or would not want to be bothered*	*Did not want to take time*	*Too confused or did not know how to report*	*Fear of reprisal*
Robbery	35%	27%	45%	9%	18%	0%
Aggravated assault	35	50	25	4	8	13
Simple assault	54	50	35	4	4	7
Burglary	42	30	63	4	2	2
Larceny ($50 and over)	40	23	62	7	7	0
Larceny (under $50)	63	31	58	7	3	(c)
Auto theft	11	[b]20	[b]60	[b]0	[b]0	[b]20
Malicious mischief	62	23	68	5	2	2
Consumer fraud	90	50	40	0	10	0
Other fraud (bad checks, swindling, etc.)	74	41	35	16	8	0
Sex offenses (other than forcible rape)	49	40	50	0	5	5
Family crimes (desertion, nonsupport, etc.)	50	65	17	10	0	7

[a] Wilful homicide, forcible rape, and a few other crimes had too few cases to be statistically useful, and they are therefore excluded.

[b] There were only 5 instances in which auto theft was not reported.

[c] Less than 0.5%.

SOURCE: President's Commission on Law Enforcement and Administration of Justice, *The Challenge of Crime in a Free Society* (Washington, D.C.: U.S. Government Printing Office, 1967), p. 22.

these means the police may and do make in behavior a reality of the order they anticipate.[51]

Making an arrest, creating a crime, is constructing a social reality.

Making the Arrest

Once the encounter has taken place, the conflicting interests of the police and the suspect continue to be important in the relationship. The question they now confront is how that encounter will be conducted. During this confrontation the police decide whether or not to impose a criminal definition by the act of arrest.

Threat of arrest is a means of conducting the encounter. But the bargaining is one-sided, with the police having the power and possessing the ultimate weapon:

> The ability to claim a given identity in an interaction involves . . . bargaining. But, as in many bargaining relations, the power is not equally distributed in police-citizen encounters. The police have one mechanism that can alter the negotiations over status claims — the arrest. By placing a citizen under arrest, the officer shifts the interaction from police-civilian to police-suspect. Arrest gives the police officer much greater protection of his role identity at the same time as it strips certain indentities held by the citizen.[52]

Many factors beyond the principal reason for the encounter between police and suspect enter into the decision to arrest. The police look for personal characteristics that may indicate criminal behavior. The outward appearance and demeanor of the suspect obviously influence the policeman in making a possible arrest. A study of the disposition of juvenile cases showed that the decision on whether or not to bring a boy to the station — and the decision made at the station — "were based largely on cues from which the officer inferred the youth's character."[53] The cues included group affiliation, age, race, grooming, and dress. Members of known delinquent gangs, older boys, blacks, and youths with well-oiled hair, black jackets, and soiled denims or jeans usually received the more serious dispositions.

But the most important cue the police used in handling juveniles was demeanor. The patrol officers themselves stated that was the major determinant in 50 to 60 per cent of the cases they processed. Youths perceived as uncooperative were more likely to be dealt with severely than those who seemed cooperative. The researchers reached this conclusion:

> The cues used by police to assess demeanor were fairly simple. Juveniles who were contrite about their infractions, respectful to officers, and fearful of the sanctions that might be employed against them tended to be viewed by patrolmen as basically law-abiding or at least "salvageable." For these youths it was usually assumed that informal or formal reprimand would suffice to guarantee their future conformity. In contrast, youthful offenders who were fractious, obdurate, or who appeared nonchalant in their encounters with patrolmen were likely to be viewed as "would-be tough guys" or "punks" who fully deserved the most severe sanction: arrest.[54]

The police, then, use symbols and behavioral cues in applying criminal definitions. They have an image of the kind of person who is a "troublemaker" or is likely to be a lawbreaker. When suspects live up to this expectation, they increase the possibility of their own arrest. And the attitude the person assumes in his or her relationship with the police affects the outcome of the encounter. Those who behave antagonistically toward the police are more likely to be treated in a hostile, authoritarian, or belittling manner by the police than are other citizens.[55] The encounter between police and citizen is, indeed, a crucial moment of interaction and assessment. It is a time when the realities of the class structure are confirmed, when unequal power distributions are played out, and when deference in personal relations becomes important.[56] All parties are involved in their personal fates. The encounter may create a crime.

Offense Situations

The police and the citizen encounter each other in a specific offense situation, the outcome of which is affected not only by their interactions, perceptions, and reactions, but also by the setting. The situations may vary in such matters as the racial context, police and community objectives in enforcing laws, and the kind of offense. Law is selectively enforced according to these variations and the person's characteristics. Law enforcement is unevenly distributed in the social structure of capitalist society.

Racism in the arrest. The police, we know from many studies, have long had differential policies toward race and minority status.[57] They are more likely to arrest blacks and third-world people on slight evidence compared with what they require for arresting whites. These two groups have also been exposed more than others to the misuse of police power. Police attitudes and policies on race were described by a police captain some time ago in a southern town, when he told a writer: "In this town there are three classes of homicide. If a nigger kills a white man, that's murder. If a white man kills a nigger, that's justifiable homicide. If a nigger kills a nigger, that's one less nigger."[58]

Official police statistics reveal that blacks are arrested between three and four times more often than whites.[59] Although blacks comprise about one-ninth of the population, they account for more than a quarter of the persons arrested for all offenses. Being black entails a greater risk of arrest than does the status of being white. In similar situations blacks are more likely than whites to be apprehended.

This selective enforcement is caused largely by prejudices of the police.[60] Blacks are often placed in the stereotype that police have of the criminal.[61] The police are more likely to arrest the black than the white in a similar offense situation. How often they use a racial image of the offender came out in a survey of police officers in Philadelphia: 75 per cent of them overestimated the percentage of arrests involving blacks made in the districts to which they were assigned.[62] With a conception of events and offenders like this, difference in law enforcement according to race is inevitable. Underlying racial discrimination in law enforcement, however, is the larger role of police force in the United States. "The police are not placed in black communities to protect the indigenous inhabitants, but to protect the property of the colonizers who live outside those communities and to restrain any black person from breaking out of the colonial wards in the event of violence."[63]

Selective objectives in the community. To accomplish objectives that may be known only to the police and some community members, an arrest may be made, possibly solving a problem that seemingly could not be resolved in any other way. A police officer might arrest a person who ordinarily would not be arrested to maintain respect for the police system.

> A police patrol stopped a car that had been traveling at 39 mph in a 30 mph zone. They decided prior to leaving the squad car that they would only issue a warning. When the deputies approached, the driver said in a sarcastic tone, "What in the hell have I done now?" Because of his belligerent attitude the driver was placed under arrest.[64]

Another kind of arrest for extralegal objectives is made to preserve an image of full enforcement. It is most often used when an offense not usually handled by arrest comes to public attention:

> The police were aware of the operation of a private card game in which there was no house "cut." Since this operation therefore qualified as mere social gambling, no action was taken against the offenders. However, the operators of the game made no attempt to conceal the operation, and it was soon apparent to the general public that the police must be aware of it. Realizing this, the police arrested the gamblers.[65]

Once an offense is widely publicized, an arrest becomes imminent. Sometimes it is intended to detain or punish someone suspected of other criminal activity:

> The police learned of a minor property theft. As the victim was not interested in prosecution, the police, in accord with their usual policy, decided not to arrest. However, when they learned that the offender was known to the police department as a "bad actor," and that the police had been unsuccessful in obtaining his conviction for other, more serious offenses, they arrested him.[66]

An arrest may also follow a minor offense when the police think a suspect is responsible for a relatively serious offense, but they need more time to gather evidence for successfully prosecuting the case.

> Officers had reasonable grounds to believe that a particular man was responsible for a recent homicide. However, desiring an opportunity to conduct a prolonged in-custody investigation, they arrested him on a vagrancy charge. He was then convicted for vagrancy, and the murder investigation was continued while he served his sentence.[67]

Offenders may be arrested too if other alternatives are lacking. The drunk may be arrested to protect him from the cold, because he has injured himself, or because he is likely to become a criminal victim; he will probably be released the next morning.[68]

Arrest charges that are used to accomplish a multitude of extralegal objectives are vagrancy and disorderly conduct. Not usually made to enforce the laws, they are intended to banish unwanted persons, prevent and control other offenses, and clear public areas.[69] Police departments may even conduct drives during the year, in the name of enforcing the vagrancy and disorderly statutes, to get "undesirables" out of town.

Enforcement of public morals. Some forms of private conduct become the business of the police. Criminal laws created primarily for reprobation are enforced (or not enforced) with a great amount of discretion. In the appropriate situations the police are expected to enforce public morals by arresting private citizens.

In general the police are not called upon to enforce laws that regulate private conduct. Although some laws are based on moral behavior, they are not usually enforced so long as the conduct is not harmful to those involved and the participating parties consent to the behavior. Enforcement is likely, however, when personal violence erupts and also when conduct becomes defined by the community as a public nuisance. Solicitation by homosexuals and prostitutes in public places may bring the police into action to enforce laws.[70]

Because the behavior of homosexuals in public is likely to be offensive to some segments of the community, numerous complaints may be registered with the police. The police are then responsible not so much for fully enforcing the law but ensuring a public order that satisfies the sensibilities of some community members: the police provide the community with an inoffensive environment.

Prostitutes are usually arrested for purposes other than prosecution. Those who are arrested, however, are the ones who come to public attention, the street walkers rather than the call girls. Prostitution may be condoned in the community, so long as it does not recruit our wives and daughters, but community members do not like to be reminded of the behavior. The police are required, therefore, to crack down on the women who publicly solicit for their favors. And the police may get information about other criminals by arresting prostitutes.[71] Most of the time, though, such arrests are meant simply to harass the prostitutes. The latter may then work out strategies that are less obvious and offensive to the public.

Enforcing dormant laws. A great many criminal laws were created to support values that have since ceased to be important. Although the laws have remained on the books, they have in essence become dormant. On occasion, however, these laws are enforced for brief periods, most often for purposes other than those intended in the original legal formulations. The sporadic enforcement of dormant laws is the ultimate use of discretion in law enforcement.

Sunday closing laws are one of the best examples of a sporadically enforced dormant law. These laws, enacted early in the history of our states, usually have been enforced by local authorities; that is, according to particular objectives.

Within communities, too, Sunday laws, when enforced, have been enforced for diverse reasons. In New York City sporadic attempts to enforce the law have been guided by different objectives. Several times in this century organized efforts have been made to enforce the closing law for business establishments, each for different reasons.[72]

In 1924 New York City police actions on Sunday closing rose 77 per cent over the previous year. The sudden enforcement policy was caused by a group known as the Lord's Day Alliance, which crusaded to get it enforced primarily on religious grounds. In the following year the arrest rate for being open on Sunday declined to its regular low level. Then in 1938 another campaign was launched in the Flatbush section of Brooklyn by the Flatbush Chamber of Commerce. Local businessmen were exercising their civic interest in keeping a law-abiding image for the community.

In 1954 in the Bedford-Stuyvesant area of Brooklyn, increased enforcement of the Sunday law was prompted by a campaign for better working conditions by a union, the American Federation of Retail Kosher Butchers, trying to abolish management-forced work on Sunday. In the next year, this time on Manhattan's West Side, police responded to pressure from unions, which were organizing the car-wash industry there. They acted upon any business establishment open on Sunday. One of the last police crackdowns on Sunday openings in New York was in August 1962 in the upper Broadway area. Behind the drive, which lasted one week, was an attempt by the large chain-store supermarkets to have the small neighborhood stores closed on Sundays. Selective law enforcement had become a way of accomplishing objectives quite apart from law enforcement itself.

Political protest. One other kind of selective law enforcement is the police reaction to political protest. The police then are sometimes used by those who hold power to resolve conflicts in their own favor. Law enforcement here consists of selectively applying criminal definitions to those who protest against the established government in ways the government thinks illegitimate and threatening to its existence; this behavior may, consequently, be defined as criminal.

Political protest almost by definition is a threat and danger to a government. The police become involved not only for the express purpose of maintaining peace, but also to preserve the society's status quo. They do as much to punish the protesters as to keep order. Police intimidation and brutality have occurred in many instances of political protest, as in the "race riots," where much of the violence may have been either prompted or initiated by the police.[73] In many other protests and demonstrations almost the only violence is that which the police inflict on the participants, the only illegalities those committed by the police themselves.[74] But the police impose criminal definitions, and are not likely to be the ones defined as criminals.

The federal government, especially, has resorted to the police to protect its own interests. In the name of national security, laws have been created and enforced to protect the government from threats it perceives. The scare about communism in this century got thousands arrested under laws especially enacted or conveniently enforced for that purpose.[75]

Selective police reaction to political protest was brought to public attention during the 1968 Democratic Convention in Chicago. That week in August, the Chicago police, arresting 668 demonstrators, committed numerous violent acts against them. A report of the events, sponsored by the National Commission on the Causes and Prevention of Violence, concluded that the police response to the demonstrators was unrestrained and indiscriminate. Furthermore, "that violence was made all the more shocking by the fact that it was often inflicted upon persons who had broken no law, disobeyed no order, made no threat. These included peaceful demonstrators, onlookers, and large numbers of residents who were simply passing through, or happened to live in, the areas where confrontations were occurring.[76]

Whether violence has been used by the police, harassment has been attempted, or arrests have been made. The police have been used to protect and help preserve the state and the interests of the capitalist class. This is to be expected, because the police are, after all, agents of the state.

Abuse in the arrest. Because of the job the police have in capitalist society, protecting the social order, they often apply harsh and illegal methods in enforcing the law.[77] Moreover, the public in the United States has traditionally provided the police with an implicit directive to use violence and other expedient methods to accomplish police goals. Police brutality finds considerable support in a public ideology that grants authority to state sovereignty.

The police continue to carry out their mandate, resorting to violence and brutality as part of their occupational activity. That they use brutality should surprise no one, because their mandate is coercing the population; they manage violence for the state. Paul Chevigny studied some abuses by the police in New York City, and says that "the one truly iron and inflexible rule we can adduce from the cases is that any person who defies the police risks the imposition of legal sanctions, commencing with a summons, on up to the use of firearms."[78] He continues, "The police may arrest *anyone* who challenges them (as they define the challenge), but they are more likely to further abuse anyone who is poor, or who belongs to an outcast group."[79] But the real problem, the author says, is that the police often provoke citizens to violence or disorderly conduct to make an arrest. Such provocation then allows the police to continue abusing the citizen.

The worst abuse, Chevigny observes, is the strong use of power, when the police not only assault people but arrest them.

> If the police simply hit a man and let him go, there would be an abuse of the authority conferred by the uniform and the stick, but not the compound abuse of hitting a man and then dragging him to court on criminal charges, really a more serious injury than a blow. One's head heals up, after all, but a criminal record never goes away. There is no more embittering experience in the legal system than to be abused by the police and then to be tried and convicted on false evidence.[80]

The police are likely to get in trouble if they let an abused person go free; therefore they make an arrest to cover the abuse, concealing their own violence.

With their private code of conduct, and complicity of the courts in accepting the criminal charges, the police continue to practice violence and abusive methods of law enforcement. And the abuses will go on as long as the police institution is accepted as the most appropriate way of handling the society's problems.

In response to events, a number of changes have been made in law enforcement in recent years. Among the proposals that have been advanced, and initiated with the support of the federal government, are those meant to strengthen and make more effective the traditional police function. Instead of examining the law-enforcement institution, proponents of these measures wish to make the police better able to perform their order-maintaining and crime-preventing functions in the community.

Programs are under way to strengthen the organization of police departments; increase their training, recruitment, and size; professionalize them; improve their deployment; and enhance their public image. With such recommendations, the President's Commission on Law Enforcement and Administration of Justice made this statement about improving the police "in a free society":

> Widespread improvement in the strength and caliber of police manpower, supported by a radical revision of personnel practices, are the basic essentials for achieving more effective and fairer law enforcement. Educational requirements should be raised to college levels and training programs improved. Recruitment and promotion should be modernized to reflect education, personality, and assessment of performance. The traditional, monolithic personnel structure must be broken up into three entry levels of varying responsibility and with different personnel requirements, and lateral entry into advanced positions encouraged.
>
> The need is urgent for the police to improve relations with the poor, minority groups, and juveniles. The establishment of strong community relations programs, review of all procedures in light of their effect on community relations, recruitment of minority group members, and strengthening of community confidence in supervision and discipline, all aim at making the police more effective in high-crime areas. Increased effectiveness also requires that law enforcement improve its facilities and techniques of management — particularly that it utilize manpower more efficiently, modernize communications and records, and formulate more explicit policy guidelines governing areas of police discretion. The pooling of services and functions by police forces in each metropolitan area can improve efficiency and effectiveness.[81]

The problem was perceived as a technical one that could be solved by money combined with manipulation of the public by community relations.

For some reformers the necessary change is definitely in "police manpower." Although improving police-community relations is important, mainly for gaining information about "the character and habits" of the

JUSTICE FOR ALL INCLUDES CHILDREN, 2.

WHAT'S GOING ON HERE?

OFFICER... SUPERMAN, MY NAME IS HARRY JONES. I *OWN* THIS BUILDING AND I *HIRED* THIS BOY TO PAINT A MURAL ON IT!

I DON'T KNOW WHY THEY RAN LIKE THAT...

BOYS, THE POLICEMAN WAS DOING HIS JOB. HE MUST INVESTIGATE POSSIBLE PROPERTY DAMAGE!

BY RUNNING AWAY, YOU HAVE MADE YOURSELVES *LOOK* GUILTY.

DAN HERE, DID THE RIGHT THING. WHEN A POLICEMAN APPROACHES, REMAIN CALM AND COOPERATE. HIS JOB IS TO ENFORCE THE LAW...

...WHICH HELPS EVERYBODY.

THE LINE OF DC SUPER-STARS

PUBLISHED AS A PUBLIC SERVICE BY NATIONAL PERIODICAL PUBLICATIONS, INC. IN COOPERATION WITH THE NATIONAL CENTER FOR JUVENILE JUSTICE, THE RESEARCH DIVISION OF THE NATIONAL COUNCIL OF JUVENILE COURT JUDGES.

people of the community, the most important problem is "improving the way in which the police perform their critical function — patrolling to prevent crime, preserve order, and enforce laws."[82] This improvement, of course, is time-consuming and costly, but the battle can be won by "deploying" large numbers of police in the community.

More liberal proposals on the police go beyond the manpower problem to "professionalizing" the police. These begin with the notion that the police must develop a professional attitude toward their work. Efficient enforcement of the law is not the sole end of the police function, but respect for "the rule of law" is essential. An argument for developing *legal* professionalism among police is presented by Jerome Skolnick:

> The needed philosophy of professionalism must rest on a set of values conveying the idea that the police are as much an institution dedicated to the achievement of legality in society as they are an official social organization designed to control misconduct through the invocation of punitive sanctions. The problem of police in a democratic society is not merely a matter of obtaining newer police cars, a higher order of technical equipment or of recruiting men who have to their credit more years of education. What must occur is a significant alteration in the ideology of police, so that police "professionalization" rests on the values of a democratic legal order, rather than on technological proficiency.[83]

The police, some argue, should be guided by "civility." A civil relationship between police and the public is needed, a feeling for the interests of others. Albert Reiss documents the prevalence of police malpractice and illegality, and then writes:

> So far as civil relations between the police and the public are concerned, the following conditions must prevail: (1) that citizens be civil in their relations with one another, including the police; (2) that citizens grant legitimacy to police authority and respect their legal intervention in the affairs of men; (3) that the police be accountable to civil authority and the citizen protected from police tyranny.[84]

The community member then must grant legitimacy to the police, and show deference to police authority.

Added to civility, especially among citizens in their relationships with the police, is the notion that the police should be "accountable" to the citizens. This "civic accountability," however, is controlled by the state and the police, not by the people of the community. And it is the "responsibility of the government," of which the police are a part, "to insure that its servants behave in a civil fashion."[85]

Finally, as the police become "professionalized," we will have to respect what they do and grant them a great deal of self-regulation as a profession. We are back to expecting misconduct, but this time the police are acting as professionals. With some negative reasoning, Bittner writes:

> It must be said, however, that the true professionalization of police work, in and of itself, is no weapon against sloth and corruption, no more than in the case of medicine, the ministry, law, teaching, and social work. That is, the professionalization of police work still leaves open the matter of its control. But if we are not willing to settle for having physicians who are merely honest, and who would frankly admit that in curing diseases and dealing with patients they have to rely entirely on "playing by ear," it is difficult to see why we would devote all our energies to trying to make the police honest without any concern whatever for whether or not they know, in a technical sense, how to do what they are supposed to do.[86]

Again, the police role is accepted; what we need is a more efficient police force. Bittner concludes: "But it is not good manners that I expect. Instead, I should like, in my dealings with policemen, to be able to perceive them as qualified to do the serious and important work I know they have to do."[87]

The Police-Community Relations Movement

Following the racial disorders in the sixties, police officials and government leaders instituted "police-community relations" programs, trying to restore order to communities, to improve the public's image of the police, and to improve the effectiveness of the police. New measures of coercive control were devised and implemented, with new equipment and increased manpower, and police departments adopted other means of manipulation as well.

> Faced with the political sensitivity of applying stringent control measures to large numbers of a disaffected minority and the sheer tactical difficulty of meeting the immense demands of civil disturbances, police also developed more conciliatory responses. Most of these noncoercive responses to the threat of civil disturbances are lumped under the label "police-community relations programs."[88]

Although these efforts were considered and sporadically practiced before, major programs have been created only in the last decade.[89] Nearly all the large cities today have police-community relations programs. All are intended to shape public opinion about the police; "community relations" is a synonym for public relations. Furthermore:

> While there are wide differences from program to program and even from time to time in individual departments, programs do have certain elements in

common. Generally they attempt to develop new relationships and new interaction with segments of the community that police identify as potential adversaries in civil disturbances. Also, there are certain common patterns in the means to be used to pursue these goals. Community relations programs depend on nonviolent, noncoercive, and communicative strategies of influence.

Thus, some aspects of community relations programs are aimed at the environment of the police. These efforts include establishing relationships with traditional minority interest groups, with newer militant interest groups, and with minority people in general. Other aspects of police community relations efforts are internal to police organizations, being directed to the departments. These include, for example, community relations training efforts, specialized positions within the police department responsible for community relations, and special efforts to recruit minority policemen.[90]

There are now several approaches to police-community relations. One is a police-community relations unit attached to the local police department. Police personnel trained in community relations administer the policies and programs, according to the department's needs.

The idea of a Community Relations Unit can scarcely be considered new. Such units have for a long time been features of most large, urban police departments. They are usually staffed by police offices of diverse ethnic backgrounds who, as part of their official duties, seek out and respond to civic groups to explain the police department's operations. In certain instances the unit may make itself available to citizens for complaints and suggestions regarding law enforcement procedures, with the implication that these complaints and suggestions might help alter unpopular police practices. What often remains unclear is precisely how the unit does or might go about correcting practices in a police department of which it is only a small part. Consequently the chief objection to it is that it is too weak and isolated within the department to serve as a real channel for responsive communication between the community and the police or that it is patent window dressing behind which police practices remain unchanged.[91]

Another approach is the community-wide citizens' group, sometimes in combination with police officials. These "civilian review boards," as they are called, deal mainly with citizen complaints of malpractice by the police. The general problem with these programs is that they are far from the citizenry's day-to-day life, giving community members little recourse for grievances, to say nothing about real control over policing of their communities.

Still another approach to police-community relations involves massive programs of education — or indoctrination — of community members. These programs are based on the liberal notion that knowledge and information — combined of course with "dialogue" — will reconcile differences and conflicts. The president's crime commission, an obvious partisan, writes about these public-education programs:

> Citizens who distrust the police will not easily be converted by information programs they consider to come from a tainted source. However, even for these groups, long-term education based upon honest and free dialogue between the police and the public can have an effect. Indeed, this is one of the basic goals of the citizen advisory committees.
>
> On the other hand, citizens who are neutral or supportive can benefit from increased understanding of the complicated problems and tasks of the police. Informational programs can also generate support for more personnel, salary increases, sufficient equipment, and other resources to improve the efficiency of police work. It can help the cooperative citizen to avoid becoming a victim of crime and show him how to work more effectively with the police. And, to the extent that the police department is genuinely working at improved community relations, dissemination of this information to the press and other media does have a positive effect on community relations.[92]

Without changing any social conditions or the economic structure, it is assumed the community-education programs can make community members understanding of and respectful toward the police. As with all the other approaches, the purpose is to make the police more efficient in maintaining the established order in the community.

Community Control

An alternative has been found for dealing with the police-community problem, going beyond police professionalization and increased manpower, or by police-community relations. It is community control over the police. This is more than community representation or community participation in police policies and practices; it is the community's determination of how it is to be policed. Community control is still heavily debated, but some recognized successes have been made in various realms of community life.[93] Few people today deny the potential of community control.

The principle behind community control of the police is community self-government. The police now in the communities can be thought of as an occupying force. In few communities are the police actually created by the residents. Instead, they are created and managed by governments outside the community. Any true relationship between the community and the police must therefore begin with the police, an integral part of the community, which necessarily involves community control of the police.

At the beginning of the seventies a number of communities began to consider and propose plans that involve some form of community control over the police. Berkeley, California voted on a community-control amendment that would have set up separate police forces in the communities within the city, the police being controlled by the respective communities.[94] Although the amendment failed, two years later other amendments were passed giving community members control over several important aspects of policing in the city.

There are, of course, several approaches to community control. Arthur I. Waskow of the Institute for Policy Studies describes three:

> There are at least three major possible directions in which to go to achieve the kind of change in police forces that seems necessary to restore democratic, civilian control over the police:
>
> 1. Formal restructuring of metropolitan police departments into federations of neighborhood police forces, with control of each neighborhood force in the hands of neighborhood people through election of commissions.
> 2. Creation of countervailing organizations (in effect, "trade unions" of those policed) responsible to a real political base, able to hear grievances and force change.
> 3. Transformation of the police "profession" and role so as to end the isolation of policemen from the rest of the community, and thus to establish de facto community control by chiefly informal means.
>
> The neighborhood control approach could be institutionalized by election of neighborhood or precinct police commissions which would (1) appoint high precinct officers (perhaps with approval of metropolitan headquarters, the mayor or a civil service commission); (2) approve the assignment in the precinct of new policemen and be able to require transfers out; (3) discipline officers, perhaps with the concurrence of a city-wide appeal board; and (4) set basic policy on law enforcement priorities in the neighborhood.[95]

Waskow suggests that many combinations of the models are possible, and that these models can be used in different ways in a strategy for achieving community control.

Those who suggest police professionalization and increased manpower dismiss the community-control movement because they are afraid that the local arrangement, "by organizing the police on a local community basis, leaves the citizen more vulnerable to a local police tyranny, since the state's right and opportunity to intervene is limited."[96] The state, though, already intervenes to establish its own tyranny when it controls the police. They also suggest that community control of the police will undermine the "rule of law."

> One of the more difficult problems in policing is the development of policy that is consistent with the democratic ideology of maintaining respect for the rule of law. The law requires universality in its application, but community standards often hold it should be otherwise. Whenever citizens are subject to

widely varying standards in the application of any law, they lose respect for it and for the rule of law. Local control of police policy and practice, therefore, runs the risk of undermining the rule of law.[97]

And lurking in the background is the fear that local control of the police will thwart development of a "professional police cadre."

Opponents of community control fear too that once the movement catches on, every community will want to control its own police. And then what would happen in periods of "civil disorder"?

If any one neighborhood obtains control over its police, all other neighborhoods will be able to make similar demands. In a period of civil disorder, the prospects for peace are not likely to be enhanced by balkanizing the city, equipping each area with its own police force, and letting the disputants, thus armed, settle their differences as best they can.[98]

This argument selectively ignores the fact that "civil disorder" and movements for change are necessary in an oppressive society.

The idea of community control of the police, a police force controlled by the people in the community, is controversial and implies a vastly different kind of society. To bring about that control is to start working toward a new society.

NOTES

1. James Q. Wilson, "Crime and Law Enforcement," in Kermit Gordon, ed., *Agenda for the Nation* (Washington, D.C.: U.S. Government Printing Office), pp. 199 and 204.

2. Center for Research on Criminal Justice, *The Iron Fist and the Velvet Glove: An Analysis of the U.S. Police,* 2nd edition, (Berkeley, Calif.: Center for Research on Criminal Justice, 1977), p. 126.

3. Allan Silver, "The Demand for Order in Civil Society: A Review of Some Themes in the History of Urban Crime, Police, and Riot," in David J. Bordua, ed., *The Police: Six Sociological Essays* (New York: John Wiley, 1967), p. 3.

4. Ibid., p. 14.

5. See Leon Radzinowicz, *A History of English Criminal Law and Its Administration from 1750* (London: Stevens, 1956), vols. 2 and 3; Alwyn Solmes, *The English Policeman, 1871–1935* (London: George Allen & Unwin, 1935); William Alfred Morris, *The Medieval English Sheriff to 1300* (Manchester, England: University Press, 1927).

6. J. L. Lymon, "The Metropolitan Police Act of 1829: An Analysis of Certain Events Influencing the Passage and Character of the Metropolitan Police Act in England," *Journal of Criminal Law, Criminology and Police Science,* 55 (March 1964), pp. 141–154.

7. Cyrus Harreld Karreker, *The Seventeenth-Century Sheriff: A Comparative Study of the Sheriff in England's Chesapeake Colonies* (Chapel Hill: University of North Carolina Press, 1930); Julius Boebel and T. Raymond Naughton, *Law Enforcement in Colonial New York* (New York: Commonwealth Fund, 1944).

8. On some of these developments, see Roger Lane, *Policing the City: Boston, 1822–1885* (Cambridge: Harvard University Press, 1967); Mark H. Haller, "Historical Roots of Police Behavior: Chicago, 1890–1925," *Law and Society Review,* 10 (Winter 1976), pp. 303–323.

9. Sidney L. Harring and Lorraine M. McMullin, "The Buffalo Police 1872–1900: Labor

Unrest, Political Power and the Creation of the Police Institution," *Crime and Social Justice,* 4 (Fall-Winter 1975), pp. 5–14.

10. Sidney L. Harring, "The Development of the Police Institution in the United States, *Crime and Social Justice,* 5 (Spring-Summer 1976), p. 54.

11. Evelyn L. Parks, "From Constabulary to Police Society: Implications for Social Control," *Catalyst* (Summer 1970), p. 80.

12. Bruce Smith, *Police Systems in the United States,* 2nd rev. ed. (New York: Harper, 1960).

13. Rita W. Cooley, "The Office of United States Marshal," *Western Political Quarterly,* 12 (March 1959), pp. 123–140.

14. Jack J. Preiss and Howard J. Ehrlich, *An Examination of Role Theory: The Case of the State Police* (Lincoln: University of Nebraska Press, 1966).

15. Bruce C. Johnson, "Taking Care of Labor: The Police in American Politics," *Theory and Society,* 3 (Spring 1976), pp. 89–117 (especially pp. 94–101). Also see J. P. Shalloo, *Private Police: With Special Reference to Pennsylvania* (Philadelphia: American Academy of Political and Social Science, Monograph No. 1, 1933); and Stephen Spitzer and Andrew T. Scull, "Privatization and Capitalist Development: The Case of the Private Police, *Social Problems,* 25 (October 1977), pp. 18–29.

16. Michael T. Klare, "The Boom in Private Police," *The Nation,* 221 (November 15, 1975), pp. 486–491; James S. Kakalik and Sorrel Wildhorn, *The Private Police Industry: Its Nature and Extent,* vol. II (Washington, D.C.: Law Enforcement Assistance Administration, 1972); Theodore M. Becker, "The Place of Private Police in Society: An Area of Research for the Social Sciences," *Social Problems,* 21 (No. 3, 1974), pp. 438–453.

17. Supreme Court decisions on law enforcement are discussed by, among others, Richard C. Donnelly, "Police Authority and Practices," *Annals of the American Academy of Political and Social Science,* 339 (January 1962), pp. 90–110; David Robinson, Jr., "Massiah, Escobedo, and Rationales for the Exclusions of Confessions," *Journal of Criminal Law, Criminology and Police Science,* 56 (December 1965), pp. 412–431; Bernard Weisberg, "Police Interrogation of Arrested Persons: A Skeptical View," *Journal of Criminal Law, Criminology and Police Science,* 52 (May-June 1961), pp. 21–46; "A Symposium on the Supreme Court and the Police: 1966," *Journal of Criminal Law, Criminology and Police Science,* 57 (September 1966), pp. 237–311. On the regulation of private police, see *The Law and Private Police,* vol. IV (Washington, D.C.: Law Enforcement Assistance Administration, 1972).

18. Albert J. Reiss, Jr., and Donald J. Black, "Interrogation and the Criminal Process," *Annals of the American Academy of Political and Social Science,* 374 (November 1967), pp. 47–57. Also see Neal A. Milner, *The Court and Local Law Enforcement* (Beverly Hills, Calif.: Sage Publications, 1970); Edwin M. Driver, "Confessions and the Social Psychology of Coercion," *Harvard Law Review,* 82 (November 1968), pp. 42–61.

19. See Egon Bittner, *The Functions of the Police in Modern Society* (Chevy Chase, Md.: National Institute of Mental Health, 1970), pp. 28–29; and Harold E. Pepinsky, "Police Decision-Making," in Don M. Gottfredson, ed., *Decision-Making in the Criminal Justice System: Reviews and Essays,* Crime and Delinquency Monograph Series, National Institute of Mental Health (Washington, D.C.: U.S. Government Printing Office, 1975), pp. 21–52.

20. Joseph Goldstein, "Police Discretion Not to Invoke the Criminal Process: Low Visibility Decisions in the Administration of Justice," *Yale Law Journal,* 69 (March 1960), pp. 543–594; Sanford H. Kadish, "Legal Norms and Discretion in the Police and Sentencing Processes," *Harvard Law Review,* 75 (March 1962), pp. 904–931; Edward L. Barrett, Jr., "Police Practices and the Law — from Arrest to Release of Charge," *California Law Review,* 50 (March 1962), pp. 11–55.

21. Wayne R. LaFave, "The Police and Nonenforcement of the Law," *Wisconsin Law Review,* 1962 (January-March, 1962), p. 239.

22. Bittner, *The Functions of the Police,* p. 40.

23. John P. Clark, "Isolation of the Police: A Comparison of the British and American Situations," *Journal of Criminal Law, Criminology and Police Science,* 56 (September 1965), pp. 307–319.

24. See Michael Banton, *The Policeman in the Community* (London: Tavistock, 1964). Also Egon Bittner, "The Police on Skid-Row: A Study of Peace Keeping," *American Sociological Review*, 2 (October 1967), pp. 699–715.

25. Elaine Cumming, Ian Cumming, and Laura Edell, "Policeman as Philosopher, Guide and Friend," *Social Problems*, 12 (Winter 1965), pp. 276–286.

26. Nathan Goldman, *The Differential Selection of Juvenile Offenders for Court Appearance* (New York: National Council on Crime and Delinquency, 1963).

27. Ibid., p. 129.

28. T. C. Esselstyn, "The Social Role of the County Sheriff," *Journal of Criminal Law, Criminology and Police Science*, 44 (July-August 1953), pp. 177–184.

29. On police in small towns, especially about protecting merchants' property and local traffic control, see John F. Galliher, L. Patrick Donovan, and David L. Adams, "Small-Town Police: Trouble, Tasks, and Publics," *Journal of Police Science and Administration*, 3 (March 1975), pp. 19–28.

30. John F. Galliher, "Explanations of Police Behavior: A Critical Review and Analysis," *Sociological Quarterly*, 12 (Summer 1971), pp. 308–318.

31. Bittner, *The Functions of the Police*, p. 53.

32. David J. Bordua and Albert J. Reiss, Jr., "Command, Control and Charisma: Reflections on Police Bureaucracy," *American Journal of Sociology*, 72 (July 1966), pp. 68–76. Further observations are in Larry L. Tifft, "Control Systems, Social Bases of Power and Power Exercise in Police Organizations," *Journal of Police Science and Administration*, 3 (March 1975), pp. 66–76.

33. Arthur L. Stinchcombe, "Institutions of Privacy in the Determination of Police Administrative Practice," *American Journal of Sociology*, 69 (September 1963), pp. 158–159.

34. John Nordheimer, "Tough Elite Police Units Useful but Controversial," *The New York Times*, July 14, 1975, p. 1; "Elite SWAT Squads Plague U.S.," *Guardian*, September 10, 1975, p. 5.

35. Robert Edward Mitchell, "Organization as a Key to Police Effectiveness," *Crime and Delinquency*, 12 (October 1966), pp. 344–353.

36. James Q. Wilson, "The Police and the Delinquent in Two Cities," in Stanton Wheeler, ed., *Controlling Delinquents* (New York: John Wiley, 1968), pp. 9–30.

37. *The New York Times*, March 15, 1966, pp. 1 and 26.

38. James Q. Wilson, *Varieties of Police Behavior* (Cambridge: Harvard University Press, 1968), pp. 95–99. Other studies of traffic-law enforcement are in John A. Gardiner, "Police Enforcement of Traffic Laws: A Comparative Analysis," in James Q. Wilson, ed., *City Politics and Public Policy* (New York: John Wiley, 1968), pp. 151–172; David M. Petersen, "Informal Norms and Public Practice: the Traffic Ticket Quota System," *Sociology and Social Research*, 55 (April 1971), pp. 354–362.

39. Peter K. Manning, "The Police: Mandate, Strategies, and Appearances," in Jack D. Douglas, ed., *Crime and Justice in American Society* (Indianapolis: Bobbs-Merrill, 1971), pp. 149–193.

40. John H. McNamara, "Uncertainties in Police Work: the Relevance of Police Recruits' Backgrounds and Training," in David J. Bordua, ed., *The Police: Six Sociological Essays* (New York: John Wiley, 1967), pp. 163–252.

41. Arthur Niederhoffer, *Behind the Shield: The Police in Urban Society* (Garden City, N.Y.: Doubleday, 1967, p. 52.

42. Jerome H. Skolnick, *Justice Without Trial: Law Enforcement in Democratic Society* (New York: John Wiley, 1966), p. 44. Additional elements of the policeman's "working personality" are discussed in Larry L. Tifft, "The 'Cop Personality' Reconsidered," *Journal of Police Science and Administration*, 2 (September 1974), pp. 266–278. Also see the excellent research and analysis in Roger Baldwin, *Inside a Cop: Tensions in the Public and Private Lives of the Police* (Pacific Grove, Calif.: The Boxwood Press, 1977).

43. Niederhoffer, *Behind the Shield*, p. 9.

44. Ibid., p. 151. On the role of the police system in one city (Philadelphia), see Jonathan Rubinstein, *City Police* (New York: Farrar, Straus and Giroux, 1973).

45. Donald J. Black and Albert J. Reiss, Jr., "Patterns of Behavior in Police and Citizen

Transactions," in the President's Commission on Law Enforcement and Administration of Justice, *Studies in Crime and Law Enforcement in Major Metropolitan Areas,* vol. 2, Field Surveys III (Washington, D.C.: U.S. Government Printing Office, 1967), pp. 4–5.

46. Ibid., p. 17.

47. Ibid., pp. 53–54.

48. Philip H. Ennis, "Criminal Victimization in the United States: A Report of a National Survey," President's Commission on Law Enforcement and Administration of Justice, Field Surveys II (Washington, D.C.: U.S. Government Printing Office, 1967), pp. 41–51.

49. Further research on reporting of offense situations is in Sarah L. Boggs and John F. Galliher, "Evaluating the Police: A Comparison of Black Street and Household Respondents," *Social Problems,* 22 (February 1975), pp. 393–406; Richard Block, "Why Notify the Police: The Victim's Decision to Notify the Police of an Assault," *Criminology,* 11 (February 1974), pp. 555–569; Michael J. Hindelang, "Decisions of Shoplifting Victims to Invoke the Criminal Justice Process," *Social Problems,* 21 (April 1974), pp. 580–593; Mary Glenn Wiley and Terry L. Hudik, "Police-Citizen Encounters: A Field Test of Exchange Theory, *Social Problems,* 22 (October 1974), pp. 119–127.

50. The gamelike conception of police-suspect relationships is found in Dean R. Smith, "Random Patrol: An Application of Game Theory to Police Problems," *Journal of Criminal Law, Criminology and Police Science,* 53 (June 1962), pp. 258–263.

51. Clayton A. Hartjen, "Police-Citizen Encounters: Social Order in Interpersonal Interaction," *Criminology,* 10 (May 1972), p. 70.

52. James R. Hudson, "Police-Citizen Encounters That Lead to Citizen Complaints," *Social Problems,* 18 (Fall 1970), p. 190.

53. Irving Piliavin and Scott Briar, "Police Encounters with Juveniles," *American Journal of Sociology,* 70 (September 1964), p. 210.

54. Ibid., pp. 210–211.

55. Black and Reiss, "Patterns of Behavior in Police and Citizen Transactions," pp. 33–37. Other research findings are reported in Donald J. Black and Albert J. Reiss, Jr., "Police Control of Juveniles," *American Sociological Review,* 35 (February 1970), pp. 63–77; Donald J. Black, "Production of Crime Rates," *American Sociological Review,* 35 (August 1970), pp. 733–748.

56. See Marcia Garrett and James F. Short, Jr., "Social Class and Delinquency: Predictions and Outcomes of Police-Juvenile Encounters," *Social Problems,* 22 (February 1975), pp. 368–383; Richard J. Lundman, "Routine Police Arrest Practices: A Commonweal Perspective," *Social Problems,* 22 (October 1974), pp. 127–141; David M. Petersen, "Police Disposition of the Petty Offender," *Sociology and Social Research,* 56 (April 1972), pp. 320–330; Richard E. Sykes, "A Theory of Deference Exchange in Police-Civilian Encounters," *American Journal of Sociology,* 81 (November 1975), pp. 584–600.

57. See Guy B. Johnson, "The Negro and Crime," *Annals of the American Academy of Political and Social Science,* 271 (September 1941), pp. 93–104; and more recently, Theodore N. Ferdinand and Elmer G. Luchterhand, "Inner-City Youth, the Police, the Juvenile Court, and Justice," *Social Problems,* 17 (Spring 1970), pp. 510–527.

58. Cited in Banton, *The Policeman in the Community,* p. 173.

59. See the discussion on Negro crime rates in Marvin E. Wolfgang, *Crime and Race: Conceptions and Misconceptions* (New York: Institute of Human Relations Press, 1964).

60. For documentation of anti-Negro attitudes among police, according to race of police and racial composition of the police precinct, see Black and Reiss, "Patterns of Behavior in Police and Citizen Transactions," pp. 132–139.

61. Piliavin and Briar, "Police Encounters with Juveniles," pp. 212–213.

62. William M. Kephart, *Racial Factors and Urban Law Enforcement* (Philadelphia: University of Pennsylvania Press, 1957), pp. 88–93.

63. Robert Staples, "White Racism, Black Crime, and American Justice: An Application of the Colonial Model to Explain Crime and Race," *Phylon,* 36 (March 1975), p. 18.

64. See Wayne R. LaFave, *Arrest: The Decision to Take a Suspect Into Custody* (Boston: Little, Brown, 1965), p. 146.

65. Ibid., p. 147.

66. Ibid., p. 149.

67. Ibid., p. 151.

68. Ibid., pp. 439–449.

69. Caleb Foote, "Vagrancy-Type Law and Its Administration," *University of Pennsylvania Law Review*, 104 (March 1956), pp. 603–650.

70. LaFave, *Arrest*, pp. 465–470.

71. Skolnick, *Justice Without Trial*, pp. 96–109.

72. The following information was obtained from the records of the New York City Police Department.

73. Allen D. Grimshaw, "Actions of Police and the Military in American Race Riots," *Phylon*, 24 (Fall 1963), pp. 271–289.

74. See Joseph C. Mouledoux, "Political Crime and the Negro Revolution," in Marshall B. Clinard and Richard Quinney, *Criminal Behavior Systems: A Typology* (New York: Holt, Rinehart and Winston, 1967), pp. 217–231.

75. Robert K. Murray, *Red Scare: A Study of National Hysteria, 1919–1920* (Minneapolis: University of Minnesota Press, 1965); William Preston, Jr., *Aliens and Dissenters: Federal Suppression of Radicals, 1903–1933* (Cambridge: Harvard University Press, 1963).

76. The Walker Report to the National Commission on the Causes and Prevention of Violence, *Rights in Conflict* (New York: Bantam Books, 1968), p. 1.

77. Albert J. Reiss, Jr., "Police Brutality — Answers to Key Questions," *Trans-action*, 5 (July-August 1968), pp. 10–19; Ellwyn R. Stoddard, "The Informal 'Code' of Police Deviancy: A Group Approach to 'Blue-Coat Crime,' " *Journal of Criminal Law, Criminology and Police Science*, 59 (June 1968), pp. 201–213; David Burnham, "Police Violence: A Changing Pattern," *The New York Times*, July 7, 1968, pp. 1 and 34.

78. Paul Chevigny, *Police Power: Police Abuses in New York City* (New York: Random House, 1969), p. 136.

79. Ibid. Further documentation of police misconduct and illegal behavior is found in Ed Cray, *The Enemy in the Streets: Police Malpractice in America* (New York: Anchor Books, 1972); Albert J. Reiss, Jr., *The Police and the Public* (New Haven: Yale University Press, 1971); and William A. Westley, *Violence and the Police: A Sociological Study of Law, Custom, and Morality* (Cambridge: MIT Press, 1970).

80. Ibid., p. 141.

81. President's Commission on Law Enforcement and Administration of Justice, *The Challenge of Crime in a Free Society* (Washington, D.C.: U.S. Government Printing Office, 1967), pp. 294–295.

82. James Q. Wilson, "The Police in the Ghetto," in Robert F. Steadman, ed., *The Police and the Community* (Baltimore: Johns Hopkins University Press, 1972), p. 80.

83. Skolnick, *Justice Without Trial*, pp. 238–239. Other aspects of professionalization are discussed in Susan O. White, "A Perspective on Police Professionalism," *Law and Society Review*, 7 (Fall 1972), pp. 61–85.

84. Reiss, *The Police and the Public*, pp. 174–175.

85. Ibid., p. 221.

86. Bittner, *The Functions of the Police*, p. 61.

87. Ibid., p. 121.

88. Gary Kreps and Jack M. Weller, "The Police-Community Relations Movement: Conciliatory Responses to Violence," *American Behavioral Scientist*, 16 (January-February 1973), p. 402.

89. Advisory Commission on Intergovernmental Relations, *State-Local Relations in Criminal Justice* (Washinton, D.C.: U.S. Government Printing Office, 1971). Also see Charles E. Reasons and Bernard A. Wirth, "Police-Community Relations Units: A National Survey," *Journal of Social Issues*, 31 (No. 1, 1975), pp. 27–34. Discussions are found in Alvin W. Cohn and Emilio C. Viano, *Police Community Relations: Images, Roles, and Realities* (Philadelphia: J. B. Lippincott, 1976).

90. Kreps and Weller, "The Police-Community Relations Movement," p. 403. Also see the research in "Citizen Interviews, Organizational Feedback, and Police-Community Relations Decisions," *Law and Society Review*, 5 (November 1977), pp. 155–182.

91. William C. Berleman, "Police and Minority Groups: The Improvement of Community Relations," *Crime and Delinquency*, 18 (April 1972), pp. 162–163.

92. President's Commission on Law Enforcement and Administration of Justice, *Task Force Report: The Police* (Washington, D.C.: U.S. Government Printing Office, 1967), p. 159.

93. See, for example, Saul D. Alinsky, *Reveille for Radicals* (New York: Random House, 1969); Alan A. Altshuler, *Community Control* (New York: Pegasus, 1970); Stanley Aronowitz, "The Dialectics of Community Control," *Social Policy*, 1 (May-June 1970), pp. 47–51; Frank Riessman and Alan Gartner, "Community Control and Radical Social Change," *Social Policy*, 1 (May-June 1970), pp. 52–55.

94. See *To Stop a Police State: The Case for Community Control of Police* (Berkeley: The Red Family, n.d.). On the implications and future strategy of community control of the police, see the excellent discussion in Center for Research on Criminal Justice, *The Iron Fist and the Velvet Glove*, pp. 149–158.

95. Arthur L. Waskow, "Community Control of the Police," *Trans-action*, 7 (December 1969), p. 4.

96. Reiss, *The Police and the Public*, p. 186.

97. Ibid., p. 208.

98. Wilson, "The Police in the Ghetto," p. 88.

POLICE COURT

Prosecution and Adjudication

9

Justice, according to the prevalent legal ideology, is achieved as the criminal law is actually administered. But the legalistic notion of justice does not take into account the whole social context in which the law is administered. A critical understanding of judicial administration requires a standard beyond our current idea of justice.[1]

Justice as we conventionally know it is the accumulated ideas and practices that have formed as capitalist society developed. Mystified, however, justice is a social norm that is a directive for guiding human action.[2] Actions are judged by the directive; and justice is dispensed according to some notion of equality for people in similar situations. But as a social norm, following our Greek heritage, justice complies with the interests of the stronger, mainly the needs of the ruling class as expressed in law.

Justice is to be applied to individual cases, but the general objective is promoting social order. Conceived in that way, individual needs and social order are combined to form the "healthy" whole: "The problem of justice is closely related to the problem of a healthy order of society. It is concerned with the healthfulness of the parts as well as with sound condition of the whole."[3] And in capitalist society the healthy order benefits the capitalist class, which owns and controls production.

To our contemporary mind, questions of justice are generally restricted to "equal justice" — and are severely limited even in that realm. Again following the Greek path, justice originates in the belief that equals should be treated equally *and* unequals unequally.[4] In practice this reading of equality has come to mean that discrimination in dispensing justice for infractions should not occur beyond that justified by relevant differences. This interpretation leaves wide open such questions as the concrete meaning of equality, the social reality of equality and inequality, the existence of class conflict and statepower, and the struggle for a better society beyond a narrow sense of justice.

Justice in contemporary capitalist society equates the limited idea of equal justice with the formulation and administration of positive law. Capitalist justice, in other words, is made concrete in the establishment of legal order. All notions of goodness, evil, and the earthly kingdom become embodied in capitalist law. And in everyday life the questions of justice are confined to whether or not the law is arbitrarily administered. Justice is grounded not in some alternative idea of the social good or natural order, but in the needs for survival of the capitalist system. Judgment is now in the hands of legal agencies of the capitalist state. Legality and the "rational" administration of the law have become the capitalist symbol of justice.

JUDICIAL ADMINISTRATION

How is justice, in the legal sense, administered in the United States? Though many believe that its administration is "above politics," it is political by its very nature. The judicial system is here in the first place to maintain order for the state; whenever decisions are made within the system — and that is what the judiciary is for — politics necessarily is involved. Criminal law is administered by and for the state.

The courts are an essential part of the political structure. The kinds of criminal cases they prosecute are influenced by local as well as national politics. Prosecuting attorneys are elected officials and often the key figures in the local political machine; they determine, according to their discretion, which law is being violated. Their actions result in getting the suspects released or indicted. If they are indicted, the prosecutor decides on the charge. Later, the fate of the accused depends on the judge's discretion; he or she too is an appointed or locally elected official sensitive to political realities.[5] People are charged, prosecuted, and convicted according to the material needs of the political system and its agents.

Much of the politics in local criminal justice is shaped by the two-party system. Political leadership is dispersed among the political parties, which are spread through the society, and local politics is influenced by party considerations. Party leaders use the judiciary as a source of patronage. Elected judges usually owe their office to favors rendered to a political party. Specific party interests inevitably enter public policy, including decisions on criminal matters. Because courts are the arena in which conflicting claims of diverse groups are presented and resolved, control over them is desired by the dominant economic class.

Within the judiciary system, the dominant groups of the capitalist class have ways of gaining access to those who make decisions: (1) influencing selection of judges, (2) influencing content of decisions, and (3) maximizing or minimizing effects of decisions as they are implemented.[6] Such methods enable dominant groups to have criminal statutes interpreted in their favor. The criminal law is administered mostly in selective interpretations of the law favoring some class interests and negating others. Under the adversary system of justice, compromise is rare: someone wins, someone else loses. And because the legal system is an institution of the capitalist class, the administration of justice naturally favors that class.

Discretion according to class interests necessarily occurs in judicial decision-making. Within the judicial proceedings different types of political decisions are made at each stage.[7] Once a case is admitted to the judicial system after an arrest, decisions are made about the suspect's fate. Some cases may be removed entirely from the system by the decision reached at the first judicial appearance, but others move sequentially, from one stage to another, before going out of the system. At each stage, the decision reached by some officials limits the alternatives for decisions in subsequent stages.

After the arrest the suspect is usually brought before a court official, the magistrate, to classify the case. A preliminary hearing may follow to establish "probable cause," and a decision is also made on detaining the suspect and setting the bail, if any. Between the first judicial appearance and the indictment, the prosecution decides what charges to press or whether to press charges at all. Once formal charges are made, pretrial proceedings are established during the arraignment. Decisions are reached on the time of trial, use of the plea, challenging the formal charge, the kind of evidence, and the defendant's mental or physical capacity. If a trial takes place, instead of settlement by guilty plea proceedings, decisions are made by judge and jury in the courtroom. Arguing their cases, the prosecuting attorney and lawyer for the defense make innumerable strategic decisions. The decisions to convict the accused and to impose a sentence are the consequences of the decisions made from the moment at which the arrest was made.

The convicted person's fate is still somewhat problematic, however, in that an appellate review may alter previous decisions. But the convicted person will probably have to continue within the judicial system until officials make decisions on his or her release. From the time suspects enter the judicial proceedings, decisions by others determine whether or not they will be defined as criminal.

The boundaries of discretion, as used by the police or in administering criminal law, are not clearly defined.[8] Obviously, judicial decisions are made, not uniformly, but according to endless extralegal factors, including age, race, and social class of the offenders. The many court systems are a major source of variation in judicial decision-making. The United States has fifty-two separate court jurisdictions in the fifty states, the District of Columbia, and the federal government.[9] The state jurisdictions have several forms of courts, known as "police" courts, "special-sessions" courts, and "quarter" courts. Some deal with minor criminal violations of local laws and ordinances and others with more serious offenses. They have specialized functions but cause much confusion by their overlapping jurisdictions.

The federal judicial system also has several types of courts with diverse activities and functions. And the federal circuit courts are divided according to geographic areas. All this complexity and diversity in the judiciary guarantees variations in judicial decision-making. The criminal law cannot be uniformly administered, but involves local discretion.

Judicial discretion shows most obviously in the way cases of those from minority groups are handled. Blacks are generally convicted with less evidence and sentenced to more severe punishment than whites. In a study of 821 homicides in several counties of North Carolina between 1930 and 1940, it was found that the fewest indictments were made when whites killed blacks and the highest proportion when blacks killed whites.[10] The courts seemed to consider slaying of a white by a black as almost prima facie or self-evident indication of guilt, but murder of a black by a white appeared to require mitigating circumstances such as provocation.

Haywood Burns writes that the law in the United States has been used against minorities "to make sure that these inferior beings stayed in their place — whatever that might be at the moment."[11] Laws have excluded Indians, Orientals, and blacks from their lands, from participation in politics, and from basic human rights. In spite of Supreme Court decisions and civil-rights legislation, racism continues in the legal system, keeping some groups subordinate. Justice for blacks is still different from that for whites; racism in law survives "institutionally" as a product of caste and class subordination.[12]

Yet, discretion operates unseen by the public. Partly by design, the public is shielded from the system's workings by the highly formal and technical language of the law. It is also organized in ways that prevent us from observing its day-to-day operations. The criminal court, in particular, has an organization and an operation outside of public scrutiny and beyind legal considerations. Abraham Blumberg, a lawyer-sociologist, writes:

> The court, unlike most other formal organizations, functions as a genuinely "closed community" in that it successfully conceals the true nature of its routine operations from the view of outsiders — and sometimes even from some of the participants themselves. It socializes its members and participants toward compliance with specific objectives which are not part of the official goals of justice and due process.[13]

The bureaucratic complexity that enshrouds the judicial system makes it difficult for the citizen to see political bias and institutionalized discrimination at work, allowing the myth of justice to prevail.

Discretion in the legal process clearly demonstrates the repressive influence of criminal justice. Discretion is not merely a function of decision-making, but a means for maintaining the class structure. As others have observed, "At every stage in the criminal justice process discretionary actions are taken which generally either benefit members of the power-advantaged group or which solidify and fix harmful effects on the politically and economically disadvantaged."[14] The political, discretionary operation of criminal justice is basic to the capitalist system of justice.

PRETRIAL PROCEEDINGS AND NONTRIAL ADJUDICATION

For the public, the focal point of criminal justice is the court trial, where the fate of the accused is decided by twelve of his or her peers. Not only is this conception incorrect about the *way* in which people are convicted, but it misleads by implying that adjudication consists *only* of the decision by judge or jury to convict or acquit. Several judicial stages precede a trial, but significantly in these pretrial proceedings most criminal cases never reach the criminal-trial stage. The decision to impose a criminal definition is usually made in the *pretrial* proceedings by *nontrial* adjudication.

Upon arrest, or after a summons or on-the-spot citation is issued, the suspect is supposed to be brought promptly before a magistrate, who reads the warrant.[15] If the offense is a minor one, triable by the magistrate, a summary trial may be held immediately. If the offense is more serious, not triable by the magistrate, the purpose of the initial appearance is more limited. The suspect will be given the opportunity of having a preliminary hearing to determine if the evidence is sufficient to justify his or her being held for possible trial. If the suspect waives a preliminary hearing, he or she is then bound over (transferred) to a court of trial jurisdiction.

The principal function of the first judicial appearance is not, however, to determine whether the evidence is sufficient for trial. Neither the prosecuting attorney nor the defense lawyer is yet ready to determine whether probable cause exists. The first appearance is meant mainly to provide for the defendant's release, pending further judicial proceedings. Release itself is a constitutional right, but the bail procedure of temporarily forfeiting money for freedom has resulted in a number of unjust practices. Ideally the only criterion for determining the amount of bail money is to make it enough to ensure that the defendant will reappear. In practice, however, the bail system discriminates against those who cannot afford to pay the bail fee, feeds a shady bail-bond business, and promotes questionable judicial procedures in setting bail.[16] Recent alternatives to the bail system, such as pretrial parole, are eliminating the deficiencies of bail, at the same time providing for both constitutional release of the defendants and assurance of their return for subsequent judicial processing.[17]

In some jurisdictions the suspect is arraigned immediately after being booked at the police station, bypassing the appearance before a magistrate. Whether arraignment is the first judicial appearance or a later one, it consists of an appearance before a judge of the trial court. There the judge reads the charge to the defendant and informs him or her of the right to counsel. The initial charge is based upon either the "information" or the "indictment," depending upon the procedures used in the jurisdiction. Some jurisdictions rely on a grand jury to return an indictment for felony and misdemeanor cases.

Whichever procedure is used for reaching a charge, the judge asks the defendant to plead to the charge, and the defendant may plead guilty, not guilty, or may stand mute. With the judge's permission, the defendant may also have the option of pleading *nolo contendere* (Latin: "I do not wish to contend"), the same as a plea of guilty except that it cannot be used as an admission in subsequent civil suits. If the defendant pleads guilty, the judge will ordinarily enter a judgment of conviction, postponing the sentence until a presentence investigation can be made by the probation department. If the defendant stands mute, the judge will enter a plea of not guilty, and a trial will follow. If the plea is not guilty, the judge asks whether the defendant desires a jury trial or prefers to be tried by the judge without a jury. A plea of not guilty places the burden on the state to prove every element of the offense beyond a reasonable doubt.

The criminal trial is about the least common method of convicting and acquitting defendants. Roughly 90 per cent of criminal convictions are based on guilty pleas that are adjudicated without a trial.[18] The judicial system in the United States has come to depend on the guilty plea. If all or even most criminal cases were to receive a trial upon a plea of not guilty, the courts simply could not handle the caseload. There are not enough, and conceivably could never be enough judges, prosecutors, and defense attorneys.

The judicial necessity for guilty pleas has given rise to the practice commonly known as "plea bargaining." A substantial portion of guilty pleas result from negotiations between prosecutor and defense lawyer or between prosecutor and defendant. The negotiated plea lightens the caseload and accomplishes other objectives:

> As the term implies, plea negotiation involves an exchange of concessions and advantages between the state and the accused. The defendant who pleads guilty is treated less severely than he would be if he were convicted of the maximum charge and assessed the most severe penalty. At the same time, he waives his right to trial, thereby losing his chance, no matter how slight, for outright acquittal. The state, at the relatively small cost of charge reduction leniency, gains the numerous administrative advantages of the guilty plea over a long, costly, and always uncertain trial. In this way the negotiated plea in a real sense answers two important objectives of criminal justice administration: the individualization of justice and the maintenance of the guilty plea system.[19]

The negotiated guilty plea is thus a compromise conviction reached by the state and the accused for the benefit of both.

Having studied this informal conviction process, Donald J. Newman reported that plea bargaining occurred in more than half the felony cases.[20] The accused, directly or through an attorney, offered to plead guilty providing the charge was reduced in kind or degree, or exchanged for a specific type or length of sentence. The subsequent agreements on conviction followed several patterns according to the types of bargains:

> 1. *Bargain Concerning the Charge.* A plea of guilty was entered by the offenders in exchange for a reduction of the charge from the one alleged in the complaint. This ordinarily occurred in cases where the offense in question carried statutory degrees of severity such as homicide, assault, and sex offenses. This type was mentioned as a major issue in 20 percent of the cases in which bargaining occurred. The majority of offenders in these instances were represented by lawyers.
>
> 2. *Bargain Concerning the Sentence.* A plea of guilty was entered by the offenders in exchange for a promise of leniency in sentencing. The most commonly accepted consideration was a promise that the offender would be placed on probation, although a less-than-maximum prison term was the basis in

certain instances. All offenses except murder, serious assault, and robbery were represented in this type of bargaining process. This was by far the most frequent consideration given in exchange for guilty pleas, occurring in almost half (45.5 percent) of the cases in which any bargaining occurred. Again, most of these offenders were represented by attorneys.

3. *Bargain for Concurrent Charges.* This type of informal process occurred chiefly among offenders pleading without counsel. These men exchanged guilty pleas for the concurrent pressing of multiple charges, generally numerous counts of the same offense or related violations such as breaking and entering and larceny. This method, of course, has much the same effect as pleading for consideration in the sentence. The offender with concurrent convictions, however, may not be serving a reduced sentence; he is merely serving one sentence for many crimes. Altogether, concurrent convictions were reported by 21.8 percent of the men who were convicted by informal methods.

4. *Bargain for Dropped Charges.* This variation occurred in about an eighth of the cases who reported bargaining. It involved an agreement on the part of the prosecution not to press formally one or more charges against the offender if he in turn pleaded guilty to (usually) the major offense. The offenses dropped were extraneous law violations contained in, or accompanying, the offense alleged in the complaint, such as auto theft accompanying armed robbery and violation of probation where a new crime had been committed. This informal method, like bargaining for concurrent charges, was reported chiefly by offenders without lawyers. If occurred in 12.6 percent of cases in which bargaining was claimed.[21]

Although most of the remainder of the sample pleaded guilty without consideration, in many of these cases the attorneys probably bargained, or attempted to bargain, without successfully achieving a compromise on conviction.

The plea-bargaining system, always controversial, is under severe attack. Recently the National Advisory Commission on Criminal Justice Standards called for totally abolishing plea bargaining by 1978. Their proposal is based on the argument that "sentences should depend not on whether the defendant has saved the state the expense of a trial but, instead, on what is needed to rehabilitate him."[22] The courts continue to protect the plea-bargaining system. The Supreme Court ruled in Brady v. U.S. that the pressures of plea bargaining do not in themselves violate the privilege against self-incrimination. This decision was followed by North Carolina v. Alford, in which the Supreme Court ruled that a person accused of a crime should be permitted to plead guilty to a lesser offense and avoid the possibility that a jury might impose a stiffer sentence, even if the defendant insists that he or she is innocent. Only one thing can be certain, no matter what the outcome of the plea-bargaining controversy: the solution will be an attempt to help preserve the prevailing social and economic system.

The defense attorney — usually court appointed for poor and minority defendants — advises a client, after suggesting a plea bargain that assures a reduced sentence but also the certainty of conviction — and reduces the court's case load at the same time.

PROSECUTION AND NEGOTIATION IN THE COURT

How the defendant will be prosecuted is decided by agents in the court system. The charges that will be brought against the defendant, and how they will be negotiated, are determined mostly beyond the accused's reach. His or her fate is decided somewhere within the interactions and relationships the judiciary has already established before this defendant ever becomes a case in the court.

The framework for negotiation has been called an "exchange system," in which linkages bind the actors in the judicial process of making decisions. In a marketlike setting, judicial decisions are made following exchanges between legal agents. In the decision to prosecute, as described in a study of the Office of the Prosecuting Attorney in King County (Seattle), the prosecutor exercises discretionary powers "within the network of exchange relationships."[23]

Curbing the flow of cases through the court is vital in the decision to prosecute. The prosecutor, in making decisions, is aware of the needs and expectations of others in the court system. As in the King County court:

> Within the limits imposed by law and the demands of the system, the prosecutor is able to regulate the flow of cases to the court. He may control the length of time between accusation and trial; hence he may hold cases until he has the evidence which will convict. Alternatively, he may seek repeated adjournment and continuances until the public's interest dies; problems such as witnesses becoming unavailable and similar difficulties make his request for dismissal of prosecution more justifiable. Further, he may determine the type of court to receive the case and the judge who will hear it. Many misdemeanors covered by state law are also violations of a city ordinance. It is a common practice for the prosecutor to send a misdemeanor case to the city prosecutor for processing in the municipal court when it is believed that a conviction may not be secured in justice court. As a deputy said, "If there is no case — send it over to the city court. Things are speedier, less formal over there."[24]

The prosecutor regulating court cases is at the same time considering the interests of those involved in administering criminal law, including his or her own political interests and the needs of the judicial system in general.[25]

The interactions and perceptions of the prosecutor and the defense, in particular, are critical in negotiating a guilty plea. David Sudnow observes that the prosecutor (district attorney) and the defense (public defender) during their interactions work out a common position on altering charges.[26] The negotiators cannot arrange a suitable reduction in charge by referring to a statutory definition of an offense, because the penal code gives too little guidance for deciding how the offender's conduct and the legal category correspond. In a charge of burglary, the prosecutor and defense negotiate about a class of "burglaries," which Sudnow calls *normal (stereotypical) burglaries.* A burglary charge can be reduced to a charge of petty theft because the negotiators are able to see the reduction as reasonable and consistent with the kinds of behaviors normally associated with that charge. During their interaction and repeated negotiations, then, the prosecutor and defense develop unstated guides for reducing original charges to lesser charges.

The reasons for plea bargaining between prosecutor and accused or defense attorney are more immediate than individualizing justice and maintaining the judicial system.[27] The charge is often reduced because the prosecutor realizes his evidence is insufficient for conviction at a trial. Reduction may be necessary too because complainants, victims, or witnesses are reluctant to testify. The prosecutor at other times may suggest reducing the charge because he believes that the judge or jury is unlikely to convict the defendant. Judges themselves may favor reducing the charge to avoid imposing the mandatory sentence (either maximum or minimum) for the original charge. A parole sentence may be possible only if the original charge is reduced to a lesser one. Whatever the bargaining agreement, though, the judge may acquit the defendant for reasons growing out of an interest in individualized justice and judicial maintenance. Acquittals are made because (1) the conduct is regarded as a minor violation, (2) the offender is thought unaccountable for his or her behavior, (3) the conduct is considered normal for the defendant's subculture, (4) the conduct is a matter of private morality, (5) specialized treatment may look more appropriate than punishment, (6) restitution is otherwise made to the victim, and (7) the judge disagrees with the purpose of the law or with the law-enforcement effort.[28]

Whether the judge convicts according to the plea negotiated by the prosecutor and defense or acquits the defendant, the judge obviously has a personal interest in the outcome of each case. Technically the judge is not supposed to enter into the bargaining, but by subtle cues and not-so-subtle demands, the judge influences negotiation of pleas. The advantages of negotiation for the judge are mentioned in a study of "Metropolitan Court":

> According to the ideology of the law, the judge is required to be not only impartial but active in seeking out and preserving the rights of all offenders. Nevertheless, he also has a vested interest in a high rate of negotiated pleas. He shares the prosecutor's earnest desire to avoid the time-consuming, expensive, unpredictable snares and pitfalls of an adversary trial. He sees an impossible backlog of cases, with their mounting delays, as possible public evidence of his "inefficiency" and failure. The defendant's plea of guilty enables the judge to engage in a social-psychological fantasy — the accused becomes an already repentant individual who has "learned his lesson" and deserves lenient treatment. Indeed, as previously indicated, many judges give a less severe sentence to a defendant who has negotiated a plea than to one who has been convicted of the same offense after a trial.[29]

No matter what the reason for negotiating a guilty plea, for the prosecutor's interest or that of the defense, the judge, or the judicial system in general, the resulting conviction is a criminal definition. Guilty-plea negotiation ultimately creates a crime.

Negotiated justice makes the judicial system possible, for without it the criminal-justice system would collapse under its own burden. The legal system in the United States and what it serves benefit by processing cases as speedily as possible through the system. Getting defendants to plead guilty to lesser charges eliminates the time and expense of further judicial processing, especially avoiding costly and time-consuming criminal trials.

The criminal-justice system, despite this shortcut, is in crisis. The backlog in criminal cases is mounting. People are recognizing too that defendants are waiting months, often in jail, to have their cases processed.[30] Officials are frantically proposing "sweeping changes" in the administration of criminal justice, including day-and-night court sessions, overhauled bail policies, more judges, and making the courts more efficient.[31] All are an attempt to make criminal justice more rational, to create an efficiently managed criminal-justice system. The problem is seen as administrative: with enough planning and engineering, the "administrative chaos" will be corrected and justice will be achieved. The survival of a legal system preserving the established order is at stake.

These reforms are being applied to deal with the heavy caseloads in the courts, and plea bargaining by itself seems incapable of handling the increased loads. Furthermore, plea negotiation is being questioned, with proposals that it at least be regularized and subjected to procedural rules. David Sternberg, examining the consequences of the radical-criminal trials of the late sixties and early seventies, suggests that the old plea-bargaining system may be in jeopardy.[32] In the future defendants and their lawyers may be less willing to bargain for justice.

Although defendants using radical strategies could disrupt the bureaucratic functioning of the courts, it is possible that the courts might make some administrative concessions, allowing a new kind of bargaining that would reduce the selection of defendants for indictments, be more lenient in bail procedures, and give better "deals" for the defendants. Another breed of reforms could be instituted to deal with defendants in more formal and insidious ways. Instead of being processed through the formal judicial system, accused persons might be "treated" and "corrected" outside the court. This appears to be the direction that criminal justice in the United States is taking, seeking to better maintain the capitalist social order.

PROSECUTION AND DEFENSE IN THE ADVERSARY SYSTEM

The administration of criminal justice in the United States is founded on the adversary principle. In this system, opposing parties — the state and the accused — are engaged in a battle. The game is right versus wrong; one side must be entirely correct and the other all wrong. One side wins when the judgment is in its favor. Rules and procedures guide the battle throughout.[33]

The adversary system arose historically to meet the needs of the new capitalist class and state. The state was made to appear as a neutral agency within which conflict and struggle could take place according to the rules of law. In effect, in England and the United States, a host of related devices were established: due process of law, independence of the judiciary, right to jury, *habeas corpus,* right to counsel, right to summon witnesses in defense, right to bail, indictment by grand jury, and the privilege against self-incrimination. This system of criminal justice, as William J. Chambliss observed, "ensured the institution of the adversary system and resolved a major conflict between competing elites without redistributing power or privilege to the lower classes."[34] The adversary system continues to secure the established order of capitalist society.

The adversary system of criminal justice is bureaucratically organized into distinct legal kinds of work with specified duties and obligations. Each position has its own definition and another relating it to the others. Expectations of performance regulate the occupational behavior of those who occupy the work roles, the principal ones being the prosecutor, the defense attorney, and the judge. Each is engaged in work that results in defining people and behaviors as criminal.

Judges act on evidence and arguments presented by the prosecuting and defense attorneys. They find the defendant guilty or innocent, sometimes by referring to a jury's decision, and then impose a sentence. The prosecutors' role is more critical in the early judicial stages. As representatives of the state, they have the authority to determine whether an alleged offender should be charged and the authority to obtain a conviction by negotiation. They have the responsibility of presenting the state's case in court, that is, of prosecuting the accused. Their skill as trial lawyers is important in convicting the defendant. Prosecutors also affect the arrest practices of the police, the volume of cases in the courts, and the number of offenders referred to the correctional system.

According to the adversary principle, the lawyer for the defense is also engaged in a battle against the other agents of the court. The defendant's lawyer represents the accused in opposition to the court's interests. In reality, however, the adversary principle does not work that way. Instead, the criminal lawyer shares in the system of criminal justice with the prosecutor and the other representatives of the court. The accused person finds that his or her interests are being overshadowed by the needs of the criminal-justice system. Everyone in the court but the defendant sees himself or herself as a colleague, not an adversary. The social reality in the judicial process, contrary to the legal ideology, is based on cooperation rather than adversary relationships. The fate of the defendant, who remains on the outside except when assisting in plea negotiation, is decided within this social reality.

The right of the accused to be represented by legal counsel has been ensured in the Sixth Amendment to the Constitution, and is essential to the adversary system of criminal justice. An individual forced to answer to a criminal charge needs assistance from one who understands the legal system and who will protect the defendant's legal rights. The defendant is not likely to understand the legal system, mainly because of its planned obscurity. For the judicial system to be effective and efficient, counsel for the defendant is necessary. An adversary system of justice depends too upon vigorous challenges to the state's accusations.

When and how to ensure or provide legal counsel for the accused has been the vital issue in the adversary system. Procedures that were inspired in part by rulings of state supreme courts and the United States Supreme Court entitle or require defendants to have legal counsel from the moment of arrest. The Supreme Court decision in the Gault case expanded the jurisdictional rights of counsel to include juvenile delinquency proceedings.

Several schemes provide defendants with legal counsel.[35] The types of legal representation include (1) court-appointed counsel, as in the legal-aid system, (2) the public-defender system, whereby the state provides its own lawyers to defend the accused, and (3) lawyer-reference plans, in which private or public agency lawyers are made known to defendants. Availability of these and other forms of legal representation varies from one jurisdiction to another. Most important for the conviction proceedings, the outcome of cases can depend on the kind of legal counsel the defendant receives.[36]

That criminal justice is differently administered according to social class is at least vaguely realized by most people. Because the poor are accused of criminal behavior more often than members of other classes, their dependence upon legal service is total. Legal services are most inadequate, however, for the class that needs legal assistance most. The poor are least likely to use lawyers; when they do they usually have access only to the least competent ones, and the legal counsel with which they are provided is generally limited. Surveys from several states indicate that about two out of three lower-class families have never employed a lawyer, compared with about one in three upper-class families.[37] Only token compliance serves the requirement that all defendants faced with a possible jail or prison term be represented by a lawyer. Moreover, the few private attorneys available to the poor, because of insecurity in their practice, often exploit their clients.[38]

To supplement private legal representation, special agencies and procedures, such as legal-aid societies and the public-defender system, have attempted to extend legal services to the poor. Nevertheless, it appears that indigents are not provided with adequate legal services, and the result is higher rates of conviction and severer sentences for the poor.

With respect to the representation of criminal defendants, there is considerable evidence to suggest that neither the assigned counsel nor public defender system as now constituted is capable of providing adequate service to the indigent accused. A large proportion of poor defendants (particularly in misdemeanor cases) are not represented at all. Moreover, when counsel is provided he frequently has neither the resources, the skill nor the incentive to defend his client effectively; and he usually enters the case too late to make any real difference in the outcome. Indeed, the generally higher rate of guilty pleas and prison sentences among defendants represented by assigned counsel or the public defender suggest that these attorneys may actually undermine their clients' position.[39]

Criminal justice in the United States, with the legalities supplied by due process, is mainly for the class that dominates and controls the social, economic, and political institutions. Even the movement to legally represent the poor in court is part of a larger regulative movement, not simply a progressive and humanitarian legal reform. The "public-defender" system is in actuality, as Gregg Barak shows, a defense system for the rich.[40] Poor people are considered incapable of defending their class interests without benevolent aid from the legal institutions of the capitalist state. The adversary form of criminal justice is consistent with the modern needs of the capitalist order.

THE CRIMINAL LAWYER

Lawyers who represent criminal defendants privately usually are engaged in a specialized type of legal practice and have distinctive career patterns. Both tendencies affect their way of handling criminal cases.

More than half the lawyers practicing in United States cities are self-employed. The other half are employed either in law firms or in corporations, governmental legal departments, and legal-aid societies. The individual practitioner or solo lawyer differs sharply from those engaged in the other types of legal practice. In a comparison of individual practitioners and firm lawyers in Detroit it was found that solo lawyers more often came from minority, religious-ethnic, entrepreneurial, and working-class homes, and had inferior educations and chaotic work histories.[41] They also restrict their practices to residual matters that the large law firms have not pre-empted. Their practice in Chicago includes these kinds of cases:

(1) Matters not large enough or remunerative enough for the large firms to handle — most generally work for small to medium-sized businesses and corporations, the smaller real estate transactions (for individuals or small businesses), and estate matters for middle-income families; (2) the undesirable cases, the dirty work, those areas of practice that have associated with them an

aura of influencing and fixing and that involve arrangements with clients and others that are felt by the large firms to be professionally damaging. The latter category includes local tax, municipal, personal injury, divorce, and criminal matters.[42]

The lawyers who privately handle the criminal cases of working-class defendants usually are individual practitioners. They are also likely to be engaged in a diversified legal practice in which criminal cases are only an occasional affair. Their practice of law generally is built on the local police court or the traffic court and is ethnic- and neighborhood-oriented. This solo lawyer in Chicago shows how diverse legal matters are related for the individual practitioner:

> I handle some small criminal cases. This year I had one case, an indictment in felony court, a bench trial. The rest would be either police court — up to the preliminary hearing, getting charges reduced to misdemeanors, and so one — assault and battery, domestic problems, mostly drunks and disorderlies, assaults, etc. Neighborhood stuff. So many domestic relations cases come out of the police court; after representing them in the police court, you get them dismissed for divorce.[43]

The individual practitioners who do specialize must maintain regular sources of case referral. They depend on close relationships with bondsmen, policemen, and community leaders for their business. Competition for criminal cases among solo lawyers who specialize in criminal law forms a legal practice built on sharp business practices more than pursuing criminal justice.

The difference between lawyers with criminal practices and those with civil practices is documented in a study of lawyers in five cities, comparing them on such characteristics as social origins, choice of legal career, preparation for law, adjustment to legal practice, and reasons for entering their field of legal practice.[44] The criminal lawyers had relatively low socioeconomic backgrounds, less professional training, had difficulty getting established, were solo practitioners engaged in an entrepreneurial career, and were not especially satisfied with criminal practice.

Using characteristics of the lawyers, the study distinguished between two types of criminal-law careers. In the first type,

> the attorney did not choose to enter criminal law, but rather he accepted criminal cases as they came his way in the process of establishing a practice or as a supplement to a meager practice in civil law. From the standpoint of the legal profession, these lawyers are among the least successful, and accordingly one may judge their morale to be correspondingly low. The second type of criminal lawyer is one who often chose this field, but in any case he enjoys the drama

and thrill of those accused of crime. He may achieve considerable success; lacking this, he is compensated by his intense absorption in the work.[45]

Only about a quarter of the criminal lawyers can be placed in the second type of criminal-law career. Of course, some criminal lawyers do not fit either of the two types, including the successful ones who do not have a welfare interest and those who strongly identify with the welfare of their clients, but whose careers may be described as failures. Many practitioners of criminal law either have failed to establish a successful practice and therefore accept criminal cases as a way of enlarging a legal practice, or relish the excitement in criminal work and feel that their practice secures justice for the accused.

The public-defender lawyer's career presents its own problems. In a study of lawyers in the Public Defender Office in California's Alameda County (which includes Oakland and Berkeley), Anthony Platt and Randi Pollock found a common career pattern among the public defenders. Most recruits regard the public-defender office as a place to develop technical skills and professional values. Very few stayed longer than two and a half years, usually leaving with a feeling of being "burned out" and often embittered by the experience. They leave to pursue a more lucrative private practice with mostly middle-class clients. Platt and Pollock conclude their analysis:

> They come to justify their role as mediators between the poor and the courts, resigned to seeking occasional loopholes in the system, softening its more explicitly repressive features, and attempting to rescue the victims of blatant injustices. But even this makeshift effort to link everyday work with liberal humanitarianism proves inadequate, since most Assistants are regarded with resentment, ingratitude or indifference by their clients. When they leave PDO [Public Defender Office], they have become cynical and embittered, alienated from politics, and preoccupied with problems of survival and success in the legal marketplace.[46]

All lawyers are subject to the controls of their occupation. Among these are (1) standards that proscribe behavior considered unethical by society in general, such as cheating, bribery, and stealing; (2) standards dealing with professional problems, such as relations among colleagues, methods of obtaining business, and conflicts of interest. Lawyers differ in conforming to these standards. Ultimately the legal assistance the client receives is influenced by the behavior and ethics of the lawyer who handles the case.

In a study on the ethical conduct of New York City bar members, it was found that characteristics of the practice influence violation of professional standards.[47] Because of the instability in their practice, lawyers with low-status clients are subject to far more temptations, opportunities, and pressure from clients to violate professional ethics than are lawyers with clients of high status. Another influence on their ethical conduct is the court setting in which they work and the constraints provided by their work group. Conformity to professional norms and ethics depends greatly on where the lawyer is in the legal profession.

For the lawyer in criminal practice, professional norms cover several subjects: "(1) confidentiality of the attorney-client relationship; (2) affective or emotional neutrality toward the merits of the case, while at the same time service in the interests of the client; and (3) participation in procedures in which a professional as opposed to a personal relationship is maintained with other participants — the police, the bondsman, the prosecutor and the judge."[48] The defense lawyer's behavior is especially complicated by confrontation with conflicting claims. Because of the legal role, the defense attorney must act as mediator between the client and judicial agents. Professional conduct, therefore, is related to the way in which the defense lawyer manages the conflicting claims imposed by the adversary system of justice.

Defendants handled by criminal lawyers are suspected of committing some offense. Because of a precarious position, the defendant is subject to much manipulation by the attorney, and the case is guided by the lawyer's personal interests. Finally, the lawyer's handling of the defendant's case is affected by the court's bureaucratic structure: "In the sense that the lawyer in the criminal court serves as a double agent, serving higher organizational rather than professional ends, he may be deemed to be engaged in bureaucratic rather than private practice."[49] In this way, criminal-law practice is actually bureaucratic practice, because the lawyer and the client are enmeshed in the authority and discipline of the judicial system. Strategies and decisions affecting the application of criminal definitions are made within the boundaries established by the adversary system of justice.

CRIMINAL TRIAL

The accused may eventually be adjudicated in a criminal trial. When negotiation between the legal agents has failed to bring the defendant to plead guilty, or the defendant pleads not guilty without any attempt at bargaining, a criminal trial will provide the setting for the remaining parts in the drama of imposing a criminal definition. The criminal trial constructs the reality of the case; it is not strictly an exercise in finding the truth, but is a product of politics and discretion ultimately for the benefit of the state.

Variations do change the trial's proceedings, but it generally follows these eight steps.[50] The arraignment and plea may be followed by: (1) selection of the jury, (2) opening statements by prosecutor and defense, (3) presentation of evidence by state and defense, (4) prosecutor's and defense's arguments to the jury, (5) prosecutor's rebuttal, (6) judge's instructions on the law, (7) rendering of the jury verdict, and (8) imposition of a sentence.

All these steps are of course not included in every trial. It may be decided that the defendant will be tried before a judge or panel of judges, not by a jury. Motions for change in procedure may be entered during the trial. Decisions may be made on waiving statements, evidence, and testimony. The defense may move for a new trial or to hold immediate judgment. Following the sentence, the case may be appealed to a higher court, or if the defense charges denial of due process further litigation may follow. In other words, the final conviction depends on many more decisions and actions once the defendant reaches the trial stage.

Extralegal Factors

In the popular mind the criminal trial is a symbol for justice in the United States. This notion suggests that justice is rationally dispensed, that all involved in the judicial process (lawyers, defendants, witnesses, jurors, judges) rest their statements, arguments, and judgments on facts, according to the rules of law. All parties supposedly are pursuing the "truth" about the case. But human actions and the organizational constraints imposed by the judicial system itself make the reality harsher. The criminal trial may be most profitably analyzed as a system of human actions that entails perceptions and behaviors like those in any social situation. Those involved in the trial are acting according to their own past, their present perspectives, and their future expectations, and their actions are adjusted according to the behavior of others.

> In a sense the courtroom may be viewed as a microcosm for the larger social world in which human beings exist, act, and interact. That the action reconstructed in court and the action-process of reconstruction are meaningful and purposive, that they involve subjective as well as objective meanings, and that they significantly hinge on human goals, purposes and motives becomes at once apparent. If some juridical writers envisage a mere mechanical application of formalized law, the participants in the ordinary court trial of a criminal case are involved in more mundane practices.[51]

The combativeness in the criminal trial ensures that judicial actions will be social and extralegal, not logical deductions from abstract principles. As a substitute for private brawls, the modern criminal trial places parties

The decorum of the courtroom, symbolizing the authority of the state, was established early in the history of the United States, as seen in this nineteenth-century woodcut of a murder trial in Superior Court, San Francisco.

in opposing camps. The adversary system of justice promotes a "fight" method rather than a "truth" method of trying cases.[52]

In other words, the criminal trial constructs a reality — a social reality. Objective facts are not gathered in a criminal trial, but decisions are reached on "evidence" that is meaningful to the interacting and conflicting participants. Subjectivity enters into arguments by the attorneys, testimony by the witnesses, deliberations by jurors, and the judge's actions. All the actors in the drama react subjectively to the actions of all others. The decisions reached during the trial, including the one that ultimately defines the defendant as a convicted criminal, are made by people as social beings. That is to say, though the criminal trial is not an exercise in fact-finding and logical deduction, it is a product of human action.

Yet, the fate of the accused is being decided here. Factors totally unrelated to the formal legal system are determining the defendant's future.

Not the least of these is the way in which the accused person presents himself or herself in the courtroom. The participants there judge not only the alleged offense of the accused but his or her demeanor in the courtroom. Studying the courtroom ceremonies, Robert M. Emerson describes the kind of performance expected of the juvenile defendant:

> A totally consistent performance is required, and this demands that the repentant delinquent convey a properly deferential and remorseful attitude by his demeanor. Deferential demeanor, expressing appreciation and respect toward both the court and the violated norm, consitutes a basic expectation in the courtroom ceremony. In this way, posture and expression should conform to the solemn and serious definition of the occasion. It is expected that the child maintain a formal, rigid, and controlled posture, both in entering the courtroom and in sitting through the course of the hearing. Facial expression must be carefully controlled in order to show worry and concern or at least serious interest in the unfolding scene. Similarly, any talking or comment must be addressed to the whole court and show respect for the officials involved.[53]

To be judged one must enter into degrading and humiliating ceremonies. No matter what the outcome, the ordeal is part of the message that the court conveys.

Testimony and Witnesses

Testimony by all types of witnesses is used by both the prosecution and the defense to argue the merits of their positions. The defense attorney has to decide whether or not it is strategically wise to put the defendant on the witness stand as a witness in his own behalf; the decision is usually based on speculation about how the jury will react to the defendant's performance. The defense will be reluctant to place a defendant with a prior criminal record on the stand.[54] Though procedurally a previous conviction should not be considered as evidence of guilt on another charge, the defendant with a previous conviction is especially vulnerable to probing by the prosecuting attorney.

Both the prosecution and defense will utilize any witness who may favorably shape the opinions of the judge and jury members. Such witnesses, however, often end up in an insecure position.[55] In spite of procedures to guarantee protection, the witnesses are subject to pressures from the public, the press, and personal contacts. They may later suffer repercussions from their testimony. The witness is most dramatically subjected to harassment during the opposition's cross-examination in the courtroom. Little wonder that the "facts" provided by witnesses are selective and subjective.

One kind of testimony that may be used in adjudicating the accused is that of the "experts." Criminal procedure today relies especially on the psychiatrist's testimony. Most states provide for preliminary observation of defendants suspected of mental disorders. If a judge decides to accept evidence provided by a psychiatrist, the accused may be declared incompetent to stand trial and then be committed indefinitely to a mental hospital.

During the criminal trial, the psychiatrist, responding about the M'Naghten test of insanity, is asked to judge the responsibility and, in essence, the guilt or innocence of the defendant.[56] In jurisdictions that have rules of the Durham type, the psychiatrist may describe the mental state of the defendant entirely in psychiatric language, deciding if the "unlawful act was the product of mental disease or mental defect." The psychiatrist's part in the criminal trial is crucial because of the information he can supposedly provide about the defendant's legal responsibility.

The psychiatrist's power in the criminal trial has been deeply criticized in recent years. A person charged with a criminal offense may be denied the right to trial because of the pretrial psychiatric examination — psychiatrists are putting people away without the guarantee of a trial. And the putting away may be inspired by adversaries who do not want the would-be defendant around.

Thomas S. Szasz describes the case of a filling station operator in Syracuse, New York, who had been pressed by real-estate developers to sell his property so that a shopping center could be built on the site.[57] When agents of the developers attempted to erect a sign on the property, the enraged operator fired warning shots from a rifle into the air. He was arrested but was never brought to trial. On the prosecuting attorney's recommendation, the operator was ordered to undergo psychiatric examination to determine his fitness to stand trial. He was held incapable and was committed to a state mental hospital. Still in a hospital after ten years, he had already served more time than he would have spent in prison had he been tried and convicted. Whether we criticize or support the use of psychiatric evidence, the defendant's fate may be directly affected by the "expert's" testimony.

Now that the dangers in psychiatric testimony and the problems in the insanity defense are recognized, changes have been proposed. In a federal case, Judge David L. Bazelon (who earlier ruled on Durham) wrote this opinion:

> It may be that psychiatry and the other social and behavioral sciences cannot provide sufficient data relevant to a determination of criminal responsibility no matter what our rules of evidence are. If so, we may be forced to eliminate the insanity defense altogether.[58]

In place of the insanity defense all technical formulations would be scrapped and the jury would be instructed simply to consider whether the defendant can "justly be held responsible for his act." The moral issue would be considered by the jury instead of being left in the hands of the expert witness.

Proposed legislation would prevent a defendant from pleading not guilty by reason of insanity as long as the prosecution can establish that all the elements of a crime are present.[59] The defendant's mental state would come up only if the condition was so serious that the prosecution could not prove criminal intent at the time of the crime. Not much will be changed by these proposals, however. Witnesses probably will continue to testify, as they have for more than a century, about the defendant's state of mind. "The battlefield may shift from the issue of right versus wrong to the equally troublesome issue of intent, but the jurors will hear testimony not substantially different from what they hear today."[60]

Trial by Jury

The cornerstone of American criminal justice is trial by a jury. In practice, about 80 per cent of the world's criminal-jury trials are held in the United States.[61] Yet the jury trial is the mode of conviction for only a small fraction of criminal prosecutions in this country. Of the cases that are tried, nearly half are tried without a jury. Only about one in seven felony prosecutions ends in a trial by jury.

The relatively small use of the jury trial for criminal conviction is accounted for by (1) legal restrictions on the right to trial by jury, (2) decision by the prosecution and defense to settle by guilty-plea conviction, and (3) choice by the defendant to be tried before a judge without a jury.[62] Although the Sixth Amendment to the Constitution guarantees the right to trial by jury, the states specify the kinds of offenses that will be tried in that way. A trial may be denied for such minor offenses as traffic violations, disorderly conduct, petty gambling, public drunkenness, and prostitution.

Where not otherwise stipulated by state laws, trial by jury is a choice that is left open to the defendant. Whether to be prosecuted without a trial or to be tried with a jury, depends on the strategy worked out by the defendant and the legal actors. The decision to avoid a jury trial varies according to the offense and local custom. About 90 per cent of forgeries but only about 30 per cent of murders are prosecuted by guilty pleas. When trials are used for murder, the jury is waived only about 15 per cent of the time, whereas for forgery the jury is waived about 50 per cent of the time. Local variations in the waiver of jury are conspicuous. In Wisconsin it is done in about three-fourths of criminal cases; in Utah in only about 5 per cent of the cases.[63]

Although the jury trial is not used as much as we might think, its influence on American criminal justice is extensive. The trial is a control on the judicial administration of cases that are not tried by a jury.

> It has become something of a commonplace to read the statistics on the impact of guilty pleas and jury waivers as gravely reducing the significance of the jury and transferring its power largely to the prosecuting attorney in the bargaining over guilty pleas. But we saw at every stage of this informal process of pre-trial dispositions that decisions are in part informed by expectations of what the jury will do. Thus, the jury is not controlling merely the immediate case before it, but the host of cases not before it which are destined to be disposed of by the pre-trial process. The jury thus controls not only the formal resolution of controversies in the criminal case, but also the informal resolution of cases that never reach the trial stage. In a sense the jury, like the visible cap of an iceberg, exposes but a fraction of its true volume.[64]

Once it has been decided to try the defendant before a jury, many social factors enter into the jury's way of arriving at a decision on the defendant's guilt or innocence. The prosecutor and defense are well aware that jurors' backgrounds and personal characteristics influence their responses to the evidence and arguments presented in the trial. In selecting the jury, during the *voir dire* (competence) examination, the attorneys try to choose jurors who will make decisions favorable to the respective sides of the case. For each attorney, a trial may be won or lost during the jury's empaneling. The composition of the jury is important in determining the kind of definition that will be imposed on the defendant.

Defendants are supposedly tried by a representative body of the citizenry, but social and economic biases are built into the methods by which jurors are selected, and the lower occupational groups are systematically excluded from juries in the United States.[65] This unrepresentative character affects the way in which juries deliberate and arrive at decisions about the defendant's innocence or guilt.

The sources of bias in jury deliberation have been commented on in several studies of jury behavior. A study of mock jury deliberations revealed that foremen are usually selected according to their social position in the community.[66] Proprietors were selected three and a half times more often than laborers, and only a fifth as many women were made foremen as would be expected by chance. Foremen are particularly important in jury deliberation because they can change the opinion of the individual jurors according to their own views.[67]

The social status and sex of the individual jurors appear to determine how much they participate in jury deliberations and influence the jury's decision. Studies of mock juries show that men and people of higher social status, not women and people of lower social status, have higher participation rates and greater influence in jury deliberations.[68] Men of the upper occupational groups act more in jury deliberation than any other type of juror. Women and people in the lower occupational groups, on the other hand, when they do participate, usually react to the contributions of the others.

Jurors also differ in things they focus on during the deliberation. In another mock jury study, it turned out that jurors spend about half their time exchanging experiences and opinions either directly or indirectly related to the trial. About a quarter of the time is spent on procedural matters, about 15 per cent on reviewing the facts in the case, and about 8 per cent on the court instructions.[69] The better educated give more emphasis to procedure and instructions; the less educated to testimony, experiences from personal and daily life, and opinions about the trial rather than procedure and instruction. The same researcher found that in insanity trials lower-class jurors are more likely to favor the defendant.[70] Women jurors, on the other hand, are more sympathetic toward the defendant than men, but are likely to qualify their verdict according to the offense.

In the end, the verdict reached by the jury may not be the same as the one the trial judge would have rendered. The differences between verdicts reached by juries and judges have been extensively researched.[71] One study investigated and analyzed 3,576 actual jury verdicts and the matching hypothetical verdicts of the judges in those cases. The major finding was that the judge and jury *agreed* in 75.4 per cent of the trials. More specifically, the judges and juries agreed to acquit in 13.4 per cent of the cases and to convict in 62.0 per cent. In the trials in which the judges and juries disagreed, the disagreement was mostly in one direction: the jury was more likely than the judge to acquit. The jury acquitted when the judge would have convicted in 16.9 per cent of the cases. But the jury convicted when the judge would have acquitted in 2.2 per cent of the cases. That is, the juries were more lenient than the judges in 16.9 per cent of the cases and less lenient than the judges in 2.2 per cent. Practically speaking, then, when the defense decided to bring the case before a jury, defendants fared better 14.7 per cent of the time than they would have in a bench trial.

The strategy in choosing the type of trial, in other words, is important in determining the probability of a criminal conviction. In manipulating the judicial process, the legal agents are able to shape the results of the criminal trial. Even in the procedure that symbolizes criminal justice in the United States — the criminal trial — the needs of the established order determine the reality of justice.

The Political Trial

The politics of justice necessarily comes to the surface in the criminal trial. The courtroom trial can be used to eliminate political foes who are a threat to the regime.[72] The wielders of state power use the courts to maintain their domination. Although this country has always had political trials, the response of the government to the challenges of the last few years has increased the number of political trials.

The United States has a rich history of political trials. Dramatic trials for such offenses against the state as treason have been rare, but the courts have been used for political purposes, from trials during the country's founding years to more recent cases involving civil rights, resistance to war, demonstrations, and conspiracy. Reviewing some of these trials, Leon Friedman dispels the myth that trials by the state are not political: "In short, the concept of a politically insulated prosecutor, a neutral court and jury and a normal trial is more an ideal than a reality, and it ceases to exist entirely when political out-groups and vociferous dissenters are brought into the judicial system."[73]

Several trials in recent times have drawn to public attention the politicality of the courts, especially in the trial of war resisters, Black Panthers, and conspiracy cases.[74] In fact, in the Chicago conspiracy trial, the defendants explicitly attempted to show how the court was being political, refusing to observe the traditional decorum of the courtroom. The severe contempt charges that followed the trial indicated the court's reaction to the defendants' political use of the trial. Friedman said: "It is total hypocrisy to attack the Chicago defendants for bringing politics into their proceeding: it was politics that brought *them* to the court room. To accuse them of tainting the trial with extraneous political considerations is to swallow the government's whitewash."[75] Courts are not "above the battle," but can be active participants, indeed instigators, of politics in administering criminal law.

The state has created a judicial structure explicitly designed to deal with threats to the social order. Modern criminal justice has a complex of judicial weapons for securing domestic order: conspiracy charges, preventive detention, grand-jury proceedings, mass prosecutions, and the like.[76] These tactics do not usually result in a successful prosecution, and often are judged to be unconstitutional, but the government is able to repress threatening thoughts and actions. Criminal justice again serves the purposes of the state. The judicial system and the political order are one.

SENTENCING

After the defendant is convicted, a decision is made on the sanction that will be attached to the newly ascribed status of "criminal." The specification of the sanction, which is known as *sentencing,* involves manipulations and discretions of many people. In some jurisdictions the type and length of sentence are determined by the jury; in others sentencing is the responsibility of an administrative board; but in most jurisdictions the judge assigns the sentence.[77]

Even when sentencing is the judge's province, other people participate in the decision. Many states provide for a presentence investigation of the convicted defendant. The decision to proceed with such an investigation depends on the defense attorney's discretion and also on maneuvers by the prosecutor and the judge. The presentence investigation is then made by the probation department attached to the court. The report, which covers the defendant's personal and social background, criminal record, and mental and physical condition, includes the probation department's recommendations for sentencing. With the report and recommendations in hand, the judge imposes a sentence. But as shown in a study of the relation between presentence reports and dispositions, most judges sentence according to recommendations by the probation department.[78] Although the final sentencing decision may belong to the judge, the decisions of others are crucial in the actual disposition.

The sentence imposed by the judge must fall within the limits provided by the penal law. The codes of penal law contain an elaborate classification of crimes with penalties graded according to seriousness of the crime.[79] Within the boundaries of penal law, however, judges may exercise a great deal of discretion in deciding upon a sentence. A range of alternative sentences and lengths of sentences are available to the judge for any crime.

Legal innovations, especially the indeterminate sentence and probation, have increased the discretionary practices in sentencing.[80] The movement toward individualizing treatment provides a rationale for using discretion in sentencing convicted offenders. The counter-movement to institute mandatory sentences would reduce some discretion, by replacing it with a practice meant to provide a certainty of control for the benefit of the current order.[81]

Most sentencing decisions are made within the framework provided by the law, including the type of crime and the offender's prior criminal record.[82] Nevertheless, within the law decisions are affected by many social considerations. The criminal sanctions ultimately imposed on the convicted defendant are influenced by such extralegal factors as the personalities of the judges who assign the sentences, the norms that regulate sentencing, the judiciary's social organization, the attorney's activities, the responses and cues provided by the defendant, and the defendant's socioeconomic and racial characteristics.

That sentencing practices of judges vary is illustrated by statistics on sentencing. A study of sentences assigned in nearly 7,500 criminal cases handled by six judges over a ten-year period in a New Jersey county reported that the judges differed considerably in the frequency, length, and type of sentences they assigned to convicted offenders.[83] The diversity was even more evident when the sentences were analyzed according to the type of crime.

An explanation for these varied practices may be found in the judges' backgrounds and attitudes. We see some indication of how background and attitude affect judges' decisions in research on the judicial decisions of state and federal supreme court judges.[84] Judges were given a decision score representing the proportion of times they favored the defense. Judges who were more defendant-minded were likely to be Democrats rather than Republicans, not members of the American Bar Association, not former prosecutors, Catholics rather than Protestants, and relatively liberal as measured by off-the-bench attitudes. Because of such attributes, then, judges often make particular kinds of decisions.

The decisions also vary geographically. Ecological variations in sentencing statistics seem to indicate that sentencing behavior of judges is normatively regulated and that the normative patterns differ from one region to another. The average sentences differ considerably from one federal court district to another.[85] Judges are influenced by local sentencing customs and local bureaucratic considerations in sentencing those who violate federal laws. For the convicted offender, the sentence received depends greatly on the sentencing patterns of the jurisdiction in which the case is tried and sentenced.

That the fate of the convicted person is in the hands of legal agents in addition to the judge is illustrated in a study of the recommendations made by probation officers to judges.[86] The researchers observed wide differences in recommendations probation officers gave on whether the convicted person should be granted probation or sentenced to prison. One probation officer recommended probation for 88.9 per cent of his cases and another in only 40 per cent. The researchers then suggest that recommendations vary because of the officer's background, training, and vocational experience. As probation officers gain experience they decrease their recommendations for probation. Again, the sanction received by the criminal is based on the discretion of others.

Discretion in sentencing goes along, of course, with awareness of the offender. It is often the offender's characteristics, not the offense, which determine the sentence, as we see in those given to blacks and third-world people. Sentencing statistics indicate that such persons are committed to prison longer than whites for the same offenses. In Table 9.1 are the average sentences of persons committed by the courts to federal prisons. Whites have an average sentence (for all offenses) of 42.1 months, but nonwhites have received an average sentence of 67.6. Moreover, the variations differ according to the offense; for many types of crimes nonwhites receive longer sentences than whites; conversely, whites receive longer sentences than nonwhites for some other types of crimes. It has also been found in a study of sentencing in Philadelphia courts that black defendants who kill white victims receive the life or the death sentence more than twice as often as black felony defendants who kill black victims.[87] No matter how you look at it, sentencing is administered differentially according to race and minority status.

In another study of prison sentences, as assigned by juries in regions of Texas, it was also found that sentences varied in length according to the offender's race.[88] Even when nonracial factors were controlled in the analysis, blacks received longer sentences than whites. The amount of the differences also varied from one region to another in Texas, indicating local biases in administration of criminal justice.

The racial and class bias of criminal justice in sentencing, as in other stages of the legal process, continues to be supported in criminological investigations. One researcher found recently that for juveniles, even when the seriousness of the offense is held constant, blacks are more likely than whites to receive a more serious disposition from the courts.[89] It was found in the same research that working-class delinquents are less likely to be put on probation and more likely to be institutionalized than delinquents from other classes. No matter what the offense, working-class juveniles receive more severe dispositions than other juveniles.

Such studies tell us that, for juveniles or adults, justice is administered according to the characteristics of those who are judged as being criminals. To be of the working class, black, of the third world, with little education, and without the "proper respect" for the law, or some combination of these, increases the likelihood that you will be processed in the criminal justice system — and more severely than others in the society. That criminal justice is dispensed by the standards of the capitalist order in the United States is the conclusion of our analysis. Criminal justice is, in fact, a device for preserving that order.

TABLE 9.1 Average Sentences of Court Commitments to Federal Prisons, by Race and Offense, 1975

Offenses in which whites have longer average sentences than nonwhites	*Average sentences (in months)*	
	Whites	*Nonwhites*
Burglary	66.6	63.0
Counterfeiting	46.0	34.0
Firearms	38.0	33.2
Larceny	42.0	34.8
Liquor laws	18.4	13.9
Extortion	79.9	55.2
Forgery	38.9	35.0
Securities	48.1	47.7
Offenses in which nonwhites have longer average sentences than whites		
Assault	60.7	70.4
Drug laws	47.9	63.8
Fraud	30.9	32.1
Robbery	139.1	140.8
Immigration	7.1	13.0
Income tax	13.4	28.1
Juvenile delinquency	31.3	35.8
Kidnapping	258.2	275.5
Selective Service acts	21.5	26.0
White-slave traffic	47.3	48.4
Average sentence for all offenses	42.1	67.6

SOURCE: Adapted from U.S. Department of Justice, Federal Bureau of Prisons, *Statistical Report, Fiscal Year 1975* (Washington, D.C., 1976), pp. 49–50.

NOTES

1. Allen W. Wood, "The Marxian Critique of Justice," *Philosophy and Public Affairs*, 1 (Spring 1972), pp. 244–282.
2. Otto A. Bird, *The Idea of Justice* (New York: Frederick A. Praeger, 1967), pp. 11–13.
3. Edgar Bodenheimer, *Treatise on Justice* (New York: Philosophical Library, 1967), p. 8.
4. Morris Ginsberg, *On Justice in Society* (Baltimore: Penguin Books, 1965), p. 7.
5. Herbert Jacob and Kenneth Vines, "The Role of the Judiciary in American State Politics," in Glendon Schubert, ed., *Judicial Decision-Making* (New York: Free Press of Glencoe, 1963), p. 250. Specific studies are found in James R. Klonoski and Robert I. Mendelsohn, eds., *The Politics of Local Justice* (Boston: Little, Brown, 1970).
6. Jack Peltason, *Federal Courts in the Political Process* (New York: Doubleday, 1955), p. 29.

7. Much of the research on discretion in the criminal-justice system is reported in George J. McCall, *Observing the Law: Applications of Field Methods to the Study of the Criminal Justice System,* Crime and Delinquency Monograph Series, National Institute of Mental Health (Washington, D.C.: U.S. Government Printing Office, 1975).

8. For a critique, see Kenneth Culp Davis, *Discretionary Justice: A Preliminary Inquiry* (Urbana: University of Illinois Press, 1971).

9. See Herbert Jacob, *Justice in America: Courts, Lawyers, and the Judicial Process* (Boston: Little, Brown, 1965), pp. 131–148.

10. Harold Garfinkel, "Research Note on Inter- and Intra-Racial Homicides," *Social Forces,* 27 (May 1949), pp. 369–381. Also see Thorsten Sellin, "Race Prejudice in the Administration of Justice," *American Journal of Sociology,* 41 (September 1935), pp. 212–217.

11. Haywood Burns, "Racism in American Law," in Robert Lefcourt, ed., *Law Against the People: Essays to Demystify Law, Order and the Courts* (New York: Random House, 1971), p. 41.

12. Ibid., p. 54. Also see Sara Blackburn, ed., *White Justice: Black Experience Today in America's Courtrooms* (New York: Harper & Row, 1971).

13. Abraham S. Blumberg, *Criminal Justice* (Chicago: Quadrangle Books, 1967), p. 70. For related research, see Maureen Mileski, "Courtroom Encounters: An Observation Study of a Lower Criminal Court," *Law and Society Review,* 5 (May 1971), pp. 473–538. Observations on the juvenile court's social organization are found in Aaron V. Cicourel, *The Social Organization of Juvenile Justice* (New York: John Wiley, 1968).

14. Raymond J. Michalowski and Edward W. Bohlander, "Repression and Criminal Justice in Capitalist America," *Sociological Inquiry,* 46 (No. 2, 1976) p. 103.

15. Frank W. Miller and Frank J. Remington, "Procedures Before Trial," *Annals of the American Academy of Political and Social Science,* 339 (January 1962), pp. 111–124. The pretrial "mediation" approach is described in Richard Danzig and Michael J. Lowy, "Everyday Disputes and Mediation in the United States," *Law and Society Review,* 9 (Summer 1975), pp. 675–694.

16. Caleb Foote, "The Bail System and Equal Justice," *Federal Probation,* 23 (September 1959), pp. 43–48; Frederic Suffet, "Bail Setting: A Study of Courtroom Interaction," *Crime and Delinquency,* 12 (October 1966), pp. 318–331; Ronald Goldfarb, *Ransom: A Critique of the American Bail System* (New York: Harper & Row, 1965; Forrest Dill, "Discretion, Exchange and Social Control: Bail Bondsmen in Criminal Courts," *Law and Society Review,* 9 (Summer 1975), pp. 639–674.

17. Charles E. Ares, Anne Rankin, and Herbert Sturz, "The Manhattan Bail Project: An Interim Report on the Use of Pre-Trial Parole," *New York University Law Review,* 38 (January 1963), pp. 67–95.

18. See Donald J. Newman, *Conviction: The Determination of Guilt or Innocence Without Trial* (Boston: Little, Brown, 1966), pp. 3–4.

19. Ibid., p. 77. Also see Donald J. Newman, *Introduction to Criminal Justice* (Philadelphia: J. B. Lippincott, 1975), pp. 187–233.

20. Donald J. Newman, "Pleading Guilty for Considerations: A Study of Bargain Justice," *Journal of Criminal Law, Criminology and Police Science,* 46 (March-April 1956), pp. 780–790.

21. Ibid., p. 787. Also see the research reported in J. A. Gilboy, "Guilty Plea Negotiations and the Exclusionary Rule of Evidence: A Case Study of Chicago Narcotics Courts," *Journal of Criminal Law and Criminology,* 67 (March 1976), pp. 89–98.

22. *The New York Times,* January 20, 1973, p. 32. Issues on the reform of plea bargaining are raised in Arthur Rosett and Donald R. Cressey, *Justice by Consent: Plea Bargains in the American Courthouse* (Philadelphia: J. B. Lippincott, 1976), pp. 161–187.

23. George F. Cole, "The Decision to Prosecute," *Law and Society Review,* 4 (February 1970), p. 342.

24. Ibid., p. 338.

25. Further discussion and research on the prosecutor's role is in Jack Kress, "Progress and Prosecution." *The Annals,* 423 (January 1976), pp. 99–116; David W. Neubauer, "After

the Arrest: The Charging Decision in Prairie City," *Law and Society Review*, 8 (Spring 1974), pp. 495–517; David W. Neubauer, "Confessions in Prairie City: Some Causes and Effects," *Journal of Criminal Law and Criminology*, 65 (March 1974), pp. 103–112.

26. David Sudnow, "Normal Crimes: Sociological Features of the Penal Code in a Public Defender Office," *Social Problems*, 12 (Winter 1965), pp. 255–276.

27. Newman, *Conviction*, pp. 67–75, 105–130, 177–187.

28. Ibid., pp. 152–172, 188–195.

29. Blumberg, *Criminal Justice*, p. 65.

30. John B. Jennings, *The Flow of Arrested Adult Defendants through the Manhattan Criminal Court in 1968 and 1969* (New York: New York City Rand Institute, 1971), pp. 8–14.

31. On proposals for New York State and New York City, see *The New York Times*, October 11, 1970, p. 1; October 18, 1970, p. 1; March 14, 1971, p. 1; April 30, 1971, p. 1; July 30, 1972, p. 1.

32. David Sternberg, "The New Radical-Criminal Trials: A Step Toward a Class-for-Itself in the American Proletariat?" *Science and Society*, 36 (Fall 1972), p. 295.

33. See Jerome H. Skolnick, "Social Control in the Adversary System," *Journal of Conflict Resolution*, 11 (March 1967), pp. 52–70.

34. William J. Chambliss, "The State, the Law, and the Definition of Behavior as Criminal or Delinquent," in Daniel Glaser, ed., *Handbook of Criminology* (Chicago: Rand McNally, 1974), p. 25.

35. Albert P. Blaustein and Charles O. Porter, *The American Lawyer: A Summary of the Survey of the Legal Profession* (Chicago: University of Chicago Press, 1954), pp. 64–96.

36. Differences in the outcomes of criminal cases according to type of legal representation are reported in Lee Silverstein, *Defense of the Poor in Criminal Cases* (Chicago: American Bar Foundation, 1965); Dallin H. Oaks and Warren Lehman, "Lawyers for the Poor," *Trans-action*, 4 (July-August 1967), pp. 25–29; Laura Banfield and C. David Anderson, "Continuances in the Cook County Criminal Courts," *University of Chicago Law Review*, 35 (Winter 1968), pp. 259–316. Differences in juvenile cases are reported in Edwin M. Lemert, "Legislating Change in the Juvenile Court," *Wisconsin Law Review* (Spring 1967), pp. 421–448.

37. Jerome E. Carlin and Jon Howard, "Legal Representation and Class Justice," *UCLA Law Review*, 12 (January 1965), pp. 382–383. Another report is summarized in Lesley Oelsner, "Study Finds Poor Unaided in Court," *The New York Times*, November 15, 1975, p. 1.

38. Jerome E. Carlin, *Lawyers' Ethics: A Survey of the New York City Bar* (New York: Russell Sage Foundation, 1966), pp. 71–73.

39. Jerome E. Carlin, Jon Howard, and Sheldon L. Messinger, "Civil Justice and the Poor: Issues for Sociological Research," *Law and Society Review*, 1 (November 1966), p. 56.

40. Gregg Barak, "In Defense of the Rich: The Emergence of the Public Defender," *Crime and Social Justice*, 3 (Summer 1975), pp. 2–14.

41. Jack Ladinsky, "Careers of Lawyers, Law Practice, and Legal Institutions," *American Sociological Review*, 28 (February 1963), pp. 47–54.

42. Jerome E. Carlin, *Lawyers on Their Own: A Study of Individual Practitioners in Chicago* (New Brunswick, N.J.: Rutgers University Press, 1962), pp. 17–18.

43. Ibid., pp. 105–106.

44. Arthur Lewis Wood, *Criminal Lawyer* (New Haven: College & University Press, 1967), pp. 34–67.

45. Ibid., p. 238. Other social characteristics of lawyers are described in Dietrich Rueschemeyer, *Lawyers and Their Society: A Comparative Study of the Legal Profession in Germany and the United States* (Cambridge: Harvard University Press, 1973).

46. Anthony Platt and Randi Pollock, "Channeling Lawyers: The Careers of Public Defenders," *Issues in Criminology*, 9 (Spring 1974), p. 27.

47. Carlin, *Lawyers' Ethics*, pp. 165–182.

48. Wood, *Criminal Lawyer*, p. 93.

49. Abraham S. Blumberg, "The Practice of Law as Confidence Game: Organizational Cooptation of a Profession," *Law and Society Review*, 1 (June 1967), pp. 15–39.

50. Robert E. Knowlton, "The Trial of Offenders," *The Annals,* 339 (January 1962), pp. 125–141.

51. Edwin M. Schur, "Scientific Method and the Criminal-Trial Decision," *Social Research,* 25 (Summer 1958), p. 178.

52. Jerome Frank, *Courts on Trial: Myth and Reality in American Justice* (Princeton: Princeton University Press, 1950), pp. 80–102.

53. Robert M. Emerson, *Judging Delinquents: Context and Process in Juvenile Court* (Chicago: Aldine, 1969), p. 192.

54. Arnold S. Trebach, *The Rationing of Justice* (New Brunswick, N.J.: Rutgers University Press, 1964), pp. 172–173.

55. See Rudolph E. Morris, "Witness Performance under Stress: A Sociological Approach," *Journal of Social Issues,* 13 (November 2, 1957), pp. 17–22; Israel Gerver, "The Social Psychology of Witness Behavior with Special Reference to Criminal Courts," *Journal of Social Issues,* 13 (November 2, 1957), pp. 23–29.

56. Seymour L. Halleck, "A Critique of Current Psychiatric Roles in the Legal Process," *Wisconsin Law Review* (Spring 1966), pp. 379–401. Also see Abraham S. Goldstein, *The Insanity Defense* (New Haven: Yale University Press, 1967).

57. Thomas S. Szasz, *Psychiatric Justice* (New York: Macmillan, 1965), pp. 85–143.

58. *The Washington Post,* April 13, 1971, p. 1.

59. *The New York Times,* March 19, 1973, p. 1.

60. Alan M. Dershowitz, "The Real Issue is 'Free Will,' " *The New York Times,* March 25, 1973, p. E6.

61. Harry Kalven, Jr., and Hans Zeisel, *The American Jury* (Boston: Little, Brown, 1966), p. 13. A survey of research on juries is in Howard S. Erlanger, "Jury Research in America: Its Past and Future," *Law and Society Review,* 4 (February 1970), pp. 345–370.

62. Ibid., pp. 14–17.

63. Ibid., pp. 19–30.

64. Ibid., pp. 31–32.

65. W. S. Robinson, "Bias, Probability, and Trial by Jury," *American Sociological Review,* 15 (February 1950), pp. 73–78.

66. Fred L. Strodtbeck, Rita M. James, and Charles Hawkins, "Social Status in Jury Deliberations," *American Sociological Review,* 22 (December 1957), pp. 713–719.

67. William Bevan, Robert S. Albert, Pierre R. Loiseaux, Peter N. Mayfield, and George Wright, "Jury Behavior as a Function of the Prestige of the Foreman and the Nature of His Leadership," *Journal of Public Law,* 7 (Fall 1958), pp. 419–449.

68. Strodtbeck, James, and Hawkins, "Social Status in Jury Deliberations," pp. 713–719; also see Fred L. Strodtbeck and Richard D. Mann, "Sex Role Differentiation in Jury Deliberations," *Sociometry,* 19 (March 1956), pp. 3–11.

69. Rita M. James, "Status and Competence of Jurors," *American Journal of Sociology,* 64 (May 1959), pp. 536–570.

70. Rita James Simon, *The Jury and the Defense of Insanity* (Boston: Little, Brown, 1967), pp. 98–119.

71. Kalven and Zeisel, *The American Jury,* especially pp. 55–65.

72. Otto Kirchheimer, *Political Justice: The Use of Legal Procedure for Political Ends* (Princeton: Princeton University Press, 1961), p. 46.

73. Leon Friedman, "Political Power and Legal Legitimacy: A Short History of Political Trials," *The Antioch Review,* 30 (Summer 1970), p. 167.

74. See *Trials of the Resistance* (New York: New York Review, 1970); Jason Epstein, *The Great Conspiracy Trial: An Essay on Law, Liberty and the Constitution* (New York: Random House, 1970).

75. Friedman, "Political Power and Legal Legitimacy," pp. 167–168.

76. See Richard Harris, *Justice: The Crisis of Law, Order, and Freedom in America* (New York: E. P. Dutton, 1970). Also Lynn Cobden, "The Grand Jury — Its Use and Misuse," *Crime and Delinquency,* 22 (April 1976), pp. 149–165.

77. See Alan M. Dershowitz, "Criminal Sentencing in the United States: An Historical and Conceptual Overview," *The Annals,* 423 (January 1976), pp. 117–132.

78. Robert M. Carter and Leslie T. Wilkins, "Some Factors in Sentencing Policy," *Journal of Criminal Law, Criminology and Police Science*, 58 (December 1967), pp. 503–514. Also see Robert M. Carter, "The Presentence Report and Decision-Making Process," *Journal of Research in Crime and Delinquency*, 4 (July 1967), pp. 203–211; Trebach, *The Rationing of Justice*, pp. 178–187.

79. On the statutory framework for sentencing, see the President's Commission on Law Enforcement and Administration of Justice, *Task Force Report: The Courts* (Washington, D.C.: U.S. Government Printing Office, 1967), pp. 14–18.

80. Leonard Cargan and Mary A. Coates, "The Indeterminate Sentence and Judicial Bias," *Crime and Delinquency*, 20 (April 1974), pp. 144–156; Martin B. Miller, "The Indeterminate Sentence Paradigm: Resocialization or Social Control," *Issues in Criminology*, 7 (Fall 1972), pp. 101–124.

81. For example, see the Report of the Twentieth Century Fund Task Force on Criminal Sentencing, *Fair and Certain Punishment* (New York: McGraw-Hill, 1976); and Andrew von Hirsch, *Doing Justice: The Choice of Punishments*, Report of the Committee for the Study of Incarceration (New York: Hill and Wang, 1976).

82. Edward Green, *Judicial Attitudes in Sentencing* (London: Macmillan, 1961).

83. Frederick J. Gaudet, "The Difference Between Judges in Granting Sentences of Probation," *Temple Law Quarterly*, 19 (April 1946), pp. 471–484; Frederick J. Gaudet, "Individual Differences in Sentencing Tendencies of Judges," *Archives of Psychology*, 32 (1938); Frederick J. Gaudet, G. S. Harris, and C. W. St. John, "Individual Differences in Penitentiary Sentences Given by Different Judges," *Journal of Applied Psychology*, 8 (October 1934), pp. 675–680.

84. Stuart S. Nagel, "Judicial Backgrounds and Criminal Cases," *Journal of Criminal Law, Criminology and Police Science*, 53 (September 1962), pp. 333–339.

85. U.S. Department of Justice, Federal Bureau of Prisons, *Statistical Report, Fiscal Year 1975* (Washington, D.C., 1976), pp. 49–50.

86. Carter and Wilkins, "Some Factors in Sentencing Policy," pp. 512–513. Related findings are reported in John Hagan, "The Social and Legal Construction of Criminal Justice: A Study of the Pre-Sentencing Process," *Social Problems*, 22 (June 1975), pp. 620–637.

87. Franklin E. Zimring, Joel Eigen, and Sheila O'Malley, "Punishing Homicide in Philadelphia: Perspectives on the Death Penalty," *University of Chicago Law Review*, 43 (Winter 1976), pp. 227–252. Also see the analysis in John Hagan, "Extra-Legal Attributes and Criminal Sentencing: An Assessment of a Sociological Viewpoint," *Law and Society Review*, 8 (Spring 1974), pp. 357–383. Also Willard Gaylin, *Partial Justice: A Study of Bias in Sentencing* (New York: Alfred A. Knopf, 1974).

88. Terence P. Thornberry, "Race, Socioeconomic Status and Sentencing in the Juvenile Justice System," *Journal of Criminal Law and Criminology*, 64 (March 1973), pp. 90–98.

89. Ibid., pp. 95–98. Also see Theodore G. Chiricos, Phillip D. Jackson, and Gordon P. Waldo, "Inequality in the Imposition of a Criminal Label," *Social Problems*, 19 (Spring 1972), pp. 553–572; Frank R. Scarpitti and Richard M. Stephenson, "Juvenile Court Dispositions: Factors in the Decision-Making Process," *Crime and Delinquency*, 17 (April 1971), pp. 142–151. Some of the same processes operate in the appeals procedure as well, as indicated in Robert B. Seidman and William J. Chambliss, "Appeals from Criminal Convictions," in Glaser, ed., *Handbook of Criminology*, pp. 651–677.

Punishment and Correction

10

Crime and the official policies on crime are two sides of the same phenomenon. Those who threaten the capitalist state and its class interests are controlled by means of the criminal law, and criminal sanctions are applied to those who are accordingly defined as criminal. The state's definition of crime thus anticipates the response. That which makes for the definition of crime also produces the policies for controlling crime. The state's control of its citizenry is rationalized and operationalized by a system of law.

The possibility of a criminal sanction exists for every citizen of the state. Indeed, the primary purpose of the criminal sanction is to warn the people that a transgression of the rules of order will lead to punishment or deprivation of some kind. Imposing the criminal sanction for an adjudicated offense is the state's retaliation against those who fail to abide by its rules. In the criminal sanction, including its administration, the state attempts to preserve the established order. As with the creation of criminal law, the reaction to crime is a political act.

The organized force of the capitalist state takes many forms as the criminal sanction is formulated and administered. In all cases the state controls the lives of the people, but the ways in which it is accomplished are diverse. In conventional language the variations are generally divided into "punishment" and "correction." Each form of criminal sanction implies divergent aims — the punitive sanction supposedly is replaced by treatment in modern times. Punishment and rehabilitation of the offender are similar in objective, however, controlling another person against his or her will. It is in the techniques by which force is accomplished that one form of criminal sanction is distinguished from another.

CUSTODY AND PUNISHMENT IN PRISON

Punishment has been, and continues to be, justified on grounds ranging from retribution, to reformation, to deterrence.[1] In the motive for retribution it is assumed that offenders must "pay" for their crimes: the individual must be changed to prevent future transgressions. And deterrence is pursued to discourage potential offenders. In spite of the differences in motive, the general intentions of punishment are the same: preserving the state's order.

Punishment, whatever its form, is deeply rooted in the society's political and economic structure. As capitalist society formed, punishment was designed to control the people who threatened the arrangements of the society.[2] Punishment to preserve capitalist order is most explicitly accomplished in the United Staes by physically confining offenders to an institution. Even when rehabilitation is attempted, it has usually been done within the punitive custodial setting. Custody has been mitigated by efforts at rehabilitation. Confinement is punishment, but rehabilitation is also part of punishment.

Confining offenders to an institution as a way of dealing with crime began in a peculiarly American historical context. After the Revolution, officials of the state thought anxiously about protecting and preserving the new order. The prison was a way of centralizing the powers of the state.[3] Leaders in the Jacksonian period continued to promote stability in the republic, eradicating any conduct that threatened the new nation.

> Legislators, philanthropists, and local officials, as well as students of poverty, crime, and insanity were convinced that the nation faced unprecedented dangers and unprecedented opportunities. The asylum, they believed, could restore a necessary social balance to the new republic, and at the same time eliminate long-standing problems. At once nervous and enthusiastic, distressed and optimistic, they set about constructing and arranging institutions.[4]

The penitentiary would rehabilitate offenders and at the same time set an example of right action for the rest of society.

The movement to confine offenders to institutions spread rapidly in the first part of the nineteenth century. Two systems for organizing prisons eventually competed as models for the whole country. In the "separate" system, as practiced in Pittsburgh and Philadelphia, prisoners were placed in solitary confinement. They could then reflect upon their crimes and gain insight for their own reformation. The "congregate" system, as practiced at Auburn, New York, emphasized common activities rather than separate confinement. The first model stressed the possibilities of personal conversion; the second, external discipline and forced rehabilitation. Gradually the Auburn system became the model for nearly all maximum-security prisons in the United States.

Custody in prisons today is essentially the same as at an earlier time. The prisons may have more programs of treatment, but the prisoner's daily life is routine and regimentation, all strictly controlled.[5] The military style of command shapes all prison life. In organization as well as in architecture the prison represents obedience and order, a model for the whole society.

A large proportion of the country's population is imprisoned, and thereby controlled, at any time.[6] The number of prisoners in custody in state and federal prisons at the end of 1976 was 283,145. By the end of 1976, as shown in Figure 10.1, the number of people in prisons rose to an all-time high. Add to these about 45,000 juveniles held in juvenile and correctional institutions. And about 165,000 people are confined to local jails, more than half of them not convicted of a crime. Considering only the adult population, about one of every 370 adults in the United States is confined at any time to a penal institution.

Prisons in this country are used mainly for those who commit a select group of crimes, primarily burglary, robbery, larceny, and assault. Criminals of the capitalist class, who cause more of an economic and social loss to the country and the society but who are not often given prison sentences, are not counted. This means that prisons are institutions of control for the working class, especially the surplus population — that portion of the working class not needed for capitalist production. Here the statistics are compared and summarized:

> Forty-one percent of the general labor force falls into white-collar employment categories (clerical and sales, managers and owners, and professional and technical workers), compared to only 14 percent of the prison population. At the other extreme, 43 percent of the prisoners are manual or service workers, com-

pared to only 17 percent of the total labor force. The same pattern is found for education: 55 percent of the prisoners have an elementary school education or less, compared to only 34 percent of the general population; 45 percent of the general population are high school graduates compared to only 18 percent of the prison population.[7]

Another consequence of this use of custody and punishment is that a very large number of prisoners are blacks. It is estimated that one in every 20 black men between the ages of 25 and 34 is either in jail or prison on any day, compared to one of every 163 white men in the same age group.[8] About one in three to four black men in their early twenties spends some time in prison, jail, or on probation. Control by the criminal-justice system is indeed a reality for a good share of the people.

The penal system is nevertheless being caught in the larger contradiction: late capitalism is producing a rising crime rate and the social expense of criminal justice is more than the capitalist state can afford. Prisons are already dangerously overcrowded; from the standpoint of the criminal-justice system, either new prisons have to be built to contain the growing number of people controlled by the system, or something has to be done to reduce the prison population at any time.[9] One direction calls for constructing roughly 1,000 new prisons, at an estimated cost of $20 billion. The other direction the capitalist state can take is to reduce the prison population by reformed sentencing.

Reforms in sentencing are mainly mandatory, fixed, and reduced sentences. These schemes, of course, apply only to crimes committed by the working class, rather than the crimes of government and corporations. Furthermore, by reducing the prison sentence, and by ensuring that a prison sentence will be administered, more people can be imprisoned with certainty. About 50 per cent more people could be sent to prison for short terms than can now be sent for long terms.

> Viewed this way, sentencing reform is a way for the criminal-justice system to have its cake and eat it too. Mandatory or fixed sentences can be introduced, sending larger numbers of people to prison while at the same time the cost of building new prisons can be avoided. Prison officials and legislators can also pose as "good guys" when shortening sentences, while also posing as "tough on crime" because more offenders will be sentenced.[10]

Prison reform actually means that control of the surplus population can be increased, for the time being at least, within the limits of social expense that the criminal-justice system can stand. Further changes in control likewise will be tied to the political economy of criminal justice. Control of the surplus population is a social expense that late capitalism must some-

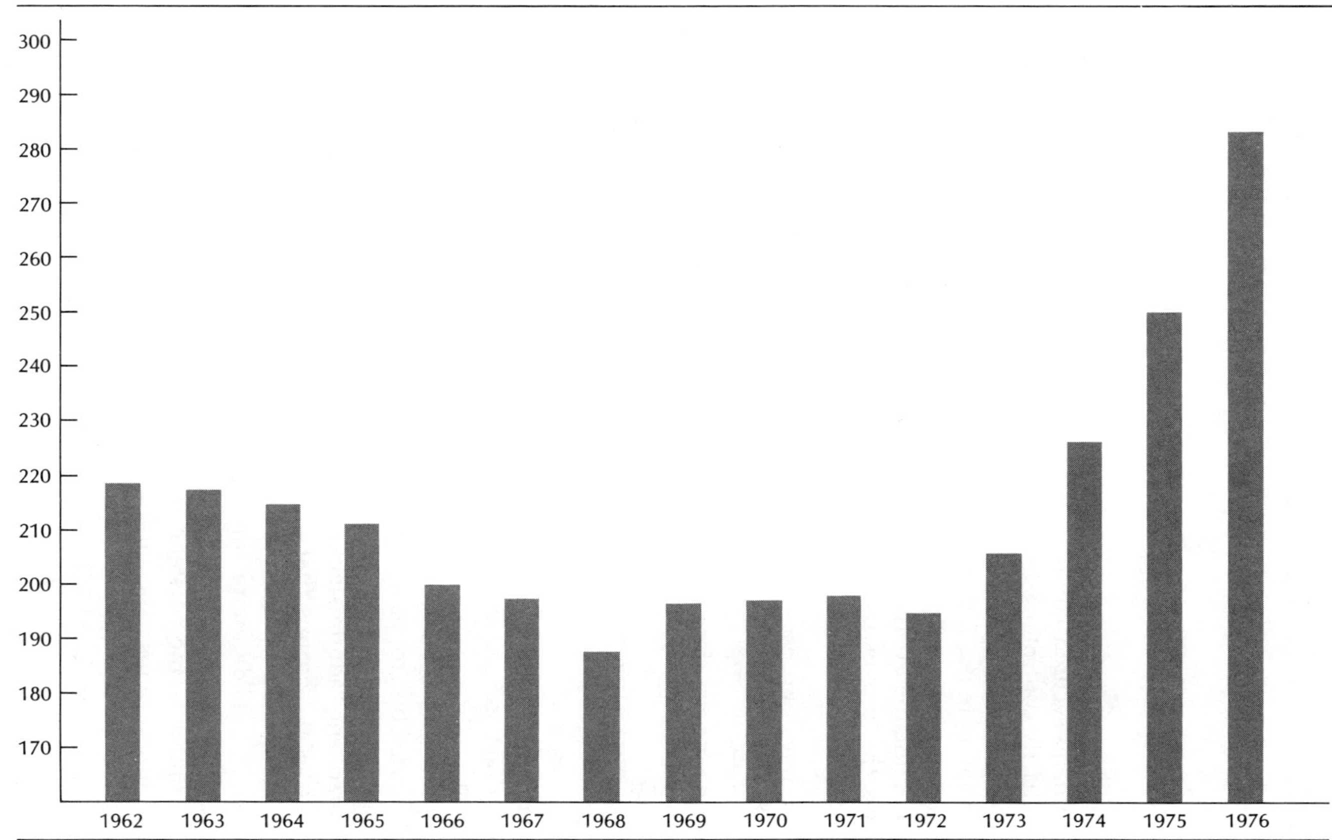

Source: Adapted from *Corrections Magazine*, March 1976.

FIGURE 10.1 Total Population of U.S. State and Federal Prisons 1962–1976 (Figures in Thousands)

how meet. Built into this control, of course, is a dialectic in which control is weakened in the class struggle and economic crisis of the capitalist state.

SOCIAL ORGANIZATION OF THE PRISON

The primary task of prisons, once they are filled, is custody. They must keep the inmates securely confined.[11] The prison's internal order is maintained by strictly controlling inmates and regimenting all functions and personnel within the prison. The prison, as a "system of total power," is an organization unto itself, which is supposed to be unaffected by external events and in which social control is paramount.[12] A distinct castelike division is maintained between those who rule and those who are ruled.

Operating the prison requires several, often contradictory, internal hierarchic organizations.

> The structure of prisons provides for three principal hierarchies — devoted to *keeping, using,* and *serving* inmates — but not for the integration of their divergent purposes. The separate organizations concerned with keeping and with serving inmates, for example, are not merely overlapping, but have entirely different and partly contradictory purposes.[13]

Each type of organization, in turn, promotes a particular kind of relationship between the staff and the inmates and a specific pattern of authority, communication, and decision-making. The people most affected by these divergent organizations are, of course, the inmates. Differences in handling their affairs are caused mostly by organizational problems inherent in the prison .

We can understand how the prison is administered if we recognize the pressures exerted by groups trying to achieve conflicting objectives. These "correctional interest groups" determine the ways in which prison policy is established and administered.[14] Some of these operate within the prison, such as the groups that make up the staff (administrative staff, custodians, professional workers) and the inmate population. Interest groups at work outside the prison include welfare agencies, educational groups, religious organizations, legal agents, and leaders of political parties. The numerous inconsistencies and contradictions in prisons are caused by these groups. The unique organization that is the prison is made by these converging, competing groups, which define their interests according to the ways in which prisons are operated.

Custody as an objective creates its own form of communication and decision-making within the prison. In an authoritarian way, the admin-

A routine body check of prisoners in this Texas penetentiary is as much a degradation ceremony as a security precaution (from the series of prison photographs by Danny Lyon titled Conversations with the Dead*).*

istrators impose a social order on the inmates, maintaining its conditions by a rigid system of communication. A massive body of regulations is passed from above to those below. Decision-making occurs at the top of the administrative structure and is communicated through well-defined channels of authority. At the bottom of the chain of command, among the inmates, decision-making is kept at a minimum: "Inmates are officially permitted to make only those types of decisions which prior study by administrators has shown to be of no danger to community safety."[15]

The custodial regime presents the inmate with personally demeaning and frustrating requirements. Being used to achieving goals, the prisoner finds it next to impossible to realize any in the prison, and is deprived too of basic liberties, goods and services, heterosexual relationships, and autonomy.[16] Imprisonment is painful. The physical deprivations are overwhelming, and having all the everyday freedoms withdrawn is also an attack against the foundations of one's sense of being.

The pains of imprisonment cannot be removed by the inmate, but only eased.

> Unable to escape either physically or psychologically, lacking the cohesion to carry through an insurrection that is bound to fail in any case, and bereft of faith in peaceful innovation, the inmate population might seem to have no recourse but the simple endurance of the pains of imprisonment. But if the rigors of confinement cannot be completely removed, they can at least be mitigated by the patterns of social interaction established among the inmates themselves. In this apparently simple fact lies the key to our understanding of the prisoner's world.[17]

This social world is an uneasy solution to the rigors of penal custody.

The inmate society is composed of related social roles, structured by an ideology, the inmate code: (1) Do not interfere with the interests of other inmates; (2) Refrain from arguments and quarrels with fellow inmates; (3) Do not exploit or take advantage of one another; (4) Maintain integrity in the face of privation; and (5) Do not side with the custodial authorities.[18] Inmate society classifies inmates by their orientation to the maxims of the code in prison argot. The *rat* is an inmate who violates the norm proscribing betrayal of a fellow inmate; the *merchant* exploits fellow inmates by manipulation; and the *tough* quarrels with other prisoners. The *square John* or *center man* makes the mistake of allying with officials. The role that most nearly fulfills the norms of the inmate code is that of the *right guy,* the *real con,* or the *real man.* But all the social roles are important for understanding this society, for they establish patterns of social interaction among inmates.[19] Only this interaction, within a society created by the inmates, can make the rigors of imprisonment bearable.

Prisoners conform to the inmate culture and oppose the expectations of the prison staff differently. In an early study it was observed that most inmates gradually assimilate the prison culture, which has been called "prisonization," suggesting that inmates increase their commitment to the prison culture with the *length* of time they serve in the prison.[20] It was found more recently that conformity to expectations of the prison staff also depends on the length of time *remaining* to be served.[21] Stanton Wheeler showed that inmates follow an adaptive, U shaped pattern of conformity. In the early and late phases of incarceration they conform to staff expectations, but those in the middle phase deviate from such expectations. Further research by others has specified these relationships: the temporal effect of the inmate code on administrative expectations varies according to the inmates' social characteristics, the type of crime committed, the experiences they had before imprisonment, and their social role in the inmate society.[22] Also evidence shows that inmates in a prison designed primarily for custody are less likely to become committed to prison objectives than those in a treatment-oriented prison.[23] And especially important in recent years are new inmate subcultures. As Leo Carroll found in a study of the Rhode Island maximum-security prison, a subculture of "cons" has developed among white inmates somewhat like the old convict subculture, and two other subcultures among blacks — "soul" and "nationalism."[24] Patterns of interaction, conflict, informal segregation, and accommodation form around these inmate subcultures. All these findings indicate how much the social organization of custody affects the administration of penal and correctional policy.

A final part of the prison's social organization is the relationship between inmates and the prison staff. Although it has an inmate system and an administrative system, prison organization also contains an informal system of inmate-staff relationships. Both inmates and staff find it necessary to establish patterns of interaction to secure their separate interests. Successful operation of the inmate society requires some cooperation from the staff. Likewise, the staff can achieve its interests only with the inmates' cooperation. In a sense, a "corruption of authority" appears among the staff.[25] The guards, under pressure to maintain smooth-running cell blocks, ignore breaches of prison rules in return for manageable conduct. The informal inmate-staff system is a response to the problem of maintaining control in a custodial institution. Informal patterns, not specified in prison regulations, are essential for administering penal and correctional policy within the confines of custody, and for the inmates' survival.

INSTITUTIONAL TREATMENT

The modern trend toward corrections continues the objectives of punishment. Correctional reform, however, involves controlling crime and criminals by modern scientific knowledge and professional management. The state's business is to maintain domestic peace; and correction is to treat or "rehabilitate" anyone who threatens public order. Prisons are to be made into theraupeutic centers, where offenders will be scientifically managed and perhaps changed, and at last reintegrated into society. Following the correctional model, eventually most offenders may be dealt with outside the prison, in the "community," with the whole society as a therapeutic environment.

The correctional movement of this century has counted on the prison serving as a center for rehabilitating offenders as well as confining and punishing them. The offenders find themselves subjected to both the punishment of custody and the punishment of treatment. Institutional treatment is not incompatible with punishment.

The rehabilitation ideal has spawned many repressive practices under the name of liberal reform and individualized treatment. Because the modern prison's purpose is to rehabilitate the offender, people are kept in prison until authorities or professional workers think they have been successfully rehabilitated. This reasoning has brought about the indeterminate sentence, which coerces the inmate into adjusting to the needs and interests of the institution's custodians and professionals; otherwise release from the institution will not be forthcoming. Furthermore, the treatment model is pursued either without examining important theoretical assumptions or according to dangerous practices by sometimes well-intentioned people.[26] Instead of dealing with the chronic problems of the society, treatment policies are designed for the victims of social and economic conditions.

In spite of the influence the rehabilitation ideal has on correctional policy, treatment programs in the prison are quite primitive. Treatment rhetoric is common, but the business of confinement still dominates the modern prison. Jessica Mitford observed:

> In prison parlance, "treatment" is an umbrella term meaning diagnosis, classification, various forms of therapy, punishment as deemed necessary, and prognosis, or the prediction of the malfeasant's future behavior: will/won't he err again? While the Corrections crowd everywhere talk a good line of "treatment" — phrases like "inadequate personalities," "borderline sociopaths," "weak superegos" come trippingly off the tongue of the latter-day prison warden, having long since replaced the sin-stained souls and fallen men or women with whom his predecessor had to cope — very few prison systems have actually done much about implementing it in practice. Nationwide, only 5 percent of the prison budget goes for services labeled "rehabilitation," and in many states there is not even the pretense of making "therapy" available to the adult offender.[27]

Nevertheless, inmates are supposed to be reformed during their prison experience. Prisoners are expected to change during confinement.

Any efforts at treating the offender within the prison are affected by its social organization, especially by the relationship of staff members to one another, relationships of inmates, and interaction between staff members and inmates. The staff in charge of treatment faces the problem of getting the inmates' respect while they are being required by other staff members to obey elaborate regulations. The regulations themselves are restrictive, and their violation results in penalties and even harsher restrictions. The therapeutic staff must maintain the restrictions, simultaneously offering treatment to the inmates. Furthermore, the therapeutic staff's attempts to administer treatment conflict with some of the custodial staff objectives.[28] Some of the specific techniques of the two staffs are contradictory. The therapeutic and custodial staffs see each other's daily activities as working at cross-purposes.

Custodial workers are concerned with maintaining control and this concern is reflected in their priorities of action in a given situation as well as in the considerations they express in planning and supervising inmates' activities. On the other hand, treatment personnel tend to be concerned with mitigating the psychological or interpersonal problems of inmates. Conflict engendered by these different priorities is exacerbated because custodial and treatment workers, by virtue of their different responsibilities, are also frequently confronted in a different manner by inmates. These workers thus develop different conceptions of the inmates and each staff group becomes convinced of the correctness of its view and derides that of the other.[29]

The relationships that inmates work out among themselves also determine how treatment programs are administered. The inmates' willingness to participate in treatment programs is influenced by involvement in the inmate system: those committed to that system are less likely to participate in treatment programs.[30] But efforts at rehabilitation are more likely to be impeded by the inmates' recognition that treatment programs are actually a coverup for control and repression in the prison. One ex-con states:

> I'd go into a room and be treated like a human being and the possibilities seemed unlimited. Then I'd leave the room and my reality was the prison. Then some hack would holler 'line up, bend over and spread your cheeks. Stand up, move out . . .' and I would be angry and resentful — as much against the people with the programs as I was against the hack. I began to resent the outsiders because they teased me. They let me think I was a human being with dignity. I stopped going to the meetings.[31]

Treatment programs within the prison are as dehumanizing as imprisonment itself.

Many treatment "techniques" have been designed and administered to change criminals into noncriminals. The punitive-oriented prisons have relied on clinical techniques, working with individual inmates in some form of counseling or psychotherapy. Treatment-oriented prisons have used a group-relations principle, trying to change the inmates' attitudes and behavior by manipulating social relationships.[32]

But how effective is institutional treatment? Imprisonment as a means of rehabilitation seems to have very little success.[33] More than half the people received into state and federal prisons and reformatories have had experience with institutional rehabilitation. Some prisons, though, may be more effective in rehabilitation than previously indicated. An analysis of several follow-up studies of inmates released from prison concludes that reimprisonment rates actually vary between 20 and 40 per cent for some correctional systems.[34] Also, it is argued, the offender's criminal career is reversed during prison experience and at least 90 per cent of the inmates released from the federal prison system seek legitimate careers for a month or more after they leave prison.[35]

Some criminologists say variations in reimprisonment rates can be accounted for by the ways in which treatment programs are implemented, structure of the inmate populations, selective use of probation, and policies of the parole officers.[36] Other researchers have suggested that some types of prisoners are better risks for rehabilitation than others. Treatment methods used with one type of inmate could be less effective with others.[37] More recently, an elaborate typology — a system of classifying forms of crime based on specific criteria — of criminal careers has been proposed, along with strategies for treating each type.[38] Group therapy or milieu forms of therapy are recommended for semiprofessional property offenders, drug addicts, joyriders, aggressive rapists, and other types. Intensive psychiatric treatment is suggested for nonviolent sex offenders, incest cases, male homosexuals, violent sex offenders, and psychopathic assaultists. Minimal treatment is recommended for statutory rapists and for "one-time loser" property or personal offenders. The implication is that inmate recidivism rates would be lowered if treatment programs were related to the offenders' special needs.

Another reason for our inconclusive evidence on recidivism is lack of systematic postrelease information and reliable follow-up studies of inmates, in part because of underdeveloped rehabilitation theories. Correctional workers also have not been trained in the skills necessary for evaluative research. But more important, those who administer institutional treatment have vested interests in specific kinds of programs. A negative evaluation of a program might mean personal loss for those associated with it.

> For example, by utilizing or advocating use of particular techniques in correctional work, a person may secure employment and income, good professional reputation, prestige as an intellectual or scholarly authority, the power stemming from being the champion of a popular ideology, and many other personal rewards. An agency organized around administration of a technique may fill such needs for dozens, even hundreds, of employees, and may itself have more general, organizational needs for survival. Hence, evaluative research results which would show that the technique is ineffective and would, thereby, seriously threaten the agency or the personnel must be avoided if possible.[39]

Ignoring the varying effectiveness of institutional treatment, we are left with a question: Why do some inmates *not* return to prison? The usual answer is that those who do not return have been rehabilitated *because of* specific treatment they have received in prison. But perhaps some do not return to prison *in spite of* institutional treatment. Some ex-prisoners may not return because of circumstances they encounter on release. This is the basis of the argument that most of those who return to prison have not been able to find legitimate opportunities during the first crucial weeks after release.[40] Those who remain outside of prison may find it is no longer necessary to engage in criminally defined activity or are able to avoid criminal definitions in some other way. If that is true, the prison is almost useless as a rehabilitative agency, serving instead as a holding device while the inmate ages and society changes. Time itself can create new circumstances for the offender. An added possibility is that prisons may radicalize the inmate. Growing revolutionary activity among prisoners can change the collective lives of the oppressed.

FROM TREATMENT TO MODIFICATION OF BEHAVIOR

Treatment programs, administered in institutions or in the community, have not produced the results desired by many authorities and professionals. Recidivism remains high and reaction by prisoners, often in political form, is growing. More repressive techniques of treatment are being developed and applied to control people who disrupt the social order.

Some of these techniques are conditioning by therapy, electronic surveillance, controlling emotions with drugs, electrical and chemical stimulation, and psychosurgery. These are more subtle and insidious than old-fashioned imprisonment and rehabilitation.

> Some aspects of behavior control technology are sufficiently established to be usefully incorporated by existing criminal justice and correction systems. Psychotherapy, mood-changing drugs, and some conditioning methods are suitable alternative or adjunctive rehabilitation procedures for a variety of offenses. They are appropriate alternative penalties for offenses where imprisonment is not necessary for the protection of society, so that probationary, voluntary correctives are in order. Precedents exist in the mandatory counseling or treatment required by some domestic and juvenile courts and the "safety classes" requied of some traffic offenders. For offenses requiring mandatory restraints, these methods are useful adjuncts which may reduce length of incarceration and/or recidivism,[41]

A few social scientists, with support from the federal government, are now involved in developing "coercive behavior-modification techniques" for controlling and manipulating those who threaten the social order. The techniques for treating and handling offenders range from classical conditioning to electronic monitoring. Ralph Schwitzgebel, one of the leading researchers and advocates of these forms of social engineering, observes: "Regardless of orientation, the basic underlying theory usually involves carefully specified changes in the environment of the person whose behavior is to be changed."[42] Scientific behavior modification is systematic and total, not limited to the "non-transferable" techniques of the individual therapist.

Scientific knowledge is being applied to the legal order, separated from morality but providing the way to a stable social order. "A science of behavior must be developed on the model of an input-output system, with adaptation to the environment as a key component."[43] The behaviorist, with "environmental design," would control information and experiences for the rest of us. "A successful crime control model must deal with behavior before the crime occurs, must deal directly with criminal behavior, and must deal with environmental design, rather than the individual offender."[44]

Technology of Behavior Control

Technology for changing and controlling human behavior is ready. Some techniques are being applied or are in the experimental stage, among them behavioral methods using computers and electronics.

> In the very near future, a computer technology will make possible alternatives to imprisonment. The development of systems for telemetering information from sensors implanted in or on the body will soon make possible the observation and control of human behavior without actual physical contact. Through such telemetric devices, it will be possible to maintain twenty-four-hour-a-day surveillance over the subject and to intervene electronically or physically to influence and control selected behavior. It will thus be possible to exercise control over human behavior from a distance without physical contact.[45]

Scientists have been experimenting with equipment for electronic surveillance and control. Schwitzgebel has devised and patented devices that can track, monitor, and modify offenders twenty-four hours a day.[46] One device, the Behavior Transmitter-Reinforcer is carried on the offender's belt; another is locked to his or her wrist. These contain batteries and transmitters that automatically send radio signals between subject and control station. The equipment can track the wearers' location and transmit information about their activities, communicating with them and modifying their behavior directly by reward and punishment.

Other experimental devices for behavior control are placed *inside* the offender, operating as internal radio-telemetry (signaling) devices, with tiny transmitters that are swallowed or implanted in the body.[47] They measure and transmit readings of gastrointestinal pressure, body temperature, blood pressure, heart rate, and oxygen level. The telemetric control systems not only monitor the activity of individual offenders, but would let the state supervise many more offenders. The advantages, we are told, are many:

> The envisioned system of telemetric control while offering many possible advantages to offenders over present penal measures also has several possible benefits for society. Society, through such systems, exercises control over behavior it defines as deviant, thus insuring its own protection. The offender, by returning to the community, can help support his dependents and share in the overall tax burden. The offender is also in a better position to make meaningful restitution. Because the control system works on conditioning principles, the offender is habituated into non-deviant behavior patterns — thus perhaps decreasing the probability of recidivism and, once the initial cost of development is absorbed, a telemetric control system might provide substantial economic advantage compared to rather costly correctional programs. All in all, the development of such a system could prove tremendously beneficial for society.[48]

By an extension of this philosophy, the whole community could be tracked and controlled, and the entire society could become a prison.

Some offenders are also being controlled by drugs. "Drug therapy" is one of the most common methods of dealing with "difficult" prisoners.[49] Such prisons or "correctional facilities" as Vacaville in California, Patuxent in Maryland, and the Illinois Security Hospital have been using powerful drugs such as Thorazine and Prolixin for many years. These are depressants used to pacify inmates. The effects can linger for weeks, altering the thoughts and emotions of the subjects.

An even more powerful drug, used in the California prison system, is Acetine, which slows the heart, causes respiratory arrest, and makes subjects feel as if they are dying. The drug is used in "aversion therapy," a technique reminding the inmates of past misdeeds, associating their negative experience with the drug with these actions. Failure to respond favorably brings more of the drug, stronger feelings of suffocation and drowning, and the sensation of death. All these drugs, Richard Speiglman concludes in investigating their use in the prison system, "find use in a program of ideological and violent repression against the working class generally and politicized prisoners in particular."[50]

Another experimental way of controlling behavior is electrically stimulating the brain by psychosurgery. Replacing massive lobotomy (removal of part of the brain) as a solution to behavioral problems, psychosurgery is the ultimate means of physiologically controlling human behavior.[51] In a number of prisons and hospitals, inmates are being subjected to these modern techniques; wires are implanted and electrodes are attached to the brain. With the electrodes the surgeon can destroy brain cells selectively and gradually while testing the conscious patient's intellectual and emotional reactions. Psychosurgeons can stimulate areas of the brain to create reactions in the patient. Researchers have devised computerized methods of mind control; by connecting the electrodes to a computer program, subjects exhibit the proper sensations and behavior. Remote mind control is a possible future for those who threaten the established order.

Modifying Behavior in the Prison

For a decade federal and state departments of correction have been trying to develop ways of changing the behavior of prisoners who threaten the prison's order and discipline. Furthermore, "the growing political consciousness of prisoners and their increased resistance to the inhumanity of prison has provided a special impetus to prison officials to establish special facilities for 'aggressive, manipulative prisoners' who are 'resistive to authority.' "[52]

The principles began to be worked out in a 1962 conference of prison administrators held in Washington, D.C., called by the director of the Federal Bureau of Prisons. The primary subject was applying newly developed brainwashing techniques to rehabilitate prisoners. Edgar H. Schein, professor at the Massachusetts Institute of Technology, explained how the North Korean brainwashing techniques used on American prisoners of war could be applied to convicts in United States prisons. In a speech entitled "Man Against Man," Schein stated:

> In order to produce marked change of behavior and/or attitudes, it is necessary to weaken, undermine, or remove the supports to the old patterns of behavior and old attitudes. Because most of the supports are the face-to-face confirmation of present behavior which are provided by those with whom close emotional ties exist, it is often necessary to break these emotional ties. This can be done by removing the individual physically and preventing any communication with those he cares about, or by providing to him that those whom he respects are not worthy of it, and indeed, should actively be mistrusted. If at the same time, the total environment inflexibly provides rewards and punishments only in terms of the new behavior to be obtained, and provides new human contacts around which to build up relationships, it is highly likely that the desired new behavior and attitudes will be learned.[53]

In his presentation Dr. Schein identified several tactics used in brainwashing that would be appropriate for modifying prisoners' behavior. A listing of these has been referred to by prisoner groups as the Manifesto of Dehumanization:

1. Physical removal of prisoners to areas sufficiently isolated to effectively break or seriously weaken close emotional ties.

2. Segregation of all natural leaders.

3. Use of cooperative prisoners as leaders.

4. Prohibition of group activities not in line with brainwashing objectives.

5. Spying on the prisoners and reporting back private material.

6. Tricking men into written statements which are then shown to others.

7. Exploitation of opportunists and informers.

8. Convincing the prisoners that they can trust no one.

9. Treating those who are willing to collaborate in far more lenient ways than those who are not.

10. Punishing those who show uncooperative attitudes.

11. Systematic withholding of mail.

12. Preventing contact with anyone unsympathetic to the method of treatment and regimen of the captive populace.

13. Building a group conviction among the prisoners that they have been abandoned by and totally isolated from their social order.

14. Disorganization of all group standards among the prisoners.

15. Undermining of all emotional supports.

16. Preventing prisoners from writing home or to friends in the community regarding the conditions of their confinement.

17. Making available and permitting access to only those publications and books that contain materials which are neutral to or supportive of the desired new attitudes.

18. Placing individuals into new and ambiguous situations for which the standards are kept deliberately unclear and then putting pressure on them to conform to what is desired in order to win favor and a reprieve from the pressure.

19. Placing individuals whose will power has been severely weakened or eroded into a living situation with several others who are more advanced in their thought-reform and whose job it is to further the undermining of the individual's emotional supports which was begun by isolating him from family and friends.

20. Using techniques of character invalidation, e.g., humiliations, revilements, shouting to induce feelings of guilt, fear and suggestibility, coupled with sleeplessness, and exacting prison regimen and periodic interrogational interviews.

21. Meeting all insincere attempts to comply with cellmates' pressures with renewed hostility.

22. Repeated pointing out to prisoner by cellmates of where he was in the past, or is in the present, not even living up to his own standards or values.

23. Rewarding of submission and subservience to the attitudes encompassing the brainwashing objectives with a lifting of pressure and acceptance as a human being.

24. Providing social and emotional supports which reinforce the new attitudes.[54]

The director of the Bureau of Prisons closed the conference by telling the assembled group of correctional officials:

> We are a group that can do a lot of experimenting and research and we can change our methods, our environments, and perhaps come up with something more specific.
>
> What I am hoping is that the audience here will believe that we here in Washington are anxious to have you understand these things. Do things on your own — undertake a little experiment with what you can do with some of the sociopathic individuals.[55]

The experimental ventures suggested by the director of the Bureau of Prisons soon began to be implemented. The program was instituted at Marion Federal Prison in Illinois, with the objective of determining how effective brainwashing techniques could be in dealing with prisoners who are "agitators," suspected militants and general troublemakers in the prison. Under the direction of Dr. Martin Groder, prison psychiatrist, the first step was severing the inmates' ties with family and friends, moving inmates to an isolated location until they agreed to participate in Groder's program. As described in a report prepared by the Federal Prisoners' Coalition at Marion, inmates who succumb are moved to new living quarters where they are confronted by members of the "prisoner thought-reform" team and subjected to intense group pressures. As the report notes:

> His emotional, behavioral, and psychic characteristics are studied by the staff and prisoner paraprofessionals to detect vulnerable points of entry to stage attack-sessions around. During these sessions, on a progressively intensified basis, he is shouted at, his fears played on, his sensitivities ridiculed, and concentrated efforts made to make him feel guilts for real or imagined characteristics or conduct. . . . Every effort is made to heighten his suggestibility and weaken his character structure so that his emotional responses and thought-flow will be brought under group and staff control as totally as possible.[56]

Another behavior modification program, initiated at the Federal Facility, Springfield, Missouri, is called START (Special Treatment and Rehabilitative Training). It has this purpose: "to provide care, custody, and correction of the long term adult offender in a setting separated from his home institution" and "to develop behavioral and attitudinal changes in offenders who have not adjusted satisfactorily to institutional settings."[57]

This program extends the one designed at Marion, providing an experimental model for future "correctional facilities" and behavior-modification programs.

These programs themselves can be called criminal. The Federal Prisoner Coalition says: "Factors of the START Program, with respect to classification of humans for compulsory participation in medical experiments, violate clearly stated World Court laws about conditions in which a civilized government can engage, and this in such a way as to constitute commission and conspiracy to commit crimes against Humanity. These comprise violations in every respect similar to those charges against the people of Germany at the conclusion of World War II during the Nuremberg Trials."[58] As the crimes of corrections continue, any prisoner is subject to these programs. The objective is to pacify those who disrupt the prison.

An institution constructed to employ and further develop the techniques of behavior modification is the Federal Center for Correctional Research at Butner, North Carolina. Costing about $14 million, it was designed originally as a federal experimental center. In addition to its own staff and facilities, it utilizes the expertise, services, and research facilities of universities within twenty miles of the center. The center was designed to include several units, a Mental Health Center, a Behavior Modification Unit, and a Training and Conference Center.[59] The programs, however, had to be changed because of public protests and because of the restriction on funds from the Law Enforcement Assistance Administration for use in behavior modification.[60] Nevertheless, Butner is to serve as the most "forward-looking" institution dedicated to further developing new forms of confinement and control.

Judging from past attempts at correction, however, combined with the increasing awareness of prisoners, behavior modification cannot ultimately be accomplished. Prisoners will be found not cooperating with the new "treatment," no matter how scientific and insidious the programs are. "They will actively resist these attempts to strip them of their humanity and their consciousness that it is society's ills rather than their own individual psychological problems which perpetrate their plight."[61]

PROBATION AND PAROLE

The state maintains control over convicted offenders in many ways. The offender is supervised outside the prison as well as inside, and may be sentenced to a period of supervision. Satisfactory completion of this probationary period depends on the offender's "good behavior" and on conforming to the stipulated conditions of probation. The other form of state supervision is parole, releasing prisoners from confinement in an institution to supervision by a parole officer. Removing the status of "criminal" from the convicted offender depends in the end on the actions and recommendations of the state and its officials.

Supervising Probation

Probation is a relatively new form of social and legal control. During the last quarter-century it has been used increasingly in sentencing offenders. Although no national statistics on probation are collected, probably about 40 per cent of adjudicated offenders are placed on probation, with wide variations from one jurisdiction to another.

Probation is usually thought of as a correctional reform measure, obscuring its punitive intentions and consequences. Nevertheless,

> implicit in probation supervision are numerous opportunities for punishment. With his awesome authority over the probationer, the probation officer may in various ways restrict his liberty. It is easily argued that restriction of liberty amounts to punishment. The probation officer, in the name of rehabilitation and under the banner of standard conditions of probation, can demand that the probationer not live in or frequent certain areas, that he not engage in certain employment, and that he refrain from a number of interpersonal associations.[62]

Probation officers work within the broader framework of the judicial system, carrying out a legal and punitive function, making decisions from the beginning of cases to their completion. The probation officer, in other words, is much like a prosecutor in the court.[63] Adjudication of criminal cases is influenced by the decisions and recommendations made by probation officers during hearings or trials. The sentence that the judge imposes is directly shaped by the interests of the court's probation department.

The probation system is "involved in a transitional period of organizational conflict as a consequence of moving from a politically oriented to a professionally career-oriented service."[64] More officers with a "professional" orientation are being drawn from social work. These more recent workers contrast with the older, politically oriented officers. The newer professional workers are liberal in ideology, recognizing the diversity of human personality, but the older workers, drawing ideological support from a conservative, middle-class philosophy of life, act as paternal counselors to the offender. The professional officers, trained in the casework approach, believe in promoting the community's welfare by changing the offender, and the politically oriented officers, relying on their common sense and experience, try to protect the community from the offender.

Probation, therefore, is beset by a conflict between types of officers and a struggle to control probation agencies; the probation officers' decisions are affected by these organizational problems. Because of several incompatible obligations in their occupation, officers have difficulty making consistent and satisfactory decisions. Officers trained in social work find their skills have not equipped them to deal with authoritative demands, and demonstrate a great deal of disagreement and confusion about the proper way of supervising cases.[65] Many regard some of the surveillance and enforcement activities as inappropriate responsibilities. Officers without training in social work, on the other hand, discover that they lack the knowledge and ability to understand the offenders they are supervising. Most probation officers, whatever their occupational direction, experience some conflict in their work.

Aside from the officers' personal inconvenience, the people ultimately affected by the organization of probation are those on probation. The divergent approaches to probation work directly affect the ways in which people on probation are handled. "Competing philosophies and working principles within the agency result in the inconsistent handling of cases and produce frustrations on the part of the workers which, in turn, affect the counseling and disposition of problem cases."[66] Like the offenders throughout the processing of their cases, the officers' fate is decided as much by the problems and actions of others as by their own volition.

Maintaining surveillance over the offender, the probation officer makes crucial decisions about the behavior of the person on probation. Probation is successfully completed only when the terms stipulated in the sentence have been met to the officer's satisfaction — or to that of any other legal agents who may come in contact with the case. If the person should be suspected of violating the terms of probation, his or her probationary status can be revoked. The officer then recommends whether or not probation should be revoked. In many jurisdictions the decision is made during a judicial hearing.[67] At that time the probation officer can testify that the person has violated probation and can also offer an appropriate course of action. Officers differ in the kinds of decisions they make in revocation proceedings.[68] The differences in recommendations are made by personal characteristics of the officers, extenuating circumstances in the cases, relationships between officers and offenders, and involvement of other legal agents in the case. Again, decisions that directly determine the offender's future are made by others, and are influenced by social and political considerations.

Supervising Parole

The major form of release from prison is parole. More than 75 per cent of the inmates released from state and federal prisons are discharged by parole or some form of mandatory supervision.[69] In principle, parole is the conditional release of an offender who has served a portion of his or her sentence in a penal or correctional institution. The decision on parole is made by the members of a parole board. Such boards may be staffed by personnel of an institution or by members of a statewide board of parole. In some jurisdictions the parole boards have the authority to administer parole as well as to grant it.[70] There is much discretion in paroling prison inmates, caused by differences in both state penal laws and the organization and administration of parole within the states.

The most obvious effect of variations in parole practice is the offender's future, settled by decisions made by others. And as the President's Commission on Law Enforcement and Administration of Justice argued, the decisions are not made fairly:

> Except for sentencing, no decision in the criminal process has more impact on the convicted offender than the parole decision, which determines how much of his maximum sentence a prisoner must serve. This again is an invisible administrative decision that is seldom open to attack or subject to review. It is made by parole board members who are often political appointees. Many are skilled and conscientious, but they generally are able to spend no more than a few minutes on a case. Parole decisions that are made in haste and on the basis of insufficient information, in the absence of parole machinery that can provide good supervision, are necessarily imperfect decisions. And since there is virtually no appeal from them, they can be made arbitrarily or discriminatorily.[71]

Decisions to release prisoners on parole are not usually made to suit the offender's interests. Though much descriptive and predictive information is available on prospective parolees, decisions are often made intuitively. Parole boards also develop their own informal procedures for processing cases.[72] Parole decisions are often based on such characteristics as original length of sentence, not individualities in the case. Inmates, when they are paroled, are likely to be released according to decisions made early in the prisoner's incarceration. Such procedures, combined with the kind of people on parole boards and the haste with which decisions must be reached, go into the decision to parole prisoners.

Once parole has been granted, satisfactory completion depends on varying regulations and supervision. Parole supervision is influenced, in particular, by the relationship between the parolee and the parole officer. One of the officer's principal duties is to observe the parolee's behavior, especially to determine if she or he is violating the conditions of parole or any other regulations and laws.[73] Such parole conditions generally forbid unauthorized association with anyone who has a criminal record, and seek to control behavior in drinking, employment, and mobility. Parolees usually must obtain permission to change their residence, to travel to another area, to marry, or to purchase some items.

The parolee is expected to fulfill many expectations, but the status of being a parolee does not correspond to the realities of being a convicted offender. Discrepancies between the legal expectations imposed on parolees and their own situation are described by John Irwin in his study of released felons:

> This status has for its underpinnings several premises which are often not shared by many deviants and ex-deviants. Two of these premises are self-evident axioms: (1) society, i.e., the existing political organization and government agencies, the laws and the government institutions, are both necessary and "good" per se; and (2) this society, especially the existing political organization and government agencies, has the right to imprison some of its members for acts which it has outlawed, to deny the ex-prisoner full citizen rights, and to impose special restrictions upon him. Furthermore, the conditions are underpinned by the belief that to be a worthy member of the society and, therefore, to be allowed to remain a free person, the ex-felon must live according to a puritanical code of conduct — he must work steadily ("steady employment is an essential for anyone's satisfactory adjustment in life"), not drink to excess ("it is conceded that total abstinence from the use of alcohol would benefit most parolees"), not use narcotics or dangerous drugs, not associate with persons of "bad" reputation, and conduct himself as a "good citizen."[74]

These prescriptions and proscriptions are derived from the pragmatic consideration of controlling the parolee. The released offenders' view of things is likely to be quite different from that which underlies their official status.

> Parolees often do not share the belief in the "goodness" of society or the existing social organizations, agencies, and persons filling positions in these organizations. Some deviants believe that conventional society, conventional people, legitimate businessmen, and public organizations are corrupt. Often they believe that the laws and the workings of the public agencies are part of a power struggle where the big and powerful are protecting what they have from the small and weak. . . . They, the deviants or ex-deviants, do not feel that the conventional society, the dominant society, the government agencies, are "right."
>
> Parolees (that is, the criminal parolees) have other definitions of good and proper conduct. Even those who have resolved to live a conventional life — resolved to "straighten up their hand" and to "make it" in terms of a conven-

tional life — are in disagreement with the conditions of parole and tend to believe that it is all right to break many of the rules. From their viewpoint, the only restrictions the agency should impose are on extreme criminal behavior.[75]

In practice the parole officer uses broad discretion in supervising the parolee. Ultimately the decisions made during interaction between officer and parolee determine when, whether, and how parole will be completed. These decisions are shaped by the parole officers' difficult role.[76] They are expected to supervise and assist the parolee and, at the same time, to protect the community from the ex-prisoner. They must fulfill the authoritarian function of representing the state, but must simultaneously try to "rehabilitate" the offender. As a person in the middle, or one who plays the "stranger," the parole officer must elicit the parolee's participation and that of the community's members in integrating the parolee into community life. The parole officer's job is both a handicap and a resource in accomplishing these diverse tasks.

The dual considerations of protecting the public and helping the parolee have inspired different types of performance by parole officers, satisfying these demands in various degrees.[77] Some parole officers emphasize both control and assistance (the "paternal" officers), and others pay little attention to either (the "passive" officers). Others emphasize assistance but not control (the "welfare" officers). Finally, some emphasize control but not assistance (the "punitive" officers). Each officer has a different way of perceiving and evaluating parolees.

The offender's fate is determined by the type of parole officer assigned to handle the case. Organizational needs as well as the broader interests of the social order shape the lives of those controlled by the criminal-justice system in the United States. In the end maintenance and survival of the capitalist legal and social order are at stake in the actions on probation and parole.

JUVENILE DELINQUENCY PROGRAMS IN THE COMMUNITY

Underlying all programs dealing with delinquency among juveniles is the effort to get the children of the poor, working class, and minorities to adjust to the conditions of capitalist society.[78] Much of the work is done in the community, focusing not on individuals but on groups or circumstances beyond individuals. When individuals are considered, they are dealt with according to their social environment. These programs, therefore, are usually located within the community or neighborhood. Such programs are administered according to the scope and comprehensiveness of social control.

One of the first community-centered juvenile delinquency programs, and the most limited in scope, was the Cambridge-Somerville Youth Study.[79] In the late thirties in those suburbs of Boston, 325 boys under twelve years of age were selected to receive preventive treatment. A matched group of the same size was selected as a control. Several community agencies cooperated in counseling, guidance for the family, medical and academic assistance, and recreational activities. The control group was given none of these services. At the end of the experimental period, in 1945, the two groups were compared for their contact with legal authorities. To the chagrin of the many involved, the offense records of the two groups were similar; 27.7 per cent of the treatment group members had appeared in court for offenses, compared to 26.1 per cent of the control group. Still later, in 1956, a follow-up study traced the adult lives of the two groups.[80] As many treated boys as control boys had been convicted of crimes in later years. The number of crimes committed too was similar for the two groups. The study indicated that behavior cannot be altered by limited change in social conditions.

A step beyond the casework approach are the programs doing participant work with *street-corner groups.* Such efforts are sometimes referred to as "detached-worker" programs, meaning that a social worker is detached from the local agency and assigned to make contact with gangs in the community, with the objective of changing the members' attitudes and behavior.

One of the earliest projects of this kind was conducted in New York City.[81] From 1947 to 1950, trained workers were attached to several street gangs in central Harlem. They tried, reporting some success, to redirect the gang's activity from fighting, stealing, sex offenses, and marijuana smoking to organized athletics, block parties, movie programs, camping trips, and the like. This approach was expanded by the New York City Youth Board to include work with gangs in several of the city's high-delinquency areas.[82] A more recent but similar project was the YMCA-sponsored program in Chicago, which produced much research.[83]

A gang-work program in Los Angeles was led by Malcolm Klein, assuming that the little "natural" cohesion gangs do have is from "external" sources.[84] Delinquency then is increased with more gang cohesion. The program was meant to reduce the gang's cohesion, but it concluded with disappointing results.

A somewhat broader project operated in Boston from 1954 to 1957.[85] Attempting to reduce juvenile offenses in a poor and working-class neighborhood, the Boston Delinquency Project tried to better coordinate community agencies and improve the family system. But the primary objective was shifting the values of street-corner groups from law-violating behavior to law-abiding behavior. Field workers established and maintained contact with 400 youths, members of twenty-one corner groups. The evaluative results were mixed. Apparently the project had negligible effect on the law-violating behavior of the gang members.[86] Nevertheless, it did confront issues of community organization.

Establishing these programs in a city usually creates or brings to the surface conflict among city agencies. A post-mortem on the prevention project in Boston documented the conflicts in administering the project.[87] About a dozen public and private organizations were interested in the city's handling of crime and delinquency. The principal public agencies were the municipal government, the recreation department, the police department, the courts, the public schools, and the state youth corrections division. The major private groups were medical and psychiatric clinics, social-work agencies, churches, universities, and special cause groups, such as ethnic associations and crime-prevention societies. Each had its own philosophy on etiology of delinquency, appropriate disposition of the delinquent, organization and procedures for prevention, and qualifications for personnel in delinquency programs. Conflicts both *between* and *within* the agencies diminished coordination and blocked efforts to administer the city's prevention program. The agencies acted as special-interest groups to get their vested interests satisfied. Prevention programs often have a major (but unstated) objective: satisfying the interests of those who determine the policies and those who administer the programs.

But some juvenile-delinquency programs do require reorganizing and developing the whole community. They treat delinquent behavior as a reflection of the social and cultural milieu; to bring about change in behavior patterns the workers understand that the community's structure must be altered. A basic procedure for implementing these programs is encouraging people in the community to lead and participate. Instead of outsiders imposing their will and techniques on the inhabitants, the residents themselves determine or help determine changes to be made in their community. Success for these programs does not necessarily mean reducing delinquent activity. Behavior patterns may eventually be changed. But in the meantime, improvements in the residents' lives and the community's social climate are much more important.

The Chicago Area Project, beginning in 1930, is the best known of these programs in community development.[88] It began in three Chicago slum areas and expanded to other parts of the city. Under Clifford R. Shaw, the Area Project used sociological assumptions about human behavior and community organization, specifically that people support and participate only in enterprises in which they have a meaningful job. The first phase of the project required knowledge about the area and its population. Local residents were encouraged to develop and administer the programs. Then residents assembled services and organizations to meet the community's welfare needs. These are the project's aims and methods:

> (1) It emphasizes the development of a program for the neighborhood as a whole. (2) It seeks to stress the autonomy of the local residents in helping to plan, support, and operate constructive programs which they may regard as their own. (3) It attaches special significance to the training and utilization of community leaders. (4) It confines the efforts of its professional staff, in large part, to consultation and planning with responsible neighborhood leaders who assume major roles in the actual development of the program. (5) It seeks to encourage the local residents to utilize to the maximum all churches, societies, clubs, and other existing institutions and agencies, and to coordinate these in a unified neighborhood program. (6) Its activities are regarded primarily as devices for enlisting the active participation of local residents in a constructive community enterprise, for creating and crystallizing neighborhood sentiment on behalf of the welfare of the children and the social and physical improvement of the community as a whole. (7) It places particular emphasis upon the importance of a continuous, objective evaluation of its effectiveness as a device for reducing delinquency, through constructive modification of the pattern of community life.[89]

Evaluations of the Area Project make it evident that some residents of low-income areas were able to organize themselves to promote their own communal interests.[90] Also, though precise measurement is not possible, apparently some delinquent and criminal activity was reduced by such efforts in community development.[91] But the major objective of the project was, in the first place, making people in the community adjust to the conditions of an industrializing society.

For some time Saul Alinsky argued that handling crime and delinquency is part of a larger program of reorganizing institutions.[92] His program was not aimed specifically at crime and delinquency, but toward eradicating unemployment, disease, inadequate housing, demoralization, and other aspects of social deterioration. He advocated forming "people's organizations" in the community. His program, variously known as Back of the Yards Project, People's Organization, and Industrial Areas Foundation, differs in several significant ways from the Chicago Area Project:

> First, the membership is wider; each local organization, such as a church, a union, an industry, a club, is represented. Second, the primary purpose is the development of groups composed of persons who are interested in their own welfare and are oganized for political action to improve their welfare. Third, the

ultimate aim is the development of a nation-wide federation of people's organizations, involving millions of people; through such a federation powerful political influence could be exerted.[93]

Putting political power into the people's hands makes this program more radical than most. Because government officials must approve programs and appropriate funds, most of these programs have remained proposals.

Through the years, then, these programs have gradually evolved into ideas building on community development, institutional reorganization, and political involvement. The culmination of some of these ideas is Mobilization for Youth, a project in a sixty-seven-block area on the Lower East Side of New York City. Beginning in the early sixties, it was founded on the theoretical proposition that obstacles to economic and social betterment are chiefly responsible for crime and delinquency among low-income groups.[94] The project's objectives were "(1) to increase the employability of youths from low-income families, (2) to improve and make more accessible training and work preparation facilities, (3) to help young people achieve employment goals equal to their capacities, (4) to increase employment opportunities for the area's youth, and (5) to help minority group youngsters overcome discrimination in hiring."[95]

Fairly orthodox remedies were designed to implement job training and work projects for unemployed youths and young adults. Specific programs included a youth job center, an urban youth service corps, on-the-job training, reading clinics, preschool education, and guidance counselors. But the rest of the project, the community-action portion, was devoted to more unorthodox procedures. Among these were a staff of lawyers for welfare clients, a housing unit that collected data on landlord violations, and a group of organizers who advised and assisted the poor to collectively change their lives.

Mobilization for Youth was distinguished from many other programs because it began to organize the poor for social protest and human betterment. The project's main hope was to "organize the unaffiliated — to overturn the status quo and replace it with a higher level of stability, without delinquents, alcoholism or drug addiction."[96] This political aspect got it into trouble with government officials. The FBI investigated those who have engaged in organized action, newspapers charged the project with subversion, its files were confiscated, and federal and local funds were questioned and altered. To provide the poor with services and assistance from above has been the traditional way of doing things; it is regarded as subversive when the poor themselves attempt to change the social pattern of their poverty.

Youths from New York's South Bronx listen to a jail guard describe the horrors of life in the old Tombs jail. In this delinquency prevention program, juveniles get a taste of prison conditions for the purpose of deterring them from delinquency and crime.

The more radical aspects of community action are imbedded in the potential of a widespread movement among the poor.

> If a movement of welfare recipients should, in fact, take form and gather strength, the ghetto and the slum will have yielded up a new political force. And it is conceivable that such a force could eventually be turned to the objective of procuring federal legislation for new programs of income redistribution (such as a guaranteed minimum income) to replace a welfare system that perpetuates poverty while it strips men of their fundamental rights as citizens.[97]

Indeed, programs within the community, when in the hands of community members, have significant implications for social change.

None of these community programs goes beyond mediating some of the needs of the community, however. Juveniles are socialized to fit into the lower end of the social and occupational world. Juvenile-delinquency programs in the community are part of the method for securing the capitalist order in the United States.

COMMUNITY-BASED CORRECTIONS

A recent kind of institutional treatment has modified the custodial setting in which treatment is administered. Among these are work-release programs outside the prison, halfway houses where offenders receive residential treatment while they also work or attend school, and community treatment centers.[98]

These techniques respond to growing pessimism about the possibilities of institutional treatment. Even some prison reformers realize that prisons are failing to rehabilitate inmates and that for most offenders treatment cannot be successful in an institution. This is the argument:

> During the past many years there has been considerable evidence justifying the increasing disillusionment with the rehabilitative and treatment effectiveness of traditional correctional institutions. It has become glaringly evident that such institutions have been designed primarily to meet the societal objectives of restraint and containment, rather than the stated concerns with treatment and rehabilitation. Indeed not only are correctional institutions generally ineffective in regard to attaining their rehabilitative objectives (which objectives they cannot be expected to meet without considerable efforts in and by the larger community), but the deleterious and destructive effects of such incarceration appear further to add to the problems of correctional clients.[99]

Efforts have grown for years to develop "community-based" treatment and correctional programs for adult offenders. Even the Bureau of Prisons, always a strong defender of the prison system, is formulating and implementing these programs. The notion of dealing with adult offenders in the community was given strong support by a director of the Bureau of Prisons in a congressional hearing:

> We in corrections know that offenders can change — can be reintegrated into the community — if provided the proper assistance, support and supervision. The focus of this effort is, of course, the community-based programs. We must continue and expand these programs and develop new ones of promise. All of us at every level of government, in public and private agencies, must share in this work.
>
> Two of the major goals of the Federal Bureau of Prisons are: to increase the program alternatives for offenders who do not require traditional institution

confinement, and expand community involvement in correctional programs and goals.

In achieving the first goal, we will attempt to minimize the corrosive effects of imprisonment, lessen the offenders' alienation from society and reduce the economic costs of the taxpayer.

We must achieve the second goal because only with the successful reintegration of the ex-offender into the community will we have fulfilled our mission — the correction of the offender.

With the help of agencies such as yours and the skilled and dedicated work of each of you, I am confident we in corrections will achieve our goals and accomplish our mission.[100]

In the movement away from complete confinement toward treatment in the community, however, the notion of "community-based" corrections has become a catch-all for assorted experiments and practices.

> Thus, almost any correctional program conducted outside the walls of traditional juvenile and adult correctional institutions has been lumped into this category. For example, probation, parole, halfway houses, noninstitutionalized boarding arrangements (such as foster and group homes), and even small institutions or residential facilities located in the community, have been included under the description "community-based correctional programs." Indeed, the impression is often obtained that the very fact of labeling or designating a program as "community-based" is supposed to connote that the effort is "innovative," "enlightened," and "progressive."[101]

To their traditional programs of probation and parole, usually supervised within the community, states are adding community treatment programs of some kind. More than half the states already have community-based correctional programs.[102] Many prisoners released from federal prisons are being sent to community treatment centers before they are released from the system. The Bureau of Prisons operates fourteen community-center programs, and the federal prison system has contracts with at least sixty other facilities for supervising federal parolees in the community. A parolee may have to reside or participate in these programs as a condition of release. The Bureau of Prisons plans to expand this form of "treatment," increasing the size and number of community-based centers.

Other community-based programs consist of noninstitutional boarding arrangements such as foster care, small-group homes, and semi-institutional cottage living. There are also community programs with forestry work and outdoor camps, nonresidential work or group-therapy programs, and a number of day-care programs. Applied to juveniles, community treatment is essentially preventive — intervention in gang activity or treatment of "predelinquents."[103] Some of these programs provide an alternative to legal processing in the criminal-justice system.

All the community-based programs, however, are administered by local, state, or federal government authorities. These are not community programs controlled by the people who are subjected to the treatment procedures. By definition, correctional programs — in the institution or in the community — are the property of the state that originally defines the behavior as criminal; community-based treatment consists of "intensive intervention in lieu of institutionalization."[104] One type of control is substituted for another and the citizen's life is still to be supervised, controlled, and manipulated. The purpose is usually to "integrate" the person into the community, not to change the community or the society in which the person found that crime was an appropriate solution.

The "success" of community-based corrections is still being evaluated and debated; the verdict will depend on the standards applied to the programs. Almost by definition, corrections in the community may be the proper alternative to institutionalization. One criminologist writes:

> In summary, from the standpoint of assessment, control, and assistance, but primarily through more timely and relevant assistance, community corrections for adults provide vast advances from traditional jailing or imprisonment. As has been indicated, these methods of graduating and deferring decision on confinement have numerous implications for the entire criminal justice system, beginning at arrest and pretrial processing. All of these implications can be consolidated well by the general maxim: never set apart from the community, any more than can possibly be avoided, those whom you wish some day to bring safely back into the community.[105]

From another point of view, the success of community-based corrections depends on whether it can handle a large number of cases in an economically feasible way; a "cost-benefit" analysis may be used to judge their merit.

> Until alternatives to institutionalization are demonstrated to be more effective than imprisonment in preventing further crime, a major rationale for the use of community programs will be that correctional costs can be considerably reduced by handling in the community setting a large number of those offenders normally institutionalized. Experimental/demonstration projects in intensive intervention have shown that for a large number of institution candidates incarceration is clearly unnecessary. Thus, if society is still determined, in the light of this evidence, to keep those offenders in prisons and training schools, it must be willing to pay the price. The central question becomes: are the goals of punishment and custodial control worth the high costs of constructing institu-

tions, and maintaining the inmate in the institution, as well as the observed and the still unknown personal and social costs incurred through exposing individuals to the institutional experience.[106]

Return on funds invested is becoming a standard by which programs of punishment, correction, and control are being evaluated and compared. This is an economic determination of criminal justice.

In the movement from putting people in institutions to handling corrections in the community, the emphasis remains on finding solutions to crime in the offender's makeup and behavior. Until we seek solutions in the social, economic, and political organization of the society, we will find no real success in handling the problem of crime.

CAPITAL PUNISHMENT

Several methods are used for releasing inmates from the prison. The original sentence may be modified by the state executive as pardon, commutation, or amnesty. Others are released on parole or simply as their sentences run out. An expiration date may be fixed by the legislature or, with an indeterminate sentence, an administrative board decides the date of release within the minimum and maximum limits set by the court.

The final and fatal solution removing the prisoner is either execution or death from other causes while in prison. Some prison deaths are caused by mistreatment or murder of inmates. Others are carried out by the state as capital punishment. Death is the most consequential aspect of the legal system. Although capital punishment is administered relatively seldom, the purpose of the death penalty is clear. As in its ancient origin, it is part of a program of legal and judicial terror by the state.[107] It stands as a warning to the citizenry that transgressions of the law may lead to death.

Administering Capital Punishment

Part of the terror of capital punishment is produced by the discretionary way in which it is administered. Although Supreme Court decisions and legislative actions have attempted to reduce this discretion, it has always taken place and continues to operate in even more subtle ways. Nearly three-quarters of the states have provisions for capital punishment.[108] The number and types of crimes that are subject to the death penalty differ, however. States differ too in stipulating whether the death penalty is mandatory upon conviction. Most of the states with capital punishment specify murder and kidnaping as capital offenses. Rape and treason are subject to the death penalty in about half. Others cover scattered offenses such as robbery, arson, dueling, illegal use of explosives, attempts on the life of the executive, and lynching. Most of the variations began as differences in regional and local customs. Although death may be a private affair, lives are taken legally by the wills and actions of others.

The extent of discretion possible in administering capital punishment is obvious from statistics on executions. The number has been decreasing though the years. Between 1900 and 1966 there were about 7,126 executions in the United States.[109] But since 1930, when statistics were first systematically compiled, executions have declined from an annual average of 167 during the thirties to 21 each year between 1960 and 1967.[110] Though 1935 had 199 executions, there were 15 in 1964, 7 in 1965, 2 in 1967. Even with the decrease in executions, at the end of 1976, 444 persons were under sentence waiting death in state and federal prisons.

Executions have always varied regionally. As shown in Table 10.1, approximately 60 per cent of the executions have occurred in the South. Of the executions between 1930 and 1967, 2,306 were in southern states, 608 in northeastern states, 509 in western states, and 403 in north central states. These regional variations are also evident according to executions for *types* of offense. Of the 455 executions for rape, 443 took place in the South. Less than 1 per cent of the executions in the northeastern region were for rape, whereas rape accounted for 15 per cent in the southern region.

Execution patterns also prevail in the *race* of victims. Statistics for 1930 to 1975, in Table 10.1, show that the majority of those executed, 2,066, were blacks, compared to 1,751 whites. For rape, in particular, far more of those executed were blacks. These figures indicate that capital punishment is highly discriminatory. Although the disproportionate percentage of blacks executed, compared to the proportion of blacks in the general population, reflects lower-class and racial involvement in violence, this disproportion *also* indicates the greater willingness of jurisdictions to apply the death penalty to blacks than to whites convicted of similar crimes. Lower-class persons from the discriminated-against racial and ethnic groups have a greater risk of being executed than their counterparts in crime.

The discriminatory character of execution operates at several stages before the final execution. Not only are blacks and the poor more likely than others to be convicted for committing similar crimes, but they are more likely to be given a death sentence than some alternative sentence. Further, once blacks are placed on death row, their sentences are less likely to be commuted.

The officials responsible for commuting sentences of execution have grave discretionary powers. The authority and procedures for granting clemency vary considerably among jurisdictions. They can be classified generally as:

> (1) A board alone; (2) a board alone, with the governor sitting as a member; (3) a board alone, the governor sitting as a member with grant, conditional on his being in the majority; (4) the governor, empowered to act only if a board makes a favorable recommendation (governor can overrule, denying commutation); (5) the governor with the advice and consent of an executive council, an elected body. Under the Federal Constitution the President alone has the power to abrogate a death sentence, derived from the power to grant reprieves and pardons.[111]

These pardoning authorities, in turn, hold differing philosophies about their responsibilities and use various criteria in making their decisions: type of crime, character of the trial, mental and physical condition of the offender, and possibilities for rehabilitation.[112] But extralegal considerations are also important in their decisions, such as publicity surrounding the case, political pressures, precedents in other cases, and personal views on capital punishment. Once a person is placed in death row, life depends on the decisions of others and on the state's actions.

The selective factors affecting commutation and execution have been documented in research. The records of capital offenders in North Carolina showed that, of those committed to North Carolina's death row since 1909, sentences of whites were commuted more often than those of blacks. Sixty-two percent of the blacks committed to death row were executed, compared to 43.8 per cent of the whites waiting for execution. Also, inmates who went to their death had less education and more menial jobs than those who were granted clemency.[113]

Of condemned inmates executed in Pennsylvania since 1914, significantly more blacks than whites were executed.[114] After finding that specific characteristics distinguished the executed inmates from those whose execution orders were commuted, such as the kind of counsel received during the trial, the researchers established that the offender's race was most important. It was concluded that blacks "have not received equal consideration for commutation of the death penalty."[115] Subsequent research continues to confirm the discriminatory character of capital punishment. When executions are carried out, blacks are executed more often

TABLE 10.1 Prisoners Executed under Civil Authority in the United States, by Race and State: 1930–1975

	All offenses			
Region and State	*Total*	*White*	*Black*	*Other*
United States	3,859	1,751	2,066	42
Percent	100.0			
Federal	33	28	3	2
State	3,826	1,723	2,063	40
Northeast	608	424	177	7
Maine	xx	xx	xx	xx
New Hampshire	1	1	0	0
Vermont	4	4	0	0
Massachusetts	27	25	2	0
Rhode Island	0	0	0	0
Connecticut	21	18	3	0
New York	329	234	90	5
New Jersey	74	47	25	2
Pennsylvania	152	95	57	0
North Central	403	257	144	2
Ohio	172	104	67	1
Indiana	41	31	10	0
Illinois	90	59	31	0
Michigan	0	0	0	0
Wisconsin	0	0	0	0
Minnesota	xx	xx	xx	xx
Iowa	18	18	0	0
Missouri	62	29	33	0
North Dakota	0	0	0	0
South Dakota	1	1	0	0
Nebraska	4	3	0	1
Kansas	15	12	3	0

South	2,306	637	1,659	10
Delaware	12	5	7	0
Maryland	68	13	55	0
District of Columbia	40	3	37	0
Virginia	92	17	75	0
West Virginia	40	31	9	0
North Carolina	263	59	199	5
South Carolina	162	35	127	0
Georgia	366	68	298	0
Florida	170	57	113	0
Kentucky	103	51	52	0
Tennessee	93	27	66	0
Alabama	135	28	107	0
Mississippi	154	30	124	0
Arkansas	118	27	90	1
Louisiana	133	30	103	0
Oklahoma	60	42	15	3
Texas	297	114	182	1
West	509	405	83	21
Montana	6	4	2	0
Idaho	3	3	0	0
Wyoming	7	6	1	0
Colorado	47	41	5	1
New Mexico	8	6	2	0
Arizona	38	28	10	0
Utah	13	13	0	0
Nevada	29	27	2	0
Washington	47	40	5	2
Oregon	19	16	3	0
California	292	221	53	18
Alaska	0	0	0	0
Hawaii	0	0	0	0

NOTE: xx Signifies that the death penalty was illegal during entire period covered by this table.

SOURCE: Adapted from National Criminal Justice Information and Statistics Service, "Capital Punishment 1975," *National Prisoner Statistics Bulletin,* No. SD-NPS-CP-4 (July 1976), pp. 18–19.

than whites, for lesser offenses, and more often without appeals and commutation of the death penalty.[116]

The Death Penalty

Despite the moral and political questions raised about administering capital punishment, several arguments for retaining statutory provisions for the death penalty are still advanced: (1) the death penalty as a deterrent to crime, (2) certainty of punishment when the death penalty is prescribed, and (3) financial economy of capital punishment. On the first argument, most evidence indicates that capital punishment does not act as a deterrent. Observations and researchers have demonstrated, first, that murder rates have remained constant despite trends away from capital punishment; second, that where one state has abolished capital punishment and another has not, the murder rate is no higher in the abolition state than in the retention state; and, third, that possible consequences are not considered by the murderer at the time of the offense.[117]

The second major argument favoring capital punishment, the certainty of being punished, is negated because the death penalty is seldom imposed. Witnesses are less willing to testify and juries are less willing to convict when the penalty can be death.[118] The argument about financial economy of the death penalty is refuted by the per capita cost for execution, which is higher than that for imprisonment.[119] Trials of capital cases are more costly and time-consuming than those for other cases, and maintenance costs for inmates on death row are higher than for inmates in the rest of the prison. Capital punishment does not perform the functions claimed by its most vociferous advocates.

Nevertheless, the issue continues to be debated. The legal status of capital punishment is more confused and uncertain than ever. In 1972 the Supreme Court in Furman v. Georgia ruled that the death penalty as carried out in the United States "constitutes cruel and unusual punishment in violation of the Eighth and Fourteenth Amendments."[120] The court was so badly split, however, that all nine judges wrote separate opinions. The decision did not eliminate capital punishment but limited the discretionary manner in which it is imposed. The consequence is that many states have enacted new capital-punishment laws.[121]

Public opinion continues to be divided on capital punishment. Aside from the moral need for eliminating the death penalty, the evidence shows that capital punishment is not a deterrent to crime, yet a president of the United States can proclaim to the public that "contrary to the social theorists, I am convinced the death penalty can be an effective deterrent."[122] The final judgment on the legality of the death penalty will depend on which set of ideas dominates, inevitably being determined by the need to maintain the advanced capitalist state. Although capital punishment may be "an archaic custom of primitive origin," it still holds its spell over the "civilized" state.[123]

The Supreme Court continues to regard the death penalty as a permissible punishment for the state to inflict at the present level of civilization in the United States, as reflected in its most recent judgments. In 1976 decisions, the Supreme Court struck down "mandatory" death-penalty laws because, in practice, the sanction is not applied mandatorily.[124] Nevertheless, the Court decided that discretionary laws are constitutional when the legislature has limited the discretion of judges and juries carefully, so that they are required to focus on the crime, the individual, and all relevant circumstances in determining sentences. It is the Court's view that when judges and juries have thought carefully about the crime and the accused, a framework of "rationality" is established sufficient to justify an official act that destroys a human life.

The decisions on the death penalty indicate in the starkest image how the capitalist ruling class uses the law to secure its order in times of economic and social crisis. The sequence in history is clear: "Death penalty laws have classically withered in times of prosperity and been reintroduced in times of economic disorder."[125] As advanced capitalism continues in crisis in the United States, capital punishment is a warning and form of legalized terror held out to the citizens. The crudest means of force and repression may be called upon in the war on crime.

POLITICS OF CUSTODY AND PUNISHMENT

Punishment is a political action taken by the state, following an explicit policy established by law, to preserve stability for the capitalist order. Punishment is totalitarian control made concrete. Custody, accompanied by legal murder, provides the state with the ultimate means of controlling that which threatens the social and economic system. The actions of those who are punished and confined by the state, however, are also becoming political — and in a revolutionary sense. The politics of custody and punishment is shared by captors and captives alike.

The state begins its political actions against the person by imposing the label "criminal" on the offender. Once that category is attached, control is established possibly for a lifetime, with legal restrictions that are never completely removed. Upon conviction for a crime an offender automatically loses rights and privileges held out to the citizenry. Unless these civil rights are restored by some formal procedure upon release from the legal system, they may be permanently forfeited. And the criminal record will be with the offender for the rest of his or her life.

Convicted persons are subject to numerous disabilities and disqualifications quite apart from the sanction imposed in the sentence. Civil rights possessed by others as citizens are lost by those convicted of felonies and some misdemeanors.[126] Most state statutes and constitutions provide for deprivation of some rights upon criminal conviction. Some states provide for blanket loss or suspension of civil rights, including the right to vote, to hold public office, to sue, to enter into contracts, to inherit property, to testify, and to serve as a juror. Where statutes provide for restoration of rights, it is often unclear which rights are restored and which disabilities and disqualifications remain. Moreover, the period for which rights are to be forfeited may depend upon the sentence. The law is complex and confusing in such matters.

Along with loss of civil rights, convicted persons are usually prohibited from participating in other activities. They may be barred from obtaining professional, occupational, and business licenses, or from other kinds of employment. The procedures for restoring such privileges are not always clear. The restoration statutes usually restore only specified rights, leaving restoration of other privileges to the discretion of various regulatory agencies. In spite of legal efforts to remove the definition of "criminal" from the convicted person, and regardless of the provisions for restoring rights and privileges, the effects of a criminal conviction are likely to be felt forever.

It is in the lawlessness of the prison that the politics of custody and punishment is more dramatically displayed. The prison, as a microcosm of the society, is an order unto itself. Screened from public visibility and control, it develops its own rules and fosters its own order of lawlessness.

> There is almost nothing the prison cannot do, and does not do to inmates, including keeping them beyond the expiration dates of their sentences (via procedures declaring them dangerous or mentally ill). It can and does transfer them far from their families; limit and restrict their visitors; censor what they read, what they may write; decide whom they may associate with inside, what medicine or other medical care they will or will not receive, what education they may or may not have, whether they will be totally locked up, for weeks, months, occasionally even years, or enjoy limited physical freedom. Inmates' personal property may be misplaced and destroyed, incoming and outgoing letters sometimes not delivered, and, in the extreme, prisoners may be starved, brutalized and killed.[127]

Not only is the prison a lawless agency, immune to the law, but its very existence is political. The prison system is both a political symbol and a device to control threats to the social and economic order outside the prison. "The prison system helps to sustain the myth that certain groups of people (for example, blacks, the Spanish-speaking, Indians, poor whites) are inferior, defective, dangerous, not to be trusted: it discourages challenges to the existing political and economic order by reminding members of those groups that the violence of the state can and will be unleashed against them if they get out of line."[128] The prison is a political arm of the capitalist state.

Social organization inside the prison maintains the political goals of imprisonment, keeping prisoners powerless. By its own lawlessness, by "classification" and segregation, by administering dehumanizing schemes of confinement, prison officials are able to establish the maximum forms of security. In fact, prison administrators keep inmates as unorganized among themselves as possible, to prevent them from joining forces.

> To this end, psychological solitary confinement is substituted, to the fullest extent possible, for physical isolation. This permits inmates to work and to participate in prescribed activities, but it minimizes the danger of violence, revolt or riot. To facilitate the state of unorganization or anomie [without norms], administrators always admonish inmates to "do your own time," and consistently, officially distribute rewards such as parole and good-time allowances to inmates who remain isolated from other prisoners.[129]

By attempting to maintain powerlessness among prisoners, the state promotes the political objectives of custody and punishment.

The new programs for prison reform extend control over prisoners. Although there are new kinds of "treatment" programs and "community correction centers," the purpose of all is to better secure control over the inmates. Instead of being used for prisoners as new opportunities offered to everyone, the reform programs are being used against prisoners as a means of control.

> On the one hand, progressive measures such as furloughs and work release are dispensed as carrots in attempts to buy off some prisoners, while on the other hand, extended segregation units are used as "treatment" for prisoners who do not cooperate with the administration. Left in the middle are the great mass of prisoners who are worse off now than they were before "reform" was institutionalized, but who are controlled by the piecemeal privileges dangled in front of them and the threat of indefinite segregation behind them.[130]

The prison-reform programs created for rehabilitation are being used as a further means of punishment.

The political intentions of the state, however, are not always successfully achieved. Within the politics of custody and punishment are the contradictions that threaten the prison's existence. Control, even under the guise of "rehabilitation," contains the seeds of its own destruction.

As observed in prison revolts, prison officials and state authorities resort to a range of repressive measures, including political transfers, torture, assassination, and authorized violence. Moreover, new techniques are being developed and applied to deal with the revolutionary movement in prisons. Tranquilizing drugs, electronic technology, surveillance, and the like are used on rebellious prisoners, just as the same devices are being used on those who threaten the social order outside the prison. At the same time, however, growing political consciousness in the United States is making it more difficult for the state to maintain its control.

The prison is an intensified form of the social and legal control that pervades the whole social and economic order; the response of the state is to control and manipulate those disruptive elements within the society. In the United States the prison and the larger society are inextricably linked.

DIVERSION FROM THE SYSTEM OF CRIMINAL JUSTICE

The current trends in corrections seem contradictory: (1) processing and manipulating offenders in the legal system and (2) diverting offenders from the criminal process. In both theory and practice, the two are related. The objective of both responses is to control in some way those who disrupt the established order. They may even be combined, as in the civil processing of offenders into compulsory commitment and treatment. Where the two responses are compatible we may understand the recent trend toward diverting cases from the criminal-justice system.

Correctional reformers have argued for some time that offenders may be more appropriately dealt with by means other than the criminal system, that there are more effective responses than those of the criminal law.

> The American system has a general tendency to rely too heavily on the law and legal process for the solution of pressing social problems. In particular, the arbitrary assignment to the criminal law and its processes of a variety of human conduct and conditions has come to be regarded as a problem of "overcriminalization."[131]

That is the reason for the recent attempts to find correctional alternatives outside the legal system.

People have always been diverted in some way from the formal system of criminal justice in the United States. Legal officials, particularly the police and prosecutors, exercise discretion at various stages in the legal system, dismissing or transferring cases during their processing. Diversion is an especially acute issue today because the judicial system cannot handle the volume of cases. The current emphasis is on "diversion of certain offenders before court processing."[132]

Hundreds of new diversion programs are being undertaken, but "because of the fragmentation of the criminal justice operations among counties, cities, states, and the federal system, it is impossible to make even a rough quantitative assessment of the extent to which offenders are being diverted out of the system."[133] Correctional reformers and many legal officials are committed to some form of diversion from the criminal process; many of them feel that diversion is an "enlightened" approach to the problem of crime.

> In effect, diversion seeks to offer the offender a set of social controls in lieu of the criminal justice system, our most drastic and overpowering form of social control. The assumption is that many who violate criminal laws are people whose lives will always be difficult and who need continuing support and that supervision and supplemental services may be more promising than the combination of a stigma and a cage. Diversion with its gentler, less debilitating controls, may offer the best hope of developing in such people a lasting capacity to deal with a complex and difficult society.[134]

Those who are threats to the society, nevertheless, are to be controlled, even "humanely" controlled, treated, and changed — reintegrated into the established order.

The basic form of diversion is eliminating some categories of offenders from the legal code, bypassing the legal system at the very beginning. Legal scholars are suggesting that some criminal laws should be repealed. This "decriminalization," it is argued, should begin by eliminating the laws that serve moralistic interests. This passage is characteristic of the discussions and conclusions being offered:

> The first principle of our cure for crime is this: we must strip off the moralistic excrescences on our criminal justice system so that it may concentrate on the essential. The prime function of the criminal law is to protect our persons and our property; these purposes are now engulfed in a mass of other distracting, inefficiently performed legislative duties. When the criminal law invades the spheres of private morality and social welfare, it exceeds its proper limits at the cost of neglecting its primary tasks. The unwarranted extension is expensive, ineffective, and criminogenic.[135]

The more specific proposals include partial or complete repeal of criminal laws that regulate drunkenness, drug use, gambling, disorderly conduct, vagrancy, abortion, adultery, prostitution, and homosexuality.[136]

The arguments for decriminalization are many. They say that the law should stay out of moral questions and that "overcriminalization" results in practices that make the law less rational and efficient. The case, in summary form, is presented by Sanford H. Kadish:

Excessive reliance upon the criminal law to perform tasks for which it is ill-suited has created acute problems for the administration of criminal justice. The use of criminal law to enforce morals, to provide social services, and to avoid legal restraints on law enforcement, to take just three examples, has tended both to be inefficient and to produce grave handicaps for enforcement of the criminal law against genuinely threatening conduct. In the case of morals offenses, it has served to reduce the criminal law's essential claim to legitimacy by inducing offensive and degrading police conduct, particularly against the poor and the subcultural, and by generating cynicism and indifference to the criminal law. It has also fostered organized criminality and has produced, possibly, more crime than it has suppressed. Used as an alternative to social services, it has diverted enormous law-enforcement resources from protecting the public against serious crime. Finally, its use to circumvent restrictions on police conduct has undermined the principle of legality and exposed the law to plausible charges of hypocrisy.[137]

By decriminalizing some of the law, the remaining laws, which regulate the public order, can be more effectively enforced. In the meantime, so the argument goes, the citizenry will gain respect for law and order.

The problem with these proposals is that law cannot be simply stripped of its moral judgments: all law is basically moral. A moral position is taken whenever any human conduct is limited and controlled. The decision to regulate some conduct, to the exclusion of other behavior, is an action to construct and protect a particular kind of social order. Some people, usually those in power, always determine which behaviors are harmful to the society. Even when individuals harm themselves, it may be argued, the whole society is morally harmed.[138] Legal reform, therefore, always involves dominance of one morality over another. And in capitalist society the morality of capitalism dominates.

A logical consequence of decriminalization in the United States is substituting civil sanctions and processing for the controls formerly applied by the legal system. An alternative to criminalization is the *civil* commitment of offenders. By channels other than the criminal procedures, those defined as drug addicts, chronic drunkenness offenders, sexual psychopaths, and juvenile delinquents are confined to institutions (such as hospitals) and forced to submit to treatment programs. Several contemporary beliefs support this form of civil intervention, although its consequences can be as dangerous as those of the criminal process:

(1) That offenders should be treated instead of punished; (2) that some conditions — alcoholism, addiction — are not criminal but manifestations of illness; (3) that some persons, because of their condition — youth, mental illness — should be given special consideration or dealt with less severely; and (4) the belief that the State has a right and obligation to intervene where the individual

or society is endangered. The quasi-criminal "civil" measures (civil commitment, juvenile court procedure, or compulsory treatment of the noncrime enforced by the prospect of penal processing for a crime) come into operation to satisfy the requirements of these beliefs. The supposed diversion of persons to civil processing whose condition or behavior is held noncriminal appears to be an attempt to have it both ways: the individual, not being criminal, is not subject to penal sanction *but,* for the protection of all concerned, he may be subjected to similar measures classified as nonpenal.[139]

Compulsory commitment and treatment of persons are in reality not much different whether carried out in a prison or a hospital. The "medical model" of dealing with those who threaten the social order offers little real alternative for someone considered deviant or "sick." Indeed, the laws on civil commitment and compulsory treatment are even more constitutionally defective than some criminal laws. These defects are "(1) that due process in these proceedings is inadequate, (2) that treatment — the rationale of the proceeding — is not provided, (3) that the statutes are unconstitutionally vague, and (4) that they permit action by the State against an individual exceeding the police powers of the State."[140] For the person subjected to civil procedures, the consequences go beyond these constitutional issues and can last a lifetime.

As long as society in the United States is based on the destructiveness of the capitalist political economy, no procedure (civil or criminal) can be appropriate. Programs formulated and implemented within the capitalist framework continue to repress those who are already oppressed. Only the far-reaching changes in movement toward a socialist society will help solve the problem of crime. The struggle today is very much related to the system of criminal justice in the United States.

NOTES

1. American Friends Service Committee, *Struggle for Justice: A Report on Crime and Punishment in America* (New York: Hill & Wang, 1971), pp. 20–33.
2. See George Rusche and Otto Kirchheimer, *Punishment and Social Structure* (New York: Columbia University Press, 1939); Barry Krisberg, *Crime and Privilege: Toward a New Criminology* (Englewood Cliffs, N.J.: Prentice-Hall, 1975), pp. 135–166; Steven Spitzer, "Punishment and Social Organization: A Study of Durkheim's Theory of Penal Evolution," *Law and Society Review,* 9 (Summer 1975), pp. 613–637; Dario Melossi, "The Penal Question in *Capital,*" *Crime and Social Justice,* 5 (Spring-Summer 1976), pp. 26–33.
3. Paul Takagi, "The Walnut Street Jail: A Penal Reform to Centralize the Powers of the State," *Federal Probation,* 40 (December 1975), pp. 18–26.
4. David J. Rothman, *The Discovery of Asylum: Social Order and Disorder in the New Republic* (Boston: Little, Brown, 1971), p. xviii.
5. See Lawrence E. Hazelrigg, ed., *Prison Within Society* (New York: Doubleday, 1968).
6. National Criminal Justice Information and Statistics Service, "Prisoners in State and

Federal Institutions on December 31, 1976," *National Prisoner Statistics Bulletin*, Advance Report, No. SD-NPS-PSF-2 (Washington, D.C.: U.S. Government Printing Office, 1976); National Criminal Justice Information and Statistics Service, *Children in Custody* (Washington, D.C.: U.S. Government Printing Office, 1975), p. 8; National Criminal Justice Information and Statistics Service, *The Nation's Jails* (Washington, D.C.: U.S. Government Printing Office, 1975), p. 1.

7. Erik Olin Wright, *The Politics of Punishment: A Critical Analysis of Prisons in America* (New York: Harper & Row, 1973), p. 26.

8. Ibid., pp. 31–34.

9. See the analysis in "Overcrowding and Sentence Reform," *NEPA News* (February, 1976), p. 3.

10. Ibid., p. 7. Related issues on penal reform are discussed in Paul Takagi, "Revising Liberal Conceptions of Penal Reform: A Bibliographic Overview," *Crime and Social Justice*, 5 (Spring-Summer 1976), pp. 60–64; Charles E. Reasons and Russell L. Kaplan, "Tear Down the Walls? Some Functions of Prisons," *Crime and Delinquency*, 21 (October 1975), pp. 360–372; Joan Smith and William Fried, *The Uses of American Prisons: Political Theory and Penal Practice* (Lexington, Mass.: Lexington Books, 1974).

11. Gresham M. Sykes, *The Society of Captives: A Study of a Maximum Security Prison* (New York: Atheneum, 1965), p. 18.

12. See Erving Goffman, "On the Characteristics of Total Institutions," in Donald R. Cressey, ed., *The Prison: Studies in Institutional Organization and Change* (New York: Holt, Rinehart and Winston, 1961), pp. 15–106; Sykes, *The Society of Captives*, pp. 40–62.

13. Donald R. Cressey, "Limitations on Organization of Treatment in the Modern Prison," in Richard A. Cloward et al., *Theoretical Studies in Social Organization of the Prison* (New York: Social Research Council, 1960), pp. 79–80.

14. Lloyd E. Ohlin, "Conflicting Interests in Correction Objectives," in Cloward et al., *Theoretical Studies in Social Organization of the Prison*, pp. 111–129.

15. Donald R. Cressey, "Prison Organizations," in James G. March, ed., *Handbook of Organizations* (Chicago: Rand McNally, 1965), p. 1044. Also see Richard McCleary, "Communication Patterns as Bases of Systems of Authority and Power," in Cloward et al., *Theoretical Studies in Social Organization of the Prison*, pp. 49–77.

16. Sykes, *The Society of Captives*, pp. 63–83.

17. Ibid., p. 82.

18. Gresham M. Sykes and Sheldon L. Messinger, "The Inmate Social System," in Cloward et al., *Theoretical Studies in Social Organization of the Prison*, pp. 5–9.

19. Sykes, *The Society of Captives*, pp. 84–108. For an excellent study of inmate roles in a women's prison, see Esther Heffernan, *Making It in Prison: The Square, the Cool, and the Life* (New York: John Wiley, 1972). Also see Gary F. Jensen and Dorothy Jones, "Perspective on Inmate Culture: A Study of Women in Prison," *Social Forces*, 54 (March 1976), pp. 590–603; Kathryn Watterson Burkhart, *Women in Prison* (New York: Doubleday, 1973).

20. Donald Clemmer, *The Prison Community* (New York: Rinehart, 1940), pp. 294–320.

21. Stanton Wheeler, "Socialization in Correctional Communities," *American Sociological Review*, 26 (October 1961), pp. 697–712.

22. See, in particular, Peter G. Garabedian, "Social Roles and Processes of Socialization in the Prison Community," *Social Problems*, 11 (Fall 1963), pp. 139–152; Daniel Glaser, *The Effectiveness of a Prison and Parole System* (Indianapolis: Bobbs-Merrill, 1964), pp. 548–583; Charles Wellford, "Factors Associated with Adoption of the Inmate Code: A Study of Normative Socialization," *Journal of Criminal Law, Criminology and Police Science*, 58 (June 1967), pp. 197–203; Charles W. Thomas, "Prisonization or Resocialization? A Study of External Factors Associated with the Impact of Imprisonment," *Journal of Research in Crime and Delinquency*, 10 (January 1973), pp. 13–21.

23. David Street, "The Inmate Group in Custodial and Treatment Settings," *American Sociological Review*, 30 (February 1965), pp. 40–55. Other research on other aspects of the inmate culture is reported in Anthony R. Harris, "Imprisonment and the Expected Value of Criminal Choice: A Specification and Test of Aspects of the Labeling Perspective," *American Sociological Review*, 40 (February 1975), pp. 71–87; Charles W. Thomas and

Matthew T. Zingraff, "Organizational Structure as a Determinant of Prisonization: An Analysis of the Consequences of Alienation," *Pacific Sociological Review,* 19 (January 1976), pp. 98–116; Charles W. Thomas and Samuel C. Foster, "Prisonization in the Inmate Contraculture," *Social Problems,* 20 (Fall 1972), pp. 229–239.

24. Leo Carroll, *Hacks, Blacks and Cons: Race Relations in a Maximum Security Prison* (Lexington, Mass.: Lexington Books, 1974). Also see the research in James B. Jacobs, "Stratification and Conflict Among Prison Inmates," *Journal of Criminal Law and Criminology,* 66 (December 1975), pp. 476–482.

25. Gresham M. Sykes, "The Corruption of Authority and Rehabilitation," *Social Forces,* 34 (March 1956), pp. 257–262. Related research is found in A. Derral Cheatwood, "The Staff in Correctional Settings: An Empirical Investigation of Frying Pans and Fires," *Journal of Research in Crime and Delinquency,* 11 (July 1974), pp. 173–179; Barry Schwartz, "Peer Versus Authority Effects in a Correctional Community," *Criminology,* 11 (August 1973), pp. 233–243; David Duffee, "The Correction Officer Subculture and Organizational Change," *Journal of Research in Crime and Delinquency,* 11 (July 1974), pp. 155–172; David B. Rottman and John R. Kimberly, "The Social Context of Jails," *Sociology and Social Research,* 59 (July 1975), pp. 344–361.

26. American Friends Service Committee, *Struggle for Justice,* pp. 34–47; Francis A. Allen, "Criminal Justice, Legal Values and the Rehabilitative Ideal," *Journal of Criminal Law, Criminology and Police Science,* 50 (September-October 1959), pp. 226–232; Robert Martinson, "The Age of Treatment: Some Implications of the Custody-Treatment Dimension," *Issues in Criminology,* 2 (Fall 1966), pp. 275–293. For a discussion about infringement of constitutional and civil rights of prisoners who are made to participate in therapy programs, see David Sternberg, "Legal Frontiers in Prison Group Psychotherapy," *Journal of Criminal Law, Criminology and Police Science,* 56 (December 1965), pp. 446–449. Also see David M. Petersen, "Some Reflections on Compulsory Treatment of Addiction," in James A. Inciardi and Carl D. Chambers, eds., *Drugs and the Criminal Justice System* (Beverly Hills: Sage, 1974), pp. 143–169; Clayton A. Hartjen, Sam M. Mitchell, and Normal F. Washburne, *Sentencing to Therapy: Some Legal, Ethical and Practical Issues,* Technical Report No. 3 (Newark: Rutgers University, 1976).

27. Jessica Miford, *Kind and Usual Punishment: The Prison Business* (New York: Alfred A. Knopf, 1973), p. 97.

28. See Gene G. Kassebaum, David A. Ward, Daniel M. Wilner, and Will C. Kennedy, "Job Related Differences in Staff Attitudes Toward Treatment in a Women's Prison," *Pacific Sociological Review,* 5 (Fall 1962), pp. 83–88; Joseph C. Mouledoux, "Organizational Goals and Structural Change: A Study of the Organization of a Prison System," *Social Forces,* 41 (March 1963), pp. 283–290; George H. Weber, "Conflicts Between Professional and Delinquency Treatment," *Journal of Criminal Law, Criminology and Police Science,* 48 (June 1957), pp. 26–43; Stanton Wheeler, "Role Conflict in Correctional Communities," in Donald R. Cressey, ed., *The Prison: Studies in Institutional Organization and Change* (New York: Holt, Rinehart and Winston, 1961), pp. 229–259; Mayer N. Zald, "Power Balance and Staff Conflict in Correctional Institutions," *Administrative Science Quarterly,* 7 (June 1962), pp. 22–49.

29. Irving Piliavin, "The Reduction of Custodian-Professional Conflict in Correctional Institutions," *Crime and Delinquency,* 12 (April 1966), pp. 125–134.

30. See Daniel Glaser and John R. Stratton, "Measuring Inmate Change in Prison," in Cressey, ed., *The Prison,* pp. 381–392; Clarence Schrag, "A Preliminary Criminal Typology," *Pacific Sociological Review,* 4 (Spring 1961), pp. 11–16; Charles R. Tittle and Drolene P. Tittle, "Structural Handicaps to Therapeutic Participation: A Case Study," *Social Problems,* 13 (Summer 1965), pp. 75–82.

31. Quoted in David Rothenberg, "Failure of Rehabilitation: A Smokescreen," *National Catholic Reporter,* 12 (April 16, 1976), p. 10.

32. The theoretical background of the "group-relations principle" is discussed in Donald R. Cressey, "Social Psychological Foundations for Using Criminals in the Rehabilitation of Criminals," *Journal of Research in Crime and Delinquency,* 2 (July 1965), pp. 49–59. For a discussion of specific programs, see Lloyd W. McCorkle, "Group Therapy in the

Treatment of Offenders," *Federal Probation,* 16 (December 1952), pp. 22–27; Lloyd W. McCorkle and Richard Korn, "Resocialization Within Walls," *Annals of the American Academy of Political and Social Science,* 293 (May 1954), pp. 88–98. For an evaluation of group-therapy programs, see Karl A. Slarkeu, "Group Treatment of Juvenile and Adult Offenders in Correctional Institutions," *Journal of Research in Crime and Delinquency,* 10 (January 1973), pp. 87–100.

33. Marshall B. Clinard, *Sociology of Deviant Behavior,* 3rd ed. (New York: Holt, Rinehart and Winston, 1968), p. 792.

34. Daniel Glaser, *The Effectiveness of a Prison and Parole System* (Indianapolis: Bobbs-Merrill, 1964), pp. 13–35.

35. Ibid., pp. 475–487.

36. Ibid., pp. 13–35. Other variations are reported in David Street, Robert D. Vinter, and Charles Perrow, *Organization for Treatment* (New York: Free Press, 1966); Mayer N. Zald, "Organizational Control Structures in Five Correctional Institutions," *American Journal of Sociology,* 68 (November 1962), pp. 335–345; Bernard B. Berk, "Organizational Goals and Inmate Organization," *American Journal of Sociology,* 71 (March 1966), pp. 522–534. Also see David Street, "The Inmate Group in Custodial and Treatment Settings," *American Sociological Review,* 30 (February 1956), pp. 40–55; Richard M. Stephenson and Frank R. Scarpitti, "Argot in a Therapeutic Correctional Milieu," *Social Problems,* 15 (Winter 1968), pp. 384–395. The "shock" treatment technique being used on some inmates is discussed in Paul C. Friday and David M. Peterson, "Shock of Imprisonment: Short-Term Incarceration as a Treatment Technique," *International Journal of Criminology and Penology,* 1 (November 1973), pp. 319–326; and David M. Petersen and Paul C. Friday, "Early Release From Incarceration: Race as a Factor in the Use of 'Shock Probation,' " *Journal of Criminal Law and Criminology,* 66 (March 1975), pp. 79–87.

37. George B. Vold, *Theoretical Criminology* (New York: Oxford University Press, 1958), pp. 296–304.

38. Don C. Gibbons, *Changing the Lawbreaker: The Treatment of Delinquents and Criminals* (Englewood Cliffs, N.J.: Prentice-Hall, 1965), pp. 228–282. Also see Daniel Glaser, *Adult Crime and Social Policy* (Englewood Cliffs, N.J.: Prentice-Hall, 1972), pp. 27–66.

39. Donald R. Cressey, "The Nature and Effectiveness of Correctional Techniques," *Law and Contemporary Problems,* 23 (Autumn 1958), p. 758. Evaluation techniques are discussed in Daniel Glaser, *Routinizing Evaluation: Getting Feedback on Effectiveness of Crime and Delinquency Programs,* Crime and Delinquency Monograph Series, National Institute of Mental Health (Washington, D.C.: U.S. Government Printing Office, 1973).

40. Glaser, *The Effectiveness of a Prison and Parole System*, pp. 487–496.

41. Perry London, "Behavior Control," in *Crimes of Violence,* vol. 12, A Staff Report Submitted to the National Commission on the Causes and Prevention of Violence, Donald J. Mulvihill and Melvin M. Tumin, Co-Directors (Washington, D.C.: U.S. Government Printing Office, 1969), p. 1374.

42. Ralph K. Schwitzgebel, *Development and Legal Regulation of Coercive Behavior Modification Techniques with Offenders* (Rockville, Md.: National Institute of Mental Health, 1971), p. 5.

43. C. Ray Jeffery, *Crime Prevention Through Environmental Design* (Beverly Hills, Calif.: Sage Publications, 1971), p. 276.

44. Ibid., p. 278.

45. Barton L. Ingraham and Gerald W. Smith, "The Use of Electronics in the Observation and Control of Human Behavior and Its Possible Use in Rehabilitation and Parole," *Issues in Criminology,* 7 (Fall 1972), p. 35.

46. Ralph K. Schwitzgebel, "Development of an Electronic Rehabilitation System for Parolees," *Law and Computer Technology,* 2 (1969), pp. 9–12; Ralph K. Schwitzgebel, "Behavioral Supervision System with Wrist Carried Transceiver," United States Patent Office, Washington, D.C., No. 3, 478, 344, November 11, 1969.

47. R. S. Mackay, "Radiotelemetering from Within the Body," *Science,* 134 (1961), p. 1196.

48. Ingraham and Smith, "The Use of Electronics in the Observation and Control of Human Behavior and Its Possible Use in Rehabilitation and Parole," p. 43.

49. See Mitford, *Kind and Usual Punishment*, pp. 95–137. Further documentation is cited in Chicago Peoples Law Office, "Check Out Your Mind: Behavior Modification, Experimentation and Control in Prison," *Chicago Connections Newsletter*, Supplement No. 1, n.d., p. 4.

50. Richard Speiglman, *Building the Walls Inside: Medicine, Corrections, and the State Apparatus for Repression* (doctoral dissertation, University of California, Berkeley, 1976), p. 471.

51. See Lee Edson, "The Psyche and the Surgeon," *The New York Times Magazine*, (September 30, 1973), pp. 14 ff.; Chicago Peoples Law Office, "Check Out Your Mind," pp. 4–5.

52. Chicago Peoples Law Office, "Check Out Your Mind," p. 1. Some of my discussion follows this source.

53. Edgar H. Schein, "Man Against Man: Brainwashing," *Correctional Psychiatry and Journal of Social Therapy*, 8 (No. 2, 1962), pp. 91–92.

54. Quoted from Federal Prisoner's Coalition, "The Mind Police," *Penal Digest International*, 2 (August 1972), pp. 4–5; "Manifesto of Dehumanization: Neo-Nazism," *Penal Digest International*, 2 (August 1972), pp. 8–10.

55. Quoted in Chicago Peoples Law Office, "Check Out Your Mind," p. 1.

56. Quoted in Mitford, *Kind and Usual Punishment*, p. 123.

57. "Operations Memorandum," Bureau of Prisons, Washington, D.C., October 25, 1972.

58. "Federal Coalition Protects Bureau's New START Program," *Prisoners' Digest International*, 2 (January 1973), p. 3.

59. Chicago Peoples Law Office, "Check Out Your Mind," p. 3. Also "Update on Butner," North Carolina Political Prisoners Committee, *Newsletter*, March 1, 1976, p. 6.

60. See Subcommittee on Constitutional Rights, *Individual Rights and the Federal Role in Behavior Modification*, Committee on the Judiciary, United States Senate, 93rd Congress (Washington, D.C.: U.S. Government Printing Office, 1974). Also see the essays in "Behavior Control in Prisons," *The Hastings Center Report*, Institute of Society, Ethics and Life Sciences, 5 (February 1975), pp. 1–56.

61. Chicago Peoples Law Office, "Check Out Your Mind," p. 4.

62. Eugene Czajkoski, "Exposing the Quasi-Judicial Role of the Probation Officer," *Federal Probation*, 37 (September 1973), p. 13.

63. Ibid., p. 11.

64. Lloyd E. Ohlin, *Sociology and the Field of Corrections* (New York: Russell Sage Foundation, 1956), p. 45.

65. See Lloyd E. Ohlin, Herman Piven, and Donnell M. Pappenfort, "Major Dilemmas of the Social Worker in Probation and Parole," *National Probation and Parole Journal*, 11 (July 1956), pp. 211–225; Dale E. Van Lanengham, Merlin Taber, and Rita Dimants, "How Adult Probation Officers View Their Job Responsibilities," *Crime and Delinquency*, 12 (April 1966), pp. 97–108; Seymour Z. Gross, "Biographical Characteristics of Juvenile Probation Officers," *Crime and Delinquency*, 12 (April 1966), pp. 109–116.

66. Ohlin, *Sociology and the Field of Corrections*, p. 47.

67. Ronald B. Sklar, "Law and Practice in Probation and Parole Revocation Hearings," *Journal of Criminal Law, Criminology and Police Science*, 55 (June 1964), pp. 175–198.

68. John P. Reed and Charles E. King, "Factors in the Decision-Making of North Carolina Probation Officers," *Journal of Research in Crime and Delinquency*, 3 (July 1966), pp. 120–128.

69. National Criminal Justice Information and Statistics Service, "Prisoners in State and Federal Institutions," *National Prisoner Statistics Bulletin*, No. SD-NPS-PSF-2 (June 1976), p. 28.

70. Information on parole boards, and on recent trends in decision-making, is in Vincent O'Leary and Joan Nuffield, "A National Survey of Parole Decision-Making," *Crime and Delinquency*, 19 (July 1973), pp. 378–393.

71. President's Commission on Law Enforcement and Administration of Justice, *The Challenge of Crime in a Free Society* (Washington, D.C.: U.S. Government Printing Office,

1967), p. 12. A critical assessment is also in Citizen's Inquiry on Parole and Criminal Justice, *Summary Report on New York Parole* (mimeographed paper, New York, n.d.).

72. Research on parole-board decisions is in Don M. Gottfredson and Kelley B. Ballard, Jr., "Differences in Decisions Associated with Decision Makers," *Journal of Research in Crime and Delinquency,* 3 (July 1966), pp. 112–119; Joseph E. Scott, "The Use of Discretion in Determining the Severity of Punishment for Incarcerated Offenders," *Journal of Criminal Law and Criminology,* 65 (June 1974), pp. 214–224; Anne M. Heinz, John P. Heinz, Stephen J. Senderowitz, and Mary Anne Vance, "Sentencing by Parole Board: An Evaluation," *Journal of Criminal Law and Criminology,* 67 (March 1976), pp. 1–31.

73. Considerable research has been done on violation of parole and parole prediction, primarily on the parolee's characteristics and behavior. See, for example, Dean V. Babst, Don M. Gottfredson, and Kelley B. Ballard, Jr., "Comparison of Multiple Regression and Configural Analysis Techniques for Developing Base Expectancy Table," *Journal of Research in Crime and Delinquency,* 5 (January 1968), pp. 72–80; Daniel Glaser, "A Reconsideration of Some Parole Prediction Factors," *American Sociological Review,* 19 (June 1954), pp. 335–341; Lloyd E. Ohlin, *Selection for Parole: A Manual of Parole Prediction* (New York: Russell Sage Foundation, 1951); Jerome H. Skolnick, "Toward a Developmental Theory of Parole," *American Sociological Review,* 25 (August 1960), pp. 542–549. For a discussion of some of the problems and issues in parole prediction, see Charles W. Dean and Thomas J. Duggan, "Problems in Parole Prediction: A Historical Analysis," *Social Problems,* 15 (Spring 1968), pp. 450–459.

74. John Irwin, *The Felon* (Englewood Cliffs, N.J.: Prentice-Hall, 1970), pp. 155–156.

75. Ibid., pp. 156–157.

76. Elmer H. Johnson, "The Parole Supervisor in the Role of Stranger," *Journal of Criminal Law, Criminology and Police Science,* 50 (May-June 1969), pp. 38–43. Research on role conflicts in the organization of parole is found in Paul Takagi, "Administrative and Professional Conflicts in Modern Corrections," *Journal of Criminal Law and Criminology,* 64 (September 1973), pp. 313–319; Paul Takagi and James Robinson, "The Parole Violator: An Organizational Report," *Journal of Research in Crime and Delinquency,* 6 (January 1969), pp. 78–86; Rodney Kingsnorth, "Decision-Making in a Parole Bureaucracy," *Journal of Research in Crime and Delinquency,* 6 (July 1969), pp. 210–218; Richard McCleary, "How Structural Variables Constrain the Parole Officer's Use of Discretionary Powers," *Social Problems,* 23 (December 1975), pp. 209–225; and Richard McCleary, "How Parole Officers Use Records," *Social Problems,* 24 (June 1977), pp. 576–598.

77. Glaser, *The Effectiveness of a Prison and Parole System,* pp. 429–442. Further research on parole-officer orientations toward parole decisions is reported in Richard Dembo, "Orientation and Activities of the Parole Officer," *Criminology,* 10 (August 1972), pp. 193–215.

78. Alexander Liaxos, "Class Oppression: The Functions of Juvenile Justice," *The Insurgent Sociologist,* 1 (Fall 1974), pp. 2–24.

79. Edwin Powers and Helen L. Witmer, *An Experiment in the Prevention of Delinquency: the Cambridge-Somerville Youth Study* (New York: Columbia University Press, 1951).

80. Joan and William McCord, "A Follow-up Report on the Cambridge-Somerville Youth Study," *Annals of the American Academy of Political and Social Science,* 322 (March 1959), pp. 89–96.

81. Paul L. Crawford, Daniel I. Malamud, and James R. Dumpson, *Working with Teen-Age Gangs* (New York: Welfare Council of New York City, 1950).

82. New York City Youth Board, *Reaching the Fighting Gang* (New York: New York City Youth Board, 1960).

83. James F. Short, Jr. and Fred L. Stodtbeck, *Group Process and Gang Delinquency* (Chicago: University of Chicago Press, 1965). For a description and analysis of other juvenile-delinquency projects, see John R. Stratton and Robert M. Terry, eds., *Prevention of Delinquency: Problems and Programs* (New York: Macmillan, 1968). A residential treatment facility within a community is described in Lamar T. Empey and Jerome Rabow, "The Provo Experiment in Delinquency Rehabilitation," *American Sociological Review,* 26 (October 1961), pp. 679–695.

84. Malcolm W. Klein, *Street Gangs and Street Workers* (Englewood Cliffs, N.J.: Prentice-Hall, 1971).

85. Walter B. Miller, "Preventive Work with Street-Corner Groups: Boston Delinquency Project," *Annals of the American Academy of Political and Social Science,* 322 (March 1959), pp. 97–106.

86. Walter B. Miller, "The Impact of a 'Total-Community Delinquency Control Project,' " *Social Problems,* 10 (Fall 1962), pp. 168–191.

87. Walter B. Miller, "Inter-Institutional Conflict as a Major Impediment to Delinquency Prevention," *Human Organization,* 17 (Fall 1958), pp. 20–23. Further documentation on the groups involved in delinquency prevention is in Robert M. MacIver, *The Prevention and Control of Delinquency* (New York: Atherton Press, 1966). Conflict between agencies in a New York community, in relation to drug programs, is described in Clayton A. Hartjen and Richard Quinney, "Social Reality of the Drug Problem: New York's Lower East Side," *Human Organization,* 30 (Winter 1971), pp. 381–391.

88. Solomon Kobrin, "The Chicago Area Project — A 25-Year Assessment," *Annals of the American Academy of Political and Social Science,* 322 (March 1959), pp. 12–29.

89. Clifford R. Shaw and Jesse A. Jacobs, "The Chicago Area Project: An Experimental Community Program for Prevention of Delinquency in Chicago" (Chicago: Institute for Juvenile Research, n.d.). Quoted in Clinard, *Sociology of Deviant Behavior,* p. 738.

90. Kobrin, "The Chicago Area Project — A 25-Year Assessment"; Anthony Sorrentino, "The Chicago Area Project after 25 Years," *Federal Probation,* 23 (June 1959), pp. 40–45; Helen L. Witmer and Edith Tufts, *The Effectiveness of Delinquency Prevention Programs,* U.S. Children's Bureau Publication No. 350 (Washington, D.C.: U.S. Government Printing Office, 1954), pp. 11–17.

91. The community-development approach has since been expanded and applied in the Delhi Project, by Marshall B. Clinard, *Slums and Community Development: Experiments in Self-Help* (New York: Free Press, 1966).

92. Saul D. Alinsky, *Reveille for Radicals* (Chicago: University of Chicago Press, 1946).

93. Edwin H. Sutherland and Donald R. Cressey, *Principles of Criminology,* 7th ed. (Philadelphia: J. B. Lippincott, 1967), p. 697.

94. Richard A. Cloward and Lloyd E. Ohlin, *Delinquency and Opportunity: A Theory of Delinquent Gangs* (New York: Free Press, 1960).

95. *Action on the Lower East Side,* Program Report: July, 1962–January, 1964 (New York: Mobilization for Youth, 1964).

96. Quoted in Murray Kempton, "When You Mobilize the Poor," *The New Republic* (December 5, 1964), p. 12. The changing goals of the project are discussed and analyzed in Joseph Helfgot, "Professional Reform Organizations and the Symbolic Representation of the Poor," *American Sociological Review,* 39 (August 1974), pp. 475–491.

97. Richard A. Cloward and Richard M. Elman, "Advocacy in the Ghetto," *Transaction,* 4 (December 1966), p. 33. Also see Richard A. Cloward and Frances Fox Piven, "The Weight of the Poor: A Strategy to End Poverty," *The Nation* (May 2, 1966), pp. 510–517.

98. See, for example, Oliver J. Keller, Jr., and Benedict S. Alper, *Halfway Houses: Community-Centered Correction and Treatment* (Lexington, Mass.: Lexington Books, 1970); President's Commission on Law Enforcement and Administration of Justice, *Task Force Report: Corrections* (Washington, D.C.: U.S. Government Printing Office, 1967), pp. 38–44; Roberta Rovner-Pieczenik, *The First Decade of Experience: A Synthesis of Manpower R & D Projects in Criminal Justice and Corrections, 1963–1973* (Cambridge, Mass.: Criminal Justice Research, 1973).

99. Saleem A. Shah, foreword to Marguerite Q. Warren, *Correctional Treatment in Community Settings: A Report of Current Research* (Rockville, Md.: National Institute of Mental Health, 1972), p. iii.

100. "Future Role of the U.S. Bureau of Prisons," *Hearings* before the Subcommittee on National Penitentiaries of the Committee of the Judiciary, United States Senate, 92nd Congress (Washington, D.C.: U.S. Government Printing Office, 1971). The President's Commission on Law Enforcement and Administration of Justice strongly recommended community-based corrections as an alternative to imprisonment — see Elmer K. Nelson,

Jr., "Community-Based Correctional Treatment: Rationale and Problems," *Annals of the American Academy of Political and Social Science*, 374 (November 1967), pp. 82–91.

101. Shah, foreword to Warren, *Correctional Treatment in Community Settings*, p. iii.

102. Bertram S. Griggs and Gary R. McCune, "Community-Based Correctional Programs: A Survey and Analysis," *Federal Probation*, 36 (June 1972), pp. 7–13.

103. Some of the specific programs are described in *Community Based Correctional Programs: Models and Practices* (Rockville, Md.: National Institute of Mental Health, 1971); and Robert D. Vinter, George Downs, and John Hall, *Juvenile Corrections in the States: Residential Programs and Deinstitutionalization: A Preliminary Report* (Ann Arbor: National Assessment of Juvenile Corrections, 1976). Research is reported in Robert D. Vinter, ed., *Time Out: A National Study of Juvenile Correctional Programs* (Ann Arbor: National Assessment of Juvenile Corrections, 1976).

104. *Community Based Correctional Programs: Models and Practices*, p. 3.

105. Daniel Glaser, "Correction of Adult Offenders in the Community," in Lloyd E. Ohlin, ed., *Prisoners in America* (Englewood Cliffs, N.J.: Prentice-Hall, 1973), p. 116. An excellent critique of community-based corrections is provided in Andrew T. Scull, *Decarceration: Community Treatment and the Deviant: A Radical View* (Englewood Cliffs, N.J.: Prentice-Hall, 1977).

106. *Community Based Correctional Programs*, pp. 33–34.

107. Douglas Hay, "Property, Authority and the Criminal Law," in Douglas Hay, Peter Linebaugh, John G. Rule, E. P. Thompson, and Cal Winslow, *Albion's Fatal Tree: Crime and Society in Eighteenth-Century England* (New York: Pantheon, 1975).

108. Bureau of Prisons, United States Department of Justice, "Capital Punishment, 1930–1970," *National Prisoner Statistics Bulletin*, No. 46 (August 1971), p. 2. See Robert H. Finkel, "A Survey of Capital Offenses," in Thorsten Sellin, ed., *Capital Punishment* (New York: Harper & Row, 1967), pp. 22–31; Leonard D. Savitz, "Capital Crimes as Defined in American Statutory Law," *Journal of Criminal Law, Criminology and Police Science*, 46 (September-October 1955), pp. 355–363.

109. Hugo Adam Bedua, "Introduction: The Laws, the Crimes, and the Executions," in Hugo Adam Bedu, ed., *The Death Penalty in America* (Garden City, N.Y.: Doubleday, 1964), p. 35.

110. National Criminal Justice Information and Statistics Service, "Capital Punishment 1975," *National Prisoner Statistics Bulletin*, No. SD-NPS-CP-4 (July, 1976), pp. 14–15.

111. Solie M. Ringold, "The Dynamics of Executive Clemency," in Sellin, ed., *Capital Punishment*, p. 227.

112. See Elkan Abramowitz and David Paget, "Executive Clemency in Capital Cases," *New York University Law Review*, 39 (January 1964), pp. 136–189.

113. Elmer H. Johnson, "Selective Factors in Capital Punishment," *Social Forces*, 36 (December 1957), pp. 165–169.

114. Marvin E. Wolfgang, Arlene Kelly, and Hans C. Nolde, "Comparison of the Executed and the Commuted among Admissions to Death Row," *Journal of Criminal Law, Criminology and Police Science*, 53 (September 1962), pp. 301–311.

115. Ibid., p. 311.

116. William J. Bowers, *Executions in America: Discrimination and Deterrence and an Inventory of 5,769 State-Imposed Executions* (Lexington, Mass.: Lexington Books, 1974); Marvin E. Wolfgang and Marc Riedel, "Race, Judicial Discretion, and the Death Penalty," *Annals of the American Academy of Political and Social Science*, 407 (May 1973), pp. 119–133.

117. See Hans Mattick, *The Unexamined Death* (Chicago: World Correctional Center for Community and Social Concerns, 1972). Also Frank E. Hartung, "Trends in the Use of Capital Punishment," *Annals of the American Academy of Political and Social Science*, 284 (November 1952), pp. 8–19; Leonard D. Savitz, "A Study in Capital Punishment," *Journal of Criminal Law, Criminology and Police Science*, 49 (December 1958), pp. 338–341; Karl F. Schuessler, "The Deterrent Influence of the Death Penalty," *Annals of the American Academy of Political and Social Science*, 284 (November 1952), pp. 54–62; Thorsten Sellin, "Capital Punishment," *Federal Probation*, 15 (September 1961), pp. 3–11; Thorsten Sellin, *The Death Penalty* (Philadelphia: American Law Institute, 1959).

118. Herbert B. Ehrmann, "The Death Penalty and the Administration of Justice," *Annals of the American Academy of Political and Social Science,* 284 (November 1952), pp. 73–84.

119. See Edwin H. Sutherland and Donald R. Cressey, *Criminology,* 9th ed. (Philadelphia: J. B. Lippincott, 1974), pp. 335–336.

120. 408 U.S. 238 (1972).

121. "Capital Punishment after Furman," *Journal of Criminal Law and Criminology,* 64 (September 1973), pp. 281–289.

122. Warren Weaver, Jr., "President Asks Law to Restore Death Penalty," *The New York Times,* March 11, 1973, p. 1.

123. Thorsten Sellin, "The Inevitable End of Capital Punishment," in Sellin, ed., *Capital Punishment,* p. 253.

124. See *The New York Times,* July 3, 1976, pp. 1, 6–7, for the Supreme Court decisions and related discussion.

125. Jeff Segal, "Court Reactivates Death Penalty," *Guardian,* July 14, 1976, p. 3.

126. See President's Commission on Law Enforcement and Administration of Justice, *Task Force Report: Corrections,* pp. 82–92; Mirjan R. Damanska, "Adverse Legal Consequences of Conviction and Their Removal: A Comparative Study," *Journal of Criminal Law, Criminology and Police Science,* 59 (September 1968), pp. 347–360, and 59 (December 1968), pp. 542–568.

127. David F. Greenberg and Fay Stender, "The Prison as a Lawless Agency," *Buffalo Law Review,* 21 (Spring 1972), p. 806.

128. Ibid., p. 820.

129. Donald R. Cressey, in the foreword to Donald Clemmer, *The Prison Community* (New York: Holt, Rinehart and Winston, 1958), p. ix.

130. "Treatment Equals Punishment," *NEPA News,* 3 (November 1975), p. 2.

131. *Diversion from the Criminal Justice System* (Rockville, Md.: National Institute of Mental Health, 1971), p. 3.

132. Ibid., p. 1.

133. Elizabeth W. Vorenberg and James Vorenberg, "Early Diversion from the Criminal Justice System: Practice in Search of a Theory," in Ohlin, ed., *Prisoners in America,* p. 154.

134. Ibid., p. 183.

135. Norval Morris and Gordon Hawkins, *The Honest Politician's Guide to Crime Control* (Chicago: University of Chicago Press, 1970), p. 2.

136. See, for example, Edwin H. Schur, *Crimes Without Victims: Deviant Behavior and Public Policy* (Englewood Cliffs, N.J.: Prentice-Hall, 1965).

137. Sanford H. Kadish, "The Crisis of Overcriminalization," *Annals of the American Academy of Political and Social Science,* 374 (November 1967), p. 157. Also see Herbert L. Packer, *The Limits of the Criminal Sanction* (Stanford, Calif.: Stanford University Press, 1968). The effect of legalization (and decriminalization) is analyzed in Austin T. Turk, *Legal Sanctioning and Social Control* (Rockville, Md.: National Institute of Mental Health, 1972).

138. This issue is considered in Gilbert Geis, *Not the Law's Business? An Examination of Homosexuality, Abortion, Prostitution, Narcotics and Gambling in the United States* (Rockville, Md.: National Institute of Mental Health, 1972).

139. *Diversion from the Criminal Justice System,* p. 8. For a critique of some of the civil procedures, see Thomas S. Szasz, *Law, Liberty and Psychiatry: An Inquiry into the Social Uses of Mental Health Practices* (New York: Macmillan, 1963).

140. *Civil Commitment of Special Categories of Offenders* (Rockville, Md.: National Institute of Mental Health, 1971), p. 11.

CRIME AND THE DEVELOPMENT OF CAPITALISM

Crime in Capitalist Society

11

What makes crime an integral part of capitalist society? For an answer we must consider larger questions: how capitalism developed; the material basis of crime (including both crime control and criminality); class structure under advanced capitalism; the capitalist state's role; and the political economy of criminal justice. Eventually our task is to document how policies of control grew in the United States, as the nation's economics and politics took shape. But theoretical questions have to be considered first.[1]

The contradiction in capitalist society today is that the state must provide a framework for continuing capitalist accumulation and at the same time legitimate the social order. It is increasingly difficult to provide resources for these services. The surplus population produced by the political economy of advanced capitalism is growing, a population that must be serviced and controlled, but financial resources are more and more limited. The criminal-justice policies of recent years are affected by this contradiction. Criminal justice has traditionally been one part of the policies of the welfare state. But as the liberal welfare state fails to resolve its own contradictions, its demise becomes imminent and criminal justice takes on new forms. A new model of criminal justice, based explicitly on punishment, reflects the economic and political crisis of late capitalism. It all takes on further meaning as the class struggle heightens and grows more political.

The future of criminal justice will be determined by changed conditions in the last stages of capitalism and by rising political consciousness in the working class, especially by the expanding portion of that class now relegated to a surplus population. Currently we are developing a theory and a practice for a transitional society, one that is moving from late capitalism to early socialism. In the transition, popular forms of action, beyond the state-sponsored programs of criminal justice, are appearing. Popular justice is the immediate alternative to criminal justice. Forms of the future will become evident only as we move to a socialist society. To understand criminal justice is to join in the struggle for a new society.

MARXIST ANALYSIS OF CRIME

A Marxist understanding of crime, as developed here, begins with the recognition that crime is a material problem. The necessary condition for any society, according to the materialist method and conception of reality, is that its members produce their material means of subsistence. Social production is primary in all social life. Moreover, in this social production we enter into relations appropriate to the forces of production.[2] It is this "economic" structure that provides the foundation for all social and political institutions, for everyday life, and for social consciousness. Our analysis begins with the *material conditions* of social life.

The *dialectical method* allows us to comprehend the world as a complex of processes, in which all things continuously come into being and pass away. All things are studied as part of their historical development. Dialectical materialism allows us to learn about things as they are in their actual connections, contradictions, and movements. In dialectical analysis we critically understand our past, informing our analysis with the possibilities for our future.

A Marxist analysis shares in the larger *socialist struggle.* One commitment is to eliminating exploitation and oppression. Being on the side of the oppressed, only those ideas are advanced which will help transform the capitalist system. The objective of the Marxist analysis is change — revolutionary change. The purpose of our intellectual labors is to assist in providing knowledge and consciousness for building a socialist society. Theories and strategies are developed to increase conscious class struggle; ideas for an alternative to capitalist society are formulated; and strategies for achieving the socialist alternative are proposed. In this intellectual-political work we engage in the activities and actions that will advance the socialist struggle.

With these notions of a Marxist analysis — encompassing a dialectical-historical analysis of the material conditions of capitalist society looking forward to socialist revolution — we begin to formulate significant substantive questions about crime. In recent years, as socialists have begun to study crime, the outline for these questions has become evident. At this stage in our intellectual development the important questions are about *the meaning of crime in capitalist society*. Furthermore, we realize that the meaning of crime changes as capitalism develops.

The basic problem in studying the meaning of crime is integrating the two sides of the phenomenon named crime; that is, placing in one framework (1) the defining of behavior as criminal (*crime control*), and (2) the behavior of those who are defined as criminal (*criminality*). Thus far our analysis of crime has been focused on one side or the other, failing to integrate them into one scheme. In pursuing a Marxist analysis, however, the dual concept of crime is resolved by *giving primacy to the underlying political economy*.

The basic question in the Marxist analysis of crime is this: What is the meaning of crime in the development of capitalism? Approaching this question, we must consider several related processes: (1) development of capitalist political economy, including the forces and relations of production, formulation of the capitalist state, and class struggle between those who do and those who do not own and control the means of production; (2) the systems of domination and repression established as capitalism develops, operating for the benefit of the capitalist class and secured by the capitalist state; (3) the forms of accommodation and resistance to the conditions of capitalism, by all people oppressed by capitalism, including the working class; and (4) the relation between the dialectics of domination and accommodation to patterns of crime in capitalist society, producing the crimes of domination and of accommodation. As indicated in Figure 11.1, all these are dialectically related to the developing political economy. Crime is to be understood as part of capitalist development.

CRIME IN THE DEVELOPMENT OF CAPITALISM

Crime is a manifestation of society's material conditions. The failure of conventional criminology is to ignore, by design, the material conditions of capitalism. Because the phenomena of crime are products of the substructure and themselves part of the superstructure, any explanation of crime using other elements of the superstructure is no explanation at all.

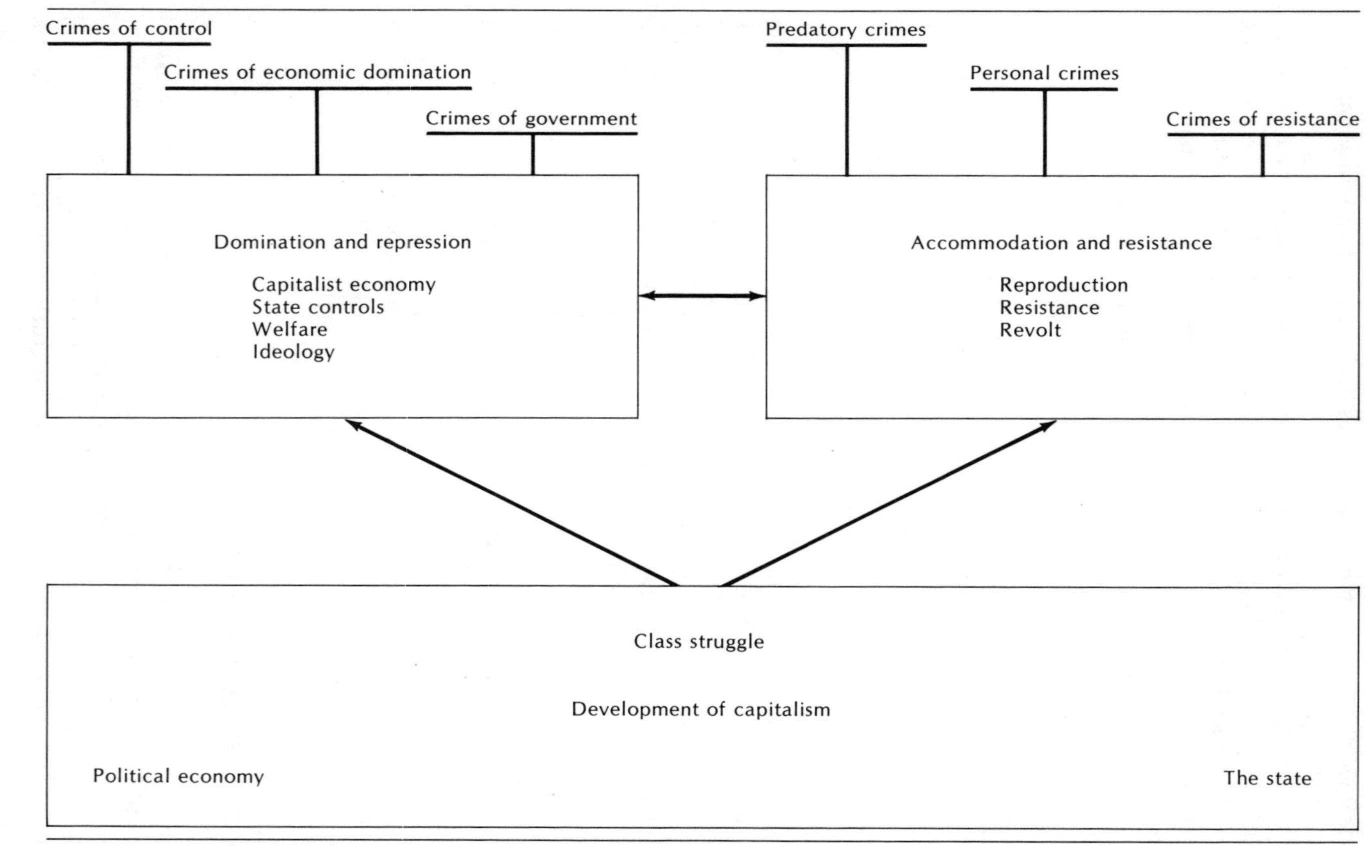

FIGURE 11.1 Crime and the Development of Capitalism

We need a general materialist framework for understanding crime, beginning with the underlying historic processes of social existence.

Production, as the necessary requirement of existence, produces its own forces and relations of social and economic life. The material factors (such as resources and technology) and personal factors (most important, the workers) present at any one time form the productive *forces* of society. During production people form definite *relations* of production with one another. These and the forces of production are the *mode* of production of a society at any time. It is the economic mode of production that furnishes society with its substructure, on which the social and political institutions (including control of crime) and supporting ideologies are built. This whole complex is the *political economy* of capitalism.[3]

The political economy of capitalism gives rise to a class society, in which the system of production is owned and controlled by one segment of the society to the exclusion of another. All social life in capitalist society, including everything associated with crime, is subject to the economic conditions of production and the struggle between classes produced by these conditions. The basic division within capitalist society is between the capitalist class that owns and controls the means of production and the working class that labors.

Therefore, it is the problem of *labor* (as the foremost human activity) that characterizes the nature and specific relationship of the classes. For the capitalist system to operate and survive, the capitalist class must exploit the labor (appropriate the *surplus labor*) of the working class. The capitalist class extracts from the worker the labor over and above that consumed by the actual producer.[4] The relationship is dialectical: the capitalist class survives by appropriating the surplus labor of the working class, and the working class as an exploited class exists as long as surplus labor is required in production. Each class depends on the other for its character and existence.

The amount of labor appropriated, techniques of exploiting labor, conditions of working-class life, and working-class consciousness have all been an integral part of capitalism's development.[5] Likewise, antagonism and conflict between classes have varied at different stages in the development. It is still the basic contradiction between classes, generalized as class conflict, that typifies the history of capitalism. Class conflict permeates its whole development, represented in the contradiction between those who own property and those who do not, and by those who oppress and those who are oppressed.[6] All history involving capitalism is the history of class struggle.

Capitalism as a system of production based on exploitation by the ruling capitalist class that owns and controls the means of production is a

Punishment — here in the form of a Delaware whipping post and pillory — served as a warning to the community and its citizens of the consequences of disturbing the established order in a developing capitalist society.

dynamic system that goes through its own stages of development. In fact, capitalism is constantly transforming its own forces and relations of production. As a result, the whole of capitalist society is constantly being altered within the capitalist political economy.

The Marxian view stresses the qualitative changes in social organization and social relations as well as (or in relation to) the quantitative changes in the economic system.[7] Capitalism transforms itself, affecting the social existence of all who live under it. This is the basic force in capitalist development: interdependence among production, relations of production, and social superstructure of institutions and ideas. "For it is a requirement of all social production that the relations which people enter into in carrying on production must be suitable to the type of production they are carrying on. Hence, it is a general law of economic development that the relations of production must necessarily be adapted to the character of the forces of production."[8]

Our analysis of the meaning of crime in capitalism's development necessarily involves investigating the relation between the concrete stage of capitalist development and social relations at that stage. This is not to argue, however, that the superstructure of social relations and culture is an automatic (directly determined) product of the economic substructure. After all, people may enter into relations of production in various ways to employ the forces of production; and it is from these relations that they create further institutions and ideas. Because human social existence is in part a product of conscious activity and struggle, conscious life must be part of any analysis.

Furthermore, the more highly developed the productive forces under capitalism the greater the discrepancy between productive forces and capitalist relations of production. Capitalist development, for which economic expansion is fundamental, exacerbates rather than mitigates the contradictions of capitalism.[9] Workers are further exploited, conditions of existence worsen, and the contradictions of capitalism increase. Capitalist development, from another vantage point, creates the conditions for transforming and abolishing capitalism, brought about in actuality by class struggle.

The periods of capitalist development, for our purposes, differ according to the ways in which surplus labor is appropriated. Capitalism itself, distinct from other modes of production, has gone through periods of utilizing various methods of production and creating social relations in association with these productive forms. Each new development in capitalism brings about its own forms of capitalist social reality and related problems of human existence. How crime — control and criminality — has its part in each stage of capitalist development is our interest in investigating the meaning of crime.

Domination and Repression

The capitalist system must continuously reproduce itself. Most explicitly it is the *state* that promotes the capitalist order. By its coercive force, embodied in law and legal repression, the social and economic order of capitalism has been traditionally secured.[10] The legal system continues to be the means of enforcing the interests of the capitalist economy.

The state's coercive force, however, is but one means of maintaining the social and economic order. A subtler way of reproducing capitalist society is to perpetuate the capitalist conception of reality, a nonviolent but equally repressive means of domination. Alan Wolfe explains below that in manipulating consciousness the social order is legitimated and secured:

> The most important reproductive mechanism which does not involve the use of state violence is consciousness-manipulation. The liberal state has an enormous amount of violence at its disposal, but is often reluctant to use it. Violence may breed counter-violence, leading to instability. It may be far better to manipulate consciousness to such an extent that most people would never think of engaging in the kinds of action which could be repressed. The most perfectly repressive (though not violently so) capitalist system, in other words, would not be a police state, but the complete opposite, one in which there were no police because there was nothing to police, everyone having accepted the legitimacy of that society and all its daily consequences.[11]

Those who rule in capitalist society, with the assistance of the state, not only accumulate capital at the expense of those who work but impose their ideology as well. Oppression and exploitation are legitimized by expropriating consciousness; labor is expropriated, consciousness must be too.[12] In fact, the *legitimacy* of the capitalist order is maintained by controlling the population's consciousness. A capitalist hegemony is established.

Moreover, a society that depends on labor exploitation for its very existence must not only control that situation but must cope with the problems that kind of economic system naturally creates. The capitalist state must therefore provide "social services" — education, health, welfare, and rehabilitation programs — to deal with the problems that could be dealt with otherwise only by changing the capitalist system. These state services are a means of securing the capitalist order.

Capitalism systematically generates a *surplus population,* an unemployed sector of the working class either dependent on fluctuations in the economy or made obsolete by new technology. As the surplus population grows, pressure builds for the welfare system to expand. Growing welfare with its host of services is designed to control the surplus population. Moreover, James O'Connor observes, "Unable to gain employment in the monopoly industries by offering their labor power at lower than going wage rates (and victimized by sexism and racism), and unemployed, underemployed, or employed at low wages in competitive industries, the surplus population increasingly becomes dependent on the state."[13] An unsteady alliance is formed between the state and the casualties it naturally produces. Only a new economic order could wipe out the need for a welfare state.

Repression through welfare is in part the history of capitalism. The kinds of services have varied with the development of economic conditions. Likewise, relief policies have changed according to specific tensions produced by unemployment and subsequent threats of disorder.[14] Control through welfare can never be a permanent solution for a system based on appropriation of labor. As with all forms of control and manipulation in capitalist society, welfare cannot completely counter the basic contradictions of a capitalist political economy.

Although the capitalist state creates and manages the institutions of control (employing physical force *and* manipulation of consciousness), the contradictions are so great that this control is not absolute and, in the long run, is subject to defeat. Because of the contradictions, the capitalist state is more weak than strong.[15] Eventually the capitalist state loses its legitimacy, no longer able to perpetuate the ideology that accumulation of capital for capitalists (at the expense of workers) is good for the nation or for human interests. The ability of the capitalist economic order to exist according to its own interests is eventually weakened.[16] The problem becomes especially acute in periods of economic crisis, unavoidable under capitalism.

As the capitalist system reproduces itself, crimes are committed. One of its contradictions is that some of its own laws must be violated in order to secure the system. The contradictions of capitalism produce their own sources of crime. Not only are these heightened in times of crisis, increasing crimes of domination, but the crimes change with further development of capitalism. Control of crime and the crimes of domination are necessary features and natural products of a developing capitalist economy.

Accommodation and Resistance

The class that does not own and control the means of production must adapt to the conditions of capitalism. Accommodation and resistance to these conditions are basic to the class struggle. The actions of those who do not own and control the means of production, who are exploited and oppressed, are mainly accommodation or resistance to the conditions produced by the capitalist political economy. Much criminality, with its many historical variations, is an integral part of class struggle in the development of capitalism.

The effects of the capitalist mode of production for the worker are all-inclusive, going far beyond the work place itself. The worker can no longer be at home anywhere in the everyday world. The alienation experienced in the work place now represents the worker's condition in all other areas of life. Ownership and control of life in general have been surrendered to alien hands.[17] The production of life itself under capitalism is alienated. The natural means of production, in which work is foremost, has become restricted in the stages of capitalist accumulation.[18]

Furthermore, a large portion of workers become expendable under advanced capitalism. For the capitalist the problem is the kind and size of labor force necessary to maximize production and realize surplus value. The physical well-being and spiritual needs of the worker are not the primary issue; rather, capitalism requires an "industrial reserve army" that can be called into action when necessary and relieved when no longer needed — but always available. Marx observed in *Capital*:

> But if a surplus laboring population is a necessary product of accumulation or of the development of wealth on a capitalist basis, this surplus population becomes, conversely, the lever of capitalist accumulation, nay, a condition of existence of the capitalist mode of production. It forms an industrial reserve army that belongs to capital quite as absolutely as if the latter had bred it at its own cost. Independently of the limits of the actual increase of population, it creates for the changing needs of the self-expansion of capital a mass of human material always ready for exploitation.[19]

Under these conditions "the labor force consists of two parts, the employed and the unemployed, with a gray area in between, containing the part-time or sporadically employed. Furthermore, all these categories of workers and potential workers continuously expand or contract with technological change, the ups and downs of the business cycle, and the vagaries of the market, all inherent characteristics of capitalist production."[20] Many workers are further exploited by being relegated to the degradations and uncertainties of a reserve army of labor.

For the unemployed, as well as for those always uncertain about their employment, the condition has its personal and social consequences. Basic human needs are thwarted when the life-giving activity of work is lost or curtailed. This form of alienation gives rise to a multiplicity of psychosocial maladjustments and psychic disorders.[21] Unemployment also means loss of personal and family income. Choices, opportunities, and even maintenance of life itself are jeopardized. For many people, the appropriate reaction is not only mental disturbance but outright acts of personal and social destruction.

Although the statistical evidence can never show conclusively the relation between unemployment and crime because such statistics are politically constructed in the beginning to obscure the failings of a capitalist economy, enough observations are available to make it obvious that unemployment produces criminality. Crimes of economic gain increase whenever the jobless seek ways to maintain themselves and their families. Crimes of violence rise when the problems of life are further inflamed by the loss of life-supporting activity. Anger and frustration at a world that punishes instead of supporting produce their own forms of destruction. Permanent unemployment — and acceptance of that condition — can form a life in which criminality is an appropriate and consistent response.

Crime under capitalism has become a response to the material conditions of life.[22] Nearly all crimes among the working class in capitalist society are actually a way to *survive,* an attempt to exist in a society where survival is not ensured by other, collective means. Crime is inevitable under capitalist conditions.

Yet, understanding crime as a reaction to capitalist conditions, whether as acts of frustration or means of survival, is only one side of the picture. The other is the problem of *consciousness* of criminality in capitalist society.[23] The history of the working class is filled with rebellion against the conditions of capitalist production, as well as those of life resulting from work under capitalism. Class struggle, after all, is a continuing war between two opposed interests: capital accumulation for the benefit of a nonworking minority class that owns and controls the means of production and, on the other hand, control and ownership of production by those who actually labor. The capitalist state regulates this struggle, so that the institutions and laws of the social order are intended to ensure victory of the capitalist class over the working class. Yet the working class constantly struggles against the capitalist class, as shown in the long history of labor battles against the conditions of capitalist production.[24] The resistance continues as long as there is need for class struggle, that is, so long as capitalism exists.

With the instruments of force and coercion on the side of the capitalist class, much of the activity in the working-class struggle is defined as criminal. Indeed, according to the legal codes, whether in simply relieving the injustices of capitalism or in taking action against class oppression, actions against the interests of the state are crimes. With growing consciousness that the state represses those who attempt to tip the scales in favor of the working class, people of that class engage in actions against the state and the capitalist class.

The movement toward a socialist society can occur only with political consciousness reached by those oppressed by capitalist society. The alternative to capitalism cannot be willed into being, but requires conscious activity by those who seek new conditions of existence. Political consciousness awakens as people realize the alienation suffered under capitalism. The contradiction of capitalism itself — the disparity between actuality and human possibility — readies large portions of the population to act in ways that will bring about a new existence. When people become conscious of how deeply they are dehumanized under the capitalist mode of production, when they realize the source and type of their alienation, they become active in a movement to build a new society. Many of their actions result in behaviors defined as criminal by the capitalist state.

The objective of Marxist analysis is to lead us to further question the capitalist system, to better understand the consequences of capitalist development. The *ultimate meaning* of crime in the development of capitalism is the need for a socialist society. And in moving toward the socialist alternative, our study of crime is necessarily based on an economic analysis of capitalist society. Crime is essentially a product of the contradictions in capitalism. Crime can be a force in social development when it becomes a part of the class struggle, increasing political consciousness. But we must continue to concentrate on the capitalist system itself. Our understanding is furthered as we investigate the nature, sources, and consequences of capitalistic development. As we engage in this work, it becomes evident that socialism is developing.

THE POLITICAL ECONOMY OF CRIMINAL JUSTICE

The capitalist state promotes the further development of the capitalist mode of production. The state, under late capitalism, must establish the framework for accumulation of capital and foster conditions for maintaining the capitalist system. In ensuring accumulation of capital, exploitative social relations are reproduced and even heightened. The social problems generated by the capitalist system are increased as capitalism develops further.

Within the political economy of late capitalism is a political economy of criminal justice, one of the fundamental characteristics of advanced capitalism. To understand its various features is to understand a crucial part of the capitalist system. Criminal justice is likely to increase as a capitalist response to the contradictions of late capitalism.

State Expenditure on Criminal Justice

The capitalist state must increasingly expend its resources on programs that secure the capitalist order. These *social expenses* of the state, as defined by O'Connor, consist of "projects and services which are required to maintain social harmony — to fulfill the state's 'legitimization' function."[25] Although *social capital* is expended in promoting profitable private accumulation, the social expenses of the state are not directly productive, producing no surplus value. They are designed, instead, to keep "social peace" among unemployed workers, or among the surplus population in general. Welfare and law enforcement are the primary forms of the state's social expenses, regulating class struggle, repressing action against the social order, and giving legitimacy to the capitalist system. Creating and administering the criminal-justice system as a whole has become a principal social expense of the capitalist state.

The state in promoting accumulation of capital in the monopoly sector stimulates overproduction and creates a surplus population and the need for state expenditures to cope with the surplus population. Such social services as education, family support, health services, and housing benefits give legitimacy to the capitalist system and satisfy some needs of the working class. These services compensate in part for the oppression and suffering caused by capitalism.[26]

The criminal-justice system, on the other hand, more explicitly controls that which cannot be remedied by available employment within the economy or by social services for the surplus population. The police, the courts, and the penal agencies — and the entire criminal-justice system — expands to cope as a last resort with the problems of the surplus population. And as the contradictions in capitalism increase, the criminal-justice system becomes a preventive institution as well as a control and corrective agency. State expenditures on criminal justice take a larger share of the state's budgetary expenses. Criminal justice as a social expense of the state necessarily expands with the further development of capitalism.

Since war was declared on crime in the mid-sixties the amount of money spent on criminal justice has climbed steadily. The federal government alone, only one portion of the state apparatus, increased its budgetary outlays from less than one-half billion dollars in 1967 to nearly $3.5 billion in 1977.[27] These increased federal expenditures are for the federal government's own efforts in enforcement and prosecution, but are also to assist law-enforcement and judicial activities of state and local governments.

With the passage of the Omnibus Crime Control and Safe Streets Act and the establishment of the Law Enforcement Assistance Administration (LEAA), the federal government created a new level of crime control, a broader and more penetrating organization of criminal justice. The mission and mandate of the newly created LEAA was stated clearly at the beginning:

> The mission of LEAA is to reduce crime and delinquency by channeling Federal financial aid to state and local governments, to conduct research in methods of improving law enforcement and criminal justice, to fund efforts to upgrade the educational level of law enforcement personnel, to develop applications of statistical research and applied systems analysis in law enforcement, and to develop broad policy guidelines for both the short- and long-range improvement of the nation's Criminal Justice System as a whole.[28]

The budget of LEAA, as one portion of federal expenditures on criminal justice, has grown sharply from a first-year expenditure of $60 million in 1969 to $880 million in 1977. The major part of LEAA's budget goes to states and localities to improve criminal-justice activities and develop new techniques of control. Funds are also provided for training law-enforcement agents and for research to improve criminal justice. The result is a coordinated system of legal control for the advanced capitalist society. All levels of the state and the agencies of the law are linked in a nationwide system of criminal justice.

Federal expenditures on criminal justice are aimed in two directions. "Direct expenditures," including cost of salaries, materials, supplies, contractual services, plus capital outlay, finance the federal government's own criminal-justice activities. But as the federal government designs and supports a nationwide criminal-justice system, "intergovernmental expenditures" are gaining importance. They consist of grants, shared revenues, and the cost of services the federal government provides for state and local governments. A major portion of federal spending on criminal justice in recent years has been on intergovernmental expenditures. These expenditures rose from $237 million in 1971 (of a federal total expenditure of $1.5 billion) to $872 million in 1976 (of a federal total of $3.3 billion).[29]

The *total expenditure* for criminal justice by the capitalist state, for *all* levels of government, is huge. According to the most recent statistics, in fiscal year 1976 nearly $20 billion was spent on criminal justice.[30] As shown in Table 11.1, well over half ($11 billion) was spent on law enforcement. The next largest amount ($4.4 billion) went to the correctional system.

At the various levels of government, the largest expenditures for criminal justice are made by state and local governments. Local governments spend more for criminal-justice activities than federal and state govern-

TABLE 11.1 Government Expenditure for Criminal Justice, Fiscal Year 1976 (Dollar Amounts in Thousands)

Criminal-justice activity	*All governments*	*Federal government*	*State governments*	*Local governments*
Total criminal-justice system	19,681,409	3,322,073	5,986,650	12,068,308
Police protection	11,028,244	1,615,714	1,789,471	7,723,588
Judicial	2,428,472	219,445	663,068	1,633,645
Legal services and prosecution	1,047,929	149,402	253,591	653,502
Public defense	331,102	103,718	78,622	157,364
Corrections	4,385,512	285,973	2,589,609	1,678,879
Other criminal-justice activity	460,150	947,821	612,289	221,329

SOURCE: National Criminal Justice Information and Statistics Service, *Expenditure and Employment Data for the Criminal Justice System, 1976* (Washington, D.C.: U.S. Government Printing Office, 1978), p. 23. The totals exclude duplicative "intergovernmental" expenditure, the amount one level of government gives another for its own subsequent "direct" expenditure. Thus, the figures for the three levels of government are not additive.

ments combined. In fiscal 1976, out of a criminal-justice expenditure of nearly $20 billion for all levels of government, the federal government spent $3.3 billion and the state governments nearly $6 billion; expenditure by local governments was over $12 billion. When we examine each type of criminal-justice activity separately, for each level of government, it becomes clear that the different levels concentrate their crime-control efforts on particular areas of criminal justice. The local governments support the police and the courts, including arrest and prosecution of cases, and corrections. The state expenditures go mainly for punishment and correction of offenders, with some attention to planning criminal justice and forming new criminal-justice programs and agencies. Half the federal government's expenditures are for law enforcement, including funds to support state and local law enforcement.

The largest share of expenditures on the criminal-justice system is obviously spent on *employment* of workers in the system. In recent years the number has grown to more than a million in the system. According to statistics for fiscal 1976, 99,553 of these workers were employed by the federal government, 272,488 by state governments, and 707,851 by local governments. Moreover, about 80 per cent of criminal-justice expenditures were for employing these criminal-justice workers. The criminal-justice system is built on the labors of the class that is itself the object of criminal justice, a fact not to be missed in understanding the political economy of criminal justice.

Workers in the criminal-justice system, then, provide in their labor "the use-value of ensuring the maintenance of the capitalist class structure."[31] They are the "repressive workers" in that they engage in actual or threatened use of physical force and legal punishment. They do not produce surplus value, but they do secure the social order (using the apparatus of the capitalist state) so that capitalists can privately accumulate capital. The concrete value of their work is to maintain domestic order, to make the society safe for capitalist accumulation, and to protect class relations. Although these workers occupy a fraction in the working class, and are not therefore members of the "ruling class," in the use-value of their labor they act against their own working-class interests. This contradiction obscures their class struggle, at the same time provoking a tension that undermines the possibility of continued repression by the capitalist state.

Beyond the contradiction of criminal-justice work is the long-term problem of financing the entire criminal-justice system. That system is meant to maintain *social peace.* State expenditure on criminal justice does not directly contribute to the accumulation of private capital and the creation of surplus value. Instead the system secures the capitalist order so that the dominant class can continue to accumulate capital. The crisis, however, becomes a fiscal one: state expenditures on criminal justice grow faster than the revenues available to support an expanding criminal-justice system.[32] Yet, as the social problems generated by the capitalist mode of production grow, repressive measures must be expanded. Criminal justice is a social expense that the capitalist state must continue to finance in order to promote the social order of advanced capitalism.

The late capitalist economy cannot be secured solely by a repressive state, however. Legitimacy has to be restored in ways that are less obviously repressive. But restoration seems unlikely at this stage of class struggle in capitalist history. Embedded in crisis and contradiction, the criminal-justice system as a last resort signals the imminent demise of the capitalist state and the capitalist mode of production. The concrete political practice for the working class appears here in late capitalism.

The Criminal Justice–Industrial Complex

The state in its efforts to stimulate accumulation of capital and stabilize the social order forms an alliance with the monopoly sector of the economy. That sector, which consists of the large and the multinational corporations that control nearly all capital-intensive industries, is the primary force of private capital accumulation in the advanced capitalist economy. The continued growth of the monopoly sector depends increasingly on the state. And in a symbiotic relationship, the continued growth of the state depends on expansion of the monopoly sector. The state provides the structure for the economic development of the monopoly sector and in turn depends on the monopoly sector for its own economic well-being as well as services and technology for maintaining social stability.

A "social-industrial complex" has appeared, an involvement of industry in the planning, production, and operation of state programs.[33] These state-financed programs (concentrating on education, welfare, and criminal justice), as social expenses necessary for maintaining social order, are furnished by monopolistic industries. The industries plan programs that simultaneously secure the social order for the state and improve productivity and profitability of the industries themselves, while attempting to make a safe environment for continued capitalist development. With the social-industrial complex, monopoly capital has a new source from which to gain profits. Social programs financed by the state provide new investment opportunities for monopoly industries. In the business community, "Companies from AT&T to Xerox have been urged to — and in many cases have willingly accepted — the challenges to educate our children, police our streets, clean up our polluted air and water, teach our disadvantaged citizens how to earn a living, rebuild our slums, and even tell us how to run our cities more efficiently."[34] A new growth industry is being sponsored by the state, for the benefit of both the state and monopoly capital — for the intended survival of the capitalist system.

A major part of the new and growing social-industrial complex is the "criminal justice–industrial" complex. Criminal justice, in all its aspects, is becoming one of the last capital-investment industries. That industry finds it profitable to invest in crime is one of the contradictions of the capitalist system.

The criminal justice–industrial complex has grown steadily since the mid-sixties, when the state elevated social control to a "war on crime." A technocratic solution to social disorder has appeared in a new and profitable alliance between the state and monopoly industries in controlling the domestic population. The special task-force report on *Science and Technology*, completed for the President's Commission on Law Enforcement and Administration of Justice, carried the explicit message that (1) crime control must become more scientific, (2) it must utilize the kind of science and technology that already serves the military, and (3) the federal government must institute and support such a program, with the assistance of private industry.[35] That a science and a technology could be developed, similar to that of the military, was the good news in the opening lines of the task-force report:

> The natural sciences and technology have long helped the police to solve specific crimes. Scientists and engineers have had very little impact, however, on the overall operations of the criminal justice system and its principal components: police, courts, and corrections. More than 200,000 scientists and engineers have applied themselves to solving military problems and hundreds of thousands more to innovation in other areas of modern life, but only a handful are working to control the crimes that injure or frighten millions of Americans each year. Yet the two communities have much to offer each other: science and technology is a valuable source of knowledge and techniques for combating crime; the criminal justice system represents a vast area of challenging problems.[35]

The kinds of equipment and tactics needed for the criminal-justice system were listed:

> In the traditional view, science and technology primarily means new equipment. And modern technology can, indeed, provide a vast array of devices beyond those now in general use to improve the operations of criminal justice agencies, particularly in helping the police deter crime and apprehend criminals. Some of the more important possibilities are:
>
> Electronic computers for processing the enormous quantities of needed data.
> Police radio networks connecting officers and neighboring departments.
> Inexpensive, light two-way portable radios for every patrolman.

> Computers for processing fingerprints.
> Instruments for identifying criminals by their voice, photographs, hair, blood, body chemistry, etc.
> Devices for automatic and continual reporting of all police car locations.
> Helicopters for airborne police patrol.
> Inexpensive, reliable burglar and robbery alarms.
> Nonlethal weapons to subdue dangerous criminals without inflicting permanent harm.
> Perimeter surveillance devices for prisoners.
> Automatic transcription devices for courtroom testimony. Many of these devices are now in existence, some as prototypes and some available commercially. Others still require basic development but are at least technically feasible and worthy of further exploration.[37]

The new technocratic approach to crime and social control has developed rapidly. Especially under the direction of LEAA, a multi-million-dollar market in domestic control has been established for hundreds of industries and research institutes.[38] The LEAA has contracted industries and institutes, directly or indirectly through state agencies, to develop and manufacture a wide range of weapons and technical devices for use in the criminal-justice system. A technology and an industry created for scientific warfare abroad is now being applied to social control at home.

In fact, the political and economic meaning of LEAA in the developing criminal justice–industrial complex is now clear. As shown by Gregory McLauchlan, LEAA is simultaneously directing the technocratic solution to social control, guiding development of the social-industrial complex in criminal justice, *and* lowering the social expense of criminal justice by making social expenditures profitable for private industry. The LEAA is attempting to reverse the economic burden, and possible crisis, of the social expense of controlling crime. Summarizing this observation, McLauchlan writes:

> LEAA represents a federal infrastructure which attempts to simultaneously rationalize the fiscal crisis of state finance, and develop a social-industrial complex in the field of law enforcement. By providing rationalized and efficient standards of organization for a nationally integrated law enforcement apparatus, LEAA can reduce social expenses over the long run. Presently, most state expenditure on law enforcement consists of social expenses (i.e., administrative costs and salaries) which do not increase productivity or reduce the cost of reproducing the labor force. However, LEAA is attempting to reverse this tendency by increasing expenditures on sophisticated technology and hardware for police operations. In so doing, the labor-to-capital ratio of law enforcement programs will be reduced, thus lowering social expenses.[39]

The criminal justice–industrial complex becomes visible as a structure in which capital accumulation is combined with the state's social expenditure. The growth of state spending on social programs is joined under advanced capitalism with growth of the monopolies. The contradiction is that even though state-financed social programs are designed to legitimate the current order, collusion between the state and monopoly industries weakens the legitimacy of the capitalist system. In the long run, in the continuing class struggle, the criminal-justice–industrial complex cannot be a lasting solution to the joint problems of accumulating capital and achieving social stability.

Nevertheless, because of limited alternatives within the capitalist framework, the complex continues to grow. As expenditures for criminal justice expand, involvement of the monopoly sector increases. Private industries are not only ever more deeply engaged in developing and manufacturing hardware for law enforcement (including guns, ammunition, gas, helmets, helicopters, electronic-detection devices, communications equipment, and the like), but they develop and manufacture more sophisticated and subtle forms of technological control. The state collaborating with private industry now plans and implements technocratic solutions to crime control that include systems analysis, managerial improvement, computerized surveillance for intelligence, and administrative reorganization. Administration of criminal justice becomes modeled on the corporate form, and the tactical operations are borrowed from the military.[40] This corporate-military approach to criminal justice meets the requirements for controlling the domestic population under advanced capitalism and readily engages monopoly capital in the state's program of criminal justice.

The private sector itself is becoming directly involved in controlling crime, adding to the criminal justice–industrial complex, and increasing in importance. Although we continue to believe that criminal justice is the sole province of the state, the fact is that private industry is engaged in aspects of criminal justice, especially in law enforcement. The private security industry, in particular, is growing steadily each year. Expenditure on uniformed guards and private detective services is about $15 million a year.[41] And, contrary to our common knowledge, private police outnumber public police in most cities and states. The benefits to private industry are contradictory, however. On the one hand, private policing is obviously beneficial to the private police industry. For the rest of private industry, though, the cost of private law enforcement takes away from profits. Private industry is in conflict within itself. The capitalist mode of production is reaching a stage at which the problems it generates cannot be adequately met by the private sector, the state sector, or both in collaboration.

As the crisis of the state and the capitalist economy accelerates, forms of control will be devised to be more pervasive and more certain and, at the same time, less of an expense for the state. The state and monopoly capital will try to create crime-control programs that do not require a major outlay of capital, capital that does not promote further capital accumulation. For example, halfway-house programs may sometimes be substituted for large and costly institutions. Surveillance may replace some other forms of confinement and control. Yet, the contradiction is only furthered: criminal justice is inevitably a losing battle under late capitalism.

In other words, spending on criminal justice is only a partial, temporary, and self-defeating resolution to capitalist economic contradictions. It is like military spending. Although expenditures on warfare and the military may have some immediate functions for the state and the economy, an economy based on such expenditure is subject to more contradictions than ultimate resolutions.[42] A substantial criminal-justice budget, like a military budget, cannot successfully solve the economic and political problems of the capitalist system. And in the long run, criminal justice as a social expenditure can only further the contradictions of capitalism.

Control of the Surplus Population

Social expenditures on criminal justice necessarily increase with developing advanced capitalism. In the late stages of capitalism the mode of production and the forms of capital accumulation accelerate the growth of the relative surplus population. The state must then provide social-expense programs, including criminal justice, both to legitimate advanced capitalism and to control the surplus population. Instead of being able to absorb the surplus population into the political economy, advanced capitalism can only supervise and control a population that is now superfluous to the system. The problem is especially acute when the surplus population threatens to disturb the system, either by overburdening it or by political action. Criminal justice is the modern way of controlling this surplus population produced by late capitalist development.

The state attempts to offset the social expense of criminal justice by supporting the growth of the criminal-justice–industrial complex. The fiscal crisis of the capitalist state is temporarily alleviated by forming an alliance between monopoly capital and state-financed social programs. The social programs of the state are transformed into social capital, providing subsidized opportunities for investment of monopoly capital and ameliorating some of the material impoverishment of the surplus population.[43] The new complex ties the surplus population to the state and to the political economy of advanced capitalism. A growing segment of the population is absorbed into the system as *indirectly productive workers* — the army of government and office workers, paraprofessionals, and those who work in one way or another in the social-expense programs — but also a large surplus population is itself *controlled* by these programs. These unemployed, underemployed, reserve army workers now find themselves dependent on the state. They are linked to the state (and to monopoly capital) for much of their economic welfare and they are linked as objects of the state's social-control programs. The criminal-justice system is the most explicit of these programs in controlling the surplus population. Criminal justice and the surplus population are symbiotically interdependent.

As the surplus population grows along with developing capitalism, the criminal-justice system or some equivalent must also grow. By expanding the system, late capitalism attempts to "integrate" the surplus population into the economic and political system. Instead, problems such as crime are dealt with as a *control* problem — controlling the population that is already oppressed by the conditions of advanced capitalism. And control becomes especially acute in periods when the economic crisis is most obvious: during depressions and recessions. It is during these periods that the surplus population is affected most, and the surplus population grows because of unemployment.

As usual during these periods, the hardest-hit groups are women, blacks, the young, and unskilled workers. The unemployment rate among nonwhites is consistently twice as high as that of whites; almost half the unemployed are women, although they occupy only about 40 per cent of the labor force; the unemployment rate of young workers (16 to 21 years) is twice the average rate of workers in general; and the unemployment rate of unskilled workers is several percentage points higher than that for all other workers.[44] Moreover, these figures drastically underestimate the extent of unemployment in the United States. Although the official statistics indicate that nearly 5 million people are unemployed during the year, this figure obscures the fact that up to 18 million people may be out of work at some time during the year. In recent years nearly 24 million people have been unemployed annually, nearly one of every four workers.

Even these figures underestimate the problem. They systematically exclude the people in the surplus population who have given up looking for jobs. Unemployment figures likewise do not count people who are employed part time but who are seeking full-time jobs. They also exclude the many people who are "subemployed," those who are not employed in jobs for which they are qualified. All these provide a picture of employment and unemployment quite different from that portrayed by the government.

A way of controlling this unemployed surplus population is simply and directly by confinement in prisons. The rhetoric of criminal justice — and that of conventional criminology — is that prisons are for incarcerating criminals. In spite of this mystification, prisons are used to control the part of the surplus population subject to the discretion of criminal law and the criminal-justice system. The figures and the conclusion that prisons are differently utilized according to the extent of economic crisis are not usually presented. The finding is clear: the prison population increases as the rate of unemployment increases.[45] Unemployment simultaneously makes necessary actions of survival and frustration by the unemployed surplus population and requires the state to control that population in some way. Containing the unemployed in prison is a certain way of controlling a threatening surplus population. Until other solutions of control are found, the capitalist state will need the prison's certainty for controlling portions of the surplus population.

The criminal-justice system continues to be developed by the state and the capitalist class as a way of controlling the problems (particularly the surplus population) that cannot be solved within advanced capitalism. The problem for us, then, is a socialist practice and a social theory that transform criminal justice during socialist revolution. As we understand criminal justice under capitalism, and as we engage in socialist struggle, we build a society that ceases to generate the crime found in capitalist society. Criminal justice ceases to be the solution to crime. Socialist solutions are to be found in the society itself — a society that neither supports nor depends on a political economy of criminal justice.

BEYOND CRIMINAL JUSTICE

Criminal justice is the characteristic form of control in advanced capitalist society. As the crisis in capitalism grows, however, as capitalist development reaches its final stages, even criminal justice fails to control the population. The crisis in capitalism at the same time produces a crisis in criminal justice. New techniques of criminal justice (in the framework of control and punishment) are constantly proposed and implemented, an indication of the increasing failure of criminal justice.

To move beyond criminal justice is to move beyond capitalism. The final development of capitalism is also the initial development of socialism. As criminal justice falters under capitalism, new socialist forms of justice appear. Rather than a justice based on the needs of the capitalist class, oppressing everyone else, a justice develops under socialism that satisfies the needs of the entire working class. We are now beginning to create the social theory and practice appropriate to socialist development, necessarily going beyond criminal justice.

Out of capitalism's final development socialist forms appear. Capitalism is transformed into socialism when capitalism can no longer reconcile the conflicts between the current mode of production and the relations of production, when the contradictions are so crippling that capitalism can no longer solve its own inherent problems. Ultimately capitalist relations become an obstacle to the further development of capitalism. New forms of productive and social relations develop. The capitalist system finally fails to control the population; criminal justice ceases to be effective; and a new social life forms. In other words, as another form becomes evident, socialism begins to develop. Marx wrote:

> No social order is ever destroyed before all the productive forces for which it is sufficient have been developed, and new superior relations of production never replace older ones before the material conditions for their existence have matured within the framework of the old society. Mankind thus inevitably sets itself only such tasks as it is able to solve, since closer examination will always show that the problem itself arises only when the material conditions for its solution are already present or at least in the course of formation.[46]

The material forces within capitalist society, combined with the socialist alternative, create the conditions for moving beyond the contradictions of capitalism. Thus begins the transition to socialism.

The transition to socialism is the ultimate trend of history in capitalist society. Transformation from capitalism to socialism depends on the prior development of capitalism. The development of socialism is, Shlomo Avineri writes, "the realization of those hidden potentialities which could not have been historically realized under the limiting conditions of capitalism."[47] Capitalism creates conditions and expectations that it cannot itself satisfy, digging its own grave. The root of the transition from capitalism to socialism is one fact: "socialism is in practice nothing but what capitalism is potentially."[48] Because the potential cannot be satisfied under capitalism, however, socialism becomes necessary.

Each transition in society is a unique historical change that must be understood as such. Nevertheless, all history is a continuous transformation. Even with the overthrow of class domination, with the eventual transition to communism, the transformation of human nature and social order never ceases. The disappearance of classes, withering away of the state, elimination of the crippling forms of the division of labor, abolition of the distinctions between city and country and between manual and mental labor — even with all these, we are moved to a higher plane where other transformations become possible. As one level of human and social development is reached, another becomes evident. Out of the seeds of the past and present, our future takes shape. We move from one historical epoch to another.

This takes us far beyond criminal justice. To transcend the capitalist economy and the capitalist state is also to transcend criminal justice. In the transition to socialism there is a dialectic between criminal justice and a popular-justice movement beyond the control of the state. Developing consciousness among the working class brings consciousness about social control. Working-class institutions will create forms of dealing with the problems that accompany class struggle, including protection from the capitalist state's repression. These forms will be in the hands of the working class, not in the jurisdiction of the state. The forms of control and human transformation will become apparent only in the movement toward socialism and from one stage of socialism to another. The only thing we can be certain of now is that the forms of "justice" — or whichever conceptualization is created — will be appropriate to the new society. The movement is clearly beyond criminal justice.

The bourgeois notion of criminal justice is replaced by the idea of popular justice. In the late stage of capitalist development people are attempting to resolve conflicts between themselves in their own communities and work places. Outside the legal institutions of the capitalist state, people are trying to deal with their own problems collectively, according to their own terms. Popular justice is an alternative to the criminal justice of the capitalist state. It is also being used as a tool in the class struggle. Working-class people are being educated about the class structure of the contemporary society.

With the transition to socialism, popular justice may become institutionalized into the society and the state. In such socialist countries as China and Cuba institutions of popular justice have been created and supported by the state.[49] These institutions protect and solidify the working class against internal and external class enemies, as well as against elitist bureaucratic tendencies in the state apparatus. The long-term use and fate of popular justice, as we progress to communism, is far from certain. Experiences will differ for every society. Only in the struggle and the transformation will future forms become evident.

A critical understanding of criminal justice as practiced in capitalist society is a necessary condition for moving beyond the theory and practice of criminal justice, indeed, for the movement to a socialist society. Theoretical analysis of the structure of criminal justice as it fits into the structure of capitalist economy is in itself a revolutionary practice. The place of theory in practical action will not vanish under socialism. On the contrary, social theory will be even more important than under capitalism, becoming a part of everyday life for the masses of people. If a social science remains, it will be one that belongs to the working class, not a social science used by the capitalist class against the workers.

The purpose of social theory — including a critical understanding of criminal justice — in the transition to socialism is to subvert the capitalist hegemony that maintains its hold over the working class. Socialist social theory provides people with an understanding of their alienation and oppressed condition, and provides a means of expression that is the beginning of socialist revolution.[50] To engage in social theory under these conditions is to engage in ideological, educational, and practical work. Social theory assists in developing class consciousness. As Theotonio Dos Santos observes: "The intellectual, considered not as an individual isolated in an ivory tower but as a militant intellectual of a class, is thus a key factor in working out and developing class consciousness."[51] A conscious working-class culture of emancipation is created.

For those who engage in this work, bourgeois ways of social science must necessarily be transcended. Social theorists, whose work has the character of critical inquiry, must be "capable of moving across the boundaries of normal science with its normal division of labor."[52] In rejecting the boundaries of normal scholarship and bourgeois paradigms, the capitalist order is critically examined and the socialist alternative is proposed. Embodied within critique and proposal is a politics of working-class struggle and socialist revolution.

Social theory, then, is to serve the working class in the struggle for a socialist society. As bourgeois social theory serves the capitalist class under capitalism, socialist social theory serves the working class under socialism and assists in the transition to socialism. In the struggle, social theory is constantly revised and practice is altered to better achieve the goal of a socialist society. The only purpose in knowing the world, Mao Tse-tung wrote, is to change it.[53]

In understanding crime in capitalist society, we provide a theory and a practice with the objective of changing the world. The importance of Marxist criminology is that it moves us dialectically to reject the capitalist order and to struggle for a new society. We are engaged in the struggle for a socialist society.

NOTES

1. The complete discussion, from which this chapter is adapted, is in my book *Class, State, and Crime: On the Theory and Practice of Criminal Justice* (New York: Longman, 1977).

2. Karl Marx, *A Contribution to the Critique of Political Economy*, ed. M. Dobb (New York: International Publishers, 1970), pp. 20–21.

3. L. Afanasyev et al., *The Political Economy of Capitalism* (Moscow: Progress Publishers, 1974), pp. 9–16.

4. Maurice Dobb, *Studies in the Development of Capitalism* (New York: International Publishers, 1963), p. 15.

5. Jurgen Kuczynski, *The Rise of the Working Class* (New York: McGraw-Hill, 1967).

6. Robert Heiss, *Engels, Kierkegaard, and Marx* (New York: Dell, 1975), p. 390.

7. Paul M. Sweezy, *The Theory of Capitalist Development* (New York: Monthly Review Press, 1968), pp. 92–95.

8. Maurice Cornforth, *Historical Materialism* (New York: International Publishers, 1962), p. 59.

9. Erik Olin Wright, "Alternative Perspectives in the Marxist Theory of Accumulation and Crisis," *The Insurgent Sociologist,* 6 (Fall 1975), pp. 5–39.

10. See Richard Quinney, *Critique of Legal Order: Crime Control in Capitalist Society* (Boston: Little, Brown, 1974), pp. 95–135.

11. Alan Wolfe, "Political Repression and the Liberal State," *Monthly Review,* 23 (December 1971), p. 20.

12. Alan Wolfe, "New Directions in the Marxist Theory of Politics," *Politics and Society,* 4 (Winter 1974), pp. 155–157.

13. James O'Connor, *The Fiscal Crisis of the State* (New York: St. Martin's Press, 1973), p. 161.

14. Frances Fox Piven and Richard A. Cloward, *Regulating the Poor: The Functions of Public Welfare* (New York: Random House, 1971), pp. 3–4.

15. Wolfe, "New Directions in the Marxist Theory of Politics," p. 155.

16. See Stanley Aronowitz, "Law, Breakdown of Order, and Revolution," in Robert Lefcourt, ed., *Law Against the People: Essays to Demystify Law, Order and the Courts* (New York: Random House, 1971), pp. 150–182; and John H. Schaar, "Legitimacy in the Modern State," in Philip Green and Sanford Levinson, ed., *Power and Community: Dissenting Essays in Political Science* (New York: Random House, 1970), pp. 276–327.

17. Karl Marx, *The Grundrisse,* ed. David McLellan (New York: Harper & Row, 1971), pp. 132–143.

18. Harry Braverman, "Work and Unemployment," *Monthly Review,* 27 (June 1975), p. 30.

19. Karl Marx, *Capital* (Chicago: C. H. Kerr, 1932), p. 693.

20. Editors, "The Economic Crisis in Historical Perspective," *Monthly Review,* 26 (June 1975), p. 2.

21. K. William Kapp, "Socio-Economic Effects of Law and High Employment," *Annals of the American Academy of Political and Social Science,* 418 (March 1975), pp. 60–71.

22. David M. Gordon, "Capitalism, Class, and Crime in America," *Crime and Delinquency,* 19 (April 1973), pp. 163–186.

23. Ian Taylor, Paul Walton, and Jock Young, *The New Criminology: For a Social Theory of Deviance* (London: Routledge & Kegan Paul, 1973), pp. 220–221.

24. Sidney Lens, *The Labor Wars: From the Molly Maguires to the Sitdowns* (New York: Doubleday, 1973); Jeremy Brecher, *Strike!* (Greenwich, Conn.: Fawcett, 1972); Samuel Yellin, *American Labor Struggles* (New York: S. A. Russell, 1936); Richard O. Boyer and Herbert M. Morais, *Labor's Untold Story* (New York: Cameron Associates, 1955).

25. O'Connor, *The Fiscal Crisis of the State,* p. 7.

26. See Ian Gough, "State Expenditure in Advanced Capitalism," *New Left Review,* No. 92 (July-August 1975), especially pp. 70–74.

27. *The New York Times,* January 22, 1976, p. 25.

28. Law Enforcement Assistance Administration, *3rd Annual Report of the Law Enforcement Assistance Administration,* Fiscal Year 1971 (Washington, D.C.: U.S. Government Printing Office, 1972), p. ii.

29. National Criminal Justice Information and Statistics Service, *Expenditure and Employment Data for the Criminal Justice System,* Advance Report 1976 (Washington, D.C.: U.S. Government Printing Office, 1978), p. 22.

30. Ibid., p. 21.

31. Francesca Freedman, "The Internal Structure of the American Proletariat: A Marxist

Analysis," *Socialist Revolution,* 5 (October-December 1975), p. 73. Also see James O'Connor's discussion of "guard labor" in his article "Productive and Unproductive Labor," *Politics and Society,* 5 (No. 3, 1975), pp. 297–336.

32. On the fiscal crisis of legitimation functions in general, see O'Connor, *The Fiscal Crisis of the State,* especially pp. 150–178.

33. See ibid., pp. 51–58.

34. "Should Business Tackle Society's Problems?" *Economic and Business News* (New York: Houghton Mifflin, 1972), p. 3. Quoted in O'Connor, *The Fiscal Crisis of the State,* p. 55.

35. President's Commission on Law Enforcement and Administration of Justice, *Science and Technology,* Task Force Report, prepared by the Institute for Defense Analysis (Washington, D.C.: U.S. Government Printing Office, 1967).

36. Ibid., p. 1.

37. Ibid.

38. Gregory McLauchlan, "LEAA: A Case Study in the Development of the Social Industrial Complex," *Crime and Social Justice,* 4 (Fall-Winter 1975), pp. 15–23.

39. Ibid., p. 21.

40. Center for Research on Criminal Justice, *The Iron Fist and the Velvet Glove: An Analysis of the U.S. Police* (Berkeley, Calif.: Center for Research on Criminal Justice, 1975), pp. 32–37.

41. Michael T. Klare, "The Boom in Private Police," *The Nation,* 221 (November 15, 1975), pp. 486–491.

42. Clarence Y. H. Lo, "The Conflicting Functions of U.S. Military Spending after World War II," *Kapitalistate,* No. 3 (Spring 1975), pp. 26–44.

43. O'Connor, *The Fiscal Crisis of the State,* p. 221.

44. "Unemployment Stays High," *Dollars & Sense,* No. 13 (January 1976), pp. 10–11.

45. *NEPA News,* February 1976, p. 15.

46. Marx, *A Contribution to the Critique of Political Economy,* p. 21.

47. Shlomo Avineri, *The Social and Political Thought of Karl Marx* (London: Cambridge University Press, 1969), p. 150.

48. Ibid., p. 181.

49. James P. Brady, "Political Contradictions and Justice Policy in People's China," *Contemporary Crises,* 1 (April 1977), pp. 127–162.

50. André Gorz, *Socialism and Revolution* (New York: Doubleday, 1973), pp. 170–174.

51. Theotonio Dos Santos, "The Concept of Social Class," *Science and Society,* 34 (Summer 1970), p. 186.

52. Alvin W. Gouldner, "Prologue to a Theory of Revolutionary Intellectuals," *Telos,* No. 26 (Winter 1975–76), p. 23.

53. Mao Tse-tung, *Where Do Correct Ideas Come from?* (Peking: Foreign Languages Press, 1966), p. 3. Also, on the role of intellectual workers, see Mao Tse-tung, *Speech at the Chinese Communist Party's National Conference on Propaganda Work* (Peking: Foreign Languages Press, 1968).

ACKNOWLEDGMENTS (Continued)

324 The Bettmann Archive, Inc. *Page 340* Danny Lyon/Magnum. *Page 347* Danny Lyon/Măgnum. *Page 369* Wide World Photos. *Page 396* Mike Goldberg/Stock, Boston. *Page 402* Library of Congress.

The following authors and publishers have granted permission to include material from their publications. Page numbers for specific citations appear in the Notes following each chapter.

Ronald L. Akers. From "The Professional Association and the Legal Regulation of Practice," *Law and Society Review,* 2, no. 3 (May 1968): 465, 467, and 476. *Law and Society Review* is the official publication of the Law and Society Association, the copyright holders. Reprinted by permission.

William C. Berleman. From "Police and Minority Groups: The Improvement of Community Relations," *Crime and Delinquency,* April 1972, pp. 162–163. Reprinted by permission.

Robert M. Carter. From "Where Have All the Crime-Fighters Gone?" *Gunsmoke Gazette,* 1 (January-February 1972), p. 9. First published in *Variety.* Reprinted by permission of the author.

Citizens Research and Investigation Committee and Louis E. Tackwood. From *The Glass House Tapes,* pp. 42, 173, and 259. Reprinted by permission.

Congressional Quarterly Almanac. From *Congressional Quarterly Almanac,* 1972, Vol. 28 (Washington D.C.: Congressional Quarterly, Inc.), p. 91. Reprinted by permission.

Donald R. Cressey. From *Theft of the Nation,* pp. 186–187 and 241–242. Copyright © 1969 by Donald R. Cressey. Reprinted by permission of Harper & Row, Publishers, Inc.

Ben A. Franklin. From "Federal Computers Amass Files on Suspect Citizens," *The New York Times,* June 28, 1970. © 1970 by The New York Times Company. Reprinted by permission.

Gilbert Geis. From "White Collar Crime: The Heavy Electrical Equipment Antitrust Cases of 1961," by Gilbert Geis in *Criminal Behavior Systems: A Topology* by Marshall B. Clinard and Richard Quinney. Copyright © 1967 by Holt, Rinehart and Winston, Inc. Reprinted by permission of Holt, Rinehart and Winston, Publishers.

Jeff Gerth. From "Nixon and the Mafia," *Sundance,* 1 (November-December 1972), p. 32. Reprinted by permission of the author.

Gus Hall. From *Ecology: Can We Survive Under Capitalism?* (New York: International Publishers Co., Inc.), pp. 7 and 34. Reprinted by permission.

Jerome Hall. Permission to reprint from *Theft, Law, and Society,* 2nd Edition, by Jerome Hall, copyright 1952 by the Bobbs-Merrill Co., Inc., granted by the publisher. All rights reserved.

Stuart L. Hills. From *Crime, Power and Morality,* pp. 121–122 and 123 (Chandler Publication). Copyright © 1971 by Harper & Row, Publishers, Inc. Reprinted by permission of Harper & Row, Publishers, Inc.

Nicholas Horrock. From "Public Disclosures of Lost Privacy," *The New York Times,* November 1, 1975. © 1975 by The New York Times Company. Reprinted by permission.

John Irwin. From *The Felon,* pp. 155–156 and 156–157, © 1970. Reprinted by permission of Prentice-Hall, Inc., Englewood Cliffs, New Jersey.

George Jackson. From *Soledad Brother: The Prison Letters of George Jackson,* pp. 30 and 32. Copyright © 1970 by World Entertainers Limited. Reprinted by permission of Bantam Books.

Paul Jacobs. From "Informers, the Enemy Within," *Ramparts* 12 (August-September 1973), pp. 53–54. Copyright 1973 by Noah's Ark, Inc., (For Ramparts Magazine). Reprinted by permission.

Donald J. Newman. From "Pleading Guilty for Considerations: A Study of Bargain Justice." Reprinted by special permission of the *Journal of Criminal Law, Criminology, and Police Science,* Vol. 46, No. 6 (March-April 1956). Copyright © 1956 by Northwestern University School of Law.

Ralph Miliband. From *The State in Capitalist Society,* © 1969 by Ralph Miliband. Basic

Books, Inc., Publishers, New York, and George Weidenfeld and Nicolson Ltd., London. Reprinted by permission.

Andrew Sinclair. From *Era of Excess: A Social History of the Prohibition Movement.* Copyright © 1962 by Andrew Sinclair. Reprinted by permission of the author and Little, Brown and Company with the Atlantic Monthly Press.

Edwin H. Sutherland and Donald R. Cressey. From *Criminology,* 9th Edition. Copyright © 1974. Reprinted by permission of the publisher, J. B. Lippincott Company.

George B. Vold. From *Theoretical Criminology,* pp. v–vi, 35–36, and 240. Reprinted by permission of Oxford University Press.

Frank Wilkinson. From "The Era of Libertarian Repression — 1948 to 1973: From Congressman to President, with Substantial Support from the Liberal Establishment," *University of Akron Law Review,* 7 (Winter 1974), pp. 280–309. Reprinted by permission.

Name Index

Subject Index